Contemporary Peacemaking

"Over the past two-decades peacemaking has become ever more urgent and complex. Scholars and practitioners grapple with the challenges of preventing and ending wars, what works and what doesn't and what we need to do differently, do better. *Contemporary Peacemaking* is an extraordinarily valuable contribution to our efforts to strengthen the way peace processes operate. A stellar cast of writers examine a full spectrum of issues that impact all stages of peace processes. This is without doubt a go to book for students, scholars, diplomats, and NGO practitioners as well as those people whose lives have been torn apart by conflict and who are working to change the opportunities for their communities."
—Jonathan Cohen, *Executive Director, Conciliation Resources*

"This volume is sure to remain a crucial reference point. The editors of this newly updated third edition have gathered together impressive insights from a wide variety of thinkers and practitioners to uncover the art and science of the essentials of classical peacemaking. The chapters are structured along phases of a peace process, a cross-cutting section assessing the participation of women, civil society, and refugees and more conceptual interventions. The analysis is clear and accessible, and a good read. Well done!"
—Thania Paffenholz, Ph.D., *Executive Director, Inclusive Peace*

"*Contemporary Peacemaking* offers an overview that is comprehensive in both sweep and detail. It shows how understanding that power lies at the heart of the peacemaking enterprise, just as it is in the core of conflict, and can open the way for a peaceful settlement. One of the most fascinating aspects of peacemaking is how pragmatic peace visionaries must be. Fittingly, the editors conclude the book with eleven propositions for successful peacemaking—propositions that are at once profoundly pragmatic and creative."
—Dan Smith, *Director, Stockholm International Peace Research Institute (SIPRI)*

"How can we make peace that can last? This is a vital question especially, as the editors note, 'the challenges to peace have become more confounding and dire'. This multi-perspective book gives us the state-of-the-art tools we need to understand the problems and the possibilities of effective peacemaking. Bringing new voices and issues into the discussion of peacemaking, this volume makes a vital contribution in explaining the state of the contemporary field. It will be of great value to those new to peacemaking and those who have long-term interests in it. The book acknowledges the multiplicity of actors involved and the

power hierarchies that implicitly and explicitly come with that, while allowing new voices and perspectives space to offer their contributions to peacemaking."
—Joanna Spear, *Director, FAO Regional Skill Sustainment Initiative & Associate Professor, The George Washington University, USA*

Roger Mac Ginty · Anthony Wanis-St. John
Editors

Contemporary Peacemaking

Peace Processes, Peacebuilding and Conflict

Third Edition

Editors
Roger Mac Ginty
Durham University
Durham, UK

Anthony Wanis-St. John
School of International Service
American University
Washington, DC, USA

ISBN 978-3-030-82961-2   ISBN 978-3-030-82962-9 (eBook)
https://doi.org/10.1007/978-3-030-82962-9

1st edition: Editorial matter and selection, Introduction and Conclusion © John Darby and Roger Mac Ginty 2003; Chapter 20 © Roger Mac Ginty 2003; Chapter 21 © John Darby 2003; Remaining chapters © Palgrave Macmillan Ltd 2003
2nd edition: Remaining chapters © respective authors 2008
3rd edition: © The Editor(s) (if applicable) and The Author(s), under exclusive license to Springer Nature Switzerland AG 2022

This work is subject to copyright. All rights are solely and exclusively licensed by the Publisher, whether the whole or part of the material is concerned, specifically the rights of translation, reprinting, reuse of illustrations, recitation, broadcasting, reproduction on microfilms or in any other physical way, and transmission or information storage and retrieval, electronic adaptation, computer software, or by similar or dissimilar methodology now known or hereafter developed.

The use of general descriptive names, registered names, trademarks, service marks, etc. in this publication does not imply, even in the absence of a specific statement, that such names are exempt from the relevant protective laws and regulations and therefore free for general use.

The publisher, the authors and the editors are safe to assume that the advice and information in this book are believed to be true and accurate at the date of publication. Neither the publisher nor the authors or the editors give a warranty, expressed or implied, with respect to the material contained herein or for any errors or omissions that may have been made. The publisher remains neutral with regard to jurisdictional claims in published maps and institutional affiliations.

Image credit: Zamurovic Brothers

This Palgrave Macmillan imprint is published by the registered company Springer Nature Switzerland AG
The registered company address is: Gewerbestrasse 11, 6330 Cham, Switzerland

Acknowledgements

We would like to acknowledge the help and encouragement of Sarah Roughley and her colleagues at Palgrave Macmillan. Anthony Wanis-St. John also gratefully recognises the support of research assistants at American University; Julian Wurpel, Kleopatra Moditsi and doctoral candidate Noah Rosen. The first and second editions of this book were edited by John Darby and Roger Mac Ginty. John passed away in 2012. As well as being a great scholar, he was a wonderful wit and mentor. He is missed. Our main thanks, of course, are due to the contributing authors.

Contents

1	**Introduction** Roger Mac Ginty and Anthony Wanis-St. John	1

Part I Preparing for Peace

2	**Understanding Ripeness: Making and Using Hurting Stalemates** I William Zartman	23
3	**Cultivating Peace: A Practitioner's View of Deadly Conflict and Negotiation** John Paul Lederach	43
4	**Conflict Analysis: A System's Approach** Lisa Schirch	55

Part II Cross Cutting Issues

5	**The United Nations and Peacemaking** Alex J. Bellamy	83
6	**Women's Participation in Peace Processes** Jana Krause and Louise Olsson	103
7	**Indigenous Approaches to Peacemaking** Douglas P. Fry and Geneviève Souillac	121

8	Peacemaking Referendums: Advantages and Challenges for Peace Processes Joana Amaral	141
9	Refugees, Peacemaking, and Durable Solutions to Displacement Maja Janmyr	159
10	Time, Sequencing and Peace Processes Roger Mac Ginty	181

Part III Negotiation and Mediation

11	Mediation and the Ending of Conflicts Christopher Mitchell	199
12	Diffusion vs. Coherence: The Competitive Environment of Multiparty Mediation Chester A. Crocker, Fen Osler Hampson, and Pamela Aall	213
13	Inclusivity in Peace Processes: Civil Society and Armed Groups Suzanne Ghais	235
14	Negotiating Peace in the Shadows Niall Ó Dochartaigh	261

Part IV Violence and Peace Processes

15	Violence and Peace Processes Kristine Höglund and Desirée Nilsson	289
16	Peacemaking and Election Violence Inken von Borzyskowski and Richard Saunders	307
17	Disarmament, Demobilisation and Reintegration of Ex-Combatants Alpaslan Özerdem	333
18	Security Sector Reform Yuji Uesugi	355

Part V Peace Accords

19	Peace Processes and Their Agreements Christine Bell and Laura Wise	381
20	Power Sharing After Civil Wars: Matching Problems to Solutions Timothy D. Sisk	407
21	Peace Accords and Human Rights Jan Pospisil	427
22	The Post-conflict Constitution as a Peace Agreement Laurie Nathan	447

Part VI Implementation and Reconstruction

23	Transitional Justice and Peacemaking/Peacebuilding Roddy Brett and Lina Malagón	475
24	Peace Education as a Peacemaking Tool in Conflict Zones Alexander Cromwell	507
25	Post-accord Crime and Violence Christina Steenkamp	533
26	Everyday Economic Experiences and Peace Processes Birte Vogel	563

Part VII Conclusion

27	Conclusion: Peace Processes, Past, Present, and Future Anthony Wanis-St. John and Roger Mac Ginty	585

Index   615

Notes on Contributors

Pamela Aall is a senior advisor for conflict prevention and management at the U.S. Institute of Peace (USIP) and an adjunct professor at American University. She serves on the board of Women in International Security and is a member of the World Refugee Council. She has co-authored and co-edited articles and books in the field of conflict management and has also written about NGOs in conflict environments. Her most recent books are *Responding to Violent Conflicts and Humanitarian Crises: A Guide to Participants* (co-edited with Dan Snodderly) and *Diplomacy and the Future of World Order*, co-edited with Chester Crocker and Fen Hampson.

Joana Amaral holds a Ph.D. in International Relations from the University of Kent, United Kingdom. The author of the book *Making Peace with Referendums: Cyprus and Northern Ireland* (Syracuse University Press: New York, 2019), her research and publications have focused on peace negotiations and mediation, particularly on issues related to inclusion and public engagement and participation. She was a Postdoctoral Research Fellow at the Centre for Conflict Studies at the University of Marburg, Germany.

Christine Bell is a Professor of Constitutional Law, Assistant Principal (Global Justice), and Director of the Political Settlements Research Programme at the University of Edinburgh. She has longstanding research interests in peace processes, constitution-making and inclusion, and has been part of the team developing the PA-X Peace Agreements Database (https://www.peacegreements.org).

Alex J. Bellamy is Professor of Peace and Conflict Studies and Director of the Asia Pacific Centre for the Responsibility to Protect at the University of Queensland, Australia. He is a Fellow of the Academy of Social Science in Australia. Recent books include 'World Peace (And How We Can Achieve It)' (Oxford, 2020) and 'East Asia's Other Miracle: Explaining the Decline of Mass Atrocities' (Oxford, 2017). His forthcoming book is 'The Betrayal of Syria: War, Atrocities, and the Failure of International Diplomacy' (Columbia, 2022).

Inken von Borzyskowski is an Assistant Professor in International Relations at University College London. Her research examines the domestic politics of international relations with an emphasis on international organisations and their effect on domestic conflict and elections. Specifically, her research falls into three areas: international organisations' membership politics, international democracy assistance, and election violence. Her book, 'The Credibility Challenge: How Democracy Aid Influences Election Violence', was published by Cornell University Press; her articles have appeared in *British Journal of Political Science*, *International Studies Quarterly*, *Review of International Organizations*, and *Journal of Peace Research*.

Roddy Brett is a Senior Lecturer in Politics and International Relations at the University of Bristol. He has published widely on the topics of political violence, genocide, peacemaking, peacebuilding and transitional justice. During thirteen years living in Guatemala and Colombia, he acted as Advisor to the United Nations and worked with the Centre for Human Rights Legal Action in Guatemala, as a member of the original team that prepared the evidence against former dictator General Ríos Montt, leading to his conviction in 2013 for genocide and crimes against humanity. He will publish *The Path Towards Reconciliation after Colombia's War: understanding the roles of victims and perpetrators* in 2021 with the University of Pennsylvania Press.

Chester A. Crocker is the James R. Schlesinger Professor of Strategic Studies at Georgetown University's Walsh School of Foreign Service. He served as chairman of the board of the United States Institute of Peace (1992–2004), and as a member of its board through 2011. From 1981 to

1989, he was U.S. assistant secretary of state for African affairs and mediated the prolonged negotiations among Angola, Cuba, and South Africa that led to Namibia's transition to independence, and to the withdrawal of Cuban forces from Angola. Dr. Crocker is a founding member of the London-based Global Leadership Foundation. He is the author or editor of numerous works on conflict management and its place in foreign policy and global politics.

Alexander Cromwell is a Professorial Lecturer and the Associate Director, Dean's Scholars and Experiential Learning at the Elliott School of International Affairs at George Washington University. His research focuses on peace education in conflict contexts, and he has investigated the impact of these programs with Pakistani, Afghan, Indonesian, and US youth. His work has been published in the *International Journal of Educational Development*, the *Journal of Peace Education*, *Action Research,* and in edited volumes. Cromwell has also trained groups from the Middle East, South Asia, Southeast Asia, Europe, and the US. He previously taught at American University and George Mason University, where he received his Ph.D.

Douglas P. Fry is Chair of the Department of Peace and Conflict Studies at the University of North Carolina at Greensboro. He holds a Ph.D. in Anthropology from Indiana University and studies topics such as peaceful societies, peace systems, cross-cultural conflict resolution, and anthropological perspectives on peace. Fry and Geneviève Souillac regularly publish together and are co-directors of the Peace Systems Project (see 'Societies within peace systems avoid war and build positive intergroup relationships', open access at: https://doi.org/10.1057/s41599-020-00692-8). Fry's books include *Nurturing Our Humanity* (co-authored with Riane Eisler, OUP, 2019), *War, Peace, and Human Nature* (OUP, 2013), and *Beyond War* (OUP, 2007).

Suzanne Ghais is the Principal of Ghais Mediation and Facilitation, LLC; co-founder and executive director of Pathfinders4Peace Inc., a nonprofit peacemaking organisation; Adjunct Professor at American University's School of International Service; and a scholar of peace processes and conflict prevention. In her 30 years in the conflict resolution field, she has provided facilitation, mediation, training, assessment, and process design in internal organisational, public policy, and other matters.

Fen Osler Hampson is Chancellor's Professor and Professor of International Affairs at The Norman Paterson School of International Affairs, Carleton University in Ottawa, Canada. He is also President of the World Refugee and Migration Council. A Fellow of the Royal Society of Canada, he is the author/coauthor of 15 books on international affairs and co-editor of 30 other volumes.

Kristine Höglund is a Professor of Peace and Conflict Research at Uppsala University. Her research pertains to the causes and consequences of electoral violence; urban violence and conflict management in cities; the causes of peace in Southern Africa; and the dynamics of peace processes, peacebuilding, and transitional justice.

Maja Janmyr is a Professor of International Migration Law at the Faculty of Law, University of Oslo and a Research Associate at the Refugee Studies Centre, University of Oxford. She is a leading authority on refugee protection in the Middle East, and has published widely on issues related to International Refugee Law. Her current work focuses on the situation of refugees and other migrants in Lebanon. Janmyr's contribution to this volume has been supported by the Research Council of Norway grant nr. 286745.

Jana Krause is an Associate Professor in the Department of Political Science at the University of Oslo. Her research focuses on the gender dimensions of peacebuilding, civilian protection, and social resilience in communal conflicts and civil wars. She holds a Ph.D. (2013) from the Graduate Institute in Geneva and has been Visiting Fellow at Yale University and King's College London. Krause is the author of *Resilient Communities: Non-Violence and Civilian Agency in Communal War* (CUP 2018) and directs the ERC Starting Grant project 'ResilienceBuilding' (2020–2025).

John Paul Lederach is an Professor Emeritus of International Peacebuilding at the Kroc Institute for International Peace Studies, University of Notre Dame. A practitioner and scholar, Lederach has been involved in mediation in Colombia, the Philippines and Nepal. He is the author of 22 books, including *The Moral Imagination: The Art and Soul of Building Peace* (Oxford University Press, 2005), *Building Peace: Sustainable Reconciliation in Divided Societies* (USIP, 1997), and *Preparing for Peace: Confliction Transformation Across Cultures* (Syracuse University Press, 1995).

Roger Mac Ginty is a Professor at the School of Government and International Affairs, and director of the Durham Global Security Institute, both at Durham University. He is co-founder of the Everyday Peace Indicators, and co-edits the journal *Peacebuilding*.

Lina Malagón is a researcher and litigant and in developing advocacy in conflict-affected and post-conflict countries, her career in balance with her academic scholarship. She was Deputy Director of the High Commissioner for Victims in Bogota (2016–2017), and Director of International Advocacy at the Colombian Commission of Jurists (2007–2012). She has worked as consultant to multiple international organisations, including the ILO and ITUC. In 2020, Lina joined the Transitional Justice Institute at Ulster University as a Research Associate in the project Socio-economic rights and Transitions, developing research on the cases study of Northern Ireland, Sri Lanka, Colombia and Sierra Leone.

Christopher Mitchell is a Professor Emeritus of Conflict Analysis and Resolution at the Jimmy and Rosalynn Carter School for Peace and Conflict Resolution, George Mason University. He has been involved in multiple track-two situations, as well as playing a leading role in the development of thinking about track-two, mediation and conflict resolution. More recently, he has headed pioneering work on Zones of Peace.

Laurie Nathan is Director of the Mediation Program and Professor of the Practice of Mediation at the Kroc Institute for International Peace Studies, University of Notre Dame. He has published extensively on mediation, regional security and security sector reform. He has served as a senior mediator advisor to the United Nations and a range of African organisations.

Desirée Nilsson is an Associate Professor at the Department of Peace and Conflict Research at Uppsala University, Sweden. Her primary research interest is conflict resolution in civil wars with a particular focus on multi-party dynamics, including topics such as inclusive peace processes, rebel fragmentation, and peacekeeping operations.

Niall Ó Dochartaigh is a Personal Professor of Political Science and Sociology at the National University of Ireland Galway. He is the author of *Deniable Contact: Back-channel Negotiation in Northern Ireland* (2021) and *Civil Rights to Armalites: Derry and the birth of the Irish Troubles* (1997; 2005) and co-editor of *Political Violence in Context* (2015) and *Dynamics of Political Change in Ireland: Making and Breaking a Divided Island* (2017). He was founding co-convener of the Standing Group on Political Violence of the European Consortium for Political Research (ECPR) and founder of the Specialist Group on Peace and Conflict of the Political Studies Association of Ireland (PSAI).

Louise Olsson (Ph.D. 2007), Senior Researcher at the Peace Research Institute Oslo. Olsson's research focuses on women's inclusion and awareness on peace agreement implementation, state strategies on gender mainstreaming, and the role of gender inequality for conflict risk. She has created and led an international Research Working Group on Women, Peace and Security and has experience in policy development and training. For example, she has been Senior Advisor on Women, Peace and Security at the Folke Bernadotte Academy, and has acted as a coach to the Supreme Commander and to the Chief of Joint Operations at the Swedish Armed Forces.

Alpaslan Özerdem is the Dean of the Carter School for Peace and Conflict Resolution and professor of peace and conflict studies at George Mason University. With 20 years of field research experience in Afghanistan, Bosnia-Herzegovina, Kosovo, Lebanon, Liberia, Nepal, Nigeria, Philippines, Sierra Leone, Sri Lanka, and Turkey, Prof Özerdem has published extensively (15 books and numerous journal articles, book chapters and op-eds), including, *Routledge Handbook of Turkish Politics* (2019), *Comparing Peace Processes* (2019), *Routledge Handbook of Peace, Security and Development* (2020). He is also a member of the Anna Lindh Foundation Scientific Committee and received his Professor Extraordinary in Politics title from Stellenbosch University in 2017.

Jan Pospisil is Research Director at the Austrian Study Centre for Peace and Conflict Resolution (ASPR) and an Associate Professor in Political Science at the University of Vienna. His work focuses on peace processes and political settlements, donor politics in peacebuilding, resilience, and South Sudanese and Sudanese politics. Jan currently heads the workstream on local peace agreements in the Political Settlements Research Programme (PSRP) at the University of Edinburgh, which is funded by UK FCDO. His monograph *Peace in Political Unsettlement* was published by Palgrave Macmillan in 2018.

Richard Saunders earned his Ph.D. at Florida State University. His research applies a behavioral perspective to explain how domestic politics affects international conflict behaviour. His work is published in *Conflict Management and Peace Science*, *Research & Politics*, and *International Interactions*, among other places.

Lisa Schirch is a Senior Research Fellow for the Toda Peace Institute, where she directs the Social Media, Technology, and Peacebuilding program. A former Fulbright Fellow in East and West Africa, Schirch is the author of eleven books, including *Conflict Assessment and Peacebuilding Planning: Toward a Participatory Approach to Human Security*. She has conducted conflict assessments in over a dozen countries. For over a decade, she directed the Alliance for Peacebuilding Policy Program to bring local civil society experts in conflict assessment from dozens of countries to share their analysis with the US Congress.

Timothy D. Sisk is a Professor of International and Comparative Politics at the Josef Korbel School of International Studies, University of Denver and Director of the Institute for Comparative and Regional Studies (ICRS) at the School. His research, teaching and policy-oriented work focuses on armed conflict and political violence together with understanding and evaluation of processes of conflict prevention, management, and peacebuilding in fragile and post-war contexts. Sisk has conducted extensive research on the role of international and regional organisations, particularly the United Nations, in peace operations, peacemaking and peacebuilding.

Geneviève Souillac is an Associate Professor in the Department of Peace and Conflict Studies at the University of North Carolina at Greensboro. Her publications explore the intersection of democratic and peace ethics, indigenous knowledge, and the theology of peace. Souillac and Douglas P. Fry regularly publish together and are co-directors of the Peace Systems Project (see 'Societies within peace systems avoid war and build positive intergroup relationships', open access at: https://doi.org/10.1057/s41599-020-00692-8). Souillac holds a Ph.D. from the University of Hong Kong in Political Philosophy.

Christina Steenkamp is a Senior Lecturer in Social and Political Change at Oxford Brookes University. She has published widely on topics related to violence and peacebuilding and is a principal investigator on several externally funded research projects addressing organised crime, public health and conflict in the Middle East. She is also writing her third book,

Organised Crime in the Middle East: Between Conflict and Peacebuilding, under contract with Cambridge University Press.

Yuji Uesugi is a Professor at the Faculty of International Research and Education, Waseda University, Japan. He has edited several books on peacebuilding in Asia, such as *Operationalisation of Hybrid Peacebuilding in Asia* (2021); *Hybrid Peacebuilding in Asia* (2020); and *Peacebuilding and Security Sector Governance in Asia* (2014), and co-authored a book called *UN Governance: Peace and Human Security in Cambodia and Timor-Leste* (2021). As a reflective practitioner, he has been involved in SSR in Timor-Leste (working for the National Directorate for Prevention of Community Conflict) and in Mindanao, the Philippines (the Japanese official representative to the Independent Commission on Policing).

Birte Vogel is a Senior Lecturer in Humanitarianism, Peace and Conflict Studies at the University of Manchester, UK. She is the Editor of the Humanitarian and Conflict Response Institute's *HCRI Policy Brief Series* that aims to make academic findings accessible to policymakers, and was previously Assistant Editor of the academic journal *Peacebuilding*. Her recently co-edited books reflect her research interest in the intersection of economics and peace and conflict studies (*Economies of Peace: Economy Formation Processes in Conflict-Affected Societies*, Routledge, 2019), as well as her interest in the ethics and methodologies of peace research (*The Companion to Peace and Conflict Fieldwork*, Palgrave, 2021).

Anthony Wanis-St. John is an Associate Professor at the School of International Service, American University. He earned his Ph.D. from The Fletcher School of Law and Diplomacy, Tufts University and was a Doctoral Fellow at Harvard Law School's Program on Negotiation. He is the author of *Back Channel Negotiation: Secrecy in Middle East Peacemaking* (Syracuse University Press, 2011). His research focuses on peace processes, ceasefires and civil society engagement. He has worked with the National Democratic Institute to unify Syrian civilian opposition groups and supported US efforts to unify the Darfuri rebel groups, among other field experiences. With the United States Institute of Peace he has supported the conflict prevention capacities of ASEAN and the Arab League. He has supported US State Department and Defense Department efforts to train civilian and military advisors. His work has appeared in outlets including the *Journal of Peace Research*, *International Negotiation* and *Negotiation Journal*.

Laura Wise is a Research Associate at the Political Settlements Research Programme (PSRP), based at the University of Edinburgh. Her research explores the intersections between minority and territorial politics in the context of peace processes and post-conflict societies. Laura has been part of the team developing the PA-X Peace Agreements Database (www.peacegreements.org) and holds an MA in Comparative Ethnic Conflict from Queen's University Belfast.

I William Zartman is the Jacob Blaustein Distinguished Professor Emeritus of International Organization and Conflict Resolution at the School of Advanced International Studies of The Johns Hopkins University in Washington, and a member of the Steering Committee of the Processes of International Negotiation (PIN) Program at the German Institute of Global and Area Studies (GIGA) in Hamburg. His doctorate is from Yale and doctorates honoris causa from Louvain and Uppsala. He is author and editor of numerous works on negotiation and mediation, including *Ripe for Resolution* (Oxford 1989), *Preventing Deadly Conflict* (Polity 2015), and (ed.) *How Negotiations End* (Cambridge 2019).

Abbreviations

ABM	Anti-Ballistic Missile
AFRC	Armed Forces Revolutionary Council
AMISOM	African Union Mission to Somalia
ANC	African National Congress
ANSA	Armed Non-Statutory Actor
AQIM	al-Qaeda in the Islamic Maghreb
AU	African Union
AVRP	Armed Violence Reduction and Prevention
BATNA	Best Alternative to a Negotiated Agreement
BICC	Bonn International Center for Conversion
BiH	Bosnia and Herzegovina
CAR	Central African Republic
CBO	Community-based Development Organization
CDA	Collaborative for Development Action
CDG	Chicken dilemma game
CMA	Coordination of Azawad Movements
CMI	Crisis Management Initiative
CNDD-FDD	National Council for the Defence of Democracy-Forces for the Defence of Democracy
CONADEP	National Commission on the Disappearance of Persons
CPA	Comprehensive Peace Accord
CPP-NPA	Communist Party of the Philippines-New People's Army
CRR	Committee on Reparations and Rehabilitation
CSO	Civil Society Organization
CSSR	Civil Society Support Room
DAAD	German Academic Exchange Service

DCAF	Geneva Centre for Security Governance
DDR	Disarmament, Demobilisation and Reintegration
DPA	Department of Political Affairs
DPKO	Department of Peacekeeping Operations
DRC	Democratic Republic of Congo
EAO	Ethnic Armed Organization
ECOWAS	Economic Community of West African States
ELN	National Liberation Army
EMB	Election Management Body
ERP	European Recovery programme
ETA	*Euskadi Ta Askatasuna*
EU	European Union
FARC-EP	Revolutionary Armed Forces of Colombia
FIB	Forced Intervention Brigade
FNL	National Forces of Liberation
GFA	Good Friday Agreement
GRP	Government of the Philippines
HD	Centre for Humanitarian Dialogue
ICAF	Interagency Conflict Assessment Framework
ICC	International Criminal Court
ICG	International Contact Group
ICJ	International Court of Justice
ICRC	International Committee of the Red Cross
ICTR	International Criminal Tribunal for Rwanda
ICTY	International Criminal Tribunal for the Former Yugoslavia
IDDRS	Integrated Disarmament, Demobilisation and Reintegration Standards
IDP	Internally Displaced Persons
IFES	International Foundation for Electoral Systems
IFI	International Financial Institution
IGAD	Intergovernmental Authority on Development
IHL	International Criminal Court
IIE	Institute of International Education
ILO	International Labour Organisation
IMF	International Monetary Fund
INGO	International Non-Governmental Organisation
IRA	Irish Republican Army
ISAF	International Security Assistance Force
JACS	Joint Analysis of Conflict and Stability
KFOR	Kosovo Force
KVM	Kosovo Verification Mission
LTTE	Liberation Tigers of Tamil Eelam
MDJT	Movement for Democracy and Justice in Chad

MENA	Middle East and North Africa
MEO	Mutually Enticing Opportunity
MHS	Mutually Hurting Stalemate
MILF	Moro Islamic Liberation Front
MINUGUA	United Nations Verification Mission in Guatemala
MINURSO	United Nations Mission for the Referendum in Western Sahara
MINUSMA	United Nations Multidimensional Integrated Stabilisation Mission in Mali
MINUSTAH	United Nations Stabilisation Mission in Haiti
MNLF	Moro National Liberation Front
MONUSCO	United Nations Organisation Stabilisation Mission in the Democratic Republic of Congo
MRG	Minority Rights Group
NATO	North Atlantic Treaty Organisation
NCA	National Ceasefire Agreement
NDC	National Demobilisation Commission
NEC	National Election Commission
NGO	Non-Governmental Organisation
NSCN	National Socialist Council of Nagalim
OECD/DAC	Organisation for Economic Cooperation and Development/Development Assistance Committee
ONUB	United Nations Office in Burundi
PCC	Post-conflict Constitution
PDG	Prisoner's Dilemma Game
PLO	Palestinian Liberation Organisation
POLISARIO	Frente Popular para la Liberación de Saguia el-Hamra y de Río de Oro
PR	Proportional Representation
PRA	Participatory Rural Appraisal
R2P	Responsibility to Protect
RPF	Rwandan Patriotic Front
RUF	Revolutionary United Front
SDG	Sustainable Development Goals
SSR	Security Sector Reform
START	Strategic Arms Reduction Treaty
TIPH	Temporary International Presence in Hebron
TJ	Transitional Justice
TJM	Transitional Justice Mechanism
TOC	Theories of Change
UK	United Kingdom
UN	United Nations
UNAMA	United Nations Assistance Mission in Afghanistan
UNAMIR	United Nations Assistance Mission for Rwanda

UNAMSIL	United Nations Mission in Sierra Leone
UNDP	United Nations Development Programme
UNHCR	United Nations Commission for Refugees
UNICEF	United National International Children's Emergency Fund
UNIFIL	United Nations Interim Force in Lebanon
UNMIK	United Nations Interim Administration Mission in Kosovo
UNMIL	United Nations Mission in Liberia
UNSCR	United Nations Security Council Resolution
UNSOM	United Nations Support Office in Somalia
URNG	Guatemalan National Revolutionary Unity
USAID	US Agency for International Development
WO	Way Out

List of Figures

Fig. 21.1	Human rights references in peace agreements and ceasefire agreements, 1990–2018	432
Fig. 21.2	Peace processes addressing human rights	435
Fig. 21.3	Types of human rights provisions in peace agreements	436
Fig. 26.1	Change of Gini Index over time	571

List of Tables

Table 7.1	Comparison of outcomes between government district courts and local village 'customary' courts among the Enga of Papua New Guinea for 2011	128
Table 12.1	Multiparty mediation	218
Table 12.2	Fragmented parties	222
Table 17.1	The typology of DDR as part of SSR frameworks	336
Table 19.1	Agreements by level of conflict and process	383
Table 19.2	Agreements by region	384
Table 19.3	Agreements by stage of process	386
Table 21.1	Regional patterns of human rights references in peace agreements	434
Table 23.1	Transitional justice provisions in peace agreements	490
Table 24.1	Peace education theories of change	511
Table 24.2	Transformations resulting from peace education	516
Table 26.1	Annual GDP growth rates in selected countries a year before (-1), the year of end of hostilities (0) and the three years after the official end of the conflict $(1-3)$	565

CHAPTER 1

Introduction

Roger Mac Ginty and Anthony Wanis-St. John

In the contemporary and ancient world, the pursuits of survival and political domination have resulted in a close encounter between the violence of warfare and the forging of peace. Our written histories of both historical and mythological struggles depict a symbiosis between peacemaking and conflict. One has to look no further than the Iliad, the Mahabharata or even the Epic of Gilgamesh to see some evidence of humanity's long preoccupation with finding a way to peace, the 'dear nurse of arts, plenties and joyful births', in order to flee from 'impious war, arrayed in flames' even if this quest does not always succeed.[1]

The art and science of peacemaking have some constant themes; mediation by a third party, rituals and gestures of reconciliation, reciprocal commitments and renewed ties with a promise of a better, shared, future.

R. Mac Ginty (✉)
Durham University, Durham, UK
e-mail: roger.macginty@durham.ac.uk

A. Wanis-St. John
School of International Service, American University, Washington, DC, USA
e-mail: wanis@american.edu

New themes constantly emerge however, and the imperative for peacemaking takes on ever greater urgency and scale in contemporary times. The depravities of interstate and civil war have been supplemented by more complex, regional warfare involving numerous states and transnational non-state armed groups, and even various forms of hybrid warfare. So too does peacemaking continue to evolve. Peacemakers embrace more sophisticated conflict analyses and ask discomforting questions about root causes: how we ended up with war. They have heeded the call to recognize the roles of civil society in both keeping things peaceful and in perpetuating exclusions that fuel political grievances. They consider referendums, elections and post-conflict constitutions; they anticipate the challenges of returning the displaced, the resurgence of post-accord violence, and the sheer plethora of uncoordinated mediators. They negotiate for more robust disarmament and demobilization, while looking ahead to security sector reforms and better roles for international agencies and organizations. They can rely now on accumulated knowledge of how armed groups prioritize their involvement in peace processes. In the pursuit of a more positive peace, they can rely on vast experience with numerous forms of transitional justice, and explicit discussions about how to design a post-conflict economy. And it is undertaken with a view towards sustaining the peace and preventing its disintegration.

No serious scholar or practitioner of peacemaking considers the signing of a peace accord to be the ultimate goal. Peace processes have come to be understood as a far broader and deeper pursuit of a better and lasting peace. Nevertheless, the advantages of a negotiated settlement in cases of civil and interstate war are self-evident. Peace processes and peace accords hold out the hope of staunching violent conflict, thereby saving and improving lives. Processes and accords also offer the possibility of grievances being addressed, fair systems of governance and rights being put in place, and communities and elites having the opportunity to forge new relationships in more constructive ways. Yet, despite the advertised benefits of negotiated settlements, warring parties often forego peace processes in pursuit of outright victory. And when they do opt for a peace process, it meets significant obstacles, not least of which are bad faith negotiation, splintering and fragmentation, perverse incentives to renew fighting and the pursuit of illicit and criminal activities.

This book is a concentrated and thematic study of the many dimensions of peace processes. It aims to showcase 'what works' but also to highlight what does not work, as well as what could work better. The ambition of the book is to present a state-of-the-art examination of peacemaking in the twenty-first century.

The book takes a thematic approach in identifying key themes in peace processes such as the role of gender, disarmament, mediation and timing. Rather than concentrating on a single case study or case studies,[2] the chapters utilise multiple examples thus providing the book with a comparative vantage point. Every peace process has unique features and so there are benefits in looking across peace processes and peace accords to see best (and suboptimal) practice.[3] While the emphasis is on 'contemporary' or recent peace processes, it is worth noting that peace and conflict are long-term endeavours. Conflicts have a long 'afterlife' and it is difficult to insert arbitrary cut-off points into timelines that often involve long-term processes such as statebuilding, decolonisation and development.[4] So while the focus of this work is on the recent past it is worth remembering that 'recent' peace processes and peace accords should be situated in a complex temporal hinterland in which people see time differently and in which peace is rarely a neatly defined endstate.

Contemporary Peacemaking draws on the expertise of mainly academic contributors, though many have practical experience in mediation, and have conducted extensive fieldwork in conflict-affected contexts. It is worth noting, however, that the published outputs of Peace and Conflict Studies show a distinct bias towards academics based in the global north. While this book reflects that bias, it does recognise the incongruity of scholars mainly from the global north writing about conflict and peace processes that mainly occur in the global south.[5] Immense peacebuilding academic expertise and practical experience exists in the global south, including in conflict-affected societies, but often this is not adequately reflected through established academic means of dissemination. Just as peace processes and the implementation of peace accords are often the site of contestation, telling the story of peace can also be contested. Some actors have more power than others in narrating their role in peacemaking or the role of their political party or militant group. For example, a small industry has developed among former prime ministers, presidents and peace process negotiators whose published memoirs seek to establish their version of peace process negotiations as the accepted version. The views from those in whose name war and peace are waged may stand in contrast to the memoirs of the elites. Several of our authors have extensive field experience researching and practicing peacemaking, and they offer perspectives often absent from the memoirs of political leaders.

As will be seen in the chapters throughout this book, the issue of power is crucial to peace processes and operates at all levels and in all domains. Some actors will have more power than others, and will wield the hard power of the military and international allies in conjunction with the soft power of diplomacy, talks and symbolic politics. The phrase 'thump and talk' dates from the era of apartheid South Africa when the apartheid regime would launch military offensives against its enemies in southern Africa and, after achieving battlefield success, would then suggest talks.[6] This strategy of establishing 'facts on the ground' and thus attempting to negotiate from an advantageous position is common with, for example, regional powers such as Turkey, Israel and Saudi Arabia attempting to use military leverage for political ends, but it was also the strategy pursued by rebel groups such as the Rwandan Patriotic Front, during the peace process in the civil war that preceded the Rwandan genocide.[7] While military and economic power is important, it is worth noting that power comes in very many forms and an over-concentration on material forms of power risks overlooking other forms of power that are vital to peace processes and the implementation of peace accords. Certainly states and international organisations are at an advantage in that they can call on the power given to them by the international order and sovereignty. Their status confers on them a structural power or a standing that allows them to designate actions and groups as illegal or 'terrorist'. This discursive or naming power is also key to the term 'international community', a group that is undefined yet the term seeks to convey a moral standing and unity that may not always be present. It is also worth bearing structural power in mind in relation to the structural violence that is common in conflict-affected contexts.

It is useful, however, to look beyond the power assumed, held or exercised by formal institutions. Crucially for the story of peace processes and peace accords, individuals and groups often have significant non-material power in the form of identity bonds, belief systems, and cultural and political preferences. This power manifests itself in multiple, often subtle, ways. For example, it might take the form of withholding consent, resisting new governing processes that create new social injustices, or continuing to support actors who are deemed 'dissident' or illegal. Organising to resist the post-accord order is a power that conflict-impacted communities assume for themselves. They are not 'empowered' by external actors to do this, but rather discern new oppressions and structural violence, and struggle against them in effort to shape the peace.[8] For the purposes of this book, it is also worth noting the importance of forms of power that are informal, non-institutional and difficult for outsiders to see. Peace processes and peace accords will spark multiple conversations in a society as individuals and groups try to assess if the process and outcome is to their advantage and worthy of support. These conversations will take place across society, in political parties and militant groups, but also in workplaces and social settings, and especially within families.

Issues of power in peace processes are not solely inter-group or between parties. They also operate at the intra-group level. It is often the case that actors in a peace process will have to manage opinion and expectations within their own camp, and perhaps face accusations that negotiating with 'the enemy' amounts to surrender or treachery. So while political and militant leaders attempt to negotiate with their out-group opponents, they might also be involved in an internal power struggle. If suffering the effects of war, or being mobilised against the 'other' during a political or military conflict tend to foster internal unity, then it can be argued that peace processes sometimes promote conditions for fragmentation as factions vie for legitimacy and contend with each other over the 'spoils' of the peace. Peace negotiators can be accused—rightly or wrongly—by their own adherents and competitors of 'betraying the cause'.

A final point to make in relation to power and peace processes is that in an optimum scenario peace processes allow conflictual forms of power (specifically attempts by one party to impose their will on another party) to be replaced with more social forms of power. Thus, the 'power over' models of authoritarian regimes and their rivals can potentially be replaced with more emancipatory forms of power along the lines of power with, power to, and power from. It is worth subjecting peace processes and peace accords to a 'power assessment' and to ask if the 'power over' model of coercion is being replaced by more consensual forms of power in the post-accord society. Surely *the ways* in which peace is made are linked to *the kind of peace* that results.

WHAT ARE PEACE PROCESSES AND PEACE ACCORDS?

Peace processes are attempts to lower the costs of conflict through negotiation that involves the main parties to a conflict. They normally sit within a conflict management framework: the actors seek to manage the conflict to acceptable limits through a range of initiatives.[9] Actors may still hold onto their beliefs, for example for territorial secession or a recalibration of power within the state, but they also agree to investigate different approaches that usually involve a lessening of violence. Some aspects of peace processes can be more ambitious than conflict management and may involve conflict resolution or even conflict transformation. These approaches may involve people-to-people activities, transitional or transformative justice, or resourcing sharing initiatives. In the main, if peace processes take root they involve hard-headed negotiation, with parties seeking to maximise advantage but not to the extent that the peace process would collapse and other parties would walk away. Clearly this is a delicate process, and parties in a peace process often have to invest significant energy in managing expectations on their own side. Indeed, the sensitivities associated with peace processes, and the possibility of compromise with parties that are regarded as 'the enemy', means that many processes are secret—at least in their early phases.

Significant variation can be found among the types and extent of peace processes and peace accords. It is useful to think in terms of a spectrum of processes and accords, with some minimalist and others maximalist. Some processes restrict themselves to security, territorial and technical issues, while others are more expansive and deal with wider issues of identity, social inclusion, and economic development. In general, there has been a trend towards more comprehensive peace processes and peace accords, possibly reflecting a recognition of the complexities of conflict and how it is often linked to wider issues of development and exclusion. There has also been significant variation in peace processes in terms of timing. Some processes are relatively brief. Others are elongated, sometimes suffering a temporary breakdown (for example, Northern Ireland) or, in other cases, with parties to the conflict using the peace process to wear down their opponents (for example, north east India). A final area of variation in peace processes and accords pertains to the complexity of the conflict. In the cases of Yemen, Syria and Libya, for example, it is difficult to conceive of a single peace process. The conflicts involve multiple actors with different external sponsors—all with different agendas, resources and timelines. Thus, in a number of cases we have seen partial rather than comprehensive peace processes that involve a limited number of actors and issues. Often these are limited to initial ceasefires that need to be expanded to include more actors and thus more issues in contention. The progression from an initial ceasefire to more comprehensive peace negotiations is neither assured nor easy, and requires different skills and strategies to effect.

Just as peace processes involve much variation and present difficulties for those tempted to generalise, peace accords vary enormously in terms of length, issues covered, and the extent to which provisions are specified (or left open-ended). In some cases, a peace accord is strictly between the conflict parties, in other cases it may involve international actors (such as the United Nations or neighbouring states), and in still other cases it may take the form of a new constitution. In most cases, peace accords will be elite-level documents, although in some cases (for example, Guatemala or Colombia) peace accords have been put to the electorate through a referendum.[10] The key issue with peace accords is, ultimately, implementation. There is a danger that parties to an accord cherry-pick those provisions that suit them and seek to ignore those issues that do not. To try to obviate this problem, some peace accords have verification processes (sometimes internationally overseen) or they have a strict sequencing to ensure that some steps can only be implemented if prior steps are already in place. Further problems arise when signatories to a peace accord are replaced by other political figures, as has been the case in Palestine-Israel, Northern Ireland and Colombia. While those who originally negotiated the peace accord may have an emotional attachment to it, and a nuanced understanding of what happened during the peace process negotiations, the same may not be true for their successors. Additionally, implementation is to some extent fraught with dilemmas. As the provisions of a peace accord become move from symbolic to substantive, implementation becomes harder. Successful implementation of, for example, a return of territory, or a repatriation of refugees, while satisfying to the 'other' side, may also generate internal rejection and discontent. At the very least, these are moments that internal rivals within the parties may leverage to delegitimise the peacemaking leadership.

The Peacemaking Landscape

The peacemaking context has always been complex and been prone to geostrategic and regional politics. In the current era a number of trends are discernible. Some of the trends overlap and some contradict each other, giving rise to a complex landscape. Firstly, there has been a withdrawal from what might be called liberal internationalism or the notion that a number of leading states and international organisations would promote their version of peace that was based on liberal ideas of rights, democracy and the free market.[11] The liberal peace was perhaps most visible in the comprehensive international interventions in the former Yugoslavia, Liberia and Sierra Leone in which there was an emphasis on statebuilding and new governance structures. These peace support interventions, and those in a number of other locations, also tended to involve extensive Security Sector Reform and Disarmament Demobilisation and Reintegration schemes, as well as measures to repatriate refugees and Internally Displaced Persons. Despite being expensive in terms of material and commitment, these 'full service' peace support interventions often marked a poor return. Cambodia, Kosovo, Bosnia-Herzegovina, El Salvador, East Timor and many other locations that have experienced peace processes, peace accords and related transitions are often the scene of sullen and disengaged populations, divided polities, and poor and ill-shared economic growth. Add to these armed groups that refuse to disarm and wartime leaders that elude accountability even as they prepare to take power in the post-war climate. Many of the international peace support actors who had championed the liberal peace in the late 1990s and early 2000s lost their enthusiasm for expensive and extensive international intervention in the wars of attrition in post-Taliban Afghanistan and post-Saddam Iraq.

The chief point is that the ambitions of liberal internationalism seem to have been chastened. The goals of democracy and rights seem to have been replaced by less emancipatory and expansive goals that are often linked to security and stabilisation. The case of Libya illustrates the point. In 2011, the United Nations Security Council mandated NATO to protect civilians from 'crimes against humanity' and the language of Responsibility to Protect was invoked. Large-scale missile strikes and air raids by the US, UK, France and Canada permitted Libyans to organise local militias which successfully routed the security forces of Colonel Gaddafi. Over two hundred such militias arose in the power vacuum, eroding the fragile space in which civil society or, for that matter, a peacekeeping mission, might have flourished.[12] After Gaddafi's downfall, instead of a sustained attempt to introduce democracy and good governance, several regional powers intervened to pick sides between competing coalitions of secular parties and Islamists.[13] Those states that had enthusiastically enjoined the regime change were conspicuous by their absence in the post-Gaddafi period. There was little enthusiasm at home for lengthy foreign entanglements that brought apparently few rewards. The primary aim of intervening states has been stabilisation and a staunching of migrant flows to Europe (Libya is regarded as an important transit point). The days of full service peace-support operations seem to be over. Instead, a decade after Gaddafi's removal, Libya continues to be the site of a civil conflict between factions who hope to form a government and the client states who sponsor them. In place of the liberal peacebuilding paradigm, the focus of current UN and regional organization peace missions seems to be divided between security-related stabilization (Central African Republic, Mali, Kosovo) and civilian protection (Darfur, Abyei, South Sudan) with a handful of traditional ceasefire monitoring missions in areas of frozen conflict, such as Cyprus, Kashmir, and the three legacy missions involving Israel and the neighbouring Arab states.[14]

Partially linked to the shrinking peacemaking ambitions of a number of states from the global north, a second trend has been discernible: the rise of other interventionist powers (although their actions could not be described as 'peacemaking'). As the US, UK and others have lost their enthusiasm for liberal internationalism and costly interventions, China, India, Turkey, Brazil and others have become more involved in interventions that can be described as 'conflict management'.[15] Just as western states patterned their preferred variety of peacemaking and gave it liberal flavour, it is unsurprising that interventions by other actors are shaping the nature of contemporary peacemaking. As de Coning and Call note, 'as their influence on global governance increases over time, their approaches to peacebuilding may significantly influence how peacebuilding will be understood and practised …'.[16] Lewis and others have identified a growing trend towards 'Authoritarian Conflict Management' or illiberal forms of stabilisation and security-led interventions that have little interest in rights and emancipation.[17] Instead, they are often motivated by regional power plays (see, for example, the actions of Iran and Saudi Arabia in relation to Yemen) or attempts by a strongman to increase his prestige (see, for example, Turkey's interventions in Libya). It is legitimate to question the extent to which any of these activities are connected to 'peace'. The government of Mahinda Rajapaksa 'ended' the long-running Sri Lankan conflict in 2009 through military force, but at the cost of an estimated 40,000 civilian lives and the incarceration of almost 300,000 Tamils.[18] The direct violence of the conflict can largely be said to have 'ended' but at a huge cost in terms of lives and rights.

While some of the alternative peacemaking actors are decidedly illiberal and authoritarian, it is worth noting another increasingly prominent and professionalised sector: peacebuilding INGOs and NGOs. There has been a significant growth in the number and portfolio of third sector mediation and peacebuilding organisations. In part, this reflects delegation by international organisations and agencies, such as the United Nations Development Programme, who fund, but often do not implement, peacebuilding. It also reflects an expansion of peacebuilding tasks and a recognition that peacebuilding is not a stand-alone task. Instead, depending on context, it is linked with a range of humanitarian, development, governance and inclusion tasks. Thus peacebuilding NGOs can work in multiple sectors and stages of a peace process. In many contexts, international intervening parties have recognised that the state and political parties may be resistant to change and so have devoted considerable attention to civil society in the hope that they can be effective agents of change.[19] Uesugi, in particular, has recognised how important peacebuilding work occurs in the 'mid-space' where connections can be made between the national and the local.[20] While many are small organisations that work locally, others are large transnational concerns that operate in multiple locations. In this respect, it is increasingly important to distinguish purely civil society-led peace work from international or even local NGO-led work. The larger non-state peacebuilding actors often have a corporate structure and have been key drivers in the professionalisation of the peacebuilding sector, the adoption of best practice, and the lending and borrowing of procedures between contexts.[21] The sums of money available in the peacebuilding and peacemaking 'industry' mean that private sector actors are also involved in peace processes and peace accord implementation, meaning that the sector is populated with an increasingly varied range of actors.[22]

A third important factor in the changing peacemaking landscape has been the increasing call for women's participation in peace negotiations and implementation, and an increased focus on gender as an important issue in peacemaking,[23] accompanied by deeper conversations about women's agentic participation in armed conflict.[24] Decades long and indefatigable campaigning by women's groups has thus led to an increased recognition of the gendered nature of peace and conflict, and how Sexual and Gender-Based Violence is a feature of violent conflict. Certainly the UN, peace-focused INGOs, and many states have adopted protocols on women's inclusion and sponsored women-focused programmes.[25]

Despite this programming, and a greater recognition of gender issues, it is worth noting that peacemaking continues to remain gendered and women face structural and direct barriers to participation. A gender analysis of societies emerging from violent conflict illustrates that issues of exclusion persist despite peace accords that often mandate gender rights and inclusion.

A fourth factor that has helped (re)shape the peacemaking and peacebuilding landscape has been an increased focus on the local level. Peacemaking, in the sense of peace negotiations and peace accords, usually occurs at the elite levels of political and militant leaders, perhaps assisted by international organisations of third parties. The expectation is that an elite-level peace, and the security and opportunities that it brings, will enable individuals and communities to enjoy and forge their own version of peace. Yet this 'trickle down' approach to peace has not always materialised and capital city-based peacebuilding will often have a limited reach.[26] Elite-level peace accords do not automatically translate into local-level harmony. Moreover, many of the issues associated with transitions away from violence (for example, refugee return, landmine clearance, livelihood training for former combatants) ultimately occur at the local level. There has been a 'local turn' in relation to peacebuilding with a number of international organisations, INGOs and NGOs recognising that local buy-in is necessary in order to increase the chances of success for peacebuilding programmes and projects.[27] This localisation agenda has manifested itself in the devolution of peacebuilding initiatives to the local level, the hiring of national and local staff, and attempts to reach partnership.[28] The extent to which an emphasis on local participation is rhetorical or meaningful has been the subject of considerable debate.

LEVEL OF ANALYSIS

For understandable reasons, most focus in peace processes is on political and militant elites, and perhaps their international sponsors. These actors have the power to shape the contexts in which others live. Yet, as has been alluded to already in this introductory chapter, peacemaking is a whole-of-society endeavour. While peace might be made nationally and endorsed internationally, it is lived and experienced locally. While a peace accord might be negotiated and agreed in a capital city, or endorsed in a parliament, to take effect it must be enacted through the everyday speech and actions of people in all walks of life. The extent to which people on-the-ground enact the provisions of a peace accord will shape the nature of the peace. It could be that individuals and communities feel empowered by a peace accord, and the security and economic situations that follow it, and so are able to develop the peace into something more expansive than envisaged by the framers of a peace accord. Or it could be that many people retain a cautious outlook following a peace accord and this is reflected in their decisions about where and with whom they live, work, play, worship, study and engage in civic activities.

What is important from the point of view of analysing peace processes and peace accords is that our studies are able to accommodate the interaction between the top-down and the bottom-up. An over-concentration on elite-level politics risks missing an important evidential trail that is cognisant of the multi-scalar nature of peace and conflict. A more balanced approach, that takes into account the local, national, international, transnational and all levels in between, will see that peace and conflict are constituted and reconstituted through constant interaction between different levels of society. While top-down and institutionalised actors have very considerable power, the contexts that they seek to create must be populated and shaped by individuals and communities.

Ultimately, peacemaking is the collection of human endeavours that resolves and prevents war. With this collection we offer analyses, reflections and proposals that, it is hoped, will strengthen the making of peace wherever and whenever it is needed.

Structure of the Book

The book is organised around six thematic areas and approximately three fourths of the material is either entirely new or significantly revised from the previous edition. We begin at Part I with Preparing for Peacemaking by looking at the timing of peacemaking, the cultivation of peace and conflict analysis. Part II addresses Cross-Cutting Issues that are found in many of the cases such as inclusion of armed groups and civil society, public consultations and referendums, as well as the roles of the United Nations. Part III focuses on Negotiation and Mediation while Part IV considers the problem of Violence and Peace Processes. In this section we augment the main discussion with a discussion of the onset and prevention of electoral violence connected to peace processes, as well as individual chapters on DDR and SSR. In Part V we consider Peace

Accords per se, including provisions found in them, trends in accord-making, power-sharing arrangements, human rights and the potential of post-conflict constitutions. Part VI closes the volume with material on transitional justice and peace education.

William Zartman, who has much contributed to thinking on international negotiation and mediation over his decades of scholarship, offers a proactive view of his classic ripeness concept, which has too often been misunderstood by practitioners, who occasionally use it as an excuse for inaction while killing goes on. In his chapter 'Understanding Ripeness', he reminds scholars and practitioners that there is both a descriptive and prescriptive application of ripeness and points to the creative possibilities peacemakers have to alter conflict parties' perceptions of both war and peace. John Paul Lederach's chapter sits well next to William Zartman's. Lederach argues that rather than wait for the 'ripe moment', those involved in conflict need to cultivate that moment. It is an argument for the long-term building of relationships and contexts and fits within the conflict transformation rather than the conflict management or resolution paradigms.

Lisa Schirch takes on the history, application and possibilities of conducting conflict analyses. Her chapter; 'Conflict Analysis: A System's Approach' explains the frameworks for and the obstacles to conducting a conflict analyses or conflict assessment, and reminds practitioners that this must be done especially by those who seek to get involved in peacemaking efforts. Flawed analyses lead to flawed peacemaking efforts. As a conflict intervention itself, it can be carried out by parties to conflict themselves, and can support their peacemaking.

Alex Bellamy provides an up-to-date overview of the international peace architecture. He points out that this architecture is in a permanent evolutionary state and that while it may be fit-for-purpose on paper, it may not be practicable. Krause and Olsson's chapter examines one element of significant development in the international peace architecture and good practice—the Women, Peace and Security agenda. They note how practice has been changing, and how strategies of inclusion deliver more sustainable and pacific outcomes. To a large extent, the Women, Peace and Security agenda has been driven by a number of states and movements based in the global north. Fry and Souillac's chapter, on indigenous approaches to peacemaking, examines agendas that are often locally based and may not connect as fully with worldviews that may be mainstreamed in the global north. Their chapter showcases indigenous approaches to dispute resolution, but also highlights some of the practical and ethical challenges when these approaches sit alongside other approaches that might be championed by states or international organisations.

Amaral considers the increasing use of referendums in peacemaking. While it is clear that referendums, despite their risks, can have an impact on the implementation of a peace agreement, she also notes how they can be used to define the scope of negotiations early on. Amaral describes how the relative inclusivity of peace negotiations can also influence the outcome of the referendum, painting a more complete picture of the interdependence between democratic consultation and peacemaking.

Suzanne Ghais' chapter not only focuses attention on the salutary effects of civil society inclusion and argues that its main benefit to peace is that civil society often keeps the focus on ameliorating the underlying grievances that led to war in the first place, unlike the armed groups. In cases where there are more than one armed group fighting the same conflict, she also makes a strong case for governments to negotiate with all of them at once, rather than sequentially, as this tends to push an erstwhile peace settlement further into the future.

In her chapter 'Refugees, Peacemaking and Durable Solutions to Displacement', Maja Janmyr illustrates the political realities that war refugees confront. Rather than merely being considered subjects in peace accords, the inclusion of refugees and repatriation issues in peacemaking holds the promise of strengthening the eventual peace. As they navigate displacement, asylum, integration and possibly even repatriation, refugees themselves will impact the implementation of peace accords. The massive number of existing refugees displaced by recent wars such as those in Myanmar and Syria loom before us as opportunities to help get the peacemaking right.

Roger Mac Ginty's chapter on timing and sequencing in peace processes examines the construction and uses of time. He notes how powerful actors are able to construct and impose timescapes that suit them, but also notes how some actors are able to ignore (or partially ignore) the imposition of formal timescapes. Chris Mitchell, one of the founders of the study of conflict resolution, gives an overview of mediation; the types of mediation and mediators, the skills required, and their relevance to different types of conflict.

Chester Crocker, Fen Hampson and Pamela Aall, building on their decades of work in international mediation research and practice, look deeply into the fragmented dynamics of conflict parties and the multiplicity of mediators that seek to intervene in contemporary civil wars. The challenges of this dual fragmentation are analysed fully and the would-be peacemaker gains insight into how mediation can be adapted to these realities in their chapter, 'Diffusion vs. Coherence: The Competitive Environment of Multiparty Mediation'.

Niall Ó Dochartaigh in his chapter entitled 'Negotiating Peace in the Shadows' explores the need for secrecy in peace negotiations, hearkening back to Weber and bringing secret peace negotiation into contemporary focus. The justifications for secrecy, as well as the potential for this secrecy to create a space for building trust among the warring parties are explained, even as several of its distortions and pitfalls are revealed.

Kristine Höglund and Desirée Nilsson contribute a chapter entitled 'Violence and Peace Processes'. Affirming that many peace processes are conducted while fighting is still occurring, they explain the reasons and causes for such violence and discuss the actors, and their targets. They then turn their attention to three paradigms within which leaders and peacemakers seek to address and mitigate such violence so that it does not up-end the peacemaking.

The chapter by Inken von Borzyskowski and Richard Saunders 'Peacemaking and Electoral Violence' offers an elegant explanation of the fragility of post-conflict elections (post-civil war elections are twice as likely to result in lethal violence) and the consequent need to protect them from such violence. They have the potential to strengthen the implementation of the peace, or reverse its gains. Helpfully, they point out that inevitable electoral problems can be easily misinterpreted by the parties, deepening mistrust unless adjudication of such issues is perceived as fair. Lowering the cost of complying with adverse electoral outcomes while raising the cost of resorting to violence, as well as assuring more inclusive political systems, can play a role in mitigating post-civil war electoral violence.

Alp Özerdem and Yugi Uesugi's chapters might be best read side-by-side. The chapters, respectively, take the reader through disarmament, demobilisation and reintegration and security sector reform. Taken together these are key tools through which the means of violence (weapons and those with the skills to use them) can be addressed, and the state—often a perpetrator of violence and repression—can be re-orientated towards more civil purposes. Both chapters show that international 'best practice' has evolved with time, and that what might initially seem like straightforward tasks are actually complex.

Christine Bell and Laura Wise take the reader through a state-of-the-art overview of peace accords—based on a large-scale study of contemporary peace accords. The study reveals trends in peacemaking, including the move towards greater complexity in peace accords (covering more issues) and the variation in the types of peace accords. Importantly, their chapter reminds us that peace accords do not just comprise of the 'handshake moments' that might attend major agreements. Also in the mix are the partial and local agreements that are common in many contexts. Timothy Sisk's revised chapter sets out one of the main approaches to negotiated peace: powersharing. He outlines the possible rewards (mainly stabilising conflict-affected contexts) but also the pitfalls—especially related to the relatively short-term 'fix' that consociationalism offers. Jan Pospisil's chapter also addresses one of the main approaches to making peace accords manifest: human rights. But as Pospisil points out, there is often a tension between making peace and the demands that human rights legislation might place on the parties to any accord. In an extension of the justice versus peace argument, human rights agendas may temper the enthusiasm of conflict parties to investigate peace. Yet without serious attention to human rights issues, there is a danger that the peace fails to deliver change and protection to vulnerable populations.

Laurie Nathan's chapter urges peacemakers to consider post-conflict constitutions to be a greater prize than a comprehensive peace agreement itself. By examining cases in which a constitution implemented the peace, he challenges us to see beyond the impermanence of peace agreements no matter how well negotiated, and to prioritise the integration of peace arrangements into a legally binding and permanent social pact that is a constitution.

Roddy Brett and Lina Malagón continue a theme touched on by many chapters in the book: the balance between peace and justice. Their focus on transitional justice examines the evolution of efforts to address 'post-conflict' issues of victimhood, perpetration and dealing with the past. They demonstrate the complex nature of the issue, but also some of the best practice as a number of contexts examine moving towards transformation justice and the need to see justice issues as connected to a wider set of issues.

Alexander Cromwell, in his chapter 'Peace Education as a Peacemaking Tool in Conflict Zones' offers a deep exploration of peace education; the theoretical underpinnings of it as well as a broad sweep of the many ways it can be transformational to individuals and societies seeking to move away from political violence. Peace education is useful for transforming the cultures, attitudes, beliefs and values that drive violent conflict, and the author lauds their utility while noting the limitations, all while noting how to strengthen peace education's transformational potential.

Finally the chapters by Christina Steenkamp and Birte Vogel can be read side-by-side. They deal with post-conflict economic issues. Steenkamp examines how, in a number of cases, conflicts have morphed from political violence to criminal violence. Crimes of acquisition, many of them violent, have become the number one issue in a number of post-peace accord societies and shape and impair the lives of millions. Steenkamp's chapter shows how peace is very much a development issue, a point echoed in Vogel's chapter on everyday economic experiences in peace processes. Building on the growing literature on the everyday and experiential analyses of peace and conflict, Vogel looks beyond the macro-economic context of many post-accord societies to see how peace is lived and experienced—especially through a developmental lens.

NOTES

1. William Shakespeare, *Henry V*, Acts 2 and 5.
2. For this approach see Özerdem, A. and R. Mac Ginty eds., 2019. *Comparing Peace Processes*. London: Routledge.
3. Darby, J. 2003. Lending and Borrowing in Peace Processes. In: J. Darby and R. Mac Ginty eds., *Contemporary Peacemaking: Conflict, Violence, and Peace Processes*. Basingstoke: Palgrave, pp. 245–255.
4. Mueller-Hirth, N. 2017. Temporalities and Victimhood: Time in the Study of Postconflict Societies. *Sociological Forum* 32(1): 186–206.
5. Njeri, S. 2020. Race, Positionality and the Researcher. In: R. Mac Ginty, R. Brett and B. Vogel eds., *The Companion to Peace and Conflict Fieldwork*. London: Palgrave Macmillan, pp. 381–394.
6. Bush, R. 1987. Book Review. *African Affairs* 86(345): 594–596 at 594.

7. Jones, Bruce. 2001. *Peacemaking in Rwanda*. Boulder CO: Lynne Rienner Publishers.
8. Mitchell, Christopher and Landon Hancock, eds. 2012. *Local Peacebuilding and National Peace: Interaction between Grassroots and Elite Processes*. Continuum Publishers; Arjona, Ana (Fall 2016). Institutions, Civilian Resistance, and Wartime Social Order: A Process Driven Natural Experiment in the Colombian Civil War. *Latin American Politics and Society* 58(3); Kaplan, Oliver. 2017. *Resisting War: How Communities Protect Themselves*. Cambridge University Press; Rosen, Noah. 2020. Doctoral dissertation, Seizing a Window of Opportunity: Converting Peace Processes into Local Peace. American University, School of International Service, in progress.
9. Ramsbotham, O., T. Woodhouse and H. Miall. 2016. *Contemporary Conflict Resolution*. Fourth edn. Cambridge: Polity, pp. 34–36.
10. Loizides, N. 2014. Negotiated Settlements and Peace Referendums. *European Journal of Political Research* 53(2): 234–249.
11. Mearsheimer, John J. 2019. Bound to Fail: The Rise and Fall of the Liberal International Order. *International Security* 43(4): 7–50; Ikenberry, G.J. 2018. The End of Liberal International Order? *International Affairs* 94(1): 7–23.
12. Perito, Robert. August 2016. Libya: A Post-Arab Spring Test for Security Sector Reform. CSG Papers, no. 8, Centre for Security Governance.
13. Bøås, M. and M. Utas. 2013. Introduction: Post-Gaddafi Repercussions in the Sahel and West Africa. *Strategic Review for Southern Africa* 35(2): 3–16; Loschi, C., L. Raineri and F. Strazzari. 2018. The Implementation of EU Crisis Response in Libya: Bridging Theory and Practice. EUNPACK Working Paper, January. Accessed at: http://www.eunpack.eu/sites/default/files/publications/2018-01-31%20D6.2%20Working%20paper%20on%20implementation%20of%20EU%20crisis%20response%20in%20Libya.pdf. Last accessed 20 July 2020.
14. As of late 2020, according to the United Nations Department of Peace Operations, https://peacekeeping.un.org/en.
15. Turkey, at least in the early years of Tayyip Erdogan's rule, did indeed have an explicitly peacemaking-orientation in some of its policies, not only with Turkey's Kurds, but also between Iran

and the United States, within Iraq, Lebanon, Somalia, Bosnia, Kosovo and elsewhere. See Eralp, Doga Ulas, ed. 2016. *Turkey as a Mediator: Stories of Success and Failure.* Lexington Books. Sadly, Erdogan's consolidation of power at home coincided with more coercive policies, such as interventions in Syria and Libya on behalf of Islamist allies.
16. De Coning, C. and C.T. Call. 2017. Introduction: Why Examine Rising Powers' Role in Peacebuilding? In C.T. Call and C. de Coning eds., *Rising Powers and Peacebuilding: Breaking the Mold?* pp. 1–12 at p. 5.
17. Lewis, D., J. Heathershaw and N. Megoran. 2018. "Illiberal Peace" Authoritarian Modes of Conflict Management. *Cooperation and Conflict* 53(4): 486–506.
18. United Nations. 2011. Report of the Secretary General's Panel of Experts on Accountability in Sri Lanka. 31 March, p. 41. Accessed at: https://www.securitycouncilreport.org/atf/cf/%7B65BF CF9B-6D27-4E9C-8CD3-CF6E4FF96FF9%7D/POC%20Rep% 20on%20Account%20in%20Sri%20Lanka.pdf. Last accessed 15 July 2020; Ganguly, M. 2016. Sri Lanka after the Tigers. *Foreign Affairs*, 17 February. Accessed at https://www.foreignaffairs. com/articles/sri-lanka/2016-02-17/sri-lanka-after-tigers. Last accessed 15 July 2020.
19. Barnes, Catherine. 2002. Democratizing Peacemaking Processes: Strategies and Dilemmas for Public Participation. In: Catherine Barnes ed., *Owning the Process: Public Participation in Peace-Making, Accord* 13. London: Conciliation Resources; McKeon, Celia. July 2004. Public Participation in Peace Processes: Comparative Experience and Relevant Principles. BADIL Expert Seminar 4 Paper; Wanis-St. John, Anthony and Darren Kew. 2008. Civil Society and Peace Negotiations: Confronting Exclusion. *International Negotiation* 13(1); Paffenholz. T. 2009. Civil Society and Peacebuilding: Summary Results for a Comparative Research Project. Geneva: CCDP Working Paper 4.
20. Uesugi, Y. 2020. Introduction. In: Y. Uesugi ed., *Hybrid Peacebuilding in Asia*. Cham: Palgrave Macmillan, pp. 1–14 at p. 10.
21. Kallman, M.E. 2020. *The Death of Idealism: Development and Anti-Politics in the Peace Corps*. New York: Columbia University Press.

22. Cornish, C. 2019. An Industry of Peacemakers Capitalises on Global Conflict. 22 October. *Financial Times*. Accessed at: https://www.ft.com/content/1ef88c8e-f0dd-11e9-bfa4-b25f11f42901. Last accessed 18 July 2020.
23. Bell, C. and C.O'Rourke. 2010. Peace Agreements or Pieces of Paper? The Impact of UNSC Resolution 1325 on Peace Processes and Their Agreements. *International and Comparative Law Quarterly* 9(3): 358–378.
24. Barsa, Michelle, Olivia Holt-Ivry, Allison Muehlenbeck et al. March 2016. Inclusive Ceasefires: Women, Gender, and a Sustainable End to Violence. Paper presented at the International Studies Association's 57th Annual Convention, Atlanta, Georgia; Miranda Allison. 2011. 'In the War Front We Never Think That We Are Women': Women, Gender, and the Liberation Tamil Tigers of Eelam. In: Laura Sjoberg, and Caron Gentry eds. *Women, Gender and Terrorism*. University of Georgia Press.
25. Olsson, L. and T.I. Gizelis eds., 2015. *Gender, Peace and Security: Implementing UN Security Council Resolution 1325*. London: Routledge.
26. Öjendal, J. and S. Ou. 2015. The 'Local Turn' Saving Liberal Peacebuilding? Unpacking Virtual Peace in Cambodia. *Third World Quarterly* 36(5): 929–949.
27. Randazzo, E. 2016. The Paradoxes of the 'Everyday': Scrutinizing the Local Turn in Peacebuilding. *Third World Quarterly* 37(8): 1351–1370.
28. Madsen, D.H. 2018. Localising the Global—Resolution 1325 as a Tool for Promoting Women's Rights and Gender Equality in Rwanda. *Women's Studies International Forum* 66: 70–78.

PART I

Preparing for Peace

CHAPTER 2

Understanding Ripeness: Making and Using Hurting Stalemates

I William Zartman

While most studies on peaceful settlement of disputes see the substance of the proposals for a solution as the key to a successful resolution of conflict, a growing focus of attention shows that a second and equally necessary key lies in the timing of efforts for resolution.[1] Parties resolve their conflict only when they are ready to do so—when alternative—usually unilateral—means of achieving a satisfactory result are blocked and the parties feel that they are in an uncomfortable and costly predicament. At that ripe moment, they are more likely to grab on to proposals, including those that have been in the air for a long time and that only now appear attractive.

The idea of a ripe moment lies at the fingertips of diplomats. "Ripeness of time is one of the absolute essences of diplomacy," wrote John Campbell.[2] "You have to do the right thing at the right time," without

I. W. Zartman (✉)
School of Advanced International Studies, Johns Hopkins University, Washington, DC, USA
e-mail: zartman@jhu.edu

© The Author(s), under exclusive license to Springer Nature Switzerland AG 2022
R. Mac Ginty and A. Wanis-St. John (eds.), *Contemporary Peacemaking*, https://doi.org/10.1007/978-3-030-82962-9_2

indicating specific causes. Henry Kissinger did better, recognizing that "stalemate is the most propitious condition for settlement."[3] Conversely, practitioners often are heard to say that certain mediation initiatives are not advisable because the conflict just is not yet ripe. In mid-1992, in the midst of ongoing conflict, the Iranian deputy foreign minister noted, "The situation in Azerbaijan is not ripe for such moves for mediation."[4]

The concept of a ripe moment centers on the parties' perception of a Mutually Hurting Stalemate (MHS), optimally associated with an impending, past or recently avoided catastrophe.[5] The concept is based on the notion that when the parties find themselves locked in a conflict which they cannot escalate to victory and this deadlock is painful to both of them (although not necessarily in equal degree or for the same reasons), they seek an alternative policy or Way Out (WO). The catastrophe provides a deadline or a lesson indicating that pain can be sharply increased if something is not done about it now; catastrophe is a useful extension of MHS but is not necessary either to its definition or to its existence. Using different images, the stalemate has been termed the Plateau, a flat and unending terrain without relief, and the catastrophe the Precipice, the point where things suddenly and predictably get worse. If the notion of mutual blockage is too static to be realistic, the concept may be stated dynamically as a moment when the upper hand slips and the lower hand rises, both parties moving toward equality, with both movements carrying pain for the parties.[6] The notion of the MHS is important because, unlike some current discussions of "readiness," it tells *why* parties are ready to envisage settlement and that is crucial to the entire dynamics of the management process.

The mutually hurting stalemate is grounded in cost–benefit analysis, fully consistent with public choice notions of rationality[7] and war termination and negotiation,[8] which assume that a party will pick the alternative which it prefers, and that a decision to change is induced by increasing pain associated with the present (conflictual) course.[9] In game theoretic terms, it marks the transformation of the situation in the parties' perception from a prisoners' dilemma (PDG) into a chicken dilemma game (CDG)[10] or, in other terms, the realization that the status quo or no negotiation (DD, the southeast corner in a game-theory matrix) is a negative-sum situation, and that to avoid the zero-sum outcomes mutually blocked (CD and DC, the northeast and southwest corners) the positive-sum outcome (CC, the northwest corner) must be explored.

Ripeness is necessarily a perceptual event, although as with any subjective perception, there are likely to be objective referents to be perceived. These can be highlighted by a mediator or an opposing party if they are not immediately recognized by the party itself, and resisted so long as the conflicting party refuses or is otherwise able to block out their perception. But it is the perception of the objective condition, not the condition itself, that makes for a MHS. If the parties do not recognize "clear evidence" (in someone else's view) that they are in an impasse, a Mutually Hurting Stalemate has not (yet) occurred, and if they do perceive themselves to be in such a situation, no matter how flimsy the "evidence," the MHS is present.

The other element necessary for a ripe moment is less complex and also perceptional: a Way Out. Parties do not have to be able to identify a specific solution, only a sense that a negotiated solution is possible for the searching and that the other party shares that sense and the willingness to search too. Without a sense of a Way Out, the push associated with the MHS would leave the parties with nowhere to go. Spokespersons often indicate whether they do or do not feel that a deal can be made with the other side and that requirement—i.e., the sense that concessions will be reciprocated, not just banked—exists, particularly when there is a change in that judgment.[11]

Ripeness is only a condition, necessary but not sufficient for the initiation of negotiations. It is not self-fulfilling or self-implementing. It must be seized, either directly by the parties or, if not, through the persuasion of a mediator. Thus, it is not identical to its results, which are not part of its definition, and is therefore not tautological. Not all ripe moments are so seized and turned into negotiations, hence the importance of specifying the meaning and evidence of ripeness so as to indicate when conflicting or third parties can fruitfully initiate negotiations.[12] Although ripeness theory is not predictive in the sense that it can tell when a given situation will become ripe, it is prognostic in the sense of identifying the elements necessary (even if not sufficient) for the productive inauguration of negotiations. This type of analytical prediction is the best that can be obtained in social science, where stronger predictions could only be ventured by eliminating free choice (including the human possibility of blindness, mistakes, and creativity). As such it is of great prescriptive value to policymakers seeking to know when and how to begin a peace process, and what to do when the requisite conditions do not now obtain.

Finding a ripe moment requires research and intelligence studies to identify the objective and subjective elements.[13] Subjective expressions of pain, impasse, and inability to bear the cost of further escalation, related to objective evidence of stalemate, data on numbers and nature of casualties and material costs, and/or other such indicators of MHS, along with expressions of a sense of a Way Out, can be researched on a regular basis in a conflict to establish whether ripeness exists. Researchers would look for evidence, for example, whether the fluid military balance in conflict—such as Mountainous Karabakh, or the Sudanese or Sri Lankan civil wars, for example—has given rise at any time to a perception of MHS by the parties, and to a perception by authoritative spokespersons that the parties ready to seek a solution to the conflict, or, to the contrary, whether indications reinforce the conclusion that any mediation is bound to fail because one or both parties believes in the possibility or necessity of escalating out of the current impasse to achieve a decisive military victory. Research and intelligence would seek to learn why Bosnia in the wartorn summer of 1994 was not ripe for a negotiated settlement and mediation would fail, and why it was in November 1995 and mediation could encourage that condition to move toward an agreement.[14] Similarly, research would indicate that there was no chance of mediating a settlement in the Ethiopia-Eritrean conflict in the early 1980s, early 1990s, or mid 1990s, or in the Sudanese conflicts in the 1990s or the early 2000s, the skills of President Carter and other mediators notwithstanding, because the components of ripeness were not present.[15] Analysts would also understand the need of skilled UN mediators Kofi Annan and Lakhdar Brahimi for decisive support from the UN Security Council that mandated their efforts in order for the warring parties in Syria to realize that they were in a MHS with a WO in 2012–2014, until a non-supporting UNSC member, Russia, broke the stalemate with direct military assistance to Bashar al-Asad.[16] They would also note that the UNSC gave the necessary support to UN mediator Jamal Benomar in October 2011 to ripen the Yemeni parties' perceptions of a MHS and enable agreement to end (one round of) the Yemeni civil war but that it did not give such backing to its own mandate given to Kofi Annan and Lakhdar Brahimi as they tried to ripen and mediate the Syrian conflict and consequently failed.[17]

While ripeness has not always been seized upon to open negotiations, there have been many occasions when it has come into play, as identified by both analysts and practitioners. A number of studies beyond the original examination[18] have used and tested the notion of ripeness in regard to negotiations in Zimbabwe, Namibia and Angola, Eritrea, South Africa, Philippines, Cyprus, Iran-Iraq, Israel, Mozambique, Cuba, Sudan, Pakistan, Northern Ireland, among others.[19] Touval's work on the Middle East was particularly important in launching the idea.[20] In general, these studies have found the concept applicable and useful as an explanation for the successful initiation of negotiations or their failure, while in some cases proposing refinements to the concept.

The most important refinements carry the theory onto a second level of questions about the effects of each side's pluralized politics on both the perceptions and uses of ripeness. What kinds of internal political conditions are helpful both for perceiving ripeness and for turning that perception into the initiation of promising negotiations? The careful case study by Stephen J. Stedman of the negotiations for Rhodesian's independence as Zimbabwe and by Dan Lieberfeld of Middle East and South African negotiations takes the concept into the complexities of internal dynamics.[21] Stedman specifies that some but not all parties must perceive the hurting stalemate, that patrons rather than parties may be the agents of perception, that the military in each party is the crucial element in perceiving the stalemate, and that the way out is as important an ingredient as the stalemate in that all parties may well see victory in the alternative outcome prepared by negotiation (although some parties will be proven wrong in that perception).[22] They also highlight the potential of leadership change for the subjective perception of a MHS where it had not been seen previously in the same objective circumstances, and of threats to incumbent leadership from domestic rivals—rather than from the enemy—as the source of impending catastrophe. In a war in Syria that has shown no signs of ripeness among the conflicting parties for 8 years, a move in November 2018 to examine negotiation possibilities may have indicated a growing sense of ripeness on the part of their sponsors (Russia, Turkey, France, and Germany).

The work of Thomas Ohlson[23] and Dean Pruitt[24] has helped push the notion of a Way Out more deeply into the negotiation process, once started. While the positive prospect of a solution does not seem, by all evidence, to have the power of a MHS in inducing negotiations, once they have begun, it is the challenge for negotiators to reinforce the push of the MHS with the pull of a WO gradually coming into view as a Mutually Enticing Opportunity (MEO).[25] MEOs are developed by negotiators in the course of negotiations. Unlike a MHS, a MEO does not depend on subjective perceptions of objective external relations but rather of perceived possibilities and creations of the negotiators themselves. The negotiators must provide or be provided with prospects for a more attractive future to pull them out of their conflict, once a MHS has pushed them into negotiations. The seeds of the pull factor begin with the Way Out that the parties vaguely perceive as part of the initial ripeness, but that general sense of possibility needs to be developed and fleshed out into the vehicle for an agreement, a formula for settlement that the negotiating parties design during negotiations. When a MEO is not developed in the negotiations, they remain truncated and unstable, even if they reach a conflict management agreement to suspend violence, as in the 1984 and 1999 Lusaka agreements or the 1994 Karabakh ceasefire.[26]

Yet, in complication, it is important for the negotiations—or their sponsors—to strengthen the objective conditions on which the perception is based. This may take diplomatic pressures to back up a mediator who is seeking to ripen the conflicting parties' perceptions, but it may also take military action to block one side to keep both parties in the vise of ripeness and to even up the sides. Later in the process, it may take measures keep alive the sense of a MHS lest its push effect wane and the pressure of ripeness dissolve—and all this while keeping the positive pull of the evolving MEO alive. Thus, the threat of a return to violence may be seen, not as a breakoff of the negotiations, but as a reinforced impulse for negotiations. This need is reinforced by a third set of contributions that come from the seminal work of Kahneman and Tversky on prospect theory, which shows that parties are more risk averse in protecting against losses than in achieving gains, and that losses are given around twice the value of gains.[27] The implications are that agreement on equivalence in a negotiated outcome becomes even more difficult than figures on the basis of intrinsic values, and also that threats and warnings are more potent to bring about a MHS (itself a locked threat) than inducements. Such findings are antithetical to the notion of negotiation as building reconciliation or as giving something to get something.

The original formulation of the theory added a third element to the definition of ripeness, the presence of a Valid Spokesman for each side.[28] As a structural element it is of a different order than the other two defining perceptual elements. Nonetheless, it remains of second level importance, as Stedman and Lieberfield have pointed out. The presence of strong leadership recognized as representative of each party and that can deliver that party's compliance to the agreement is a necessary (while alone insufficient) condition for productive negotiations to begin, or indeed to end successfully. Often the difference between continued conflict and perception of a ripe moment and follow-through involves the change of leadership, in part to save the first leader from having to reverse his policy stand before his followers and his public.

Diplomatic memoirs have explicitly referred to ripeness by its MHS component. Chester A. Crocker, US Assistant Secretary of State for Africa between 1981 and 1989, patiently mediated an agreement for the withdrawal of Cuban troops from Angola and of South African troops from Namibia, then to become independent. For years a mutual hurting stalemate, and hence productive negotiations, had eluded the parties. "The second half of 1987 was ... the moment when the situation 'ripened'."[29] Military escalations on both sides and bloody confrontations in southeastern Angola beginning in November 1987 and in southwestern Angola in May 1988 ended in a draw. "By late June 1988, the ... Techipa-Calueque clashes in southwestern Angola confirmed a precarious military stalemate. That stalemate was both the reflection and the cause of underlying political decisions. By early May, my colleagues and I convened representatives of Angola, Cuba, and South Africa in London for face-to-face, tripartite talks. The political decisions leading to the London meeting formed a distinct sequence, paralleling military events on the ground, like planets moving one by one into a certain alignment."[30] In his conclusion, Crocker identifies specific signs of ripeness, while qualifying that "correct timing is a matter of feel and instinct."[31] The American mediation involved building diplomatic moves that paralleled the growing awareness of the parties, observed by the mediator, of the hurting stalemate in which they found themselves.

Alvaro de Soto, Assistant Secretary General for Political Affairs at the United Nations, also endorsed the necessity of ripeness in his mission to mediate a peace in El Salvador. After chronicling a series of failed initiatives, he points to the importance of the FMLN's November 1989 offensive, the largest of the war, which penetrated the main cities including the capital but failed to dislodge the government. "The silver lining was that it was, almost literally, a defining moment—the point at which it became possible to seriously envisage a negotiation. The offensive showed the FMLN that they could not spark a popular uprising, ... The offensive also showed the rightist elements in government, and elites in general, that the armed forces could not defend them, let alone crush the insurgents ... Neither side could defeat the other. As the dust settled, the notion that the conflict could not be solved by military means, and that its persistence was causing pain that could no longer be endured, began to take shape. The offensive codified the existence of a mutually hurting stalemate. The conflict was ripe for a negotiated solution."[32]

In Yugoslavia, Secretary of State James Baker looked for a ripe moment during his quick trip to Belgrade in June 1991 and reported the same day to President George Bush that he did not find it: "My gut feeling is that we won't produce a serious dialogue on the future of Yugoslavia until all the parties have a greater sense of urgency and danger."[33] Richard Holbrooke calls this "a crucial misreading," and had his own image of the MHS (or the upper hand slipping and the underdog rising). "The best time to hit a serve is when the ball is suspended in the air, neither rising nor falling. We felt this equilibrium had arrived, or was about to, on the battlefield [in October 1995]."[34] He saw a better moment created by the Croatian Krajina offensive in August 1995.[35] It took the offensive, coupled with NATO bombing, to create a mutually hurting stalemate composed of a temporary Serb setback and a temporary and unsustainable Croat advance to instill a perception of the ripe moment in the mind of Bosnian President Izetbegovic. A State Department official stated, "Events on the ground have made it propitious to try again to get the negotiations started. The Serbs are on the run a bit. That won't last forever. So we are taking the obvious major step ...."[36]

In his parting report as Under-Secretary-General of the United Nations, Marrack Goulding specifically cited the literature on ripeness in discussing the selection of conflicts to be handled by an overburdened UN. "Not all conflicts are 'ripe' for action by the United Nations (or any other third party) .... It therefore behooves the Secretary-General to be selective and to recommend action only in situations where he judges that the investment of scarce resources is likely to produce a good return (in terms of preventing, managing and resolving conflict.)."[37]

Some practitioners have given a more nuanced endorsement of the concept, although not all have read the conceptual fine print carefully. Itamar Rabinovich, the careful historian and skilful ambassador in the failed negotiations between Israel and Syria, terms the concept "a very useful analytical tool ... but ... less valuable as an operational tool," but he expects that "ripeness will account for the success of negotiations" rather than simply provide a necessary but insufficient condition for their initiation.[38]

Other commentators have also missed the point. John Paul Lederach, a good analyst and Track 2 practitioner, confuses the mediator's hopes with the protagonists' "unripe" perceptions; he misses the value of the theory in alerting the mediator to the difficulties of instilling a perception (as Holbrooke did), grasping a moment (as deSoto did), or pursuing a long-term change once the negotiation/mediation process is begun (as Crocker did). Happily Lederach then turns around and provides a good understanding of the ripening process, as discussed below.[39]

Resistant Reactions

Ripeness is not just waiting for the apple to fall. One complication with the operation of a hurting stalemate arises when increased pain increases resistance rather than reducing it (it must be remembered that while ripeness is a necessary precondition for negotiation, not all ripeness leads to negotiation). Although this may be considered "bad," irrational, or even adolescent behavior, it is a common reaction and one that may be natural and functional. Reinforcement is the normal response to opposition: "don't give up without a fight," "no gain without pain," "hold the course, whatever the cost," "when the going gets tough, the tough get going," and "if at first you don't succeed, try, try again."[40] When the impasse became tighter in 2012 in Syria, it only led the government and the rebels to dig in deeper and look for outside support. Asad found it in the Russians, whereas the resistance came away empty from the US.

The imposition of pain to a present course in conflict is not likely to lead to a search for alternative measures without first being tested. The theory takes this into account by referring to the parties' perception that they cannot escalate an exit from their stalemate, implying efforts to break out before giving in, but it cannot predict when the realization will sink in. There are indications of the type of test required to be decisive: a sharp confrontation that leaves both sides reeling. The military confrontation in early 1988 in Angola or in late 1989 in San Salvador, plus the return of white body bags to South Africa, both referred to above, brought the parties to their senses. It often takes quite a while for parties wholly committed to a struggle to see that they are stuck in a stalemate and need to seek other ways to get out of it. There do not appear to be any similarly effective sharp and indecisive combats to date in the twenty-first century; loss of troops and massacres of civilians in Syria, Afghanistan,

Yemen, or Gaza did not dissuade authorities or rebels that "it can just go on like it is," in the words of an Israeli diplomat.

Furthermore, pressure on a party in conflict often leads to the psychological reaction of worsening the image of the opponent, a natural tendency that has the functional advantage of justifying resistance, but while lessening chances of reconciliation. Particular types of adversaries such as "true believers," "warriors," or "hardliners" are unlikely to be led to compromise by increased pain; instead, pain is likely to justify renewed struggle.[41] Similarly, qualifying all opponents as "terrorist" raises barriers to negotiation, empathy, or concessions. Justified struggles call for greater sacrifices, which absorb increased pain and strengthen determination. The cycle is functional and self-protecting. To this type of reaction, it is the other side's release of pain or its admission of its own pain that justifies relaxation; when the opponent admits the error of its ways, the true believer can claim the vindication of its efforts which permits a management of the conflict.[42] Yet, escalation can lead to the perception of ripeness, when it shows that the cycle has reached its end and has actually produced awareness of the MHS.[43]

Implications

Inescapable as it may be, the most unfortunate implications of the notion of a hurting stalemate lie in its dependence on conflict. In itself, the concept explains the difficulty of achieving preemptive conflict resolution and preventive diplomacy, even though nothing in the definition of the MHS requires it to take place at the height of the conflict or at a high level of violence. The internal (and unmediated) negotiations in South Africa between 1990 and 1994 stand out as a striking case of negotiations opened (and pursued) on the basis of a MHS perceived by both sides aware of impending catastrophe, not of present casualties.[44]

Indeed, nothing in the idea of ripeness calls for the necessity of present conflict at all. Conflict may be future of impending, or may even be a problem, heavy with consequences but not necessarily violent. Parties in a "trade war" may escalate to the point of imposing pain and damage on each other; at some point they realize such efforts would require more escalation and pain than they deem desirable, and they turn to negotiation. The course of hardline bargaining during 2017 and 2018 between US, Mexico, and Canada yielding the formation of a post-NAFTA US-Mexico-Canada Agreement are a rich example, and the similar relations between US and China will produce similar material for analysis, whatever the outcome. Even further afield, most countries feel themselves stalemated by a nature bent on changing its climate and they perceive a future pain descending on generations to come, which leads them to negotiate, somewhat; the US is of two minds on both the pain vs cost and on the possibility of a WO, let alone a MEO. The notion is a powerful and focusing tool of analysis.

Despite the absence of a linear relationship, the greater the objective evidence, the greater the potential for a subjective perception of the stalemate and its pain, and this evidence is more likely to come late, when all other courses of action and possibilities of escalation have been exhausted. In notable cases, a long period of conflict is required before the MHS sinks in.[45] Yet, given the infinite number of potential conflicts which have not reached "the heights," evidence would suggest that perception of an MHS occurs either (and optimally) at a low level of conflict, where it is relatively easy to begin preemptive problem-solving, or, in salient cases, at rather high levels of conflict. The ozone issue was handled relatively early, in the 1987 Montreal Protocol, before the pain had descended on the world[46]; arms control treaties, from the Anti-Ballistic Missile Treaty (ABM) to the Strategic Arms Limitation Treaty (SALT I) and the Strategic Arms Reduction Treaty (START I) all were preemptive measures by parties who felt a dangerously hurting stalemate looming ahead, a sense often made more acute by punctual crises in other areas of the parties' relationship; and in 1989 Zambia and Zaire undertook a series of technical adjustments of their border along a winding river and local roads to prevent embitterment of local hurt and stalemate. These are a highly diverse collection of cases where negotiations took place early to head off the perspective of MHSs in the foreseeable future if nothing were to be done.

A set of counterexamples comes from Namibia: President Carter launched a preventive mediation effort of conflict management under Secretary Cyrus Vance in the late 1970s before the violent conflict had actually broken out but was unable to attract attention to the need for a solution, whereas President Reagan relaunched the effort under Assistant Secretary Chester Crocker throughout the 1980s, when the conflict had become heated, with the process and results described above. Early negotiation before ripeness was more difficult than when the MHS clearly came to a head. Thus, conflicts not treated "early" appear to require a high level of intensity for a MHS perception to kick in and negotiations toward a solution to begin. To ripen for resolution at least those conflicts that have not been managed early, one must raise the level of conflict until a stalemate is reached, and then further until it begins to hurt, and then still more, to ensure the perception of pain, and then still more yet, to create the perception of an impending catastrophe as well. The ripe moment becomes the godchild of brinkmanship.

As the (misleading) image of ripeness implies, MHS can be a very fleeting opportunity, a moment to be seized lest it pass, but it can be of a long duration, waiting to be noticed and acted upon by mediators. The moment was brief in Bosnia but longer in Angola; it is claimed that is was only potentially (objectively) present in 2011 in Syria but it was present for perhaps a year in 2001 in Cyprus until the precondition of an agreement in order for Cyprus to accede to the EU was lifted at the end of the year.[47] In fact, failure to seize the moment often hastens its passing, as parties lose faith in the possibility of a negotiated Way Out or regain hope in the possibility of unilateral escalation. Worse yet, when a moment of joint perception of a hurting stalemate passes without producing any results, parties frequently fall back on their previous perceptions that the other side will never be ready and the only course left is to hope and fight for a total realization of one's goals, no matter how long it takes: "Nothing is acceptable but a Palestinian/Israeli state with Jerusalem as its capital." By the same token, the possibility of long duration often dulls the urgency of rapid seizure.

Yet, it must be clear: there may be no subjective ripeness whatever the objective signs may indicate, if the party does not want to or feels it cannot negotiate, that is make compromises and give something to get something. In Syria, there was never a ripe moment because President Asad felt that he *must* win, for his people (whom he killed), his father, and himself, and the resistance felt it *must* win because in its disorganization it was afraid to negotiate with a steely, united Asad, who had always tricked the opposition in previous negotiations. So there were no negotiations, despite the tireless efforts of the Personal Envoys of the UN Secretary-General.[48] Even the best of mediators could not arouse a sense that the war was unwinnable.

Practitioners and students of conflict management would also like to think that there could be a more positive prelude to negotiation, through the pull of an attractive outcome without the push of a mutually hurting stalemate. Real cases are rare, as explained by prospect theory that shows prevented losses are valued more than possible gains.[49] In any case, even positive inducements appear positive only against the unpleasant or hurting situation in which the parties find themselves. As in other ripe moments, these occasions provided an opportunity for improvement, but from a tiring rather than more strongly painful deadlock.[50] In some views, the attraction lies in a possibility of winning more cheaply than by conflict (paradoxically, a shared perception), or else a possibility of sharing power that did not exist before.[51] In other views, enticement comes in the form of a new ingredient, the chance for improved relations with the mediating third party, that helps the parties out of their previous stalemate.[52] In other instances, the opportunity for a settlement grows more attractive because the issue of the conflict becomes depassé, no longer justifying the bad relations with the other party or the mediator that it imposed. These types of perception are similar to those that accompany preemptive negotiation faced with a future MHS.

Unripeness should not constitute an excuse for second or third parties' inaction, even if one or both of the conflicting parties are mired in their hopes of escalation and victory. It is a rich advantage of ripeness theory that it emphasizes subjective perceptions, not just objective elements. When a conflict or problem is not ripe—no MHS and no WO—the job of third parties is to ripen. "If you go the other route, letting things happen and you only move when it's ripe you're role is relatively passive," Kofi Annan summarized on his Syrian experience. "There are moments in a crisis when things are ripe, but before you get there, there are options. You can help create the moments, you can help create the environment."[53] Only when this is accomplished can mediators turn to what is considered to be their basic task—helping the parties find an outcome agreeable to both sides. And as seen in the role of the MHS in the negotiations, the mediator must continue to keep the parties' aware of the hurting stalemate that brought them into negotiations and will return if they let the process drop. If ripeness were a matter of objective conditions alone, ripening would be out of the mandate of the mediators and in the hands of hard pressures and changed facts on the ground.

Basically, ripening involves inculcating the perception in each party that it cannot win, that persistence is costly, that this perception is shared on the other side, and that a joint search for a solution is possible. Unfortunately, the first message is not a welcome one and may cost the mediator its entry into upper chambers.[54] Involving Friends of the Mediator and friends of the conflicting parties, encouraging comparisons with (and differences from) other conflicts, and emphasizing the harmful effect of passing time are adjuncts to persuasion.[55] Although not within the mediator's mandate, objective ripening is part of the possibilities of the mandators. Diplomatic pressures and sanctions, economic inducements and disincentives, even military measures can change facts on the ground sufficiently to attract the parties' attention to pain and stalemate. These are ultimate measures, but may be necessary for effective ripening, as Sinai, Dayton, and even Namibia showed, and Syria also did, in the negative.

The other possibility for interested parties in yet-unripe conflicts is to position themselves for eventual involvement. Crocker states very forcefully (in boldface in the original) that "the absence of 'ripeness' does not tell us to walk away and do nothing. Rather, it helps us to identify obstacles and suggests ways of handling them and managing the problem until resolution becomes possible."[56] Crocker's own experience indicates, before and above all, the importance of being present and available to the contestants while waiting for the moment to ripen in their perception, so as to be able to seize it when it occurs, listing a number of important insights for positioning[57]:

- Give the parties some fresh ideas to shake them up;
- Play the "what-if" game to loosen thinking;
- Keep new ideas flexible to avoid getting bogged down in details;
- Establish basic principles to form building blocks of a settlement;
- Become an indispensable channel of communication for negotiation;
- Establish an acceptable mechanism for negotiation; and
- Cultivate long-term relationships.

Other strategies include preliminary explorations of items identified with diagnosis and pre-negotiations[58]:

- Identify the parties necessary to a settlement;
- Identify the issues to be resolved, and separate out issues not now resolvable;
- Air alternatives to the current conflict course;
- Establish contacts and bridges between the parties;
- Clarify costs and risks involved in seeking settlement;
- Establish requirements; and

- Develop support for settlement within each party's domestic constituency.

Since ripeness results from a combination of objective and subjective elements, both need attention. If some objective elements are present, persuasion is the obvious diplomatic challenge. Such was the message of Kissinger in the Sinai withdrawal negotiations, Crocker in the Angolan negotiations, Holbrooke in the Bosnian mediation, and Annan and Brahimi in the Syrian mediation, among many others, emphasizing the absence of real alternatives (stalemate) and the high cost of the current conflict course (pain).[59]

Practitioners need to employ all their skills and apply all the concepts of negotiation and mediation to take advantage of the necessary but insufficient condition of ripeness in order to turn it into a successful peacemaking process when it exists, or to help produce it or stand ready to act on it when it does not as yet.

NOTES

1. I W Zartman, "Ripeness: The Hurting Stalemate and Beyond," in Paul Stern and Daniel Druckman, eds., *International Conflict Resolution after the Cold War* (Washington, DC: National Academy Press, 2000).
2. John Campbell, *Successful Negotiation: Trieste* (Princeton: Princeton University Press, 1976), p 73.
3. Henry Kissinger, *New York Times*, 12 October 1974.
4. Agence France Presse, 17 May 1992.
5. I W Zartman & Maureen Berman, *The Practical Negotiator* (New Haven: Yale University Press, 1982), pp 66–78; I W Zartman, "The Strategy of Preventive Diplomacy in Third World Conflicts," in Alexander George, ed., *Managing US-Soviet Rivalry* (Boulder: Westview, 1983); Saadia Touval & I W Zartman, eds., *International Mediation in Theory and Reality* (Boulder: Westview, 1985), pp 11, 258–60; I W Zartman, *Ripe for Resolution* (New York: Oxford University Press, 1985/1989).
6. The same logic has been identified in regard to domestic elite settlements, produced by costly and inconclusive conflict; "Precisely because no single faction has been a clear winner and all factions have more nearly been losers, elites are disposed to

compromise if at all possible" (M Burton & J Higley, "Elite Settlement," *American Sociological Review* LII 2:295–307 (1992) at p 298).
7. A Sen, *Collective Choice and Social Welfare* (San Francisco: Aldine, 1970); K Arrow, *Social Change and Individual Values* (New Haven: Yale University Press, 1963); M Olson, *The Logic of Collective Action* (New York: Schocken, 1965).
8. S Brams, *Negotiation Games* (New York: Routledge, 1990); Q Wright, "The Escalation of Conflict," *Journal of Conflict Resolution* IX 4:434–49 (1965).
9. Timing can refer to many things other than costs and benefits, including domestic political schedules, generational socialization, and attitudinal maturation, among others. For an excellent analysis based on the first, see William B Quandt, *Camp David* (Washington: Brookings, 1986); on the second, see R Samuels et al., *Political Generations and Political Development* (Boston: Lexington, 1977). These are perfectly valid approaches, but ultimately they can be reduced to cost/benefits, calculated or affected by different referents. To note this is not to deny their separate value, but simply to justify the conceptual focus used here.
10. S Brams, *Superpower Games* (New Haven: Yale University Press, 1985); Joshua Goldstein, "The Game of Chicken in International Relations," School of International Service, American University, 1998.
11. I W Zartman & J Aurik, "Power Strategies in De-Escalation," in L Kriesberg & J Thornson, eds., *Timing the De-Escalation of International Conflicts* (Syracuse: Syracuse University Press, 1991).
12. At the outset, confusion may arise from the fact that not all "negotiations" appear to be the result of a ripe moment. Negotiation may be a tactical interlude, a breather for rest and rearmament, a sop to external pressure, without any intent of opening a sincere search for a joint outcome (F C Ikle, *How Nations Negotiate* [New York: Harper & Row, 1964]). Thus the need for quotation marks, or for some elusive modifier such as "serious" or "sincere" negotiations. It is difficult at the outset to determine whether negotiations are indeed serious or sincere, and indeed "true" and "false" motives may be indistinguishably mixed in the minds of the actors themselves at the beginning. Yet, it is the outset which is the subject of

the theory. The best that can be done is to note that many theories contain a reference to a "false" event or an event in appearance only, to distinguish it from an event that has a defined purpose. Indeed, a sense of ripeness may be required to turn negotiations for side effects into negotiations to resolve conflict.

13. I W Zartman & A de Soto, *Timing Mediation Initiatives* (USIP for the UN Mission Support Unit, 2010).
14. S Touval "Coercive Mediation on the Road to Geneva," in S Touval & I William Zartman, eds., *Negotiations in the Former Soviet Union and Former Yugoslavia, International Negotiation* I 3:547–70 (1996); J Goodby "When War Won Out: Bosnian Peace Plans Before Dayton," *International Negotiation* l 3:501–23 (1996); R Holbrooke *To End a War* (New York: Random House, 1998).
15. M Ottaway, "Eritrea and Ethiopia: Negotiations in a Transitional Conflict," and F Deng, "Negotiating a Hidden Agenda: Sudan's Conflict of Identities," both in I W Zartman, ed., *Elusive Peace: Negotiating an End to Civil Wars* (Washington: Brookings, 1995).
16. R Hinnebusch & I W Zartman, *UN Mediation in the Syrian Crisis: From Kofi Annan to Lakhdar Brahimi* (NY: IPI, 2016).
17. A Hamidaddin, "Yemen: Negotitions with Tribes, States and Memories," in I W Zartman, ed., *Arab Spring: Negotiating in the Shadow of the Intifadat* (Athens: University of Georgia Press, 2015).'
18. Zartman & Berman, op.cit.; S Touval, *The Peace Brokers* (Princeton: Princeton University Press, 1982); Zartman 1983, op.cit.; Touval & Zartman op.cit.; Zartman 1985/1989, op.cit.; Zartman, "Ripening Conflict, Ripe Moment, Formula and Mediation," in Diane BenDahmane & John McDonald, eds., *Perspectives on Negotiation.* (Washington: Government Printing Office, 1986); Zartman & Aurik, op. cit.
19. Touval, op.cit.; Haass, *Conflicts Unending* (Yale University Press, 1990); S J Stedman, *Peacemaking in Civil War* (Lynne Rienner, 1991); T Sisk, *Democratization in South Africa: The Elusive Social Contract* (Princeton: Princeton University Press, 1995); I W Zartman, ed., *Elusive Peace: Negotiating to End Civil* War (Washington: Brookings, 1995); Druckman & J Green, "Playing Two Games" in Zartman, ed.. 1995; T Norlen, *A Study of the Ripe Moment foir Conflict Resolution and Its Applicability to Two Periods*

in the Israeli-Palestinian Conflict (Uppsala: Uppsala University Conflict Resolution Program, 1995); F O Hampson, *Nurturing Peace* (US Institute of Peace, 1996); J Goodby op.cit.; T Ali & R Matthews, eds. *Civil Wars in Africa* (Montreal: McGill-Queens University Press, 1999); M Sala, "Creating the 'Ripe Moment' in the East Timor Conflict," *Journal of Peace Research* XXXIV 4:449–66 (1997); D G Pruitt, ed., *The Oslo Negotiations, International Negotiation* II 2, 1997; K Aggestam & C Jönson, "(Un)ending Conflict," *Millennium* XXXVI 3:771–94 (1997); C A Crocker, F O Hampson, & P Aall, eds, *Herding Cats: The Management of Complex International Mediation* (Washington: US Institute of Peace, 1999); M Mooradian & D Druckman "Hurting Stalemate or Mediation? The Conflict Over Nagorno-Karabakh, 1990–95," *Journal of Peace Research* XXXVI 6:709–27 (1999); N Sambanis, 'Conflict Resolution Ripeness and Spoiler Problems in Cyprus: from the Intercommunal Talks (1968–1974) to the Present', paper presented to the American Political Science Association (25 September 1998).

20. S Touval, *The Peace Brokers* (Princeton: Princeton University Press, 1982), esp pp 228–32, 328.
21. Stedman, op.cit.; D Lieberfeld, *Talking with the Enemy* (New York: Praeger, 1999), and "Conflict 'Ripeness' Revisited," *Negotiation Journal* XV 1:63–82 (1999).
22. Stedman, op.cit., passim, ch. 7 esp pp 238, 241–42.
23. T Ohlson, *Power Politics and Peace Politics* (Uppsla University, 1998).
24. D G Pruitt & O Olczak, "Beyond Hope: Approaches to Resolving Seemingly Intractable Conflict," in B B Bunker & J Z Rubin, eds., *Conflict, Cooperation and Justice* (Jossey-Bass).
25. I W Zartman, "MEOs and Durable Settlements," paper presented to the American Political Science Association, 2006; S Vukovic, "Mediating Closure: Driving Toward a MEO," in I W Zartman, ed. *How Negotiations End*, (Cambridge 2019).
26. Zartman, op.cit., 1989; Mooradian & Druckman op.cit.
27. D Kahneman & A Tversky, "Prospect Theory: An Analysis of Decision Under Risk," *Econometrica* and "Conflict Resolution: A Cognitive Perspective," in K Arrow et al., eds., *Barriers to Negotiation* (Standford Center on Conflict &Negotiation, 1995); Rose McDermott, "Prospect Theory and Negotiation," in Rudolf

Avenhaus & Gunar Sjøstedt, eds., *Negotiated Risks* (Springer, 2009).
28. Zartman 1989, op.cit.
29. C A Crocker, *High Noon in Southern Africa* (New York: Norton, 1992), p 363.
30. Ibid., p 373.
31. Ibid., p 481.
32. A deSoto, "Multiparty Mediation: El Salvador," in Crocker, Hampson & Aall op.cit., p 356.
33. J Baker & T de Franck, *The Politics of Diplomacy* (New York: Putnam, 1995).
34. Holbrooke, op.cit., pp 27, 193.
35. Ibid., p 73.
36. *New York Times*, 9 August 1995, A7.
37. M Goulding, *Enhancing the United Nations' Effectiveness in Peace and Security* (New York: UN Secretariat), Report to the Secretary-General, 30 June 1997, p 20.
38. I Rabinovich, *The Brink of Peace: The Israeli-Syrian Negotiations* (Princeton: Princeton University Press, 1998), p 251.
39. J P Lederach, "Cultivating Peace," in J Darby & R Mac Ginty, eds., *Contemporary Peacemaking* (New York: Palgrave, 2003), pp 32–34, 34–37.
40. D G Pruitt & S Kim, *Social Conflict* (New York: McGraw-Hill, 2003).
41. E Hoffer, *The True Believer* (New York: Harper, 1951); Nicolson, *Diplomacy* (New York: Oxford University Press, 1960); G Snyder & P Diesing, *Conflict Among Nations* (Princeton: Princeton University Press, 1977); Pruitt & Kim, op.cit.
42. R L Moses, *Freeing the Hostages* (Pittsburgh: University of Pittsburgh Press, 1996).
43. I W Zartman & G O Faure, eds., *Escalation and International Negotiation* (Cambridge, UK: Cambridge University Press, 2005).
44. T Ohlson & S J Stedman, *The New Is Not Yet Born* (Washington: Brookings, 1994); Sisk, op.cit.; Zartman 1995, op.cit.; Lieberfeld op.cit.
45. B Steiner *Collective Preventive Diplomacy* (SUNY Press, 2004).
46. Richard Benedick, *Ozone Diplomacy* (Harvard University Press, 1991).

47. Claire Palley, *An International Relations Debacle: The UN Secretary-General's Mission of Good Offices in Cyprus 1999–2004* (Hart Publishing, 2005).
48. Raymond Hinnebusch and I William Zartman, "UN Mediation in the Syrian Crisis: From Kofi Annan to Lakhdar Brahimi," IPI.
49. D Kahneman & A Tversky, "Prospect Theory: An Analysis of Decisions Under Risk," *Econometrica* IIIL 3:263–91 (1979).
50. C Mitchell, "Cutting Losses," Working Paper 9, Institute for Conflict Analysis & Resolution, George Mason University, appearing in a shorter version in *Paradigms: Kent Journal of International Relations* IX 2 1995, p 3 (2); Zartman 1995, op.cit.
51. Mitchell, op.cit., p 7.
52. Touval & Zartman, op.cit.; H. Saunders, "Guidelines B," unpublished manuscript. 1991.
53. Kofi Annan, interview, 26 October 2013.
54. Hinnebusch & Zartman, op. cit.
55. Zartman & de Soto, op.cit.
56. Crocker, op.cit., 471.
57. Ibid., pp 471–72; R Haass, op.cit., 1990; M Goulding, op.cit.; Lederach, op.cit., 2003; Zartman & de Soto, op.cit.
58. J Stein, ed., *Getting to the Table* (Johns Hopkins University Press, 1994).
59. M Golan, *The Secret Conversations of Henry Kissinger* (New York: Bantam, 1976), p 52; Crocker, op.cit., pp 381–82.

CHAPTER 3

Cultivating Peace: A Practitioner's View of Deadly Conflict and Negotiation

John Paul Lederach

INTRODUCTION

'So do you think it may be possible to move toward dialogue, maybe initial, off record contacts to see what obstacles or possibilities exist for a negotiated process to end the conflict?' The question posed by our peace research team to the representatives of the Basque separatist movement was genuine though intuitively we knew the response. The heads shook slowly and the inevitable short answer emerged, 'No. It is going to be a hard two years', followed by a much more detailed justification and rationale.

The year of this conversation could have been 1991 prior to the Barcelona Olympic Games, or 1994 following the Olympics. On the other hand, it could have been January 2021, for the answer was much the same. The counterparts could just as well have been representatives of the Spanish Government rather than the separatists. For that matter,

---

J. P. Lederach (✉)
Kroc Institute for International Peace Studies, University of Notre Dame, Notre Dame, IN, USA

the conversation could have taken place in Northern Ireland, Somalia, or Colombia. In protracted conflict, the horizon of expectation is not the rise of peaceful change. The horizon is the regeneration of violence, steady and sure as the rising sun.

The conversation, much repeated in my experience as a conciliator, poses a dilemma that I often hear framed as a significant doubt and question from students in seminars and journalists in interviews. Is it possible to negotiate while the fighting is still raging, and when, for all practical purposes, neither side is expecting or even preparing for any significant change in the cycle of deadly conflict?

In this chapter, I will formulate some initial responses to that question from the standpoint and perspective of a practitioner. Theoretically, the field abounds with suggestions. Most well known is the idea of 'ripeness' first articulated by Zartman in his important book Ripe for Resolution.[1] Since 1995 research and writing have focused on lessons gained from peace processes and the question of timing.[2] The arguments have suggested that negotiations, and in particular mediation and conciliation, need to read a situation with a capacity to determine whether the timing is right for nudging the conflict from violence to dialogue, and more specifically to agreements that end the open violence. Conditions, patterns and criteria have emerged to further develop this capacity, but in the end, the metaphor created by 'ripeness' points towards a single important premise: change from cycles of deadly violence to negotiation is possible only when the conflict and its perpetrating actors have reached a certain maturation point; then conciliation and negotiation efforts can be introduced with greater effectiveness and success.

This chapter is not aimed at refuting the important research gained from the studies of peace processes in reference to criteria and patterns for successful intervention and negotiation in deadly conflict. I will provide a critique of the guiding metaphor—ripeness—and propose a re-orientation of the practice of developing negotiated peace processes with particular reference to time periods prior to and following the opening of formal talks. These are reflections that emerge from my own direct experiences and I believe that while they provide an alternative view to the metaphor of ripeness they are complementary to the existing body of literature.

A Critique of Ripeness

I start with three observations as to why I have found ripeness a limited metaphor for practice and then suggest several alternative metaphors or guiding perspectives in reference to how practitioners might align their work when faced with the question of whether it is possible to work for peace and negotiations when fighting is still raging. Let me start with what I consider to be a few of the practical limitations of ripeness.

Ripeness Is a Rear-View Mirror

From the standpoint of practice ripeness theory and approaches present an awkward challenge and paradox. On the one hand, much of this theoretical emphasis has been pursued in order to create a 'predictive' capacity useful to conciliators and mediators as they engage with people involved in negotiation processes. Such a capacity offers the promise that if, as practitioners, we can recognize factors, conditions and characteristics of negotiation situations in settings of violent conflict we can effectively increase our capacity to achieve a settlement, or inversely, to know when it is not effective to proceed with the effort. In other words, ripeness proposes to provide a predictive capacity. This is a forward-looking skill orientation, one that assumes linearity of process capable of foretelling outcomes from conditions. To draw the metaphor, ripeness should serve as a large windshield in a car providing a clear and expansive view of what is coming on the horizon such that the driver can adjust the manoeuvres to match the challenges of the approaching road.

However on the other side of the paradox, as I look back across my practical experience, unlike what the metaphor suggests, peacebuilding generally, and negotiations, in particular, have not entailed a 'ripeness' process where I have watched the process develop, like the seasonal maturation of an apple moving from blossom to red, juicy, and ready to eat fruit. In fact, more often than not the opposite has been true. I have only recognized the keys to transformative change in retrospect and in differing ways in each context. For example, on several occasions in the Miskito/Sandinista negotiations, the times when all the conditions pointed to successfully opening the talks were precisely the moments when all our efforts as conciliators failed. They were, in fact, called off at least three times, and once within a day of starting. On the other hand, when they finally opened, what appeared to be a long drawn-out entry in the airport where nearly everything fell apart again and seemed to point to a complete lack of ripeness, the talks that followed lasted about a week and were highly successful. 'Who would have known?' we commented time and again to ourselves.

To draw out the metaphor, 'ripeness' (as in recognizing that potential for change happened) was more like a rear-view mirror than a windshield. The roadway of protracted conflict, it seems, may be more akin to dynamic, nearly amoeba-like spaces than the linear and predictable development of fruit. Moreover, herein lies the limitation. Ripeness may be most useful in retrospective (as we look back we can account for things in our interpretation of the history), but is extremely weak in its predictive capacity from the standpoint of a practitioner and in fact, may provide us with lenses that are not helpful for adapting constructively to the pathways of peacebuilding.

Repeatedly, in situations as varied as Northern Ireland, the Basque Country, or the negotiations between the Philippine government and the communist insurgency, the moments when I thought there was the greatest potential for a significant move forward have been stagnant and even counterproductive. For a practitioner, these periods create an emotional roller coaster. The predictive view suggests significant change is near. Then just when hopes are high, everything collapses leading to a deep sense of despair, and often urgent, at times inappropriate responses to save the moment. Other times, exactly when all the predictive characteristics pointed to complete stagnation and even highly escalated cycles of violence, turned out to be the periods when by way of some unexpected suggestion or event, a significant move forward was created. These experiences have led me towards an attitude not driven by a predictive lens of visible factors but rather towards the development of a lens that does not focus excessively on what appears at any given moment to be the limitations of temporal conditions. In protracted conflict, temporal conditions are ephemeral and nonlinear, requiring paradoxical intentionality: a set of mediative attitudes that keeps your feet on the ground (a realist view of the situation) and your head in the clouds (a hope driven idealist view of the possible). Therefore, rather than orienting my action around predictive ripeness, I find the opposite is increasingly true in my work. I am carefully cautious when all appears ripe for settlement and innoculatingly naive when all appears hopelessly lost in the grip of calamity.

Ripeness Is in the Eye of the Beholder

Among the many things I have learnt in the school of hard knocks of protracted conflict is a simple idea with wide-ranging implications: the prevailing system is set up to create a permanently emerging crisis. This essentially has to do with time and response. I find that in situations with a long history of social division and violence the focus of attention is on the immediate situation and the crisis, event, or impending disaster that just happened. This is accompanied by the common view that once this 'crisis' is dealt with we can move on to the deeper and longer range concerns and needs. The tendency across the board is to be driven by the crisis. This I have found particularly true of people who are directly involved on one side or the other of the conflict, and as such, there is a prevailing attitude that the situation is not ripe. In other words, ripeness is more often than not something perceived by outsiders with the luxury of dispassionate facts and factors. In the midst of week-to-week and month-to-month emergencies, people rarely see their situations as 'ripe' for peace. Ripeness is in the eye of the beholder and few who live in the settings have the luxury of such vision.

This leads to practical and attitudinal dilemmas for the peacebuilder. The most critical shift required is to understand the process not as linear but circular and linear. Ripeness, however, depends exclusively on a linear metaphor of time and change. Circular and linear can be visualized like a horizontal spiral where there is circular movement creating at any given moment forward, upward, backward and downward movements and the whole of the circles is moving forward across time. These actually are the temporal experiences from within the situation that I have commonly experienced: things feel like they may be moving forward, then a crisis comes and it feels like everything has come to a standstill. At other times, it can easily feel like it is moving backwards, or even collapsing. This is the immediate time circle, and it is continuous, a permanent feature of the system. The challenge is how to visualize the possibility of sustaining an overall forward movement over time visible in the lens of decades, not months. This requires a capacity to envision a long-term process and recognize opportunities for constructive change in the midst of a crisis. In other words, it is a shift towards being crisis-responsive rather than crisis-driven. The key attitude and skill shift is that of adaptation of process that assumes and takes account of constant crisis rather than a linear view of maturation that assumes step-wise progression to resolution.

Ripeness Sees Mediator Action as Cherry-Picking

When I played basketball many years ago, our coach had a phrase with which he provoked us whenever we missed an easy shot, 'I can't believe you missed that cherry picker'. Essentially, it meant that a lot of work had gone into place and then just when everything was right and a give-away opportunity was presented, the basket was missed.

There are times when I have the impression that the metaphor of ripeness leads towards an emphasis on mediator action as if it were 'cherry picking'. The impression emerges from two understandings about mediation that I believe have significant limitations and implications.

The first commonly held belief is that mediation lies primarily in the person, and often the personality of the mediator-as-the-actor rather than mediation as-process with multiple roles, functions and activities carried out by a wide array of people.[3] Particularly critical to our discussion here is the idea that the mediator comes from outside the setting and outside the relationships in conflict, or what I have referred to as the 'outside-neutral' view of mediator role.[4] When the mediator provides an outside and neutral role in many cases they are 'in' and 'out' of the setting in terms of their actual physical presence. Ripeness is oriented towards providing terms of reference for this kind of action such that the mediator can gauge when it is most effective to push for agreement or renewed negotiation. What the ripeness metaphor does not provide is a sense of the long-term nature of the process, the building and sustaining of the relationships, nor the multiplicity of roles, activities and functions that may be necessary to make a sustained dialogue and change in the relationships possible.

The second commonly held belief is that the success of mediation is primarily judged by whether it produced an agreement rather than whether it helped create a space for constructive change in people, perceptions and relationships that are not always captured in the confines of a written negotiated document. Ripeness suggests the cherry is the agreement and that picking the cherry is like a mediation harvest. In my practical experience in conciliation work, this tends to promote a measuring stick of success based on what is often the least important element for gauging the sustainability of the change process necessary actually to create the transformation from deadly conflict to respect, cooperation, and increased peaceful interdependence. It is not a metaphor that provides a vision of cultivating the soil, planting the seeds or nourishing the seedling in the face of winds, burning sun or icy storms, all of which speak to process, relationship and sustainability rather than a momentary action.

ALTERNATIVE METAPHORS TO RIPENESS

What I just outlined suggests that from the standpoint of practice the ripeness metaphor has some limitations when applied to contexts of protracted deadly conflict. The metaphor suggests a focus on content and agreement making rather than being relationship and change-oriented. It places emphasis on the mediator's action and perception rather than on the mediation-as-process with multiple sets of action and people. It tends to have a short-term view of action in mind aimed at intense action in specific timeframes (harvest) but not necessarily the slower and painstaking process of preparing and sustaining process. This suggests a need for additional and complementary metaphors emerging from and oriented towards the experience of practice. As I reflect on my own experience several come to mind.

Cultivation: The Building of Long-Term Authentic Relationships

Since the early 1990s, my efforts at peacebuilding and conciliation have led me to the metaphor of cultivator more than harvester, towards nourishment of soil and plant more than picking the fruit. The images that accompany this complementary metaphor suggest an organic connection to context, the building of relationships and a commitment to process over time. Each of the images provides an avenue towards answering the question posed at the beginning of the chapter: is it possible to pursue negotiations while deadly conflict is raging?

The cultivation metaphor suggests that a deep respect for and connection to the context is critical for sustaining a change process that is moving from deadly expressions of conflict to increased justice and peace in relationships. The context of protracted deadly conflict, like soil, is the people, commonly shared geographies but often sharply differing views of history, rights and responsibilities, and the formation of perceptions and understandings based on cultural meaning structures. Cultivation is recognizing that ultimately the change process must be taken up, embraced and sustained by people in these contexts. The cultivator, as a connected but outside element in the system, approaches this soil with a great deal of respect, the suspension of quick judgement in favour of the wisdom of adaptation, and an orientation towards supporting the change process through highs and lows, ebbs and flows of violence and thawing of tensions, whether or not the situation appears ripe. The cultivator gives attention to the well-being of the eco-system not just the quick production of a given fruit.

A relationship-centric orientation naturally emerges from the metaphor. This is built on a genuine concern for relationships, not an instrumentalist approach to people in order to achieve an external goal. This suggests a criterion of authenticity, which cannot be overstated from the perspective of cultivation. A relationship-centric orientation keeps the focus on people, realities of histories, and perceptions as the source that generates and regenerates cycles of deadly conflict. The contentious content of specific agreements is often symbolic of this deeper level. In essence, you can resolve an issue but you till the soils of relationships if you are interested in sustained transformation and systemic health.

Both of the above images require a long-term commitment. I think this may be the single most important lesson learnt over the years, a shift from thinking about negotiations as a 'ripe' moment in time to an understanding of the preparation and support for a change process over a much longer period.[5] It requires you to shift from thinking in weeks and months to thinking in decades. If you have ever talked with a farmer about their land, you will hear them talking about years—decades and even a lifetime of relationship to the soil and the climate.

Accompaniment: The Pace of Presence

To understand accompaniment as a metaphor of peacebuilding and conciliation it is useful to break it down to its Latin origins. The word is built on two primary concepts 'com' or with—and 'pani' or bread. A literal translation would be 'with bread'. In other words, this is a table metaphor. To accompany is to sit and share bread with another. In my mind, there are a number of important images this metaphor places before us as practical guidelines.

First, sharing a table provides a sense of intimacy, of being inside a shared space of humanity with another. This takes us back to our earlier idea of relationship. Nevertheless, it goes further because the image suggests presence with another, a quality of what I once called 'alongsideness'.[6] This of course is very much a part of the image that the word 'accompany' creates; we walk alongside the journey of another. The image it suggests is a respect for the journey of others. It represents presence with others as they travel on their way. The second intriguing aspect of this image is the idea of pace. When it is the journey of the other, the pace is not forced or prescribed from outside, but must, if it is to be authentic, be directed from sources of leading that come from within. In reference to peacebuilding, this poses numerous difficult dilemmas, for more often than not the pace of moving from deadly cycles of conflict to more constructive, mutually beneficial and respectful cycles is extremely slow. In addition, much of peacebuilding from outside is oriented towards getting that movement to happen more rapidly. However, if movement or compromise happens because one is obligated or forced, then the change is rarely authentic and sustainable, and plants the seeds of renewed destructive conflict that sprout later. This becomes even more complex when the accompaniment is with people across the lines of division, and when slowness towards change means a great deal of suffering for many people.

Ripeness seems to answer this dilemma by suggesting that if we read the situation correctly we can determine when the greatest potential for change could happen and can then push for this change to take place. Accompaniment suggests an ongoing presence motivated by an interest in supporting a sustainable change process built on making opportunities available for genuine change motivated from within but not under obligation or external time frames. If we were to put this in detail that is more concrete it would suggest that conciliation work is not about moving in and out of a situation according to a measure of the potential for success. Rather, the activities of conciliation are about ongoing presence, a constancy of availability and a regularity of connection.

Naïveté: The Art of the Possible

Naïveté in the world of realpolitik is generally seen as foolishness, gullibility and weakness of understanding about the true character of politics, power relationships, and even basic human nature. Those who are naïve are those with a Pollyannaish attitude who make things worse and are usually taken advantage of and eaten up in the process. Applied to peacebuilding, this is a common critique of those who pursue peace, particularly at times when things appear to be falling apart and getting worse.

When I look back at my own experiences, I should like to suggest the inverse may be true, that the key to significant change came not when I was capable of producing a hard, factual, objective view of a situation and the predictable outcomes. Rather it seemed to come from a kind of naïveté that suspended the lens of presented reality and with a commonsensical approach asked questions and pursued ideas that seemed out of line with reality as presented. Paradoxically, naïveté cuts in both directions. It is equally naïve for the little boy alongside the parade to point a finger and say out loud, 'the emperor has no clothes' (which is exactly what I felt when the Dayton Peace Accords were hatched) or the sustaining of hope and pursuing of a 'couple of ideas' as I heard from Irish colleagues when on numerous occasions the bombs in the ceasefire period seemed to bring everything to a halt.

For my own edification as a peacebuilder, I have come to embrace the utility of naïveté as the art of the possible. Naïveté does not take what is presented on the surface and is generally accepted as final truth as the primary measuring stick of how things work, are held together, or fall apart. Naïveté is unafraid of being perceived as stupid and has the courage to raise basic questions, both of optimism when all seems impossible and of common sense realism when everybody expects peace to happen because a paper was signed. In both instances, the art is in seeking a way to reach towards a deeper source of what is possible and needed to keep a constructive change process alive and healthy.

Epilogue

Therefore, what do I say when the journalist asks, 'And do you really believe it is possible to talk about negotiation and peace when war is raging?' I say hope is not negotiated. It is kept alive by people who understand the depth of suffering and know the cost of keeping a horizon of change as a possibility for their children and grandchildren. Quick fixes to a long-standing violent conflict are like growing a garden with no understanding of seeds, soils and sweat. This conflict traces back across decades even generations. It will take that long to sort out.

Journalists generally do not quote me in their papers. Soundbites about ripeness, people coming to their senses, and the need for realism and pressure seem to find their way to print more often. However, I believe in cultivation. Cultivation as a metaphor suggests that the core of the peacebuilding work—fostering and sustaining committed, authentic relationships across the lines of conflict over time—does not rise and fall with the temporal vicissitudes of the conflict cycles. It answers the question—is it possible to pursue peace when things are bad—with a resounding 'Yes!' Just as it also suggests that when things are suddenly headed towards an agreement the work is hardly over. It has only begun.

NOTES

1. I.W. Zartman, *Ripe for Resolution: Conflict and Intervention in Africa* (New York: Oxford University Press, 1985/1989).
2. See, for example, L. Kriesberg & S.J. Thorson (eds), *Timing the De-escalation of International Conflicts* (Syracuse, NY: Syracuse University Press, 1991).
3. C. Mitchell, 'External Peace-Making Initiatives and Intranational Conflict', in M.I. Midlarsky (ed.), *The Internationalization of Communal Strife* (New York: Routledge, 1992).
4. P. Wehr & J.P. Lederach, 'Mediating in Central America', *Journal of Peace Research*, 28, 1 (February 1991), 86–98.
5. J.P. Lederach, *Building Peace: Sustainable Reconciliation in Divided Societies* (Washingtonc, DC: United States Institute of Peace, 1997).
6. J.P. Lederach, 'Qualities of Practice for Reconciliation', in R. Helmick (ed.), *Reconciliation* (New York: Templeton Press, 2001).

CHAPTER 4

Conflict Analysis: A System's Approach

Lisa Schirch

Robust and ongoing conflict analysis is an essential foundation for effective peace efforts. This chapter reviews the evolution of conflict analysis practices used by community organizations, international NGOs, donor countries, and even military agencies.[1] Next a summary of conflict analysis tools and frameworks provides a taste for what an actual conflict analysis process looks like. Throughout this chapter, a system's approach to conflict analysis strives to address past problems and describe best practices. A system's approach views conflict analysis as an essential part of program planning, and linking directly with self-assessment, theories of change, and the design, monitoring, and evaluation of peace efforts.

The chapter then describes the various functions of conflict analysis in peacebuilding. Based on extensive experience in implementing conflict analysis on the ground, the chapter details some of the most prevalent challenges and obstacles to effective conflict analysis and how this hampers effective peacebuilding. The chapter concludes by making the

L. Schirch (✉)
Toda Peace Institute, Tokyo, Japan
e-mail: schirchl@emu.edu

case for robust research involving a combination of insiders and outsiders coordinated with donors funding peacebuilding efforts.

History of Conflict Analysis

Modern conflict analysis tools date back to the foundational work of local level social justice, development, and peace practitioners in the 1970s and 1980s in various regions of the world. Paulo Freire, Augusto Boal, and other Latin American community leaders believed local people could analyze their own context by using their own life experience, languages, and cultural, political, economic, and social knowledge.[2] Freire's *Pedagogy of the Oppressed* argued that empowerment and transformation of conflict begins with local people analyzing their own context.

Around the same time, local people in India, Kenya and then other countries developed the "Participatory Rural Appraisal" (PRA) methodology to replace the top-down "Rapid Rural Appraisal" methodology.[3] Instead of outside experts analyzing development needs and telling local people what was needed, the PRA put local people in the driver's seat of their own social change, including both improving development outcomes and building peace. For example, the "problem tree" or "conflict tree" analysis tool was a simple and widely used early PRA conflict analysis tool to help communities distinguish between symptoms (such as street riots) and root causes (such as structural inequalities and political exclusion.) As the field of conflict transformation grew in the 1980s and 1990s, academics and practitioners published collections of conflict analysis tools that grew out of the PRA methodology.[4]

Next, peace and development practitioners began to realize that some of their interventions were causing unintended negative impacts on communities and that conflict analysis was a necessary step in preventing harm. The "Do No Harm" and "Conflict Sensitivity" frameworks partially emerged from and were deepened by a project of the Collaborative for Development Action (CDA) "Reflecting on Peace Practice," an ongoing series of case studies on what works in peacebuilding, but also what causes harm.[5]

At the same time, there was a growing recognition that the military and intelligence communities were conducting forms of conflict analysis that were similar but distinct from peace and development civil society groups and universities.[6] The fundamental assumption that conflicts in places like

Iraq and Afghanistan are a simple matter of who has the strongest military force came into question. Widespread recognition of the failures of the US-led wars in Iraq and Afghanistan prompted military leaders to make astonishing claims that there was "no military solution" to these complex political conflicts. Military leaders came to see that these conflicts stemmed from complex political challenges.[7]

As the number of people and resources devoted to peace efforts increases, there has been a rapid growth in the number and type of conflict analysis methods and schools of thought.

Many organizations began institutionalizing conflict analysis as a requirement before deciding on a particular type of peacebuilding intervention, such as intergroup economic development programs, peace education, or dialogue.[8] The United Nations, Regional Organizations, International NGOs, and government diplomatic, development and defense agencies began developing their own conflict analysis processes. For example, the US Agency for International Development (USAID) developed the Conflict Assessment Framework[9] and the US State Department developed the Interagency Conflict Assessment Framework (ICAF)[10] The latter is used to help people from different U.S. government departments and agencies work together to reach a shared understanding of a country's conflict dynamics and consensus on potential entry points for additional U.S. government efforts. In the UK, various government agencies participated in developing the Joint Analysis of Conflict and Stability (JACS) Guidance Note[11] The United Nations developed a conflict analysis handbook in 2016.[12]

A System's Approach to Conflict Analysis

The elements of a conflict interact like a system or machine where each part of the conflict interacts and reinforces other parts of the system. There are no quick fixes or impacts in most complex conflicts. Often, multiple parts of a system need to change before the system of conflict changes.

A system's approach to conflict analysis takes a wider view than the typical attempts to single out one or two "causes" of conflict. A system's approach examines *multiple interacting factors*. Most conflicts have multiple factors that interact with each other, driving a cycle of dynamic causes and effects.

A systems approach moves away from a "blame" orientation in conflict that isolates specific leaders (Bin Laden) or groups (Al-Qaeda). A systems approach recognizes that a simple identification and removal of an "enemy" is unlikely to change the dynamics of a conflict if underlying driving factors still remain. In most cases, no one part of the conflict system is responsible for conflict and each part of the system plays a part in the perpetuation of conflictual relationship patterns.

A systems approach to conflict analysis maps both conflict drivers and mitigators, or resources for peace. Conflict drivers are people, institutions, or forces that increase divisions and threaten political, economic, security, justice, and social factors related to human security.[13] A conflict driver can be something like a famine, unemployment, easy access to weapons, or religious extremism that motivates individuals or groups to engage in conflict. Conflict drivers tap into and mobilize grievances related to the root causes of conflict in existing political, economic, and social relations.

Many conflict analysis lenses and assessment frameworks focus on the roots of conflict without looking at the resources supporting peace. A positive approach to peace is not just problem focused. It assumes that there is a local capacity for peace that can be supported and expanded. Conflict mitigators are people, institutions, or forces that support political, economic, security, justice, and social factors related to human security. These are also referred to as "Local Capacities for Peace" and are connected to the concept of "social resilience." Resilience refers to the capacity of a system to survive, adapt, absorb, or respond to a crisis or severe change. An individual, community, and institutional is resilient in as much as they can adapt, be agile, learn quickly and improvise new survival methods in a changed environment. Some communities experience political exclusion, environmental changes, economic inequality, easy access to weapons, repressive government forces, or an impending election, and do not experience violent conflict while other communities experience the same challenges and are devastated by intercommunal violence. Resilience is the existing capacity within a community to manage hardships, humanitarian crises, and intercommunal tensions through skilled leadership, community volunteer work, and intercommunal dialogue, problem-solving, and coordination to respond to these challenges.

Conflicts are always changing. New actors emerge. Events change relationships. Analysis is not a one-time event. A systems approach to conflict analysis involves robust research, with a wide range of diverse stakeholders, iterating over time as new events happen and relationships shift.

Psychological Challenges to Conflict Analysis

A joint process of conflict analysis involving diverse stakeholders is necessary because humans perceive only a small part of a conflict system on their own. The psychological processes of perception shape and limit what people see of a conflict in a variety of ways. First, people reinforce preexisting views of what the conflict is about based on personal experience or professional expertise. Second, cognitive dissonance, denial, and a range of other psychological factors make it difficult to be open to potential solutions offered by the other side. Third, humans tend to attribute existential causes (they are evil) to actions taken by our adversaries, while excusing our own similar actions. And finally, people tend to jump to conclusions about what is best to do in a conflict based on the programs or resources we already have available or what our organization would like to do.

Conflict analysis can help to provide a more unbiased picture of all the elements that perpetuate or fuel conflict. There are dozens of conflict analysis tools, exercises, and lenses helpful for gathering and analyzing data to help people expand their perceptions and understand the more complex conflict system.

A lens on a camera helps to capture an image or view. Photographers use different lenses to "see" different facets of the world. In the same way different conflict analysis lenses help to provide different points of view on a conflict. A diversity of conflict analysis tools and lenses provides the greatest insight into the conflict system. Focusing on only one element can create a skewed or inadequate understanding of the conflict.

Functions of Conflict Analysis

Conflict analysis is a distinct discipline. Unlike humanitarian needs assessments that focus on access to water, food, shelter, and healthcare, conflict analysis explores factors influencing conflict in order to be able to prevent, mitigate, or transform conflict. Unlike intelligence and military assessments that identify "the enemy" and their weaknesses to identify targets for violent action, conflict assessment processes aim to inform peacebuilding efforts.[14]

Conflict analysis plays a range of roles. First, it simply helps people to understand conflict dynamics, both factors that are supporting a conflict (drivers) and factors that are supporting peace (mitigators, or asset-based analysis). Conflict analysis conceptually organizes factors driving conflict and supporting peace to enable more effective peace and security policies, programs, and projects.

Second, conflict analysis is a method of *intervening* into conflict. Peace practitioners began using conflict analysis tools as a central part of intergroup dialogue, negotiation, and mediation efforts, to create joint understanding of the dynamics of conflict between groups in conflict.[15] By creating a structured process, often led by a facilitator, conflict analysis seems to create a method for helping people move from an emotional state with automatic reactions toward a thoughtful state where people can discern a variety of different possible responses.

Advances in neuroscience contribute to understanding the importance of conflict analysis as a method of peacemaking. The older part of the brain is an automatic crisis center in the brain that activates a "fight, flight or freeze" response to threats. In the midst of conflict, it is often difficult to achieve high cognitive functioning using the frontal lobe of the brain. Emotions play important roles in conflict to alert us to the importance of a potential threat, and to prepare the body to respond. But emotions can also hijack the parts of the brain involved in solving complex problems and addressing ambiguous situations where humans may not be able to survive by simply fighting or fleeing. The frontal cortex helps people regulate their behavior and engage in critical thinking, anticipate potential outcomes of different behavior choices, and achieve a high level of cognitive functioning that enables creative problem-solving to develop mutually satisfying solutions. Humans, like other animals tend to overestimate potential threats since to underestimate may result in death, while overestimating threats has a lower cost to wellbeing. In the midst of negotiation, overestimating threats from an adversary can make problem-solving difficult. A structured conflict analysis process as part of a negotiation can provide a safe space to allow the frontal lobe to engage more fully to assess more information, despite emotions of fear or anger that might inhibit complex thought without such a structured process.[16]

Third, conflict analysis functions as a mechanism to prevent costly mistakes. Conflict analysis can save money and time by preventing mistakes in programming that stem from unexamined assumptions. Fear of "analysis paralysis" can lead to skimping on conflict analysis. In any intervention to alter conflict dynamics, it is wiser to "go slow to go fast." Attempting to find a quick solution without robust analysis almost always leads to unintended negative impacts that reinforce rather than transform conflict dynamics. Wasteful and ineffective aid programs do real harm. Conflict analysis ultimately saves both time and money by preventing mistakes and misguided theories of change. For example, Western countries spent millions of dollars on job creation in Afghanistan, Somalia, and other countries with the goal of preventing violent extremism and stemming recruitment to violent groups. But research has shown that unemployment is not often a major factor in young men joining these groups.[17]

As more institutions began to use conflict analysis to inform their peace and development programming, they also realized that some programs not only do not work, they may actually do harm. There is often a significant gap between the "intent" of a peace effort and its actual "impact." Even when people set out to do good, they may inadvertently harm others. For example, an NGO providing humanitarian assistance to refugee communities without adequate conflict analysis may unintentionally enable an armed group within the refugee community to sell aid to buy weapons.[18] A government program providing solar ovens to communities may not understand the impact of choosing a local woman of one ethnic group to make decisions about which families in the community receive a solar oven. In both of these real-life cases, good intentions resulted in increased conflict because of a lack of robust conflict analysis.

Conflict Analysis Tools and Framework

Governments, universities, and NGOs around the world all use similar conflict analysis tools, though package these tools together in different conceptual frameworks. A conflict analysis framework is a collection of conflict analysis tools and lenses. A synthesis of these frameworks in *Conflict Assessment and Peacebuilding Planning* boils down to six lines of inquiry similar to questions used by journalists: Where, Who, Why, What, How, and When.[19]

> **WHERE** is the conflict taking place?
> **WHO** is driving the conflict and who is supporting peace?
> **WHY** are the key actors' motivated?
> **WHAT** are the driving and mitigating factors?
> **HOW** are key actors mobilizing their sources of power to drive or mitigate conflict?

WHEN did the conflict escalate or deescalate in the past and what is the forecast for future windows of opportunity or vulnerability?

There are dozens of tools useful for exploring these six questions. (An extensive and detailed list of conflict analysis tools and greater instructions on how to use them can be found in *Conflict Assessment and Peacebuilding Planning*.) Each tool or "lens" offers an insight into one facet of a conflict. These tools also provide interactive methods for small groups of people to carry out an analytical process together. Not only does the tool become a helpful focal point for discussion and mutual exploration of conflict dynamics. As noted earlier, these tools create opportunities for people in conflict to further understand other points of view, and to begin to envision mutually satisfying solutions to conflict.

Some conflict analysis tools are visual. In rural settings, these drawings can be done on simple chalk boards or large sheets of paper with people sitting in a circle working together to use the tool in small groups of 4–8 people. For example, the stakeholder mapping tool asks a small group to draw a map of the relationships between people or groups that have a stake in the conflict. For example, in a conflict analysis of the conflict between the US and Iran, each of these countries would be drawn with circles around their names, and a jagged line between them representing conflict. Other stakeholders such as Russia, the European Union, Iraq, Israel, and Turkey, for example, would be drawn in smaller circles. Solid lines or green colored lines indicating alliances would be drawn between allies. And jagged or red colored lines would be drawn between these broader stakeholders and the two main ones.

The conflict tree exercise asks a small group to draw the roots, trunk, and branches of a tree. The group then decides what are the "root" causes of the conflict, what is the main issue (the trunk), and what are the symptoms or results of the conflict (the leaves). For example, if civil war is the main issue, then colonial divide and conquer strategies, corrupt governance, and loss of traditional dispute resolution mechanisms may be the root causes, while unemployment, crime, and internally displaced peoples may be the results.

Other conflict analysis tools take the form of charts. For example, the chart below illustrates a combination of the "onion tool" which aims to distinguish between the outer layer of an onion which represents the stated public positions of each stakeholder, and the core of the onion which represents the stakeholders' underlying interests and needs. The point of this tool is to understand the deeper motivations each stakeholder is attempting to address. While stakeholders may publicly insist on one solution, often there are other solutions that address their core interests. This tool helps to reveal potential ways of satisfying those basic human interests such as dignity, respect, identity, belonging, and so on. These deeper interests are at the heart of most conflicts. Yet stakeholders often make public statements that make it difficult to discover or understand these deeper interests.

This chart also adds a column including the "power analysis" tool, which aims to analyze each stakeholder's sources of power including, for example, the network of relationships, their charisma and ability to influence others, their access to information and education, and, of course, their physical or military power.

Name of Stakeholder	Public Position	Underlying Interest or Human Need	Source of Power

Finally, the timeline tool asks small groups to identify key points in history for each stakeholder that were significant. These could be markers of historical traumas or significant events that were celebrated. If the key stakeholders in a conflict create an historical timeline for themselves, this can be compared with and help to educate other stakeholders on historical narratives that inform the present conflict. Each stakeholder group would write each positive or negative historical event for their group on a single normal size sheet of photocopy paper. Ideally, this exercise can create a large timeline on the floor or ground by then asking each group to place these "event sheets" along a string or rope with dates marking years or decades.

A conflict analysis process at the community level may simply end with some diagrams and verbal identification of common ground, differences, and new understanding. In more formal processes, a conflict analysis process ends with a short report or document summarizing the key factors in the Where, Who, Why, What, How, and When into short statements or narratives that contain the condensed information from the entire process.

From Conflict Analysis to Peacebuilding Planning

Many conflict analysis tools produce long lists of "factors" or "actors" involved in a conflict without a way of prioritizing their importance or identifying how they should inform peacebuilding planning. Conflict analysis is most helpful when information can be categorized, synthesized, connected with other information and sorted out by priorities for its relevance to peace efforts. The lack of methods for linking conflict analysis to planning sparked new publications linking the two.[20]

The chart below is an example of a comprehensive conflict analysis framework that links conflict analysis to self-assessment, theories of change, and planning for peace efforts. This framework aims to enable a system's view of conflict while helping to prioritize possible theories of change and interventions with the addition of self-assessment questions that narrow the scope of possibility for any potential intervenor.

	Conflict assessment lenses	Self-assessment	Theory of change	Planning
WHERE	Where is the conflict taking place - in what cultural, social, economic, justice, and political context or system?	How well do you understand the local context, language, cultures, religions, etc.? Where will you work?	If x parts of the context are at the root of conflict or provide a foundation of resilience and connection between people, what will influence these factors?	**How will the context interact with your efforts?** Given your self-assessment, identify your capacity to impact the elements of the context that drive conflict and your ability to foster institutional and cultural resilience

(continued)

(continued)

	Conflict assessment lenses	Self-assessment	Theory of change	Planning
WHO	Who are the stakeholders – the people who have a stake or interest in the conflict or its resolution?	Where are you in the stakeholder map? What social capital do you have? To which key actors do you relate?	If x individual or group is driving or mitigating conflict, who can help mobilize or incentivize change?	**Who will you work with?** Given your self-assessment, decide whom to work with to improve relationships between key stakeholders or support key actors who could play a peacebuilding role
WHY	Why are the stakeholders acting the way they do? What are their motivations?	How do stakeholders perceive your motivations?	If x group is motivated to drive or mitigate conflict, what will you do to support or challenge these motivations?	**Why will you work?** Given your self-assessment of your motivations and how stakeholders perceive your motivations, identify how these align with the motivations of the key stakeholders in the context
WHAT	What factors are driving or mitigating conflict?	What are you capable of doing to address the key drivers and mitigators of conflict?	If x is driving and mitigating conflict, what actions can you take that will influence these factors?	**What will you do?** Given your self-assessment, identify which driving and mitigating factors you will address

(continued)

(continued)

	Conflict assessment lenses	Self-assessment	Theory of change	Planning
HOW	How is conflict manifested? What are the stakeholders' means and sources of power?	What are your resources, or sources of power? How do these enable or limit your ability to work?	If x power sources are driving conflict or mitigating conflict, what can you do to address these sources of power?	**How will you shift power sources in support of peace?** Given your self-assessment, identify and prioritize your capacities to reduce conflict drivers and to increase local capacities for peace
WHEN	Are historical patterns or cycles of the conflict evident?	Do you have an ability to respond quickly to windows of vulnerability or opportunity?	If x times are conducive to violence or peace, what actions will influence windows of vulnerability or opportunity?	**When is the best timing for your peace efforts?** Given historical patterns, identify possible windows of opportunity or vulnerability and potential triggers and trends of future scenarios

SELF-ASSESSMENT

All too often, groups carrying out conflict analysis choose not to or forget to analyze themselves. Self-assessment is a process of identifying one's own cultural biases, perspectives, interests, and assumptions about a conflict, and then identifying one's own resources, capacities, and networks to prioritize planning on what is possible and pragmatic. Self-assessment is an ongoing process throughout the entire cycle of assessment planning, and evaluation. Conducting a self-assessment identifies your own cultural biases and perspectives on the conflict. A set of self-assessment questions help to both examine the potential strengths and challenges of the group planning a peace effort while also narrowing and prioritizing the range of possibilities for intervention. Questions include:

WHERE will you work? Where are you already involved in this context?
WHO will you work with? Who are you related to already? How do they perceive you?
WHY will you do what you do? What are your motivations?
WHAT will you do? What are your capacities and lack of capacities for action?
HOW will you intervene? What are your sources of power?
WHEN is the best timing for your peace efforts?

Self-assessment requires an honest appraisal of one's own lack of capacity. Self-assessment requires coming to terms with how one's own group contributes to conflict dynamics. Each part of the system is involved in either sustaining or changing existing patterns of relationship. Both action and inaction can bring changes in systems. An event or person that creates "positive feedback" changes the patterns of relationships in systems. Negative feedback sustains current patterns of relationships in systems. Negative feedback loops operate to keep the system the same. Positive feedback loops operate to change the system.

The easiest way to shift a conflict system is to focus on those parts of the system closest to us. Each of us has most control over our own behavior in a system. Rather than focusing on how to change the other parts of a system, most of our efforts in peacebuilding should go into identifying the wisest, most emotionally intelligent ways for ourselves to behave in our systems. In conflicts, a peacebuilding approach spends far more time examining the endogenous question of "why do they hate us?" rather than the exogenous question of "what can we do to reform them?".

THEORIES OF CHANGE

A *theory of change* or a *program rationale* is a statement about how a program hopes to foster change to produce intended outcomes and impacts. Theories of change can be either implicit or explicit assumptions about how peace efforts will affect a conflict-affected context. Theories of change (ToCs) have two parts. First a ToC is a theory about what factors are driving or mitigating conflict. Second a ToC is a theory about what can be done about conflict. A theory of change describes how some driving or mitigating factor of the context (factor) can be changed with some peacebuilding action (action) to achieve an impact that prevents violence or builds peace.

Theories of change can be written as a formula: If **X is** driving or mitigating violence, then **X types of** actions will achieve **X** impacts to reduce violence, foster perceptions of justice, or strengthen peaceful relations between groups. There are three parts of this Theory of Change: conflict analysis factors, types of peace efforts, and impacts on the conflict.

For example, if competition over land is driving conflict, then a negotiation between key leaders may be an important intervention to reduce conflict. If religious leaders are mitigating conflict, then a possible intervention could be to provide resources and training to religious leaders. If human rights violations carried out by security forces are driving violent conflict, then a possible intervention is security sector reform. If a political and economic disenfranchisement is driving conflict, then supporting civil society and social movements supporting democracy may be an important intervention. If youth exchange programs are mitigating conflict between ethnic groups, supporting youth activities may.

If, for example, an analysis of white nationalist groups in Charlottesville, Virginia found that young men joining these violent extremist groups tended to desire to belong to a group that boosted their self-esteem, this would be a *conflict analysis factor*. To address this factor, a *peace effort* might be the creation of a positive identity groups through community group formation that did not rely on putting other groups down or using violence and aggression to prove manhood. The *impact* this intervention might have would be to weaken the level of recruiting by white nationalist groups.

Theories of change rely heavily on conflict analysis. Most theories of change are hypotheses or guesses that need testing. Monitoring and evaluation gather evidence to assess whether the theory of change is accurate. Some theories of change emphasize *who* needs to change, such as a specific individual or group that is driving a violent conflict or key people who could play a positive peacebuilding role. Other theories of change focus on *what* needs to change in the context, such as a specific policy or institution, or a problem like corruption or lack of a free press.

ROBUST CONFLICT-SENSITIVE RESEARCH

Conflict analysis is always shaped by our own experiences and beliefs. In the parable of the five blind people and the elephant, each blind person describes the elephant differently. One views the elephant by holding the trunk, another the tail, and others hold the leg, or the side of the elephant. They describe the elephant according to their personal experience: as a water hose, a rope, a tree, or a wall, respectively. Similarly, people have different perceptions of what is driving the conflict or what is supporting peace. Five different conflict analysis teams could all research the same conflict and design five different interventions based on their analysis. Conflict analysis requires listening to diverse points of view to approach a more complex and full understanding of conflict. Conflict analysis is a process, not a destination. A conflict analysis will never be final.

Conflict analysis requires a research methodology that is valid, reliable, accurate, and triangulated.[21] Data is *valid* if it is relevant and informs the conflict analysis framework. Data is *reliable* if it comes from a dependable, respected source such as a primary source such as an interview or focus group with person living in the conflict region. Data is *accurate* if it can be replicated by repeating the research process and finding similar information. Accuracy also relates to whether researchers are transparent, clear, and logical about whom they choose to interview. Data is less accurate if researchers interview only a small sample and are not explicit about reasons for choosing that group. Data is *triangulated* if it comes from three or more reliable sources and can be fact-checked by comparison.

Data sources include books, reports, blogs, news articles, twitter feeds, polling, interviews, focus groups, observations, and the interactive methods such as the conflict analysis tools and frameworks referenced here. Data sources vary in quality and relevance. Identifying the gaps in data or the places where there is uncertain or contradictory data can be helpful to understand why there may be conflicting data. Researchers should identify missing information, missing perspectives of key stakeholders who might provide greater understanding of key themes in the conflict analysis research.

Unlike other types of research, in conflict analysis, the goal is both to triangulate data to find where there is common ground and agreement in analysis; but also to find the areas of disagreement or different ways that different groups of people answer the questions in the framework.

People in conflict have different experiences and perceptions that shape their different points of view. Conflict analysis can help to identify these important differences, often a necessary step in building understanding for negotiation and other peace efforts.

Ironically conflict analysis processes can also create conflict. Research processes are interventions that change conflict dynamics based on who is involved in designing and participating in the process. Conflict analysis research can be a form of conflict transformation. Researchers should be transparent about the purposes and interests that are funding and carrying out conflict analysis. This transparency ethic is essential to any research process involving human beings. Local groups that carry out conflict analysis with local communities need to be just as transparent as foreign governments carrying out research. All researchers need to have a clear statement and communication strategy for explaining the purpose of their research.

In addition, it is important that researchers are aware that asking questions about conflict can re-open trauma for people who have experienced great loss. Research questions may feel re-victimizing to people who do not want to remember painful parts of their experience. When researchers ask about ethnic divisions, inequality, gender-based violence, or human rights violations, people may experience strong negative emotions. Pilot testing research questions and exercises can help researchers determine whether their research is trauma sensitive.

Insider–Outsider Conflict Analysis Teams

Conflict analysis requires a diverse array of skills. Key skills include:

a. Knowledge of local language, cultures and social, economic, and political history in order to develop relevant and conflict-sensitive research questions
b. Ability to travel to collect data across diverse regions in a country
c. Ability to identify and engage relevant stakeholders that represent a wide range of experiences and groups
d. Ability to organize a variety of data collection methods, including interviews, focus groups, and surveys to ensure data is valid

It is unlikely any one group will have all of these capacities. Insiders and outsiders tend to be stronger in different key capacities, which is one reason why coordinated teams of insiders and outsiders are important.

The Organization for Economic Co-operation and Development (OECD) called for an "inclusive approach" that respects "local ownership" of the development process starting in 1996.[22] Since then many organizations have documented the ethical necessity and strategic benefits of local ownership. Conflict analysis processes work best when they include collaborative, participatory processes involving diverse insiders and outsiders. "Insiders" are those who live in a conflict-affected region. They hold a variety of capacities, including knowledge of local languages, and understanding the local history, including deep knowledge of political, economic, social, religious, cultural, and media aspects. Local civil society includes religious leaders, non-governmental groups such as charities, community-based development organizations (CBOs), women's groups, media, business associations, faith-based organizations, professional associations, trade unions, self-help groups, coalitions and advocacy groups.

Because people with different backgrounds view a conflict in different ways, conflict analysis should draw on a diverse range of people from within a community or region complemented by outsiders who bring inter-disciplinary and comparative insights from outside the region. Leaving local people out of conflict assessments is disempowering and leads to ineffective programs. Multi-stakeholder conflict analysis forums that include diverse sectors of civil society, business, media, government and outsider/foreigners provide an ongoing insight into shifting local dynamics and function as peacebuilding interventions that can positively impact the conflict. On the ground teams of insiders and outsiders can also work together to monitor local media, conduct polling, conduct focus groups, and interviews to produce rolling conflict assessment report for donor communities.

Inclusive, respectful processes where diverse stakeholders discuss, decide, and implement programs together demonstrate democratic decision-making about what peace efforts to pursue. Peace efforts do not work when local people are left out of conflict analysis processes but are then asked to "implement" the programs designed by outsiders.

While it is necessary to consider the necessity of local ownership and local leadership in conflict analysis processes, it is also important not to idealize insiders. Most insiders will have strong opinions supporting one side of the conflict or another, or may be protagonists in the conflict. There are also power dynamics within local groups. Insiders of different socioeconomic, ethnic, religious, or linguistic groups may censor themselves, or defer to other groups in public settings. Again, recognizing power dynamics is important. Rumors, misinformation, and outright deception are common in place affected by conflict. Fears and threats impact those who stand to gain or lose in the conflict. Setting up interviews and identity caucus focus groups helps to ensure that conflict analysis processes come out with valid results. It may be the quality of the listening rather than the quantity of time that is most important.

But conversely, the assumption that there is no "local capacity for peace" has been widely denounced and dispelled.[24] It is possible to find insiders at all levels of society who are bridge-builders and who have already built healthy relationships with people on other sides of the conflict. Local capacities for conflict analysis, including local people trained in using conflict analysis tools and holding Mas and Ph.D.s in conflict transformation exist in most conflict-affected countries.[25] These bridge-building insiders are critical to conflict analysis processes, as they can help to ensure that the research includes diverse points of view.

CURRENT PROBLEMS IN CONFLICT ANALYSIS RESEARCH

In a reversal of the PRA methodology and the OECD principles on local ownership or insider–outsider partnerships, many government and international organizations still rely on outsider-based, expert-oriented conflict analysis processes that limit local participation rather than being led and directed by insiders.

One of the most common forms of conflict analysis occurs when an external donor pays for an "expert" team of academics to fly into a country and conduct a two-week conflict analysis. Reliant on translators and often oblivious to the perceptions that locals may have of them and their interests in conducting research, they write up a conflict analysis report which then sets a blueprint for how donors will spend millions of dollars.

There are deep flaws in many of these outsider-led conflict analysis processes. In my own practice in conflict analysis in over twenty countries and two decades, local people have repeatedly told me that they are often not consulted in the design or process of outside donor-funded conflict analysis processes. Civil society organizations in many regions of the world report that governments cite a "lack of local capacity" even when there are highly skilled NGOs led by teams of local experts with graduate degrees in conflict analysis and peacebuilding. They report that governments and some international NGOs treat them as "implementing partners" of projects rather than having their own insights into peacebuilding programming. This is backed up by other researchers who have heard the same critique of western-led conflict analysis processes.[26]

First, outsiders often seem to believe they are neutral, or objective, even if they are coming from countries funding one or more armed groups or governments involved in the conflict. Outsiders express distrust of local people's biases and political affiliations to justify not allowing full local leadership of a conflict analysis process, while at the same time often not taking into account their own biased identities. When conducting conflict analysis exercises such as the "stakeholder mapping," outsiders may inhibit local people from fully articulating the role they see outside countries as playing in local conflict dynamics. In general outsiders often fail to recognize how outsider's countries' policies are contributing to local conflict.

Second, few conflict analysis teams account for how their own identity disrupts accurate data collection. When Western conflict analysis teams drop into a country, local people will often tell data collectors what they want to hear so that they can benefit from aid money, because they fear for their safety, or because they want to be polite to outsiders. The identity of the group collecting the data impacts the quality of the data. Local people tend to be savvy and suspicious of the motivations of donor countries and outside researchers, even suspecting them of being intelligence agents.

Third, teams rarely conduct a self-assessment to identify their own biases and assumptions about the local context. Locals report that outsiders often show a lack of sensitivity to local cultures and religious values including arrogance and a "we know what is best for you" attitude. Outsider teams may simply hear what they want to hear, or selectively consider information according to that which confirms their prior beliefs. Insiders report that outsiders often fail to listen to their ideas about the design of the conflict analysis process and use neocolonial attitudes that seek only "implementing partners" of foreign-designed projects.

Fourth, outsiders often do not speak the local languages. Many important nuances and issues that come out of interviews are lost through translation or lack of the cultural knowledge to interpret local metaphors or references. Out of their own lack of contextual understanding, Western experts may also develop research questions that may unintentionally cause insult or stir up conflict and tension. In some places, for example, even the words "conflict" or "peacebuilding" are highly charged and create tension. Furthermore, translators can misinterpret research questions, and may, in some cases, intentionally misinterpret a response to reflect the priorities from a particular ethnic or ideological group.

Fifth, most outsiders do not have a deep understanding of the local religion, economy, political or social history. Outsiders may be tempted to oversimplify local conflict dynamics by failing to appreciate the complexity of the local context. Outsiders representing donor interests may be looking for quick-fix solutions rather than exploring the historical and systemic roots of conflict.

Sixth, these expert teams conduct interviews or focus groups, often with a select group of elite government and civil society leaders. Often these same local elites participate in the conflict analysis processes for many different countries. If a conflict analysis involves mostly elite academics or religious leaders, their point of view may be radically different from interviews with women, youth, or minority groups. In any conflict, there will be wildly different perceptions about who is to blame, what is happening, and what motivations are driving people's behaviors. Listening to diverse voices is an essential part of identifying not the "one" truth, but the variations of perceptions among different parts of society. Therefore, no select group of elites can "speak for" those with less power in a society. And it is essential for local people aware of complex dynamics within a country to design a conflict analysis research process that involves traveling to diverse regions of the country and listening to disempowered and minority groups.

Multiple countries and international organizations may all be conducting separate conflict analysis in the same country, with the same elite group of people being interviewed. This can also tax local leadership, as it requires them to spend a great deal of time providing insights to their international partners. This lack of international coordination consumes local leader's energy and wastes international resources. The experts then write up a report, often recommending similar types of programs. But this replication of the research process is not a sign that the data gathered is valuable or complete.

Seventh, too often, conflict analysis is a simplistic exercise undertaken one time, and in a short time frame due to the large cost of flying in foreign experts rather than supporting a diverse, local conflict analysis team to conduct ongoing analysis of rapidly changing conflict dynamics. The goal seems to mirror the mainstream media's packaging of simple "cause-effect" analyses of complex issues. Some conflict analysis processes are just a self-fulfilling prophecy for outsiders that come in looking for evidence that their branded peacebuilding method could work.[27] Outside researchers may simply "hear what they want to hear" or carry out a conflict analysis to "check a box" on a donor's list. Local civil society actors report that donors come to them with projects in hand and a box to tick for "consulting with civil society" rather than taking the time to listen and assess the conflict with diverse local voices.

Conflict analysis may just serve to justify their program resources with neat and tidy lists of factors driving conflict.

Given their short amount of time to write a conflict analysis report, teams may dismiss or ignore data that contradicts their assumptions about local drivers of conflict. Data warping and distorting often go undetected. Peacebuilding planners first and foremost need humility to "know what you don't know." Over-confidence in understanding complex dynamics in a conflict-affected context creates a chain of problems, including ineffective programs, wasted funding, and lack of addressing actual conflict drivers.

Eighth, most conflict analysis research processes fail to analyze and address implicit power relationships that affect data quality. The research process can implicitly convey whose goals and voices are most important and whose opinions are most trusted. Local people often view external donor-driven peace efforts without local input as illegitimate, wasteful, and even neocolonial—reflecting a "we-know-what's-best-for-you" approach. Civil society insiders often report that outside expert teams in conflict analysis "came to do an assessment already knowing what they wanted to do."[28] They also not that outsiders often leave if a crisis emerges, indicating a lack accountability to local people.

Finally, conflict analysis exercises sometimes seem to place confidence in the tools themselves without understanding the need for robust research that involves including diverse points of view and sources of data. The conflict analysis tools on their own cannot magically produce insight. Quality conflict analysis depends upon the diversity and accuracy of the sources of the information.

The often-flawed conflict analysis processes lead to ineffective, wasteful, and even harmful peace efforts.

For example, in Afghanistan, insiders and outsiders carried out conflict analysis processes separately. Their results were quite different. Imagine being an Afghan villager with a knock on the door by two separate researchers: one a US citizen with a translator, the other a local Afghan from a neighboring village who speaks Dari and Pashto, the local languages. Interviewees answer research questions not only based on the question, but also on who is asking, what they think that researcher wants to hear, and the possible implications of telling the truth.

The conflict analysis processes carried out by outside donors such as USAID found that unemployment was driving conflict, and thus devoted large sums of aid money to job creation projects.[29] Local Afghan researchers in local peacebuilding NGOs found that unemployment was only weakly linked to growing support for the insurgency. These local researchers found that government corruption and negative experiences with foreign troops in night raids and house searches[30] were driving the insurgency. They recommended addressing these drivers of conflict.[31]

In a number of east African countries, local NGO and think tank reports saw government corruption and the need for land reform as major drivers of conflict, while foreign donors pushed interethnic dialogue. Local NGOs who had deep knowledge of the local context and clear ideas about what needed to be done to foster peace were largely left out of conflict analysis processes or were asked for their approval of the assessment after donors had already decided what they wanted to do. Donor-funded conflict analysis teams were reluctant to listen to local NGOs since they had already gone through a long process of developing policy goals, getting budget lines approved and sending out request for proposals for local "implementing partners" who would carry out donor priorities. The disparity between local and foreign conflict analysis meant that relationships between donors and implementers suffered, preventing coordinated action.[33]

SUMMARY AND CONCLUSION

Conflict analysis is an essential element in building peace, both because it improves the quality and effectiveness of peace efforts, and because it is an intervention between conflicting groups that can support their ability to find mutually satisfying solutions. The methods and practices of conflict analysis have evolved over the last half century. Today there is an abundance of publications outlining conflict analysis tools and frameworks, as well as methods for moving from analysis to planning, and including self-assessment and theories of change.

While originating in local communities to empower local action, conflict analysis processes have become contested spaces where outsiders often assume local people lack capacity to carry out their own analysis. Robust, ongoing, and coordinated conflict analysis can support strategic and coordinated peace efforts with a variety of different actors working for peace, from the top, middle, and community levels of society. A systems approach to conflict analysis can help to identify a range of potential peace efforts. These might include a variety of different activities including economic development, human rights advocacy, and participatory governance programs, all sensitive to reducing divisions and fostering peaceful and just relations between groups, a short-term focus on immediate issues as well as a long-term focus on systemic change, and a balance between stopping conflict drivers and starting or supporting conflict mitigators. A coordinated conflict analysis process can lay the foundation for greater coordination of peace efforts, ensuring that activities complement and synergize with each other. Donors can incentivize coordination of conflict analysis and fund a repository of conflict analysis research to improve data quality, reduce duplication, and maximize complementary research that produces accurate and balanced results with triangulated data.

NOTES

1. This chapter draws on my book on this same topic. The research included extensive participation in conflict assessment exercises at the local level as well as with donor states and international organizations like the World Bank and United Nations, interviews, and a literature review. L. Schirch (2013) *Conflict Assessment and Peacebuilding Planning: Toward a Participatory Approach to Human Security* (Boulder, CO: Lynne Rienner Publishers).
2. P. Freire (1972) *Pedagogy of the Oppressed* (New York: Herder and Herder); A. Boal (1985) *Theatre of the oppressed* (New York: Theatre Communications Group).
3. K. Singh (2001) "Handing over the stick: The global spread of participatory approaches to development". In Edwards, Michael; Gaventa, John (eds.). *Global citizen action* (Boulder, CO: Lynne Rienner Publishers) pp. 175–187.

4. Mennonite Conciliation Service (1992) *Mediation and Facilitation Training Manual: Foundations and Skills for Constructive Conflict Transformation* (Akron, PA: Mennonite Central Committee). And S. Fisher (2000) *Working with Conflict: Skills and Strategies for Action* (London: Zed Books).
5. Collaborative for Development Action (2009) *Reflecting on Peace Practice* (Boston, MA: CDA Collaborative Learning Projects).
6. L. Woocher (June 2011) *Conflict Assessment and Intelligence Analysis Commonality, Convergence, and Complementarity* (Washington, DC: US Institute of Peace).
7. I. Villelabeitia (March 8, 2007) U.S. Commander Says No Military Solution in Iraq (Reuters).
8. See the websites of Conciliation Resources (http://www.c-r.org/PPP) and SaferWorld (http://www.saferworld.org.uk) for copies of locally-driven conflict assessments and policy recommendations.
9. US Agency for International Development (2012) *Conflict Assessment Framework 2.0* (Washington, DC: USAID).
10. Department of State (DOS). (2008) *Interagency Conflict Assessment Framework (ICAF)* (Washington, DC: Bureau of Conflict and Stabilization Operations).
11. Stabilization Unit (2017) *Joint Analysis of Conflict and Stability (JACS) Guidance Note* (London: UK Government).
12. See United Nations Systems Staff College. (2016) *Conflict Analysis Handbook: A Field and Headquarter Guide to Conflict Assessments* (Turin, Italy: United Nations).
13. The term "conflict driver" has gained wide acceptance in the research literature as a better way of identifying a "factor" that influences conflict as opposed to a "cause" of conflict. Scholars have moved away from talking about "causes" of conflict because of the rejection that any one cause is responsible for conflict. See for example an early use of the term conflict driver in this publication. M. Kett and M. Rowson (2007) 'Drivers of violent conflict,' *Journal of the Royal Society for Medicine*, 100(9): 403–406.
14. L. Woocher (June 2011) *Conflict Assessment and Intelligence Analysis Commonality, Convergence, and Complementarity* (Washington, DC: US Institute of Peace).
15. See for example C. Moore (2004) *The Mediation Process: Practical Strategies for Resolving Conflict*, 3rd. (San Francisco: Jossey-Bass Publishers).

16. For more on the role of neuroscience and conflict see L. Schirch (2004) *Ritual, Symbol, and Peacebuilding* (Connecticut: Kumarian Press); L. Schirch (2013) *Conflict Assessment and Peacebuilding Planning*.
17. Mercy Corps (2015) *Youth and Consequences: Unemployment, Injustice and Violence* (Portland, OR: Mercy Corps).
18. See M.B. Anderson (1999) Mary B. *Do No Harm: How Aid Can Support Peace—Or War* (Boulder, CO: Lynne Rienner Publishers).
19. L. Schirch (2013) *Conflict Assessment and Peacebuilding Planning*.
20. See for example L. Schirch (2013) *Conflict Assessment and Peacebuilding Planning*. And See also D. Hiscock and T. Dumasy (March 2012) *From Conflict Analysis to Peacebuilding Impact: Lessons Learned from People's Peacemaking Perspectives* (London: Conciliation Resources and SaferWorld).
21. See for example L. Schirch (2013) *Conflict Assessment and Peacebuilding Planning*.
22. Organization for Economic Co-operation and Development (OECD)—Development Assistance Committee (DAC) (1996) *Shaping the 21st Century: The Contribution of Development Co-operation*.
23. L. Schirch with D. Mancini-Griffoli (2015) *Local Ownership in Security: Case Studies of Peacebuilding Approaches* (The Hague: Alliance for Peacebuilding, GPPAC, Kroc Institute).
24. See for example the "Capacities for Peace" initiative by Conciliation Resources and Saferworld to document local capacities for early warning and conflict prevention at https://www.c-r.org/where-we-work/capacities-peace; accessed 1 January 2020.
25. At Eastern Mennonite University's Summer Peacebuilding Institute, where I am a faculty member, we have hosted participants from approximately 120 countries over the last 25 years. In each of the 22 countries I have worked in, I have worked side by side with local experts with extensive experience in conflict analysis. And in some countries, like Afghanistan, I worked with dozens of local Afghans holding advanced degrees in conflict resolution. Yet I could not find even one European or North American in the compounds at the International Security Assistance Force who held a degree or competency in conflict analysis.

26. Adapted from "Reflecting on Peace Practice and the Peacebuilding Effective Partnerships Forum" held by Interpeace and the International Peace Academy, Geneva, Switzerland, 2004.
27. M.B. Anderson and L.Olson (2003) *Confronting War: Critical Lessons for Peace Practitioners* (Cambridge, MA: Collaborative for Development Action).
28. Konraad Van Brabant. Peacebuilding How? "Insiders"—"Outsiders" and Peacebuilding Partnerships. Geneva, Switzerland, Interpeace, 2010.
29. See for example, USAID Afghanistan. Community Development Program (CDP) Fact Sheet. June 2011. http://afghanistan.usaid.gov/en/USAID/Activity/147/Community_Development_Program__South_East__West_CDPSEW.
30. In this situation, the two drivers of conflict found repeatedly by researchers outside of government were both the two parts of the system that outside governments had most control over. While foreign troops did aim to decrease the negative impacts of night raids and house searches, the communication strategies around these tactics either were inadequate, or the degree of change in the house searches (from less respectful involving dogs and body searches on women to more respectful of local culture and religion) the degree of perceived change in the behavior of foreign forces worsened over time, increasing antagonism against foreign forces. The presence of forces then became a primary driver of "fence-sitters" to support the insurgent groups. International policy in Afghanistan became a "wicked problem" where the solution (military forces) to the identified problem (Taliban and other insurgent groups) actually reinforced the problem.
31. See for example, P. Fishstein and A. Wilder (2012) *Winning Hearts and Minds? Examining the Relationship between Aid and Security in Afghanistan* (Medford, MA: Feinstein International Center at Tufts University).
32. K. Kanyinga (2009) "The legacy of the white highlands: Land rights, ethnicity and the post-2007 election violence in Kenya," *Journal of Contemporary African Studies*, 27(3): 325–344.
33. Interviews by this author with peacebuilding NGOs in Kenya, Uganda and those working in parts of Somalia between January 2002 and October 2011.

PART II

Cross Cutting Issues

CHAPTER 5

The United Nations and Peacemaking

Alex J. Bellamy

INTRODUCTION

The United Nations was established to 'save succeeding generations from the scourge of war'. Limited by great power politics and influenced by some key innovators, the UN's approach to peacemaking developed as a series of ad hoc responses to pressing issues. It has been subject to the shifting sands of political interests but also to the bitter lessons of lived experience. As a result, whilst concepts such as peacemaking, mediation, preventive diplomacy, peacekeeping, and peacebuilding—among others—have been developed to describe and explain different facets of the UN's work, in practice there have rarely been such neat distinctions. Peacemaking at the UN was always to some extent multidimensional, comprising many different aspects of peace that overlapped with one another. Most obviously, from the UN's perspective, peacemaking has almost always gone hand in hand with peacebuilding. Likewise, peacekeeping has *always* entailed a degree of peacemaking.

A. J. Bellamy (✉)
University of Queensland, Brisbane, QLD, Australia
e-mail: a.bellamy@uq.edu.au

This multidimensional quality has become more pronounced in the last two decades largely as a result of lessons learned from the past. Traditionally, peacemaking in theory involved the use of negotiations to persuade parties to negotiate an agreement. Whilst this work acquired a relatively good track record of reducing violence in the near-term it often produced shallow agreements that left key problems unresolved. As a result, there was a high incidence of conflict reignition. In response to this, since the early 1990s especially, the UN has significantly widened its' approach to peacemaking, blurring still further conceptual distinctions between peacemaking, peacebuilding, peacekeeping and even—sometimes—peace enforcement, and broadening the range of activities thought necessary to supporting effective peacemaking. What is more, whilst the problem of conflict reignition has increased the UN's focus on continuing peacemaking *after* war, the commitment of successive Secretaries-General to promoting prevention has driven action towards peacemaking to *prevent* war.

This chapter aims to provide a sense of the breadth of the UN's engagement with peacemaking and its evolution. It shows that there is no single approach to peacemaking in the UN—no one ideology, institutional architecture, or method of acting guides the whole range of UN activity in this field. Take elections, for example. Commonly regarded as a defining feature of what some see as the UN's 'liberal peacebuilding', in reality only some of the UN's peacemaking activities include, let alone prioritise, the holding of elections. Elections were not, for example, part of the power-sharing agreement brokered by Kofi Annan in Kenya. Nor did they feature in any of the plans brought forward by the UN's Special Envoys for Syria (Kofi Annan, Lakhdar Brahimi, Staffan de Mistura). Election support is part of the mandate for some, but by no means all, of the UN's Special Political Missions and regional offices. The point I want to make in this chapter is that not only can we see significant change over time in UN practice, but that at any given time there is great variation across the UN's peacemaking activities. There are two main reasons for this. First, because UN activities tend be to ad hoc reactions to specific situations, and each situation really is different. Second, because the international political configurations around each situation is also different. Thus, what may be achievable in one situation, may not be achievable in another. Often, we see conformity in UN practices only because we do not look at the whole picture. This chapter tries to provide a necessarily brief snapshot of that wider picture.

It proceeds in three main parts. The first briefly describes the evolution of the UN's peacemaking role, showing how it evolved as the global political context changed. The second reviews the Organization's contemporary peacemaking activities, focusing on the 'primacy of politics' in peacekeeping, special political missions, the use of envoys, the role of regional offices, and the range of ad hoc activities undertaken to support peacemaking. The third part briefly identifies some of the factors that have made UN mediation more—or less—effective.

THE EVOLUTION OF UN PEACEMAKING

Wrought amidst the turmoil of the Second World War, the United Nations was established, the first line of its Charter tells us, to 'save succeeding generations from the scourge of war'. It would do so through a system of collective security that would deter and respond to armed aggression, by promoting and (eventually) protecting fundamental human rights, by fostering international cooperation to advance economic development and social progress for 'better standards of life in larger freedom' (Charter of the United Nations, Preamble), and by facilitating the expansion of international law and the adjudication of disputes between states by the International Court of Justice. It was a system designed to address the causes of the Second World War and prevent a repeat of its worst excesses, one that assumed that states would continue to be the world's principal war-makers. Article 24 of the UN Charter conferred upon the Security Council 'primary responsibility to international peace and security'. The Council's responsibility being primary, not exclusive, means that it has no obligation to assume responsibility for *every* problem of international security. Indeed, aware that it was impossible to predict the security challenges of the future, the Charter's drafters showed considerable foresight in granting the Council latitude to determine its own agenda and adopt whatever measures it deemed appropriate, allowing the Council to adapt to the challenges, power configurations, and norms of the day. Article 24(2) requires only that the Council discharge its duties in accordance with the purposes and principles of the UN, identified in Article 1 of the Charter, and that it utilizes the powers set out in Chapters VI, VII, VIII, and XII of the Charter.

Though this latitude has produced a selective and uneven approach to peacemaking, it has ensured the continuing cooperation of the major powers (US, Soviet Union/Russia, and China) whilst allowing the

Council to respond to problems when consensus was possible. When the Council is at its best, it is this latitude that partly explains its capacity for innovation and ability to tailor measures to specific situations. But this has come at the cost of inaction and inconsistency by allowing the permanent members to further their own interests and protect their friends. For example, during the Cold War, two decades of bloody fighting in Vietnam and a decade of war in Afghanistan failed to elicit a Council response because both wars involved permanent members prepared to use their veto to block collective action. But it is the very fact that the Council—as a political body all the way down—provides the major powers with reassurance that explains its endurance, authority, and centrality in contemporary peacemaking.

The Council's powers are laid out in Chapters VI (on the peaceful settlement of disputes), VII (actions with respect to breaches of the peace and acts of aggression), VIII (regional arrangements), and XII (international trusteeship) of the Charter. Although most attention is paid to its Chapter VII authority, the Council's peacemaking role stems more from Chapter VI. Indeed, in his landmark report of 1992, *Agenda for Peace*, Secretary-General Boutros-Ghali defined peacemaking as 'action to bring hostile parties to agreement, essentially through peaceful means as those foreseen in Chapter VI...'. Things are never quite so clear-cut in practice, however. Specifically, Chapter VI permits the Security Council to investigate any dispute or situation likely to give rise to international friction (Article 34) and allows the Council to recommend remedies (Article 36), terms of settlement (Article 37) or recommendations about the pacific settlement of the dispute (Article 38). Chapter VI also allows any Member State to refer any such situation to the Council (Article 35 [1]) and requires that parties to a dispute unable to resolve their differences by arbitration bring the matter to the Security Council (Article 37). Among other things, these provisions have facilitated the mandating of diplomacy, commissions of inquiry, special political missions, civilian observation missions, police missions, and peacekeeping operations by the Security Council.

Chapter VII bestows upon the Council its unique authority to authorize enforcement actions. Article 39 states that the Council 'shall determine the existence of any threat to the peace, breach of the peace, or act of aggression' and shall decide what 'recommendations to make' or measures to adopt to maintain or restore international peace and security. There are three important points worth stressing here. First, it is for the Council itself to determine when a threat or breach of the peace exists. This is a political, not a legal, decision and is not subject to judicial review. Second, Article 39 awards the Council an explicitly preventive function by referring to *threats* to international peace and security and requiring action to *maintain* the peace: the Council need not wait for threats to materialize (i.e. for the peace to be broken) before it acts. This preventive function is reinforced by Article 40, which permits the Council to adopt 'provisional measures' to 'prevent an aggravation of the situation' prior to the adoption of recommendations about the resolution of a dispute. Third, Article 39 awards the Council a discretionary *right* to adopt measures to maintain international peace and insecurity but does not impose any *obligation* upon it to do so.[1]

Chapter VIII of the Charter, which addresses the role of regional arrangements in the maintenance of international peace and security, also refers to the Security Council. In particular, the Security Council is to encourage the pacific settlement of disputes by regional arrangements (Article 52 [3]) and is entitled to utilize such arrangements for enforcement action under its authority (Article 53 [1]), whilst the often-overlooked Chapter VIII points to the important role played by regional organizations. This is a role that has grown more important with time, not least because of the growing peacemaking partnerships between the UN and regional bodies such as the African Union (the UN and AU worked together to make peace in Kenya in 2007–8) and League of Arab States (which together appointed a joint envoy for Syria in 2011).

Things did not pan out as the Charter's drafters thought they would. The Cold War put collective security into a deep freeze, whilst decolonization and wars of secession presented the new organization with new challenges that it was not well-equipped to deal with. In the field of peace and security, the UN was forced to innovate, and it did so in at least three ways.

First, the UN General Assembly began to play a more active role in peacemaking than was initially envisaged. Thus, in May 1948, it was the General Assembly, not the Security Council, that appointed Folke Bernadotte as 'United Nations Mediator in Palestine' tasked with negotiating an end to violence between the new state of Israel and its Arab neighbours. Influenced by Ralph Bunche, an African American who played a critically important role in helping to establish the UN Secretariat and the Organization's role in peacemaking, Bernadotte initially proposed a one state solution. Recognizing that Jews and Palestinians were too intermixed to make partition viable, the UN's mediator proposed a confederal state that would protect the rights of all. Both sides rejected the plan, and the Security Council was also divided on the matter. Bernadotte changed tack and proposed a two-state solution instead. That too was torpedoed, this time by the US which wanted a deal more favourable to the Zionists, which created a rift between it and the UK (which favoured Bernadotte's proposal) and the Arab world. (The Soviet Union, it should be noted, also supported the Zionists' rejection of Bernadotte's plan). Just a day after presenting this second plan, on 17 September 1948, Bernadotte was murdered by a Zionist terrorist organization known as the Stern Gang. He was replaced by Bunche who attempted to secure the return of displaced Palestinians and later negotiated a ceasefire in 1949, but the underlying political dispute that Bernadotte had tried to address remains with us today.[2] The General Assembly continued to play a proactive role in peacemaking, for example authorizing the UN Temporary Executive Authority in 1962 to oversee the transition of authority in West Irian/West Papua from the Netherlands to Indonesia.[3]

The General Assembly's role in peacemaking has developed over time, giving rise to significant parts of the UN's architecture for peace and security. For example, the UN's Peacebuilding Commission, Support Office, and Fund, established at the 2005 World Summit sit partly under the General Assembly. The Assembly has also continued to appoint envoys or to recommend that the Secretary-General offer good offices, especially in situations where the Security Council is deadlocked. More recently, it has begun to innovate in other ways too. Confronted by Security Council deadlock over Syria, the General Assembly took the step of establishing its own independent mechanism for collecting evidence of war crimes and crimes against humanity that might be used in future prosecutions.[4]

Second, and partly in response to pressure from the General Assembly, the Secretary-General developed an independent role as a mediator, a role envisaged nowhere in the Charter. This was first articulated by the Organization's second Secretary-General, U Thant, who argued that 'the Secretary-General's obligations under the Charter must include any humanitarian action that he can take to save the lives of large numbers of human beings'.[5] It was developed further by his successor, Dag Hammarskjold, who conceived the idea of making 'preventive diplomacy' a core function of the organization. By that, Hammarskjold meant that the UN Secretary-General should use his good offices to help parties to a dispute resolve their differences peacefully. The 'preventive' aspect was a nod to the realities of Cold War politics and recognition that local proxy conflicts could escalate into wider conflagrations.[6] The UN's role, as Hammarskjold saw it, was to prevent that from happening. It was a cause for which Hammarskjold gave his life, as in September 1961 he was killed in when his airplane crashed on his way to mediate a resolution to a secessionist war in the Congo between the Congolese government (backed by the Soviet Union), and Western-supported separatists in Katanga.[7] To this day, questions remain about whether the Secretary-General's plane was shot down or whether the crash was accidental. Bunche would also have been aboard had the Secretary-General not asked him at the last moment to perform another task.

Initially, the Secretary-General's role in peacemaking was entirely ad hoc, staffed from within the Secretary-General's own administrative office. After all, this was not a role envisaged by the UN Charter.[8] But since the end of the Cold War, especially, much of the UN's institutional architecture for peacemaking has come from the initiative of the Secretary-General. In particular, as this peacemaking function grew, so too did the demand for expertise and analysis. To respond to this growing need, in 1992 Secretary-General Boutros Boutros-Ghali established the Department of Political Affairs (DPA) to support the UN's work by providing political analysis, engaging with national and local actors, and supporting mediation and political processes. In the 2000s, the DPA began establishing 'Special Political Missions', civilian missions aimed at supporting peacemaking and helping states and societies implement peace agreements, and in 2006 established a Mediation Support Unit to support a team of expert mediators who could be deployed by the Secretary-General into a crisis setting at very short notice.

The third innovation was the development of a range of new practices by the Security Council, General Assembly, and Secretariat to support peace processes. Foremost among these was the innovation of peacekeeping—UN military operations deployed, initially at least, to separate forces and observe ceasefires whilst parties negotiated a political settlement. Like every other aspect of the UN's role in peacemaking, peacekeeping emerged as an ad hoc response to immediate crises. In this case, the need to find a way of facilitating a British and French withdrawal from the Suez, whilst keeping Egyptian and Israeli forces apart, provided a catalyst for the development of peacekeeping and its core principles of consent, impartiality, and minimum force. Over time, peacekeeping operations have become larger and more complex. Sometimes, as in East Timor and Kosovo, the UN assumed responsibility for transitional administrations. Increasingly, UN peacekeeping operations are primarily concerned with the protection of civilians and are deployed into situations of ongoing armed conflict, raising important questions about the relationship between peacekeeping and peacemaking and drawing calls for a new, more strategic and comprehensive approach that better aligns these different modes of action.[9] However, in practice the mediation of local disputes and prevention of escalation through negotiation remains a core part of the peacekeepers' daily practice, as a recent study of the United Nations Interim Force in Lebanon (UNIFIL) in southern Lebanon demonstrates.[10]

The critical point in all of this is that both the institutional architecture and the UN's practices of peacemaking evolved over time as largely ad hoc responses to pressing challenges. There is therefore no single template, nor organizing ideology for the UN's peacemaking activities. Whilst the Organization has tried to become more systematic to its approach—notably through formalizing the role of the DPA and establishing the Mediation Support Unit—it remains hostage to the demands of its political organs and the limits of political support for both the UN's actions in general but, perhaps more significantly, the UN's role in particular situations.

UN Peacemaking Today

The UN's institutional architecture for peacemaking is a product of its historical evolution and attempts by past Secretaries-General to strengthen the UN's capacity, not all of which proved successful. The current Secretary-General, Antonio Guterres has proposed his own set of reforms designed to better integrate the organization's different functional areas and thus improve its capacity to engage with individual crises in a coordinated fashion. In particular, Guterres proposes to bring the UN's peacemaking and peacebuilding work together into a single department of Political and Peacebuilding Affairs, whilst giving the Department of Peace Operations responsibility for all field missions, be they military, police, or civilian.[11] Yet, like those of his predecessors, these proposals have already met with resistance from the UN's Member States. Some, including major donors such as the US, prefer to maintain budgetary discretion over individual missions and thus do not want the UN's civilian political missions funded in the same way as its peacekeeping missions. Many states, including Russia, China, and India are wary of extending peacebuilding into areas other than physical reconstruction after armed conflict and prefer to treat it separately from other issues. Still others, mainly European and Latin American states complain that human rights seem to have been excluded from the agenda.

To get a good sense of the sheer diversity of the types of peacemaking engagement undertaken by the UN it is best to look beyond institutional architecture, at the actual activities themselves. At the time of writing, this comprised 24 distinct peacemaking endeavours (in addition to peacekeeping and peacebuilding) covering close to 50 different countries. We can cluster them into five types.

Peace Operations

Because peacekeeping operations are distinct from the UN's peacemaking missions, it is often overlooked that all of the UN's peace operations have a peacemaking dimension. Within the UN, however, the centrality of peacemaking to the achievement of peacekeeping goals is being increasingly recognized.[12] In its early years, UN peacekeeping was conceptualized as an instrument for monitoring ceasefires and overseeing the implementation of peace agreements between parties to conflict. In this sense, it was always understood to be deployed *in support of* a political process already underway, not as a substitute for one. In theory at least, peacekeeping operated on the assumption that the parties to the conflict were already committed to the peace—and it has always been successful when that assumption has proven more or less right (for example, in Namibia, Mozambique, and El Salvador). That changed after the end of the Cold War as the role of peacekeeping expanded and peacekeepers found themselves expected to sometimes enforce the peace (as in Somalia) or achieve more limited goals (such as delivering aid or protecting civilians) in conditions on ongoing violence. It became increasingly obvious that political settlements could not be imposed by peacekeepers but that peacekeepers could help to alleviate suffering in situations where the conflict parties were unwilling to broker peace. Partly as a result, peacekeeping became more heavily focused on protecting civilians in conditions of armed conflict than on supporting peace processes. There were notable successes in Sierra Leone (UNAMSIL) and Liberia (UNMIL) but by the 2010s the UN was confronting a situation where its largest peacekeeping operations—deployed in the Democratic Republic of Congo, South Sudan, Darfur, Mali, and the Central African Republic—were operating in the absence of a viable political process.[13]

The UN has tried to respond by reinforcing the role of peacemaking in peacekeeping operations—something referred to as the 'primacy of politics', which the UN Security Council resolved should be central to the UN's approach (Resolution 2378 [2018]). As a result, the UN is integrating effective preventive diplomacy, peacemaking, peacekeeping and peacebuilding into its peacekeeping missions. Each one of those missions therefore has a dedicated team working on political affairs. The logic behind this approach was identified by the High-Level Panel on Peace Operations in 2015, which concluded that: 'Lasting peace is achieved not through military and technical engagements but through political solutions. Political solutions should always guide the design and deployment of UN peace operations. When the momentum behind peace falters, the United Nations, and particularly Member States, must help to mobilize renewed political efforts to keep peace processes on track'.[14]

Similarly, the Review of the Peacebuilding Architecture 2015 and the 'Sustaining Peace' agenda developed by the General Assembly in 2017 have reinforced the importance of integrating peacemaking into peacekeeping operations.[15] These initiatives have begun to filter down into the way that the UN does business on the ground. For example, internal reviews of the UN's missions in the DRC (MONUSCO) and Mali (MINUSMA) have given rise to new mission strategies that prioritize support for national political processes. In this model, UN mediators on the ground negotiate political agreements around issues such as the disarmament, demobilization, and reintegration of armed groups, the conducting of elections, or the management of local ceasefires, and the peacekeepers follow-up to support implementation. This new approach to peacekeeping was signalled clearly in the 2018 Action for Peacekeeping (A4P) initiative. A4P emphasizes the importance of advancing political solutions to conflict and enhancing the political impact of peacekeeping. It calls for more action to better connect the UN's peacekeeping activities with its peacemaking goals.[16]

Political Missions

Special political missions were initially developed in the 1990s and early 2000s, they have since developed into one of the principal means by which the UN supports peacemaking.[17] One of the first political missions, was the UN Office in Burundi (ONUB), established alongside the ill-fated UNAMIR mission in Rwanda, to support implementation of the Arusha accords and the transfer of power. Although ONUB fared a little better than its counterpart, it too was unable to prevent the country sliding towards civil war and the mission was eventually replaced by a peacekeeping operation. The emergence of political missions gathered pace after 2007. When Ban Ki-moon became UN Secretary-General in that year, he expressed concern that peacekeeping had become the UN's default response to emerging crises.[18] This had been evident, for example, in the Security Council's response to the crisis in Darfur which had focused on creating the conditions necessary for the deployment of peacekeepers, arguably at the expense of a more comprehensive and inclusive approach to peacemaking. Ban was also concerned that peacekeeping was an essentially reactive tool, deployed after an armed conflict broke out. Ban championed the idea of 'Special Political Missions'—*civilian* missions, tailored to address specific problems or concerns ahead of escalation into war.

In 2018, the UN had special political missions deployed in Afghanistan, Angola, Burundi, Central African Republic, Cote d'Ivoire, Guinea, Iraq, Liberia, Libya, Sierra Leone, and Somalia. They are typically used in one of three settings—to continue political, humanitarian, and development cooperation after the withdrawal of a peacekeeping operation (as in Liberia and Sierra Leone), to fulfil political tasks alongside other multinational operations (as in Afghanistan and Iraq alongside coalition operations, Somalia alongside the AU's AMISOM mission, and the Central African Republic alongside French and UN forces), and in preventive mode in situations at risk of armed conflict or the escalation of existing conflicts (as in Burundi, Guinea, and Libya). Each of these missions is different in terms of their mandate and composition. One of the largest is the UN Assistance Mission in Afghanistan (UNAMA). Comprising some 1200 people, UNAMA's work focuses on three core areas: supporting mediation efforts to reconcile the country's parties, negotiate local agreements, and encourage participation in national processes; human rights promotion, reporting, and protection—including support for elections and capacity building for national human rights institutions; and technical support and assistance in economic development—an agenda driven by the Afghan government's priorities. By contrast, the UN's support office in Guinea Bissau is much smaller, comprising around 140 staff. A good example of how the UN's peacemaking is connected to other areas of work—in this case, peacebuilding—the Guinea office is focused primarily on supporting projects developed by the Peacebuilding Commission and resourced by the Peacebuilding Fund. This includes national dialogue focused on reconciliation, supporting capacity building in the media to support peace, improving the capacity and legitimacy of the justice sectors, and promoting opportunities and inclusiveness for women and youth. The UN's support office in Somalia (UNSOM) is significantly different in that it was established to complement and support a large AU peacekeeping mission (AMISOM). Comprising around 275 staff, UNSOM's mandate has a distinct political focus centred on providing support to the fledgling federal government, especially in the fields of security sector governance, including the justice sector, and economic development. The Office also provides support for elections and other political processes as needed, and also supports local and national mediation efforts when conflicts arise. Of course, anticipating conflict and preventing escalation is something that all the special political missions attempt to do. Indeed, part of the logic behind positioning political offices in-country is that they are better able to anticipate and respond to emerging crises and conflicts.

A third type of UN peacemaking is the despatch of envoys to help mediate ceasefires of political agreements. Envoys may be despatched at the request of the General Assembly (as in the case of Bernadotte in Palestine) or Security Council (as in the case of Kofi Annan in Syria in 2012). In 2018, the UN had six such mandates, covering Burundi, the African Great Lakes, Sudan/South Sudan, Cyprus, Myanmar, Syria, and Yemen (recall that these are in addition to the political functions in 18 peacekeeping missions and the special political missions). Envoys may also be appointed under the personal initiative of the Secretary-General. For example, in 2017 Antonio Guterres appointed Horst Koehler as his personal envoy to Western Sahara, charged with continuing efforts to negotiate an agreement that would allow the exercising of self-determination there. Likewise, the recent agreement between Greece and Macedonia over the latter's formal name was in part facilitated by the

Secretary-General's personal envoy, Matthew Nimetz. In a salutary lesson about the virtue of patience in peacemaking, Nimetz held the role for nearly twenty years before an agreement was finally reached.[19]

To get a sense of the complexities of this role, it is worth considering Annan's experience as joint UN-Arab League envoy for Syria. In 2007–8, the Secretary-General had asked Kofi Annan to serve as joint UN-African Union mediator to broker a deal between Kenya's divided leaders in the wake of a disputed election that had led to ethnic violence. Then, Annan had succeeded in forging an agreement and stemming the escalation to violence. But the situation confronting Syria in early 2012 was far worse and the international community far more divided. Annan accepted that Syria's President Assad would not be easily dislodged from power but also understood that a process that left Assad in power would never be acceptable to the opposition.[20] A managed transition of some sorts would be necessary: the question was how that would be achieved. Annan first focused on international opinion, seeking the views of key capitals and developing a plan that he hoped would command international support. It involved immediate steps to reduce violence and de-escalate tensions, overseen by UN observers, and talks on a political process. Annan would then use what international support he had to persuade the Syria's government and opposition to participate. 'For a challenge as great as this, only a united international community can compel both sides to engage in a peaceful political transition', he explained.[21] As the parties talked, Annan hoped that the reduction of violence would help ease tensions and build support for peace on Syria's streets.[22] If violence could be reduced, Annan thought the parties could be persuaded to agree on a Yemen-style orderly transition of power that preserved the state itself intact. Just three weeks into his mandate, Annan proposed a new six-point plan. He persuaded the US and Russia to back the plan, and they helped bring Syria's parties on board. A ceasefire was agreed and UN monitors deployed to observe compliance. But the deal soon fell apart, as government forces refused to comply with key parts of their agreement and the opposition, in turn, stepped up its non-compliance.

Regional offices. As I noted earlier, the UN now understands that peacemaking is done best when it is based as close as possible to where it is needed. In addition to in-country missions, therefore, the UN has tried to establish a network of regional offices with three principal purposes: strengthening the UN's preventive diplomacy (including mediation), promoting functional cooperation with regional organizations, and managing responses to emerging crises, and facilitating coordinated action to transnational crises that cross-national boundaries. The UN's Regional Centre for Preventive Diplomacy in Central Asia, for example, is a small office (comprising around 25 staff) focused on promoting preventive dialogue between the region's governments, providing early warning of imminent crises, facilitating UN action on prevention, and encouraging engagement between Afghanistan and the rest of the region. Similarly, its office in West Africa and Sahel supports preventive diplomacy and mediation, but also works to help sub-regional organizations such as ECOWAS to build their capacities for mediation. More specifically, this office oversees a regional plan for addressing the cross-border flow of arms and militia in the Sahel and a boundary commission aimed at resolving a dispute between Nigeria and Cameroon. Thus far, besides the central Asia and West Africa/Sahel offices, the UN has also established regional offices to the African Union and Central Africa.

Special activities. The fifth type of activity relates to peacemaking efforts that do not fit neatly into the other categories, but which are important to include not only because of their own value but also as a reminder of the variety of activities associated with peacemaking and the many different approaches that the UN alone can adopt. There is a surprisingly large number of examples of this kind of activity, but I will briefly mention three that were operating in 2018. In Guatemala, the UN oversees an International Commission Against Impunity designed to support efforts to ensure accountability for atrocity crimes committed during the country's civil war by people who may now be in positions of power and authority. This initiative was developed in partnership with the government of Guatemala which recognized that impunity for past crimes was impeding contemporary efforts to reconcile divided communities and improve accountability. In Colombia, meanwhile, the UN has deployed a civilian verification mission to monitor and report on ceasefire and human rights violations under the terms of a UN brokered agreement between the government and FARC rebels. In Lebanon, a UN envoy is charged with overseeing and reporting on the disarmament and demobilization of non-state armed groups, and especially non-Lebanese armed groups, a process that at the time of writing had not progressed far.

EVALUATION

There is no space here to perform a thorough assessment of the UN's performance in peacemaking. Besides, such evaluations are fraught given the breadth of activities that contribute to peacemaking and the range of intervening variables that influence the outcome. As both Kofi Annan and Lakhdar Brahimi found, seasoned mediators with strong track records of success can sometimes fail even when they apply strategies and practices that worked in other situations. There is, however, quantitative evidence that the UN's activities do help to prevent conflict, reduce its duration, reduce civilian victimization, and encourage the sustainability of peace. Such generalizations might help reassure sceptical observers that the peace industry has value, but it provides little succour to those living in places that see little positive effect. It would be remiss, then, to not reflect briefly on the some of the conditions that seem to make UN peacemaking more, or less, effective.

First, the receptiveness of national leaders matters. As Edward Luck argued recently, it helps if local, group and national leaders 'are willing to listen to international appeals and are concerned about how their reputations are likely to be affected by escalating violence'.[23] By itself, peacemaking is unlikely to forge peace in places where leaders with access to arms prefer war. Some degree of goodwill is necessary. UN mediators like Folke Bernadotte—and Sergio Vieira de Mello, who was killed by al-Qaeda in Iraq in 2003—have paid the ultimate price for arguing the case for peace among armed groups who retain a preference for violence.

Second, as other chapters in this volume demonstrate, the timing of peacemaking matters. When conflicts are so intense as to give rise to major wars or atrocities, the window for effective peacemaking is already quite small. As violence escalates and parties resort to violence on a more widespread and systematic basis, that window closes almost entirely until either one party prevails or all the major parties recognize that they have reached a stalemate—a realization that can be many years in the making. To have good practical effect, peacemaking measures need to be mobilized in the early stages of a crisis. We should expect limited success when peacemakers are despatched during or after the escalation of violence.

Third, quantity sometimes has a quality all of its own. Individually, none of the measures associated with peacemaking that I described above would likely tilt societies away from war and towards peace. That is precisely why the UN's approach to peacemaking has become broader and more multi-faceted. What is needed now is more coordinated, multi-level, and simultaneous action by a range of different actors, utilizing all of the appropriate instruments. When multiple parties are engaged in protective action, those activities work better when they are coordinated. Coordination reduces the capacity of armed groups to go forum shopping and prioritize the international mechanisms that work best for them whilst buying time by exploiting ambiguities and gaps. Coordination also has a multiplier effect on individual actions. For example, the effect of determined private sector action to prevent election violence in Kenya in 2013 was multiplied by the fact that it was accompanied by intense bilateral diplomacy by influential states and concerted efforts by the UN and its partners. No one of these actors could have achieved the same effect working alone. Because violence can be triggered and perpetrated at different levels, it is important that peacemaking occurs at different levels too—ranging from international forums and the state leadership down to individual localities. The UN is obviously better suited to operating at the regional and national levels, and through its offices is looking to improve its admittedly modest capacity to support sub-national mediation. Not only is this necessary to deal with different sorts of conflicts, but top-down and bottom-up work can be mutually reinforcing. Finally, peacemaking action needs to be 'simultaneous' to some extent. Whilst the logical sequencing of measures can prove useful, peacemaking tends to work best when a range of actions are pursued simultaneously on a number of different fronts. For example, difficult negotiations can be assisted by reporting from the ground by monitors, which can help establish the facts of the matter between conflicting parties based on independent evidence. Likewise, the UN's efforts can be amplified by regional efforts, which may be more consequential for leaders keen to preserve their reputation among their peers. The obverse might also be true in that global efforts might amplify efforts led by the region. It is no coincidence that some of the best recent results have been seen in sub-Saharan Africa where the UN has worked closely with the AU and ECOWAS.

Fourth, the resilience of affected societies matters. A community's resilience to violence can be found in many places, including within national institutions, faith-based groupings, civil society, the private sector, the media, traditional means of maintaining order and resolving disputes, and cultures of peace. Anecdotally, UN peacemakers have often explained that their efforts are more likely to have good effect when they can relate to and build upon existing sources of local resilience and capacities for conflict resolution. Conversely, where institutions or civil society are weak, as for example, they were in Libya under Gaddafi, societies are more prone towards fragmentation.

Fifth, the political and material resources dedicated to supporting peacemaking matter. It is one thing for the Security Council or General Assembly to pass resolutions and create mandates, it is another thing entirely for it to back those decisions with determined and well-resourced action. UN peacemakers have, historically, achieved much with limited resources. States need to understand that if they want a more comprehensive approach to peacemaking, one that draws on all the UN's capacities and partnerships, they have to properly resource these efforts. That is something they have not yet been willing to do. Two examples suffice to make the point. As I mentioned earlier, some Western and other governments oppose the Secretary-General's proposal to better finance special political missions by funding them in the same way that peacekeeping operations are funded, rather than—as they are now—through entirely ad hoc means. Likewise, although the General Assembly champions mediation as the best way of resolving conflicts, the UN's Mediation Support Unit is not fully financed out of the UN's regular budget. Instead, it relies on voluntary contributions by states for some of its basic operations.[24]

Sixth, it matters whether the UN's Member States signal their support for the UN's peacemaking efforts. It is a well-known rule of thumb that the UN does best when its Member States are united, and regional partnerships are utilized, and that the chances of success are much more limited when states are divided. Peacemaking often fails because political or military leaders judge that their interests are better served by violence. Persuading leaders to change course includes steps such as reframing the conflict, finding practical solutions to clashes of interest, convincing them either that their chances of success are limited or that the costs associated with continuing the violence are prohibitive, and calling attention to their legacy. A central part of doing that entails providing groups with peaceful ways of resolving their disputes and protecting their legitimate interests, through mediation, trust building, and conflict resolution. Part of shaping leaders' calculations involves persuading them that there is little to be gained by continuing down the path of violence. Like most things, signalling credibility is most straightforward in the early stages of a crisis and, once lost, credibility is difficult to recover. Peace efforts are undermined when states fail to signal support to the UN's peacemakers.

Conclusion

Peacemaking is among the core functions of the UN system. In practice, there are no neat distinctions between peacemaking and other aspects of the organizations work supporting peace. What is more, with growing recognition of the fact that sustainable peace requires sustained engagement, so the UN's approach to peacemaking has begun to incorporate areas such as human rights, institutional capacity building, and economic development. Variation across UN activities is only likely to grow as the organization implements lessons learned from bitter experience, which shows that peacemaking is best done quickly and by those closest to the conflict. The proliferation of national missions and regional offices offers one way in which UN peacemaking is becoming more adaptive to regional, national, and local conditions. Ultimately, though, if states want the UN to improve on its mixed record when it comes to peacemaking they have to be better prepared to support the Organization's efforts and to properly resource them. But that, after all, is what 'we the peoples' demanded in 1945.

Notes

1. See Edward C. Luck, *UN Security Council: Promise and Practice* (London: Routledge, 2006), pp. 22–23.
2. Brian Urquhart, *Ralph Bunche: An American Odyssey* (New York: W.W. Norton, 1993), pp. 139–232.
3. Alan James, *The Politics of Peace-Keeping* (London: Chatto and Windus, 1969), pp. 159–169.
4. Melinda Rankin, 'The Future of International Criminal Evidence in New Wars? The Evolution of the Commission for International Justice and Accountability', *Journal of Genocide Research*, 20 (3), 2018, pp. 392–411.
5. U. Thant, *View From the United Nations* (New York: David and Charles, 1978), p. 27.
6. Bertrand G. Ramcharan, *Preventive Diplomacy at the UN* (Bloomington: Indiana University Press, 2008), pp. 79–104.
7. Brian Urquhart, *Hammarskjold* (New York: W.W. Norton, 1994), pp. 545–589.
8. Brian Urquhart, *A Life in Peace and War* (New York: W.W. Norton, 1991).

9. On the evolution of peacekeeping as a tool of mediation see Lise Morje Howard, *Power in Peacekeeping* (Cambridge: Cambridge University Press, 2019).
10. Vanessa F. Newby, *Peacekeeping in Southern Lebanon: Credibility and Local Cooperation* (New York: Syracuse University Press, 2018).
11. Bertrand G. Ramcharan, 'Antonio Guteress' Strategy for Reforming the UN', *Global Governance*, 25 (1), 2019, pp. 13–21.
12. See *Report of the High-Level Independent Panel on Peace Operations on uniting our strengths for peace: Politics, partnerships, and people*, A/70/95-S/2015/446, 17 June 2015.
13. Mats Berdal, 'What are the Limits to the Use of Force in UN Peacekeeping?', in Cedric de Coning and Mateja Peter (eds.), *United Nations Peace Operations in a Changing Global Order* (New York: Springer, 2018), pp. 113–132.
14. *Report of the High-Level Independent Panel on Peace Operations*, para. 15.
15. Advisory Group of Experts on the Review of the Peacebuilding Architecture (AGE) 2015.
16. *Action for Peacekeeping: Declaration of Shared Commitments on UN Peacekeeping Operations*, New York, 18 June 2018.
17. Ian Johnstone, 'Emerging Doctrine for Special Political Missions', *Annual Review of United Nations Peace Operations* (New York: Centre for International Cooperation, 2010), pp. 15–27.
18. Richard Gowan, 'Less Bound to the Desk: Ban Ki-Moon, the UN, and Preventive Diplomacy', *Global Governance*, 18 (2), 2012, pp. 387–404.
19. 'The Man Who Has Focused on One Word for 23 years', *BBC News*, 2 August 2017.
20. Richard Gowan, 'Kofi Annan, Syria and the Uses of Uncertainty in Mediation', *Stability*, 2 (1), 2013, p. 3.
21. Kofi Annan, 'My Departing Advice on How the World Can Yet Save Syria', *Financial Times*, 3 August 2012.
22. Tom H. J. Hill, 'Kofi Annan's Multilateral Strategy of Mediation and the Syrian Crisis: The Future of Peacemaking in a Multipolar World?', *International Negotiation*, 20 (3), 2015, pp. 444–478.
23. Edward C. Luck, 'The Responsibility to Protect at Ten: The Challenges Ahead', Policy Analysis Brief for the Stanley Foundation, June 2015, p. 6.
24. *United Nations Activities in Support of Mediation*, A/72/115, 27 June 2017, paras. 46–49.

CHAPTER 6

Women's Participation in Peace Processes

Jana Krause and Louise Olsson

INTRODUCTION

Engendered in a peace tent and then driven forcefully by women's organizations from conflict areas, the argument on the importance of improving women's participation in peace processes was translated into an explicit objective in the Beijing Declaration and Platform for Action in 1995. In October 2000, this objective was declared important for international peace and security by the UN Security Council in Resolution (UNSCR) 1325, adopted under Namibia's Presidency. This thematic resolution, and the additional ones on Women, Peace and Security which have been adopted since, stressed two points. First, the importance of women's participation in the formal stages of a peace process. Second, the centrality

---

J. Krause (✉)
University of Oslo, Oslo, Norway
e-mail: jana.krause@stv.uio.no

L. Olsson
PRIO, Oslo, Norway
e-mail: louise@prio.org

of recognizing more informal contributions to peace by women's organizations. Unfortunately, however, there is near consensus that progress on reaching these objectives has remained extremely slow. For example, between 1990 and 2017, women have constituted only five per cent of signatories of, and witnesses to, peace agreements.[1] Consultations with women's organizations and support of their ongoing work in societies in war have progressed but still constitute a very limited, and sometimes marginalized, dimension of a peace process. This is despite the fact that women's inclusion in peace negotiations and peacebuilding appear to contribute to a decrease in the risk of a return to war.[2] In relation to the 15-year anniversary of UNSCR 1325 in 2015, women's continued lack of access and influence on peace processes therefore became a central theme.[3]

A post-2015 wave of policy efforts followed as outlined in the UN Secretary-General's yearly reports on Women and Peace and Security. This time, there was an increased emphasis on seeking to turn words into actions. This meant creating and utilizing more concrete approaches to including women, such as rapid response mechanisms to allow women to join peace negotiations even if these were announced on short notice.[4] Other examples include Women's Advisory Boards or Women Mediator Networks. The Secretary-General's reports further recognized the need for practical steps in eliminating barriers for women's participation, such as providing travel expenses and child care. While these practical aspects are difficult but solvable, a more fundamental aspect unearthed by these efforts was the difficulties of 'token' representation, a critique that was regularly levelled against women participants whether or not they had been symbolically appointed members or relations from the warring parties. As a response, the Secretary General introduced the term 'meaningful participation'. This is meant to challenge superficial efforts of participation without voice and influence, demanding instead participation that can shape the content of negotiations.[5]

The debate on meaningful participation highlighted further questions about what and who women represent and why representation is important, centring around two core points. First, peace agreements do set in place the foundation for transformative political, legal, social, and economic reforms that have the potential to affect the trajectory of women's empowerment and to shift gender hierarchies.[6] Hence, if women are included in peace negotiations to represent 'women's interests' for change, what do such interests entail? This debate on the relationship between women's representation and women's interests is not unique for peace processes. A similar discussion has ranged in relation to regular political processes ever since Hanna Arendt differentiated between formal, descriptive, symbolic, and substantive representation already in 1967. Even though women hold many different political standpoints and interactive identities research has found that women's inclusion does result in more gender equal political choices.[7] Peace agreements with women signatories include more provisions that address social inequality and women's rights and also demonstrate higher implementation rates for these provisions than agreements without direct women's participation.[8] Consequently, women's meaningful inclusion is relevant for the quality of the peace.[9] Second, research indicates that women's exclusion from peace negotiations undermines the durability of peace.[10] Women's inclusion is thereby important for ensuring a positive development trajectory for the whole of society. The reason is that women's representation broadens public support for peace processes through an interaction between women negotiators and women's groups. This increases the quality and legitimacy of an agreement and can assist its implementation.[11] This finding puts the spotlight on the fact that women constitute mobilized political actors in many contexts. Furthermore, we need to recognize that the core of this debate concerns how we should understand representation in peace processes and its role for ensuring a positive overall trajectory for a society over time.[12] With the exception of cases such as Northern Ireland where parties to the negotiations were selected through a popular vote, the representativeness of all parties in a process—both male and female-dominated ones—can be debated.

Elaborating further on these points, this chapter will proceed as follows. The first part of the chapter will identify and discuss key issues for a more nuanced understanding of women's participation. We begin by discussing challenges in the different stages of a process—pre-negotiations, negotiations, peace agreement formulation (i.e. bargaining), and peace agreement implementation—providing examples of what these can mean for women's participation. We then further problematize this in light of the fact that many processes do not progress in a *linear manner*. Thereafter, we will look closer at women's participation per se, both in terms of representation issues and practical approaches to their inclusion. The second part of the chapter will then focus on the last two stages of a peace process, that of the bargaining of the peace agreement and of the implementation and peacebuilding. This debate includes central considerations of the role of women's participation for the quality of the peace outcome as regards gender equality, transformation of hierarchical or patriarchal power structures, and why it is relevant for understanding peace durability. We conclude by highlighting future venues for research and policy.

1. Understanding Participation in Peace Processes

Previous research highlights three key areas where we need to improve our understandings of women's participation: (a) We need to be able to differentiate between different stages of a process and recognize that many processes do not follow a linear development. Rather, they should be perceived as repetitive; (b) We need to start from the perception of women as a diverse category of political actors and better connect that to a discussion on what 'women' are expected to represent. In so doing, we need to (c) consider the implications of the practical and technical approaches used to promote women's inclusion and if that contributes to forming 'women' as one consisted group rather than ensuring a more diverse representation.

Stages of a Peace Process

Stages of a peace process can range from pre-negotiations, negotiations, peace agreement formulation (i.e. bargaining), to peace agreement implementation.[13] A critique directed at existing international efforts to improve women's meaningful participation in a peace process is that they too generally span all stages of a process without recognizing important differences between each stage.[14] For example, supporting women's inclusion in pre-negotiations—a stage often surrounded by secrecy and restricted inclusion—can require different forms of support than seeking to promote participation during bargaining of the agreement—a stage with a high level of competition and often a rising number of involved actors.[15] In addition, each stage has its own practical and technical complexities requiring specific forms of expertise. For instance, the bargaining stage can include the formulation of a wide set of various legal and policy documents. Notably, the Peace Agreements Database, PAX,[16] include declarations of intent, substantive agreements, process agreements, and new constitutions.

It is important to recognize that women's participation is embedded within a broader peace process with multiple negotiations on specific documents and decisions. These processes can span months or years and few follow a linear development. The number of protracted conflicts with their equally protracted, or repetitive, peace negotiations is substantial. In recent years, negotiations have taken place or continue in Afghanistan, the Central African Republic (CAR), Colombia, Myanmar, the Philippines/Mindanao, Mali, Syria, South Sudan, and Yemen. These peace processes overwhelmingly concern conflicts with repeated cycles of negotiations and renewed peace agreements. Protracted conflicts are complex. They frequently do not only involve the government and a well-organized opposition group but a high fragmentation within the armed opposition and numerous armed actors on the sub-state level. The latter may not be fully controlled by either the government or rebel organizations but pursue their own agenda. Such 'multi-level conflicts' demand innovation in peace process design for 'multi-level peace processes'.[17]

For women's peace organizations, the nature of protracted conflicts and repeated negotiations require continuous mobilization and lobbying for inclusion at various stages of the peace process, often over years. This presents a significant cost to these organizations, often already burdened by survival struggles in conflict zones or situations of displacement. The implications for their ability to support peace can thereby decrease.[18] An informative example is the 2003 all-inclusive peace agreement in the Democratic Republic of the Congo (DRC). This included women's organizations who mobilized their own members in addition to being supported by international feminist networks. This combination of internal resources and external support enabled the women's organization to take part in the negotiations which were placed outside of the country, in the exclusive Sun City in South Africa. In addition to the cost of mobilization and participation, these women invested much resources into training of their members and time in agenda building to push for their meaningful participation in the negotiations. However, the 2003 peace agreement failed and new negotiations started in 2008. Women's organizations had to invest into mobilizing again while suffering from internal tensions and a struggle over leadership, thereby being unable to capitalize on their momentum and pressure the warring parties to include substantial women's representation and their political positions in the negotiations.[19] Consequently, in protracted conflicts, women's organizations may gain as well as lose access and influence to the negotiations over time.

Women's Agency—Who Do 'Women' Represent?

Women's civil society organizations were central for pushing for the recognition that women are political actors and that they have a right to be included in peace processes at both Beijing in 1995 and in the adoption of UNSCR 1325.[20] Further, research has demonstrated that more inclusive peace processes in which civil society groups[21] and women's organizations in particular[22] can shape the negotiations are more likely to lead to durable peace. Civil society participation increases public representation, broad population support, and brings local context-sensitive knowledge to the table.

Currently, the debate about women's participation is increasingly characterized by recognition of the need to move beyond essentialist stereotypes of 'peace women' and 'women' as a homogenous category. Instead, it is important to note the diversity of women, including women civil society activists, female combatants and women within the political wing of armed groups, as well as female government representatives; all of which could be vital for building peace.[23] This means that their situation and ability to affect different stages of the peace processes can differ but also that they are likely to represent different interests. Recognizing such diversity and intersectionality is particularly important in the context of protracted and multi-level conflicts. Women from different ethnic, religious, or political groups; women from urban and rural areas; and women from the civil society sector versus women in government or within the rebel group may hold substantially different understandings of the conflict, the main perpetrators, obstacles to resolution, and the very meaning of peace. Recognizing diversity among women leads to the question of who should be involved in peace negotiations and 'represent women'. Although the questioning of women's participation has often been criticized by feminist NGOs, the question is legitimate from a bottom-up point of view. National-level civil society and women groups can be disconnected to local-level groups or perceived as 'out-of-touch' and tokenistic.[24]

Recognizing the diversity of women and their views further means acknowledging women as political actors influenced by political agendas, group interests, as well as the trauma and hardship of civil war. An illuminating example of the complex composition of women regards their participation in South Sudan's peace process. Since the outbreak of civil war in 2013, the country's peace process included numerous rounds of negotiations. In the fall of 2017, South Sudanese women groups, who have a long history of mobilizing for peace and supporting peace negotiations (e.g. see the 1999 Wunlit peace agreement), met in Uganda, to prepare their participation in renewed peace negotiations in 2018. This brought together an impressive array of women representatives. Their discussions produced a statement signed by 40 South Sudanese women's organizations from within the country and those displaced in the region. This was a major achievement given that the country's diversity and deep conflict divides challenge women's mobilization and peacebuilding.[25] The illiteracy rate for women in South Sudan is at about 80 per cent of the population.[26] For the South Sudanese women groups, agreeing on a joint political agenda, selecting representatives to take part in the negotiations, establishing priorities for the negotiation process to jointly advocate for gender-related provisions was hard work and should be understood as an important act of reconciliation and good will that is fundamental for political collaboration and peacebuilding.

How Can women's Participation Be Strengthened?

The 2018 Secretary-General's report acknowledged the need to turn words into actions and implement more concrete steps to include women, eliminate barriers for their participation, and institutionalize rapid response mechanisms.[27] Since 2015, we can observe several forms of attempts, where the peace negotiations on Syria is an illuminating example. The first Syria peace talks under mediator Kofi Annan in 2012 in Geneva (Geneva I), while failing to result in any progress, excluded civil society and women representatives. The Geneva II talks, led by Lakhdar Brahimi in 2014, again saw no formal participation of women and civil society representatives. This time, there was more of an active exclusion as UN Women had brought women representatives from Syria to Geneva to take part in consultations. The talks broke down after a few days. A third round of negotiations then took place in 2016 under then mediator Staffan de Mistura. While Annan and Brahimi led 'exclusionary processes',[28] de Mistura institutionalized civil society's participation. Practically, this meant establishing the Civil Society Support

Room (CSSR), which developed into a platform of Syrian civil society actors to influence the political process. As for women's participation, this process demonstrated a concrete example of methods and rapid response mechanisms. Women were organized into a Women's Advisory Board to participate as third-party observers, at the time heralded as an innovative solution for women's inclusion in peacemaking.

The Syrian process also unearthed a debate on women as political representatives. Criticism arose as to whether the members 'represented Syrian women'. Here, the visible cooperation between women supporting the Assad government and women supporting opposition groups seemed to ignite strong reactions.[29] Still, the political 'inclusiveness' of the Women's Advisory Board demonstrated that women could find common ground across the conflict divides despite severe tensions. After the January 2016 negotiations in Geneva, members of the Women's Advisory Board met with members from the Syrian Women Initiative for Peace and Democracy in Beirut and produced a statement of unity.[30] Two years later, almost 200 Syrian women leaders met again in Beirut to discuss ways to safeguard and advance women's rights in Syria, and participants identified some key elements for a common framework for the Syrian women's movement. However, after more than two years of collaboration, members of the advisory board found themselves 'depoliticized' and unable to represent a constituency of women.[31] Under the Russian-led diplomatic initiative for Syria, civil society and the Women's Advisory Board were excluded from the 2018 negotiations in Sochi, where negotiating parties agreed on a new constitution.

2. Participation and the Peace Agreement

Peace agreements have been noted to increasingly include not only the interests of the warring parties but the population's concerns, even if the latter can meet with specific challenges during the implementation. It is in this context important to raise questions as to the inclusion and realization of women's interest.[32] In fact, a number of surveys have found that women, on average, hold more negative attitudes to peace outcomes than men. One reason is argued to be that the manner in which women have been affected by the conflict has not been prioritized in the post-war period.[33] In combination with (a) armed conflict constituting a shock to society with the propensity to upset gender hierarchies, (b) increased levels of local women's mobilization for improved power and resources access, and (c) rising global calls related to women, peace and security, arguably make a latent demand for improvements in women's rights a factor that is relevant to all post-conflict settings.[34] To take that demand seriously can contribute to ensuring that the peace has legitimacy among the women. In extension, this can be important for peace durability.[35]

This raises two central points. First, that the bargaining of the peace agreement sets in place reforms and institutions which can have both short-term and long-term effects on gender equality, women's empowerment, and peace. Second, while a peace agreement creates the foundation, the implementation and peacebuilding stages are central for realizing actual social change. Women's inclusion is critical for ensuring progress.

Peace Agreement Bargaining and Women's Inclusion

Joshi et al. have shown that a comprehensive peace agreement, on average, contains provisions for 21 multi-sectoral reforms.[36] This means that peace agreements constitute a roadmap for future political and constitutional processes as well as for significant socio-economic changes. Being able to affect the bargaining of this 'roadmap' is therefore imperative. The exclusion of women might perpetuate a marginalization in the post-war period i.e., the peace might entail a lower quality for women than men in terms of less access to resources and security.[37] For example, armed conflicts involving human rights abuse or systematic sexual violence, such as those in Timor-Leste, Bosnia-Herzegovina, and the Democratic Republic of Congo, have highlighted that women and men need different forms of protection in order to become equally secure when peace is to be created after war. New legislation and provisions for transitional justice need to cover crimes, such as sexual violence and discrimination, if women's security is to be improved.[38] A positive example was the peace process in Colombia where victims of violence were given a voice in the negotiations. This resulted in the inclusion of provisions related to many different forms of violence, including violence against women.[39]

Bell (2015) argues that we need to distinguish between processes which include 'a robust "gender perspective" in the formulation of the agreement and those which only give symbolic recognition to gender dynamics.[40] She notes some learning among the international community as 'substantive measures on equality for women and sexual violence have improved over time', particularly regarding the role of women's participation.[41] While the inclusion of women in bargaining has also often come after international pressure, it is important to connect international support to ongoing local mobilization processes. In many conflict zones, women's political representation and economic participation have been improving as a result of women's mobilization, the questioning of existing gender norms, and changes in the structures of society.[42]

One example is the peace process in the Philippines resulting in the 2014 Comprehensive Agreement on the Bangsamoro conflict. In this process, women and women's organizations came to play key roles in the formulation of the agreement, not least through the actions of the organization We Act 1325. This organization had originated as a women's network that aimed to monitor and support the implementation of the National Action Plan on Women, Peace and Security adopted by the government for the 2010–2016 period. A former chair of this network, Miriam Coronel-Ferrer, later came to play a key role in the peace negotiations where she also became instrumental for promoting women's rights. She contributed to so-called gender provisions being included in the agreement: clauses which focus specifically on improving women's rights post-war and on addressing gender aspects of the conflict. In the subsequent process, We Act 1325 together with two other women's organizations and supported by Conciliation Resources, pushed for women's rights to be included as the agreement's clauses were translated into implementable actions. In addition, women's organizations prioritized seeking to be included in the mechanisms created to monitor an implementation process.[43]

Women in Implementation and Peacebuilding

The implementation of a peace agreement after a civil war is central for the peace to hold.[44] That said, implementation and peacebuilding are challenging and costly processes with a substantial risk for a return to war. Women's inclusion could be essential for increasing legitimacy and social capital, thereby improving the chance for peace durability.[45] Due to the challenges of the implementation stage, however, research has found that different categories of clauses in an agreement tend to be prioritized differently. Those related to security tend to take priority in the eyes of the former warring parties whereas social aspects rank the lowest. This can have a detrimental effect on implementation related to gender equality and could help explain why women have more negative attitudes to peace than men.[46]

One method to promote women's interests, as displayed in the case of the Philippines, would be to ensure the implementation of any gender provisions adopted in the agreement. Such provisions can come in many different forms. One form focuses on core issues for the post-war society, such as improving protection from sexual violence, strengthened land rights, or increased political representation of women. Other clauses are process related, that is, used to formalize the implementation process, including dictating women's formal participation. Research suggests that both these forms of gender provisions meet with challenges in the implementation stage, such as being deprioritized or suffer from low state capacity on gender equality.[47] Bell further proposes that in agreements where the gender provisions have merely been added on—without much buy-in or understanding of the warring parties—the chance of the clauses resulting in actual change is slim.[48]

An example of this dynamic can be found in the Colombian Final Agreement from 2016 where 130 out of 578 stipulations recognize gender differences.[49] Unfortunately, data from the University of Notre Dame's Kroc Institute Barometer project show that the implementation of gender provisions is lagging behind the other, non-gendered—provisions. As of August, 2019, the Barometer project find that 42% of the gender provisions had not been initiated. This can be compared to 27% of the general commitments.[50] A possible explanation, as discussed by Bell, concerns the ownership of these provisions—who had an interest in them being included and who can promote their realization?[51] As noted by the Kroc Institute: 'Women's organizations and actors pushing for gender equality often start from a weaker power-base and their efforts challenge existing power hierarchies at the national and local levels'. They also note that resistance to many of the gender provisions in the Colombian agreement became visible already in the political debate leading up to the public referendum in 2016.[52]

While gender provisions can be one tool for including women's interests, it is important to observe that research has yet to examine their role for actual advancements in gender equality post-war. In fact, Krause et al. and Joshi and Olsson[53] do not find that gender quotas or other provisions included in the peace agreement necessarily have an effect. That does not mean that we should remove gender provisions—these bring in critical issues for women. However, we need to ensure that these are implemented and work in tandem with the entire agreement towards an equal peace.[54] The study by Joshi and Olsson further underlines this and suggests that women's rights can actually improve post-war due to how the broader political reforms set in place by an agreement are realized.[55] While Anderson (2013) argues that the warring parties often categorically resist change in gender equality, Joshi and Olsson instead propose that we should nuance the understanding to consider the opportunity, willingness, and capacity of the former warring actors in instituting and realizing positive effects on women's rights and in addressing gender hierarchies post-war. Ensuring women's formal inclusion in the core implementation processes and recognizing and supporting women's informal efforts for peace instead remained central. As advocated by the lessons learned from the UN Decade for Women and the Beijing Conference—all issues are in fact women's issues.

Conclusions and Future Research

While at a first glance, increasing women's participation in a peace process might seem straight forward, research has started to highlight that we need to consider a number of core issues in order to comprehend this fully. First, it is important to consider the different conditions which exist under each stage of a peace process. These can provide different openings and present different challenges for inclusion. Importantly, as highlighted in many of the examples, just because women managed to obtain entry during one stage does not necessarily entail that they will be included in the next. Second, many peace processes are protracted and non-linear, requiring long-term investments for women. This might be particularly challenging for women's civil society organizations which might have very limited resources. Third, women do not represent one group or one interest. Women, like men, come from various political standpoints. In some conflicts, we see women unite on common gender equality interests across the conflict divide, as in Syria. Still, we must develop a much better understanding of women as political actors in order to fully understand what conditions shape their participation. Fourth, we are currently seeing the development of new forms of mechanisms to include women in peace processes, again demonstrated by the Syrian process. Yet, we have limited knowledge of what the effects are for women's influence on the outcome.

As regards the last stages of a peace process, peace agreement bargaining and implementation, research is under development but suggests a number of key areas for further investigation. First, as the peace agreement will constitute the road map for future societal development—politically, legally, and socio-economically—UNSRC 1325 argues that it is central to ensure that women's participation is promoted and that the agreement addresses gender dynamics in the post-war state. For research, an improved understanding is important for measuring the quality of the peace and when examining the conditions for creating a durable peace. Second, the implementation of an agreement is central for creating peace but also for the post-war trajectory of women's rights. The manner in which peace is created and if provisions specifically targeting gender equality dynamics are realized, are therefore central. Future research should here consider women's formal and informal efforts but also variations in the former warring parties' willingness and opportunity to realize gender equal reforms. In conclusion, it remains imperative that research clearly connect women's involvement and the understanding of gender dynamics to core processes in contemporary peacemaking. Recent research findings underline the importance of the norms established in UNSCR 1325 that women should be considered as political actors indispensable for societal development.

Notes

1. Council on Foreign Relations (2019) *Women's Participation in Peace Processes*. Available online https://www.cfr.org/womens-participation-in-peace-processes/.
2. Theodora-Ismene Gizelis (2009) 'Gender Empowerment and United Nations Peacebuilding', *Journal of Peace Research* 46(4): 505–523; Theodora-Ismene Gizelis (2011) 'A Country of their Own: Women and Peacebuilding', *Conflict Management and Peace Science* 28(5): 522–542; J. Krause, W. Krause and P. Bränfors (2018) 'Women's Participation in Peace Negotiations and the Durability of Peace', *International Interactions* 44(6): 985–1016.
3. Karin Aggestam (2019) 'WPS, Peace Negotiations, and Peace Agreements', in S. Davies and J. True (Eds.) *The Oxford Handbook of Women, Peace and Security* (Oxford: Oxford University Press); R. Coomaraswamy et al. (2015) *Preventing Conflict, Transforming Justice, Securing the Peace: A Global Study on the Implementation of UNSCR 1325* (New York: UN Women); Louise Olsson and Theodora-Ismene Gizelis (2019) 'The Production of the Global

Study', in Sara Davies and Jacqui True (Eds.) *Oxford University Press Handbook on Women, Peace and Security (WPS)* (Oxford: Oxford: Oxford University Press); T. Paffenholz, N. Ross, S. Dixon, A.-L. Schluchter, and J. True (2016) *Making Women Count-not Just Counting Women: Assessing Women's Inclusion and Influence on Peace Negotiations* (New York: UN Women).
4. UN Secretary General (2018) 'Report of the Secretary General: Peacebuilding and Sustaining Peace', 18 January. Available at: https://www.un.org/peacebuilding/content/report-secretary-general-peacebuilding-and-sustaining-peace.
5. Ibid.
6. Madhav Joshi and Louise Olsson (2019) *War Termination and Women's Political Rights*. Research Working paper, Department of Peace and Conflict Research, Uppsala University, September 26; Jana Krause, Werner Krause and Piia Braenfors (2018) 'Women's Participation in Peace Negotiations and the Durability of Peace', *International Interactions* 44(6): 985–1016.
7. Valeriya Mechkova and Ruth Carlitz (2019). Gendered Accountability: When and Why Do Women's Policy Priorities Get Implemented? V-DEM Working Paper SERIES 2019: 88.
8. Krause et al., op. cit.
9. Erik Melander (2018) 'A Procedural Approach to Quality Peace', in C. Davenport, E. Melander, and P.M.Regan (Eds.)*The Peace Continuum: What It Is and How to Study It* (New York, NY: Oxford University Press); Louise Olsson (2018) 'Same Peace, Different Quality? The importance of Security Equality for Quality Peace', in Madhav Joshi and Peter Wallensteen (Eds.) *Understanding Quality Peace* (Milton Park and New York: Routledge).
10. Krause et al., op. cit.
11. Ibid.
12. D. Nilsson (2012) 'Anchoring the Peace: Civil Society Actors in Peace Accords and Durable Peace', *International Interactions*, 38(2): 243–266. https://doi.org/10.1080/03050629.2012.659139; D. Nilsson, I. Svensson, B. Teixeira, L. Lorenzo, and A. Ruus (2020) 'In the Streets and at the Table: Civil Society Coordination during Peace Negotiations', *International Negotiation* 25(2): 225–251. https://doi-org.ezproxy.its.uu.se/10.1163/15718069-25131241.

13. In a basic form, but different forms of categorizations exist. For example, PAX categorizes peace processes into seven distinct stages, ranging from pre-negotiations and process agreements to framework and partial agreement of substantive issues, to comprehensive agreements that address the whole conflict, to implementation and renegotiation agreements, and finally renewal or revitalization agreements.
14. Olsson and Gizelis (2019), op. cit.
15. Manuela Nilsson (2018) 'Civil Society Actors in Peace Negotiations in Central America', *Journal of Civil Society*, 14(2): 135–152. https://doi.org/10.1080/17448689.2018.1484004.
16. PAX uses a broad understanding of peace agreements and defines them as "formal, publicly-available documents, produced after discussion with conflict protagonists and mutually agreed by some or all of them, addressing conflict with a view to ending it". Peace Agreement Definitions. https://www.peaceagreements.org/files/Definitions_v3.pdf.
17. C. Bell (2019) 'New Inclusion Project: Building Inclusive Peace Settlements', *Accord: Navigating Inclusion in Peace Processes*, (28).
18. N.J. Mai, and N. James (2015) *The Role of Women in Peace-Building in South Sudan*. Policy Brief: The Sudd Institute, Juba, South Sudan.
19. Jane Freedman (2016) *Gender, Violence and Politics in the Democratic Republic of the Congo* (London: Routledge); Catherine Odimba, Paul Robain Namegabe and Julienne Baseke Nzabandora (2012) *La participation des femmes dans les processus de paix et la prise de décision politique end République Démocratique du Congo* (London and Kampala: International Alert and EASSI).
20. T.L. Tryggestad (2009) 'Trick or Treat? the UN and Implementation of Security Council Resolution 1325 on Women, Peace, and Security', *Global Governance* 15(4): 539–557; Olsson and Gizelis (2019) op. cit.
21. Nilsson (2019) op. cit.
22. Krause et al. (2018) op. cit.
23. Olsson and Gizelis (2019) op. cit.
24. J. Aulin (2019) 'Civil Society Inclusion in Peacebuilding. Who, How and So What?', *Accord: Navigating Inclusion in Peace Processes* (28).

25. https://www.cordaid.org/en/wp-content/uploads/sites/3/2017/09/South-Sudan-Women-Position-on-the-Promotion-of-Durable-Peace-and-Reconciliation-in-South-Sudan-Final.pdf.
26. Mai and James (2015) op. cit.
27. UN Secretary General (2018) op. cit.
28. S. Hellmueller and M.J. Zahar (2019) 'UN-Led Mediation in Syria and Civil Society', *Accord: Navigating Inclusion in Peace Processes*, 28.
29. https://www.passblue.com/2016/05/10/how-syrian-women-landed-at-the-un-peace-talks-and-what-it-all-means/.
30. http://www.unwomen.org/-/media/headquarters/attachments/sections/news%20and%20events/stories/2016/syriawomen-conference-statement-en.pdf?la=en&vs=5009.
31. See Mouna Ghanem's statement. https://www.independent.co.uk/voices/syria-conflict-resolution-women-sexism-war-a8792271.html.
32. M. Joshi, J.M. Quinn and P.M. Regan (2015) 'Annualized Implementation Data on Comprehensive Intrastate Peace Accords, 1989–2012', *Journal of Peace Research* 52(4): 551–562; M. Joshi and J.M. Quinn (2017) 'Implementing the Peace: The Aggregate Implementation of Comprehensive Peace Agreements and Peace Duration After Intrastate Armed Conflict', *British Journal of Political Science* 47(4): 869–892.
33. Karen Brounéus, Erika Forsberg, Karin Dyrstad, Helga Malmin Binningsbø (2017) 'The Gendered Links between War-Related Trauma and Attitudes to Peace: Exploring Survey Data from Guatemala, Nepal, and Northern Ireland', ISA 2017, International Studies Association, February 22–25, 2017, Baltimore, USA.
34. Louise Olsson and Madhav Joshi, 'Where are the Women in Peace Agreement Implementation?', Political Violence at a Glance, blog post. October 26, 2018; K. Webster, C. Chen, and K. Beardsley (2019) 'Conflict, Peace, and the Evolution of Women's Empowerment', *International Organization* 73(2): 255–289.
35. Krause et al. (2018) op. cit.
36. Josh et al. (2015) op. cit.
37. Krause et al. (2018) op. cit; Olsson (2018) op. cit.; Melander et al. (2018) op. cit.
38. Olsson (2009) op. cit; Brouneus et al. (2017) op. cit.

39. Isabela Marín Carvajal and Eduardo Álvarez-Vanegas (2019) 'Securing Participation and Protection in Peace Agreements: The Case of Colombia', in Sara E. Davies and Jacqui True (Eds.) *The Oxford Handbook of Women, Peace, and Security* (Oxford: Oxford University Press).
40. C. Bell (2015) Text and Context: Evaluating Peace Agreements for their Gender Perspective. *PSRP Report*.
41. Ibid.
42. Marie E. Berry, *War, Women, and Power: From Violence to Mobilization in Rwanda and Bosnia-Herzegovina* (Cambridge: Cambridge University Press, 2018).
43. Juan Diego Duque-Salazar, Erika Forsberg and Louise Olsson. Exploring the Conditions of Gender Provision Implementation: The Comprehensive Agreement on the Bangsamoro in the Philippines. Working paper, Department of Peace and Conflict Research, Uppsala University, 2020.
44. Joshi and Quinn (2016 and 2017) op. cit.
45. Gizelis (2009 and 2011) op. cit and Krause et al. (2018) op. cit.
46. Brouneus et al. (2017) op. cit. and Duque-Salazar et al. (2020) op. cit.
47. Gindele, Rebecca et al. *Implementing the Final Colombian Peace Agreement, 2016–2018: Are gender stipulations and women's inclusion lagging behind?* GPS Policy Brief 1, 2018.
48. Bell (2015) op. cit.
49. Gindele et al. (2018) op. cit.
50. Kroc Institute Second Special Report of the Kroc Institute and the International Accompaniment Component—UN Women, Women's International Democratic Federation, and Sweden—on the Monitoring of the Gender Perspective in the Implementation of the Colombian Final Peace Accord Executive Summary. https://kroc.nd.edu/assets/345130/final_english_executive_summary_four_logos.pdf.
51. Bell (2015) op. cit.
52. Gindele et al. (2018) op. cit.
53. Krause et al. (2018) op. cit., and Joshi and Olsson (2019) op. cit.
54. Joshi and Olsson (2019) op. cit.
55. Ibid.

CHAPTER 7

Indigenous Approaches to Peacemaking

Douglas P. Fry and Geneviève Souillac

We will start with the question: Why is Indigenous peacemaking important? This chapter explores five answers to this question. First, a culturally comparative vantage point that includes Indigenous peacemaking can contribute to an understanding of general peacemaking principles. Second, knowledge of Indigenous forms of peacemaking can help to expand the available options beyond Western methods and models. Third, Indigenous peacemaking is important because, very often, it works. A central implication is that in situations where colonial or national policies and practices have disrupted local Indigenous paths toward peacemaking, it may be wise to return to tried-and-true Indigenous systems that have an effective record of restoring the peace within particular cultural milieus. Fourth, understanding the wealth of Indigenous approaches to conflict prevention, management, transformation, and reconciliation can inform

D. P. Fry (✉) · G. Souillac
Department of Peace and Conflict Studies, University of North Carolina, Greensboro, NC, USA
e-mail: dpfry@uncg.edu

G. Souillac
e-mail: gsouillac@uncg.edu

a broader view of humanity and human nature. In other words, an appreciation of Indigenous peacemaking practices may counter and even contradict presumptions in Western thought that competition, violence, and mayhem are the default reactions of *Homo sapiens* to conflict. Finally, attention to and respect for Indigenous peacemaking in the twenty-first-century global community can be seen as but one manifestation of equalizing relationships, perceptions, and practices away from the domination of some peoples by others and toward the promotion of values, norms, institutions, and ethics of egalitarian participation, justice, and human rights for humanity as a whole.

Indigenous knowledge and practice are worthy of study both in terms of the theoretical insights they may offer and also for the practical lessons they may suggest for the modern world. But such an approach requires suspending any notions of cultural superiority or ethnocentric arrogance that perpetuate exploitation, cultural appropriation, and objectification—whether explicit or implicit. Remaining open to exploring difference along the ethno-horizon requires much care to prevent existing inegalitarian and exploitative worldviews from persisting into the future.

INDIGENOUS PEACEMAKING AND THE SEARCH FOR OVERARCHING PRINCIPLES

Taking a cross-cultural perspective can help to 'discover general conflict resolution principles'.[1] One recurring principle is the focus on restoring relationships damaged by conflict.[2] For instance, the emphasis on mending relationships is apparent when Lederach[3] discusses the metaphor of repairing the fishing net, which is "frequently torn leaving holes that must be sewn back together, knotting once again the separate loose ends. Nothing describes conflict resolution at the interpersonal level in Central America better than this folk metaphor." Similarly, Pinto[4] explains that "The Navajo philosophy and system of justice focuses on healing both the wrongdoer and all the people that may have been affected—directly and indirectly." The contrast is stark between the recurrent Indigenous focus on restoring relationships and the central focus of the Western courtroom that is not concerned with psychosocial healing and reconciliation of people.[5] By contrast, as a generalization, the key elements in Indigenous peacemaking are restoring relationships and reconciling disputants, a process that draws on such metaphors as untangling and mending the nets, restoring the balance, unjamming the blocked flow of energy between those in a conflict, and so on.[6]

Recently, Tuso[7] proposes a list of principles typically found in Indigenous peacemaking, inclusive of the aforementioned focus on healing relationships. Another main principle is that conflict resolution is mandatory, which showcases how Indigenous peoples often develop a "system to identify conflicts early, prevent them from escalating, and create culturally based mechanisms of resolution that allow healing to take place."[8] Some of the other principles on Tuso's list include frequent involvement of elders, who are respected for their experience and wisdom, the use of storytelling as part of an overall package of the peacemaking process, the integration of spirituality and the supernatural within peacemaking processes and beliefs, and the use of rituals to repair damaged relationships and solidify reconciliation.[9]

Another line of research draws upon comparative ethnographic methods to examine the peacemaking principles operating in nonwarring social systems. In focusing on such peace systems, one goal is to understand how clusters of neighboring societies that do not make war on each other successfully manage to keep the peace. Examples of Indigenous peace systems include the Iroquois Confederation that endured for over three hundred years, the tribes of the Upper Xingu River basin in Brazil, the peoples of the Nilgiri and Wynaad Plateaus in India, and the Aborigines of Australia's Great Western Desert. Salient features of nonwarring peace systems seem to include an overarching social identity; interconnections among subgroups; interdependence among the subunits; nonwarring values and norms; rituals, symbols, and ceremonies that reinforce peace; superordinate institutions; and visionary leadership for peace.[10] In sum, one reason Indigenous peacemaking is important is because it allows for the understanding of recurring principles such as the emphasis on mending relationships, the centrality of restoring the balance among those in conflict and the whole community, the promotion of common identities and interconnections, the valuation of the skills, experience, impartiality, and wisdom of third-party mediators such as elders or leaders, and the impact of rituals, ceremonies, symbols, and narratives in creating and preserving the peace.

Expanding the Options

Indigenous knowledge and practice in peacemaking hold lessons for the prevention and reduction of enmity in the modern world. Harnessing existing Indigenous knowledge about the creation and maintenance of peace can shed light on foundational paths to local, regional, and global peace. We are not advocating the grabbing of specific conflict prevention or conflict resolution mechanisms from other cultures with the idea of simply applying them out of their original emic context.[11] Rather, we propose that one value of examining Indigenous cases is to "look outside the box" of the Western tradition with its culturally specific beliefs, values, and assumptions about the nature of humanity, society, and politics in order to gain new perspectives on democracy, peacemaking, and peacebuilding.[12]

"An implication of conflict being a cultural phenomenon is that the culturally typical ways of perceiving and responding to conflict remain in some ways invisible to the members of any given society as unquestioned assumptions within their social universe."[13] In other words, when an individual is born, raised, and remains in her native culture, she will tend to take her cultural beliefs, including those pertaining to how to deal with conflict, for granted. We suggest that a second reason for valuing and studying Indigenous peacemaking is that it has the potential for expanding our understanding of our own cultural presumptions and, in so doing, to open our minds to new approaches to conflict transformation.

A few examples may illustrate the value of Indigenous knowledge and peacemaking for prompting awareness and reflection about one's own assumptions. Values and beliefs are inextricably intertwined with how conflict is perceived and handled. For example, a Western presumption is that an attack merits a counterattack. Consider, however, that Indigenous peoples may simply pack up and leave, employing a "discretion is the better part of valor" approach to aggressive neighbors. Among the tribes of the Upper Xingu River basin in Brazil, self-control is valued over aggressiveness. Warriors gain no special rewards. Should a chief behave aggressively, his actions are viewed as failed leadership, rather than as courageous or admirable.[14] Similarly, Harris and Wasilewski note that in many North American Indigenous societies, good leadership entails taking responsibility rather than control.[15]

To take another example, some Indigenous cultures emphasize the importance of satisfying the needs of other people, which has the effect of preventing conflict in the first place.[16] Such thinking may catch many Westerners by surprise, but this awareness can be viewed as an Indigenous peacemaking gem. Preventing conflict by seeing that the needs of others are satisfied, as well as being attuned to the needs of adversaries during peacemaking processes, can in the first scenario halt bloodshed before it begins and in the second contribute to establishing not merely a truce but an enduring sustainable peace.

An understanding of Indigenous peacemaking suggests that values and cultural beliefs really do play a role in how conflicts are perceived, handled, and resolved. For the Comanche, the concept of *mabitsiaruh* wraps respect, honor, and care into one key concept.[17] Ideally, people should show respect/honor/care for each other, even if enemies. "You can even value your enemies. Utes and Comanches were traditional rivals. We warred against each other. But we never wanted to exterminate each other."[18]

Some very peaceful societies hold a concept of respect as a core value that guides civil, nonviolent social interaction.[19] Kemp and Fry include nine case studies of peaceful societies and how they manage to keep the peace.[20] One observation is that the peaceful societies described in the collection as well as many others tend to have core values that promote nonviolence. Violence is simply unacceptable. A second recurring pattern is the cultural emphasis on avoidance of confrontation in societies with low levels of violence. Whereas people in most if not all societies sometimes avoid rivals and confrontation, some Indigenous societies place a great cultural emphasis on avoidance. Additionally, a theme in the case studies of peaceful societies examined in Kemp and Fry is the exercise of self-control.[21] During conflict situations, and generally, people are not supposed to lose their tempers, express anger, or act out. A study of peaceful societies leads to the conclusion that through cultural mechanisms that place a strong value on nonviolence, avoidance, respect, and/or self-control, aggressive acts, whether of the interpersonal type or between groups, can be much reduced in both frequency and severity.[22]

We do not want to imply that Indigenous methods of handling conflict and engaging in peacemaking are always superior to Western approaches.[23] Sometimes local Indigenous methods have their pitfalls or are constructed around the principle of self-redress.[24] However, the converse presumption that Western methods of conflict resolution are inherently superior to Indigenous peacemaking overall is equally untrue.

Our two conclusions for this section are that, first, a comparative exploration of peacemaking across cultural contexts can cause us to question our own assumptions and to rethink whether our own culturally familiar peacemaking approaches are the only ways or the best ways to deal with conflict. The second conclusion is that Indigenous knowledge in its variety and wisdom presents a treasure trove of peacemaking lessons from which to learn, including how values, worldviews, practices, institutions, and affects are culturally intertwined and how Indigenous knowledge can be applied in various ways to promote the peace. We would all do well to listen to the peacemaking wisdom of the elders and include Indigenous voices across the human cultural landscape.

RETURNING TO WHAT WORKS: REJUVENATION OF LOCAL PEACEMAKING

Some societies tolerate more violence than do others.[25] However, mechanisms and practices for violence prevention, conflict management, peacemaking, and reconciliation exist across human societies.[26] Mac Ginty points out that in situations where colonial powers or more recently the international community impose external peacemaking practices, "having little conception of state sovereignty, modern bureaucracy, written covenants, formal participation structures and linear sequential notions of time, it is unsurprising that traditional societies found and still find Western versions of peace alien."[27]

Furthermore, when given a choice, local people prefer to handle their own disputes without the involvement of outsiders such as colonial, national, or international actors.[28] Imposition of procedures by cultural outsiders who may be unaware of local beliefs, values, and practices represents a problematic approach to peacemaking. Peacemaking processes do not exist *sui generis*, but are embedded in the cultural settings in which they have developed and operate.[29] Therefore, rather than ignoring or discarding Indigenous forms of conflict management and resolution, it would be important for external actors to encourage and facilitate effective local peacemaking practices, as Yousaf and Poncian illustrate drawing on Indigenous practices used in Pakistan and Tanzania.[30] "Indigenous strategies can go a long way in resolving conflicts because they have deep roots in societies themselves and they are generally accepted and respected."[31]

The mediation process among the Navajo, for example, reflects core elements of the culture and thus differs from a Western model of mediation in notable ways.[32] The goal of the Peacemaker Ceremony is to promote healing and the mending of relationships, as contrasted with the Western emphasis on arriving at an agreement. Among the Navajo, the mediator typically knows the disputants—as contrasted to the Western model reliant on trained outsiders—and is a respected elder and perhaps a family member. Pinto points out that rather than focusing narrowly on the interests of the disputants, Navajo mediation focuses on the concept called *k'e*—the harmony of the person and the community.[33] Furthermore, the Navajo core value of harmony entails a central emphasis on respect, responsibility, and relationship as guiding principles that lead to a resolution seen as best for all members of the community, not merely the parties to the conflict. Pinto explains that "the sense of relationship of one thing to another is evident in the process of the Peacemaker Ceremony because it promotes the balance of one person to another, one person to the group, and the group to the larger community. It also aids in restoring the balance of body, mind, and spirit within the individual."[34] Application of the standard Western approach to mediation as a disputant-centered process with the primary goal of reaching an agreement would be seen by the Navajo as insufficient for many reasons.

Another case that illustrates how local means of peacemaking are effective and valuable because they are familiar and deeply embedded in the values, practices, and ethos of particular local cultures comes from the Enga of Papua New Guinea, who number some half-a-million people. In the 1990s, the Enga replaced their bows-and-arrows with semiautomatic weapons, shotguns, and M-16s in interclan disputes, and this resulted in a bloodbath.[35] For about 15 years, the Enga engaged in approximately 250 interclan wars, as gangs of mercenaries wreaked havoc, destroying gardens, homes, schools, and killing many victims.[36]

Wiessner and Pupu explain that traditionally, the Enga fought wars "to restore balance and so that exchange could flow. Most Enga who have experienced recent wars have incurred unprecedented losses with no gains for exchange."[37] By about 2010, the Enga were fed up with war and managed to curtail the violence. Three factors contributed to peacemaking: exhaustion and economic hardships caused by the chronic fighting, influences of the church, and a focus on local village courts in place of war.[38] The Enga see the village courts, as contrasted with District Courts, as their own institutions. Local Enga "own" the village courts,

Table 7.1 Comparison of outcomes between government district courts and local village 'customary' courts among the Enga of Papua New Guinea for 2011

Outcome	Non-Indigenous district courts (n = 42 cases) (%)	Local 'customary' courts (n = 39 cases) (%)
Fine/Jail	10	2
Case Struck from Record	43	0
Case Withdrawn	47	0
Ordered Compensation	0	40
Mediated Compensation	0	29
Mediated Out-of-Court Agreement	0	29

Source Table constructed from data in Wiessner and Pupu (2012)

because they themselves appoint Enga magistrates and the judicial decisions are not controlled or enforced by the New Guinea government. Wiessner and Pupu report that the village court magistrates "speak the language, know the hearts of people, and do not just read from some law book" and thus they make decisions in accordance with local conditions, custom, and values.[39]

As shown in Table 7.1, the village courts proved to be a very effective alternative to culturally external District Courts for bringing about peaceful resolution of violent conflicts. The payment of compensation has long been a cultural mechanism for peacemaking among the Enga, stemming from the time when wars were fought periodically with bows-and-arrows. As shown in Table 7.1, the village courts drew heavily upon the culturally known and preferred mechanism of restoring the balance in relationships among warring groups through the payment of compensation and mediated agreements. The Enga case clearly illustrates the effectiveness of what Yousaf and Poncian call the decolonization of the field of conflict resolution through "recognising, strengthening, and formalising indigenous conflict resolution strategies."[40]

THE HUMAN POTENTIAL FOR PEACEMAKING

A fourth reason that Indigenous peacemaking is important is because a broader comparative perspective that goes beyond the confines of Western models contributes to our understandings of human nature. A common refrain in the West is that conflict and violence are ingrained in human nature, but a consideration of indigenous approaches leads to a different view.[41] It becomes apparent that resolving disputes in ways that do not entail violence occurs in even the most conflictual societies and that the application of peacemaking mechanisms constitutes a human universal. Across cultural settings, most conflicts are prevented, resolved, or transformed without any violence, although such peaceable and peacemaking events are typically taken for granted, whereas the violence that does occur receives abundant commentary from the public, politicians, the media, and scholars as being the inevitable outcome of humans simply being humans.

Taking Indigenous peacemaking seriously, not only as a subject worthy of study but also as a topic with practical significance, can reveal the diversity of successful approaches to peacemaking that humans regularly employ. Human nature is not solely about making war and perpetrating violence, and we suggest that an assessment of human behavior across cultural circumstances reveals the overwhelming centrality of human conflict prevention, avoidance, resolution, third-party interventions, reconciliation, forgiveness, and restoration of relationships, or, in a word, of peacemaking. Ongoing conflict bothers people, causes disruptions, and induces fear, and consequently across cultural situations people engage in peacemaking. Hence peacemaking, not merely violence, is an integral feature of human nature.

Further, conflicts arise within any social order, but conflict is not synonymous with aggression.[42] A study of Indigenous peacemaking shows substantial variation in how conflicts are addressed.[43] At one cross-cultural extreme, peaceful societies, and nonwarring societies exist. At the other end of the continuum, violent acts occur more regularly. Most societies span the middle ground.[44] Values, norms, practices, and social institutions can support structural and direct violence or, conversely, they can promote nonviolence, social equity, and just conflict resolution. Thus, violence and warfare are options, but they are not the only options, and to construct a view of humanity with violence at the heart of the image is a distortion. First, it ignores internally peaceful societies, nonwarring cultures, and peace systems. Second, it sidesteps the fact that the overwhelming majority of human social interaction is peaceful. Third, it overlooks the plethora of effective conflict management and peacemaking in use by societies around the world in many Indigenous contexts.

Indigenous peacemaking practices demonstrate that time and again humans are capable of resolving both intra-group and inter-group conflicts without bloodshed.[45] The study of the prevention of conflict can be challenging because it entails in some instances reconstructing the reasons that something did not happen. Conflict prevention can involve mechanisms that lower the chances that conflict develops in the first place. Prevention also can involve reactions that curtail the spread of conflict to others and escalation in the severity of conflict. Prevention is a term that applies across social levels from individual conflict to group-level phenomena.

Fry reviews Indigenous practices and suggests various mechanisms that may contribute to prevention, including the socialization and enculturation of cultural patterns of self-control regarding emotional expression generally or showing anger more particularly; self-restraint regarding violence; the maintenance at a psychosocial level of positive, empathy-based relationships with others; reduction of dissatisfaction in others, demonstration of remorse, and responsibility-taking for any harm caused to other people; active involvement of third parties in roles such as friendly peacemaker, a person who distracts or separates antagonists, or as mediator, an individual who steps in to help disputants work out a peaceful solution; and a variety of other cultural mechanisms such as song duels, mock battles, or competitive wealth displays that allow for effective resolutions of conflict with a minimum of harm.[47] Additionally, the presence of features such as viable conflict resolution procedures, cross-cutting ties that bind subgroups and groups, mutual dependencies, and peace values, norms, symbols, rituals, and narratives can be seen as preventing violence including war.[48] A cross-cultural perspective that includes Indigenous practices not only reveals the widespread occurrence and impressive variety of human conflict management mechanisms but also suggests that preventing violence and promoting peacemaking are strong human tendencies.

As noted earlier during the discussion of principles, restoring relations, reconciling adversaries, and reinstating a harmonious atmosphere are central goals of much Indigenous peacemaking. Bountiful evidence exists from various fields that the preponderance of human interaction and behavior is geared toward getting along with others without using violence, showing restraint against serious aggression, cooperating to achieve shared goals, expressing empathy toward the plight of others, and employing apologies, reconciliation rituals, and forgiveness as critical ingredients in peacemaking processes. When the peacemaking capacities, even tendencies, used by people from many diverse geographical and Indigenous cultural settings are recognized, then the common narrative that humanity is naturally competitive, aggression-prone, and warlike receives a counterbalancing adjustment.[49] Thus, a realization that human nature does not block the possibility of reducing, even eliminating, armed conflict, boosts the impetus to work toward peace. On the other hand, harboring the pessimistic views of human nature, as are common in Western tradition, can contribute to their own realization and perpetuation.[50]

WALKING THE TALK: PROMOTING RESPECT, EQUALITY, AND PARTNERSHIP AMONG PLANETARY CITIZENS

In the twenty-first century, the peoples of the planet are part of the same interdependent socioeconomic–ecological system. We propose that an Indigenous-style relational, reciprocal, cooperative, and normative system, which has served numerous societies well for millennia at lower levels of organization, is now needed at the planetary level. This is the fifth reason that Indigenous knowledge on peacemaking has a vital role to play in today's world.

Traditional forms of knowledge about governance and peacemaking have relevance for human wellbeing and ultimately survival on a crowded interdependent planet. Current global conditions, some positive but many threatening, position humanity in similar survival scenarios as those repeatedly faced and met by Indigenous societies over the course of our species' biocultural evolution. Our human forbearers developed material and cultural toolkits to help them meet the challenges of social life and of survival, including the control of violence. The current global crises of unprecedented environmental degradation, unsustainable population growth, presence of weapons of mass destruction, paucity of effective governance at the global level, and recurrence of war and violence, among other threats, are challenges that could benefit from an awareness of an ancient Indigenous ethos. Indeed, this ethos emphasizes cooperation over competition, relationships over raw individualism, and responsibility for others rather than their exploitation, and supports a sustainable way of living within the shared and endangered global ecosystem.[51] Appreciation, inclusion, and application of ancestral wisdom for peacemaking, including how to balance relationships with one another and the living world, when they are virtues grounded in reflexivity and balanced reciprocity can be part of a new planetary ethos.

We suggest that Indigenous knowledge thus be included in a global vision that formalizes continuity between humanity, other species, and the environment into one biocultural evolutionary whole. Two features would characterize this vision. First, it would be oriented toward common responsibility regarding conflict prevention, resolution, and transformation, as well as with regard to the delegitimization of violence toward humans, other species, and the ecosystem generally. Second, an inclusive vision, by drawing upon Indigenous knowledge, would contribute to the critique of a global system rooted in inequality, exploitation, and a self-interested material ethos characterized by historically entrenched patterns of domination. Maintaining dichotomies between Indigenous and modern knowledge enshrines asymmetrical power relationships and consolidates the exclusion of Indigenous actors. Divides in worldviews relative to community, human nature, and the sacred can be perceived as obstacles between Indigenous and industrial/postindustrial societies. Therefore, integrating traditional forms of knowledge for the purpose of peace entails cultivating awareness about both the destruction and exclusion of Indigenous societies since the earliest colonizing conquests and acknowledging the importance of cultural recognition in the implementation of human rights and, in particular, Indigenous cultural rights.

Acknowledging the struggles of Indigenous communities to retain their livelihood, cultural memory, traditional ways of life, and governance that are all now endangered begins the path toward recognizing the relevance of traditional knowledge in a modern world facing an existential crisis of social, political, cultural, and spiritual dimensions. Consider what humanity might learn from Indigenous philosophy and approaches to conflict such as Navajo peacemaking. Pinto explains:

> The Peacemaker Ceremony illustrates the Navajo perception of connection between spiritual beliefs and law. The law then becomes more than maxims applied to certain situations; it is a way of conducting oneself in day-to-day activities. The effectiveness and success of the Peacemaker Division is dependent on a shared conception of this sense of interconnectedness in all things. In this way, the application of Navajo common law using the Peacemaker process transcends the notion of a method of resolving disputes and becomes a powerful tool for healing the inner processes of the individual and the group that contribute to the production of conflict.[52]

Since the end of the twentieth century, Indigenous forms of knowledge about peace increasingly have been recruited for the purpose of local conflict transformation alongside the deployment of peacebuilding projects led by the international community. Iconic examples in the post-Cold War history of peacebuilding include the post-Apartheid Truth and Reconciliation Commission that mobilized the concept of *ubuntu* in South Africa; the community court system of *gacaca* meetings in post-genocidal Rwanda to supplement transitional justice mechanisms such as the International Criminal Tribunal for Rwanda; and the practice of *nahe biti*, or "stretching the mat," for grassroots reconciliation in the Democratic Republic of Timor-Leste (formerly East Timor) in the context of the post-conflict state-building effort led by the United Nations Transitional Authority in East Timor. Critics of the liberal peace[53] draw attention to the ways in which initiatives for peace led by global institutions alienate local agents, denying them the opportunity to own the peacebuilding process subsequent to the cessation of hostilities. But some efforts have generated community-driven peace initiatives that target women, youth, and other marginalized constituencies. In these cases, state or internationally based actors and structures reinforced community-engaged practices and beliefs, amplifying the legitimacy and effectiveness of peacemaking as a whole despite post-conflict environments highly fraught with imperfections and global processes echoing historical inequalities.

Resorting to local forms of peacemaking may overcome the limitations of state-based interventions and be more effective because they are grounded in cultural ownership. As noted earlier, Enga's sense of cultural and institutional identity regarding the traditional village courts, as compared with District Courts, underpinned the effectiveness of this conflict resolution strategy. But deeply hybridized peacemaking processes combining state institutions with local practices may also shed light on how local identity can be enhanced in transformational ways by applying local knowledge against a backdrop of broader geopolitics and national or global dynamics. In the historic cases mentioned above, a meaningful continuity between the abstract ideals of justice and popular sovereignty and local identities was ultimately established in the wake of traumatic conflict. The transition to a new democratic society facilitated and strengthened local actors' sense of place in the broader world. As Babo-Soares argues in the case of Timor-Leste's democratic transition, *nahe biti* "forms part of a grand process that aims to link the past and the future and to bring society into an ultimate state of social stability where peace, tranquility and honesty prevail."[54] The psychosocial dimensions of peacemaking, such as the formation, reinforcement, and transformation of historical identities, emerge clearly when local communities seeking to rebuild social relationships draw from virtuous identities in a positively reinforcing cycle in which the effects ripple inwards and outwards onto shared civic life.[55]

The convergence of civic engagement with meaningful practices, rituals, narrations, symbolizations and commemorations demonstrate the long-term, collective and complex nature of peacemaking into the future. On an interstate scale, Kadir argues that the village council system for conflict resolution in the Asian subcontinent named *panchayat* provides an overarching psycho-social framework to manage the India-Pakistan conflict that solicits the structural and moral dimensions of this system through which India and Pakistan are linked historically.[56] In another example, Aboriginal and Torres Strait Islander peoples in Australia have resourced the words *makarrata, makarata* or *makarta*, and *narragunnawali* in advocating for national reconciliation on the basis of Indigenous empowerment and education. For the Ngunnawal people, the traditional owners of the land on which Reconciliation Australia's office is located, *narragunnawali* connotes well-being, coming together, and peace. The creation of a *Makarrata* Commission was called for to evoke the complex notion of conflict resolution, peacemaking, and justice of the same name, as "the coming together after a struggle" and to "supervise a process of agreement-making between governments and First Nations and truth-telling about our history."[57] It echoes the Murngin (or Yolngu) of Arnhem Land's ceremonial peacemaking ritual reaching to a rich ceremonial and normative heritage that prioritized elaborate processes of conflict resolution against actual warfare.[58]

Examples of Indigenous mechanisms such as *ubuntu, gacaca, nahe biti, panchayat*, and *makarrata* that we have considered in this section, as people-based traditions of peacemaking whose resonance, legitimacy, and often universal appeal arise from centuries of cultural memory, enhance the effectiveness of state-driven governance in peacemaking. An inclusive and egalitarian dialogue between Indigenous and modern approaches to the conceptual and institutional foundations of a global society oriented toward peace require a multi-scalar, multidimensional approach to actors, institutions, and processes.[59] We advocate egalitarian sharing of both knowledge and practice followed by collaborative problem solving along the lines of the structured dialogue process described by Harris and Wasilewski.[60] The structured dialogue process illustrates how the medium can be part of the message, meaning concretely that the undergirding ethos, methods, and applications of conflict resolution and dialogic engagement are conducted on an even playing field in an inclusive and respectful manner among all the participants. Cooperative and inclusive paths of collaboration achieve mutually beneficial outcomes, whether the social scale involves local communities, nations, or the entire global community.[61] In large part, it is the scale of the challenges that determines the level of participation in dialogic and peacemaking processes, but the fundamental principles of inclusiveness, equality, respect, responsibility, and cooperation need not change dramatically across social levels. Indeed, it could be argued that many issues that seem at first to be local in nature in fact are transborder in their consequences and correspondingly require a wide net of collaboration for problem-solving that stretches beyond local epicenters.[62]

Indigenous wisdom on peacemaking can be successfully and respectfully applied in the modern world, premised upon a recognition of the inherent value of Indigenous knowledge and its powerful contribution to an inclusive global community for generations to come. We encourage readers to envision a participatory global world that nonviolently employs the collective wisdom of peacemaking, Indigenous as well as modern. The sharing of knowledge resources for common peace and ecological purposes is in the interest of all of humanity. We propose that a wealth of Indigenous practices for dealing with conflict without violence as well as a cross-cultural comparative view can offer important insights for the global community as it struggles to create international laws, norms, ethics, and institutions for a pluralistic, interdependent, emergent global society. Such a global challenge of this scale and importance has never before been faced, and developing ways of harnessing collective wisdom in a manner that is grounded in inclusive cultural reflexivity can provide vital insights for how to accomplish the necessary transitions. The scale is immense but there are reasons to think successful enmity prevention and reduction may indeed be possible, even at the planetary level. Acknowledging the ancestral contribution of Indigenous peoples to our common humanity and respecting Indigenous actors today as full and equal partners are vital steps toward healing relationships across every sector of the global community.

Notes

1. D.P. Fry and K. Björkqvist, 'Introduction: Conflict Resolution Themes' in D.P. Fry and K. Björkqvist (eds.) *Cultural Variation in Conflict Resolution: Alternatives to Violence* (Mahwah, NJ: Erlbaum, 1997), p. 5.
2. B.E. Barnes and F.V. Magdalena 'Traditional Peacemaking Processes among Indigenous Populations in the Northern and Southern Philippines' in H. Tuso and M.P. Flaherty (eds.) *Creating the Third Force: Indigenous Processes of Peacemaking* (Lanham, MD: Lexington, 2016); R.M. Berndt, 'Law and Order in Aboriginal Australia' in R.M. Berndt and C.H. Berndt (eds.) *Aboriginal Man in Australi*a (London: Angus & Robertson, 1965); D.P. Fry, 'Conflict Management in Cross-Cultural Perspective' in F. Aureli and F. de Waal (eds.) *Natural Conflict Resolution* (Berkeley, CA: University of California Press, 2000); D.P. Fry, 'Anthropological Examples of Peacemaking: Practice and Theory' in S. Allen Nan, Z.C. Mampilly, and A. Bartoli (eds.) *Peacemaking: From Practice to Theory*, volume 2 (Santa Barbara, CA: Praeger Security International, 2012a); R. Mac Ginty 'Indigenous Peace-Making versus the Liberal Peace'. *Cooperation and Conflict*, 43 (2008) 139–163; G. Souillac and D.P. Fry, 'Indigenous Lessons for Conflict Resolution' in P.T. Coleman, M. Deutsch, and E.C. Marcus (eds.) *The Handbook of Conflict Resolution: Theory and Practice* (San Francisco, CA: Josey Bass, 2014); S. Stobbe 'Respecting Identity, Creating Justice, and Building Peaceful Relationships in Laos through Traditional Conflict Resolution Processes' in H. Tuso and M.P. Flaherty (eds.) *Creating the Third Force: Indigenous Processes of Peacemaking* (Lanham, MD: Lexington, 2016); G. Souillac and D.P. Fry, 'Anthropology: Implications for Peace' in O.P. Richmond, S. Pogodda, and J. Ramović (eds.) *The Palgrave Handbook of Disciplinary and Regional Approaches to Peace* (Hampshire, UK: Palgrave Macmillan, 2016).
3. J.P. Lederach 'Of Nets, Nails, and Problems: The Folk Language of Conflict Resolution in a Central American Setting,' in K. Avruch, P.W. Black, and J.A Scimecca (eds.) *Conflict Resolution: Cross-Cultural Perspectives* (New York, NY: Greenwood Press, 1991), p. 168.

4. J. Pinto, 'Case Study: Peacemaking as Ceremony: The Mediation Model of the Navajo Nation' in H. Tuso and M.P. Flaherty (eds.) *Creating the Third Force: Indigenous Processes of Peacemaking* (Lanham, MD: Lexington, 2016), p. 163.
5. Mac Ginty, op. cit.; H. Tuso, 'Creating the Third Side: Some Common Features in Indigenous Processes of Peacemaking, and Some Preliminary Observations' in H. Tuso and M.P. Flaherty (eds.) *Creating the Third Force: Indigenous Processes of Peacemaking* (Lanham, MD: Lexington, 2016b).
6. Berndt, op. cit.; Fry (2000), op. cit.; L. Nader, 'Styles of Court Procedure: To Make the Balance' in L. Nader (ed.) *Law and Culture in Society* (Chicago, IL: Aldine, 1969).
7. H. Tuso, 'Indigenous Processes of Conflict Resolution: Neglected Methods of Peacemaking by the New Field of Conflict Resolution' in H. Tuso and M.P. Flaherty (eds.) *Creating the Third Force: Indigenous Processes of Peacemaking* (Lanham, MD: Lexington 2016a); Tuso (2016b), op. cit.
8. Tuso (2016b), op. cit., p. 514.
9. Fry (2000), op. cit., A. Gohar and L. Schirch, 'Ritual and Symbol in Justice and Peacemaking: Lessons from Pukhtoon Tribes on the Jirga,' in H. Tuso and M.P. Flaherty (eds.) *Creating the Third Force: Indigenous Processes of Peacemaking* (Lanham, MD: Lexington, 2016); Tuso (2016a, 2016b), op. cit.
10. D.P. Fry, 'Life without War,' *Science*, 336 (2012b) 879–884; D.P. Fry and G. Souillac, 'Peace by Other Means,' *Common Knowledge*, 22 (2016) 8–24; G. Souillac and D.P. Fry, 'The Human Quest for Peace, Rights, and Justice: Convergence of the Traditional and the Modern' in J. Seibt and J. Garsdal (eds.) *How is Global Dialogue Possible?* (Berlin: de Gruyter, 2015), Souillac and Fry (2016), op. cit; D.P. Fry et al., 'Societies within Peace Systems Avoid War and Build Positive Intergroup Relationships'. *Humanities and Social Sciences Communications* 8, 17 (2021). https://doi.org/10.1057/s41599-020-00692-8.
11. D.P. Fry and K. Björkqvist (eds.) *Cultural Variation in Conflict Resolution: Alternatives to Violence* (Mahwah, NJ: Erlbaum, 1997).
12. A. Christakis and K. Bausch, *How People Harness Their Collective Wisdom and Power to Construct the Future* (Charlotte, NC: Information Age, 2006); Souillac and Fry (2014) and (2016), op. cit.

13. D.P. Fry and C.B. Fry, 'Culture and Conflict Resolution Models: Exploring Alternatives to Violence' in D.P. Fry and K. Björkqvist (eds.) *Cultural Variation in Conflict Resolution: Alternatives to Violence* (Mahwah, NJ: Erlbaum, 1997), p. 10.
14. Souillac and Fry (2015), op. cit; Souillac and Fry (2016), op cit.
15. L. Harris and J. Wasilewski, 'Indigeneity, an Alternative Worldview—Four Rs (Relationship, Responsibility, Reciprocity, Redistribution) vs. Two Ps (Power and Profit): Sharing the Journey Towards Conscious Evolution,' *Systems Research and Behavioral Science*, 21 (2004) 489–503, at p. 497.
16. G. Kemp and D.P. Fry, *Keeping the Peace: Conflict Resolution and Peaceful Societies around the World* (New York, NY: Routledge, 2004); Fry (2000), op. cit.
17. Harris and Wasilewski, op. cit.
18. Ibid. p. 496.
19. Fry and Souillac (2016), op. cit.
20. Kemp and Fry, op. cit.
21. Ibid.
22. Fry and Fry, op. cit; Kemp and Fry (2004), op. cit; Souillac and Fry (2015), op. cit; G. Souillac, *A Study in Transborder Ethics: Justice, Citizenship, Civility* (Brussels: Lang, 2012).
23. Mac Ginty (2008), op. cit; R. Mac Ginty, 'Indigenous Peacemaking in Northern Ireland,' in H. Tuso and M.P. Flaherty (eds.) *Creating the Third Force: Indigenous Processes of Peacemaking* (Lanham, MD: Lexington, 2016).
24. Fry (2000), op. cit; Mac Ginty (2016), op. cit; P. Wiessner and N. Pupu, 'Toward Peace: Foreign Arms and Indigenous Institutions in Papua New Guinea Society', *Science*, 337 (2012) 1651–1654.
25. Fry (2012), op. cit.
26. Fry (2000), op. cit; Mac Ginty (2008), op. cit; Souillac and Fry (2015 and 2016), op. cit.
27. Mac Ginty (2008), p. 149.
28. Nader (1969), op. cit.
29. Fry and Björkqvist (1997), op. cit; Fry and Fry (1997), op. cit.
30. F. Yousaf and J. Poncian, 'Detriments of Colonialism on Indigenous Conflict Resolution: An Analysis of Pakistan and Tanzania,' *Contemporary Justice Review* (2018) published online: https://doi.org/10.1080/10282580.2018.1532795.
31. Ibid., p. 14.

32. Pinto, op. cit.
33. Ibid.
34. Ibid., p. 179.
35. Wiessner and Pupu, op. cit.
36. Ibid.
37. Ibid, p. 1653.
38. Ibid.
39. Ibid.
40. Yousaf and Poncian, op. cit., p. 14.
41. Kemp and Fry, op. cit.; Souillac and Fry (2016), op. cit.
42. Fry (2000), op. cit.
43. Fry (2000, 2012a), op. cit.; Fry and Björkqvist, op. cit; Fry and Souillac (2016), op. cit.
44. Souillac and Fry (2016), op. cit.
45. Ibid.
46. Fry (2000), op. cit.
47. Ibid.
48. Fry (2012a, 2012b), op. cit.; Souillac and Fry (2014, 2016), op. cit; D.P. Fry, G. Souillac, L. Liebovitch, L. et al. 'Societies within peace systems avoid war and build positive intergroup relationships,' *Humanities and Social Sciences Communications*, 8, 17 (2021). https://doi.org/10.1057/s41599-020-00692-8.
49. Souillac and Fry (2016), op. cit.
50. Fry and Fry (1997), op. cit; Fry and Souillac (2016), op. cit.
51. Harris and Wasilewski (2004), op. cit.; Pinto (2016), op. cit.; Souillac and Fry (2014), op. cit.
52. Pinto, op. cit., 179–180.
53. R. Mac Ginty and O. Richmond (eds.) *The Liberal Peace and Post-War Reconstruction: Myth or reality?* (New York, NY: Routledge, 2013).
54. D. Babo-Soares, '*Nahe Biti:* The Philosophy and Process of Grassroots Reconciliation (and Justice) in East Timor,' *The Asia Pacific Journal of Anthropology*, 5 (2004) 15–33 at p. 15.
55. Souillac (2012), op. cit.
56. J. Kadir, 'The Utility of Traditional Justice System of "Panchayat" in Resolving Pakistan-India Interstate Conflict,' *Journal of Living Together*, 6 (2019) 133–143.
57. Uluru Statement (2017). The Uluru Statement from the Heart. Published online: https://ulurustatement.org/the-statement.

58. D.P. Fry, *The Human Potential for Peace: An Anthropological Challenge to Assumptions about War and Violence* (New York: Oxford University Press, 2006).
59. Fry and Fry (1997), op. cit.; G. Souillac, *The Burden of Democracy: The Claims of Cultures, Public Culture, and Democratic Memory* (Lanham, MD: Lexington, 2011) and 2012; op. cit.; Souillac and Fry (2014 and 2015), op. cit.
60. Harris and Wasilewski, op. cit.
61. Souillac and Fry (2014), op. cit.
62. Souillac (2012), op. cit.

CHAPTER 8

Peacemaking Referendums: Advantages and Challenges for Peace Processes

Joana Amaral

Introduction

In the past three decades, referendums have become a significant part of conflict resolution around the world: 1992 in South Africa, 1998 in Northern Ireland, 1999 in East Timor and Guatemala, 2001 in Somaliland, 2003 in Rwanda, 2004 in Cyprus, 2005 in Iraq, 2011 in South Sudan, 2016 in Colombia, and again in Guatemala in 2018. Some of these have represented important milestones in their respective peace processes. For example, the 1992 referendum in South Africa paved the way to the end of the decades-long apartheid regime, while the 1998 Good Friday Agreement referendum in Northern Ireland marked a point of no return in the province's path away from violence. In ongoing peace processes elsewhere, referendums are being discussed or negotiated as a means to help resolve disputes, suggesting more will take place in the future.

J. Amaral (✉)
Berghof Foundation, Berlin, Germany
e-mail: j.amaral@berghof-foundation.org

© The Author(s), under exclusive license to Springer Nature Switzerland AG 2022
R. Mac Ginty and A. Wanis-St. John (eds.), *Contemporary Peacemaking*,
https://doi.org/10.1007/978-3-030-82962-9_8

Because the use of referendums in peace processes is relatively new, comprehensive discussion of this type of referendum has just begun. In this chapter, I propose a definition of *peacemaking referendums* based on when, how, and why referendums have taken place in support of peace processes. Although peacemaking has come to refer to a variety of ways of resolving and transforming conflict, I draw on its definition in the United Nations charter as a category of instruments used by parties in conflict, and eventually with the support of a third party, in the peaceful search for a solution to conflict; peacemaking instruments include negotiation, enquiry, mediation, conciliation, arbitration, or judicial settlement. To this list, I add peacemaking referendums.

Given the specificities of the processes and contexts within which they take place, peacemaking referendums require a distinct *praxis* from referendums held for other purposes and, as such, a distinct and specialized study. In this chapter, I identify four attributes in peacemaking referendums: their issues, purpose, scope, and outcome. I then discuss the many advantages of employing referendums as a peacemaking tool and note the specific challenges of preparing and organizing a referendum in a conflict context. I conclude with a reflection on whether referendums are beneficial or counterproductive to peace processes, a question at the epicentre of this field of research.

Peacemaking Referendums: Definition and Characterization

Referendums have been used to manage conflict and deal with ethnic and nationalistic divisions for centuries and contemporary referendums are really no different in that sense.[1] However, with their increasing popularity, *peacemaking* referendums are emerging as a distinct category within the universe of all types of referendums that merits and requires specialized study. Exercising referendums in conflict settings presents very specific challenges when compared to peaceful settings. In addition, they are used in peace processes for unique purposes and in pursuit of very singular benefits.

I define *peacemaking referendums* as those held to consult the public on matters specifically related to an ongoing peacemaking process, with a view to aiding in the resolution of a conflict.[2] This excludes referendums that, even though take place to manage ethnonational differences between communities, are not held with the consent of the main parties to the conflict and/or to deal with issues related to the content, process, or outcome of a peacemaking process. Since a peacemaking initiative presupposes the collaborative search by the parties to find a solution to their conflict, any kind of unilateral referendum, such as the referendums in Quebec in 1995 and Congo-Brazzaville in 2015, fall outside the concept. I characterize a referendum as peacemaking based on the issue it addresses, the purpose of the consultation, the scope of the consultation, and the implications of the outcome.

First, peacemaking referendums have been generally held on issues related to power-sharing, territory, and self-determination. The 2018 referendum in Guatemala over the country's territorial claim to Belize is an example of a referendum held on a territorial dispute. This referendum took place after Belize, Guatemala, and the Organization of American States agreed to allow the International Court of Justice (ICJ) to arbitrate the dispute. With the referendum, the Guatemalan government sought popular support for the government to follow through on its commitment and submit the issue to the ICJ. In addition, in contemporary peace negotiations, consociational solutions are typically negotiated and agreed-upon by the parties in conflict and call for the establishment of power-sharing institutions. Peacemaking referendums have been held on the approval/rejection of this new constitutional order. This was the case in Northern Ireland in 1998, Guatemala in 1999, Rwanda 2003, Cyprus 2004, and Iraq in 2005. Finally, self-determination referendums are common in peacemaking processes; in these, voters opt to remain part of an existing state or to secede. In East Timor in 1999 and in South Sudan in 2011, voters massively voted in favour of independence.

Second, the purpose, in the sense of the function or aim, for which referendums are most often used in peacemaking processes is to ratify a peace agreement. This type of peacemaking referendum took place in Northern Ireland in 1998, Guatemala in 1999, Rwanda in 2003, Cyprus in 2004, Iraq in 2005, and in Colombia in 2016. Peace agreement, or peace settlement, referendums have profound implications for a peace process. Since the new institutions that will function post-conflict are generally enshrined in peace agreements, peacemaking referendums are often, but not always, constitutional referendums. An exception is the 2016 referendum in Colombia on the ratification of the peace agreement between the Santos government and the Revolutionary Armed Forces of Colombia (FARC). The agreement was not constitutional in nature, although some of its provisions required constitutional changes for implementation.

Peace agreement referendums take place at the end of the peace negotiations, but similar referendums have been used to consult the public while the negotiations are ongoing. These procedural or mandate peacemaking referendums are held to consult the public on a specific issue, or set of issues, related to negotiation proceedings. Loizides defines mandate referendums as those where 'a leader presents a general idea or a framework for a peace arrangement to the public in an attempt to secure early approval for the nascent agreement'.[3] This was the case in Guatemala in 2018 and South Africa in 1992. In South Africa, President De Klerk held a referendum asking the white community whether it supported his negotiating position, which envisioned the end of apartheid. Procedural or mandate referendums, I would add, can only be considered peacemaking referendums if the other parties to the negotiations do not oppose them and if they are in line with the framework for agreement. A referendum that does not comply with these requirements is more likely to exacerbate than contribute to the peaceful resolution of a conflict.

The third aspect is the scope of the consultation: some peacemaking referendums are universal plebiscites, while in others only a specific community is asked to vote, as in South Africa. Who is allowed to vote in a peacemaking referendum can be a thorny issue in the peace negotiations simply because the society is likely to be deeply divided. For example, although the 2004 peace agreement referendum in Cyprus was, in the end, a universal plebiscite, it was a contentious issue in the negotiations whether the community of Turkish settlers living in northern Cyprus should be allowed to vote. In the worst cases, peace negotiations have stalled over this issue. The most paradigmatic case is that of the negotiations between Morocco and the POLISARIO (Frente Popular para la Liberación de Saguia el-Hamra y de Río de Oro) over Western Sahara. While the parties agreed in 1991 to hold a self-determination referendum and a United Nations Mission for the Referendum in Western Sahara (MINURSO) was established to oversee it, the referendum is yet to take place. Because the outcome of a referendum is unavoidably tied to who is allowed to vote, this question has been the main sticking point in negotiations for decades. A similar issue has beset negotiations over the Nagorno-Karabakh conflict, in this case, whether or not displaced Azerbaijanis would be allowed to vote in an independence referendum. While their participation would likely favour a pro-independence result, the opposite outcome is likely if they are excluded.[4] The decision on what population to include in the consultation is, therefore, bound to be a delicate one. In principle, inclusive consultations that bring to the vote all the population that will be affected by the referendum result will provide greater legitimacy to the outcome. Nevertheless, to agree on holding a referendum to resolve some of the most difficult issues and/or sticking points in the negotiations can be a significant leap forward. The parties' agreement to hold an independence referendum at a later date allowed peace negotiations in New Caledonia and Bougainville to progress.[5]

Finally, peacemaking referendum results may differ in the implications they have. Some referendums are binding and, therefore, their outcome is necessarily implemented, while others are merely consultative. Peacemaking referendums tend to be binding, especially when they are held to ratify a peace agreement. The 1992 referendum in South Africa, for example, was a consultative referendum, where the implementation of the referendum result was not compulsory. This is not to say that the result did not have significant repercussions since De Klerk had promised to resign if his proposal for reform did not receive the white community's support.

Advantages and Challenges for Peacemaking

As the cases mentioned above suggest, peacemaking referendums present some significant challenges—and not only to peacemaking processes specifically, but more generally to peace processes. Some of these challenges are inherent to the fact that peacemaking referendums take place in conflict contexts. One important challenge that specifically afflicts peacemaking referendums is insecurity. On the one hand, holding a referendum can put voters at risk while, on the other, a sense of insecurity, mistrust or fear can influence their voting.[6] For example, insecurity can make voters wary that the referendum result will lead to a resurgence of violence, and this fear can instigate rejection. Issues of (in)security are believed to have reduced support for the peace settlements in the referendums in Guatemala, Cyprus and Iraq. On a more practical note, areas destroyed by conflict may not have the infrastructure required to carry out the electoral process or simply not have the democratic institutions and traditions that would make a referendum suitable. In such cases, other forms of deliberation should be considered that can provide for wide political or group representation and societal inclusion in the decision-making process as possible.

Referendums are bound to heighten political and public debate. While this in itself is not a negative factor, the referendum can revive tensions and further divide a highly polarized society along existing conflict lines. When stakes are high, and the outcome has significant political implications, referendum campaigns can be highly competitive, establishing a new field where the conflict is played out. This is highly problematic in conflict because a referendum campaign can be used as a platform for those who oppose the peace process to influence public opinion with campaign messaging that reignites the deep-rooted fears, insecurities, and hatreds that fuelled the conflict in the first place.[7] For example, 'No' campaign leaflets against the Good Friday Agreement (GFA) in Northern Ireland sought to raise the Unionist community's fears that the GFA was a slippery slope to Northern Ireland's departure from the UK. Some leaflets read 'The Agreement will lead to a United Ireland' and called it an 'abject surrender to IRA/Sinn Feín's "terrorist gangsters"'.[8] Finally, when referendums present voters with a zero-sum dichotomous choice, there is a higher risk that the outcome will be regarded as a loss/victory, to the detriment of reconciliation.[9] Peacemaking referendums have so far only posed voters questions with binary answers. Presenting voters with different options, or preferences, to choose from, could be a feasible alternative, although it would demand more flexibility from negotiators in agreeing to the implementation of different outcomes, which would add complexity to the negotiation.

For all these reasons, the ultimate challenge or danger of a peace-making referendum is a resurgence of violence. This was the case in East Timor in 1999; anti-independence militias backed by Indonesia opposed the result of the self-determination referendum and began a bloody intimidation campaign in the capital, Dili. Although a referendum can present serious dangers when held in conflict contexts, there is a growing understanding among scholars that the referendums themselves are not the source of the problem. Qvortrup points out that violence in referendums is a rarity and argues that the escalation in East Timor was the result of the lack of a clear agreement between the parties for the use of the referendum to determine the status of the territory and the poor administration of the referendum.[10] In fact, it is not that referendums are unsuitable for conflict resolution; rather, they must be employed in certain ways for peace processes to benefit. For instance, there needs to be clear agreement between the conflicting parties on the legitimacy of a referendum,[11] and it must be carefully considered whether the conflict context is sufficiently taken into consideration and, in the best-case scenario, sufficiently transformed to prevent further polarization due to the referendum.[12] In peace agreement referendums, for example, there should be a certain amount of reconciliation during the negotiations, so that communities can say 'Yes' to a future together. To this end, groundwork is needed prior to the referendum that mobilizes popular support for peace and, in the case of an agreement referendum, it is important that the agreement is seen as a step in a longer term process, and not the end of the road. In essence, the referendum should be deployed and publicly understood as an (important) step in the longer term process of achieving peace.

Aside from contextual challenges, referendums can throw significant roadblocks in the way of the peacemaking process. As previously mentioned, deciding the conditions and rules under which the referendum will take place has led to difficulties and prolonged stalemates in peace negotiations. Interpretation of the results can be another problem. There is an inherent risk in peacemaking referendums that the results will generate a perception that one side 'won' and the other 'lost', which can be profoundly harmful to the reconciliation process. The turnout can have an impact on the perceived legitimacy and implication of the results as well. Peacemaking referendums have had varying degrees of participation, from the very low 19 per cent in Guatemala in 1999, to the 37 per cent in Colombia in 2016, to the surprisingly high over 80 per cent turnout in Northern Ireland in 1998 and Cyprus in 2004. The reasons behind why turnouts are so different are multiple, and not yet fully understood. In the Colombian referendum, for example, geography was an important factor. With the exception of the capital, Bogotá, support for the agreement was low among urban populations and higher among the rural population more directly affected by the conflict. Voter turnout among this population was highly supressed by a tropical storm that hit Colombia's Caribbean coast on the day of the referendum.[13] Independent of the causes, the turnout and the percentage of support for the 'winning' outcome will likely have important repercussions on the implementation of whatever was decided in the referendum. Typically, the results of referendums with a turnout lower than 50 per cent cast serious doubt on the legitimacy of implementing an outcome that did not receive the support of a significant share of the population.

Despite the challenges, under the right circumstances, peacemaking referendums can boost peace processes and be a powerful peacemaking tool. Some of the benefits derive from the democratic exercise itself. The referendum experience has the potential to increase public debate and awareness, educating citizens, and encouraging civic engagement in the political process, creating a sense of ownership of, and responsibility for, the peace being made at the negotiations table. A more educated and engaged public is better able to hold its political representatives accountable for their commitments and compromises. Mandate referendums, in particular, can help political leaders make difficult concessions or commitments by gaining public support for them, and create momentum for agreement.[14] Holding a referendum at an earlier stage of the peace negotiations, as in a procedural or mandate referendum, can familiarize the public with, and prepare it for, a final agreement or settlement. One of the most important benefits of peacemaking referendums is their ability to legitimize a negotiating process and its outcome. Because peacemaking referendums typically take place in societies where power is contested, and for which power-sharing solutions are negotiated, they are an important means of granting legitimacy to newly devised political institutions.[15]

The way peace negotiations are conducted can shape the referendum campaign experience and the referendum outcome, particularly in peace agreement referendums.[16] The degree of secrecy in which the negotiations are held, and whether political stakeholders and civil society are included, are particularly important factors influencing the results. Secrecy and inclusion influence whether leaders publicly endorse the agreement, affect the organization and comparative strength of the 'Yes' and 'No' campaigns, and shape the information available to the public on what is, or will be, at stake in the referendum.

To begin with, there is growing consensus that the political inclusivity of the negotiations process[17] and the consequent inclusivity of the political institutions enshrined in peace agreements[18] are essential to peace agreements being supported in referendums. Whether a political party or leader is included in the negotiations is likely to affect the party's endorsement of a peace agreement and whether and the extent to which it will mobilize its economic and human resources to campaign for or against it. Referendum voters tend to be highly influenced by political leaderships and even more so in conflict contexts where party lines are typically drawn along the differences that fuelled the conflict. In addition, political leaders and parties are able to mobilize considerable economic and human resources—and sometimes use the media—to build influential referendum campaigns. The fact that the Good Friday Agreement was negotiated by a majority of the political parties in Northern Ireland meant they all had a stake in it and supported and campaigned for its endorsement, which deeply shaped the referendum's historical outcome. The ambiguity of the agreement was also a facilitating factor in allowing the parties to interpret it somewhat differently and better 'sell' it to their constituencies.[19] However, this also led to the existence of multiple 'yes' campaigns with mutually exclusive interpretations of the agreement and adversarial campaign messages which have endured in the public psyche and harmed the reconciliation process.

Political parties or groups excluded from negotiations are likely to have an incentive to *spoil* a peacemaking referendum for political gain and may actively campaign against a peace agreement. Exclusionist, typically secretive, negotiations tend to feed negative reactions to the agreement from those who were outside the negotiations, exacerbating spoiler problems and negatively influencing public opinion.[20] Therefore, while excluding certain actors from the negotiations may favour the creation of an agreement by those at the table (for example, by reducing contention) it may be counterproductive if a referendum is used to ratify the agreement. Returning to the Good Friday Agreement referendum example, the 'No' campaign was exclusively led by two smaller and hardliner unionist political parties who initially participated in the negotiations but walked out a year before the agreement was reached.[21] The Colombian experience provides another example. There, the 2016 referendum put to a vote a peace agreement reached exclusively by President Santos' government and the FARC. The low turnout and the marginal victory of the 'No' vote was a surprise to many in Colombia and abroad. Although transparency and inclusion were unprecedentedly a concern during the negotiations, former President Uribe and his new party, the Democratic Centre, opposed the agreement from the side-lines from the start. Campaigning for the 'No' vote in the referendum, he and his party exploited Colombian fears that the amnesty provided in the agreement meant impunity for the FARC. The rejection of the agreement forced Santos to include the opposition in the renegotiations that started shortly after the referendum, bringing the Democratic Centre's proposals to the negotiations with the FARC. Instead of a new referendum, the new version of the agreement was ratified by a vote in the Parliament, where the Santos government held a majority of seats.

The outcome that political leaders and parties support and campaign for can strongly affect any referendum. But such political advocacy can be especially influential in peacemaking referendums. This is due to the fact that peace negotiations often take place exclusively between political elites and with secrecy. Under these circumstances, political leaders become the major sources of information to both the media and the public on the content and potential outcomes of the negotiations, strengthening their ability to shape public opinion. Secrecy also impacts when, what, and how much voters get to know about what is being negotiated. When negotiations are secretive, the final agreement easily becomes the first contact the public has with the content of the negotiations—and their leaders' opinions on it can make a difference in how they vote. At the same time, this leaves voters with little time to understand the content and implications of agreements that are typically complex, fuelling their suspicion and enabling misinformation during the referendum campaigns. While this is a general malady of all referendums, peacemaking referendums are especially prone to it because they take place in a societal context of distrust and polarization.

It is especially important that the public be, as far as possible, educated on the issues and the potential forms of agreement. This requires a less secretive negotiation process that allows public debate to start at earlier stages of the process—not just in the weeks leading up to a referendum—and encourages leaders, civil society and even the mediators to educate the public throughout. The secrecy of the negotiations on a comprehensive solution to the Cyprus conflict (or *problem*), commonly known as the Annan Plan, left an unengaged and poorly informed Greek Cypriot community with less than a month to grasp the lengthy, complex and legalistic language of an agreement which would bring about a new federal United Cyprus Republic. The 'No' campaign, headed by the President himself, capitalized on the lack of public understanding of the implications of the agreement and sought to feed Greek Cypriot anxieties about Turkey's military presence on the island and agitate Greek Cypriot nationalistic sentiments. Requiring majority support from both communities to be implemented, the Annan Plan was rejected with an overwhelming 'No' vote from the Greek Cypriot community. Interestingly, the majority of Turkish Cypriots voted 'Yes', even though the Turkish Cypriot leader also led a 'No' campaign and similarly played on Turkish Cypriot fears. Yet the Turkish Cypriot community was considerably more engaged and informed at an earlier stage of the process. In this community, the promise of accession to the European Union and the end of international isolation embedded in the negotiations galvanized civil society groups and pro-Annan Plan political parties; they mobilized the community and discussed the negotiations at an early stage of the process. Some of the important work done by the 'This Country is Ours' platform, which included dozens of civil society groups, was to inform and discuss with citizens the benefits and shortcomings of the Annan Plan. Later becoming the core of the 'Yes' campaign in the referendum, its efforts helped curb misinformation and fearmongering in the community during the referendum campaign period.[22]

Civil society plays an important role in peace referendum campaigns, and including it in the negotiations can be crucial to the 'Yes' vote. Including civil society actors in the negotiations increases public support for the peace negotiation process—particularly by enhancing public perceptions of the legitimacy of the process—and lead to more durable agreements.[23] Because civil society actors who engage with the negotiations will potentially be highly mobilized in a referendum campaign, negotiation processes that include them in some capacity can generate stronger 'Yes' campaigns down the line. Campaigns organized by civil society groups can make up for risk-averse and less enthusiastic campaigns led by political leaders and parties.[24] For example, despite their support for an agreement, leaders may be fearful of the cost of openly committing to an outcome if their constituencies do not support it in a referendum. This is heightened in peace agreement referendums where supporting the agreement can be seen as a betrayal or capitulation. In many cases, the process of negotiations can lead to splits within political parties, who then tend to have less effusive campaigns to avoid alienating segments of its delegates and constituency.

In addition, as peace agreement referendums are often followed by elections, politicians may be cautious in their support and refrained in their campaign spending on the referendum. Campaigns led by civil society are also less divisive and better able to deliver reconciliatory messages that can help reduce polarization in the referendum. In Northern Ireland, a well-resourced and organized civil society-led 'Yes' campaign played a crucial role in rallying support for the Good Friday Agreement, especially among unionist voters. Using professional campaign techniques that conveyed the dangers of a 'No' vote and its consequences for a new peaceful future,[25] civil society was able to convey a more inclusive reasoning for voting 'Yes' to the agreement, one that crossed community and party lines.

For all the above reasons, peace agreement referendums challenge the way peace negotiations and mediation have traditionally taken place—in secret, between political elites. Thus, they require a new paradigm of peacemaking *praxis* that allows for less secretive and more inclusive negotiations.[26]

Conclusion

Referendums can have surprising twists and turns and offer a less-than-democratic experience. If anything, the increase in the use of referendums has highlighted some of their paradoxical risks. For one thing, there is a danger that the public will be manipulated during the referendum campaigns. For another, referendums can be deployed to serve certain political interests and establish an inherently undemocratic centralization of power.[27] Ironically, in these situations, an artifice created for the greater representation of people in democratic societies has been used to ask those same people to give up that power to certain political figures. Given their flaws and paradoxes, should we welcome referendums as a new feature of contemporary peacemaking?

While an inherent problem of referendums is that the public can be manipulated by political and other special interest forces, they offer an unmatched opportunity for people to effect change.[28] In conflict contexts, this can signify a powerful shift in the status quo and symbolic step towards a more peaceful future. Referendums are an undeniably important and perhaps essential tool in contemporary peacemaking. In a world where power is increasingly a function of legitimacy, peacemaking referendums, or more specifically, a peace agreement, may well become a requirement for the legitimacy of a peace process. Referendums have become such a powerful legitimizing force that it is increasingly uncommon for an agreement referendum not to follow the announcement of a peace agreement. Despite the significant challenges and risks, peacemaking referendums are probably here to stay. Therefore, the more central question to researchers and practitioners is not whether referendums should be held in peace processes, but how peacemaking referendums can best be used to serve a peace process.

On the bright side, peacemaking referendums potentially have less risk of misuse because they take place within a peacemaking process.

Ideally, the negotiations process provides a neutral arena for the resolution of conflict, so peacemaking referendums are less likely to be used for undemocratic purposes. Further, when a referendum is part of a peacemaking process led or supported by international or regional organizations, or that otherwise enjoys the support of the international community, this support can provide greater legitimacy to the process and the outcome of the referendum. Finally, devices can be put in place to monitor the voting.

More than simply one-off events, peacemaking referendums are formative experiences in peace processes. Referendum campaign periods are potentially a first opportunity for societies in conflict to experience and play out their political disagreements without violence. Referendums are an opportunity for new visions and possibilities for the future to be publicly discussed. Communities in conflict can come together in support of a common future, in spite of their disagreements on the details of that imagined future. While peacemaking referendums pose the risks discussed in this chapter, the referendum experience itself has the potential to positively shape society in an enduring way and be a crucial positive step towards peace.

Notes

1. M. Qvortrup (2012) 'The History of Ethno-National Referendums 1791–2011', *Nationalism and Ethnic Politics*, 18:1, 129.
2. Peacemaking referendums have previously been defined more strictly as referring to sovereignty referendums held on issues of *stateness* by K. Collin in 'Do Referendums Resolve or Perpetuate Contention?' in Pippa Norris, Richard W. Frank, and Ferran Martínez i Coma (eds.) *Contentious Elections: From Ballots to Barricades* (New York and Oxon: Routledge), p. 112.
3. N. Loizides (2014) 'Negotiated Settlements and Peace Referendums', *European Journal of Political Research*, 53:2, 237.
4. P. Johansson (2009) 'Putting Peace to the Vote: Displaced Persons and a Future Referendum on Nagorno-Karabakh', *Refugee Survey Quarterly*, 28:1, 123.
5. K. Collin (2018) 'Peacemaking Referendums in Oceania: Making or Delaying Peace in New Caledonia and Bougainville', *Ethnopolitics*, 18:2, 2.

6. S. Y. Lee and R. Mac Ginty (2012) 'Context and Postconflict Referendums', *Nationalism and Ethnic Politics*, 18:1, 50–58.
7. B. Reilly (2008) 'Democratic Validation', in J. Darby and R. Mac Ginty (eds) *Contemporary Peacemaking*, 2nd edn (London and New York: Palgrave Macmillan), p. 233.
8. I. Somerville and S. Kirby (2012) 'Public Relations and the Northern Ireland Peace Process: Dissemination, Reconciliation and the "Good Friday Agreement" Referendum Campaign', *Public Relations Inquiry*, 1:3, 249.
9. R. Mac Ginty (2003) 'Constitutional Referendums and Ethnonational Conflict: The Case of Northern Ireland', *Nationalism and Ethnic Politics*, 9:2.
10. M. Qvortrup (2014) *Referendums and Ethnic Conflict* (Philadelphia: University of Pennsylvania Press), p. 157.
11. M. Qvortrup, *Referendums and Ethnic Conflict*, p. 154.
12. S. Y. Lee and Roger Mac Ginty (2012) 'Context and Postconflict Referendums', p. 63; K. Collin (2018) 'Peacemaking Referendums in Oceania', p. 60.
13. E. Dávalos et al. (2018) 'Opposition Support and the Experience of Violence Explain Colombian Peace Referendum Results', *Journal of Politics in Latin America*, 10:2, 188.
14. N. Loizides (2014) 'Negotiated Settlements and Peace Referendums', p. 237.
15. J. McEvoy (2018) 'Letting "The People(s)" Decide: Peace Referendums and Power-Sharing Settlements', *Democratization*, 25:5, 865.
16. J. Amaral (2018) 'Do Peace Negotiations Shape Settlement Referendums? The Annan Plan and Good Friday Agreement Experiences Compared', *Cooperation and Conflict*, 53:3, 356–74.
17. J. Amaral (2019) *Making Peace with Referendums: Cyprus and Northern Ireland* (Syracuse, New York: Syracuse University Press), pp. 111–15.
18. N. Loizides (2015) *Designing Peace: Cyprus and Institutional Innovations in Divided Societies* (Pennsylvania: University of Pennsylvania Press); J. McEvoy (2018) 'Letting "The People(s)" Decide'.
19. J. Tonge and J. Evans (2002) 'Party Members and the Good Friday Agreement in Northern Ireland.' *Irish Political Studies*, 17:2, 62;

P. Dixon (2013) 'An Honourable Deception? The Labour Government, the Good Friday Agreement and the Northern Ireland Peace Process', *British Politics*, 8:2, 114.
20. A. Wanis-St. John (2011) *Back Channel Negotiation: Secrecy in the Middle East Peace Process* (Syracuse, New York: Syracuse University Press), pp. 271–72, 286.
21. The Democratic Unionist Party (DUP) and the United Kingdom Unionist Party (UKUP) left the negotiations in 1997 objecting to negotiating with Sinn Féin. The republican nationalist party was allowed to join the multi-party negotiations when the Provisional Irish Republican Army (PIRA) paramilitaries re-committed to a ceasefire.
22. J. Amaral (2019) *Making Peace with Referendums*, pp. 66–69.
23. D. Nilsson (2012). 'Anchoring the Peace: Civil Society Actors in Peace Accords and Durable Peace', *International Interactions*, 38:2, 243–266; D. Kew and A. Wanis-St. John (2008) 'Civil Society and Peace Negotiations: Confronting Exclusion', *International Negotiation*, 13:1, 11–36; T. Paffenholz (2014) 'Civil Society and Peace Negotiations: Beyond the Inclusion–Exclusion Dichotomy', *Negotiation Journal*, 30:1, 69–91.
24. S. Rao (2010) 'Citizen's Role in Political Settlements', Helpdesk Research Report, GSDRC Applied Government Knowledge Services, Birmingham, p. 10. Available at: http://www.gsdrc.org/docs/open/hdq1014.pdf.
25. L. E. Hancock (2011) 'There Is No Alternative: Prospect Theory, the Yes Campaign and Selling the Good Friday Agreement', *Irish Political Studies*, 26:1, 95–116.
26. J. Amaral (2019) *Making Peace with Referendums*, pp. 122–29.
27. M. Qvortrup, B. O'Leary, and R. Wintrobe (2018) 'Explaining the Paradox of Plebiscites', *Government and Opposition*, 1–18.
28. K. Collin (2015) 'Do Referendums Resolve or Perpetuate Contention?' p. 116.

Bibliography

Amaral, J. (2018) 'Do Peace Negotiations Shape Settlement Referendums? The Annan Plan and Good Friday Agreement Experiences Compared', *Cooperation and Conflict*, 53:3, 356–74. https://doi.org/10.1177/0010836717737569.

———. (2019) *Making Peace with Referendums: Cyprus and Northern Ireland* (Syracuse, New York: Syracuse University Press).

Collin, K. (2015) 'Do Referendums Resolve or Perpetuate Contention?' in Pippa Norris, Richard W. Frank, and Ferran Martínez i Coma (eds.) *Contentious Elections: From Ballots to Barricades* (New York and Oxon: Routledge), pp. 111–30.

———. (2018) 'Peacemaking Referendums in Oceania: Making or Delaying Peace in New Caledonia and Bougainville', *Ethnopolitics*, 18:2, 139–57. https://doi.org/10.1080/17449057.2018.1513726.

Dávalos, E., L. F. Morales, J. S. Holmes, and L. M. Dávalos (2018) 'Opposition Support and the Experience of Violence Explain Colombian Peace Referendum Results', *Journal of Politics in Latin America*, 10:2, 99–122. https://doi.org/10.1177/1866802X1801000204.

Dixon, P. (2013) 'An Honourable Deception? The Labour Government, the Good Friday Agreement and the Northern Ireland Peace Process.' *British Politics*, 8:2, 108–37. https://doi.org/10.1057/bp.2012.30.

Hancock, L. (2011) 'There Is No Alternative: Prospect Theory, the Yes Campaign and Selling the Good Friday Agreement', *Irish Political Studies*, 26:1, 95–116. https://doi.org/10.1080/07907184.2011.531107.

Johansson, P. (2009) 'Putting Peace to the Vote: Displaced Persons and a Future Referendum on Nagorno-Karabakh', *Refugee Survey Quarterly*, 28:1, 122–39. https://doi.org/10.1093/rsq/hdp013.

Lee, S. Y., and R. Mac Ginty (2012) 'Context and Postconflict Referendums', *Nationalism and Ethnic Politics*, 18:1, 43–64. https://doi.org/10.1080/13537113.2012.654085.

Loizides, N. (2014) 'Negotiated Settlements and Peace Referendums', *European Journal of Political Research*, 53:2, 234–49. https://doi.org/10.1111/1475-6765.12043.

———. (2015) *Designing Peace: Cyprus and Institutional Innovations in Divided Societies* (Pennsylvania: University of Pennsylvania Press).

Mac Ginty, R. (2003) 'Constitutional Referendums and Ethnonational Conflict: The Case of Northern Ireland', *Nationalism and Ethnic Politics*, 9:2, 1–22. https://doi.org/10.1080/13537110412331301395.

McEvoy, J. (2018) 'Letting 'The People(s)' Decide: Peace Referendums and Power-Sharing Settlements', *Democratization*, 25:5, 864–81. https://doi.org/10.1080/13510347.2018.1426568.

Nilsson, D. (2012) 'Anchoring the Peace: Civil Society Actors in Peace Accords and Durable Peace', *International Interactions*, 38:2, 243–66.

Paffenholz, T. (2014) 'Civil Society and Peace Negotiations: Beyond the Inclusion-Exclusion Dichotomy', *Negotiation Journal*, 30:1, 69–91.

Qvortrup, M. (2012) 'The History of Ethno-National Referendums 1791–2011', *Nationalism and Ethnic Politics*, 18:1, 129–50. https://doi.org/10.1080/13537113.2012.654081.

———. (2014) *Referendums and Ethnic Conflict* (Philadelphia: University of Pennsylvania Press).

Qvortrup, M., B. O'Leary, and R. Wintrobe. 2018. 'Explaining the Paradox of Plebiscites', *Government and Opposition*, 1–18. https://doi.org/10.1017/gov.2018.16.

Rao, S. (2010) 'Citizen's Role in Political Settlements', Helpdesk Research Report, GSDRC Applied Government Knowledge Services, Birmingham, p. 10. Available at: http://www.gsdrc.org/docs/open/hdq1014.pdf.

Reilly, B. (2008) 'Democratic Validation', in J. Darby and R. Mac Guinty (eds) *Contemporary Peacemaking*, 2nd ed. (London and New York: Palgrave Macmillan), pp. 230–41.

Somerville, I., and S. Kirby (2012) 'Public Relations and the Northern Ireland Peace Process: Dissemination, Reconciliation and the "Good Friday Agreement" Referendum Campaign', *Public Relations Inquiry*, 1:3, 231–55. https://doi.org/10.1177/2046147X12448370.

Tonge, J., and J. Evans (2002) 'Party Members and the Good Friday Agreement in Northern Ireland', *Irish Political Studies*, 17:2, 59–73. https://doi.org/10.1080/714003201.

Wanis-St. John, A. (2011) *Back Channel Negotiation: Secrecy in the Middle East Peace Process* (Syracuse, New York: Syracuse University Press).

Wanis-St. John, A., and D. Kew (2008) 'Civil Society and Peace Negotiations: Confronting Exclusion', *International Negotiation*, 13:1, 11–36.

CHAPTER 9

Refugees, Peacemaking, and Durable Solutions to Displacement

Maja Janmyr

Introduction

Armed conflicts and other situations of violence have long been the major reasons for the involuntary displacement of people across borders.[1] In fact, the majority of today's approximately 26 million refugees originate from regions experiencing protracted armed conflict, and about half come from just three countries: Syria, Afghanistan and South Sudan. 84 per cent of the world's refugees are hosted by countries in the Majority World—with Turkey accommodating the greatest number, followed by Pakistan, Colombia, and Uganda. The protracted nature of many refugee situations across the globe are testaments to the difficulty of resolving displacement.[2]

Throughout history, people living as refugees have widely been seen as a marginalized and disempowered group with little impact on peace-building[3] and the resolution of conflict. Being viewed as passive recipients

M. Janmyr (✉)
University of Oslo, Oslo, Norway
e-mail: maja.janmyr@jus.uio.no

of outcomes that are negotiated in distant arenas of power, refugees have only rarely been consulted or represented in peace processes.[4] As this chapter intends to show, however, the exclusion of refugees as actors in peacemaking is an approach that is fundamentally flawed; people living as refugees can be important political actors whose actions and interests greatly affect the outcome of a conflict.

While refugees are far from a homogenous group—and cannot therefore be prima facie regarded as either 'agents of peace' or 'agents of war'[5]—there is a growing recognition that refugees are able to influence conflict and peace outcomes.[6] The forms of political action refugees engage in ranges from conventional—i.e. in arenas of formal consultation and institutionalized processes—to nonconventional—i.e. through protests, demonstrations, sit-ins, and so on.[7] Conflict is no longer (if ever) a predominantly place-specific experience.[8] Contemporary changes, not the least advances in communications technology, are giving refugees more prominent roles.[9] A growing body of scholarship focuses precisely on how social media platforms and the associated communication technologies facilitate political transnational lives.[10] Thus, in exile, refugees may exacerbate conflict or frustrate efforts to find peace,[11] but refugee participation in peacebuilding efforts has also proved to be crucial in many attempts to achieve peace in the country of origin.[12] As James Milner has argued, 'effective peacebuilding initiatives must incorporate a full consideration of the potential role that refugees and the regional dynamics of conflict can play both in undermining and supporting peacebuilding activities in the country of origin'.[13]

This chapter demonstrates how resolving displacement is intrinsically linked to achieving peace. In light of international refugee law's three durable solutions to refugee situations—voluntary repatriation, resettlement and local integration—I address refugee participation in peacebuilding in exile. First, the chapter considers the fundamental principle of asylum as peaceful and humanitarian, followed by an examination of the three formal durable solutions. It thereafter explores refugee involvement in peace negotiations and agreements, as well as in peacebuilding elections and referenda. Following this, the chapter discusses how the observance of refugee rights in countries of asylum may contribute to peacemaking, before finally examining how skills training and education in exile allows refugees to make important contributions to peacebuilding in their countries of origin.

Asylum—Peaceful and Humanitarian

The notion of refugees actively contributing to violent resistance predates the contemporary international refugee regime and has existed for as long as individuals have been forced into exile.[14] Rather than serving as safe havens, on a number of occasions, camps for refugees have become notorious for serious problems of insecurity, including armed attacks—against the camps but sometimes also from the camps—arbitrary killings, torture, exploitation, and military recruitment.[15] International refugee law developed in the early and mid-twentieth century precisely against this backdrop, prompting the international community to ever since emphasize the peaceful and humanitarian nature of asylum.

In 1967, the UN General Assembly unanimously adopted the United Nations Declaration on Territorial Asylum, which provided that 'States granting asylum shall not permit persons who have received asylum to engage in activities contrary to the purposes and principles of the United Nations', and, more importantly, recognized that the grant of asylum is 'a peaceful and humanitarian act and... as such, cannot be regarded as unfriendly by another State'.[16] This notion is also reflected in important legal instruments such as the 1951 Refugee Convention, the Preamble of which expresses the wish that 'all States, recognizing the social and humanitarian nature of the problem of refugees, will do everything within their power to prevent this problem from becoming a cause of tension between States'.[17]

In 1987, UNHCR's Executive Committee furthermore coined the principle of the civilian and humanitarian character of refugee camps in its Conclusion No. 48 on military or armed attacks on refugee camps and settlements.[18] The Principle's importance has since been repeatedly emphasized, first under the auspices of the UNHCR, and later by the UN General Assembly and UN Security Council.[19] Most important among a number of Council Resolutions concerning refugee camp security are those recognizing that a breach of the refugee camps' civilian and humanitarian character may develop into threats against international peace and security.[20] Despite these important milestones, there are numerous examples of situations where these principles have been violated; probably the most well-known example is the Rwandan refugee camps in Zaïre (today the Democratic Republic of the Congo) during the mid-1990s. Here, the camps were used as a base from which the former Rwandan extremist government, army, and *Interahamwe* militias launched raids on Rwanda with the intention to regain the power that they lost to the Rwandan Patriotic Front (RPF) following the 1994 Rwandan genocide.[21]

The establishment of the principle of the civilian and humanitarian character of asylum/camps has arguably also had fundamental implications for refugee participation in peacebuilding initiatives. While the principle primarily aims to prevent refugees contributing to violent resistance and thereby risk drawing their country of asylum into armed conflict, some host states have interpreted the principle as precluding all forms of political participation directed towards the refugee's country of asylum. In Uganda, for example, refugees are explicitly discouraged from engaging in *any* political activities related to their country of origin in order to avoid the replication of ethnic or tribal divisions in the country of asylum.[22] As this chapter will show throughout, such a blanket ban may not only be unwarranted—and sometimes also in contradiction to fundamental human rights standards relating to freedom of association and expression—it is often counter-productive to the resolution of both the armed conflict *and* displacement. Where opportunities for political participation are not guaranteed, refugees in exile risk becoming politicized or militarized.[23] This means that disregarding refugees' interests may be explicitly destructive to peace processes and, as we shall see, the resolution of displacement.

Durable Solutions and Peace

International refugee law provides three options for the resolution of displacement—voluntary repatriation, local integration in the country of first asylum, or resettlement in a third country.[24] There is to be no hierarchy in the application of the durable solutions; UNHCR rather advises an integrated approach including, for example, countries of origin and asylum, donor states, and refugees themselves. The restoration of citizenship and the remaking of state–citizen bonds lie at the heart of all of these solutions—the search for solutions to refugee situations is, to paraphrase Katy Long, very much a struggle of the politically excluded for political inclusion.[25] This is particularly important as, in most countries of first asylum, refugees are admitted under some form of temporary protection, and this status generally means refugees are excluded from formal political institutions and the political rights that come with citizenship.[26]

Resettlement involves 'the selection and transfer of refugees from a state in which they have sought protection to a third state which has agreed to admit them – as refugees – with permanent residence status'.[27] It provides individual refugees with legal and physical protection, and, as UNHCR has pointed out, the planned or strategic use of resettlement can also maximize the benefit of resettlement, either directly or indirectly, other than to those being resettled.[28] For example, the strategic use of resettlement can impact the situation in the first country of asylum by decongesting camps and reduce demands on assistance programmes and scarce environmental resources. However, on average, a mere 1 per cent of the global number of refugees are resettled each year, and only a handful of countries receive the majority of resettled refugees: the United States (38 per cent of global refugees resettled in 2017), Canada (14 per cent), the United Kingdom (10 per cent), and Australia (6 per cent).[29] This is largely due to the fact that resettlement is not formally codified in international law, and with no positive legal obligation on states to participate, only a few 'core' countries have voluntarily participated in UNHCR's resettlement programmes.

On occasion, the desire to further peacebuilding in countries of origin has also led to the local integration or naturalization of refugees in their countries of asylum. This appears to have been the case behind Tanzania's decision in 2007 to consider the naturalization of approximately 220,000 Burundians who had been in exile in Tanzania since 1972.[30] In essence, local integration means that 'a refugee is granted some form of durable legal status that allows him or her to remain in the country of first asylum on an indefinite basis, and to fully participate in the social, economic, and cultural life of the host community'.[31] As with resettlement, local integration also has considerable limitations. Many states hosting large refugee populations oppose any form of local integration or naturalization of refugees. By arguing that it is not a country of asylum, Lebanon, for example, opposes the local integration of any of the 1.5 million refugees that it is currently hosting.[32] The difficulties in securing resettlement and local integration for more than a small portion of refugees has notably meant that, for international protection agencies like UNHCR, voluntary repatriation to the country of origin is in practice the above all preferred durable solution.

Refugee repatriation and peacebuilding are linked in a number of ways. First, considering that the existence of refugees is the very manifestation of the collapse of state protection, refugee repatriation—if voluntary—can be seen as an indicator that national protection is re-established, and, consequently, of successful peacebuilding.[33] In addressing the UN Security Council in January 2009, the UN High Commissioner for Refugees explained how 'the scale of return and success of reintegration are two of the most tangible indicators of progress in any peace-building process'.[34] On the other hand, the fact that not all refugees are repatriated may demonstrate that problems still persist, and suggests that there can be no sustainable peace as long as a substantial number of citizens are excluded from the process and no durable solutions have been found.

Second, the repatriation of refugees legitimizes and gives credibility to the new post-conflict regime. Indeed, it is a significant part of the peace process that can indicate changes to the international community.[35] Refugee return can moreover be a precondition for peace if these refugees are politically and/or militarily active in the conflict. Their peaceful integration and inclusion is as such necessary for conflict resolution. A similar argument is that refugee participation in formal political negotiations will lead to a more sustainable return, and particularly so because refugees become more inclined to see themselves as stakeholders in the peacebuilding and reconstruction process.[36]

At the same time, return in the context of protracted conflict may be difficult, where physical infrastructure, homes, and social services have been damaged, and prolonged exile may complicate issues of access to land and property, and reintegration into the local economy.[37] This is exemplified in the case of Burundi, where approximately two-thirds of the returnees in 2008 had limited or no access to land.[38] In some cases, the circumstances of repatriation have rendered returning refugees to become internally displaced persons, thereby casting doubt about the achievement of a sustainable durable solution.

While the durable solutions described in this section are part and parcel of the international refugee regime's toolkit for resolving displacement, it is important to note that people living as refugees have at times found the imposition of these solutions at odds with their own desires and concerns. In the context of Ghana, for example, Liberian refugees protested the lack of realistic repatriation to Liberia or the possibility of third-country resettlement. They were opposed to local integration in Ghana, and demanded larger financial grants for repatriation or resettlement to a third country. In a similar vein, in Uganda and Tanzania, Congolese refugees have strategically navigated the resettlement process in ways obscured by UNHCR's static resettlement categories.[39] Additionally, it is important to keep in mind that people living as refugees sometimes make their own way out of displacement, outside the realm of the formal solutions.[40]

PEACE NEGOTIATIONS AND AGREEMENTS

Negotiated peace settlements and ceasefires have become increasingly important to ending armed conflict.[41] Civilians, including refugees, are taking more prominent roles, and the achievement of lasting peace has often shown to require the support of civilian communities. While people living as refugees are increasingly acknowledged to be important contributors to the development of peace agreements that more comprehensively address the causes and consequences of conflicts, the practice of refugee involvement in these processes varies greatly.[42] With regard to refugees from Myanmar, for example, recent scholarship has found that there has been essentially no effort made by the Myanmar government to ensure the participation of refugees in the peace process generally or in discussions concerning repatriation.[43]

In contrast, many major peace agreements in the last decades have included references to, and often more detailed provisions on, refugees or other displaced populations. These agreements often incorporate legal protections for returning refugees with a view both to address past injustices and to prevent future rights violations. A well-known example concerns Guatemalan refugees in Mexico, who organized themselves into Permanent Commissions focused on refugee repatriation and in 1992 negotiated the October 8 Accord with the government of Guatemala.[44] This Accord not only reiterated a number of constitutional rights, but also focused specifically on land acquisition for returnees.

Similarly, Burundian refugees participated in the Arusha Peace Process consultations where they promoted refugees' interests in the negotiations.[45] Issues put forward by refugees that were subsequently included in the peace agreement included the recovery of land and property, and procedures to guarantee the voluntary and safe return and reintegration of refugees into Burundian society. Along this same line, Liberian civil society, backed by refugees, formally participated in the 2003 peace negotiations.[46] Their participation contributed to the establishment of a Truth and Reconciliation Commission.

Ensuring sustainable peace notably requires in any peace agreement, a more focused attention on the challenges for voluntary repatriation of refugees. Goal 5 of UNHCR's Agenda for Protection ('Redoubling the search for durable solutions') explicitly encourages states 'to facilitate the participation of refugees, including women, in peace and reconciliation processes to ensure that such agreements duly recognise the right to return and contemplate measures to encourage repatriation, reintegration, and reconciliation'.[47] Returnees may notably contribute to the implementation of peace agreements and to the economic recovery of the country. As then High Commissioner Antonio Guterres remarked in 2006, speaking to the UN Security Council about South Sudanese peacebuilding, 'Over and over, we see that [refugees'] participation is necessary for the consolidation of both peace and post-conflict economic recovery. Sustainable peace and recovery are necessary to allow refugee returns. Yes. But refugee returns are every bit as essential to sustained peace and recovery'.[48] As is highlighted below, refugees frequently return with schooling and new skills that help facilitate post-conflict recovery.

In the Syrian context, a sustainable political settlement appears unlikely without a real focus on the challenges of refugee return.[49] Such a refugee-focused approach entails that any peace agreement would need to not only actively address communal and sectarian dynamics and guarantee security to returning populations, but also establish a transitional justice mechanism that guarantees the housing, land and property rights of refugees.[50] As of early 2021, Syrian refugees in countries neighbouring Syria are under continued pressure to return, notwithstanding UNHCR's position that conditions in Syria are not conducive for voluntary repatriation in safety and dignity.[51]

PEACEBUILDING ELECTIONS AND REFERENDA

Refugees may also participate in peacebuilding elections and referenda without being forced to first physically repatriate.[52] Recent years have seen a dramatic increase in out-of-country voting; according to International IDEA's Voting from Abroad Database, 146 countries had by 2018 enacted legislation allowing their citizens to vote from abroad.[53] As these regulations encompass all citizens irrespective of the circumstances that have led them abroad, in principle, out-of-country voting also applies to people living as refugees.

Noteworthy, historical examples of successful refugee out-of-country participation include the Eritrean independence referendum (1993), and elections in Bosnia (1996 and 1997), Kosovo (1999), Afghanistan (2004), Iraq (2005 and 2010), and South Sudan (2010 and 2011).[54] The Eritrean referendum, in which 99.7 per cent voted for independence, can be considered a highly successful example of refugee participation in peacebuilding through out-of-country voting. Some 300,000 Eritreans in exile, out of approximately 1.2 million (including children), registered for out-of-country voting—which amounted to around a third of the total electorate.[55] In the Bosnian context, the Dayton Agreement furthermore explicitly linked refugee participation to refugee repatriation, confirming that 'the exercise of a refugee's right to vote shall be interpreted as confirmation of his or her intention to return to Bosnia and Herzegovina'.[56]

However, exile may also effectively exclude refugees from participation in the political life of their country of origin.[57] A legal or administrative framework to ensure out-of-country voting may simply be lacking, whereas in other cases, refugees have had reasons to be reluctant to register with the authorities of a persecutory or unprotective country even when they are formally entitled to vote from abroad.[58] While host states may encourage refugees' participation in country-of-origin elections as a first step towards their repatriation,[59] in other situations, refugee participation may be interpreted as an indication that they have reavailed themselves of the protection of their country of origin. This may prompt the host state to prematurely revoke refugee status and insist upon repatriation.

Two of the world's current largest producers of refugees—Syria and Afghanistan—both have out-of-country voting regulations, but are also illustrative of many of the challenges of refugee participation. In the historic first democratic elections in Afghanistan in 2004, the opportunity for out-of-country voting was considered for the nearly 3 million refugees living in Pakistan and the 1 million refugees in Iran. Despite a lack of funding as well as bureaucratic and political obstacles in negotiations with the host countries, Afghan refugee voters made up a notable 10 per cent of the total 2004 electorate.[60] But host states Iran and Pakistan had also tried to influence Afghan refugee voting along ethnic lines to protect their political interests in Afghanistan, and no arrangement was made for refugees abroad to cast their votes remotely in the 2009 and 2014 elections. This is also reminiscent of the 2010 election in Iraq, where the nature and form of refugee participation were subject to fierce disputes, including because of continued sectarian struggles for political power.[61]

The 2014 Syrian presidential election as it played out in neighbouring Lebanon is another example of how highly politicized refugee out-of-country voting can be. During this election, the Syrian Embassy in Beirut was one of the very few places across the Arab region where it was possible to cast a vote. Tens of thousands of refugees participated, and the result showed huge support for President Assad among Syrian refugees in Lebanon.[62] Syrian opposition activists denounced the election as a sham, even claiming that the main reason Syrian refugees cast their vote for the incumbent president was a fear of reprisals by the Syrian regime and its powerful supporters in Lebanon.[63]

Observance of Refugee Rights

Despite the clear linkage between refugee participation in peacebuilding efforts and sustainable repatriation and peace, refugees across the world face crackdowns on their fundamental rights. Refugees are among the most marginalized groups in society, not only facing persecution in the country of origin but also new dangers and insecurities in their countries of refuge. The refugee issue is widely securitized, often driven by a political and media narrative that portrays refugees as a potential source of instability. Fearful of altered domestic demographics, in Lebanon, for example, President Michel Aoun, a Maronite Christian, has argued that the predominantly Sunni Muslim Syrian refugee presence is an 'existential threat' for the country.[64] Approaches such as this have brought about a number of restrictive measures towards refugees with a detrimental impact on their abilities and willingness to engage in processes of peacebuilding.

For many people living as refugees, the main preoccupations are related to grappling with the daily challenges of survival and integration. As Bekaj and Antara have noted, '[c]ompared to more pressing humanitarian and livelihood-related concerns, political engagement might seem to be an extravagant commodity that can hardly be afforded'.[65] In Lebanon, for example, 74 per cent of Syrian refugees over the age of 15 did not have legal residency in 2017.[66] This irregular legal status is a cross-cutting issue that affects other sources of vulnerabilities, including freedom of movement, threats of deportation, difficulty in accessing security and justice mechanisms as well as registering marriages and births. This is exasperated by unlawful evictions, extreme economic marginalization, intimidation of Syrian refugees without legal status, and raids by security forces.

The marginalization of refugees in countries of asylum often affects their freedom of expression and results in avoidance of political discussion or mobilization. The 2017 kidnap and forced return of South Sudanese political activists carried out by agents of South Sudan in Nairobi, for example, served as a warning to other refugees in Kenya and halted any political discussion on the situation in South Sudan.[67] In Sweden, mobilization among Syrian refugees has similarly been hindered 'significantly by surveillance, intelligence reports, and threats against activists abroad and their family members still living in their country of origin'.[68] In Lebanon, many Syrian political activists have been arrested by Lebanese political entities sympathetic to the Syrian regime. Fearing reprisals, Syrian refugees rarely voice their opinion on Syrian politics.[69] The lack of basic means for survival and the precarious legal status of Syrian refugees in Lebanon has, more precisely, had negative consequences for their willingness to openly engage in democracy- and peacebuilding in Syria.[70]

Skills Training and Education

One way refugees may make an important contribution to peacebuilding in their country of origin is by benefitting from skills training and education while in exile. In a 2006 statement to the UN Security Council, the UN High Commissioner for Refugees noted that 'refugees return with schooling and new skills... Over and over, we see that their participation is necessary for the consolidation of both peace and post-conflict economic recovery.'[71] These new skills and qualifications could, for example, address specific gaps in the provision of basic services in their country of origin, such as focusing on health and education. Teacher-training programmes in Kakuma refugee camp in Kenya have notably mitigated the shortage of teachers in South Sudan.[72]

Education is in particular seen as 'a core component of building sustainable peace'.[73] Indeed, common schooling is key in the establishment of a modern political community, and thus in the creation modern citizens.[74] While schools can play an important role in mitigating factors that can exacerbate conflict by promoting democratic environments,[75] the literature has also emphasized how education in conflict settings does not always contribute to creating spaces for inclusion and engagement. By actively promoting prejudice and conflict, education risks playing a major role in sustaining conflict in ways that make peacebuilding a distant goal.[76] In Rwanda and Burundi, for example, education has been argued to fuel conflicts by promoting ethnic divisions and discrimination of particular groups.[77]

An equally pressing issue is that only half of school-aged refugee children actually have access to schools.[78] At primary level, the number of refugee children enrolled in school in 2018 was 63 per cent, compared with a global figure for all children of 91 per cent.[79] The likelihood of a refugee child progressing to the next academic grade drops sharply as each year passes, and is especially marked in the transition to secondary school. Less than one-quarter of refugee adolescents make it to secondary school, compared with 84 per cent globally. There is thus great potential for improving both the quantity and quality of educational opportunities for those living as refugees.

Higher education for refugees has also been considered to be 'an invaluable peacebuilding tool'.[80] In the Syrian refugee situation, 'university graduates ... include Syria's brightest and most ambitious young people ... the human capital that will be critical to the rebuilding of Syrian society after the conflict has ended'.[81] Thus, in order to tackle the lack of educational opportunities for Syrian refugee youths, a wide range of initiatives have recently been taken. The Institute of International Education (IIE) works on the issue of Syrian refugees and higher education in Jordan and Lebanon,[82] and, in Turkey, the Free Syrian University was established 'to prepare educated generations who seek to build a country of law and justice and institutions'.[83] Indeed, this training may assist in the actual implementation of peace agreements, where one major reason for their lack of implementation has been suggested to be a lack of local capacity to do so.[84]

Other initiatives include the IIE Scholar Rescue Fund, the Syria Consortium for Higher Education in Crisis, and university scholarships promoted by organizations like the German Academic Exchange Service-DAAD.[85] While such efforts are important, significant barriers to refugees continuing higher education include financial constraints and a lack of documents needed for academic study.

Specific peace education programmes for refugees in exile could furthermore enhance prospects of reconciliation and conflict resolution upon return. UNHCR's Executive Committee has emphasized education for peace and the promotion of a culture of peace.[86] Returnees will be better equipped to reconcile with former community members and mediate conflicts during fragile post-conflict and reintegration processes. As UNHCR has also noted: 'While living in exile, long-term refugees also have an ideal opportunity to acquire valuable skills in areas such as leadership, advocacy, mediation and conflict resolution, which will again enable them to contribute to the rebuilding of their communities once return becomes possible'.[87] In a similar vein, recent scholarship has pointed to the role of legal empowerment and legal conscientization—i.e. the process of coming to know how the law affects one's life, and the role law and legal institutions may play in both oppression and as tools for change—among refugees in opening up opportunities for refugees' active participation in peacebuilding and reconciliation processes.[88]

Conclusions

This chapter has explored the close linkage between refugees and peacebuilding, and has shown how refugees engage in diverse practices of peacemaking, sometimes but not always linked to the formal durable solutions framework—resettlement, local integration, and voluntary repatriation. The chapter has also emphasized how contemporary displacement generates many challenges to achieving durable peace. This includes refugee participation (or lack thereof) in peacebuilding elections and peace negotiations, where legal protections for returning refugees are potentially incorporated.

One of the most pressing issues is nevertheless the growing trend of coerced returns—rather than voluntary repatriation in safety and dignity—to the country of origin. Various forms of coercion is being placed on refugees to ensure that mass repatriation movements take place; Bangladesh, Myanmar, and key donor states have long been in discussions of what arguably must be seen as a premature return of an estimated 700,000 Rohingya refugees, while a similar growing international effort is taking place to set in motion large-scale refugee returns to Syria.[89] In countries like Lebanon, refugees face such extreme marginalization and exploitation that many refugees see no other option but to return to Syria despite conditions for many not being ripe for return.

Developments such as these have clear implications for peacemaking; not only does force return goes against the core principles of international refugee law, but being pressured to return in the face of obvious danger negatively impacts upon refugees' ability and willingness to engage in the peaceful resolution of conflicts. In any discussions of refugees' role in peacemaking, there is therefore a pressing need to consider the strong linkage between protecting the human rights of refugees during all phases of displacement, and the extent to which refugees are able and willing to openly engage in democracy- and peacebuilding.

Notes

1. See for example S. K. Lischer (2007) 'Causes and Consequences of Conflict-Induced Displacement', 9 *Civil Wars* 2, 142–155; W. Hayden (1999) 'The Kosovo Conflict: The Strategic Use of Displacement and the Obstacles to International Protection' 2 *Civil Wars* 1, 35–68.
2. A protracted refugee situation is where refugees have been in exile for more than five years. G. Loescher and J. Milner (2013) *Protracted Refugee Situations: Domestic and International Security Implications* (Florence: Taylor and Francis).
3. Peace-building is here understood as intending to create positive peace and consists of a wide range of activities—capacity building, reconciliation, and societal transformation—focusing on the social conditions that foster violent conflict. It is seen as a process of positive and sustainable change. See UN, Report of the UN Secretary-General (1992) 'An Agenda for Peace: Preventative Diplomacy, Peacemaking and Peace-Keeping', UN Doc A/47/277-S/24111; J. P. Lederach (2005) *The Moral Imagination: The Art and Soul of Building Peace* (Oxford: Oxford University Press).
4. K. Jacobsen, H. Young, and A. Osman, 'Refugees and IDPs in Peacemaking Processes' (2008) in J. Darby and R. MacGinty (eds) *Contemporary Peacemaking: Conflict, Peace Processes and Post-War Reconstruction* (Basingstoke; New York: Palgrave Macmillan), 313–327; K. Koser (2008) 'Introduction: Integrating Displacement in Peace Processes and Peacebuilding' 28 *Refugee Survey Quarterly* 1, 5–12.
5. A. Bekaj and L. Antara (2018) *Political Participation of Refugees: Bridging the Gaps* (Stockholm: International IDEA), 18–19.
6. M. Bradley, J. Milner, and B. Peruniak (eds. 2019) *Refugees' Roles in Resolving Displacement and Building Peace: Beyond Beneficiaries* (Washington, DC: Georgetown University Press).
7. J. Hyndman (2018) 'Durable Solutions and the Political Action of Refugees' in Bradley, Milner and Peruniak, *Refugees' Roles*; P.

Nyers and K. Rygiel (2014) *Citizenship, Migrant Activism and the Politics of Movement* (London: Routledge); A. Betts and W. Jones (2016) *Mobilising the Diaspora How Refugees Challenge Authoritarianism* (Cambridge: Cambridge University Press).
8. E. van der Dussen Toukan (2019) 'Refugee Youth in Settlement, Schooling and Social Action: Reviewing Current Research Through a Transnational Lens' 16 *Journal of Peace Education* 1, 1–20.
9. Jacobsen, Young and Osman (2008), 315.
10. See for example R. Dekker, G. Engbersen, and J. Klaver (2018) 'Smart Refugees: How Syrian Asylum Migrants Use Social Media Information in Migration Decision-Making' 4 *Social Media and Society* 1, 1–11; J. Marlowe (2019) 'Social Media and Forced Migration: The Subversion and Subjugation of Political Life' 7 *Media and Communication* 2, 173–183.
11. H. Smith and P. Stares (2007) *Diasporas in Conflict: Peace-Makers or Peace-Wreckers?* (Tokyo: United Nations University Press).
12. UNSC Res 1325 (2000) UN Doc S/RES/1325(2000), para 8(a); UN Sub-Commission on the Prevention of Discrimination and Protection of Minorities (1998), Res 1998/26.
13. J. Milner (2011) *Refugees and the Peacebuilding Process* (Geneva: UNHCR New Issues in Refugee Research), 29.
14. See generally K. B. Harpviken (2008) *From "Refugee Warriors" to "Returnee Warriors": Militant Homecoming in Afghanistan and Beyond* (Arlington, VA: Center for Global Studies, George Mason University, Global Migration and Transnational Politics Working Paper 5).
15. M. Janmyr, (2014) 'Revisiting the Civilian and Humanitarian Character of Refugee Camps', in D. Cantor and J. F. Durieux, *Refuge from Inhumanity: War Refugees and International Humanitarian Law* (Leiden: Brill Nijhoff), 225–246.
16. UNGA (1967) Res. 2312 (XXII), UN Doc A/RES/2312(XXII), Article 4 and preamble.
17. UN Convention Relating to the Status of Refugees, 28 July 1951, United Nations, Treaty Series, vol. 189, p. 137, preamble.
18. UNHCR (1987) 'Military attacks on refugee camps and settlements in Southern Africa and elsewhere', EXCOM Conclusion no 48 (XXXVIII), preamble.
19. Janmyr, 'Revisiting the Civilian'.

20. For an overview, see Janmyr, 'Revisiting the Civilian'.
21. UN, Report of the Secretary General of the United Nations on Security in the Rwandese Camps (1994), UN Doc. no. S/1994/1308 para. 30.
22. T. Zakaryan (2018) *Political Participation of Refugees: The Case of Congolese and South Sudanese Refugees in Uganda* (Stockholm: International IDEA).
23. I. Saleyhan and K. Gleditsch (2006) 'Refugees and the Spread of Civil War' 60 *International Organization* 2, 335–366. See also J. Milner (2009) 'Refugees and the Regional Dynamics of Peacebuilding' 28 *Refugee Survey Quarterly* 1, 13–30 at 17; T. Sharpe and S. Cordova (2009) 'Peacebuilding in Displacement' (2009) 33 *Forced Migration Review*, 46–48; G. Loescher, J. Milner, E. Newman, and G. G. Troeller (eds. 2008) *Protracted Refugee Situations: Political, Human Rights and Security Implications* (Tokyo: United Nations University Press).
24. The search for durable solutions is a central part of UNHCR's mandate. See Statute of the Office of the United Nations High Commissioner for Refugees (14 December 1950) UNGA Res 428 (V), annex, 5 UN GAOR Supp (No 20) 46, UN Doc A/177, Chapter 1 para. 1.
25. K. Long (2010) *Voting with Their Feet: A Review of Refugee Participation and the Role of UNHCR in Country of Origin Elections and Other Political Processes* (Geneva: UNHCR Policy Development and Evaluation Service), 1.
26. Hyndman 'Durable Solutions', 24–25.
27. UNHCR (2011) *Resettlement Handbook* (Geneva: UNHCR).
28. UNHCR (2003) 'Convention Plus: Framework of Understandings on Resettlement', UN Doc FORUM/CG/RES/04.
29. UNHCR (2017) *Resettlement in a Glance: 2017 in Review*, https://www.unhcr.org/protection/resettlement/5a9d507f7/resettlement-fact-sheet-2017.html.
30. Milner, 'Refugees and the Regional', 8.
31. See J. Hathaway (2005) *The Rights of Refugees under International Law* (Cambridge: Cambridge University Press), 977.
32. M. Janmyr (2017) 'No Country of Asylum: "Legitimizing" Lebanon's Rejection of the 1951 Refugee Convention' 29 *International Journal of Refugee Law* 3, 438–465.

33. UNHCR (1997) *The State of the World's Refugees—A Humanitarian Agenda* (Oxford: Oxford University Press), 160–163.
34. Statement by António Guterres to the UNSC (2009), https://www.unhcr.org/admin/hcspeeches/496625484/statement-mr-antonio-guterres-united-nations-high-commissioner-refugees.html.
35. J. Crisp (2000) *Africa's Refugees: Patterns, Problems and Policy Challenges*' (UNHCR New Issues in Refugee Research Working Paper 28); R. Black and S. Gent (2006) 'Sustainable Return in Post-Conflict Contexts' 44 *International Migration*, 15–36.
36. Long, *Voting with Their Feet*, 6.
37. Koser, 'Introduction', 6; Milner, 'Refugees and the Regional', 7.
38. Milner, 'Refugees and the Regional', 8.
39. C. Clark-Kazak C., and M. J. Thomson (2019) 'Refugees' Role in Resettlement from Uganda and Tanzania: Agency, Intersectionality and Relationships', in Bradley, Milner and Peruniak, *Refugees' Roles*.
40. For examples, see generally Bradley, Milner, and Peruniak, *Refugees Roles*.
41. C. A. Hartzell (2018) 'Civil War Termination', in W. R. Thompson (ed), *The Oxford Encyclopedia of Empirical International Relations Theory* (Oxford: Oxford University Press).
42. For an overview, see C. Bell (2000) *Peace Agreements and Human Rights* (Oxford: Oxford University Press). See also Koser, 'Introduction'.
43. A. Purkey (2019) 'Transformative Justice and Legal Conscientization: Refugee Participation in Peace Processes, Repatriation, and Reconciliation', in Bradley, Milner and Peruniak, *Refugees' Roles*, 75–97 at 82.
44. Hyndman 'Durable Solutions', 33.
45. Sharpe and Cordova, 'Peacebuilding in Displacement'.
46. P. Hayner (2007) *Negotiating Peace in Liberia: Preserving the Possibility for Justice* (Geneva: Henry Dunant Centre for Humanitarian Dialogue).
47. 'Agenda for Protection' (2002), UNHCR EXCOM, UN Doc. A/AC.96/965/Add.1.
48. UNHCR, 'Guterres Warns UN Security Council of Possible "Catastrophe" in Darfur' (24 January 2006), UNHCR Press Release.

49. M. Yahya and J. Kassir (2017) *Coming Home? A Political Settlement in Syria Must Focus on Refugees* (Carnegie Policy Outlook); D. Suber and RDe Stone (2018), *Return to Syria: A Proposal from Syrian Refugees in Lebanon* (Jadaliyya, May 8), http://www.jadaliyya.com/Details/37513/Return-to-Syria-A-Proposal-from-Syrian-Refugees-in-Lebanon.
50. Yahya and Kassir (2017) *Coming Home?*
51. UNHCR (2018) *Comprehensive Protection and Solutions Strategy: Protection Thresholds and Parameters for Refugee Return to Syria*, https://data2.unhcr.org/en/documents/download/63223.
52. See generally, Long, *Voting with their Feet*, 17ff. See also J. Grace and E. Mooney (2009) 'Peacebuilding Through the Electoral Participation of Displaced Populations' 28 *Refugee Survey Quarterly* 1, 95–121; P. Johansson (2009) 'Putting Peace to the Vote: Displaced Persons and a Future Referendum on Nagorno-Karabakh' 28 *Refugee Survey Quarterly* 1, 122–139.
53. Bekaj and Antara, *Political Participation*, 73.
54. International Organization for Migration (2003) *Case Studies on the Participation of Conflict Forced Migrants in Elections: Participatory Elections Project (PEP)* (Geneva: IOM).
55. International Organization for Migration, *Case Studies*, 74.
56. Dayton Peace Agreement (adopted 14 December 1995), Article 4.
57. Ziegler 2017; Long, 'Voting with their Feet', 1.
58. Bekaj and Antara, *Political Participation*.
59. Bekaj and Antara, *Political Participation*, 75–76.
60. Bekaj and Antara, *Political Participation*, 74. C. Slavu (2007) 'Afghanistan's 2004 Presidential Election: External Voting for a Large Displaced Population', in A. Ellis and others (eds), *Voting from Abroad: The International IDEA Handbook* (Stockholm and Mexico City: International IDEA and Federal Electoral Institute of Mexico), 158–162.
61. Long, *Voting with Their Feet*, 30.
62. Z. El –Helou (2018), *Political Participation of Refugees: The Case of Syrian Refugees in Lebanon* (Stockholm: International IDEA), 12.
63. H. Haid (2014) *The Syrian President Is Being Made in Lebanon? Rumours and the Syrian Presidential Election in Lebanon* (Beirut: Heinrich Böll Stiftung), https://lb.boell.org/en/2014/11/05/

syrian-president-being-made-lebanon-rumours-and-syrian-presidential-election-lebanon.
64. The Daily Star Lebanon (2017) 'Aoun: Refugee Crisis an "Existential Threat"', http://www.dailystar.com.lb/News/Lebanon-News/2017/Oct-31/424548-aoun-refugee-crisis-an-existential-threat.ashx.
65. Bekaj and Antara, *Political Participation*.
66. UNHCR and others (2017) *VASYR 2017: Vulnerability Assessment of Syrian Refugees in Lebanon*, https://reliefweb.int/report/lebanon/vasyr-2017-vulnerability-assessment-syrian-refugees-lebanon.
67. K. Houreld (2017) 'South Sudanese Exiles Fear Kidnap After Activists Disappear in Kenya', Reuters, https://www.reuters.com/article/uk-southsudan-security-kenya-idUKKBN1611U0.
68. J. E. Lundgren (2015) 'Repression Across Borders: Homeland Response to Anti-Regime Mobilization Among Syrians in Sweden', 8 *Diaspora Studies* 2, 104–119.
69. Saferworld and Lebanese Center for Policy Studies (2018), *Building Peace into Refugee Responses: Syrian refugees in Lebanon*, 17. El –Helou, *Political Participation*.
70. Bekaj and Antara, *Political Participation*, 18–19.
71. Statement by Mr. António Guterres, United Nations High Commissioner for Refugees to the United Nations Security Council (New York, 24 January 2006), http://www.unhcr.org/43d643334.html, accessed 12 December 2019.
72. Milner, 'Refugees and the Regional', 6.
73. M. Noveli and A. Smith (2011) *The Role of Education in Peacebuilding: A Synthesis Report of Findings from Lebanon, Nepal, and Sierra Leone* (New York: UNICEF).
74. T. Waters and K. LeBlanc (2005) 'Refugees and Education: Mass Public Schooling Without a Nation-State' 49 *Comparative Education Review* 2, 129–147.
75. van der Dussen Toukan, 'Refugee Youth', 11.
76. M. Matsumoto (2015) 'Schooling's "Contribution" to Contemporary Violent Conflict: Review of Theoretical Ideas and Case Studies in the Field of Education and Conflict' 10 *Research in Comparative and International Education* 2, 238–256.
77. Matsumoto, 'Schooling's "Contribution"'.

78. UNHCR (2019) *Stepping Up: Refugee Education in Crisis* (Geneva: UNHCR), https://www.unhcr.org/steppingup/wp-con tent/uploads/sites/76/2019/09/Education-Report-2019-Final-web-9.pdf.
79. UNHCR, *Stepping Up*.
80. R. A. Rasheed and A. Munoz (2016) 'Higher Education and Peacebuilding—A Bridge Between Communities?' 13 *Journal of Peace Education* 2, 172–185 at 172. See also B. Zeus (2009) *Exploring Paradoxes Around Higher Education in Protracted Refugee Situations: The Case of Burmese Refugees in Thailand* (London: Institute of Education, University of London).
81. K. D. Watenpaugh, A. L. Fricke, and T. Siegel (2013) *Uncounted and Unacknowledged: Syria's Refugee University Students and Academics in Jordan* (California: UC Davis Human Rights Initiative and the Institute of International Education).
82. Watenpaugh, Fricke and Siegel, *Uncounted and Unacknowledged*; J. King (2014) 'The Syrian Refugee Crisis and Higher Education: A View from Lebanon' (Institute of International Education Blog), https://www.iie.org/en/Learn/Blog/2014/04/2014-April-The-Syrian-Refugee-Crisis-And-Higher-Education-A-View-From-Lebanon.
83. D. Seckman and M. Trevithick (2014) 'The Scholar-Rebels of the Free Syrian University' (The Atlantic), http://www.theatlantic.com/international/archive/2014/01/the-scholar-rebels-of-the-free-syrian-university/283175/.
84. P. Weiss Fagen (2009) 'Peace Processes and IDP Solutions' 28 *Refugee Survey Quarterly* 1, 31–58; G. T. Tinde (2009) 'Top United Nations Peacebuilders and Advocacy for Women, Peace and Security' 28 *Refugee Survey Quarterly* 1, 140–150.
85. A. Young-Powell (2015) '"University Is One Place You're Not Labelled": Refugees Who Flee War to Study' (The Guardian), https://www.theguardian.com/education/2015/dec/17/uni versity-is-one-place-youre-not-labelled-refugees-who-flee-war-to-study.
86. See for example UNHCR (1996) 'Comprehensive and Regional Approaches Within a Protection Framework' (Geneva: UNHCR), para (e)(xi); UNHCR (2007) 'Children at Risk' (Geneva: UNHCR), para (h).

87. UNHCR (2008) 'Protracted Refugee Situations: A Discussion Paper Prepared for the High Commissioner's Dialogue on Protection Challenges' (Geneva: UNHCR), https://www.unhcr.org/protection/hcdialogue%20/492ad3782/protracted-refugee-situations-discussion-paper-prepared-high-commissioners.html. See also Jacobsen, Young, and Osman (2008), 318–319.
88. Purkey, 'Transformative Justice'.
89. J. Crisp (2019) 'Unwilling and Fearful Refugees Should Not Be Forced to Return Home' (The Guardian), https://www.theguardian.com/global-development/2019/oct/07/unwilling-and-fearful-refugees-should-not-be-forced-to-return-home.

CHAPTER 10

Time, Sequencing and Peace Processes

Roger Mac Ginty

Introduction

Peace processes and peace accords are full of references to time. There may be deadlines by which time agreements must be reached or conditions met. There may be exit strategies or other aims and dynamics that, it is hoped, will occur according to a particular timetable. A peace process, or the implementation of elements of a peace accord, may be linked to sequencing with actions or actors following, or hoping to follow, an order. This order may be reciprocal and thus vital to the notion and practices of compromise that lie at the heart of a functional peace process. More generally, peace processes operate in the present but often have an eye on the past (in order to deal with injustices) and on the future (in order to prevent conflict recidivism). This chapter will unpack the notion and practice of time in relation to peace processes and peace accords. It will begin conceptually, by making the point that time is often linked to power: some actors have the power to impose deadlines or their understanding

R. Mac Ginty (✉)
Durham University, Durham, UK
e-mail: roger.macginty@durham.ac.uk

of urgency and crisis on others. The chapter then moves on to examine some of the specific roles that time can play in peace processes and the implementation of peace accords.

The Concept of Time

The concept of temporality can be taken for granted, but it is worth unpacking the concept of time to understand that it is a social and political construct and as such should not be thought of as fixed or static. A good starting point is to highlight the differences between what might be called sociological time and political time.[1] Sociological time can be understood as those notions of time that are embedded in how people live and interact in cultural, social and economic settings.[2] Here we might regard time in terms of lifecycles, coming of age milestones (from a bar mitzvah to a mid-life crisis), agricultural cycles, or daily routines linked with bodily needs (such as hunger, thirst or toileting). Sociological time may be organic, bottom-up, culturally constructed and linked with natural cycles. It may be highly localised and understandable in that format to a relatively small group of people.[3] These understandings of time are not without power and the weight of tradition, and should not be romanticised. Think, for example, of the power of religious organisations in some societies to impose observance of religious dates or festivals. But much of this sociological time can be private, familial and outside of the surveillance of the state or other institutions. It can be vague, and rather than fixed according to the clock and defined units of hours, days and years, it can be loose and malleable. Sociological time is vital for our understanding of conflict and peace processes. Individuals, families and communities may feel that it is time to act, for example, to up arms, to protest against an authoritarian regime or to urge a political group to sue for peace. Similarly, they may need time to grieve, to comprehend acts of violence or to come to terms with new circumstances of peace or conflict. It is impossible to prescribe how long such processes may take and they will differ from individual to individual or community to community.

Political time can be regarded, on the other hand, as formal, top-down, and sometimes legally enshrined. States and international bodies, for example, have coordinated in order to define and fix time-zones.[4] Many domestic laws—enforced by states—have a time element: births and deaths must be registered within a time limit, taxes must be paid by a particular date, etc. In many states, a political timetable will be an important fixture and will be marked by the electoral cycle, budgets and demarcated anniversaries. The political and state timetable is entirely a construction, but it might become a social and cultural fixture that is embedded in how people map out their days and years. For example, school holidays may be set by the state, thus steering families with children towards particular dates for vacations. The very minutia of life, for example, when people can buy particular products or access services, might be legislated by the state.

We should not see political and sociological time as entirely separate. They constitute an assemblage with the two leaching into one another. The hybrid between sociological and political time is a construction that is permanently being negotiated, built and re-built. The key to this on-going process is power with some actors having more power than others. Just as parents set bed-time for children and can impose penalties if it is not adhered to, states can impose deadlines, fix-dates and mandate anniversaries. It is worth bearing this issue of power in mind when thinking of peace processes. The possession and use of power in peace processes are often linked to which actors can impose and enforce deadlines and time limits.

A final point to be made when thinking conceptually about time in relation to peace processes is that our analytical time-lines are often quite short. Certainly it is useful to think of peace as a process rather than as an event. That is, it is prudent to consider peace as a series of multiple interactions over the long term rather than as an event such as the signing ceremony of a peace accord. Yet, even when we think of a peace process we might be tempted to think of the process in terms of the period beginning from negotiations and pre-negotiations to a peace accord and then with an implementation period. For analytical comprehension, it is useful to think of time in terms of neatly packaged units. Indeed, many aspects of a peace process and peace accord implementation invite us to think along the lines of peace compressed into fixed time units. International organisations and INGOs who might be engaging in peace-support activities usually operate according to log-frames and time-limited programmes and projects. They might establish a number of milestones that help them judge the success of the implementation of a peace accord. For example, this might include the holding of elections, the completion of a Security Sector Reform process or the recruitment and training of a post-conflict police force. Yet, it is worth considering the adequacy of the relatively short time frame associated with this view of peace processes. Many conflicts last for generations or have very long-lasting impacts. Consider, for example, the Lebanese civil war that is often given a date range of 1975–1991, with the peace accord dated to 1989.[5] While these dates are useful for our comprehension, and allow us to place the Lebanese civil war within regional and global dynamics of that time period, the date range seems somewhat artificial. The Lebanese civil war, peace process and peace accord were the products of long-term processes of colonialism, sectarianism, regional competition, and the political economies of dynastic politics. Despite the 1989 peace accord, fighting continued through 1990 and militias (with the exception of Hezbollah) only disbanded in 1991. To corral such a complex series of processes into a neat and relatively compressed date range seems artificial. Instead, it is worth thinking about peace processes within the longue durée of history—something that is quite difficult given the a-historicism that is associated with much of the policy and practitioner world, but also with Peace and Conflict Studies. The experience of individuals and families in the civil war is also difficult to place within a short time frame. While some individuals might be able to say that their active service in a militia lasted from one date to another, that decision to join a militia was probably moulded by a series of longer-term factors, often stretching deep into family history. The necessity of the long-term view is also clear when we think of the bereaved or injured—impacts that last well beyond a peace process implementation period of a few years.

The chief point here is that peace processes and conflicts are unlikely to have neat endpoints. Instead, they have an afterlife. In an optimal situation, memories of the conflict fade and forms of politics less marked by violence and division take over. Yet given that most of the cases covered in this book are concerned with identity politics, this is likely to be a long-term process. Northern Ireland's Good Friday Agreement was reached in 1998 but, a generation later, identity politics are still firmly entrenched and so it is prudent to be circumspect when thinking about dates associated with conflict beginnings or endings.

Sequencing

The notion of sequencing in peace processes rests on the view that peace processes have a linear or step-by-step sequence. An abstraction of a linear peace process might take the following form: pre-negotiations, ceasefire, negotiations, peace accord, and post-accord implementation. Of course, peace processes rarely have such a neat sequence. They may become stuck at a particular phase, make progress on some issues but little on others or may collapse and have to go to the pre-ceasefire stage again. In short, peace processes will likely be messy, difficult to read and inconclusive.

Central to the notion of sequencing is confidence-building. A key feature of violent conflict is the building and reinforcement of negative images of 'the other'. This negative image may be based on demonstrable evidence; for example, an enemy may have engaged in atrocities or may have proven untrustworthy in previous peace processes. Parties to a conflict may also invest heavily in the demonisation of 'the other', perhaps using a variety of propaganda methods to paint them as (inherently) untrustworthy and violent. A peace process, therefore, will challenge perceptions of 'the other' among political and military elites and publics. Those involved in a peace process may seek evidence of the *bona fides* of the other side: Are they serious about investigating a peace process? Can militants or security forces be trusted to abide by a ceasefire or a lessening of violence as talks begin? Can others involved in negotiations be trusted to respect the confidentiality of negotiations? Can opponents be trusted to implement what they have agreed to?

Questions around trust are complex. All sides in a peace process work with incomplete information and are likely to hold negative assumptions about their opponents. For political elites involved in negotiations, it is not simply a case of trusting their opponents to negotiate in good faith and to implement what they have agreed to. There is also the issue of expectation management within their own constituency. Deciding to instigate a peace process involves significant risks, including being branded naïve or traitorous by your own side. President Santos in Colombia, for example, risked being outflanked by former President Uribe who accused Santos of being weak in the face of insurgency. Militant groups who investigate peace processes also risk splinter groups who accuse them of betraying the cause and accepting less than their core aim.

One way of dealing with issues of trust—both at the inter and intra-group levels—is to sequence interactions and concessions. The advantage of this approach is that the peace process ceases to become a zero-sum game. Instead, concessions and interactions are graduated and risks are lowered. In this model, a peace process can be seen as a series of trade-offs. Rather than a take it or leave it single agreement, it is a series of trades that breaks the peace process down into a number of sequenced interactions. Parties to the peace process are awarded multiple opportunities to prove their trustworthiness. Again, this operates at the inter and intra-group levels. A government engaging with a militant group may be able to satisfy itself that the militant group is cooperating with the peace process, and demonstrate to its own constituency that it has been prudent in its interactions with a militant group.

Perhaps the most obvious sequencing trade-off in peace processes relates to ceasefires and negotiations, with many parties to a peace process insisting that a ceasefire must be in place before there can be substantive negotiations.[6] The rationale behind the ceasefire-then-negotiations sequence is understandable in that negotiations are likely to have a better chance of making progress if negotiators are able to concentrate on conflict-wide issues rather than feel the need to respond to the latest atrocity. Yet, calling a ceasefire is a significant step. For many militant groups, violence, or the threat of violence, is their main point of leverage. Militant groups that surrender this leverage risk becoming toothless and irrelevant—especially if a government wishes to stretch out a peace process as is the case in Myanmar. Parties to a conflict may also be tempted to 'change the facts on the ground' prior to negotiations by escalating violence. This 'thump and talk' approach is dangerous in that an escalation of conflict may merely reinforce grievances and a determination, on the other side, not to make concessions on core goals.[7] In an optimum scenario, a ceasefire allows space for parties to engage in substantive negotiations. If the ceasefire is observed, then this sends out important signals regarding the extent to which parties are disciplined and unitary. Such confidence-building, again in an optimum scenario, may allow parties to engage in ever more substantive negotiations and reach a peace accord.

A final point to make in relation to sequencing is to remind ourselves of the points made in the Introduction to this chapter on the role of power in the temporality of peace processes. Some parties to a peace process, perhaps international arbiters or a government, may have the power to demand a particular sequence (for example, that weapons must be disarmed prior to a further stage in the peace process). The sequencing trade-offs are unlikely to be part of a completely free 'market'. Instead, some actors may be able to use their power to demand that a particular sequence is followed.

DEADLINES

Peace processes and the implementation of peace accords can be long-drawn out. This is unsurprising as these are complex political and social processes that may involve significant technical and legal, as well as political, cultural and emotional challenges. For example, the disarmament of militant groups and the reform of state security forces, the drafting of a new constitution and the safe disposable of unexploded ordinance are all likely to take considerable lengths of time. Moreover, the emotional and identity-related dispositions related to the conflict are likely to change only in the longer term. Aside from the 'natural' pace of a peace process, there is also the possibility that parties to the peace process deliberately try to slow the speed of a peace process or the implementation of a peace accord.

There may be numerous reasons for delay in peace processes. For example, a militant group may be reluctant to decommission its weapons as, without them, they would lose their principal point of leverage. A government may regulate its involvement in a peace process according to the electoral cycle—with the peace process being of secondary importance to the key aim of remaining in power. A government may also wish to elongate negotiations or pre-negotiations as they calculate that the longer that a militant group is on ceasefire then it is more likely to lose its fighting edge. Or, conversely, a militant group may wish to stretch out a period of negotiations so that it can re-arm (as was the case in Sri Lanka during one of its peace processes). In the case of separatists groups in both India and Myanmar, the governments have been content to secure ceasefires with militant groups but have little intention of moving towards substantive talks.[8] Many of the militant groups are quite content with these 'no war, no peace' situations as they diversify into business and profit from ceasefire economies.[9] 'No war, no peace' situations can be prolonged but are clearly dysfunctional in that the identity divisions in society persist.[10]

One way of attempting to accelerate movement in a peace process is through the use of deadlines. A deadline may concentrate minds, and encourage peace process participants to move beyond recriminations and focus on practical or actionable outcomes. George Mitchell, the US chair of the multi-party talks in Northern Ireland grew tired of talks delegations recounting historical grievances and took action by reducing the numbers of each delegation and showing little patience for history.

The issue of deadlines, however, comes back to power: does any party in the peace process have the ability to impose a deadline, and are there penalties for failure to meet deadlines? Usually, those with the power to impose and police deadlines will be governments or the international sponsors of peace processes. This is not always the case, however. Repeated UN attempts to kick-start talks in relation to Yemen have been rebuffed by Saudi Arabia and its attempts to find a military solution to the conflict.[11] In all cases, deadlines will be arbitrary, but they may help talks participants to focus. In a number of peace processes, there have been attempts to 'hothouse' the negotiations by bringing together a small number of talks participants and seeking to intensify the talks against the backdrop of a deadline.[12] While deadlines are arbitrary social constructions, they may be accompanied by a moral pressure to keep the momentum going, meet public or international expectations, or to be seen to be acting in a way that will keep the peace process going. This last point is important. A significant aspect of many peace processes concerns optics and perceptions. Parties to peace processes often have to engage in expectation management in their own constituencies to ensure that populations do not exceed expectations of benefits and the speed of those benefits.[13] Deadlines can have the effect of creating a public expectation of a breakthrough in negotiations with benefits to follow, with a possible downside should the expected benefits fail to materialise.

Deadlines or time limits often feature in peace accords as a way to encourage compliance. The risk with many peace accords is that parties will implement those peace accord provisions that suit them, and ignore or delay the implementation of those provisions that do not suit. This can be addressed by sequencing (discussed in the section above), and through deadlines for implementation that are accompanied by penalties for non-implementation. In some peace accords, the implementation of provisions might be linked with a schedule, while in others they might be open-ended or vague. The risk with the latter is that the implementation of the peace accord becomes a new site of contestation or conflict by other means. Grievances might develop if one party feels that another party is dragging its heels on implementing some provisions.

In addition to announced deadlines and time limits linked with peace accords, there is also a 'natural' time cycle in relation to international attention and associated largesse. International peace support is faddish and can be likened to a caravan that moves from peace process to peace process.[14] At any one time, a particular conflict and peace process, or a select few of them, will receive considerable international attention and financial and practical support. Over the past few decades, we have seen the caravan of INGOs and bilateral donors move through Cambodia, Bosnia, Croatia, Kosovo, Rwanda, Sierra Leone, Liberia, Iraq, Afghanistan, Myanmar and Colombia. In all cases, international attention stays for a few years but then moves on. Local actors must act fast to capitalise on this international attention before the window closes and the caravan moves on.

A final (and rather morbid) point to make in relation to deadlines is that peace processes, at the elite level, rely on individuals and those individuals, like anything biological, face an ultimate clock of mortality. Some peace processes have been associated with totemic individuals whose strength of personality and conviction has pushed through barriers. It is difficult to think of the demise of South Africa's apartheid in the absence of Nelson Mandela. In other cases though, key figures died at inopportune moments and it is difficult not to wonder what might have happened if they had lived. For example, John Garang, the leader of the Sudan People's Liberation Army died in a helicopter crash in July 2005. It is difficult to wonder if South Sudan's post-independence story might have been different (and more peaceful) if he survived.

Exit Strategies

The final time-related factor to be covered in this chapter relates to exit strategies, or the aim of international actors to withdraw from, or lessen their involvement in, peace-support operations. In an ideal scenario, a peace process may lead to a peace accord and an implementation period in which international actors play a role in supporting statebuilding, reconstruction, Security Sector Reform and other initiatives that might support the peace. The post-conflict state and civil society may develop or rebuild capacities so that international support is no longer required (or required in such large amounts) and so international actors can withdraw. In such a scenario—admittedly an ideal type—the post-conflict state has become sustainable as a polity and is no longer seen as a threat to its citizens or the region.

Exit strategies can be seen as connected to 'the local turn' in peace interventions, or the notion that local rather than international actors are best equipped to push forward war to peace transitions.[15] In the heyday of liberal peace interventions in the late 1990s and early 2000s,[16] many international peace-support actors held what could be called neo-colonial views on the righteousness of liberalism and democracy and its applicability to non-western societies. In this view, local actors were often seen as backward and in need of 'enlightenment' through good governance training and intrusive forms of mentorship. Yet the hubris and 'we can fix it' attitude of many liberal peace champions was punctured by the wars of attrition that followed regime change in Iraq and Afghanistan, and poor results from massive peace investments in Cambodia, Sierra Leone, Bosnia and elsewhere. Since then, international organisations, bilateral donors, INGOs and many others have engaged in extensive work to try to perfect their own modes of intervention and practice. This has involved turning to local actors who were once seen as an impediment to peace.

The 'local turn' has placed a renewed emphasis on local actors—governments, NGOs and civil society, and citizens—to be the engines of change and stabilisation. Rather than being regarded as backward, obsessed with identity politics, and corrupt, many international actors have 'rediscovered' the virtues of local actors as possessing indigenous technical knowledge. In this view, local actors are the key to the exit strategy. If 'properly' trained, capable of ensuring stability, and cognisant of the virtues of good governance (increasingly watered down to good enough governance), then international actors can draw down their involvement. The advantages of local actors over international actors are manifold; they are cheaper, speak the language, understand the context, and do not require the same security protection.

It is worth noting that in recent years, many western states have rowed back on the rhetoric of democracy, liberalism and human rights in relation to the peace-support and statebuilding operations. Instead the emphasis has been on stability—of the post-conflict country and the region. This has meant—as witnessed in Afghanistan, Iraq, Rwanda, Libya and elsewhere—finding a reasonably reliable client ruler who can secure the capital city and much of the state and then supporting this ruler. This tougher version of the exit strategy has had negative implications for human rights and the transparency of governance, but has been relatively easy to justify among western publics who have been jaded by lengthy overseas involvements that have brought what are, at best, mixed results. These lighter touch interventions meant that there is less emphasis on an exit strategy—quite simply there are fewer personnel and resources to exit.

A final point to make in relation to exit strategies, and one that resonates with the conceptual comments on temporality in the first section, is that an exit strategy is based on the notion that there can be a definitive exit or clean break from intervention. It is worth reminding ourselves of the complexity and extent of many peace-support interventions (notwithstanding the trend towards lighter touch interventions) and thus the impossibility of a full exit. Many peace-support interventions, particularly in the heyday of the liberal peace, have witnessed very extensive intervention across multiple sectors; government and law-making, justice, security, education and other public service provision. This often involved tens of thousands of international and national peace-support personnel, to the extent that local economies became distorted.[17] In some cases, international staff 'went native' and formed relationships with national staff. The key point is that international peace-support interventions take the form of multiple interventions in multiple spheres of life. Many of these interventions are subtle and can have an extensive afterlife. For example, bilateral donors and INGOs may invest heavily in curriculum development in a state emerging from violent conflict. The new curriculum may address the violent and contested past of the country. The impact of the language used to describe the past might, over time, filter its way into narratives and how young people describe themselves and the country. This impact—or afterlife—might persist decades after the curriculum development programme ended and international actors had, notionally, 'exited' from the country.

Another form of afterlife or peace implementation legacy comes in the form of the lessons learned from one peace process to another. Shrewd observers of peace processes have long been aware of the possibility of one peace process informing another—both positively and negatively—and so have been keen to observe lessons learned.[18] On top of this, a cadre of increasingly professional peacebuilders has honed their skills in one context (perhaps as a project officer) and transfer these skills to another location (perhaps as a programme manager). The result is that there has been considerable lending and borrowing between peace processes and peace implementation, some of it conscious but much of it unconscious in the sense that it has become hardwired into how organisations operate.

Concluding Discussion

The essential point in this chapter is that time relates to power. Some actors have the power to impose deadlines and sequences and to decree an exit strategy. Those actors are often international or government actors who have the material (often economic and coercive) power to incentivise or compel timeliness among others. But wielding this power is not always straightforward. Peace processes can develop a rhythm and pace of their own. Moreover, the timescale of the formal peace process may not be reflected in the temporal rhythms of non-elites. It could be the case that communities are more willing to embrace peace than their political leaders (or vice versa) and act accordingly either by foot-dragging or anticipating change from political leaders. Or it could be that many community members see change related to peace in the long term. This contrasts, for example, with the attitude of the US and its allies in relation to the interventions in Iraq and Afghanistan. Here the intervening parties have had technocratic milestones that—theoretically—indicated that the intervention has been successful and a drawdown could take place.[19] This has involved, variously, the numbers of national police and military members trained or the number of judges appointed under a reformed judicial system. Yet, in both Afghanistan, Iraq and elsewhere, there is a sense that the society is working according to a different timescale that is unrelated to the technocratic milestones of the intervening party. Certainly in the years after the removal of the Ba'athist and Taliban regimes, there was a sense that many Iraqis and Afghans were 'waiting in the long grass'. They were aware that the intervening parties would one day withdraw, or at least scale down their presence, and it was wisest to keep a low profile until that time. This brings us back to the differences between political and sociological time and the need to look behind the façade and understand what it is that makes intervening actors, national actors and all others interpret (and impose) time in the ways that they do.

In terms of advice for practitioners and theorists, it would be to stress the necessity of standing back from the time tactics of deadlines and project cycles and instead to take a more strategic, and necessarily longer term, view of time and temporality. While it is tempting to think of peace processes in terms of political time and deadlines, start and end dates, and other time segments, this chapter argues that the picture is messier. Political time is only one way of interpreting time and it must be seen in conjunction with other versions of time that are sympathetic to how people actually experience war, conflict and peace processes. This involves building notions of anticipation, grief and withholding judgement, into our calculations.

Notes

1. This is explored in greater detail in Roger Mac Ginty. 2016. Political versus sociological time: The fraught world of timelines and deadlines. In: Arnim Langer and Graham K. Brown eds., Building Sustainable Peace: Timing and sequencing of post-conflict reconstruction and peacebuilding. Oxford: Oxford University Press, pp. 15–31.
2. This argument is influenced by thinking on the concept of the everyday. See, for example, Andrew Smith. 2015. Rethinking the 'Everyday' in 'Ethnicity' and Everyday Life. Ethnic and Racial Studies 38(7): 1137–1151; Niras Yuval-Davis, Geogia Wemyss, and Kathryn Cassidy. 2018. Everyday Bordering: Belonging and the Reorientation of British Immigration Legislation. Sociology 52(2): 228–244; Michael Foucault. 1980. 'Body/Power' in Power/Knowledge: Selected Interviews and Other Writings 1972–1977. New York: Pantheon; and John D. Brewer, Bernadette C. Hayes, Francis Teeney, Katrin Dudgeon, Natascha Mueller-Hirth, Shirley Lal Wijesinghe. 2018. The Sociology of Everyday Life Peacebuilding. Basingstoke: Palgrave Macmillan.
3. S. Hogben. 2006. Life's on Hold: Missing People, Private Calendars and Waiting. Time and Society 15(2–3): 327–342.
4. V. Ogle. 2015. The Global Transformation of Time 1870–1950. Harvard, MA: Harvard University Press.
5. For background on this case, see: Fawaaz Traboulsi. 2007. A History of Modern Lebanon, London: Pluto; Marie-Joëlle Zahar. 2012. Peace by Unconventional Means: Lebanon's Ta'if Agreement. In Stephen John Stedman, Donald Rothchild; and Elizabeth M. Cousens eds., Ending Civil Wars: The Implementation of Peace Agreements, Boulder, CO: Lynne Rienner, 567–597, and Robert Fisk. 1990. Pity the Nation: Lebanon at War. Oxford: Oxford University Press.
6. Nir Eisikovots. 2016. A Theory of Truces. Houndmills: Palgrave.
7. In the case of Rwanda, the rebels were able to combine fighting and talking to extract significant concessions from the government.

See, Bruce Jones. 2001. Peacemaking in Rwanda: The Dynamics of Failure. Boulder, CO: Lynne Rienner.
8. Gurinder Singh. 2007. A Decade of Ceasefire in Nagaland. Strategic Analysis 31(5): 815–832; and Samrat Sinha. 2017. The Strategic Use of Peace: Non-State Armed Groups and Subnational Peacebuilding Mechanisms in Northeastern India. Democracy and Security 13(4): 273–303.
9. David Brenner. 2015. Ashes of Co-Optation: From Armed Group Fragmentation to the Rebuilding of Popular Insurgency in Myanmar. Conflict, Security & Development 15(4): 337–358 at 338.
10. Roger Mac Ginty. 2006. No War, No Peace: The Rejuvenation of Stalled Peace Processes and Peace Accords. Basingstoke: Palgrave.
11. Julian Borger. 2018. Yemen Ceasefire Resolution Blocked at UN After Saudi UAE 'Blackmail'. Guardian, 29 November. Accessed at: https://www.theguardian.com/world/2018/nov/29/un-yemen-ceasefire-resolution-blocked-saudi-uae-blackmail. Last Accessed 6 January 2020.
12. John Paul Rathbone and Andres Schipani. 2015. Insights into Negotiations from Colombia's Peace Talks with Farc. Financial Times, 4 May. Accessed at: https://www.ft.com/content/ecfac32e-ef3c-11e4-87dc-00144feab7de. Last Accessed 6 January 2020.
13. Ariel Hernandez. 2014. Nation-Building and Identity Conflicts: Facilitating the Mediation Process in Southern Philippines. Berlin: Springer VS, pp. 245–247.
14. Susan Moeller. 1999. Compassion Fatigue: How the Media Sells Disease, Famine, War and Death. New York: Routledge.
15. Roger Mac Ginty and Oliver P. Richmond. 2013. The Local Turn in Peace Building: A Critical Agenda for Peace. Third World Quarterly 34(5): 763–783.
16. Oliver P. Richmond. 2006. The Problem of Peace: Understanding the 'Liberal Peace'. Conflict, Security & Development 6(3): 291–314; and David Roberts. 2011. Liberal Peacebuilding and Global Governance: Beyond the Metropolis. London: Routledge.
17. See, Kathleen M., and Jennings, K. M. 2014. 'Service, Sex, and Security: Gendered Peacekeeping Economies in Liberia and the Democratic Republic of the Congo'. Security Dialogue 45(4): 313–330; and Kathleen M. Jennings and Morten Bøås. 2015.

Transactions and Interactions: Everyday Life in the Peacekeeping Economy. Journal of Intervention and Statebuilding 9(3): 281–295.
18. John Darby. 2008. Lending and Borrowing in Peace Processes. In John Darby and Roger Mac Ginty eds., 2003. Contemporary Peace Making: Conflict, Peace Processes and Post-War Reconstruction. Basingstoke: Palgrave, pp. 339–351.
19. There is a fascinating literature on measuring 'success' in relation to peace and other political projects. In relation to Afghanistan, see, for example, Anthony H. Cordesman. 2009. The New Metrics of Afghanistan. CSIS Accessed at: https://www.csis.org/analysis/new-metrics-afghanistan. Last Accessed 6 January 2020.

PART III

Negotiation and Mediation

CHAPTER 11

Mediation and the Ending of Conflicts

Christopher Mitchell

Progress towards the settlement of protracted and violent social conflicts usually takes one of two basic forms. In one, the adversaries manage to arrive at some solution through direct, interparty discussion of the issues in contention. They then bargain towards an accommodation of their competing goals that, at the very least, satisfies enough of their underlying interests to make the resultant settlement acceptable to leaders and rank and file followers, and thus durable over time. This process of negotiation is usually an extremely complex one, subject to many vicissitudes, and liable, because of its fragility, to break down frequently and disastrously, as in the Basque country, in the Philippines and in Sri Lanka. Perhaps for this last reason, a directly negotiated bilateral settlement is something of a rarity.

Far more usually, the adversaries in any protracted conflict find themselves in need of the assistance of others to begin, conduct, and conclude successfully what has fashionably become known as a 'peace process'.

C. Mitchell (✉)
Jimmy & Rosalyn Carter School for Peace & Conflict Resolution,
George Mason University, Arlington, VA, USA
e-mail: cmitchel@gmu.edu

Hence, what is often seen as a bilateral negotiating process becomes trilateral, with the introduction of some third party as a 'go-between', 'facilitator', or 'mediator'. Again, the actual mediation of historic protracted conflicts usually turns out, on examination, to be a much more complex process than a simple interaction between two clearly defined and well-articulated adversaries plus one mediating party. In many kinds of conflict, the term 'mediation' has come to be used far from precisely, and to cover a wide variety of activities otherwise labelled informal contacts, conciliation, good offices, brokering, or intermediary initiatives. This seems especially to be the case in violent and protracted conflicts that take place between communities or ethnicities within the formal boundaries of so-called 'nation states'—the Somalias, Sri Lankas and Colombias of today's world. It is possibly for this reason that sure and systematic knowledge about the nature and dynamics of 'mediation processes' in protracted social conflicts is relatively scarce, compared with, for example, our understanding of the work of mediators in other fields, such as industrial or intra-family conflicts. What follows is a brief discussion of some of the issues in the current debate about appropriate and effective mediation practices in protracted social conflicts[1]—otherwise somewhat loosely described as 'civil strife', 'intra-state conflicts', or 'ethnopolitical conflict'.

Mediation: The Dominant Model

Much current thinking about mediation processes in protracted social conflicts remains strongly influenced by the kind of mediation that has, throughout history, been practised in violent conflicts between formally independent 'sovereign' societies. In these, leaders from other societies 'outside' the conflict offer intermediary services to help bring the adversaries together with the aim of concluding an acceptable agreement to end the violence and to compromise on the issues. In the world of Classical Greece, leading city states such as Sparta, Athens, and Corinth frequently acted as powerful intermediaries in conflict between their lesser neighbours, thus providing a classical model for mediators with considerable leverage on the adversaries—'outsider' intermediaries whose offer of services could not easily be rebuffed, whose advice could not easily be ignored, and whose blueprints for a settlement could not simply be rejected or amended. The model of the 'Great Power' mediator was thus first constructed in the world of the Greek city states.

Similar types of mediator and mediatory processes can be seen operating in the world of separate and formally equal states that came into being in Europe and elsewhere following the end of the 30 Years War, although the reality of the powerful and influential mediator tended to be politely masked on many occasions. The best known of these was Bismarck's use of the concept of the 'honest broker' to describe Germany's role at the Congress of Berlin in 1878, and his claim of disinterested activity for the good of Europe—against which one can set the more cynical but probably more accurate comment of Nikita Krushchev that 'There are no neutral men!'.

The world of nineteenth and twentieth-century diplomacy, however, saw the development of other mediatory models than that of the Great Power 'intermediary with leverage'. Intermediary action by a group of governments—what might be termed the multi-government model—can be traced to the post-Napoleonic conception of 'the Concert of Europe' and exemplified in the late twentieth century by the successful activities of the Contadora Group in Central America and the less successful efforts of the Western Contact Group in attempting to assist the search for a solution in the conflict over Namibia.[2] Similarly, the same period has seen the frequent use of major international figures as intermediaries, utilizing reputation and prestige to accomplish ceasefires and settlements in violent and volatile situations—Theodore Roosevelt helping to end the Russo–Japanese War in 1905, the Emperor of Ethiopia presiding over the process resulting in the 1972 agreement ending the First Sudanese Civil War, Presidents Nyerere and Mandela brokering an agreement between antagonistic factions in Burundi at the very end of the twentieth century. The 'eminent persons' model is another variant of the theme of outside mediation developed to deal with wars and even—on occasions—with civil wars.

However, while it is clearly the case that both thinking about and practice of mediation in protracted social conflicts has been much influenced by the various models of appropriate mediator activity derived from international practice, questions have been raised about the utility of any of these models or approaches. This is especially so when the conflict in question takes place within the formal boundaries of one of the 'members of the international community' (i.e. a territorial state); when it involves the formal government of the state as one of the parties to the conflict opposed by ethnic or other types of insurgent; and when the issues in conflict revolve around the preservation of the unity of the state as opposed to its division or disintegration. In such circumstances, it becomes even more difficult to discover an appropriate government as 'honest broker', given the tendency of the governments of existing states—and those international organizations such as the United Nations, the Organization of African Unity (OAU), or the Organization of American States (OAS), that consist of the representatives of the governments of existing states—to be somewhat biased in favour of the principles of continuing territorial integrity and of non-interference in the internal affairs of any other country, unless genocide clearly threatens. Both these principles raise major barriers to intermediary action even in situations where the effects of protracted social conflicts spill over borders and disrupt neighbours through raids, refugees, reinforcements, routes for arms, and general mayhem.

Much of the current intellectual and practical debate about the role of mediation in protracted social conflicts thus revolves around the question of who—or more accurately, what type of entity—might be most appropriate to perform mediatory tasks. This is particularly true in conflicts that are violent, protracted, and dangerous to a region, but which take place within the confines of an existing state or country, no matter how collapsed or disintegrated. Three aspects of this debate currently predominate, and the next sections of this paper will briefly discuss each of these in turn. They are the debates about (1) the timing of mediation (2) 'external neutrals' vs 'insider-partials' as effective intermediaries, and (3) appropriate forms of intermediary activity and their relation to various stages of a 'peace process'.

WHEN CAN MEDIATION HELP?

Since William Zartman wrote his pioneering work on the timing of interventions into protracted social conflicts,[3] the issues of timing or a conflict's 'ripeness' for resolution have been much discussed and written about. One focus for debate has naturally taken the form of asking when there exist appropriate conditions for successful intermediary actions. Much of the writing of Ron Fisher and Loraleigh Keashley has concentrated on developing a contingency approach to peacemaking interventions.[4] They argue that the type of initiative (whether from benevolently inclined outsiders or indirectly involved insiders) most likely to have a positive impact on a conflict depends on the stage that particular conflict has reached. For example, Fisher and Keashley suggest that once conflicts have crossed the threshold from hostility and threats to direct violence, only low-key efforts to dampen the violence and—perhaps—restore non-provocative communications between the adversaries are likely to be effective, although, in another work on the issue of timing, Jeff Rubin takes a more hopeful view of what might be attempted.[5]

In spite of this body of work, the dominant concepts about 'ripeness' and when third parties might best intervene remain firmly those initially proposed and later elaborated by Zartman[6] himself and his colleague Stephen Stedman.[7] Mediators and other types of third-party intermediaries should best await the development of a 'hurting stalemate' for both adversaries, perhaps accompanied by an approaching mutual catastrophe. Such circumstances offer the best context for mediatory activity, as they will have set leaders on at least the intellectual course of considering alternatives and searching for a way out. In such circumstances, mediators are less likely to encounter a discouraging—if conceptually ambiguous—'lack of will' on the part of the adversaries and are more likely to be able to move the conflict nearer a solution.

There seem to have been many protracted social conflicts that bear out Zartman's contentions that only mutual pain and a sense of 'no end in sight' will make parties in violent conflict open to the possibilities of mediation and a brokered solution. However, there are clearly other cases that do not fit this model and where mediators have been able to move adversaries towards an alternative process to continuing mutual coercion and harm. In another paper, I have suggested alternative ideas about 'ripe moments', arguing that circumstances that enable leaders to abandon entrapping commitments or to envisage creative alternatives may also provide openings for well-crafted intermediary initiatives.[8]

More generally, it might be that while a situation of stalemate and cost may bring about a change of mind on the part of the leaders of embattled adversaries, other external forms of change can also produce rethinking and reconsideration so that those leaders thus become more receptive to offers of mediation, conciliation, good offices, or facilitation. Now, there seems to be very little systematic examination of the relationship between contextual changes affecting a conflict system and reconsiderations on the part of decision-makers therein. However, both anecdotal evidence and some theoretical formulations suggest that such a link does exist and should be explored. Change does beget change, as the old saying has it, and it seems only commonsensical to argue that major alterations in circumstances can become the occasion for leaders locked in a conflict to ask whether alternative courses of action—perhaps involving help from third parties—might exist.

For example, it seems clear to have been the case that the ending of the Cold War and the collapse of the Soviet Union had a not unimportant effect on British strategic thinking about the conflict in Northern Ireland, while the growing importance of the European Union and the progressive integration of Western Europe did much to affect nationalist thinking about the whole set of relationships involving north-western Europe's off-shore islands. We need to know more about the dynamics of this kind of linked change.

Elsewhere, I have argued that three levels or types of change can have a profound effect upon the thinking of both leaders and constituents of parties in conflict.[9] Changes at the systemic, structural, and tactical levels of a conflict system can all bring about a situation in which leaders jerk themselves out of an incremental continuation mode of decision-making and into a comprehensive reconsideration mode. The latter is not unlikely to involve a search for alternatives and a potential opportunity for mediators to become involved in a search for such alternatives. At the moment, unfortunately, we know too little about the types of contextual change which lead towards the search for new ideas about solutions and those which lead to decisions about 'more of the same' and an intensification of struggle. However, the idea that change can provide mediators with an opening does seem to offer an interesting alternative to the idea that openings only open when parties recognize hurt.

Appropriate Mediators

A second major intellectual puzzle currently being faced is the whole issue about whether it is more appropriate that mediatory tasks are carried out by outsiders, rather on the 'classical' model of international mediation discussed above, or whether success is more likely when insiders—individuals and organization that are themselves part of the society or community within which the conflict is being fought out—act as intermediaries between warring factions. The 'outsider-neutral' vs 'insider-partial' debate is too frequently carried out as though the existence of these two types of intermediary presented an 'either-or' choice, at least in those situations where choice is possible. More fruitfully, enquiry might well start with the assumption that there are circumstances in which one rather than the other is more likely to be successful, while the reverse is true in other circumstances.

Of course, a preliminary question ought to be whether the distinction is as clear-cut as the ongoing debate implies. Where is the dividing line between those who are genuinely 'insiders' and those who, for some unambiguous reason, can be regarded as 'outside' the conflict, in the sense that they are not even a 'peripheral' as opposed to a 'core' party to that conflict? For example, it is clearly the case that the US government is not exactly 'neutral' in the protracted Israeli/Palestinian conflict, but is it even 'outside' that conflict, given the substantial influence on domestic US politics wielded by the Jewish community in the United States of America and by the number of Florida registered voters that appear to reside normally in Tel Aviv and its environs?

A similar definitional dilemma arises from the intermediary activities of many successful third parties. For example, Kare Loder reports on the successful mediatory role played by Norwegian Church Aid (NCA) in helping to end the civil war in Mali in 1996.[10] He notes that NCA had been working in northern Mali on drought relief since 1984 had 'saved the various communities in the area from disintegration and the nomads in particular from extinction'[11] and had made a point of using Malians rather than Norwegian expatriates in senior positions. Thus, the 'NCA team' that began to act as facilitators of a traditional peacemaking dialogue in the autumn of 1995 consisted of four individuals, three of whom were respected Malians and only one a Norwegian. Was this a case of an outsider-neutral or an insider-partial initiative? On the other hand, might it have been a hybrid case of an insider-neutral? Similar questions might even be asked about the Norwegian team from The Institute for Applied Social Sciences (FAFO) that had been working in the Gaza Strip for over ten years before some of its members launched the informal talks that made up the Oslo Process and led, in 1993, to the tragically undermined Oslo Accords.[12]

Nevertheless, the issue of what kind of mediators are most appropriate for what circumstances remains a baffling and contentious one. Outsiders have problems obtaining access to intra-state conflicts, although the doctrine of non-interference in the internal affairs of an independent state is beginning to fray at the edges, especially when it is hard to argue that a state still exists, as in the cases of Somalia, Rwanda, or parts of former-Yugoslavia. Still, the steadfast refusal of the Madrid government to allow outsiders to act as intermediaries in the Spanish–Basque conflict indicates that in many situations only insiders (or, at the most, relatively powerless and unofficial 'Track Two' intermediaries) can even obtain access to the parties involved in a protracted intra-state conflict. Although the Sri Lankan conflict did see external mediation, in the end, the Sri Lankan government was able to assert its 'domestic jurisdiction' and pursue a military termination of the conflict.[13]

Wehr and Lederach[14] have argued persuasively that in many protracted conflicts, only intermediaries that understand the cultural nuances of the society and who enjoy the *confianza* (something more than simply 'trust') of the antagonists can hope to carry out intermediary roles successfully. Certainly, experiences of the success of local intermediaries in developing peace at least at the local level in parts of north-eastern Kenya,[15] in northern Ghana, and in the Atlantic provinces of Nicaragua[16] back up the claim that insider partials have advantages that are denied to outsiders. On the other hand, there are enough cases of outsiders—usually outsiders who do not conform to the classical model of an 'outsider with leverage'—playing a successful part in processes achieving peace at the national level to raise again the question of what circumstances do favour one type of mediator over the other. Obvious examples of effective outsider mediation range from the work of the San Egidio Community in helping to bring about the Mozambique peace accords[17] to the Vatican's role in helping to arrange an agreement between Argentina and Chile over their disputed boundary in the Beagle Channel.[18] However, the examples are many, the overall picture is a confusing one, and any precise matching of type of intermediary to set of circumstances so that success is likely seems a long way off, even at the theoretical level.

Mediator Roles and Functions

The final puzzle for students and practitioners of mediation is a variant of the traditional query: What do mediators actually do? In this connection, it has been clear for some considerable time that the answer to this apparently simple query is that it depends on when a mediator chooses to take an initiative—that is, that there are clearly appropriate roles and functions—tasks to be undertaken, in plain language—depending upon what stage a peace process has achieved.

Even 40 years ago the then sparse literature on mediation recognized that mediators would be called upon to do different things for the conflicting parties, depending on the recent history of their conflict. If negotiations had taken place but had broken down then the task of an effective intermediary was to restore communications between the adversaries and explore the conditions each was imposing for the resumption of talks. If the antagonists had yet to explore even the possibility of conversations, then the task of the mediator was to sound out both sides to see if there might be any readiness to engage in talks—if the elusive 'will' existed on both sides, and if it did what conditions for meeting might be imposed.

At this time, and subsequently, the vast preponderance of attention was paid to the tasks of mediators once representatives of the parties in conflict were 'at the table' and much time and effort was spent in delineating what skills a mediator required in the role of chairperson or moderator of the actual face-to-face talks. Issues over the appropriate place for third-party 'power' or 'leverage' developed out of these analyses and still occupy a central place in today's diverse and controversial literature about what makes a successful mediator, and whether adroitness and creativity can make up for the absence of resources to be promised or withheld as ways of inducing agreement between rivals. The debates over 'pure' vs 'power' mediation have been well summarized by Ron Fisher,[19] while Marieke Kleiboer has proposed a sophisticated explanation of why different analysts take up very different positions on this and other debates on the nature of appropriate and successful mediation practices.[20]

The publication of Hal Saunders's[21] seminal article on pre-negotiation and of James Wall's[22] analyses of mediation systems derived from his studies of industrial and organization mediation further complicated ideas about mediators' tasks and roles from the early 1980s. Both analyses suggested that mediators could and do carry out a far wider range of tasks than merely acting as a go-between for parties unwilling— perhaps temporarily—to meet face-to-face or moderating face-to-face exchanges when these became a possibility. Wall's analysis suggested strongly that one of the tasks facing many mediators involved dealing not merely with the relationships between negotiators or between negotiators and their own decision-makers 'back home' but also between negotiators, their leaders and their constituents. Hence, this became a further complicating task for mediators aiming for success in ending a conflict. Saunders, in turn, raised questions of what mediators needed to do in the pre-negotiation stages of any peace process, and how various types of intermediary might best prepare parties to be ready to conduct a fruitful negotiation by bringing the most appropriate attitudes, expectations, and skills to any formal, 'table'.

Finally, some of the contemporary literature on conflict transformation and the aftermath of achieving an agreement has added a list of still further roles for third parties. Mediators' tasks now do not end with the signing of the agreement or a set of accords. Part of the result of all this has been the suggestion that it might be helpful to think of a mediator less as a single person or organization and more as a set of roles to be fulfilled or tasks to be performed. Furthermore, these necessary tasks may actually be carried out by a variety of individuals or organizations, acting—one hopes—in concert with one another, a hope that Susan Allen Nan has characterized as involving 'complementarity' of intermediary initiatives.[23]

All these writings clearly support the suggestion that answering questions about what mediators do depends very much on the answer to a prior question: When do mediators become involved? The answer to the first question is complicated enough, even simply focussing on the traditional view that a mediator's main tasks occur during face-to-face meetings between the adversaries. However, even at this stage of a conflict, there are likely to be a variety of very different circumstances calling forth a very different set of mediatory tasks. How do mediator roles differ during smoothly proceeding talks from those needed during a tough but (hopefully) temporary impasse? What do mediators do—apart from shoulder the blame—in the aftermath of a complete breakdown of negotiations and a threatened return to violence?

The picture becomes even more complex when we consider other stages and sub-stages of a protracted conflict. Literature on conflict prevention suggests the need for mediator involvement in a variety of situations; in the development of long-term conflict-avoidance strategies, in times of developing tensions, at points of imminent crisis, and even following the actual outbreak of violence. Possible work at the height of conflict involves efforts to diminish reactive violence or to arrange cease-fires or humanitarian pauses while searching for opportunities for 'talks about talk', especially when stalemate has led to a search for face-saving, non-violent alternatives, a stage often marked by face-saving bluster. As noted previously, mediators can also be deeply involved in post-agreement tasks, some concerned with overcoming immediate problems of implementation, others with longer-term reconciliation processes that try to avoid a repetition of the same conflict by future generations.

Hence, the list of appropriate mediator activities grows as our understanding of the dynamics of conflict grows. My own summary list (below) clearly contains some tasks that would not have been regarded as proper for classical mediators even 40 years ago. However, I would argue that all have an important impact on the likely success of mediation in moving a conflict towards a resolution. Moreover, this list has become somewhat less startling with the recognition—again brought about by recent work on peacebuilding at the grassroots and opinion leader levels—of the importance of multi-level intermediary tasks that need to be carried out so as to improve the chances of a lasting and generally accepted resolution of a conflict.

CORE MEDIATOR TASKS IN CONFLICT RESOLUTION[24]

Pre-Negotiation

Explorer Determines adversaries' readiness for contacts; sketches range of possible solutions.

Reassurer Reassures adversaries that others are not wholly bent on 'victory'.

Decoupler Assists external patrons to withdraw from core conflict; enlists patrons in other positive tasks.

Unifier Repairs intra-party cleavages and encourages consensus on interests, core values, concessions.

Enskiller Develops skills and competencies needed to enable adversaries to reach a durable solution.

Convener Initiates process of talks, provides venue, and legitimizes contacts and meetings.

During Talks or Negotiations

Facilitator Fulfils functions within meetings to enable a fruitful exchange of versions, aims, and visions.

Envisioner Provides new data, ideas, theories, and options for adversaries to adapt; creates fresh thinking.

Enhancer Provides additional resources to assist in search for positive sum solution.

Guarantor Provides insurance against talks breaking down and offers to guarantee any durable solution.

Legitimizer Adds prestige and legitimacy to any agreed solution.

Post-Agreement

Verifier Reassures adversaries that terms of agreement are being fulfilled.

Implementer Imposes sanctions for non-performance of agreement.

Reconciler Assists in long-term actions to build new relationships among and within adversaries.

CONCLUSION

The list of mediator tasks—what mediators do and when—will undoubtedly be modified and extended as we analyse more examples of successful and unsuccessful initiatives, and then draw some general lessons from the wealth of case material currently becoming available. This book is clearly part of this necessary consolidation of knowledge about mediators and mediation, and equally clearly will contribute to our obtaining a better understanding of the nature of mediation work and its role in resolving protracted and dangerous social conflicts. I can only hope that this present chapter contributes to the task of understanding what we know and, more importantly, what we still need to know about these issues.

NOTES

1. E.E. Azar, The Management of Protracted Social Conflict (Aldershot: Dartmouth Publishing, 1990).
2. V. Jabri, Mediating Conflict: Decision Making and Western Intervention in Namibia (Manchester, NH: Manchester University Press, 1990).
3. I.W. Zartman, Ripe for Resolution: Conflict and Intervention in Africa (New York: Oxford University Press, 1985).
4. R.J. Fisher & L. Keashley, 'The Potential Complimentarity of Mediation and Consultation Within a Contingency Model of Third Party Consultation', Journal of Peace Research, 28, 1 (1991), pp. 21–42.
5. J.Z. Rubin, 'The Timing of Ripeness and the Ripeness of Timing', in L. Kriesberg & S.J. Thornson (eds), Timing the De-escalation of International Conflicts (New York: Syracuse University Press, 1991).
6. Zartman (1985), op. cit.

7. S.J. Stedman, Peacemaking in Civil Wars: International Mediation in Zimbabwe, 1974–1980 (Boulder, CO: Lynne Rienner, 1991).
8. C. Mitchell, 'The Right Moments: Notes on Four Models of "Ripeness"', Paradigms, 9, 2 (Winter 1995), pp. 38–52.
9. C. Mitchell, Gestures of Conciliation (London: Macmillan, 2000).
10. K. Loder, 'The Peace Process in Mali', Security Dialogue, 28, 4 (1997), pp. 409–424.
11. Ibid., p. 416.
12. J. Corbin, The Norway Channel (New York: Atlantic Monthly Press, 1994).
13. P. Saravanamuttu, 'Sri Lanka: The Intractability of Ethnic Conflict', in J. Darby & R. Mac Ginty (eds), The Management of Peace Processes (London: Macmillan, 2000), pp. 195–227.
14. P. Wehr & J.P. Lederach, 'Mediating Conflict in Central America', Journal of Peace Research, 28, 1 (February 1991).
15. D. Ibrahim & J. Jenner, 'Breaking the Cycle of Violence in Wajir', Chapter 10 in R. Herr & J.Z. Herr (eds), Transforming Violence (Scottdale, PA: Herald Press, 1998).
16. Wehr & Lederach (1991), op. cit., pp. 85–98.
17. C. Hume, Mozambique's War: The Role of Mediation and Good Offices (Washington, DC: USIP Press, 1994).
18. T. Princen, 'Mediation by a Transnational Organization: The Case of the Vatican', Chapter 7 in J. Bercovitch & J.Z. Rubin (eds), Mediation in International Relations (New York: St. Martin's Press, 1992), pp. 149–175.
19. R. Fisher, Inter-Active Conflict Resolution (New York: Syracuse University Press, 1997).
20. M. Kleiboer, International Mediation: The Multiple Realities of Third Party Intervention (Boulder, CO: Lynne Rienner, 1997); and M. Kleiboer & P. t'Hart, 'Time to Talk? Multiple Perspectives on Timing of International Mediation', Cooperation and Conflict, 30 (1995), pp. 307–348.
21. H.H. Saunders, 'We Need a Larger Theory of Negotiation: The Importance of the Pre-Negotiation Phase', Negotiation Journal, 1, 1 (July 1985), pp. 249–262.
22. J.A. Wall, 'Mediation: An Analysis, Review and Proposed Research', Journal of Conflict Studies, 25, 1 (March 1981), pp. 157–180; and J.A. Wall & A. Lynn, 'Mediation: A Current

Review', Journal of Conflict Resolution, 37, 1 (March 1993), pp. 160–194.
23. S. Allen-Nan, Complementarity and Coordination of Conflict Resolution Efforts in the Conflicts in Abkhazia, South Ossetia and TransDniestria (PhD Dissertation, George Mason University, 1999).
24. Adapted from C. Mitchell, 'The Process and Stages of Mediation: Two Sudanese Cases', Chapter 6 in D. R. Smock (ed), Making War and Waging Peace (Washington, DC: USIP Press, 1993), pp. 128–141.

CHAPTER 12

Diffusion vs. Coherence: The Competitive Environment of Multiparty Mediation

Chester A. Crocker, Fen Osler Hampson, and Pamela Aall

INTRODUCTION

Over the past 30 years, mediation has become a common tool of conflict management and peacemaking. We have moved from a world where conflicts ended in victory by one side or a draw, to a situation in

---

Parts of this paper were presented at the FBA Research Workshop on Mediation for Prevention and Peacemaking, June 7–8, 2017.

C. A. Crocker
Institute for the Study of Diplomacy, Georgetown University,
Washington, DC, USA
e-mail: crockerc@georgetown.edu

F. O. Hampson
School of International Affairs, Carleton University, Ottawa,
ON, Canada
e-mail: fen.hampson@carleton.ca

P. Aall (✉)
United States Institute of Peace, Washington, DC, USA

which some form of negotiated settlements has become accepted practice.[1] These are often seen as three-sided negotiations in which a single mediator helps two conflict parties find a solution to their disputes—the Vatican in the Beagle Channel dispute between Chile and Argentina in the 1970s, the Community of Sant'Egidio in Mozambique in the 1990s, former UN Secretary-General Kofi Annan in Kenya in 2008.

In reality, even in these examples, neither conflict parties nor mediators are monolithic, but represent many different parties, interests, and issues. Mediators are rarely on their own as they contend with differing interests within their sponsoring institution and their coalition partners, as well as several other third parties eager to play a role in the peacemaking process. The presence of multiple mediators in a conflict resolution process raises the question of whether this state of affairs makes mediation more or less effective. Some argue that sharing the burden among several third parties increases the chances for a successful outcome. Others warn that the engagement of multiple mediators simply raises the opportunities for forum shopping among the conflict parties and miscommunication among the peacemakers.

Complicating matters even more is the impact of party or factional fracture. In a number of current and recent conflicts—Darfur, Mali, Myanmar, South Sudan, Syria, Yemen—one of the sides is composed of rival factions which are deeply divided and unified only by their opposition to the government. These divisions present a particular challenge for reaching a negotiated settlement: who negotiates, what is on the agenda, and what might be a mutually acceptable outcome to many different actors. A major challenge for conflict parties and the mediator(s) is to develop a unified political narrative out of these differences.

Dealing with fragmented parties could be viewed as a collective action problem, insofar as producing a sense of cohesion among disparate interests is concerned.[2] Much of the examination of collective behavior has focused on the free rider problem: in those associations where the membership number is large, there is an incentive for members to avoid paying their full share and simply free-riding on the efforts of others. Overcoming the free rider problem often depends on the willingness of a dominant member (hegemon) to bear the burden of association because the benefit to the dominant member exceeds the cost of keeping the association together.[3] A third party in this case could support the peacemaking process by encouraging one of the parties to take on a leadership role.[4] This is the part that UN special envoy Alvaro de Soto played in the 1980s when he backed Costa Rican President Oscar Arias' leadership in drafting the Esquipulas agreement settling the conflict in and among the Central American countries of Guatemala, El Salvador, Nicaragua, Honduras, and Costa Rica.[5]

A basic assumption behind promoting collective behavior is that the actors act in their own self-interest, and that self-interest includes allowing another member to take the lead for the whole group. In a conflict featuring fragmented parties, it is more likely that each subgroup will feel too strongly about its identity to allow another group to represent its interest. Similarly, it would be unlikely for subgroups to coalesce around similar issues because of distrust and suspicions of their opponent or of each other. The twenty-one ethnic armed organizations (EAOs) in Myanmar have shown this reluctance in their desire to carve out separate deals with the government rather than unite under a large and more powerful collectivity. Outside third parties have worked to encourage unity among the EAOs. However, the international community has also been split in its approach to Myanmar, largely over the response to the Rohingya crisis. The lack of unity and cohesion on the part of outside third parties has reduced their impact. No leading actor willing to bear the costs of coordination has emerged in the opposition parties or the interested third parties.

This chapter will examine the consequences for mediation of the proliferation of actors in peace processes through multiparty mediation and fragmentation of conflict parties. The chapter explores this diffusion in mediation and conflict party actors, assessing the consequences for the peacemaking process of a splintering of players on both sides. While a number of approaches such as collective action and multilateral negotiations shed light on how to make multiparty mediation more effective, these approaches do not necessarily help to understand the dynamics of fragmented parties. The paper concludes, however, that multiparty mediation can help to deal with the challenge of fragmented parties if it maintains a strong element of coherence as the mediators engage with the conflict parties.

Multiparty Mediation: Varieties and Impact

Multiparty mediation is a mediation process in which more than one mediator engages in a peace process, working either in collaboration with or independently of each other. Multiparty mediation can arise out of deliberate third party planning to share the responsibility for supporting a peace process, or it can develop when conflict parties seek out different mediators on their own. It can also be the result of different third parties vying to be accepted as mediators who are attempting to "sell their wares" to the conflict parties and, perhaps, the international community. In this section, we examine a typology of different types of multiparty mediation as well as the impact of multiparty mediation on peace processes.

There are three major types of multiparty mediation: sequential, simultaneous, and composite.

Sequential mediation refers to situations in which one mediation effort is followed by another. In some cases, the same institution continues to support the mediation while the principal mediator changes. In the mediation of the Syrian civil conflict, for instance, the UN sponsored the peacemaking effort more or less continually since 2012. Nevertheless, by 2018, the mediator position had been taken up by three different people—Kofi Annan, Lakhdar Brahimi, and Steffan de Mistura. While the process broke down briefly between mediators, the fact that the sponsoring institution remained constant arguably brought an element of continuity to the three separate efforts. In other cases, however, the sequential mediation efforts are not linked, by institution or other means. In the Bosnia–Herzegovina conflict following the break-up of the former Yugoslavia during the 1991–1995 period, for instance, a variety of overlapping, sequential, and sometimes competitive efforts made by European and American diplomats sought to prevent or terminate the conflict (EC (Carrington-Cutileiro), UN (Vance-Owen and Owen Stoltenberg), US–EU–Russia at Dayton (Christopher-Holbrooke, Carl Bildt, Ivan Ivanov). Some estimate no less than 144 mediators of different stripes and political persuasions participated in peacemaking in the Bosnia conflict over its history.[6] Another example of sequential mediation practice occurred between two NGOs in Indonesia's Aceh region, starting with Martin Griffiths' work based at the Centre for Humanitarian Dialogue (HD) followed by the Crisis Management Initiative (CMI) headed by former Finnish President Martti Ahtisaari during the period 2000–2005.

Simultaneous mediation occurs when more than one person or institution engages in a mediation process roughly at the same time. Such mediations can be coordinated or competitive. In coordinated simultaneous mediations, there is generally a tacit agreement among the mediators on which institution takes the lead and which institutions should fall into line to support the process. For instance, the Inter-Tajik

Dialogue, a project of the Dartmouth Conference Regional Conflicts Task Force (a collaborative effort of Russian and American citizens) was established with the express purpose of preparing participants for the official UN peace process.[7] However, some simultaneous mediations operate on separate tracks without overlapping with each other. During the early months of the Central African Republic conflict that erupted in 2013, the African Union and the country's neighbors, Angola and Chad, launched independent mediation efforts. These were eventually brought together (under pressure from the AU and the UN) in 2016, but the ensuing fragile electoral and constitutional accord has been repeatedly challenged by armed groups. The Centre for Humanitarian Dialogue has assisted in organizing the country's national dialogue process, while Sant'Egidio mediation efforts were credited with arranging a peace deal between the government and over a dozen armed groups.[8] In practice, the government's writ has been regularly challenged due to the prevalence of multiple armed groups, the complex relations between the African Union mediation effort and the UN peacekeeping mission, and the arrival on the scene of Russian mediators creating their own parallel process while offering arms to the weak national authorities.[9]

Composite mediations comprise mediations carried out by intergovernmental institutions or other membership organizations. Mediations carried out by representatives of the UN Secretary-General under Security Council authorization are by their nature composite, as the 15 members of the Security Council—and especially the P-5—conduct their foreign policy through the international organization. This is also true of mediations by regional organizations—the African Union, IGAD, ECOWAS, the European Union—to varying degrees. At times, these organizations can act as relatively unified entities, for example the EU in the Kosovo–Serbia normalization agreement in 2013. Often, however, intergovernmental organizations are the battlegrounds for the strongest members about issues that they feel strongly about. The US-Russian antagonism in the UN Security Council does not only reflect their entire troubled relations but it also spills over into mediation efforts, for example in Syria.

Multiparty mediation, then, refers to a variety of circumstances in which multiple third parties engage in a peacemaking process, attempting to help the parties in their negotiations with each other. It includes competitive efforts where third party institutions vie with one another for the conflict parties' attention, non-competitive but unconnected efforts, collaborative efforts among institutions that work closely with one another, and somewhat collaborative, layered efforts in which subnational and sectoral efforts of mediation and facilitation are sponsored by experts in various fields of conflict management practice. Layered efforts are not competitive but may only be loosely coordinated with each other and with larger processes. An example of such tradecraft occurred in the genesis of the Oslo process between Israel and the Palestinians, starting with the initiative of FAFO, a Norwegian non-governmental research organization, and linking to key ministries of the Norwegian government which transmitted the resulting accords to the US and other members of the international community in 1993. Another example of a layered effort is the Crisis Management Initiative's (CMI) work in support of the larger mediation process in South Sudan, led by the Intergovernmental Authority on Development (IGAD) (Table 12.1).

Multiparty mediation does not refer to third party engagements through humanitarian aid, development assistance, and diplomatic initiatives unless these are tied specifically to the negotiation process in some way. Nor does it refer to actions taken by third parties to fuel the conflict except in those cases in which outsiders are playing a dual role as mediators and partisans, a role that Russia has played in the Syrian conflict.

Impact of Multiparty Mediation It would be misleading in the extreme to pronounce an over-arching verdict on the impact of multiparty processes of mediation. As we have argued elsewhere, the conclusion

Table 12.1 Multiparty mediation

	Simultaneous	*Sequential*
Competitive	Bosnia Central African Republic (African Union, Angola, Chad, Centre for Humanitarian Dialogue, Community of Sant'Egidio)	Russia and UN in Syria
Non-competitive	Malaysia and ICG in Philippines Central America–Esquiipulas	HD and CMI in Aceh
Collaborative	Mitchell group in Northern Ireland Madrid Process	Tajikistan
Layered	IGAD and CMI in South Sudan	Israeli–Palestinian conflict—Track 2 mediation

depends on a variety of complex conditions and contexts.[10] To illustrate, a multiparty process can gain depth and breadth when there is regional and broader international consensus that the problem requires a negotiated solution and that diplomatic and political investments in an ongoing process are acceptable. This means that no external party will attempt to undermine or sabotage the mediation by competing directly with it or influencing one or more of the direct conflict parties to block it or refuse to cooperate. It is possible for a complex mediation of the composite/layered type to effectively corral the fragmented parties into the same ring and get them to commit to a negotiating process that eventually leads to a negotiated political outcome. In the Northern Ireland case (discussed below) George Mitchell and his Finnish and Canadian colleagues (in the International Body created by the British and Irish governments) succeeded in negotiating the 1998 Good Friday Accord. The process worked because of their skilled approach but crucially also because the US, EU, UK, and the Republic of Ireland wanted it to work—and no one else was able to intervene to undermine it.

A far more complex and still successful form of multiparty mediation developed in the case of the deeply fragmented conflict between the government of the Philippines and the Moro Islamic Liberation Front (MILF). The government of Malaysia has been the official mediator of this process since 2001. In 2009, with the agreement of both parties, the process was joined by the International Contact Group (ICG) whose function is to offer advice to the mediation process and to help verify that agreements are implemented. The ICG, made up of four countries and four international NGOs, works in support of the Malaysian process but also adds heft to the procedure through its state-based and expert membership.[11] This example suggests that elaborate forms of multiparty process (composite/layered, sequenced, and even simultaneous at various levels of authority) can provide some ingredients for consensus and movement toward settlement.

On the other hand, the Geneva I and Geneva II Middle East peace conferences on Syria (the first led by Kofi Annan and the second by Lakhdar Brahimi), which was a composite process mandated by a divided UN Security Council faced rival proxy interventions by regional and global powers (notably Russia and Iran), and struggled to gain any useful traction. Such a process only aggravated the divisions among the warring parties each of which maneuvered for ways to exploit the open divisions in the international community.

The conclusion is that a mediator facing fragmented warring parties, which splinter and morph as factions collapse and new alliances and leaders emerge, should recognize that additional help may be needed to broaden the base of the process in a fashion akin to player-to-player coverage in a sports game like soccer. Accordingly, the mediator may look for third party allies that can be recruited to help on the basis of their ties to and knowledge of different factions and their leaders. This is borrowing leverage and building a mediatory coalition. A cautionary note, however, is to resist recruiting extra third parties that are simply partisan allies of different factions since this would only replicate the confusion and divisions in the conflict arena itself. There is evidence that the creation of "friends groups" or "contact groups" around a UN-led process can sometimes help, but at other times be a negative because the selection of supposed "friends" was ill-considered.[12]

Fragmented Parties and Shifting Coalitions

Drivers of fragmentation may include leadership or personal rivalry; splits between generations or sectarian groups; destabilizing fresh incentives from peacemaking initiatives (media coverage, opportunities for recognition, "outbidding" opportunities by defining oneself as "ultra" or "real"); or potential availability of external support from an outsider looking for a role in the conflict. Fragmentation may also be triggered by elections, or by the death of a senior leader (for instance, South Sudan's John Garang and FARC leader Manuel Marulanda). The peace process itself can trigger such rivalries, both at the beginning of talks when the parties negotiate around the agenda or at the endgame when decisions about the division of power, resources, and legitimacy become apparent to all the stakeholders and elites jostle to secure advantage. The ways that conflict parties can fragment are numerous. This chapter focuses on two predominant scenarios: leadership fractures and competitive factions within a party. Leadership fractures occur when the leadership of one or more of the parties divide over issues (objectives and means) or over the division of power among the leaders. Competitive factions within a party may be a consequence of leadership fractures, but they also may occur when many smaller parties join together in a side but find that they do not share sufficient interests to bind them together.

Fractured Leadership: A dynamic that increasingly characterizes current conflict is the instability of local parties and groupings in terms of their political leadership. The resulting internal divisions that come from the struggle for power in an any given political grouping or factions can present insuperable problems to a mediator. Internal division is a fairly consistent characteristic of opposition groups stretching back through history, often tied to a battle between aspiring leaders. In the eighteenth century, for instance, the French Revolution was marked by internal power struggles between Maximilien Robespierre and Jacques Danton. The twentieth-century Soviet Union saw the same dynamic in the fight between Joseph Stalin and Leon Trotsky. There have been acute leadership struggles within the ETA, in Kosovo, and in South Sudan.[13] At various points in the long history of peace talks in Cyprus, divisions within both the leadership and the Greek and Turkish Cypriot communities have severely hampered the work of peacemakers, causing talks to break down and ripeness to evaporate.[14] The South Sudan civil war exploded in 2013 as a contest between rival governmental leaders and their ethnic constituencies, leading to a major humanitarian disaster and a number of unsuccessful efforts to stitch the polity back together again.[15] Leadership fractures occur among conflict parties as well. In 1984, the MILF (Moro Islamic Liberation Front) broke away from the Moro National Liberation Front over ideological differences and continued the fight against the Filipino government well beyond the 1996 peace agreement. Similarly, in Mali in 2013, the Islamic Movement for the Azawad broke off from Tuareg rebel group Ansar Dine.

Competitive Factions: Fragmented conflict parties can be subgroups of a single party riven by splits that make it difficult for one subgroup to maintain ascendency over the others, as was the case in the early days of post-Gaddafi Libya. Just as often, they are coalitions of groups that unite under a single banner of opposition (to the regime or other hostile party), but that otherwise have different objectives, leadership, and philosophies. The lines of cleavage may be along with political, ideological, confessional, geographic, ethnic, or tribal divisions or a combination of these factors, or they can be the result of a power struggle among factions looking to expand their base.[16] The ongoing conflicts in Syria offer an example of this type of factionalized conflict.

These cases highlight fragmentation that grows out of a competitive environment in which each group believes that another's win is its loss. This is fragmentation driven by fear of being left out or marginalized by the process. However, another source of fragmentation may arise out of another scenario—the desire by the third party or the conflict parties to

Table 12.2 Fragmented parties

	Government	Opposition groups
Fractured leadership (split within one or more of the parties to the conflict)	Cyrus Philippines South Sudan	MNLF and MILF in the Philippines Ansar Dine and the Islamic Movement for the Azawad in Mali Yemen
Multiple, competitive factions on one side of the conflict	Palestine (West Bank and Gaza)	Darfur–Sudan Myanmar Syria Yemen

include a variety of peoples and groups in a peace process, or the desire to limit that engagement. In Myanmar, for instance, the peace process by design is inclusive both of the ethnic armed organizations and of civil society. However, the government does make a distinction among the EAOs in terms of which of the twenty-two armed groups may participate in the process. Those EAOs which have signed the National Ceasefire Agreement are invited into the process; those that have not signed are more or less excluded. Therefore, the nature of the peace process itself emphasizes the separate status of the armed groups. By and large, inclusion in the process does not depend on relative size and influence of the groups or on common interests, but a willingness to lay down arms. In this way, the process itself preserves the parties' separate identities (Table 12.2).

Impact of Conflict Party Fragmentation

Conflict party fragmentation introduces several layers of complexity in a peace process. Instead of bilateral negotiations between the government and the rebels, for instance, a process might entail bilateral negotiations between many groups leading up—in the best of circumstances—to a multilateral negotiation process over peace agreement terms. Some of these complexities will have a direct impact on the negotiation process itself. Parties will have different positions and interests as well as different goals. Consequently, agenda-setting is made more complex by party fragmentation. The challenges of developing a negotiable agenda have always been difficult, with much time spent on deciding what is on and off the agenda and who can represent the sides at the negotiating table. But in the circumstances in which multiple parties are engaged in the process, setting a negotiating agenda is often beyond of reach of all involved.[17] Most opposition parties in Syria share the goal of overthrowing Syrian President Bashar al-Asad but do not agree on much else. Non-state actors ISIS and al-Qaeda may share a common goal but have very different negotiating positions and show a fair amount of hostility toward each other.

Another complication involves timing, a critical element of mediation. Ripeness—the moment when productive negotiations might begin—has been the subject of a number of foundational studies on mediation.[18] According to Zartman, ripeness occurs when both or all parties to a conflict are in a mutually hurting stalemate (MHS) and are presented with a mutually enticing opportunity (MEO), or "way out" of a seemingly locked battle.[19] Each of the subgroups, however, will have its own perception of an MHS and MEO, which may not be in step with the other groups in a fragmented peace process. In Darfur, for instance, mediators from the United Nations, US, and African Union struggled to find a basis for cohesion among various rebel factions as they sought to stop ugly fighting between the government and rebels in this contested Sudanese province.[20]

It is quite likely that the parties will also have a variety of BATNA or best alternatives to a negotiation agreement,[21] which invariably will affect their own calculus whether they are prepared to walk away from the negotiation table or not. Another example from the Myanmar peace process highlights this challenge. In Myanmar's fraught history, the Kachin—an ethnic armed group from northern Myanmar—signed an early ceasefire in 1994. This ceasefire was held until 2011 and broke down shortly before eight other EAOs agreed to sign the National Ceasefire Agreement (NCA) with the government. Why they chose this moment of an emerging national consensus to repudiate the arrangement ending years of conflict is due to intra-Kachin relations and disagreements about the future where some believed the contours of a new peace agreement would be disadvantageous to the Kachin.[22] Their BATNA—their calculations of the costs and benefits of agreement—changed in the interim period. Nonetheless, their refusal to sign the NCA was a blow to national process and has made reaching a national agreement a more complicated process.

The groups may have quite different capabilities and levels of support, which may be hard to gauge in terms of relative importance. For instance, the Communist Party of the Philippines–New People's Army (CPP–NPA)—one of the several opposition groups active in the Philippines—had armed troops of approximately 5000 in 2009, half the size of the more widely acknowledged Moro Islamic Liberation Front. Nevertheless, the Armed Forces of the Philippines has named CPP–NPA the most serious terrorist threat facing the country: in 2013 the CPP–NPA attacks caused around 30 percent of the deaths in the Philippines through terror group activity that year.[23]

It may be difficult with fragmented parties to identify who the key decision-makers are. Negotiations in the seemingly intractable conflict between the government and insurgents in southern Thailand, for instance, have been hampered by uncertainty about who speaks for the rebel groups.[24] This is complicated by internal divisions within and shifting alliances between rival groups. Fragmentation means that each of the subgroups is negotiating in conditions of uncertainty and may or may not know what other side-deals the other subgroups have made. Suspicion and fear—already endemic in a conflict negotiation–are heightened by this uncertainty with the consequence that it makes coalition building all that more difficult to achieve. The parties stay fragmented because it is not clear that it is in their interests to team up together and work as a coalition.

Fragmentation also has an important external dimension that also has to be managed by mediators. In an increasingly globalized world, those conflicts that occur within the boundaries of a nation-state or even within a particular region or sub-region of the world cannot be considered to be "closed" systems. Arms and financial assistance tend to flow relatively freely across borders.[25] Groups can promote their cause through social media and recruit followers. Many such groups have spawned social, cultural, economic, and political networks that tend to reinforce group-based affiliations and loyalties across space and time.[26] ISIS's participation in the Iraq and Syrian conflicts, for instance, fits the mold of a local insurgent group with the training and resources to constitute a long-term challenge to the sitting governments. However, its transnational network and ability to launch terrorist attacks far from its base of power introduce a different kind of model. ISIS's motives differ from the traditional profile as well. While their wish to control territory and dominate the political landscape in the Middle East was similar to other insurgent groups' goals, their desire to create a caliphate set them apart. It also broadened their recruitment base to include potential adherents who otherwise shared a few of their goals.

Finally, there is the issue of implementation. The problem of credible commitment focuses on the incentives structure of the parties to conclude a lasting political settlement.[27] Parties always have some incentive to agree to a settlement that will satisfy their demands for political autonomy or some degree of independence in secessionist struggles. But when rebel groups are certain that they have strong external sponsors or backers, they are more likely to escalate their demands and seek major concessions from the other side as opposed to those situations where rebel sources of external support are limited or weak and the presence of a mutually hurting stalemate forces them to look for a political "way out" of the conflict. As Fearon explains, "when rebels do better day-to-day in a civil war (due to contraband or outside support, for instance) they need to be given more in a regional autonomy deal to be willing to accept it. But the more the government has to give away, the more tempted it will be to renege when it is again in a strong position, which makes it harder to construct a credible negotiated settlement."[28] To the extent that external third parties intervene on the side of opposition forces and become involved in the extraction and illicit marketing of lootable resources, like diamonds, this too will adversely affect conflict dynamics and the prospects for successful negotiation.[29]

Multiparty Mediators, Fragmented Conflict Parties, and the Mediation Process

When multiparty mediators engage with conflicts that incorporate fragmented parties, the complexities of peacemaking multiply. Problems of multiparty mediation (forum shopping, loss of leverage, lack of coherence) can easily exacerbate conflict rather than resolve it, especially when multiparty mediation meets the challenges of fragmented parties in the areas of agenda-setting, leadership struggles, uneven capabilities, and providing credible commitment.

Improving Conflict Party Coherence

The issue of deciding who needs to be at the table is a central part of the peace process. In a democracy, party fragmentation can be an unintended consequence of an inclusive democratic system. This was a major challenge for George Mitchell, Harri Holkeri, and John de Chastelain in the Northern Ireland peace process, where over a dozen political parties had a strong interest in the outcome. The International Body (as the 3-person mediation team was called) developed several mechanisms to deal with the fragmentation: (1) creating a "centrist coalition" by choosing ten parties to participate in the Elected Forum for Debate, provided they accepted the Mitchell Principles of dialogue, democracy, and non-violence; (2) introducing the notion of "sufficient consensus" defined as enjoying majority support on multiple levels (inside the forum, in each community, in the overall population, and with the UK and Irish Governments); (3) using variable negotiating geometry by allowing parties to vote against things they did not like but in favor of the overall resulting package; and (4) breaking up the agenda so that weapons decommissioning was addressed separately. In other words, they created a political center, an approach most applicable in open and democratic societies.[30]

There are other approaches to building consensus among disparate parties: individual negotiations with each party in order to identify some negotiating ground; stacking the deck in favor of one or several subgroups in order to create pressure on a more recalcitrant actor; a type of conditional bargaining as practiced by James A. Baker III in the Middle East before the Madrid Conference; and bridging extremes.[31] It is important to note that this last approach rarely works on violent conflicts unless a durable deal can be constructed between armed factions operating more or less autonomously. In the case of the process leading to the 1988 Namibia–Angola peace accords, it was necessary, first, to create a mediating coalition or contact group to work with African regional partners; second, to motivate African "frontline states" to persuade the Namibian insurgent movement SWAPO to go along; third, to table proposals that would bridge the core interests and asymmetrical priorities of South Africa, Angola, and Cuba; fourth, to explore the parameters of potential common ground through lengthy pre-negotiations with the separate sides; and, fifth, to assure the coherence of negotiating teams from three sovereign governments as well as the mediator's own team.[32]

Building Up Leadership

Another important element of peacemaking is the quality of leadership among the conflict parties. What may make a difference in these circumstances is leadership, i.e., the emergence of an individual or set of individuals who can project a sense of common vision and unite the subgroups around a similar positions or interests. Mahatma Gandhi, Nelson Mandela, and John Garang were such leaders and were able to unify their fractious followers. I. William Zartman points out, however, a more common phenomenon, especially in lengthy conflicts: "The long ebb and flow of the conflict washes out soft-liners, leaving the hardliners in charge to turn inward to their small group interests. Fragmentation eats up the moderates and opens up the fissures among identity claims – ethnic, religious, regional, generational, personal – with little 'interest in maintaining each other'."[33]

The lack of strong leaders may pose a serious obstacle to a mediated process. Unstable/weak leadership contributes to the problem of a lack of ripeness. This is different from the hurting stalemate/war-weariness argument. The issue here is that without strong leaders who can effectively manage their own constituencies, enjoy political legitimacy, and are in a position to make concessions at the negotiating table, it is very hard for a mediator to gain traction. Shifting/fluid and floating alliances among different factions may also contribute to instability and complicate negotiations. It takes time to form viable coalitions, which have valid representatives to speak and negotiate for their coalition partners and it is difficult for mediators today to find the time and resources to shepherd the conflict parties forward for this long game. As fragmentation is often within a single party's decision-making apparatus, the mediator's task is to create unity within a party's team. In the Northern Ireland example, the three-member mediation team's adroit marginalization of opponents to the peace process is a textbook case of how to deal with those who want to block progress.[34]

Managing Risk

It is not just the costs of negotiation and settlement that matter to the parties but also the perceived "risks" of negotiation, i.e., the probabilities that are associated with negative outcomes.[35] Because the parties in civil conflict situations are distrustful of each other and refuse to cooperate even if there are powerful incentives to consider negotiations. Ways have to be found to reduce the risks of defection so that the parties can entertain the possibility of a negotiated, reciprocal exchange of concessions. The theoretical basis for this position is spelled out in "prisoner's dilemma" and "games of chicken" in which defection is the dominant bargaining strategy and cooperative solutions are confounded in the first instance by information problems (because of the absence of proper and reliable channels of communication between the parties), and the problems of credible commitment.[36]

With factionalized/fractured parties, the challenges of managing the security dilemma of the parties multiply with the number of different factions. The persistence of high levels of mutual distrust need not pose an insurmountable obstacle to negotiations if ways can be found to effectively reduce compliance risks and "insure" the parties against the costs of negotiation failure. In terms of mediation tactics, there are a number of different risk management options that are available such as: (1) developing deliberately ambiguous commitments during the course of negotiations that can be reinterpreted, manipulated, or even withdrawn as circumstances change (also known as hedging); (2) sharing risks so that potential losses if a negotiation fails are more or less equally distributed among the parties; and (3) segregating assets to limit liability, by, for example, separating issues and taking a step-by-step or incremental approach to negotiations.[37] Agreements can be structured so the risks of any kind of default—deliberate or inadvertent—are manageable and spread out and that if there is compliance failure it does not destroy the entire peace process. In the southern African case discussed above, the mediator and conflict parties established an implementing commission with the participation of observers from the US, Soviet Union, and UN in order to serve as the primary court of appeal when issues arose.

As with the other aspects of dealing with fragmented parties, the issue of how to manage spoilers is more complex than in mediating a two- or three-party dispute. Spoilers abound when parties are split into factions (or for that matter the government) in a sectarian/ethnic conflict. In these cases, the problem is simply not mediation, but how to situate mediation within a broader conflict management and security framework. In the end, coercion may be the only way to deal with total spoilers who see the world in all-or-nothing terms and seek a violent transformation of society.[38] This is, however, a further challenge for multiparty mediation efforts which often break down around the use of force in a peacemaking process. The UN Security Council has been split over this issue on a number of occasions, most recently with the mediation process for the Syrian conflict.

Conclusion

As the preceding discussion suggests, there are implications for mediation practice at various levels. We offer a few concluding thoughts. First, the severity of the challenges facing modern mediators calls for particular skills that might have been less important in the past, e.g., skills in networking and coalition building; in connecting the top levels of decision to lower societal layers where constituencies live, vote, and (when necessary) fight; and understanding the strengths and limitations of their own biases.[39] While it continues to face challenges, the mediation experience of various third party interventions in the Philippines/Mindanao offers a compelling portrait of the possibilities. The case of Tajikistan in the 1990s offers another portrait of the potential for diverse third party tracks to cooperate in pulling the strands of a fragmented political universe toward a modus vivendi.

Secondly, successful mediation in violent conflict often depends on skilful practice on the mediator's part, accompanied in some measure by persuasive leverage.[40] If leverage in its various forms is the "ticket" to effective mediation, coherence of the mediation process is the key to acquiring and maintaining leverage.[41] This point is especially critical in an era of growing geopolitical competition at the global level. Each region may have its own poles of influence and lines of cleavage that demarcate the hurdles facing mediators. Conflicts in geopolitically contested regions such as the Middle East appear more challenging for mediators than others that are less prone to such divisions.

Thirdly, there are times when third parties behave as if there was an imperative to "do something," or a "responsibility to mediate."[42] This dynamic is unhelpful, especially amidst hot conflicts in fragmented polities where the gun will naturally and inevitably dominate consideration of political initiatives in the conference room. Practitioners may need to think consciously about identifying circumstances when mediation is not the answer, and other measures would be more appropriate.

Finally, it is important to remember that there are risks in drawing general conclusions about mediation challenges across the vast spectrum of contemporary conflict environments. Prospects for multiparty mediation among fragmented parties in the Philippines differ in basic ways from the outlook for the case of Colombia or South Sudan. Peacemakers need to look deeply into each polity to assess who (if anyone) controls the guns, how much authority leaders have within their constituencies, or whether civilians and civil society organizations have the voice and the capacity to shape negotiation outcomes vis-à-vis assorted strongmen and potential spoilers. The Mitchell approach of strengthening the center and marginalizing the extremes can work in polities that have a center and where civil society has or can be given a voice. Where these conditions do not exist, this approach will run into difficulties, requiring much effort to build that center. We know what will and will not work in specific circumstances through careful conflict analysis. This aspect of conflict management is often overlooked—the press of time, the scarcity of resources, the overwhelming need of the conflict parties urge us to commit to action before we thoroughly understand the situation. Conflict analysis is slow and deliberate rather than quick and flexible, but it is critical to the successful practice of multiparty mediation.

Notes

1. Communities in Transition. (2014). "Statistics about International Mediation," March 21, 2014, http://www.communitiesintransition.com/StatisticsaboutInternationalMediation. Accessed 1/21/2016).
2. Olsen, Mancur. (1971). *The Logic of Collective Action: Public Goods and the Theory of Groups*. Cambridge, MA: Harvard University Press (revised edition).
3. Ikenberry, G. John. (1999). "Institutions, Strategic Restraint, and the Persistence of American Postwar Order." *International Security* 23(3): 43–78.
4. Jones, Bruce. (2002). "Strategic Coordination and Peace Implementation," in S. Stedman, E. Cousens, and D. Rothchild (eds.) *Strategies, Organizations, and Consequences: Evaluating the Implementation of Peace Agreements in Civil Wars*. Boulder, CO: Lynne Reinner.
5. UN General Assembly. (1987). Doc A/42/541; S19085 of 31 August 1987.
6. Greig, J. Michael, and Paul F. Diehl. (2012). *International Mediation: War and Conflict in the Modern World*. Cambridge, UK: Polity Books; Vukovic, Sinisa. (2017). *International Multiparty Mediation and Conflict Management: Challenges of Cooperation and Coordination*. Abingdon-on-Thames: Taylor and Francis.

7. Saunders, Harold H. with Teddy Nemeroff, Priya Narayan Parker, Randa M. Slim, and Philip D. Stewart. (2011). *Sustained Dialogue in Conflicts: Transformation and Change.* Palgrave Macmillan.
8. Centre for Humanitarian Dialogue, website. (2018). "Central African Republic 2007–2008." https://www.hdcentre.org/activities/central-african-republic-2. Accessed 10/21/18; Community of Sant'Egidio. (2017). "Central African Republic: An Agreement for Immediate Cease-Fire and a Roadmap to Peace was Signed at Sant'Egidio." https://www.santegidio.org/pageID/30284/langID/en/itemID/21492/Central-African-Republic-an-agreement-for-immediate-ceasefire-and-a-road-map-to-peace-was-signed-at-Sant-Egidio.html. Accessed 10/21/18.
9. International Crisis Group. (2017). "Avoiding the Worst in the Central African Republic." *Report No. 253/Africa.*
10. Crocker, Chester A., Fen Osler Hampson, and Pamela Aall, eds. (1999). *Herding Cats: Multiparty Mediation in a Complex World.* US Institute of Peace Press.
11. Johns Hopkins School of Advanced International Studies. (2014). "Mindanao: Understanding Conflict 2014." https://www.sais-jhu.edu/sites/default/files/2014%20Mindanao-Final%20Report_April%202b_0.pdf. Accessed 10/21/18.
12. Whitfield, Teresa. (2007). *Friends Indeed? The United Nations, Groups of Friends and the Resolution of Conflict.* US Institute of Peace Press.
13. Murua, Imanol. (2017). "No More Bullets for ETA: The Loss of Internal Support as a Key Factor in the End of the Basque Group's Campaign." *Critical Studies on Terrorism* 10(1): 93–114; Whitfield, Teresa. (2014). *Endgame for ETA: Elusive Peace in the Basque Country.* Oxford University Press; Zabyelina, Y., & Arsovska, J. (2013). "Rediscovering Corruption's Other side: Bribing for Peace in Post-Conflict Kosovo and Chechnya." *Crime, Law and Social Change* 60(1): 1–24. http://dx.doi.org.proxyau.wrlc.org/10.1007/s10611-013-9446-x; Van der Borgh, Chris. (2012). "Resisting International State Building in Kosovo." *Problems of Post-Communism*, 59(2): 31–42.
14. Congressional Research Service. (2018). "Cyprus: Reunification Proving Elusive." https://fas.org/sgp/crs/row/R41136.pdf. Accessed 10/24/18.

15. Council on Foreign Relations. (2016). "Ending South Sudan's Civil War." *Council Special Report No. 77.* https://www.cfr.org/report/ending-south-sudans-civil-war. Accessed 10/25/18.
16. Pischedda, Costantino. (2018). "Wars Within Wars: Why Windows of Opportunity and Vulnerability Cause Inter-rebel Fighting in Internal Conflict." *International Security* 43(1): 138–176.
17. Zartman, I. William. (2009). "Negotiation as a Choice of Partners." *PINPoints Network Newsletter* 33: 13–16.
18. Zartman, I. William. (1989). *Ripe for Resolution.* New York: Oxford University Press; Haass, Richard N. (1988). *Conflicts Unending: The United States and Regional Disputes.* New Haven: Yale University Press.
19. Zartman, I. William. (1989). *Ripe for Resolution.* New York: Oxford University Press.
20. Zartman, I. William. (1995). *Elusive Peace: Negotiating an End to Civil Wars.* Washington, DC: Brookings Institution; Pruitt, Dean G. (2005). "Whither Ripeness Theory?" *Working Paper No. 25.* Institute for Conflict Analysis and Resolution, George Mason University, at http://scar.gmu.edu/wp_25_pruitt.pdf.
21. Fisher, Roger, William Ury, and Bill Patton. (1991). *Getting to Yes: Negotiating Agreements Without Giving In*, 2nd edn. New York: Penguin.
22. Sadan, Mandy, ed. (2016). *War and Peace in the Borderlands of Myanmar: The Kachin Ceasefire 1994–2011.* NIAS Press.
23. Stanford University. (2017). *Mapping Militant Organizations* webpage. http://web.stanford.edu/group/mappingmilitants/cgi-bin/groups/view/149. Accessed 5/25/17.
24. Stratfor Worldview. (2016). "A New Phase in Thailand's Age-old Insurgency." https://www.stratfor.com/analysis/new-phase-thailands-age-old-insurgency. Accessed 5/26/17.
25. Berdal, Mats, and David M. Malone, eds. (2001). *Greed and Grievance: Economic Agendas in Civil Wars.* Boulder, CO: Lynne Rienner; Van Hear, Nicholas. (2003). "Refugee Diasporas, Remittances, Development, and Conflict." *Migration Information Source* (June 1). http://www.migrationinformation.org/feature/print.cfm?ID=125.
26. Brinkerhoff, Jennifer M. (2005). "Digital Diasporas and Governance in Semi-Authoritarian States: The Case of the Egyptian Copts." *Public Administration and Development* 25: 193–204;

Brinkerhoff, Jennifer M. (2006). "Digital Diasporas and Conflict Prevention: The Case of Somalinet.com." *Review of International Studies* 32: 25–47; Stanfield II, John H. (1996). "Multiethnic Societies and Regions." *American Behavioral Scientist* 40(1): 8–17.
27. Walter, Barbara F. (1997). "The Critical Barrier to Civil War Settlement." *International Organization* 51(3): 335–364; Zartman, I. William. (1989). *Ripe for Resolution*. New York: Oxford University Press; Zartman, I. William. (2008). "Ripeness Revisited: The Push and Pull of Conflict Management." I. William Zartman (2007). *Negotiation and Conflict Management: Essays on Theory and Practice*. London: Routledge: 232–244; Fearon, James D. (2004). "Why Do Some Civil Wars Last so Much Longer Than Others?" *Journal of Peace Research* 41(3): 275–301.
28. Fearon, James D. (2004), 295–296.
29. Päivi Lujala, Nils Petter Gleditsch, and Elisabeth Gilmore. (2005). "A Diamond Curse? Civil War and a Lootable Resource." *Journal of Conflict Resolution* 49: 538; Michael G. Findley, Josiah F. Marineau. (2014). "Lootable Resources and Third-Party Intervention into Civil Wars." *Conflict Management and Peace Science* 32(5): 465–486.
30. Curran, Daniel F., and James K. Sebenius. (2003). "The Mediator as Coalition-Builder: George Mitchell in Northern Ireland." *International Negotiation* 8(1): 111–147; de Chastain, John. (1999). "The Good Friday Agreement in Northern Ireland," in Crocker, Chester A., Fen Osler Hampson, and Pamela Aall, eds. *Herding Cats: Multiparty Mediation in a Complex World*. US Institute of Peace Press.
31. Curran, Daniel F., and James K. Sebenius. (2003). "The Mediator as Coalition-Builder: George Mitchell in Northern Ireland." *International Negotiation* 8(1): 111–147; Crocker, Chester A., Fen Osler Hampson, and Pamela Aall, eds. (1999). *Herding Cats: Multiparty Mediation in a Complex World*. US Institute of Peace Press.
32. Crocker, Chester A. (1993). *High Noon in Southern Africa: Making Peace in a Rough Neighborhood*. W. W. Norton and Co.
33. Zartman, I. William. (2015). "Negotiation and the Intifada." *International Negotiation* 20(1): 109–128, p. 118.

34. Mitchell, George. (2015). *The Negotiator.* Simon and Schuster: 239–256.
35. Hampson, Fen Osler. (2006). "The Risks of Peace: Implications for International Mediation." *Negotiation Journal* 22(1): 13–30. Tingley, D. (2011). "The Dark Side of the Future: An Experimental Test of Commitment Problems in Bargaining." *International Studies Quarterly* 55: 521–554.
36. Fearon, James D. (2004); Walter, Barbara F. (1997). "The Critical Barrier to Civil War Settlement." *International Organization* 51(3) (Summer, 1997): 335–364; Walter, Barbara. (2002). *Committing to Peace: The Successful Settlement of Civil Wars.* Princeton, NJ: Princeton University Press; Walter, Barbara. (2004). "Does Conflict Beget Conflict? Explaining Recurring Civil War." *Journal of Peace Research* 41: 371–388. Whitfield, Teresa (2007). *Friends Indeed? The United Nations, Groups of Friends and the Resolution of Conflict.* US Institute of Peace Press.
37. Hampson, Fen Osler. (2006). "The Risks of Peace: Implications for International Mediation." *Negotiation Journal* 22(1): 13–30.
38. Stedman, Stephen John. (1997). "Spoiler Problems in Peace Processes." *International Security* 22(2): 5–53.
39. Svensson, Isak. (2009). "Who Brings Which Peace? Neutral Versus Biased Mediation and Institutuional Peace Arrangements in Civil Wars." *Journal of Conflict Resolution* 53(3): 446–469.
40. Beardsley, Kyle. (2011). *The Mediation Dilemma.* Ithaca, NY: Cornell University Press; Beardsley, Kyle, David E. Cunningham, and Peter B. White. (2019). "Mediation, Peacekeeping, and the Severity of Civil War." With Kyle Beardsley and Peter B. White. *Journal of Conflict Resolution* 63(7): 1682–1709; Reid, Lindsay. (2017). "Finding a Peace That Lasts: Mediator Leverage and the Durable Resolution of Civil Wars." *Journal of Conflict Resolution* 61(7): 1401–1431; Wilkenfeld, Jonathan, Kile Beardsley, and David Quinn. (2019). *Research Handbook on Mediating International Crises.* Cheltenham UK and Northampton US: Edward Elgar Publishing.
41. Zartman, I. William, and Saadia Touval, eds. (2005). *International Cooperation: The Extents and Limits of Multilateralism.* Cambridge, UK: Cambridge University Press.
42. Crocker, Chester A., Fen Osler Hampson, and Pamela Aall. (2015). "The Shifting Sands of Peacemaking: Challenges of Multiparty Mediation." *International Negotiation* 20 (2015): 363–388.

CHAPTER 13

Inclusivity in Peace Processes: Civil Society and Armed Groups

Suzanne Ghais

The consensus in recent years among individuals and organizations that support peace processes has favored greater inclusivity.[1] The landscape of contemporary conflicts, meanwhile, has featured increasing fragmentation of armed groups and a proliferation of armed non-state actors, with conflict sometimes occurring among these rather than strictly between rebels and government.[2] Mediators and international supporters of peace processes may rightly feel bewildered as to how inclusive is inclusive enough, whether there is some limit to the utility of inclusion, and how to sort through the cacophony of voices that might seek a voice in the peace negotiations. In general, the rhetoric on inclusivity is not fully met by the practice, although there are many examples of relatively inclusive peace processes in recent years.

This chapter seeks to take a closer look at inclusivity with respect to two particular aspects: civil society organizations (CSOs) and armed groups.

S. Ghais (✉)
School of International Service, American University, Washington, DC, USA
e-mail: suzanne@sghais.com

Of course, there are other aspects that might be considered, particularly the inclusion of women (explored elsewhere in this volume), youth, and so forth; these are outside the scope of this chapter, except to the extent that CSOs often represent these interests. Drawing heavily from three cases and lightly from others, I will argue that groups included in a peace process are more likely to support the peace agreement (and carry the support of their followers), and less likely to seek to undermine it, than those who are excluded. This is because people who participate in a decision-making process are generally more committed to its outcome, having had a chance to shape it and to listen to the competing concerns that also shaped it. Additionally, civil society groups press for the negotiations to address underlying sources of conflict and not to reward armed actors. Broad participation of armed and unarmed groups—particularly those who represent large constituencies—makes peace agreements more complete and durable by maximizing commitment to the peace and ensuring the grievances that generated conflict are addressed. Inclusive processes do bring practical challenges, but these are by and large manageable, as this chapter also explains.

What Is 'Inclusion'?

Inclusion may take various forms, with different gradations of influence over the agreement.[3] The strongest form is participation as a full, equal negotiating party in a process in which any party has veto power. Close to this would be direct participation in negotiation, but without veto power. For example, both the South Africa and Northern Ireland peace processes utilized 'sufficient consensus' rules which effectively allowed the major parties (in South Africa, the African National Congress and the government, and in Northern Ireland, the Social Democratic Labour Party and the Ulster Unionist Party) to conclude an accord if they were to reach agreement even while some smaller parties had not.[4] Proceeding to less direct forms of inclusion, a consultative forum designed to channel recommendations to peace negotiators can be surprisingly influential. For example, in Guatemala, an Assembly of Civil Society formed to make recommendations on each issue in the peace negotiations; most of these were adopted in the 1996 final accord.[5] There may also be more cursory consultations in which participants express opinions and organizers may note common themes among the comments, but there is no attempt to bring opposing views into agreement—instead, the various views may (or may not) be taken into account by peace negotiators. Such consultations were used frequently in the Philippines to get input from particular constituencies in between rounds of negotiations.[6] Because there is no negotiation needed during such forums, they are suitable for obtaining input from the general public (as opposed to organized stakeholder groups). There are additional forms of inclusion, especially for civil society participation: one is having civil society representatives as members of negotiating teams of the government or armed opponents; another is permitting such representatives to observe the negotiations but not to participate, an arrangement which still allows them to influence negotiators informally on the sidelines of the negotiations, such as during breaks.

It is not at all clear whose role it is to determine who gets to be included and who does not. The most common gatekeeper seems to be the mediator. For example, it was the mediator in the Liberia peace negotiations in 2003 who determined which civil society groups could participate in negotiations. The UN urges mediators to 'gauge the comfort levels of conflict parties and convince them of the value of broadening participation',[7] implying the decision should be consensual. However, it could simply come down to power in some circumstances, such as if one crucial actor says it will only participate if some other particular actor is excluded, or if powerful foreign actors pressure parties to include civil society or women. Needless to say, some groups may not want to be part of a peace negotiation and thus may exclude themselves. Such self-exclusion may make peace negotiations impossible, as was the case with the Taliban of Afghanistan and the U.S. government for years before negotiations finally began in Doha. On the other hand, some civil society groups gain a role in negotiations only after generating considerable public pressure to admit them into the talks through demonstrations and other activism, as was the case with women's groups in Liberia in 2003.

This cool analysis of types and extent of inclusion masks how tremendously emotional, political, and controversial these decisions can be—especially when the issue is whether to include groups that have been labeled, accurately or not, as terrorists. In the late 1980s, for example, it was not only illegal but unthinkable for Israelis to have contact with the Palestine Liberation Organization (PLO), despite the maximal legitimacy the organization had among Palestinians at the time. The Israeli government and the PLO saw each other as the embodiment of evil. Organizers of the Madrid Peace Conference of 1991 went to great lengths to find Palestinians *other* than the PLO to participate. After the two parties finally negotiated directly in Norway, leading to the Oslo Accords, Yitzhak Rabin was assassinated for his role in the peacemaking effort. To sit across the table from the people one views as responsible for untold death and misery can create both internal, psychological dissonance and dissension within the ranks of one's side. Colombian President Juan Manuel Santos likened negotiating with the Revolutionary Armed Forces of Colombia to 'swallowing toads'.[8]

There may also be emotions, albeit less intense ones, surrounding the inclusion of civil society. Government officials and leaders of armed groups alike are accustomed to being treated with deference and endowed with status. If CSOs are admitted into the negotiating room (even as observers), officials and leaders may argue that their status is diminished.

Civil Society

There is considerable research indicating that peace processes that include civil society in some way are more likely to reach a full and durable peace.[9] This either/or dichotomy (included or excluded) belies the wide variety of ways the voices of civil society actors are brought into different peace processes.[10] In practice, it is rare that CSOs are represented at the table with equal standing as the armed parties—one of the other arrangements described above is far more likely. One may rightly ask whether this is as it should be. On the one hand, the question of ending war necessitates ensuring that those with the weapons are somehow either persuaded or forced to lay them down; hence the logic of making armed groups the key interlocutors. On the other hand, civil wars, as distinct from interstate wars, involve questions of governance, politics, economics, and even social norms within a country—questions which civil society groups are at least as qualified to address as armed actors.

To be clear, most discussion of 'civil society' refers to *organized* civil society actors. This is still broad—it could include informal groups of activists, for instance, or traditional structures such as tribal councils or religious orders, in addition to registered non-governmental organizations—but it does not refer to the general public. 'Inclusion' thus means participation of such groups' *representatives*. This does, however, raise the interesting question of how the general public is brought into play, which will be addressed below.

While a number of theories have been put forth as to why inclusion of CSOs leads to more durable peace,[11] the most compelling—based on cases I have examined in depth[12]—is that CSOs help keep attention focused on addressing the sources of conflict rather than on negotiating power-sharing arrangements in which rebel leaders are brought into the government. The latter is not necessarily a bad solution, but the danger is that discussions revolve around who gets what post rather than how the country will solve the issues that prompted some to rebel in the first place.

Liberia's Comprehensive Peace Agreement, 2003

The case of Liberia illustrates how CSOs can be included and how their inclusion influenced the peace process. Rebellion in Liberia emerged in reaction to brutal repression of political dissent and economic decline linked to severe corruption and the government's hoarding of natural resource wealth. By the time of Liberia's second civil war (1999–2003), several CSOs including women's groups and interfaith religious groups were actively pressing for peace and for a role in the peace negotiations. The mediator of the 2003 peace negotiations, Nigerian Gen. Abdulsalami Abubakar, chose to admit five CSOs as official observers. He also welcomed political parties, which generally had stances similar to those of the CSOs. Despite their 'observer' status, the CSOs in fact spoke up during the negotiations and engaged with the negotiators.[13] There were also women peace activists demonstrating outside the hotel where the negotiations were taking place, which perhaps emboldened the CSO representatives inside the room to do more than observe.

During the negotiations, the civil society representatives advocated not only for peace but for political reforms and for limiting the roles of the armed leaders in the transitional government. Although they did not achieve all their aims, the Comprehensive Peace Agreement reached in August 2003[14] included several measures for political reform: the creation of a Governance Reform Commission, an Independent National Commission on Human Rights, and a Contract and Monopolies Commission (to combat corruption in government contracting), as well as measures for making the National Elections Commission more independent. Civil society groups were given authority to name seats in the new commissions as well as to name a list of three candidates for interim head of state from which the armed parties would then choose one.[15] Furthermore, key figures in the interim government (which was formed after the agreement was complete) were barred from running for any post-transition elected office in the 2005 elections. The armed-faction leaders chose immediate power over the prospects of running for office two years later, so in effect, the agreement took these leaders out of politics (in some cases permanently) by the end of the transition period.[16]

The civil society actors also pressed for accountability for war crimes, proposing a war crimes tribunal. The rebel groups supported the idea initially, until the mediator reminded them that they, too, might be accused of war crimes. The creation of a truth and reconciliation commission was agreed as a compromise.[17] This outcome still stands in contrast to the blanket amnesty provided by the 1990s peace agreements that ended Liberia's first civil war. Liberia's 2003 agreement was largely implemented, and with the help of a multidimensional UN peace operation, the country has remained at peace.

Comparison with Other Cases

Chad's peace negotiations illustrate the opposite of the inclusive dynamics of Liberia. The country had numerous rebellions in the 1990s and well into the 2000s, often with different rebel groups fighting simultaneously in different regions, and numerous bilateral peace agreements between the government and one rebel group at a time.[18] One such conflict and peace agreement involved the Movement for Democracy and Justice in Chad (MDJT). The rebels' demands were not very clearly articulated, but they were reacting to the government's brutal repression of dissent and the reversal of the steps toward democracy taken in the early 1990s. In peace negotiations in early 2002, no civil society representatives were present—only representatives of the government, the rebels, and their host the Libyan government. The key agreement provisions were a ceasefire, general amnesty for all combatants, participation of MDJT leaders in the government (with specifics to be determined by a committee), and integration of rebel fighters into the national army—no serious reforms to address the original grievances.[19]

The Philippines case differs from the above two African examples in that it involved a separatist movement; civil society did have some involvement in the peace process. The Muslims or *Moro* of the Philippines were systematically marginalized for centuries starting with the conquest of the islands by Spain in the 1500s. A separatist movement began in the late 1960s after the Jabidah massacre in which dozens of young Moro recruits to the military were killed after a mutiny. The separatist movement became embodied in the Moro National Liberation Front (MNLF). The government and the MNLF reached a peace agreement, called the Tripoli Agreement, in December 1976 in Libya, but it soon broke down.

In the early 1990s then-President Ramos began a new peace process in earnest, beginning with a massive public consultation process involving numerous sectors of civil society at provincial, regional, and national levels.[20] This process was managed by the National Unification Commission, a government entity chaired by Haydee Yorac, a widely respected, independent-minded human rights lawyer. The consultation created the Six Paths to Peace, a set of recommendations that addressed the underlying poverty and marginalization of the Moro as well as security and impacts of armed conflict. The Six Paths informed peace agreements leading all the way up to the most recent one, the Comprehensive Agreement on the Bangsamoro of 2014, for which implementing legislation was passed in July 2018. This agreement, like its predecessors,[21] addressed underlying issues including humanitarian needs, economic development, and the distinct Moro cultural heritage.

There was some additional civil society involvement in later negotiations. For example, in negotiations in the early 2000s, the five-person government delegation included two women from civil society, one Muslim and one Christian.[22] Civil society representatives were also admitted as observers. However, the greatest evident impact of civil society influence came in the form of the Six Paths to Peace, to which President Gloria Macapagal-Arroyo recommitted her government upon taking office in January 2001, and which influenced all the subsequent peace agreements.

Discussion and Caveats

The above cases support the notion that civil society participation in peace processes serves the cause of peace by focusing negotiators on addressing underlying grievances and sources of conflict. Nevertheless, peacemakers (mediators and officials who host or encourage peace negotiations) should resist the temptation to blindly copy the Liberian or Philippine model in other contexts. First, in the Liberian case, and increasingly over time in the Philippines case, civil society was already robust and included a strong peace movement. In Chad, by contrast, at the time of the government-MDJT agreement, civil society was relatively weak.[23] Additionally, especially in the Liberian case, the peace movement transcended ethnic, religious, and regional identities. In both countries, peace-oriented CSOs helped bring about peace not only through their inclusion in the peace process, but also through their activism, their dialogues with armed actors urging them to negotiate, and their efforts to promote the peace agreements once achieved and to aid in implementation (such as, in the Liberian case, by escorting rebel combatants to turn in their guns for cash in the DDR program). In a setting without a strong, unified peace movement, it is not clear what would be achieved by searching for civil society groups such as charities or unions to include in the peace process. It is also unlikely in a case of a divided civil society— that is, a situation where each warring party has civic groups aligned with it—that bringing such partisans to the table would advance the goal of peace.

Second, the research on civil society participation[24] indicates that the benefit of bringing civil society into the peace process is highest in the most undemocratic settings. In democracies, mechanisms already exist for both organized civil society groups and members of the general public to voice their needs and concerns through the political process. Therefore, there is less need to overtly include civil society in peace negotiations in democracies. Moreover, there are also cases in which a rebel group is itself democratic, even if the government is not. Blaydes and DeMaio[25] describe the Polisario movement in Western Sahara as inclusive and democratic; to the extent this is true, bringing that group to the negotiating table would bring the voices of the population it represents, without, perhaps, the need for separate civil society inclusion mechanisms.

Still, the cases suggest that civil society voices—whether in the negotiating room or elsewhere—can bring profound benefits to a peace process. First and foremost, civic actors help ensure negotiators address the underlying causes of conflict in the agreement. Additionally, civil society actors can serve as champions for peace. Where armed group leaders (government and rebel alike) may get caught up in their quest to maintain or acquire power, civil society groups can remind them of the severe humanitarian impacts of war and push them to find a peace agreement. This clearly happened in Liberia, the Philippines, and other cases. Finally, CSO representatives can help ensure the benefits of peace accrue to the broader society rather than to the armed actors. In Chad, where the peace talks lacked civil society involvement, the government more or less purchased peace from the rebels by offering government posts for rebel leaders and integration into the military for rank-and-file rebels, as well as a general amnesty.

ARMED GROUPS

We turn now to the inclusion of armed groups, both government and rebel. Here the issue is not whether they should be included in peace negotiations—they usually are the main interlocutors, barring some intriguing exceptions such as the 1989 Ta'if Accords in which Lebanese parliamentarians spoke for the various confessional groups in ending Lebanon's civil war. Assuming, though, that at least one rebel group enters into dialogue with the government, the question is: how comprehensive is the selection of armed groups at the table? In many civil wars or even lower-intensity armed conflicts, there are factions or splinter groups, such that more than one rebel group is fighting the government over more or less the same issues. The inclination of many governments seems to be to simplify matters by negotiating with only one rebel group at a time, reasoning that other rebel groups can be brought into the fold of peace later (or that one group in isolation can be more easily appeased). While acknowledging that some governments enter peace agreements only to placate the international community, I will argue here that if the goal is truly a lasting peace, the separate, sequential negotiating approach is a mistake.

Armed groups left out of peace negotiations are more likely to become spoilers. One study found that if a rebel group is excluded from a peace process, the chance of post-agreement violence increases by 84 percent.[26] Another found that spoiling—defined as violence aimed at undermining or altering a peace accord—is committed by parties excluded from the agreement almost twice as often as by included parties.[27] These results are consistent with earlier theoretical arguments[28] that excluded parties cannot advocate for their desired outcomes at the negotiating table and therefore are more likely than included parties to resort to violence to achieve their political goals.

Despite the obviousness of this argument, there remain numerous explanations for why mediators, governments, or rebel groups might prefer two-party negotiations rather than more inclusive ones. It is natural, of course, to assume that two-party negotiations will reach agreement more easily, but research finds otherwise. One study on international negotiations found that multilateral negotiations took only slightly more time than bilateral ones[29]; a study of peace processes found that more inclusive negotiations are just as likely to reach agreement.[30] This may seem surprising—but not to those familiar with the dynamics of consensus building. Although having more parties represented in a negotiation certainly adds a layer of complexity, it also adds more possibilities for creative, joint-gain solutions; it may permit a moderate middle to emerge on a polarizing issue; and it may add pressure on dissenting parties to join the emerging consensus.[31]

One caveat to this argument is that it applies only when the different rebel groups can be said to be involved in the same conflict. For instance, I do not consider the 'reds' or Communist insurgents of the Philippines to be engaged in the same conflict as the Moro groups. While contested state legitimacy may broadly link the two, the former seek a change in government type while the latter seek separation or autonomy for a minority. Similarly, in large countries, there can be armed opposition movements in different parts of the country (such as struggles for autonomy in northeastern India and the Maoist insurgency in central and eastern India) that have little to do with each other. However, in Chad, although there were many rebellions originating in different parts of the country, they shared an aim to replace the government with one less brutal and more democratic. Admittedly, the determination of 'same conflict' versus 'separate conflict' may be debatable in some cases, but in concept at least, my argument for inclusive rather than separate, sequential negotiations applies to the cases where more than one rebel group is fighting the government in the same conflict.

The Philippines, MNLF and MILF

The case of the Philippine government's negotiations with, first, the Moro National Liberation Front and later the Moro Islamic Liberation Front (MILF) illustrates the problems with the separate, sequential approach. In the 1970s, the MNLF was recognized by the Organization of the Islamic Conference as the legitimate representative of the Moro people, and the government reached the 'Final Peace Agreement' with the MNLF in 1996, intended to revive and complete an earlier agreement (signed in 1976) between the same two parties. Meanwhile, in 1984, the MILF split off from the MNLF. The government was aware of this and held preliminary, pre-negotiation discussions with both groups in the early 1990s.

The government's National Unification Commission recommended that the government form one delegation to negotiate with both groups.[32] Then, without explanation, the government proceeded to negotiate only with the MNLF.[33] The MILF, according to one of its members, launched an assault in 1987 in direct protest of this exclusion[34]—a vivid illustration of the link between exclusion and spoiling.

The parties struggled to implement the 1996 government-MNLF agreement—which provided for a fairly weak form of autonomy—while the government and the excluded MILF continued to clash. Many MNLF fighters also joined the MILF after the peace agreement.[35] The agreement suffered from a lack of popular support—Christians in Mindanao 'expressed exaggerated fears that they would be subjected to Muslim dominance', while in the Philippine Congress, there were 'accusations that President Ramos had "sold out" to the militant Muslims'.[36] Perhaps it is harder to support a peace agreement that seems to give new rights to a minority group but fails to bring peace. Reflecting the popular skepticism, the Philippine Congress weakened the autonomy arrangement further in the implementing legislation which was passed, after delays, in 2001.

Nearly as soon as the ink on the 1996 agreement was dry, the government began years of on-and-off talks with the MILF, the erstwhile excluded armed group. The MILF was at the time still demanding independence—another vivid illustration of the consequences of their exclusion, in that there had been no opportunity as yet for the government or intermediaries to persuade them to accept autonomy. There were numerous partial agreements and relapses into conflict. In the meantime, while some MNLF fighters had been integrated into the national army or police and others had joined the MILF, a rump of remaining MNLF fighters launched attacks in 2001, 2005, 2007, and 2013. Part of the problem was the negotiations with the MILF were rehashing the same issues on which agreement had already been reached with the MNLF, most centrally the form of an autonomous government and territory.

A comprehensive agreement with the MILF was not reached until 2014—over 16 years after talks began—and the implementing legislation, after delays, was finally passed in July 2018. We cannot know how long this process would have taken had the MILF been included in the 1990s negotiations between the government and the MNLF, but the facts are sufficient to make clear some consequences of the separate, sequential approach. In summary, it prompted renewed MILF violence in reaction to its exclusion; it allowed the MILF forces to swell with erstwhile MNLF fighters (though a robust DDR program might have prevented this); it detracted from public support and thus the implementation of the 1996 agreement; it necessitated reworking the same issues with the MILF that had already been negotiated with the MNLF; and once the MILF was the main negotiating partner, the remaining MNLF fighters protested violently. A single negotiating process that included the government and both Moro groups would have had at least the prospect of attaining peace much sooner.

Other Cases

A cursory review of other cases, what armed groups they included and excluded and the results, allows us to further test the proposition that broader inclusion leads to more lasting peace than does the separate, sequential approach. Liberia's 2003 negotiations were inclusive not only of civil society but also both major armed groups active in the second civil war. Similar to the Philippines, one group had split off from the other. As indicated above, the inclusiveness seems to have contributed to a durable peace agreement. The negotiations were intense and lasted a grueling three months (June 4 to August 18, 2003), but this is still a fraction of the 16 years the Philippine government and the MILF spent in on-and-off negotiations.

In Chad, the government conducted numerous separate, sequential peace negotiations with various rebel groups over the 1990s and well into the 2000s. There were several calls for more comprehensive political negotiations that would include multiple armed groups and/or unarmed political opposition groups—indeed, one such request was made by the MDJT leader during his first meeting with President Déby in 2000[37]—but such calls were not answered. Soon after each peace agreement, the country relapsed into a new armed conflict. The string of rebellions finally ended by 2010 after several things occurred: a coalition of numerous opposition parties and the government held a political dialogue, facilitated by the EU, in 2007 and agreed on democratic reforms[38]; the French government helped repel a rebel assault on N'Djamena in 2008; the Chadian government succeeded in defeating a rebel offensive in 2009; and the governments of Chad and Sudan reached agreement in 2010 to stop supporting the rebels in each other's countries.[39] These cases are consistent with the argument that the separate, sequential approach delays the achievement of durable peace.

I searched for an example of a recent (but not ongoing) peace process that used a separate, sequential approach but still attained durable peace. One possible example is the Burundi peace process culminating in the Arusha agreement of 2000. The talks were intended to be all-inclusive, with political parties representing their corresponding armed factions. However, in reality, the two major armed factions (CNDD-FDD and PALIPEHUTU-FNL) were splitting off from their respective political parties while talks were ongoing. Consequently, the signing of the accord did not end the violence. However, further negotiations took place between these two groups and the Burundian government after the main accord. The larger group, CNDD-FDD, joined the transitional government in 2002, while the other did not lay down its arms until 2006, after the transition period and subsequent elections.[40] Thus, similar to the Philippines situation, the exclusion of these armed groups did not prevent peace entirely but does seem to have delayed it.

Extremists

The most compelling reason to exclude some armed parties may be their extremist ideologies or tactics that deliberately target civilians. (Of course, governments frequently label any armed opponents 'terrorists' to delegitimize them when they do not meet any established definition of the term; here, in any case, I am speaking somewhat more broadly.) Most would agree that peace processes should not reward such actors, and many argue that one cannot reason with extremists, or at least certain subsets of them, such as 'total spoilers'[41] or 'absolute terrorists'.[42] However, it is debatable whether the act of talking in itself rewards extremists or serves to legitimize them. Zartman argues it does not, the main question being not so much whether negotiations occur but rather what concessions are made and by whom. The terrorists may only gain a small symbolic victory through negotiation in exchange for substantive concessions to the government, or they may have to renounce terrorist tactics in order to gain anything.[43]

Still, since in the popular imagination, negotiations occur between equals, negotiation (unless it is of the secretive, backchannel sort) does seem to lend at least some symbolic victory to the actor sitting across from a government. Powell argues that if a group using terrorism has a 'serious political base', the government in question will have to negotiate with it eventually[44]; moreover, the negotiations themselves may moderate the extremists' stance when they are 'confronted with hard reality'.[45] He cites many examples, such as the Irish Republican Army and the Basque group ETA. Blum and Heymann[46] distinguish between negotiating to end a particular incident (such as a hostage taking), which they caution against (especially against ransom payments), versus negotiating to transform the larger political relationship between the government and the terrorist group. In this latter kind of case, negotiating with extremists may, in some cases, be the best option (assuming of course the group is interested in such negotiation).

Here, our focus being peace processes, the topic is certainly in the realm of negotiations to change the political relationship rather than to end a particular terrorist incident. Many peace processes have included a range of parties from the more mainstream to the more extreme. Rules for 'sufficient consensus' as described earlier are one way to include more extreme actors without blocking the path to a peace agreement.

It remains unclear whether excluding extremist armed groups serves peace in the long run. Is it worth the risk of rewarding and encouraging such groups in order to try to persuade them to moderate their ideology and trade terrorist tactics for political engagement? One key criterion for determining whom to include may be the amount of public support the group has. Powell argues it is only terrorist groups with broad political support that governments should engage in discussions. In the Philippines case, my research as of 2015 suggested that the government had safely excluded the extremist Abu Sayyaf Group from peace negotiations—'safely' in the sense that the group was unable to seriously spoil the peace process. This group sustained itself mostly through kidnapping ransoms, committed gruesome violence against civilians, and consequently had little public support. By 2014, the group had lost most of its fighting force and had been substantially weakened through military and police action. That outcome seemed to vindicate the government's decision to exclude the group from the peace process and to seek only its defeat. However, the same year, the Abu Sayyaf Group pledged allegiance to the Islamic State and has since experienced a modest revival, engaging in fighting and bombings of civilian targets in recent years.

Would the government have bought itself a more comprehensive peace by including even this reviled group in negotiations? There may have been a missed opportunity to do so. In January 2001, Gloria Macapagal-Arroyo was beginning her term as president of the Philippines, and declared a policy of 'all-out peace', reversing her predecessor's policy of 'all-out war'. At this time, the Abu Sayyaf Group indicated its willingness to release its hostages and negotiate with the new government if its conditions were met. The president, however, was unmoved: she ordered the military to 'neutralize' the Abu Sayyaf 'bandits'.[47] While the nature of the conditions was not publicized, just eight months earlier the group had made political demands for the release of its hostages in Sipadan, Malaysia: Moro independence, a commission on the plight of ethnic Filipinos in Malaysia, and the release of Ramzi Yousef, the Pakistani imprisoned for his role in the 1993 World Trade Center bombing.[48] They ended up settling instead for a large ransom (paid by a mysterious third party, probably Libya, possibly on behalf of France and Germany, although these countries deny it).[49] As years passed, the group splintered and its demands veered toward money more than ideology, making any peace overture futile. But as things stood in January 2001, there may conceivably have been conditions for negotiation: a relatively coherent organization (by that time there were two factions, but they later fragmented even further) and demands that, while extreme, were mostly political in nature and not inherently nonnegotiable. Perhaps backchannel talks could have focused on securing agreement from the group to end violence in exchange for a seat in the peace talks. It is impossible, of course, to know whether this approach would have succeeded in transforming the group into a nonviolent political movement, but as Powell has argued, many terrorist groups have undergone such a transformation.

Thus at this point, the best guidance to mediators and governments as to whether to invite extremist groups to peace negotiations might be (a) give more serious consideration to those groups that have broad public support; (b) begin with backchannel talks—so as to minimize political fallout and the possible legitimizing effect—until the groups renounce terrorist tactics; and (c) consider a decision rule that allows the moderate groups to carry the day even if extremist groups disagree. However, more research is needed on this topic.

Practical Issues

Even if inclusive negotiations enhance chances for durable peace and do not detract from the chances of agreement as much as feared, it may still be daunting to manage so many parties to one negotiation. The challenges are many. In a large-group setting compared to a small, intimate one, participants are more likely to grandstand rather than engage in the kind of frank dialogue that can help enhance mutual understanding and empathy. Moreover, a number of commonplace problems are more likely with more people in the room: a few individuals dominating the conversation, tangential or distracting comments, inefficiency in getting to decisions, and so on.[50]

There are, however, practical approaches to help manage the complexity of an inclusive negotiation. Group facilitation is a well-established area of practice from which mediators or other hosts of peace processes can learn. Simple tactics like pre-agreed ground rules, use of small groups, and well-defined objectives and agendas can help, and there are also subtler methods concerning how questions are asked and how participants are interviewed before the group meeting to help put them in the right mind frame. There are techniques for quickly polling a group at key moments and for closing disagreements on the way to consensus.

An area of practice related to peace negotiations is multilateral negotiations on other topics such as climate or trade. Cross-fertilization between these two arenas would be helpful, as multilateral negotiations may include well over 100 countries. Techniques such as the 'take it or change it' method used in the 2012 climate negotiation[51] or the *indaba* method used in the 2015 Paris climate negotiations[52] might prove useful in peace negotiations as well. *Indaba* (a southern African practice) involves delegates getting away from the formal tables to meet in a standing circle, speaking personally rather than repeating prepared positions, and exchanging 'red lines' as well as ideas for bridging differences. The practice has succeeded in generating agreements to break impasses.

It is also important to remember that peace processes are rarely limited to one event, one room, and one table; on the contrary, there are working groups, public consultations, and more. For civil society engagement in particular, multiple forums may be used. One approach would be a parallel, separate civil society forum that develops proposals to feed to the peace negotiations. The Guatemalan Assembly of Civil Society and the Philippines' National Unification Commission consultations were both examples of this.

We should also consider that broader publics—as distinct from civil society *organizations*—may or may not share the views of the CSOs. Publics are sometimes more conservative than the organized civic groups, which are often led by educated, urban elites. In the Philippines, for example, while numerous civil society groups advocated for peace with the Moro rebels, the broader Christian public tended for many years to regard the Moro cause with more hostility. Moreover, in conflict or post-conflict zones receiving foreign financial support, CSOs may spring up in response to donor funds, reflecting the donors' priorities more than those of the general population.

Thus, initiatives that involve the broader public are also worth considering in peace processes. Public involvement (synonymous with other terms such as 'community engagement') typically involves use of (a) a variety of communication tools to inform the public, (b) a variety of mechanisms to receive input from the public, ranging from quick commenting opportunities via social or other media to in-depth public meetings, and (c) some feedback loop wherein decision-makers (which here would be the peace negotiators) characterize the input received and how it affected the decisions made. Referendums might also be considered a form of public involvement, and indeed they have been used to generate legitimacy for peace agreements. Caution is warranted in that a referendum is, like any vote, an adversarial process, and it typically offers only two choices—yes or no. The Northern Ireland peace agreement passed its referendum after an active 'yes campaign' to promote it; the Colombia-FARC peace agreement failed its referendum in 2016, but the negotiators went back to the table and revised the agreement based on the public's objections. (See the chapter by Joana Amaral in this volume on peacemaking referendums for a fuller discussion.)

In the design of complex, inclusive peace processes, cultural factors must be considered. While a full exploration of this topic is beyond the scope of this chapter, one example emerges in the comparison of the Liberia and Philippines cases. In the Liberian negotiations, representatives of the government, armed groups, political parties, and civil society were all in the same room. As mentioned above, civil society representatives spoke up and addressed the gathering even when not invited to do so. This is easy to imagine in the direct-dealing cultures of West Africa, but harder to imagine in Southeast Asia. During negotiations in the Philippines in the early 2000s, civil society observers never spoke up during plenary sessions as far as I could find. However, the government and MILF delegations had civil society representatives in them, which allowed, perhaps, for behind-the-scenes influence. Additionally, the Philippines peace process involved many more small-group meetings and less time in plenary sessions. These arrangements are perhaps better suited to Southeast Asian cultures, where open confrontation is less common.

Many questions remain about inclusiveness of peace processes. First, is it truly impossible for a government to proceed with a smaller number of willing participants and bring in others over time? The government of Colombia undertook this experiment, negotiating with the smaller ELN after having concluded a peace agreement with the FARC. Those talks are moribund at the time of writing. My argument above, based on the cases I have examined, is that this separate, sequential approach pushes peace farther into the future, but time will tell in Colombia. Similarly, the government of Myanmar conducted political negotiations with only those ethnic armed organizations (EAOs) that had signed the Nationwide Ceasefire Agreement (NCA), leaving out several others that had not. However, the February 2021 military coup in Myanmar effectively ended these peace negotiations and thus the experiment in partial inclusion. If any peace process reaches comprehensive peace with the separate, sequential approach,—my argument will have to be revised.

Second, if all armed groups are welcome to the peace table, will that encourage further fragmentation of rebel groups?[53] If a rebel group is internally divided, it may be tempting for a faction to split off and act as a spoiler in hopes of an invitation to negotiations as a distinct entity. There may be other factors that incentivize rebel groups to stay together—the main one being strength through solidarity—but these have not prevented the considerable fractionation that already is common.

A larger question concerns nonviolent movements. Much scholarly attention (including my own) has been directed toward armed conflicts because of the human costs of violence, but one could argue that researchers and policymakers are indirectly encouraging violence by focusing so much on the groups who commit it. Chenoweth and Stephan[54] have demonstrated that when efforts to end a regime or an occupation come from nonviolent movements rather than violent ones, they are more effective and more likely to result in an increase in democracy. One of many questions is to what extent the lessons of peace processes can be applied to negotiations involving governments and mass, nonviolent movements. There are excellent examinations of the asymmetries between governments and armed rebels,[55] but the asymmetries between governments and mass movements might be even more challenging to analyze, as mass movements often lack a clear, singular leadership. If there are negotiations at all, who would be the interlocutors on the side of the mass movement? How would anyone ensure the talks are adequately inclusive?

Conclusion

I have argued that peace processes that integrate the voices of civil society and the full array of armed groups (at least those representing a substantial constituency) in a given conflict are more conducive to durable peace than more exclusive ones. There are many pathways by which both organized civil society and the unorganized, general public may have their voices heard, but the key value of civil society inclusion is to maintain focus on the underlying sources of conflict, as well as the impacts of conflict on the population, as opposed to a narrow focus on configurations of power among the armed leaders. The rationale for inclusion of all major armed groups rests on prevention of spoiling behavior, the difficulty of bringing peace by negotiating with one group at a time while another group continues armed action, and the tendency of engagement in negotiation to moderate extreme positions. Questions remain concerning inclusion of terrorist or other extremist groups, as well as on other areas such as mass, nonviolent movements, and fragmentation of armed groups.

Conflict and peace are complex human processes, and hard-and-fast rules should be regarded with skepticism. For this reason, my arguments are not framed as absolute. In recent years, the practice of making peace has become more sophisticated and institutionalized: there are United Nations special envoys, multidimensional peace operations, regional organizations with increasingly robust conflict management capacity, NGOs and others offering mediation support, an assortment of training seminars, and so on. These are welcome developments, as long as this practice area does not devolve into one-size-fits-all prescriptions, with models copied and pasted mindlessly from one setting to another. Context specificity is paramount, and lessons gleaned from comparative examination of numerous cases must be tempered with rich understanding of the local context.

Notes

1. For example, Paffenholz 2015; UN Peacemaker 2012, 11–13.
2. Melander et al. 2016.
3. My thinking here is influenced by Paffenholz 2014 and the IAP2 Spectrum of Public Participation, available at https://cdn.ymaws.com/www.iap2.org/resource/resmgr/pillars/Spectrum_8.5x11_Print.pdf.

4. Mnookin 2003.
5. Jonas 2000, 12–13; Alvarez and Prado 2002, 41.
6. Iribani 2006.
7. UN Peacemaker 2012, 12.
8. Miroff 2014, np.
9. Wanis-St John and Kew 2008, Nilsson 2012, Paffenholz 2015.
10. Paffenholz 2014.
11. For example, Nilsson 2012; Wanis-St. John and Kew 2008.
12. Ghais 2016.
13. Hayner 2007, 11.
14. 'Peace Agreement between the Government of Liberia, the Liberians United for Reconciliation and Democracy, the Movement for Democracy in Liberia and the political parties, Accra, Ghana, 18 August 2003,' https://peaceaccords.nd.edu/matrix/accord/58.
15. Annex 2 of the peace agreement.
16. Some tried to run for office in 2005 but were thwarted—see Cook 2010, 9, and the Peace Accords Matrix tracking of implementation (https://peaceaccords.nd.edu/accord/accra-peace-agreement).
17. Hayner 2007, 15.
18. See for example Cornwell 1999; International Crisis Group 2006; Human Rights Watch 2007; Bessell and Campbell 2008; Bekoe 2010; Ploch 2010.
19. There are no insider accounts that I can find on what was discussed during the negotiations and whether there were any attempts to address these underlying issues.
20. Ferrer 2002.
21. The Comprehensive Agreement on the Bangsamoro can be found at https://peace.gov.ph/2014/03/comprehensive-agreement-bangsamoro/. This agreement incorporated many earlier agreements by reference; one important one was the 2001 Agreement on Peace Between the Government of the Republic of the Philippines and the Moro Islamic Liberation Front, which can be found at https://peacemaker.un.org/philippines-agreementonpeace2001.
22. Cagoco-Guiam 2003, 6; Rood 2004, 19.
23. Bessell and Campbell 2008, 2; Bertelsmann Fdn. 2003, 5.
24. Wanis-St John and Kew 2008, Nilsson 2012.
25. Blaydes and De Maio 2010, 15–17.

26. Nilsson 2008, 489.
27. Reiter 2011, 89.
28. Such as Darby and Mac Ginty 2003, 266; Hampson 1996, 217; and Licklider 2001, 701.
29. Simonelli 2011, 165.
30. Paffenholz 2015, 3.
31. See also Touval 1989, 356–359 for factors that overcome impediments and facilitate agreement in multiparty negotiations.
32. National Unification Commission 1993, 50.
33. Jubair 1999, 198.
34. Jubair 1999, 194.
35. Santos Jr 2010, 179.
36. May 2001, 267.
37. Lanne 2003, 210.
38. Djiraibe 2002, 1.
39. Ploch 2010, 4; Bekoe 2010, 3.
40. Wolpe 2011; McClintock and Tahimana 2008.
41. Stedman 1997.
42. Zartman 2003.
43. Zartman 2003, 448–449.
44. Powell 2015, 29.
45. Powell 2015, 28.
46. Blum and Heymann 2010, 157.
47. Waran 2001.
48. Parry 2001.
49. Parry 2001.
50. Raiffa et al. 2003, 390–392.
51. Wagner 2013, 347 and 351.
52. Rathi 2015.
53. Thanks to Nicholas Ross of the Inclusive Peace and Transition Initiative, Graduate Institute Geneva for this question.
54. Chenoweth and Stephan 2011.
55. Such as Zartman 1995.

Bibliography

Alvarez, E., and T. P. Prado (2002) 'Guatemala's Peace Process: Context, Analysis, and Evaluation', *Accord 13: Owning the Process: Public Participation in Peacemaking*, 38–43 (London: Conciliation Resources).

Barnes, C. (2002) 'Democratizing Peacemaking Processes: Strategies and Dilemmas for Public Participation', *Accord 13: Owning the Process: Public Participation in Peacemaking*, 6–12 (London: Conciliation Resources).

Bekoe, D. (2010) 'Stabilizing Chad: Security, Governance, and Development Challenges' (Washington: United States Institute of Peace) October 21.

Bertelsmann Foundation (2003) *Bertelsmann Transformation Index 2003 Country Reports: Chad* (Gütersloh, Germany: Bertelsmann Stiftung).

Bessell, S., and Campbell (2008) *Toward Resolving Chad's Interlocking Conflicts* (Washington: United States Institute of Peace) December.

Blaydes, L., and J. De Maio (2010) 'Spoiling the Peace? Peace Process Exclusivity and Political Violence in North-Central Africa', *Civil Wars* 12(1–2), 3–28.

Blum, G., and P. B. Heymann (2010) *Laws, Outlaws, and Terrorists: Lessons from the War on Terrorism* (Cambridge, MA: MIT Press).

Cagoco-Guiam, R. (2003) 'Negotiations and Detours: The Rocky Road to Peace in Mindanao' Accord: The Mindanao Peace Process, Supplement to Issue 6, *Compromising on Autonomy*, pp. 4–11 (London: Conciliation Resources).

Chenoweth, E., and M. J. Stephan (2011) *Why Civil Resistance Works* (New York: Columbia University).

Cook, N. (2010) *Liberia's Post-War Development: Key Issues and U.S. Assistance* (Washington: Congressional Research Service).

Cornwell, R. (1999) 'Chad: Fuelling the Flames?' *African Security Review* 8(5), 76–81.

Darby, J., and R. Mac Ginty, eds (2003) *Contemporary Peacemaking: Conflict, Violence, and Peace Processes* (Basingstoke and New York: Palgrave Macmillan).

Djiraibe, D. (2002) 'Chad Oil: Why Develop It?' *Review of African Political Economy* 29(91), 170–173.

Ferrer, M. C. (2002) 'Philippines National Unification Commission: National Consultations and the "Six Paths to Peace"', *Accord 13: Owning the Process: Public Participation in Peacemaking*, 82–85 (London: Conciliation Resources).

Ghais, S. (2016) *Inclusivity and Peacemaking in Internal Armed Conflicts*, doctoral dissertation (Washington: American University).

Ghais, S. (2019) 'Consequences of Excluding Armed Groups from Peace Negotiations: Chad and the Philippines, *International Negotiation* 24(1), 61–90.

Hampson, F. O. (1996) *Nurturing Peace: Why Peace Settlements Succeed or Fail* (Washington: United States Institute of Peace).

Hayner, P. (2007) *Negotiating Peace in Liberia: Preserving the Possibility for Justice* (Geneva: Centre for Humanitarian Dialogue).
Human Rights Watch (2007) 'Early to War: Child Soldiers in the Chad Conflict' *Human Rights Watch* 19(9A).
International Crisis Group (2006) 'Chad: Back Towards War?' *Africa Report* No. 111, June 1.
Iribani, A. (2006) *Give Peace a Chance: The Story of the GRP-MNLF Peace Talks* (Mandaluyong City, Philippines: Magbasa Kita Foundation/Philippine Council for Islam and Democracy).
Jonas, S. (2000) 'Democratization through Peace: The Difficult Case of Guatemala', *Journal of Interamerican Studies and World Affairs*, 42(2), v–38.
Jubair, S. (1999) *Bangsamoro: A Nation under Endless Tyranny*, 3rd edn (Kuala Lumpur: IQ Marin).
Lanne, B. (2003) 'Chad: Recent History', in K. Murison (ed.) *Africa South of the Sahara 2003* (London: Europa/Taylor and Francis), pp. 203–212.
Licklider, R. (2001) 'Obstacles to Peace Settlement', in C. A. Crocker, F. O. Hampson, and P. Aall (eds) *Turbulent Peace: The Challenges of Managing International Conflict* (Washington: United States Institute of Peace), pp. 697–718.
May, R. J. (2001) 'Muslim Mindanao: Four Years after the Peace Agreement', *Southeast Asian Affairs*, 263–275.
McClintock, E. A. and T. Nahimana (2008) 'Managing the Tension between Inclusionary and Exclusionary Processes: Building Peace in Burundi', *International Negotiation* 13, 73–91.
Melander, E., T. Pettersson, and L. Themnér (2016) 'Organized Violence, 1989–2015', *Journal of Peace Research* 53(5), 727–742.
Miroff, N. (2014). 'Colombia Peace Talks Enter "Toad Swallowing" Phase', *Washington Post*, 29 October. https://www.washingtonpost.com/news/worldviews/wp/2014/10/29/colombia-peace-talks-enter-toad-swallowing-phase/.
Mnookin, R. H. (2003) 'Strategic Barriers to Dispute Resolution: A Comparison of Bilateral and Multilateral Negotiations', *Journal of Institutional and Theoretical Economics* 159(1), 199–220.
National Unification Commission (1993) *National Unification Commission Report to President Fidel V. Ramos on the Pursuit of a Comprehensive Peace Process* (Quezon City, Philippines).
Nilsson, D. (2008) 'Partial Peace: Rebel Groups Inside and Outside of Civil War Settlements', *Journal of Peace Research* 45(4), 479–495.
Nilsson, D. (2012) 'Anchoring the Peace: Civil Society Actors in Peace Accords and Durable Peace', *International Interactions: Empirical and Theoretical Research in International Relations* 38, 243–266.

Paffenholz, T. (2014) 'Civil Society and Peace Negotiations: Beyond the Inclusion-Exclusion Dichotomy', *Negotiation Journal*, January, 69–91.

Paffenholz, T. (2015) *Can Inclusive Peace Processes Work? New Evidence from a Multi-Year Research Project: Policy Brief* (Geneva: Graduate Institute of Geneva, Centre on Conflict, Development and Peacebuilding) https://www.inclusivepeace.org/sites/default/files/IPTI-CCDP-Can-Inclusive-Processes-Work.pdf.

Parry, R. L. (2001) 'Treasure Island', *The Independent* (London), accessed through LexisNexis Academic.

Ploch, L. (2010) Instability in Chad (Washington: Congressional Research Service).

Powell, J. (2015) *Terrorists at the Table: Why Negotiating Is the Only Way to Peace* (Basingstoke and New York: Palgrave Macmillan).

Raiffa, H., J. Richardson, and D. Metcalfe (2003) *Negotiation Analysis* (Cambridge: Harvard University).

Rathi, A. (2015) 'This Simple Negotiation Tactic Brought 195 Countries to Consensus', *Quartz*, https://qz.com/572623/this-simple-negotiation-tactic-brought-195-countries-to-consensus-in-the-paris-climate-talks/.

Reiter, A. G. (2011) *Fighting Over Peace: Spoilers, Peace Agreements, and the Strategic Use of Violence*, Ph.D. dissertation (University of Wisconsin-Madison).

Rood, S. (2004) *Civil Society and Conflict Management*, Paper Presented at The Dynamics and Management of Internal Conflicts in Asia, Third Study Group Meeting, February 27–March 3, Washington.

Santos Jr, S. M. (2010) 'MNLF Integration into the AFP and PNP: Successful Co-optation or Failed Transformation? (Case Study)', in D. Rodriguez (ed.) *Primed and Purposeful: Armed Groups and Human Security Efforts in the Philippines* (Geneva: Small Arms Survey), pp. 162–184.

Simonelli, N. M. (2011) 'Bargaining over International Multilateral Agreements: The Duration of Negotiations', *International Interactions* 37, 147–169.

Stedman, S. J. (1997) 'Spoiler Problems in Peace Processes', *International Security* 22(2), 5–53.

Touval, S. (1989) 'Multilateral Negotiation: An Analytic Approach', *Negotiation Journal* 5(2), 159–173.

United Nations Peacemaker (2012) *United Nations Guidance for Effective Mediation*, https://peacemaker.un.org/guidance-effective-mediation (New York: United Nations Mediation Support Unit).

Wagner, L. (2013) 'A Forty-Year Search for a Single Negotiating Text', *International Negotiation* 18(3), 333–356.

Wanis-St John, A., and D. Kew (2008) 'Civil Society and Peace Negotiations: Confronting Exclusion', *International Negotiation* 13(1), 11–36.

Waran, K. P. (30 January 2001) 'Abu Sayyaf: We Are Ready to Talk', *New Straits Times* (Malaysia) (accessed through LexisNexis Academic).

Wolpe. H. (2011) *Making Peace After Genocide: Anatomy of the Burundi Process* (Washington: US Institute of Peace).

Zartman, I. W., ed. (1995) *Elusive Peace: Negotiating an End to Civil Wars* (Washington: Brookings Institution).

Zartman, I. W. (2003) 'Negotiating with Terrorists', *International Negotiation* 8(3), 443–450.

CHAPTER 14

Negotiating Peace in the Shadows

Niall Ó Dochartaigh

Discretion and Deceit

The sharply dualistic character of secrecy provokes polarised debate. On the one hand we value discretion and the keeping of confidences: we respect those who guard our secrets and those values are woven into our lexicon of secrecy and disclosure. Information leaks; people spill the beans. To be able to keep a secret is part of the definition of maturity, an indicator of trustworthiness and reliability.[1] The virtue of discretion is embedded in the professional codes of diplomacy. And in the negotiated settlement of intractable conflicts, secret negotiation through back channels has been a vital means of reaching an agreement between ostensibly irreconcilable enemies.

But the keeping of a secret is both a sacred *and* a profane act: secrecy may 'conceal wrongdoing of every kind'.[2] Secret diplomacy has been a

N. Ó Dochartaigh (✉)
School of Political Science & Sociology, National University of Ireland Galway, Galway, Ireland
e-mail: Niall.odochartaigh@nuigalway.ie

particular target of criticism. It has connotations of deceit and manipulation that stoke conspiracy theories and agitate advocates of transparency and public scrutiny. For the critics, secret negotiations and hidden back channels are inimical to democracy and undermine the public sphere. Thomas More was blunt about how his perfect society, Utopia, would deal with the use of such back channels: 'it is death to have any consultation for the commonwealth out of the council or the place of the common election' he wrote.[3] Those who conferred in secret would be killed.

The First World War, which many politicians, historians and commentators attributed to the 'evils of secret diplomacy' sparked an outcry against diplomacy behind closed doors.[4] Millions had marched to their deaths, due in part to secret treaties of which they knew nothing. Condemnation of secret diplomacy took a place at the heart of debates on democracy and self-determination at this high point of liberal internationalism.[5] The critique retains force today, argued most vigorously by intelligence whistleblowers who advocate close public scrutiny of warfare and foreign policy as part of a broader project to transform the political, and by organisations such as Wikileaks who argue that they seek to hold those in power to their word in a spirit of transparency and disclosure.[6] When secrecy is used to conceal bargains that are regarded as unfair, or even shameful, it adds insult to injury.

Critics contend that secrecy undermines democratic legitimacy. An honest, open, public politics without hidden agendas and secret deals will restore it.[7] It's important to note however that even the strongest advocates of transparency approve of certain kinds of concealment. Intelligence whistleblowers such as Edward Snowden, for example, are strongly supportive of individual privacy and argue against the massification of data and the intensification of surveillance.[8]

Advocates of transparency in peace negotiations argue that openness serves the cause of peace. But what if transparency makes it harder to achieve peace and increases the risks of war? Writing as defeat loomed for Germany in the First World War, sociologist and theorist of power Max Weber advocated increased transparency in domestic politics and blamed Germany's disastrous conduct of the war partly on its lack of democracy. But he had a different attitude to secrecy in the realm of foreign relations and peacemaking. He criticised the view of many democrats 'that *conducting things in public*, particularly diplomacy, is a panacea and, above all, one which will always operate in favour of peace', arguing instead that 'making things public… can seriously *interfere* with the *objectivity* and unprejudiced character of current deliberations, thus actually endangering or preventing peace'.[9]

And even those who fiercely criticised secret treaties after the First World War recognised the necessity of negotiating in secret. Maurice Low may have been caustically critical of 'the vice of secret diplomacy' but he insisted on the validity of certain kinds of secrecy:

> Secret negotiation is not only proper, but, in many cases, absolutely essential; it is so necessary that if negotiations were not kept secret few treaties could be concluded and the negotiators would always be hampered... Secrecy, therefore, in the early stages of negotiation is perfectly proper.[10]

While secrecy is no more a panacea than transparency, Weber's argument for the use of secrecy in the pursuit of peace is largely confirmed by the scholarship on back-channel negotiation in peace processes.[11] It can be extraordinarily difficult to make peace in the glare of public attention or even if knowledge is shared with all of one's own senior colleagues, or with other Government ministries or one's own military leadership. Back-channel negotiation is ubiquitous in peace processes for this very reason.

This chapter examines the debate on secret diplomacy from the late twentieth century onwards, tracing its intertwining with debates on the role of secrecy in peace processes and peace agreements. Secret diplomacy came back into favour in the 1970s with Richard Nixon's secret rapprochement with China, and then again in the 1990s when it was crucial to three high-profile peace agreements in Israel/Palestine, Northern Ireland and South Africa. The War on Terror disrupted this pattern by stigmatising any negotiation with 'terrorists' but by the beginning of the 2020s back-channel links were once again a taken for granted tool of conflict management even in highly ideologically charged conflicts such as those in Syria and Afghanistan.[12] The chapter discusses the motivations for covert contact, outlining how it increases the clarity of communication and provides a way for long-time enemies to establish the authority of opposing leaders, to discuss proposals without making strong public commitments and to develop the limited trust on which a settlement can ultimately be built.

Back Channels to Peace

Secret diplomacy and back-channel negotiation abruptly came back into favour in the summer of 1971 with the high drama of a secret night-time flight over the Himalayas to Beijing by Henry Kissinger. The US National Security Advisor faked a stomach illness in Pakistan and his team organised a decoy convoy with drawn curtains in order to allow him to slip away unnoticed. He reappeared 36 hours later to announce a historic rapprochement with China that shifted the global balance of power.[13] It showed in the most dramatic way that secrecy, rather than simply stoking confrontation as had occurred before the First World War, was a valuable tool in de-escalation and building cooperative relationships with adversaries in the face of hardline domestic opposition. In 1988 Klieman wrote one of the first studies of back-channel diplomacy between states, examining in detail the way in which Israel routinely, and effectively, managed its relations in a sensitive region through secret contact with states that were publicly hostile.[14] The case for secret contact with sworn enemies was given a further powerful boost in the early 1990s when three separate peace processes were nurtured through back-channel negotiations. In South Africa, in Ireland and in Israel/Palestine, secret talks were decisive in securing the transition from seemingly intractable conflicts to open, public (if varyingly successful) peace processes and negotiated compromise agreements.[15] Parties who had seemed incapable of compromise or even of talking to one another turned out to be capable of building cooperative, if strictly limited, relationships in secret and creating a foundation for public compromise. It was a high point for the hopes of peace. It opened the way for a validation of back-channel links as a liberating if high-risk means of overcoming seemingly impossible obstacles, celebrated in the 2016 Broadway play 'Oslo' about the Norwegian facilitation of secret talks between the PLO and Israel.[16]

In two of these three cases secret exchanges between governments and their militant opponents took place in parallel with high-profile public talks that pointedly and very publicly excluded these same opposition groups: the Madrid peace talks on the Middle East in 1991–1993 and the Brooke/Mayhew talks in Belfast in 1991–1992. It is a measure of the importance of secrecy that both the British and Israeli leaders concealed their back-channel talks from their most important allies in the public talks—the Irish and US governments respectively—as well as from almost all of their own government ministers and senior security force commanders.[17] When the secret talks culminated in public rapprochement between apparently irreconcilable forces it did a great deal to validate the use of covert diplomacy in the most intractable of conflicts. Crucially, back-channel contact created a shared project—maintaining the secrecy of the channel—around which cooperation and trust could be built. It provided a means to communicate without conceding the legitimacy of adversaries, while bypassing internal opponents of compromise.[18] Secrecy is no guarantee of success of course, and the varying outcomes of these three processes indicate some of the weaknesses of back channels, even if we can't blame all of the disappointments on the secret origins of these processes.

The September 11 attacks on New York and Washington DC in 2001 marked the onset of a 'War on Terror' that seemed to sweep aside the possibilities for compromise with non-state armed groups. Six months after the attacks US President George Bush declared 'No nation can negotiate with terrorists. For there is no way to make peace with those whose only goal is death'.[19] But the freezing effect on engagement turned out to be short-lived and the logic of negotiation with armed opponents was subsequently reasserted in Iraq, in Afghanistan and in Syria. Over the past decade secret contact has again come to be taken for granted as an essential tool of diplomacy in civil wars and insurgencies, even with those labelled terrorists.[20]

One way to get around the taboo against talking to 'terrorists' is to change the terminology and speak instead of 'insurgents' or simply avoid referring to them constantly as terrorists, even if they remain on an official terrorist list. In Iraq in the early 2000s, for example, the US distinguished between reconcilable and irreconcilable 'insurgents' to pave the way for compromise and engagement with hostile armed groups.[21] Their success in coopting a section of the Sunni insurgents (framed as a 'Sunni Awakening') was a boost for the principle of engagement with sworn militant opponents, even if it led in this case to cooption rather than a compromise peace agreement—a useful reminder of the sometimes blurred boundary between peace processes and counter-insurgency efforts. Perhaps the most remarkable transition was that from 'War on Terror' in Afghanistan to back-channel negotiation with the Taliban and subsequently an open engagement that is now treated as quite unremarkable.[22] It is a measure of the normalisation of such contact—despite strong resistance in some US military and policy circles, and friction surrounding the exclusion of the Afghan government from talks—that US President Donald Trump could casually announce on Twitter in September 2019 that he had been planning to meet secretly with Taliban leaders at Camp David.[23]

WHY SECRECY?

One of the most powerful reasons to talk in secret is to insulate negotiations from domestic political struggles. Secrecy ensures that domestic audiences are unaware of what is being said and often—particularly in cases of intractable conflict—remain unaware that contact is taking place at all. The pressures for secrecy are greatest when governments communicate with groups they themselves have placed beyond the pale through public commitments to never negotiate. The Israeli Prime Minister, for example, was in secret contact with the PLO at a time when it was a criminal offence for an Israeli citizen to have such contact.[24] At the same time as the British Government was in contact with the IRA through an intermediary British Prime Minister John Major told Parliament it would 'turn my stomach' to talk to the leader of its political wing.[25] A government that openly began talks with such opponents would not only suffer severe political damage, it would be stopped before it could even start. The taboo against engagement in some cases is so powerful that public contact is simply impossible. The choice is secret talks or no talks at all.[26] Compromise with opponents can be pursued to a limited degree without direct contact—through tacit communication[27] and public statements, for example—but direct communication is needed if it is to move to a more serious level.

Secrecy allows leaders to protect these sensitive talks from political opponents in parliament and in the public arena who might see short-term advantage in using them to topple or discredit a government. It allows leaders to bypass powerful sections of public opinion opposed to compromise who might mobilise to prevent talks. The key aim of secret talks is to make enough progress and achieve sufficient movement in the positions of both sides that domestic opponents will see the value of engagement because it will already have proved itself. Thus, if Kissinger's 1971 mission to Beijing to pursue a geopolitical rapprochement with China had been publicised in advance, it would have provided a lightning-rod for opposition in Congress and the process might have been stopped. And it might have been so surrounded by unrealistic expectations that the outcome could not be presented as a success but would have been accounted a disappointing failure.[28] Viewed in terms of Putnam's model of international negotiations as two-level games conducted simultaneously at domestic and international level, secrecy allows for one level of the game to be insulated from the other level during the most sensitive and difficult phase.[29] It can be 'played' at the international level without becoming hopelessly entangled in the domestic level until enough progress has been made to win the game at the latter level. The corollary is that if talks are exposed prematurely before sufficient progress has been made, there is a high risk of their ending in scandal and severe political damage. Hence, when a party enters secret talks it is often entrusting its political fate to a sworn enemy, making it all the more remarkable that such contacts take place.

But political opponents and hardline public opinion are not the most important audiences from which contact is concealed in such cases. As theorists of negotiation pointed out long ago fierce intra-party struggles take place on either side of the negotiating divide.[30] These can be so serious that negotiators representing the opposing parties not infrequently find themselves cooperating to help their opponent manage internal divisions on the other side. Those in the middle become allies of a sort, pursuing the shared goal of a successful, mutually acceptable settlement.[31] These internal divisions provide one of the strongest motivations for secret peacemaking: to conceal contact from those within the same organisation who might undermine, expose or hinder engagement. Internal opponents may also try to prevent the implementation of agreements, acting as internal 'spoilers'.[32] Thus, Kissinger's secret contacts with China were aimed partly at bypassing the State Department where there was resistance to compromise and a shift in policy. US Secretary of State William Rogers was only informed of Kissinger's secret visit to Beijing at the last minute.[33]

Secret channels tend to be characterised by the direct involvement of principals and by short chains that involve few people. As Anthony Wanis-St. John notes, back-channel negotiators tend to have better access to decision makers than front-channel negotiators.[34]

They often report directly to senior figures who enjoy privileged access to the top decision makers. The short chain often includes an intermediary who provides a crucial connection at the centre of the chain. In the case of Britain and the IRA those in the back channel reported directly to the British Prime Minister from the earliest stages and various Prime Ministers were directly involved in approving and editing messages to be conveyed through the channel.[35] Given the political sensitivity, a back channel of this kind can only operate effectively if the highest executive authority is available to authorise the bold and risky gestures and statements that are sometimes necessary to sustain contact. Back channels may originate with low-level contacts or track two diplomacy but if they are to develop further, high-level authorisation and support is essential.

In limiting knowledge of contact to a tiny group surrounding the head of the executive, back-channel contact is often screened even from the inner circles at the highest levels of government. In all three of the prominent peace processes of the early 1990s, in South Africa, Israel-Palestine and Northern Ireland, contacts were concealed not only from government ministers but also from senior figures in the military, intelligence and police services.[36]

This reduces the risk that hostile ministers and civil servants will prevent progress and the possibility that security forces focused on winning the 'armed struggle' will oppose or disrupt engagement. Concealing contact from the security forces has other purposes too. Most importantly, it effects some insulation between the struggle for military advantage on the one hand and the efforts to transform relationships and end violent confrontation on the other. It reduces the danger that a back channel's primary purpose could be undermined by the efforts of victory-oriented forces within the state to use it for military advantage. One of the starkest examples comes from the long history of US back channels to Cuba. Members of the CIA's 'executive action' unit learned in 1963 that US envoy James Donovan–a US lawyer who had negotiated prisoner exchange agreements between the United States and the Soviet Union and Cuba in the early 1960s—was to meet secretly with Fidel Castro as an unofficial emissary from the Kennedy Administration and planned to give Castro a present of a scuba diving suit. The CIA unit devised a plan to impregnate the wetsuit with poison, contaminate the snorkel and use the contact as an opportunity to assassinate Castro. It was only the intervention of the two CIA agents who worked with Donovan that prevented the plot.[37]

In every back channel there is a danger that the other side will take advantage of contact to gain a short-term military advantage. Secret meetings might be used as an opportunity to arrest or abduct people; evidence of secret negotiation with illegal organisations could be used to prosecute those involved in talks. For this reason, it is vital that these channels be insulated from agencies or sections of an organisation who might be driven by organisational priorities and policy preferences to use them for military advantage.

Another reason to limit knowledge to a small circle is more prosaic: avoiding leaks. Intelligence and security agencies engage in wide-ranging surveillance. Much of the information they gather circulates widely enough that it may reach people either politically opposed to engagement or inclined to leak for other reasons. Hence, one of the main purposes of secret back channels is to conceal information from one's own security and intelligence agencies. When MI6 officers communicated with the IRA in Northern Ireland through intermediaries from the early 1970s onwards a top priority was to conceal communication from other British intelligence agencies, including the domestic intelligence service, MI5. Speaking to the Bloody Sunday Inquiry[38] in the early 2000s 'David', the MI5 officer who was Director and Coordinator of Intelligence in Northern Ireland in the early 1970s, commented somewhat unhappily:

> I had no contact with the MI6 set-up ... they were operating on a separate brief and I did not control their operation or activities in any way ... I have no knowledge of their activities ... and I was certainly never consulted or asked to clear any of their operations.'[39]

Concealing contact from other state agencies helps to prevent leaks and sustain the process, but implementing any agreement made through back channels ultimately requires the assistance and support of these agencies and of the wider public. While this is often forthcoming when talks come into the open it has been argued that keeping secrets from other state agencies is one of the weaknesses of back-channel deals, and one of the reasons why implementation of a peace agreement can be so difficult.[40] State agencies, particularly security forces, play a leading role in implementation: withdrawing troops, returning territory, safeguarding rights and carrying out changes that may threaten powerful interests. Having been left out of negotiations they may feel little sense of ownership or responsibility. In the Israeli case the Oslo accords that were surrounded by so many high hopes are said to have collapsed partly because of this issue. The argument implies that if contact had been in the open these various forces would have developed a greater sense of ownership and might have been more enthusiastic about implementation. Given the sensitivity of the process, however, we might equally well conclude that if the agencies that were reluctant to implement the deal had been involved at an earlier stage they might have prevented any compromise in the first place.

It is also argued that peace agreements that originate in secret back channels without civil society participation can undermine public confidence and may be rejected by the public:

> Although the exclusion of civil society from peace negotiations may streamline the process, the absence of civil society voices and interests at the negotiating table can negatively impact the sustainability of a peace agreement during peacebuilding.[41]

One way to bolster the legitimacy of such agreements is by submitting them to public approval in a referendum, as was done successfully in Northern Ireland in 1998 and unsuccessfully in Colombia in 2016. The role of peace referendums is discussed by Joana Amaral in her chapter in this volume.

CONTROLLING COMMUNICATION

Clarity is another advantage of back-channel communication. Even where they don't oppose talks, audiences have a powerful shaping effect on communication, making it more difficult to compromise or to explore new possibilities, and reducing clarity. This is partly a result of the 'audience effect'.[42] Speakers tailor their messages to the audiences they are addressing, and it can be difficult to simultaneously address several very different audiences, as is necessary when one speaks at the same time to domestic supporters and external antagonists.

Nicholson provides the example of the ancient Greek city states which insisted that all addresses to foreign monarchs and negotiations with them be conducted in public.[43] This was born of suspicion of secret contact and a fear of treachery by political leaders.[44] The main consequence was that communication that might have been oriented to reaching an agreement with the opponent was addressed instead to a domestic audience with the aim of advancing the speaker's position in internal struggles. Instructions to negotiators became so restrictive that compromise was rendered impossible. It was so ineffective that the practice was abandoned.[45] Apart from the tug away from compromise that public communication exerts, it distorts communication and makes it difficult to distinguish internally directed messages from those directed to the opponent.

When speakers attempt to address an armed opponent in a public speech it can be difficult for the opponent to disentangle those signals meant for them from the others, to divine whether an ambiguous statement is intended as a rejection of compromise or might in fact be a conciliatory gesture bundled up with a statement of firmness intended for a domestic audience. The audience effect is important at the microlevel too. As Walton and McKersie have noted, if there are more people in the negotiating room they often start to perform for the other representatives on their own side, seeking to shore up their position within the group rather than focusing on constructive engagement with those on the other side. This is another reason why the most sensitive negotiations are often conducted by just two or three people on each side.[46] It reduces intra-group struggles and internally oriented communication, making for greater clarity of communication and easing the path to compromise. It also helps to create a sense of common purpose and cooperation in managing intra-party struggles on both sides of the divide.[47]

But secrecy can also undermine the effectiveness of communication across the divide. If neither side can publicly acknowledge contact, it makes it much more difficult to judge the commitment and authority of those at the other end of the line or indeed to confirm whether there is anyone at the other end of the line at all. This is particularly difficult when intermediaries are involved. Research on a US backchannel to Soviet premier Nikita Khrushchev during the Cuban Missile crisis now shows the back channel didn't actually reach as far as Khrushchev: the KGB intermediary's key report on contact with the US made it as far as the KGB Chairman but no further.[48] PLO officials in the Oslo process believed that their interlocutors were acting on behalf of the Israeli Prime Minister Rabin and Foreign Minister Peres from the beginning. In fact, the back channel had been opened without the knowledge of either man and two rounds of negotiation had been completed by the time they were made aware of it.[49] In one well-known incident, an Afghan intermediary put the US and Afghan Governments in contact with a senior Taliban leader. After three secret meetings with Afghan and NATO officials, and after paying him sizeable sums of money, the Americans realised the supposed Taliban leader was an imposter.[50] Secret negotiation creates distinctive barriers of its own to clarity and accuracy of communication, providing fertile ground for Walter Mittys, self-promoters and fantasists of every description.

In assessing the accuracy of messages received through a back channel, the first step is to establish the legitimacy of the channel. Does it actually connect to those it claims to connect to? Both sides need clear signs that their interlocutors have access to, and can get a response from, the highest levels of power on the other side. Legitimacy is often established through the coordination of private and public communication. Thus, a message whose text is secretly agreed between the parties through the back channel can be inserted into a public speech by a government minister as happened in Northern Ireland in 1972.[51] Or one party might provide a copy of a public speech in advance, highlighting the passages that are intended as a message to the opponent. The very fact of giving the text in advance of public delivery is a signal in its own right, a confidence-building measure that points up the importance of the temporalities of communication. If the message is communicated privately in advance of public distribution, and the specific lines that are meant to be conciliatory are pointed out, it gives clarity to the message that is lost if parties attempt to explain or spin the message in retrospect. The clarity that comes with direct confidential communication without an audience is one of the greatest strengths of secret communication. Combining it with public statements allows both sides to demonstrate they are willing to say in public the things they say in private.

Another way to demonstrate the legitimacy of a channel is through action. In 1981 for example, the British Prime Minister secretly authorised a visit by a senior Irish Republican leader to IRA prisoners on hunger strike.[52] It demonstrated to the IRA that the channel involved the highest levels of the British state. Importantly, both statements and actions have to be communicated through secret channels *before* they take place.

This testing of legitimacy of the channel is closely allied to the testing of authority.[53] Do your interlocutors have sufficient control over their own forces to take authoritative decisions? Do they have the capacity to implement their side of any agreement, and will they be willing to stand by their positions when it comes time to make them public? A central feature of covert diplomacy is the gradual building of trust in the other's legitimacy, authority and discretion. It is a cumulative process in which increasing levels of trust facilitate increasing communication. That said, there is often a measure of deception involved. Channels can be built by an intermediary who initially exaggerates their level of access to party A in order to get access to party B. Having secured access to party B, the intermediary can then use this genuine access to get access to party

A. Beginning with an exaggerated claim may be essential to realising the claim.

One further aspect of private communication is worthy of mention here—its impact on commitment. Condemning the controversial and disruptive effect of Kaiser Wilhelm II's public pronouncements on sensitive diplomatic issues in the approach to the First World War Max Weber pointed out the damaging impact of such public statements:

> once he [the Kaiser] has committed himself personally in *public*, any attempt to take back his words, as required by the changed situation, will be in vain. Passions and the *sense of honour* have been aroused… Both at home and abroad people cling *permanently* to the words once they have been uttered, and the situation become intractable.[54]

It might have been valuable to make the same points in private through diplomatic channels, Weber argues, but public communication casually, and sometimes unintentionally, established strong commitments that limited the German government's room for manoeuvre and helped to produce the opposite outcome to the one they sought. The problem is exacerbated in the twentieth-first century by the use of social networking tools that provide multiple new platforms on which leaders can make rash and unwise commitments. Avoiding public commitments makes it easier to modify positions as relationships develop and circumstances change. Private contact behind the scenes has the advantage of lowering the public commitment attached to the expression of views and exchange of positions. It is one of the reasons why a figure such as Kennedy's envoy to Cuba, James Donovan, could negotiate so effectively. Operating with the knowledge of the CIA but acting alone and as a private citizen, he could negotiate compromises without committing the US government in any way until a deal had been agreed,[55] an approach dramatised in Steven Spielberg's 2015 film *Bridge of Spies*, based on Donovan's 1964 memoir *Strangers on a Bridge*.[56]

LEGITIMACY AND INTERMEDIARIES

Back-channel communication has particular benefits in asymmetric conflicts where states face non-state armed groups. Governments are inhibited from publicly engaging with such groups because engagement risks according them a kind of recognition as legitimate interlocutors and combatants. This undermines state framing of armed opponents as criminal and illegitimate, a framing that is important to sustaining public support for the state as well as the motivation and morale of the armed forces. Engaging publicly with armed opponents also makes an important political concession that a government might want to withhold until they are more certain of reaching agreement.[57] Back-channel contact allows states to communicate and negotiate with violent oppositional forces without conceding legitimacy. In agreeing to maintain secrecy about these contacts, rebel groups sacrifice the political gains that would come with public recognition.

This brings us to the role of mediators and intermediaries, one of whose vital functions is to permit communication without direct contact and thus ensure that contact remains deniable and legitimacy is not conceded.[58] Intermediaries and mediators were crucial in Nixon's 1971 engagement with China and they were vital to the three peace processes of the 1990s discussed above. The first qualification of an intermediary is discretion.

It can also help if the intermediary has little power of their own because they don't then bring the same public interests as a politician or public figure might, and they don't have the capacity or profile to damage the parties to negotiation by attaching blame to one or the other if talks break down.[59] Secrecy enhances the influence an intermediary can wield because each party relies on him or her for information about the position of the other. An intermediary can promote agreement by delicately managing the flow of information between the parties: for example, passing on one element of a communication while holding back another element until it has the potential to make a greater positive impact. If negotiations become deadlocked and both sides are refusing to move, the intermediary can pass on the delayed information and thereby give one side the impression that the other side has made a move, stimulating a response and thereby restarting engagement without either side having to make the first move. Where a mediator is committed to the process and does not distort the substance of positions, this can be to the benefit of both sides, allowing them to move forward without conceding ground. It can be useful to remain ignorant of why the other party moved if it brings both parties to a point they wanted to reach. Thus, when IRA and British government representatives met in 1976 for the first time in several months the British began by noting that the IRA had requested the meeting. The IRA corrected them, stating that it was the British who had asked for the meeting. In fact, the intermediary, businessman Brendan Duddy, had told both sides that the other side wanted to meet. But now that they were there in the room together they simply glided past this issue and moved on to substantive discussion.[60]

Conclusion: Peace and Secrecy

Secret contact takes place now in a radically different, and rapidly changing, information environment. It was always difficult to hide sensitive meetings from prying eyes but with the greater penetration of space and the acceleration of time brought about by new technologies, secrets cannot be kept as long, and hidden spaces are more exposed to surveillance. Some argue that the time of secrecy is over, and that it is no longer viable.[61] The view that secrecy is less and less feasible is allied to a continuing condemnation of secrecy that echoes the rhetoric of the early twentieth century.[62] But announcements of the death of secrecy are premature. Every leak alerts states to their vulnerabilities and prompts them to tighten up security, and new technologies of concealment are under constant development.[63] In certain ways the level of transparency in public life has never been lower. With the growth of 'algorithmic governance' biases are built into governance structures and it becomes increasingly difficult to identify the assumptions and decisions that inform the software.[64] With ever more complex and opaque ICT systems transparency becomes even harder to achieve.

In many ways the new technologies make secrecy more important than ever. If the information does leak it can be disseminated worldwide within seconds, making it all the more important to control it tightly. Conflict can escalate much more rapidly, stoked by the rapid circulation of news media and the manipulation of opinion online. It is ever more important that delicate negotiations be allowed to continue without being disrupted by struggles for short-term political advantage.

Back-channel negotiators have always had to concern themselves with leaks and these channels have never been completely watertight. Many of the benefits of secrecy do not in fact depend on its completeness. A 'shared secret' may leak beyond those who are meant to know but the fact that everyone decides not to talk about it in public keeps it a secret of sorts and maintains many of the benefits of secrecy. Even if public opponents of engagement learn of secret contacts, they may allow talks to continue if they think the outcome might ultimately benefit them. In such cases the value of secrecy is that parties whose supporters might expect them to oppose compromise are not forced to take up hostile stances opposing engagement. Back-channel contacts may deliver goals that even the most hardline opponents of contact value and would wish to see pursued and achieved. If compromise and conciliation is exposed it forces them to take a public position on the matter and demonstrate their toughness to their own constituents. If contact proceeds secretly, they can benefit from the developments without ever being implicated in supporting them.

Weber's argument that full transparency in peace negotiations can be a danger to peace has stood the test of time. Secret contact eases the pressures for escalation and over-commitment. It allows short-term struggles for political advantage, efforts to sway people with escalatory rhetoric, and intra-party struggles, to be bracketed long enough to establish whether a compromise is possible and to make enough progress that those who might have opposed engagement can come to see its value.

It doesn't always work, and it is no more certain to produce peace than transparency is. But it allows for a clarity of communication that has immense practical value and allows states to engage without conceding legitimacy to non-state opponents. It allows all sides to test the other side's reliability, trustworthiness and authority. Ultimately however it is much more than just a mechanism for ensuring clear communication between parties to the conflict. It is a site at which struggles within parties crystallise, a site at which parties themselves gradually learn how far they can move and are forced to finalise their own positions, making sure they stay aligned with their public positions but moving gradually away from extreme and uncompromising public rhetoric. Above all, back-channel communication, when it works, contributes to transforming the broader relationships between opponents in the most intractable conflicts.[65] They can begin to work together on a shared project of secrecy, develop limited trust, learn about the limits the opponent can go to and ultimately begin to develop a new and less violently confrontational relationship.

Notes

1. S. Bok, *Secrets: On the Ethics of Concealment and Revelation* (New York: Pantheon Books, 1982).
2. Ibid.
3. T. More, *Utopia* (Cambridge: Cambridge University Press, 1989 [1516]).

4. A.M. Low, 'The vice of secret diplomacy', *The North American Review*, 207, 747 (1918) pp. 209–220, p. 210.
5. A.S. Klieman, *Statecraft in the Dark: Israel's Practice of Quiet Diplomacy* (Boulder: Westview, 1988), p. 9.
6. M. Fenster, 'Disclosure's effects: WikiLeaks and transparency', *Iowa Law Review*, 97, 3 (2012) pp. 753–807, pp. 755–756; D. Leigh & L. Harding, *WikiLeaks: Inside Julian Assange's War on Secrecy* (London: Guardian Books, 2011); W.E. Scheuerman, 'Whistleblowing as civil disobedience: the case of Edward Snowden', *Philosophy & Social Criticism*, 40, 7 (2014) pp. 609–628.
7. J. Jarvis, 'Welcome to the end of secrecy', *The Guardian* (13 April 2013). www.theguardian.com/commentisfree/2013/sep/06/nsa-surveillance-welcome-end-secrecy; A. Roberts, 'WikiLeaks: the illusion of transparency', *International Review of Administrative Sciences*, 78, 1 (2012) pp. 116–133.
8. D.P. Fidler, *The Snowden Reader* (Bloomington: Indiana University Press, 2015).
9. M. Weber, 'Parliament and government in Germany under a new political order'. In P. Lassman & R. Speirs (eds), *Weber: Political Writings* (Cambridge: Cambridge University Press, 1994 [1918]) pp. 130–271, p. 186. Emphasis in the original.
10. R. Low (1918), op. cit., p. 212.
11. C. Bjola & S. Murray, *Secret Diplomacy: Concepts, Contexts and Cases* (London: Routledge, 2016); D. Lieberfeld, 'Secrecy and "two-level games" in the Oslo Accord: What the primary sources tell us', *International Negotiation*, 13, 1 (2008) pp. 133–146; N. Ó Dochartaigh, 'Together in the middle: Back-channel negotiation in the Irish peace process', *Journal of Peace Research*, 48, 6 (2011) pp. 767–780; N. Ó Dochartaigh, *Deniable Contact: Back-Channel Negotiation in Northern Ireland* (Oxford: Oxford University Press: 2021); D.G. Pruitt, 'Back-channel communication in the settlement of conflict', *International Negotiation* 13, 1 (2008) pp. 37–54; A. Wanis-St. John, 'Back-channel negotiation: International bargaining in the shadows', *Negotiation Journal* 22, 2 (2006) pp. 119–144; A. Wanis-St. John, *Back Channel Negotiation: Secrecy in the Middle East Peace Process* (Syracuse: Syracuse University Press, 2011).
12. M. Lundgren, 'Mediation in Syria: Initiatives, strategies, and obstacles, 2011–2016', *Contemporary Security Policy*, 37, 2 (2016)

pp. 273–288; B.R. Rubin, 'Negotiations Are the Best Way to End the War in Afghanistan', *Foreign Affairs* (1 March 2019).
13. H. Kissinger, *White House Years* (Boston: Little Brown and Co, 1979); A.S. Klieman (1988) op. cit., p. 23.
14. A.S. Klieman (1988) op. cit.
15. B. Gidron, S.N. Katz & Y. Hasenfeld, *Mobilizing for Peace: Conflict Resolution in Northern Ireland, Israel/Palestine, and South Africa* (Oxford: Oxford University Press, 2002); D. Lieberfeld, 'Evaluating the contributions of track-two diplomacy to conflict termination in South Africa, 1984–90', *Journal of Peace Research*, 39, 3 (2002) pp. 355–372; R. Mac Ginty & J. Darby, *Guns and Government: The Management of the Northern Ireland Peace Process* (Basingstoke: Palgrave, 2002); D. Makovsky, *Making Peace with the PLO: The Rabin Government's Road to the Oslo Accord* (London: Routledge, 1996). A. Wanis-St. John (2011) op. cit.
16. J.T. Rogers, *Oslo: A Play* (New York: Theatre Communications Group, 2017).
17. L. Kriesberg, 'Mediation and the transformation of the Israeli–Palestinian conflict', *Journal of Peace Research*, 38, 3 (2001) pp. 373–392; E. Mallie & D. McKittrick (1996) *The Fight for Peace: The Secret Story Behind the Irish Peace Process* (London: Heinemann, 1996); H. Waage, '"Peacemaking is a risky business": Norway's role in the peace process in the Middle East, 1993–96' (Oslo: International Peace Research Institute Oslo, 2004); A. Wanis-St. John (2011) op. cit.
18. N. Ó Dochartaigh (2011) op. cit.; D.G. Pruitt, 'Negotiation with terrorists', *International Negotiation*, 11, 2 (2006) pp. 371–394. D.G. Pruitt (2008) op. cit.; L. Putnam, & M. Carcasson 'Communication and the Oslo Negotiation: contacts, patterns, and modes', *International Negotiation*, 2, 2 (1997) pp. 251–278; A. Wanis-St. John (2006, 2011) op. cit.
19. G.W. Bush, 'President to send Secretary Powell to Middle East', *Vital Speeches of the Day*, 68, 13 (2002) p. 388.
20. J. Dobbins, & C. Malkasian, 'Time to negotiate in Afghanistan: how to talk to the Taliban', *Foreign Affairs*, 94, 4 (2015) pp. 53–64; T. Farrell & M. Semple, 'Making peace with the Taliban', *Survival*, 57, 6 (2015) pp. 79–110; Lundgrun (2016) op. cit.; Rubin (2019) op. cit.

21. J.A. McCary, 'The Anbar Awakening: An alliance of incentives', *The Washington Quarterly*, 32, 1 (2009) pp. 43–59.
22. M. Mashal, 'U.S. and Taliban agree in principle to peace framework, envoy says', *New York Times* (28 Jan 2019); Rubin (2019) op. cit.
23. BBC News, 'Trump cancels secret US meeting with Afghan Taliban', *BBC News* (8 September 2019), https://www.bbc.com/news/world-asia-49624132.
24. Wanis-St. John (2011) op. cit., p. 36.
25. Mallie & McKittrick (1996) op. cit., p. 212.
26. Lieberfeld (2008) op. cit., p. 138.
27. T.C. Schelling, *The Strategy of Conflict* (Cambridge, MA: Harvard University Press, 1980).
28. Klieman (1988) op. cit., p. 21.
29. D. Lieberfeld (2008) op. cit.: R.D. Putnam, 'Diplomacy and domestic politics: the logic of two-level games', *International Organization*, 42, 3 (1988) pp. 427–460.
30. R.E. Walton & R.B. McKersie, *A Behavioral Theory of Labor Negotiations: An Analysis of a Social Interaction System* (Ithaca: Cornell University Press, 1991).
31. N. Ó Dochartaigh (2011) op. cit.; R.E. Walton & R.B. McKersie (1991) op. cit., p. 299.
32. S.J. Stedman, 'Spoiler problems in peace processes', *International Security*, 22, 2 (1997) pp. 5–53.
33. Klieman (1988) op. cit., p. 23.
34. A. Wanis-St. John (2011) op. cit., p. 267.
35. N. Ó Dochartaigh (2021) op. cit.
36. E. Mallie & D. McKittrick (1996) op. cit.; L. Putnam & M. Carcasson (1997) op. cit.; A. Wanis-St. John (2006) op. cit.
37. P.J. Bigger, *Negotiator: The Life and Career of James B. Donovan* (Bethlehem, PA: Lehigh University Press, 2006) pp. 154–155; W.M. LeoGrande & P. Kornbluh, *Back channel to Cuba: The Hidden History of Negotiations Between Washington and Havana* (Chapel Hill: University of North Carolina Press, 2015) pp. 1–2.
38. An Official Inquiry into the events of Bloody Sunday in Derry, Northern Ireland in January 1972 when British soldiers shot dead 13 people at a Civil Rights demonstration.
39. Statement of 'David' to the Bloody Sunday Inquiry, 17 Feb 2000. https://webarchive.nationalarchives.gov.uk/201010170

60841/ http://report.bloody-sunday-inquiry.org/evidence-index/; 'David', oral evidence at the Bloody Sunday Inquiry, 13 May 2003.
40. D. Lieberfeld (2008) op. cit.; D.G. Pruitt (2008) op. cit.; A. Wanis-St. John, 'Peace processes, secret negotiations and civil society', *International Negotiation*, 13 (2008) pp. 443–445; A. Wanis-St. John (2006) op. cit.; A. Wanis-St. John (2011) p. 271.
41. A. Wanis-St. John (2008) op. cit.
42. D.G. Pruitt (2008) op. cit., pp. 41–42; J.Z. Rubin, D.G. Pruitt & S.H. Kim, *Social Conflict: Escalation, Stalemate, and Settlement* (2nd edn) (New York: McGraw-Hill, 1994); A. Wanis-St. John (2011) op. cit., pp. 274–275.
43. H. Nicolson, *The Evolution of Diplomatic Method* (Leicester: University of Leicester Press, 1998) p. 7.
44. S. Murray, 'Secret "versus" open diplomacy across the ages', In C. Bjola and S. Murray (eds) *Secret Diplomacy* (London: Routledge, 2016) pp. 29–45, pp. 15–16.
45. S. Murray (2016) op. cit., p. 16.
46. R.E. Walton & R.B. McKersie (1991) op. cit.
47. N. Ó Dochartaigh (2011) op. cit.; R.E. Walton & R.B. McKersie (1991) op. cit.
48. A. Fursenko & T. Naftali, 'Using KGB documents: The Scali-Feklisov channel in the Cuban missile crisis', *Cold War International History Project Bulletin*, 5, 2 (1995) pp. 58–62; L. Scott, 'Secret intelligence, covert action and clandestine diplomacy', *Intelligence & National Security*, 19, 2 (2004) pp. 322–341.
49. L. Lehrs, 'Private peace entrepreneurs in conflict resolution processes', *International Negotiation*, 21, 3 (2016) pp. 381–408, pp. 389–390.
50. D. Filkins & C. Gall, 'Taliban leader in secret talks was an impostor', *The New York Times* (22 November 2010).
51. Interview by the author with former Sinn Féin President Ruairí Ó Brádaigh, 27 June 2005.
52. D. Beresford, *Ten Men Dead: the Story of the 1981 Irish Hunger Strike* (London: Grafton, 1987).
53. L. Putnam & M. Carcasson (1997) p. 253.
54. M. Weber (1994 [1918]) op. cit., pp. 198–199.
55. P.J. Bigger (2006) op. cit.

56. J.B. Donovan, *Strangers on a Bridge* (New York: Simon & Schuster, 2015), re-print of the 1964 original edition.
57. J. Browne & E.S. Dickson, '"We don't talk to terrorists": On the rhetoric and practice of secret negotiations. *Journal of Conflict Resolution*, 54, 3 (2010) pp. 379–407. D.G. Pruitt (2008) op. cit.; A. Wanis-St. John (2011) op. cit., pp. 277–278.
58. J. Bercovitch, *Resolving International Conflicts: The Theory and Practice of Mediation* (Boulder CO: Lynne Rienner, 1996); T. Princen, *Intermediaries in International Conflict* (Princeton: Princeton University Press, 2014); P. Wallensteen & I. Svensson, 'Talking peace: International mediation in armed conflicts', *Journal of Peace Research*, 51, 2 (2014) pp. 315–327.
59. L. Lehrs (2016) op. cit.; N. Ó Dochartaigh & I. Svensson, 'The exit option: mediation and the termination of negotiations in the Northern Ireland conflict', *International Journal of Conflict Management*, 24, 1 (2013) pp. 40–55.
60. Spun Sugar 10: Meeting with O'Brady [Ó Brádaigh], McKee and McCallion, 10 February 1976, PREM 16/960, UK National Archives.
61. S. Murray, 'Secret "versus" open diplomacy across the ages', In C. Bjola and S. Murray (eds) *Secret Diplomacy* (London: Routledge, 2016) pp. 29–45.
62. C. Bjola, 'Introduction: the theory and practice of secret diplomacy', in C. Bjola and S. Murray (eds) *Secret Diplomacy* (London: Routledge, 2016) pp. 17–26, p. 22.
63. Roberts (2012) op. cit., pp. 128–129.
64. J. Danaher, M.J. Hogan, C. Noone, R. Kennedy, A. Behan, A. de Paor, A. et al., 'Algorithmic governance: Developing a research agenda through the power of collective intelligence', *Big Data & Society*, 4, 2 (2017).
65. J.P. Lederach 'Cultivating peace: A practitioners view of deadly conflict and negotiation'. In J. Darby & R. Mac Ginty (eds), *Contemporary Peacemaking: Conflict, Violence and Peace Processes* (Basingstoke: Palgrave, 2003) pp. 30–37.

Bibliography

BBC News, 'Trump cancels secret US meeting with Afghan Taliban', *BBC News* (8 September 2019), https://www.bbc.com/news/world-asia-49624132.

J. Bercovitch, *Resolving International Conflicts: The Theory and Practice of Mediation* (Boulder, CO: Lynne Rienner, 1996).

D. Beresford, *Ten Men Dead: The Story of the 1981 Irish Hunger Strike* (London: Grafton, 1987).

P.J. Bigger, *Negotiator: The Life and Career of James B. Donovan* (Bethlehem, PA: Lehigh University Press, 2006).

C. Bjola, 'Introduction: the theory and practice of secret diplomacy', in C. Bjola and S. Murray (eds) *Secret Diplomacy* (London: Routledge, 2016), pp. 17–26.

C. Bjola & S. Murray, *Secret Diplomacy: Concepts, Contexts and Cases* (London: Routledge, 2016).

S. Bok, *Secrets: On the Ethics of Concealment and Revelation* (New York: Pantheon Books, 1982).

J. Browne & E.S. Dickson, '"We don't talk to terrorists": On the rhetoric and practice of secret negotiations', *Journal of Conflict Resolution*, 54, 3 (2010), pp. 379–407.

G.W. Bush, 'President to send Secretary Powell to Middle East', *Vital Speeches of the Day*, 68, 13 (2002), p. 388.

J. Danaher, M.J. Hogan, C. Noone, R. Kennedy, A. Behan, A. de Paor, A. et al., 'Algorithmic governance: developing a research agenda through the power of collective intelligence', *Big Data & Society*, 4, 2 (2017).

J. Dobbins, & C. Malkasian, 'Time to negotiate in Afghanistan: how to talk to the Taliban', *Foreign Affairs*, 94, 4 (2015) pp. 53–64.

T. Farrell & M. Semple, 'Making peace with the Taliban', *Survival*, 57, 6 (2015) pp. 79–110.

M. Fenster, 'Disclosure's effects: WikiLeaks and transparency', *Iowa Law Review*, 97, 3 (2012) pp. 753–807.

D.P. Fidler, *The Snowden Reader* (Bloomington: Indiana University Press, 2015).

D. Filkins & C. Gall, 'Taliban leader in secret talks was an impostor', *The New York Times* (22 November 2010).

A. Fursenko & T. Naftali, 'Using KGB documents: The Scali-Feklisov channel in the Cuban missile crisis', *Cold War International History Project Bulletin*, 5, 2 (1995) pp. 58–62.

B. Gidron, S.N. Katz & Y. Hasenfeld, *Mobilizing for Peace: Conflict Resolution in Northern Ireland, Israel/Palestine, and South Africa* (Oxford: Oxford University Press, 2002).

J. Jarvis, 'Welcome to the end of secrecy', *The Guardian* (13 April 2013). www.theguardian.com/commentisfree/2013/sep/06/nsa-surveillance-welcome-end-secrecy.

H. Kissinger, *White House Years* (Boston: Little Brown and Co, 1979).

A.S. Klieman, *Statecraft in the Dark: Israel's Practice of Quiet Diplomacy* (Boulder: Westview, 1988).

L. Kriesberg, 'Mediation and the transformation of the Israeli–Palestinian conflict', *Journal of Peace Research* 38, 3 (2001) pp. 373–392.

J.P. Lederach 'Cultivating peace: A practitioners view of deadly conflict and negotiation'. In J. Darby & R. Mac Ginty (eds), *Contemporary Peacemaking: Conflict, Violence and Peace Processes* (Basingstoke: Palgrave, 2003) pp. 30–37.

L. Lehrs, 'Private Peace Entrepreneurs in conflict resolution processes', *International Negotiation*, 21, 3 (2016) pp. 381–408.

D. Leigh & L. Harding, *WikiLeaks: Inside Julian Assange's War on Secrecy* (London: Guardian Books, 2011).

W.M. LeoGrande & P. Kornbluh, *Back Channel to Cuba: The Hidden History of Negotiations Between Washington and Havana* (Chapel Hill: University of North Carolina Press, 2015).

D. Lieberfeld, 'Evaluating the contributions of track-two diplomacy to conflict termination in South Africa, 1984–90', *Journal of Peace Research* 39, 3 (2002) pp. 355–372.

D. Lieberfeld, 'Secrecy and "two-level games" in the Oslo Accord: What the primary sources tell us', *International Negotiation*, 13, 1 (2008) pp. 133–146.

A.M. Low, 'The vice of secret diplomacy', *The North American Review*, 207, 747 (1918) pp. 209–220.

M. Lundgren, 'Mediation in Syria: Initiatives, strategies, and obstacles, 2011–2016', *Contemporary Security Policy*, 37, 2 (2016) pp. 273–288.

J.A. McCary, 'The Anbar Awakening: an alliance of incentives', *The Washington Quarterly* 32, 1 (2009) pp. 43–59.

R. Mac Ginty & J. Darby, *Guns and Government: The Management of the Northern Ireland Peace Process* (Basingstoke: Palgrave, 2002).

D. Makovsky, *Making Peace with the PLO: The Rabin Government's Road to the Oslo Accord* (London: Routledge, 1996).

E. Mallie & D. McKittrick (1996) *The Fight for Peace: The Secret Story Behind the Irish Peace Process* (London: Heinemann, 1996).

M. Mashal, 'U.S. and Taliban Agree in Principle to Peace Framework, Envoy Says'. *New York Times* (28 Jan 2019).

T. More, *Utopia* (Cambridge: Cambridge University Press, 1989 [1516]).

S. Murray, 'Secret "versus" open diplomacy across the ages'. In C. Bjola & S. Murray (eds) *Secret Diplomacy* (London: Routledge, 2016) pp. 29–45.

H. Nicolson, *The Evolution of Diplomatic Method* (Leicester: University of Leicester Press, 1998)

N. Ó Dochartaigh, 'Together in the middle: Back-channel negotiation in the Irish peace process', *Journal of Peace Research*, 48, 6 (2011) pp. 767–780.

N. Ó Dochartaigh, *Deniable Contact: Back-Channel Negotiation in Northern Ireland* (Oxford: Oxford University Press, 2021).

N. Ó Dochartaigh & I. Svensson, 'The Exit Option: Mediation and the Termination of Negotiations in the Northern Ireland Conflict', *International Journal of Conflict Management*, 24, 1 (2013) pp. 40–55.

T. Princen, *Intermediaries in International Conflict* (Princeton: Princeton University Press, 2014).

D.G. Pruitt, 'Negotiation with terrorists', *International Negotiation* 11, 2 (2006) pp. 371–394.

D.G. Pruitt, 'Back-channel communication in the settlement of conflict', *International Negotiation* 13, 1 (2008) pp. 37–54.

R.D. Putnam, 'Diplomacy and domestic politics: the logic of two-level games', *International Organization*, 42, 3 (1988) pp. 427–460.

L. Putnam, & M. Carcasson 'Communication and the Oslo Negotiation: contacts, patterns, and modes', *International Negotiation* 2, 2 (1997) pp. 251–278.

A. Roberts, 'WikiLeaks: the illusion of transparency', *International Review of Administrative Sciences*, 78, 1 (2012) pp. 116–133.

J.T. Rogers, *Oslo: A Play* (New York: Theatre Communications Group, 2017).

J.Z. Rubin, D.G. Pruitt & S.H. Kim, *Social Conflict: Escalation, Stalemate, and Settlement* (2nd edn) (New York: McGraw-Hill, 1994).

B.R. Rubin, 'Negotiations are the best way to end the war in Afghanistan', *Foreign Affairs* (1 March 2019).

T.C. Schelling, *The Strategy of Conflict* (Cambridge, MA: Harvard University Press, 1980).

W.E. Scheuerman, 'Whistleblowing as civil disobedience: the case of Edward Snowden', *Philosophy & Social Criticism*, 40, 7 (2014) pp. 609–628.

L. Scott, 'Secret intelligence, covert action and clandestine diplomacy', *Intelligence & National Security*, 19, 2 (2004) pp. 322–341.

S.J. Stedman, 'Spoiler Problems in Peace Processes', *International Security*, 22, 2 (1997) pp. 5–53.

H. Waage, '"Peacemaking is a risky business": Norway's role in the peace process in the Middle East, 1993–96' (Oslo: International Peace Research Institute Oslo, 2004).

P. Wallensteen & I. Svensson, 'Talking peace: International mediation in armed conflicts', *Journal of Peace Research*, 51, 2 (2014) pp. 315–327.

R.E. Walton & R.B. McKersie, *A Behavioral Theory of Labor Negotiations: An Analysis of a Social Interaction System* (Ithaca: Cornell University Press, 1991).

A. Wanis-St. John, 'Back-channel negotiation: International bargaining in the shadows', *Negotiation Journal* 22, 2 (2006) pp. 119–144.

A. Wanis-St. John, 'Peace processes, secret negotiations and civil society', *International Negotiation*, 13 (2008) pp. 443–445.

A. Wanis-St. John, *Back Channel Negotiation: Secrecy in the Middle East Peace Process* (Syracuse: Syracuse University Press, 2011).

M. Weber, 'Parliament and government in Germany under a new political order'. In P. Lassman & R. Speirs (eds), *Weber: Political Writings* (Cambridge: Cambridge University Press, 1994 [1918]) pp. 130–271.

PART IV

Violence and Peace Processes

CHAPTER 15

Violence and Peace Processes

Kristine Höglund and Desirée Nilsson

INTRODUCTION

Car bombings, kidnappings, political assassinations, conventional battles and street protests. These are all types of violence that can occur conjointly with efforts to negotiate and implement peace. This chapter addresses the role of violence as an influence on peace negotiations. We look at its main characteristics in terms of the actors involved, targets and motives, as well as chart the main modes by which domestic and international actors seek to prevent and stop violence that threaten to undermine peace efforts.

We approach this topic from the perspective that most peace agreements are negotiated and implemented in the midst of violence. Eradicating violence and building peace are what motivate a peace process in

---

K. Höglund (✉) · D. Nilsson
Department of Peace and Conflict Research, Uppsala University, Uppsala, Sweden
e-mail: Kristine.Hoglund@pcr.uu.se

D. Nilsson
e-mail: desiree.nilsson@pcr.uu.se

the first place. However, as peace talks begin violence tend to continue because it can be used strategically to influence the conduct and outcome of negotiations. While violence in different forms can fester long after the warring parties have laid down their arms, our focal point is violence taking place in conjunction to the peace negotiations and the direct efforts to close the war, including the implementation of peace agreements.[1]

Violence occurring parallel to peace negotiations can effectively hinder advancement to agreement and consolidation of peace by reducing trust between negotiating parties and causing crises in a negotiation process. On rare instances, it can also remind parties of the costs associated with failure to reach agreement: basically inspiring cooler heads to prevail and motivating parties to try harder to reach an agreement.[2] Violence is sometimes regulated by significant efforts by the parties to the negotiations and thus managed within the peace processes.[3] However, here we focus primarily on how other domestic and international actors—mediators, INGOs and NGOs, neighbouring or concerned countries—seek to manage violence that is carried out during a peace process and how they seek to minimize its destructive effects.

In this chapter, we identify and discuss three main approaches used by domestic and international actors that seek to address violence in the context of a peace process. A first approach is to influence violence makers via dialogue and negotiation, the *conflict resolution* approach. A second is to pursue a coercive approach commonly involving the use of force to compel actors into refraining from violence, here labelled the *security* approach. Third, is the *rights-based* approach where any type of violence is considered a human rights problem and perpetrators of violence must be held accountable. Before outlining these modes of violence management in more detail, we describe some of the key characteristics of the violence occurring within peace processes with a particular focus on the actors, targets, and motives for violence occurring in the context of negotiations.

Forms of Violence: Actors, Targets and Motives

Violence may take place before, during or after a period of negotiations and can take many different forms during a peace process. Scholars interested in the dynamics of violence in peace processes have long focused on understanding patterns of violence between the main belligerents in civil war. Yet, the scholarly field has broadened to more carefully consider and explore also other forms of violence. The termination of battlefield violence between a government and one or more rebel groups—measured in terms of the intensity of such violence—is often seen to mark the ending of a civil war.[4] While a ceasefire agreement is sometimes a prerequisite for the warring parties to enter peace talks, violence involving these actors frequently occurs in parallel to peace negotiations, regardless of whether a ceasefire is in place or not. Peace processes can, thus, see the continuation of violence on the battlefield, but frequently also include a varied set of violent behaviours, such as attacks on civilians, sexual violence, kidnappings, car bombings, attacks on peacekeepers, electoral violence or various forms of criminal violence.

Two types of influences of violence on peace processes are important to consider. First, there are specific incidents of violence, usually of a high-profile kind. Such incidents include the assassination of political leaders, massacres, attacks on buildings of strategic or symbolic value (e.g. religious buildings or economic centres), but also repressive actions by governments, such as Israel's detention of activists aboard the Ship to Gaza, a vessel shipping humanitarian goods to Gaza in a civil obedience action intended to break the blockade on Gaza. Second, peace processes are also impacted by the broader trends of violence. For instance, all peace efforts in Afghanistan over the past decade have taken place in the shadow of ongoing Taliban violence against civilians. Similarly, negotiations to end the armed conflicts that have engulfed Sudan's Darfur region since 2003, have been taking place against the backdrop of large-scale violence targeting civilians.

Diverse motivations underlie the various forms of violence during peace processes. A key driving force behind violence during negotiations relates to attempts to spoil the peace effort. Stephen Stedman coined the concept of spoilers, referring to 'leaders and factions who view a particular peace as opposed to their interests and who are willing to use violence to undermine it'.[5] While some violent attacks occur due to strategic or tactical motivations and are related to the main fault lines in the civil war, at other times violence during peace processes can be driven by leaders' individual motivation to remain in power or be based on economic gains generated by a continuation of violence, enjoyed by both top leaders and their followers. In many instances, the parties have a vested interest in violence; and therefore envisage few benefits with a move towards peace.

According to Stedman, spoilers can be found on the *inside* as well as the *outside* of a peace process, an important distinction for understanding the motives of violence. Whereas actors participating in the negotiations have made some form of commitment to pursue peace talks, or even signed on to a peace agreement, actors who do not partake may either have deliberately opted out of the peace process, or have been excluded by the parties already committed to the peace process.[6] It is not uncommon for excluded rebel factions to continue to fight following the signing of a peace deal. In Burundi in 2003, the Palipehutu-National Forces of Liberation (FNL) continued to fight after the National Council for the Defence of Democracy–Forces for the Defence of Democracy (CNDD–FDD) had joined the peace process and signed a peace deal with the government. In Colombia, the peace agreement reached in 2016 between the government and the rebel movement Revolutionary Armed Forces of Colombia (FARC), left out the rebel group National Liberation Army (ELN). While the ELN also has engaged in peace talks with the government, violent attacks have continued to occur in parallel to such negotiation attempts.[7] Violence is, however, also perpetrated by actors who partake in the negotiations. Sometimes, such violence serves as a deliberate strategy to renegotiate the terms of the deal. In other cases, the violence can be accidents or pre-emptive attacks, or be driven by the parties' concerns for their own security, or be economically motivated.[8] For instance, in August 1996, Guatemala's peace process almost came to a complete halt due to the kidnapping of a wealthy businesswoman, Olga Alvarado de Novella. She was taken hostage by one of the factions of the rebel group URNG that had been negotiating for peace with the government for years and which had already resulted in a series of partial agreements. The economically motivated incident caused a major dent in the relationship between the negotiating parties and the negotiations could only be brought back on track after intense shuttle diplomacy by the UN mediator Jean Arnault.[9]

The set of actors perpetrating violent events can also be very diverse and may include government and rebel factions, paramilitary groups, militias, criminal networks, militaries of foreign governments, as well as peacekeepers. Just as the perpetrators of violence are manifold, so are the targets of violence. While some violence is carried out between the government, on the one hand, and the rebel side, on the other, or between different rebel factions, the targets of violence frequently include also other types of armed actors, as well as non-armed groups. For example, we know that a significant proportion of the violence occurring in many civil wars is carried out against civilians, both indiscriminate violence and targeted violence against certain collectives, such as an ethnic group. Peacekeepers are sometimes perpetrators of violence directed at armed actors and in some cases against civilians, and may also become the deliberate targets of violent attacks.[10]

In civil wars consisting of many actors engaging in violence, the increased complexity involved can make peace negotiations more vulnerable and risk reducing the prospects for peace. This is partly due to the multiple sources from which violence can arise.[11] The peace processes in Mali and Syria are in many ways illustrative of these dynamics. In Mali, following the signing of the Bamako agreement between the Government of Mali and the two coalitions on the rebel side—Coordination of Azawad Movements (CMA) and Platform—the process has been fraught with various forms of violence such as terrorist attacks, violence against peacekeepers, clashes between the main warring actors, as well as violent events involving Islamist extremist groups such as AQIM (al-Qaeda in the Islamic Maghreb), but also criminal groups.[12] In Syria, the large-scale violence has been extremely multifaceted and involved the Assad regime and a severely fractionalized rebel side where the many rebel factions have been fighting alongside as well as against each other. In addition, many foreign governments have been active as warring parties to the conflict. Throughout the civil war and the tenuous peace talks, civilians have been targets of various forms of violence, including aerial bombings, battle violence, as well as sexual violence. In the Syrian case, one of the many challenges in the different rounds of peace talks has been to identify and include valid spokespersons for all armed as well as unarmed actors. The problem of valid spokespersons[13] is, however, only partly the result of a larger number of actors, and even in contexts where fragmentation does not permeate the situation, the question of valid spokespersons is central for the negotiations.

In sum, across peace processes there is great diversity, not only in terms of the type of actors involved and the degree of fragmentation among the warring parties, but also in the forms of violence and the targets of attacks, as well as the reasons and motives underlying the violence. Violence during peace efforts is thus a multifaceted challenge, and next we discuss common approaches to manage it.

Managing Violence

How is violence managed within a peace process? Based on how domestic and international actors perceive and address violence in peace processes, three distinct approaches can be discerned. We refer to these as (1) the conflict resolution approach, (2) the security approach and, finally, (3) the rights-based approach.[14] Domestic and international actors—mediators, INGOs and NGOs, neighbouring or concerned countries—frequently become engaged in peace processes and their roles vary from being directly involved as mediators and facilitators of the peace talks, to being supporters of the peace efforts by providing political and material support. For instance, a number of peace processes have witnessed the existence of groups of countries, donors or organisations coming together as custodians of specific peace initiatives. As an example, the peace talks to end violence between the Philippine government and the MILF (Moro Islamic Liberation Front), leading up to the Comprehensive Agreement on the Bangsamoro in 2015, involved a wide range of actors: the Malaysian facilitator, the International Monitoring Team (consisting of several countries as well as the EU) and the International Contact Group which was made up of Japan, Saudi Arabia, Turkey, the UK, as well as four international NGOs.

The conflict resolution approach, the security approach and the rights-based approach all feature in the realm of practice, policy and research and here we will specifically problematize implications of each approach for how violence is managed within a negotiation process. For analytical purposes, the three approaches are presented in a stylized and simplified way. In reality, these different approaches can all be present at the same time within the same peace process. There are obvious tensions between the modes of violence management, both in terms of their underlying logic in how to best promote peace and in terms of the most appropriate policy tools. For instance, the conflict resolution approach and rights-based approach involve long-standing debates on peace versus justice, as well as debates between idealists and realists.[15] However, a security approach has increasingly come to dominate the international response to internal violent conflicts in the wake of the war on terrorism, with the military tool partly replacing negotiation and compromise-based solutions. We conclude by raising some of the issues which constitute challenges in relation to the management of violence in peace processes, taking these approaches into consideration.

The Conflict Resolution Approach

The first approach to manage violence in a peace process is firmly rooted within the *conflict resolution* paradigm. Based on the assumption that violence is a political problem, the approach is characterized by dialogue and pragmatism, where the importance of bringing the warring parties to the table is emphasized as an essential requirement to end violence. From this perspective, it is the warring parties who hold the power to end violence and are therefore absolutely necessary to involve in the peace negotiations, even at the cost of negotiating with perpetrators of violence.[16] Within this approach, violence is commonly managed via three different mechanisms.

This first avenue for actors to address violence during peace negotiations is by making use of the conventional tools of diplomacy. When violence-induced crises arise shuttle diplomacy and dialogue are used to put the peace process back on track, as illustrated by the example above where the UN mediator in the Guatemalan peace process Jean Arnault engaged in dialogue with the main parties to put the process back on track after a kidnapping incident. While mediation efforts frequently involve regional or international organizations, or states, different types of civil society actors sometimes also become involved as mediators. Moreover, in addition to these more conventional tools of diplomacy, there are other means of addressing violence, such as informal consultations, or track-two facilitation in the form of problem-solving workshops, sometimes facilitated by civil society actors or representatives of states or INGOs.[17] Such initiatives may take place in the pre-negotiation phase in the midst of violence, or in direct response to violence that occurs during peace negotiations.

Ceasefires and other violence-regulating mechanisms are another preferred means of managing violence. These are frequently invoked to create a climate conducive for negotiation and to build confidence. The peace process in Northern Ireland was only possible after the Irish Republican Army (IRA) had declared a ceasefire in 1994; a long-standing demand from the British government in order for negotiations to begin. Ceasefires thus sometimes serve as critical steps for building trust between belligerents and as 'test balloons' for negotiations over substantive issues, or to probe whether the insurgents have sufficient control over their forces to prevent spoiler violence. While ceasefires can help pave the way for transitions from war to peace, there are also potential shortcomings involved.[18] Ceasefires sometimes have unintended negative effects, such as fuelling rivalries and intergroup fighting. For instance, in north-eastern India, ceasefires between the government and factions of the National Socialist Council of Nagalim (NSCN) have contributed to 'an escalation of factional and intergroup fighting and violent politics in the region, while poor monitoring and reduced threat of prosecution has enabled armed groups to operate more easily after entering into ceasefire agreements'.[19] Thus, in the worst-case scenario ceasefires may create conditions where the armed actors favour the status quo over a transition towards a more comprehensive peace settlement. The government also faces certain risks by negotiating with groups labelled as violence makers; initiatives for ceasefires may be perceived as a sign of weakness and can even be met with violence from within their own ranks.[20]

Finally, monitoring missions or consent-based peacekeeping missions can be used to prevent violence from occurring and also to oversee, monitor and sometimes guarantee ceasefires.[21] Field presence is a common denominator of these missions, but their mandates, capacity and compositions can vary significantly. They range from civilian monitoring missions such as the Temporary International Presence in Hebron (TIPH, 1994 to date), the Kosovo Verification Mission (KVM, 1998–99) under the OSCE and the UN Mission for the Verification of Human Rights and of Compliance with the Commitments of the Comprehensive Agreement on Human Rights in Guatemala (MINUGUA, 1994–96), to armed peace operations authorized to use force to uphold security and the mission mandate, such as Forced Intervention Brigade (FIB) in the UN Stabilization Mission to the Democratic Republic of the Congo (MONUSCO) or United Nations Assistance Mission for Rwanda (UNAMIR) in Rwanda. Contingent on a mission's mandate and set-up, the logic of its violence-reducing function will be different. Armed missions with an enforcement mandate can have a direct deterrent function and sanction breaches of a ceasefire and quell violent outbreaks. For instance, when riots threatened the fragile peace process in Liberia in October 2004, UNMIL (United Nations Mission in Liberia) responded by showcasing the strength of their military presence, for instance, through cordon and search patrols, redeployment of forces, and UNMIL undertook '…both aerial reconnaissance and show-of-force patrols over the city', and the disturbances were shortly thereafter brought under control.[22] By contrast, a civilian mission will by necessity rest more on its ability to monitor and report violence with credibility to enable 'naming and shaming' of violence perpetrators, as well as to solve disputes regarding implementation of a ceasefire before they escalate into violence. Admittedly, there is here a certain degree of overlap between our proposed categorization, as some peacekeeping operations feature elements of the conflict resolution approach, as well as the security approach. The balance in the tasks and approach of a peace operation may also vary over time.

The conflict resolution approach is criticized as being too soft on violence makers. Rather than punishing them for their violent behaviour, dialogue may be seen as a way of rewarding violence. In their efforts to make sure that the peace process stays on course, domestic and international actors may be prepared to tolerate some violence, and therefore look the other way. The approach may also preserve a status quo and can contribute to cementing existing power relations—power relations that in the first place may have caused the violence. Another criticism is that by giving violence makers a stake in the negotiations, it fosters impunity and will make it more difficult to hold perpetrators—both on the rebel and government side—accountable for atrocities committed during the war. Hence, peace negotiations sometimes involve, or are perceived to involve, a trade-off in terms of pursuing a ceasefire with belligerents that may risk cementing injustices, or seek a solution that better addresses injustices.[23]

The Security Approach

A second approach to manage violence within a peace process is to look at violence primarily as a terrorist and security problem, where violence makers should not be negotiated with. The *security* approach has existed alongside the conflict resolution approach, but gained more resonance within large parts of the international community after the 9/11 attacks and the ensuing war on terror.

From this perspective, the tools used to manage violence are, first, through the criminalization of violence in the form of terrorist listings and proscriptions. Such measures entail the freezing of assets, banning of membership and broadcast and travel bans for those involved in terrorist activities. The logic of these types of sanctions is that by raising the costs of pursuing terrorist activities, individuals and groups will be forced to abandon violence. By extension, such measures should also encourage insurgents and other armed actors to seek a negotiated settlement with the government. A second tool is an increased reliance on the military instrument to control violence. A recurring theme—or even policy-prescription in relation to peacebuilding—is the insistence on security often expressed as a strong peacekeeping force willing to use violence to enforce peace.

There are several criticisms of the security-focused approach. First, it largely fails to recognize the political nature of conflict. In particular, labelling an actor as a 'terrorist group' denies the group legitimacy, possibly pushing it towards further reliance on violence.[24] As a consequence, such groups may be less inclined to seek negotiation, since issues related to recognition are often at the core of internal armed conflict. Moreover, criminalization and bans of entire insurgent groups can prevent the strengthening of moderates within such organizations who otherwise might embrace negotiations. Whether or not groups using terrorist activities should be allowed to work politically poses an important dilemma for governments facing armed resistance, since political activity can be misused for militant mobilization. Terrorist bans also make it increasingly difficult for both domestic and international actors to engage constructively with proscribed groups. Individuals or organizations who work with the listed groups can easily be labelled as 'terrorist sympathizers'.[25] The insurgent groups, on their part, are unlikely to accept a mediator who has listed them as terrorists. However, analyses also indicate that proscription and de-proscription of terrorist groups can be used instrumentally in negotiation processes. The removal of a group from a terrorist list can provide a positive incentive by granting it legitimacy.

Second, the military tool is not an easy instrument to apply. There are many examples where international interventions have had a dismal human rights record, which has led to problems related to legitimacy of the intervention, and increased support for armed opposition. The effectiveness of deploying peace operations in contexts where there is really no peace to keep has also been questioned. The NATO-led International Security Assistance Force (ISAF) in Afghanistan, for instance, was authorized by the UN to assist in the stabilization of Afghanistan in the wake of the Bonn Agreement in 2001. While assisting in the rebuilding of Afghan state institutions, including its armed forces, peace in Afghanistan was undermined by violence by the Taliban, with ISAF increasingly becoming involved in combat with the insurgents. ISAF failed to curtail the violence and disbanded in 2014, but the war in has Afghanistan persisted. In addition, international actors are sometimes inadequately equipped to deal with the new forms of violence that emerge during a peace process or in a post-war society. For instance, in March 2004 violent riots targeting the Serb minority, religious sites and the international presence engulfed Kosovo leaving 19 people dead and several thousands of people displaced. The spate of violence caught the international peacekeepers (the NATO-led Kosovo Force—KFOR) and police (under the United Mission in Kosovo—UNMIK) by surprise and demonstrated that the international peace operation was neither adequately equipped nor trained to deal with large scale and rapidly spreading riots. At the same time, there is important research nuancing this picture with many studies showing positive effects of peacekeeping. For example, a study of UN peacekeeping covering all civil wars in Africa demonstrates that increases in military personnel are associated with lower battlefield violence, whereas police or observers are not.[26]

The Rights-Based Approach

The third approach to violence within a peace process is what can be called a right-based approach. Violence is—from this perspective—mainly seen as a human rights problem. This is a normative approach to violence that sees human rights as non-negotiable, universal and codified by international law and treaties.

Adherents of this approach would demand accountability of perpetrators of violence as a key component of a peace process and an issue that cannot be compromised. It is with this perspective in mind that temporary international or hybrid tribunals in various parts of the world have been established to promote peace and hold war criminals accountable. Such efforts stand in contrast to the reality of many peace negotiations, where amnesties are considered a practical solution to a difficult problem and sometimes seen as the only way forward if the goal is to reach a peace deal. In many instances, amnesties are demanded by the armed actors in exchange for concession on, for example, disarmament. Indeed, a significant number of peace agreements contains provisions for amnesties. One study showed that of 188 peace agreements in the time period 1989–2007, 28 per cent included provisions on amnesties.[27]

The approach is also embedded in and based on treaties and principles which have broad international consensus. The International Criminal Court for example has sought to prosecute individuals for war crimes in cases like Bosnia, Kosovo, Sudan and Uganda, not just to punish, but as a long-term violence deterrent, sending a signal to future warring parties that crimes against humanity will not go unpunished.

The main criticism with regard to the rights-based approach is that it is too confrontational and unrealistic in the context of war.[28] If principles of accountability are strictly adhered to, negotiations may risk falling apart before they have begun, as government and rebel leaders may seek to minimize their own costs. If the warring factions and their leaders perceive a risk of prosecution, negotiations may not be seen as an attractive option. Another criticism is that war creates a blurring of lines between perpetrators and victims, and regarding who should be held accountable for actions committed during wartime. In the wake of the 1999 Lomé peace accord, which sought to end the Sierra Leone civil war, a war crimes tribunal—The Special Court for Sierra Leone—was set up in Freetown with a mandate to try those 'who bear the gravest responsibility' for the war crimes committed—thereby focusing more on leaders of the warring factions than the rank and file.[29] The additional critique against the rights-based approach is that where justice is prioritized this could have the unintended consequence of weakening processes aimed at truth telling and reconciliation.[30] It has also been suggested that the rights-based approach largely is a Western ideal that goes against local preferences in many parts of the world.[31]

The Three Approaches Combined

The three perspectives on how to manage violence during peace processes—the conflict resolution, the security and the human rights approach—each come with their respective pros and cons. In reality, in many contemporary peace processes they appear simultaneously, with different sections of local and international society promoting their own approaches. One example is Sri Lanka's peace process in the mid-2000s, which preceded the resumption of armed conflict that in 2009 led to the government's victory over the Liberation Tigers of Tamil Eelam (LTTE). A Norwegian mediation effort with support from other Nordic countries and the European Union (EU), sought to address violence through political dialogue, and a ceasefire was overseen via the unarmed Sri Lanka Monitoring Mission. At the same time, there were a number of countries that had already proscribed the LTTE as a terrorist group before the peace process. In response to violent incidents during the peace process, the EU eventually listed the LTTE as a terrorist organization. Finally, there were a number of actors who were critical of the Norwegian approach, claiming that they compromised their own legitimacy and rewarded violence makers by being too closely associated with both the government and the LTTE who were still committing major human rights abuses. Ultimately, none of the approaches by the international community proved apt enough to prevent the return to open war.

In contrast, Northern Ireland is a case where important shifts in the approach to managing violence contributed to the successful conclusion of negotiations and the signing of the 1998 comprehensive peace agreement, which led to the formal ending of the long-standing conflict between the British government and the Irish Republican Army (IRA). The start of negotiations had only been possible after the IRA declared a ceasefire in 1994. However, this decision, in turn, was facilitated by the US move to—after years of denied entry—authorize Sinn Fein leader (IRA's political wing) Gerry Adams a travel visa to the US in early 1994, which gave IRA long-awaited international legitimacy.

Ways Forward

The research on violence and peace processes takes into account the numerous complexities involved in the commission of violence during peace processes, its main motives and targets and what can be done to prevent violence from undermining peace efforts. However, there are several questions in need of further inquiry.

A first question concerns the multifaceted nature of violence. Traditionally, concerned domestic and international actors have largely focused on how to put an end to the battlefield violence between the main belligerents. However, there is an increased awareness of the challenges that external actors and internal stakeholders face. A myriad of actors engages in different forms of violence against diverse targets, not just armed actors, but also civilian populations and peacekeepers. The field needs to incorporate more specificity about the measures to prevent, deter and suppress such different forms of violence within the context of a peace process.

Another question relates to how mediation and negotiation fit with other types of policy tools to address violence during peace processes. How can the best possible balance between sticks and carrots be struck to manage violence and move peace processes along? While the overview above has highlighted some of the potential problems of different measures to discourage violence—such as anti-terrorist measures and proscription—we need to know more about how different strategies and tactics affect one another and how they best can be combined. This point also raises the question of implications for the role of the international community in these processes in terms of whether the same actors who are banning groups as terrorists also can and should serve as mediators in negotiations with the same groups.

As negotiations to end civil war ensue, violence is more likely to continue than to come to a complete halt. Many actors stand to lose from a transition from war to peace due to vested interest in violence. This means that negotiations will only be able to see peace through if domestic and international actors can find methods to reduce, regulate and minimize the destructive effects of violence.

NOTES

1. On post-war violence, see e.g. Michael J. Boyle (2014) *Violence after War: Explaining Instability in Post-Conflict States* (Baltimore: JHU Press); Sebastian van Baalen & Kristine Höglund (2017) '"So, the Killings Continued": Wartime Mobilization and Post-War Violence in KwaZulu-Natal, South Africa', *Terrorism and Political Violence* 31(6): 1168–1186; and Steenkamp in this volume. For a review of research on post-war crime, see Rosemary Gartner & Liam Kennedy (2018) 'War and Postwar Violence', *Crime and Justice* 47(1): 1–67.
2. John Darby (2001) *The Effects of Violence on Peace Processes* (Washington, DC: United States Institute of Peace); John Darby & Roger Mac Ginty (2000) *The Management of Peace Processes* (London: Macmillan Press Ltd.); Kristine Höglund (2008) *Peace Negotiations in the Shadow of Violence* (Leiden: Martinus Nijhoff Publishers); Timothy D. Sisk (2009) *International mediation in civil wars: bargaining with bullets* (London: Routledge).
3. Thomas Ohlson (1998) *Power Politics and Peace Policies: Intra-State Conflict Resolution in Southern Africa* Uppsala: Report Nr. 50, Department of Peace and Conflict Research, Uppsala University; Stephen John Stedman (2003) 'Peace Processes and the Challenges of Violence'. In: John Darby & Roger Mac Ginty (eds) *Contemporary Peace Making: Conflict, Violence, and Peace Processes* (Basingstoke: Macmillan Press Ltd).
4. Roy Licklider (1995) 'The Consequences of Negotiated Settlements in Civil Wars, 1945–1993', *American Political Science*

Review 89(3): 681–690; Barbara F. Walter (2002) *Committing to Peace: The Successful Settlement of Civil Wars* (Princeton and Oxford: Princeton University Press).
5. Stedman, op. cit.; For a review of the spoiler debate, see Desirée Nilsson & Mimmi Söderberg Kovacs (2011) 'Revisiting an Elusive Concept: A Review of the Debate on Spoilers in Peace Processes', *International Studies Review* 13(4): 606–626 and Andrew G. Reiter (2016) *Fighting Over Peace: Spoilers, Peace Agreements, and the Strategic Use of Violence* (Cham: Springer).
6. Stedman, op. cit.; Desirée Nilsson (2008) 'Partial Peace: Rebel Groups Inside and Outside of Civil War Settlements', *Journal of Peace Research* 45(4): 479–495.
7. Wes Michael Tomaselli (2018) 'Colombia Is Trying to End 50 Years of War, but One Rebel Group Won't Stop Its Attacks', *The Washington Post* (11 January). Accessed at: https://www.washingtonpost.com/world/rebel-cease-fire-breakdown-could-imperil-colombias-ruling-party-election-chances/2018/01/11/0e33299e-f64e-11e7-9af7-a50bc3300042_story.html.
8. On the commitment problem and security concerns of the actors, see Walter (2002) op. cit.
9. David Holiday (1997) 'Guatemala's Long Road to Peace', *Current History* 96(607): 68–74 at p. 73.
10. Sabine C. Carey, Neil J. Mitchell, & Will Lowe (2013) 'States, the Security Sector, and the Monopoly of Violence: A New Database on Pro-government Militias', *Journal of Peace Research* 50(2): 249–258; Sabrine Karim & Kyle Beardsley (2017) *Equal Opportunity Peacekeeping: Women, Peace, and Security in Post-Conflict States* (Oxford: Oxford University Press); Dara Kay Cohen & Ragnhild Nordås (2014) 'Sexual Violence in Armed Conflict Introducing the SVAC Dataset, 1989–2009', *Journal of Peace Research* 51(3): 418–428; Sara Lindberg Bromley (2018) 'Introducing the UCDP Peacemakers at Risk Dataset, Sub-Saharan Africa 1989–2009', *Journal of Peace Research* 55(1): 122–131.
11. David Cunningham (2011) *Barriers to Peace in Civil War* (Cambridge: Cambridge University Press); Peter Rudloff & Michael G. Findley (2016) 'The Downstream Effects of Combatant Fragmentation on Civil War Recurrence', *Journal of Peace Research* 53(1): 19–32; Nilsson (2008) op. cit.

12. Sara Lindberg Bromley (2017) MINUSMA and Mali's Precarious Peace: Current-day UN Peacekeeping in Contexts of Insecurity. In: *Keeping Peace While Under Fire: The Causes, Characteristics and Consequences of Violence against Peacekeepers.* Department of Peace and Conflict Research, pp. 16–17.
13. I. William Zartman (1989) *Ripe for Resolution: Conflict and Intervention in Africa* (New York: Oxford University Press).
14. Stedman (1997) op. cit., identifies three strategies to deal with spoilers: *inducement* (giving the actor what it wants), *socialization* (changing the behaviour of the actor in line with a set of established norms) and *coercion* ('the use or threat of punishment' of spoiler behaviour). He argues that these strategies are to be matched with different spoiler types (limited, greedy and total spoilers). In contrast to Stedman, we identify overarching approaches commonly used to manage violence, but there are also some similarities and overlap, for example, the coercive strategy identified by Stedman could be used as part of an overall security approach to addressing violence.
15. Pauline H. Baker (2001) 'Conflict Resolution versus Democratic Governance: Divergent Paths to Peace?' In: Chester Crocker, Fen Osler Hampson, & Pamela Aall (eds) *Turbulent Peace: The Challenges of Managing International Conflict* (Washington, DC: United States Institute of Peace Press) pp. 753–764; Roy Licklider (2008) 'Ethical Advice: Conflict Management vs. Human Rights in Ending Civil Wars', *Journal of Human Rights* 7(4): 376–387.
16. Baker (2001), ibid.
17. Thania Paffenholz (2014) 'Civil Society and Peace Negotiations: Beyond the Inclusion–Exclusion Dichotomy', *Negotiation Journal* 30: 69–91.
18. Kristine Höglund (2011) 'Tactics in Negotiations between States and Extremists: The Role of Cease-Fires and Counterterrorist Measures'. In: I. William Zartman & Guy Olivier Faure (eds) *Engaging Extremists: Trade-offs, Timing and Diplomacy* (Washington, DC: United States Institute of Peace Press).
19. Åshild Kolås (2011) 'Naga Militancy and Violent Politics in the Shadow of Ceasefire', *Journal of Peace Research* 48(6): 781–792, p. 783.

20. Corinne Bara, Govinda Clayton & Siri Aas Rustad (2021) 'Understanding Ceasefires', *International Peacekeeping*, 28(3): 329–340; Höglund (2011), op. cit.
21. Virginia Page Fortna (2008) *Does Peacekeeping Work: Shaping Belligerents' Choices after Civil War* (Princeton: Princeton University Press); Ryan Grist (2001) 'More Than Eunuchs at the Orgy: Observation and Monitoring Reconsidered', *International Peacekeeping* 8(3): 59–78.
22. United Nations. Fifth progress report of the Secretary-General on the United Nations Mission in Liberia (S/2004/972). 972); Desirée Nilsson & Mimmi Söderberg Kovacs (2005) 'Breaking the Cycle of Violence? Promises and Pitfalls of the Liberian Peace Process', *Civil Wars*, 7(4): 396–14.
23. Saadia Touval (1995) 'Ethical Dilemmas in International Mediation', *Negotiation Journal* 11(4): 333–337.
24. Michael V. Bhatia (2005) 'Fighting Words: Naming Terrorists, Bandits, Rebels and Other Violent Actors', *Third World Quarterly* 26(1): 5–22; Sophie Haspeslagh (2021) *Proscribing Peace*. Manchester: Manchester University Press.
25. To counter this problem, the group Geneva Call actively engages with non-state armed actors to respect humanitarian norms. https://www.genevacall.org (accessed 8 November 2019).
26. Lisa Hultman, Jacob Kathman, & Megan Shannon (2014) 'Beyond Keeping Peace: United Nations Effectiveness in the Midst of Fighting', *American Political Science Review* 108(4): 737–753. On the positive effects of peacekeeping, see also e.g. Walter (2002) op. cit.; Fortna (2008) op. cit.; Lisa Hultman, Jacob D. Kathman, & Megan Shannon (2016) 'United Nations Peacekeeping Dynamics and the Duration of Post-civil Conflict Peace', *Conflict Management and Peace Science* 33(3): 231–249; Andrea Ruggeri, Han Dorussen, & Theodora-Ismene Gizelis (2017) 'Winning the Peace Locally: UN Peacekeeping and Local Conflict', *International Organization* 71(1): 163–185; Hanne Fjelde, Lisa Hultman, & Desirée Nilsson (2019) 'Protection Through Presence: UN Peacekeeping and the Costs of Targeting Civilians', *International Organization* 73(1): 103–131.
27. Peter Wallensteen, et al. (2012) 'Peace Agreements, Justice and Durable Peace'. In: Karin Aggestam & Annika Björkdahl (eds)

Rethinking Peacebuilding: The Quest for Just Peace in the Middle East and the Western Balkans (London: Routledge), p. 133.
28. Licklider (2008) op. cit.
29. The Residual Special Court for Sierra Leone. http://www.rscsl.org (accessed 24 September 2018).
30. Priscilla B. Hayner (2011) *Unspeakable Truths. Confronting State Terror and Atrocity* (New York & London: Routledge).
31. Rosalind Shaw, Lars Waldorf, & Pierre Hazan (2010) *Localizing Transitional Justice: Interventions and Priorities After Mass Violence* (Stanford: Stanford University Press).

CHAPTER 16

Peacemaking and Election Violence

Inken von Borzyskowski and Richard Saunders

INTRODUCTION

Elections in post-conflict states serve a dual role. The first role, as in most countries, is to select leaders and lend legitimacy to the elected government and its policies. The second role, specific to post-conflict states, is for elections to help implement and consolidate an often fragile peace in the wake of ceasefires and in the context of destruction and mistrust; in this context, elections are part of a longer term peacebuilding process centred around re-establishing the rule of law and political participation.[1] It is also worth noting that civil war does not necessarily mean elections stop: India, Colombia, Philippines, and Sri Lanka are cases in point.

I. von Borzyskowski (✉)
Department of Political Science, University College London, London, UK
e-mail: i.Borzyskowski@ucl.ac.uk

R. Saunders
Department of Political Science, Tulane University, New Orleans, Louisiana, USA
e-mail: rsaunders@tulane.edu

In this chapter we explore the reasons why post-conflict elections seem prone to election-related violence and civil war recurrence, and we outline strategies for peacemaking. Scholarship has mixed findings on the effect of previous civil war on election violence[2] but shows that delaying the holding of elections after civil war for a few years can reduce the risk of reigniting civil war.[3] We begin by discussing general causes and consequences of election violence. Next we proceed to examine the unique challenges in post-conflict environments. We then examine strategies for election violence prevention and mitigation, drawing on existing studies and field research around the 2017 elections in Liberia and Kenya conducted by one of the authors. Based on these studies, we note that improved election administration and security sector engagement are promising strategies for mitigating election-related violence.

ELECTION VIOLENCE BACKGROUND

Election violence is political violence intended to influence the process or outcome of an election, or to prevent elections from taking place. It can be directed against people or property, and ranges from low-level harassment, threats, intimidation, and hate speech to physical force (including arbitrary arrest), injuries, and fatalities (i.e. casualties).[4]

Election-related violence affects about a quarter of elections worldwide and is even more widespread in the developing world.[5] In Africa, Latin America, and Asia, election-related casualties occurred in around 30 per cent of elections between 1990 and 2012.[6] In developing democracies, politicians often have a larger menu of strategies at their disposal because they face fewer institutional constraints than in advanced democracies. In addition to the usual tools of influencing electoral processes and outcomes through positioning, advertising, and mobilizing, politicians in developing democracies can also resort to fraud, vote buying, and violence.[7]

Election violence follows different logics before and after Election Day. Campaign violence, i.e. the use of force as a strategic tool prior to Election Day, is often used to shape turnout or vote choice or to keep elections from happening.[8] This violence can be directed against (potential) candidates, voters, election officials, and election events (e.g. rallies) and materials (e.g. posters, ballots, and polling stations). While election violence is usually *between* parties, it can also occur *within* a party very early in the electoral cycle when contenders of the same party vie for a spot on the ballot during the party and candidate nomination period.[9] In contrast to pre-election violence, post-election violence usually arises in response to an announced result and is an attempt to overturn the official result and change the status quo. As such, it often arises after election losers have challenged election results.

Who are the perpetrators and victims of election violence? While election violence can be (or appear) spontaneous, most studies point to it being orchestrated by politicians, particularly incumbent politicians or their affiliates. By one count, about 75 per cent of election violence in sub-Saharan Africa is orchestrated by incumbents.[10] Both opposition and incumbent forces are involved in about 20 per cent of election violence, and the remaining five per cent is perpetrated by the opposition alone.[11] Of course, politicians themselves rarely implement violence directly. Instead, politicians usually activate party youth wings or hire thugs for implementation, drawn from vulnerable sections of society (poor, unemployed, and often young male citizens).[12] In a post-conflict context (which we explore further below), parties may also be the political arm of (former) military forces,[13] thus recruiting from a pool of individuals with military skills.

As for the victims of election violence, research is still scarce. Targets and types of violence seem to vary widely and include the assassination of candidates, intimidation of their families and supporters, mob violence against certain communities, and impact on bystanders. In terms of who gets targeted by campaign violence, some theoretical studies (formal models) identify partisanship[14] but empirically the primary targets of campaign violence vary: sometimes it is opposition partisans, at other times it is non-partisans.[15] Incumbent partisans are usually the least likely to fear or be exposed to campaign violence, which again points to incumbent politicians as the main perpetrator. Others argue that more informed citizens, who are least likely to be swayed by vote buying, ethnic appeals, and promises, are more prone to being attacked in order to reduce their turnout.[16]

Turning to the causes and consequences of election violence, most research has focused on the former. The causes of electoral violence can be usefully grouped into more immediate, election-specific triggers, and more long-term, underlying root causes.[17] The first group of short-term triggers include competition, fraud, poll type, and past election violence. Competition or close elections have been shown to be associated with higher violence risk and intensity in cross-national[18] and some sub-national studies.[19] Theoretically, the link between electoral competition and election violence rests on the notion that competition on the streets and at the ballot box are linked. The number of people a candidate or party is able to mobilize in one venue correlates with the number they are able to mobilize in the other.[20]

Real or perceived fraud is another common trigger of election violence. Stolen elections—or the perceptions of stolen elections—often ignite tensions on the ground. These perceptions can stem from irregularities in the campaigning period and on Election Day or from the vote counting process. Technical glitches (due to capacity issues) are often interpreted by political actors as signs of intentional manipulation and malintent. While these dynamics are usually discussed in the context of post-election violence, pre-election violence can also be triggered by perceived fraud, such as biases during the registration of candidates and voters. If aggrieved parties cannot channel their appeals to the processes through capable and unbiased institutional channels (which promise a fair decision), they are more likely to take their frustration to the streets. That is why institutions in charge of election administration—usually election management bodies (EMBs) such as national election commissions (NECs)—play a central role in election quality, public trust in the process and outcome (i.e. election credibility), and ultimately violence risks.[21] NEC capacity and credibility can go a long way in assuring people and candidates that the election is conducted fairly and smoothly, that shortcomings are addressed, and that potential disputes are adjudicated in a fair and transparent manner.

Two other short-term, election-specific correlates of election violence are poll type and previous election violence. The type of the poll—whether it is for the legislature, executive, or both—can shape the stakes of elections, as does the electoral system.[22] In theory, higher stakes elections should increase incentives of actors to use costly means (such as violence) to influence elections. On the sub-national level, devolution of political power and budgets can also increase the stakes surrounding sub-national contests for power. Lastly, election violence at previous elections may influence violence at the current election. Empirical findings here diverge, with some studies finding a relationship and others not.[23]

In addition to short-term, election-specific conflict triggers, there are also more deep-seated, country-level root causes. These include levels of democracy and development, natural resources, conflict history, ethnic heterogeneity, and population size. Regime type—or the level of democracy—clearly matter for election violence, as advanced democracies rarely experience election-related violence. In contrast, developing democracies, hybrid regimes, and autocracies are more prone to election violence. This is because more democratic countries place higher constraints on political elites and are more likely to hold actors accountable for (violent or non-violent) manipulation. This increases the costs of using violence from the perpetrator's perspective and thus makes it a less attractive strategy to pursue. Economic development also plays a role. Some argue that elections cause conflict in poor societies.[24] Empirically, though, poor countries vary widely in whether they experience election violence. Some places, such as Liberia and Mozambique, are poor but have held fairly peaceful elections. Nevertheless, elections in poor countries are more likely to turn violent than in rich countries. This might be because institutions are usually weak in poor countries, so that democratic constraints on political actors (as discussed above) are low. It might also be because elections in poorer societies are more likely to be perceived as "do or die" affairs, where the winner gets everything and losers might be excluded from power and resources for the foreseeable future. By a similar logic, natural resources can increase the size of the "pie" and make winning elections even more attractive, and thus more conflict-prone.[25]

A country's history of civil war can be crucial for whether elections turn violent, and we explore this aspect in greater detail in the subsequent section below. Like economic and democratic development, though, this is not an inescapable determinant. While many post-conflict countries struggle to hold peaceful elections, some post-conflict countries have beaten the odds. For example, Sierra Leone and Liberia—which both are recovering from more than decade long civil wars—have held fairly peaceful elections in their post-conflict period. Some of this may be attributed to the extensive role played by international election support (which we address in the third section below). But regardless of the explanation, it is worth noting that some post-conflict societies are escaping the conflict trap and have managed to hold relatively peaceful, free, and fair elections. Yet, even in some of these "successful" post-conflict societies, the "peace dividend" often remains unrealized, as consecutive peaceful elections and democratic procedures often are not accompanied by substantive improvements in life quality.

Lastly, election violence tends to be higher in more ethnically heterogeneous and more populous countries. One explanation for this pattern is that political elites increase the salience of ethnic identity over other identities in the campaigning period in order to shore up support and enable an ethnic head count to build coalitions.[26] The role of a country's population size for election violence is often weakly theorized. The link seems to be largely a function of numbers, as countries with larger populations tend to have a greater conflict potential simply because more people might have conflicts with each other than in smaller countries.

Compared to the variety of studies on the causes of election violence, the consequences of election violence remain largely unchartered territory. Interestingly, most studies in this realm rely on case material and survey data, in contrast to the wealth of large scale, national-level studies on the causes of election violence. Studies show that election violence can have detrimental consequences not only in terms of the loss of human lives but also for human and social capital more broadly, economic development, and for public opinion towards democracy and autocracy. As with any conflict, election violence tends to rupture social bonds between people and generate lasting mistrust and suspicion towards the "other."

Election violence can also have detrimental consequences for democracy. Studies using public opinion data have shown that people fearing election violence are less supportive of democracy.[27] More worryingly, this frustration extends to core democratic institutions (multi-party competition), and people who fear and experience more election violence are also more supportive of returning to the country's previous autocratic regime.[28] That is, election violence can undermine public support for democratic governance. When citizens come to associate elections with unrest, intimidation, and violence, they may (legitimately) begin to prioritize safety and stability over democratic rights. This has grave implications for democratic stability and further deepens the call for policy interventions to prevent election violence, which we detail in our final section.

Elections, Violence, and Post-Conflict Challenges

In addition to selecting a government, elections in post-conflict states are also meant to consolidate an often fragile peace. In this context, elections are particularly prone to violence.[29] Worldwide since 1970, elections held during civil war or within 10 years after the end of a civil war have been twice as likely to involve significant violence leading to civilian deaths immediately around the election than elections not held in the shadow of civil war (specifically, 35 versus 14 per cent of elections).[30] Moreover, election violence in post-conflict societies can escalate, leading to the failure of the peace processes they are meant to support and to the resumption of civil war. Examples of these election-related peace failures include Angola in 1992 and Côte d'Ivoire in 2010. In Angola, electoral irregularities and the lack of a clear majority victor led to protracted disputes that ended a month later with a government-backed assault on opposition officials and supporters. Opposition forces fought back, reigniting the previous civil war and ultimately leading to a series of purges, revenge killings, and ethnic cleansing by both sides. More than 300,000 were killed in the fighting.[31] A similar fate befell Côte d'Ivoire following the ceasefire in the First Ivorian Civil War in 2007. In this case, the election results of 2010 were disputed with both sides claiming victory, and international actors supporting the opposition. This sparked the Second Ivorian Civil War of 2010–2011 in which opposition forces under Alassane Ouattara launched a new military assault to break the electoral deadlock. This conflict displaced almost one million Ivorians and resulted in an estimated 3000 deaths.[32]

Why are elections in post-conflict states more prone to violence? Elections held in the shadow of civil war can turn violent for some of the same reasons that peacetime elections can descend into violence. Low economic development, ethnic fractionalization, and natural resource wealth can drive election violence in post-conflict societies as well. However, the post-conflict context also introduces some unique drivers of conflict (such as the existence of former or current armed militants) and can drastically increase the prevalence of other drivers, like weak infrastructure, low institutional capacity, and low government accountability. Such characteristics make elections in post-conflict states more prone to violence. Elections tend to be high-stakes event, but holding them in weakly institutionalized and conflict-prone environment heightens the risk of violence.

Recent scholarship has identified a number of factors that can drive election violence in a post-conflict setting; we group these factors into three categories: motive, means, and timing. Factors which increase the motive (incentive) for violence make it more attractive to use violence over alternative means to achieve political goals (secure victory). For example, losing elections and accepting adverse election outcomes may be more costly in post-conflict contexts. Losing elections is usually disappointing and means exclusion from political power and economic resources; in some places, losers may also fear punishment, i.e. fear that they will be imprisoned or killed by the electoral victor in retribution for activities during the previous civil war or the electoral process.[33] However, some actors are shielded by the presence of amnesty.[34]

While a possible concern in any context, the fear of exclusion or punishment is particularly acute in post-conflict environments. States experiencing civil war often emerge with weakened institutions and few checks on executive power.[35] Thus, in many cases, the winner of the first post-conflict election wins the means to consolidate power under herself and her political allies while excluding rivals from access—or eliminating them outright, as occurred to many opposition figures in the wake of Charles Taylor's victory in Liberia's post-conflict elections of 1997.[36] This increases the benefit of winning elections, motivating candidates to engage in irregular practices in hopes of influencing election outcomes in their favor.

Another factor influencing the motive for violence is weak institutions. Key electoral institutions (election management bodies such as election commissions) are often weakened during civil war due to the destruction of physical infrastructure (roads and headquarters), the loss of human resources (skilled staff), and low operating budgets. Whether due to lack of competence or independence, such electoral institutions often struggle to administer credible elections. The civil war experience usually also affects other institutions, such as judiciary, civil society, and security forces.[37] This weakening and politicization of core governance institutions reduces election credibility overall, reduces the ability of government bodies to contain or mitigate irregular practices, and reduces the ability and willingness of electoral losers to challenge election results through such weak institutions.

Finally, the aforementioned lack of executive constraints that is common in post-conflict contexts may make it difficult even for electoral winners who are sincerely committed to democratic norms to be able to credibly guarantee, ex-ante, that election results will not be manipulated, nor that electoral losers will not be marginalized or persecuted.[38] These factors combine to create an even greater perception in post-conflict states of elections as high-stakes and winner-take-all contests, incentivizing contenders to use more extreme measures in the hope of ensuring victory. These include intimidation of voters and rival candidates and forcibly denying political rivals the ability to campaign.

In addition to this first set of drivers surrounding *motives* for violence, the second set of drivers includes factors increasing the *means* of violence, such as a supply of weapons and trained fighters. In the immediate wake of civil war there are large numbers of unsecured weapons and experienced militants who hold strong loyalties to one or the other side of the formerly warring factions.[39] Worse, the contesting parties themselves are at times little more than these same formerly warring factions, now transitioning from the battlefield struggle to political competition (examples include Guatemala's National Revolutionary Unity and Colombia's M-19).[40] These armed groups can serve the interests of parties by providing them violent means to influence or overturn electoral outcomes. Armed groups may also serve as patrons to "front" parties that they create as a means of supporting or legitimizing their battlefield activities through political action.[41] In both cases, electoral participation and violence serve as complements in achieving actors' goals.

Armed groups need not be linked to a political party to contribute to election violence. In many cases armed groups—such as current or former rebel factions—are explicitly excluded from the political process or face levels of public support that are too low to make electoral participation a viable strategy (examples include Colombia's Revolutionary Armed Forces/FARC who were banned from electoral participation until 2016 and the Afghan Taliban who were banned from politics from 2001 until their military victory in 2021). When electoral participation is not a viable option, some groups may use violence to keep the election from happening at all in some regions (e.g. Taliban in Afghanistan) or to undermine the legitimacy of the election and thus the elected government.[42] Further, armed groups employed in perpetrating violence possess varying levels of autonomy from their political patrons and may escape the control of the political actors to continue carrying out acts of violence after the election in service of their own goals, possibly prompting a government crackdown or the resumption of fighting.[43] Finally, as mentioned above, police and security forces can be weakened at times and face difficulty in responding to violence or may themselves be perpetrators of violence as police and security forces often make up the combatant arm of the government during the war.[44]

When contestants in an election have both strong *motives* to engage in violent manipulation (due to the high-stakes, perceived threats of exclusion and punishment, or perceived illegitimacy of the electoral process) and the *means* to employ violence easily and cheaply by calling upon the wartime loyalties of armed ex-militant supporters, then elections are more likely to be characterized by violence during the pre-electoral period.

Further, when the stakes are high and violence is easy to employ, it is similarly likely that electoral losers will resort to violence as a means of holding on to power and resources that would be lost if the outcome of winner-take-all elections were honored.

In addition to *motives* and *means* of violence, the *timing* of post-conflict elections appears to be salient for election violence and peace failure. The first post-conflict elections are more prone to conflict/war recurrence than elections held after a longer delay from the end of active combat.[45] Elections have been held increasingly soon after the end of fighting, with the average delay falling from five and a half years in 1989 to just over two and a half years in the late 2000s.[46]

Note that election timing likely exercises an indirect rather than direct effect on election violence and the propensity for violent elections to lead to peace failure/war recurrence. That is, timing likely affects motive and means, which in turn affect violence. When elections are held in the immediate aftermath of civil war, little time has passed to allow for militant formations to disperse, for arms to be collected and disposed of (means); or for institutions, civil society, electoral management bodies, and political constraints to be designed or strengthened (motives).[47] Thus, when elections are held soon after the cessation of hostilities, many of the risk factors discussed above are likely to be present, so that elections are more likely to turn violent.

PEACEMAKING AND ELECTION VIOLENCE MITIGATION

The issue of peacemaking in the electoral process and of mitigating election violence in particular has only recently been addressed. This is perhaps surprising, as the international community has greatly invested in election aid and conflict prevention. For United Nations' election support, one of three core goals is the prevention of election-related violence.[48] Many other international organizations have issued guides on best practices to mitigate election violence and improve election security.[49] Other organizations offer training workshops for policymakers and practitioners to better address election violence.[50] While funding and implementing organizations conduct their own studies on prevention (such as project evaluations), these are often case studies using qualitative material,[51] and they tend to evaluate implementation (e.g. how many people were reached and how many leaflets were distributed) instead of effectiveness (whether these people or leaflets actually lead to changes in behavior and violence outcomes). As a result, many evaluations are of limited help for assessing the effectiveness of violence prevention strategies.

Research lags behind practitioner interest with only a handful of systematic studies focused on election violence mitigation. Part of the issue is that many of the causes, triggers, and structural risk factors we have discussed change rather slowly and are difficult to address through outside intervention. For example, the level of economic and democratic development changes slowly over time. The degree of ethnic heterogeneity also changes slowly over time and is usually (and for good reason) outside actors' control. Further, changes in electoral systems, such as from majority to proportional representation are rare. Finally, the existence of previous election violence cannot be washed away by intervention. In other words, many of the causes of violence cannot be easily addressed in a short time.

Here we discuss both peacemaking (i.e. how to reduce the risk of post-conflict elections spurring *civil war* recurrence) and *election violence* mitigation (which often stays below civil war thresholds). First, how can post-conflict challenges surrounding elections be addressed to prevent the recurrence of civil war? One mitigation strategy is to diminish the prevalence of the aforementioned drivers of election violence[52] through disarmament, demobilization, and reintegration (DDR) to break up militant units, security sector reform (SSR) efforts to integrate ex-combatants from both sides into the new security forces, thus strengthening state institutions and the rule of law while placing neither group of former combatants entirely at the mercy of the other.[53] It should be noted, however, that DDR and SSR efforts are frequently imperfect (failing to disarm all militants) and in some instances may strengthen militant unit structures and loyalties when unit leaders are responsible for leading their fighters through the DDR process,[54] which can make these approaches ineffective.

Another peacemaking strategy is to craft agreements that reduce the winner-take-all nature of elections through including some form of proportional representation or power-sharing arrangement which may mitigate the conflict-inducing effect of post-conflict elections.[55] Empirically, about half of peace agreements that promise elections also provide for political power-sharing, compared to one fifth in the whole body of peace agreement documents.[56] Of course, the pressing policy question is how to get contestants to craft peace agreements with such features, and the underlying political contexts with and without such agreement features likely differ in a number of ways that influence the odds of peace. In other words, it is not just words on paper but also underlying power dynamics which influence violence.

These arrangements provide assurance to minority groups and electoral losers that they will not be excluded from power and economic resources due to a single electoral loss, reducing the stakes of the election and thus the incentives to use violence.[57] Peace agreements can also be crafted to attract external involvement, and thus external enforcement of agreed-upon electoral participation provisions that also serve to reassure the losing side.[58] Prior experience with democracy can serve a similar role in reducing the expectations of all actors that an electoral loss would result in permanent disadvantage or persecution.[59] One important and still open question is which types of external interventions can best help countries recovering from civil war to overcome these multi-faceted challenges.

Second, what works in mitigating election-related violence (often short of civil war recurrence)? The handful of studies on this issue suggest that competent election administration and security sector engagement are promising instruments to influence the prospects of electoral peace. With regard to election management, several studies have documented a link between improved election administration and reduced violence. They focus on United Nations (UN), IFES, and domestic efforts to improve election administration and lower election-related violence in recipient countries.[60] For example, Birch and Muchlinski (2018) find that capacity-building strategies are associated with reduced violence by non-state actors, and that attitude-transforming strategies are associated with reduced violence by state actors.

These findings are all the more noteworthy because of the selection behind assistance programs: country requests for and UN provision of assistance is not randomly distributed. UN technical election assistance is more likely to be requested by developing democracies that are poorer, more conflict-prone, and have weaker election administrative capacity. The UN, in turn, is more likely to provide such assistance to countries in need and those with a willingness for political reform. This means that UN technical election assistance tends to select into more administratively weak and conflict-prone elections[61] and yet manages to boost capacity and prospects for peace under difficult circumstances.

Another study finds similar results for capacity-building/technical election assistance while distinguishing between pre- and post-election violence and testing the underlying mechanism. Specifically, von Borzyskowski (2019a) examines the influence of the two major forms of international election support—technical assistance and election observation—on election violence in national elections in Africa and Latin America between 1990 and 2012, accounting for the selection issue noted above. Technical election assistance is associated with reduced electoral violence both before and after voting. This mainly works through building the capacity and credibility of the election commission. Months before voting begins, technical election assistance can remove conflict triggers—such as during party nomination and voter registration—and thus make the run-up to the election less error prone. Technical assistance can also help mitigate post-election violence in a few ways. First, it can improve (perceived) election quality. Post-election violence often breaks out when the result is not seen as credible. By making the NEC more capable and credible, the result that it announces should also be more trustworthy, reducing incentives for electoral losers to reject the election outcome violently, and thus keeping violence from erupting or escalating. If citizens and contestants trust the institution to administer elections without technical glitches and biases, they should also trust the election result that this institution announces. Second, capacity assistance can reduce the delay between voting and results announcement, reducing room for rumors to spread. Third, technical assistance can also help strengthen and spread information about dispute resolution, which should make contestants more likely to channel their complaints through the courts or institutions instead of into the streets. All of these should reduce incentives of the electoral loser to challenge the announced result violently.

These insights about the importance of election administration for election violence are also supported by a recent sub-national study about the 2017 elections in Kenya and Liberia.[62] Based on extensive field research with over 2000 survey interviews before and after the elections in 300 locations across Kenya and Liberia, this study evaluated seven common tools to mitigate election violence. It used a practice evaluation to assess the collective impact of a given type of intervention instead of focusing on a single program by a single organization. For example, instead of evaluating a voter education effort supported by the National Democratic Institute (as in a project evaluation), practice evaluations evaluate all voter education efforts in a given location, regardless of whether they were supported by domestic institutions, domestic civil society, or internationally funded. A practice evaluation asks whether and how the local population experienced this type of programming (regardless of implementer), and whether this affected their attitudes and behavior. Taking this approach, Claes and von Borzyskowski (2018) find that election administration and security sector engagement are promising tools for conflict mitigation in towns at risk of conflict in Kenya's and Liberia's recent elections.

In the 2017 elections in Kenya and Liberia, the quality of election administration clearly mattered, both for the integrity of the process and for the promotion of peaceful elections. The study finds that better election administration is associated with more trust in institutions, more confidence in the credibility of elections, and less election violence. At the same time, poorly performing election institutions are often responsible for much of the violence.[63] As part of the election management system, the Supreme Courts of both countries also played an important role in these elections, as both elections were challenged in the Court—and in the case of Kenya, results were nullified and a repeat election held.

Liberia illustrates the stabilizing influence that a pragmatic election commission and Supreme Court can have. The Supreme Court handled challenges to the code of conduct and candidate registration before the election as well as post-election challenges about election quality in a pragmatic and transparent way. Although tensions rose as Liberians waited for a final verdict, widespread confidence in the functioning of the electoral institutions kept tensions from further escalating.

In Kenya, real and perceived irregularities triggered violence before, during, and after the election. On Election Day, delays reduced trust in the election commission, flawed voter identification procedures created tensions, and irregularities in the transmission and publication of local results triggered incendiary statements and provoked much of the violence. Respondents who reported fewer delays and irregularities in the local election process also increased their trust in the election management (compared to before the election) and experienced less election violence in their locations. Thus, the role of election integrity for peacemaking is promising.

In addition to election administration, the study also found that sound security sector engagement can mitigate election violence. While just increasing the number of police officers on the ground had mixed results, adequate resources and improved dialogue between police officers and local communities were promising. Respondents who engaged more closely with police were inclined to believe that police make elections safer and protect voters equally, and that the police are more trustworthy. On the other side, poor police engagement was also a significant source of violence in both countries. Distrust of police is high among locals, which points both to missed opportunities and to great potential for improved relations, if such substantial investments are made long before the next electoral cycle begins. This finding emphasizes the need for high-quality SSR efforts as a means of professionalizing police and security forces and promoting citizens' trust in them.

It is also important to note which prevention tools have not been effective. This is often difficult to assess both because "no effects" are difficult to prove conclusively and because publication bias is pervasive in the social sciences, so that we are more likely to learn about effective programming than failed interventions and null effects. In the Kenya and Liberia study mentioned above, most programming types had only mixed or no support in terms of mitigating election violence. These were civic and voter education, voter consultation, youth programming, and peace messaging. That does not mean that these programming types never work or should be disbanded. It simply provides an insight that in the context of these two elections with varying risk profiles, those policy tools as implemented did not have the desired effects. It is also important to keep in mind that most of these studies rely on observational data; well-designed experimental research using surveys or small-scale community policing projects are promising ways to deepen this growing body of knowledge.

Lastly, election observation has received mixed results with regard to election violence. Some studies find that it can reduce election violence particularly before elections[64] while other studies find that it increases pre-election conflict events.[65] After elections, observer criticism can exacerbate election violence,[66] and the presence of observers at fraudulent elections is also associated with more conflict events.[67]

Conclusion

In this chapter, we have explored peacemaking in the context of elections. Holding peaceful and credible elections is often a significant challenge for developing countries. Election violence is a threat to the development and consolidation of democracy in any country, but especially so in post-conflict countries. Years of investment in ceasefires, peace agreements, peacekeeping, and peacebuilding often risk being shattered by a high-stakes election where violence could erupt and lead to conflict recurrence.

Because elections are key for political power in most countries, warring parties often start thinking about the rules of the game while negotiating peace. Many peace agreements include provisions for elections, their rules, and institutions. Negotiations at all stages of a peace process often produce agreements that prescribe elections: 351 of 1789 or roughly 20 per cent of agreement documents signed since 1990 have a provision for elections.[68] National election commissions are often directly prescribed in negotiated documents.[69] It may be, as argued by Brancati and Snyder, that insisting on early elections is what sets them up to fail—but often this insistence has its roots very early in the peace process and is not simply imposed by an external organization as a precondition for keeping the peace once the agreement is signed.

It is noteworthy that the country with the highest proportion of peace agreements that mention elections is Liberia: 22 of 30 or about 73 per cent of peace agreements between 1990 and 2003.[70] Liberia has been beating the odds of election violence: although it is a perfect candidate for election violence due to the post-conflict context, low development, and institutional challenges, its 2005, 2011, and 2017 elections have seen low or no violence, thanks in no small part to international election support.[71]

An interesting question for future research is whether including the details of a future electoral system in peace agreements lengthens the duration of civil war and/or post-conflict peace. Bargaining theories of war suggest that bargaining over goods that influence the future power distribution—such as future electoral rules—prolongs fighting.[72] Warring parties are unlikely to accept peace until they believe that they can gain no additional future power (at a sufficiently low cost) through continued fighting. Thus, while the war might last longer, the peace might be more stable.

Holding peaceful and credible elections in this context is no easy task and requires a modicum of peaceful cooperation from former adversaries and, usually, strong international support. Militant forces on both sides must be demobilized to reduce the ease of returning to violence and must be integrated into new state security forces to provide assurances to former combatants that they are protected by the state. But DDR and SSR are only a small part of the solution. Technical election assistance is also needed to aid in building (or bridging the gap for) the infrastructure for elections as well as the domestic institutions that administer elections. At best, election observation can deter fraud and violent manipulation and provide external legitimacy when elections are run fairly. Over a series of elections, a cycle of peaceful contestation can be built as war-weary citizens are empowered and societal sections re-learn to participate in governance, ideally with peace dividends emerging under newly democratic rule.

NOTES

1. United Nations (2008, 25–28).
2. In cross-national studies, there does not seem to be a significant association between post-conflict countries and post-election violence (von Borzyskowski 2019a, b; Hafner-Burton et al. 2014). For pre-election violence, post-conflict has a positive or no effect on *onset* (Hafner-Burton et al. 2014) and a negative effect on *intensity* of pre-election violence (von Borzyskowski 2019a), perhaps because war-torn societies are tired of fighting. Post-conflict is linked to a lower risk of opposition violence but no change in the risk of government violence (Fjelde and Höglund 2016a).
3. Brancati and Snyder (2013), Flores and Nooruddin (2012).
4. This section draws on a longer discussion in von Borzyskowski (2019a, 32–47). For another recent overview, see Fjelde and Höglund (2016b), and Birch et al. (2020). While its forms can vary widely, many studies focus on physical force because that is easier to document and capture systematically. For a recent exception, see Birch (2011), Claes and Borzyskowski (2018).
5. Fischer (2002, 11), Straus and Taylor (2012), Hafner-Burton et al. (2014, 151), von Borzyskowski (2019a, 44–45).
6. von Borzyskowski (2019a, 24). For (violent and non-violent) event estimates, see Daxecker et al. (2019) and Fjelde and Höglund (2021).
7. Schedler (2002), Southall (2013), von Borzyskowski and Kuhn (2020).
8. Wilkinson and Haid (2009), Straus and Taylor (2012, 20).
9. Seeberg et al. (2018).
10. Straus and Taylor (2012, 29–30), Sachikonye (2011, 19), International Crisis Group (2007, 4).

11. Straus and Taylor (2012, 29–30).
12. Laakso (2009, 231–232, 243–244), Mehler (2009, 204–206), Makumbe (2002, 91), Masunungure (2011, 55–57).
13. Matanock and Staniland (2018).
14. Chaturvedi (2005), Collier and Vicente (2012), Robinson and Torvik (2009).
15. Kuhn (2015), Bratton (2008, 624), Wallsworth (2016, 101).
16. von Borzyskowski and Kuhn (2020).
17. von Borzyskowski (2019a, 55).
18. Hafner-Burton et al. (2014, 2018), Daxecker (2014, 2012), von Borzyskowski (2019a).
19. Asunka et al. (2018), Gutierrez-Romero (2014). Other subnational studies find no significant association (von Borzyskowski and Wahman 2021).
20. Londregan and Vindigni (2006, 25).
21. von Borzyskowski (2019a).
22. Fjelde and Höglund (2016).
23. Hafner-Burton et al. (2014, 172); Taylor et al. (2017, 21).
24. Collier (2009).
25. Englebert and Ron (2004).
26. Arriola (2013), Laakso (2009), Straus (2011), Wilkinson (2004), Wilkinson and Haid (2009).
27. Burchard (2015).
28. von Borzyskowski, Daxecker and Kuhn (2021).
29. Kumar (1998), Flores and Nooruddin (2012), Reilly (2017).
30. When considering only elections taking place within ten years after a civil war but not during civil war, the percentage drops from 35 to 28 per cent. Authors' calculation based on data from Gleditsch et al. (2002) and Hyde and Marinov (2012).
31. Roque (2009).
32. United Nations (2013).
33. Bjarnesen (2018), Keels (2017), Hartzell and Hoddie (2015), Linder and Bachtiger (2005).
34. Mallinder (2019).
35. Flores and Nooruddin (2012, 2018), Höglund et al. (2009), Kumar (1998).
36. Nilsson and Kovacs (2005).
37. Höglund et al. (2009), Kumar (1998).
38. Joshi et al. (2017), Walter (1999).

39. Bjarnesen (2018), Ebiede (2018), Höglund et al. (2009), Kumar (1998).
40. Acosta (2014), Dresden (2017), Höglund et al. (2009).
41. Matanock and Staniland (2018).
42. Matanock and Staniland (2018).
43. Staniland (2015).
44. Höglund et al. (2009), Kumar (1998).
45. Joshi et al. (2017), Brancati and Snyder (2011, 2013), Flores and Nooruddin (2012).
46. Brancati and Snyder (2011).
47. Brancati and Snyder (2013, 826–827).
48. United Nations (2010, 1).
49. United Nations (2009, 2011b), USAID (2010, 2013), ECDPM (2012), Atwood (2012).
50. United Nations (2011a), USIP (N.d).
51. Claes (2016), United Nations (2009, 51–93), Kumar and Ottaway (1998), Kumar (1998), Gillies (2011).
52. Joshi et al. (2017, 17–18), Brancati and Snyder (2013, 828–831).
53. Brancati and Snyder (2013, 828–829), USIP (2010).
54. Bjarnesen (2018), Ebiede (2018).
55. Joshi et al. (2017), Fjelde and Höglund (2016), Ottmann and Vüllers (2015, 344–346), Hartzell and Hoddie (2015).
56. Authors' analysis based on data in Bell and Badanjak (2019).
57. Hartzell and Hoddie (2015).
58. Matanock and Staniland (2018), Matanock (2018).
59. Flores and Nooruddin (2012).
60. Kammerud (2011), Opitz et al. (2013), Claes (2016), Claes and von Borzyskowski (2018), Birch and Muchlinski (2018), von Borzyskowski (2019a), Birch (2020, Chapter 6).
61. von Borzyskowski (2016).
62. Claes and Borzyskowski (2018).
63. Claes and Borzyskowski (2018, 28).
64. Asunka et al. (2018), von Borzyskowski (2019a, Chapter 2).
65. Daxecker 2014.
66. von Borzyskowski (2019a; 2019b, Chapter 3).
67. Daxecker (2012).
68. Bell and Badanjak (2019).
69. Bell and Badanjak (2019). URL: https://www.peaceagreements.org/search?SearchForm%5Bregion%5D=&SearchForm%5Bc

ountry_entity%5D=&SearchForm%5Bname%5D=&SearchForm%5Bcategory_addressed%5D%5B%5D=104&SearchForm%5Bcategory_mode%5D=any&SearchForm%5Bagreement_text%5D=&s=Search+Database.
70. Bell and Badanjak (2019). URL: https://www.peaceagreements.org/search?SearchForm%5Bregion%5D=&SearchForm%5Bcountry_entity%5D=76&SearchForm%5Bname%5D=&SearchForm%5Bcategory_addressed%5D%5B0%5D=59&SearchForm%5Bcategory_mode%5D=any&SearchForm%5Bagreement_text%5D=&SearchForm%5Border%5D=date_signed_desc&s=Search+Database.
71. Burchard (2015).
72. Reiter (2009).

References

Acosta, Benjamin. 2014. "From Bombs to Ballots: When Militant Organizations Transition to Political Parties." Journal of Politics 76(3):666–683.

Arriola, Leonardo. 2013. "Protesting and Policing in a Multiethnic Authoritarian State: Evidence from Ethiopia." Comparative Politics 45(2):147–168.

Asunka, Joseph, Sarah Brierley, Eric Kramon and George Ofosu. 2018. "Electoral Fraud or Violence: The Effect of Observers on Party Manipulation Strategies." British Journal of Political Science 49(1):129–151.

Atwood, Brian. 2012. "How the EU Can Support Peaceful Post-Election Transitions of Power: Lessons from Africa."

Bell, Christine and Sanja Badanjak. 2019. "Introducing PA-X: A New Peace Agreement Database and Dataset." Journal of Peace Research 56(3):452–466.

Birch, Sarah. 2011. Electoral Malpractice. Oxford University Press.

———. 2020. Electoral Violence, Corruption, and Political Order. Princeton University Press.

Birch, Sarah and David Muchlinski. 2018. "Electoral Violence Prevention: What Works?" Democratization 25(3):385–403.

Birch, Sarah, Ursula Daxecker, Kristine Höglund. 2020. Electoral violence: An introduction. Journal of Peace Research 57(1):3–14. https://doi.org/10.1177/0022343319889657.

Bjarnesen, Mariam. 2018. The Winner Takes It All: Post-War Rebel Networks; Big Man Politics, and the Threat of Violence in the 2011 Liberian Elections. In Violence in African Elections, ed. Mimmi Soderberg and Jesper Bjarnesen. University of Chicago Press, Chapter 7.

von Borzyskowski, Inken. 2016. "Resisting Democracy Assistance: Who Seeks and Receives Technical Election Assistance?" Review of International Organizations 11(2):247–282.

———. 2019a. The Credibility Challenge: How Democracy Aid Influences Election Violence. Cornell University Press.

———. 2019b. "The Risks of Election Observation: International Condemnation and Post-Election Violence." International Studies Quarterly 63(3):654–667.

von Borzyskowski, Inken and Michael Wahman. 2021. "Systematic Measurement Error in Election Violence Data: Causes and Consequences." British Journal of Political Science 51(1): 230-252.

von Borzyskowski, Inken and Patrick Kuhn. 2020. "Dangerously Informed: Voter Information and Pre-Electoral Violence in Africa." Journal of Peace Research 57(1):15-29.

von Borzyskowski, Inken, Ursula Daxecker and Patrick Kuhn. 2021. "Fear of Campaign Violence and Support for Democracy and Autocracy." Conflict Management and Peace Science. https://doi.org/10.1177/07388942211026319.

Brancati, Dawn and Jack Snyder. 2011. "Rushing to the Polls: The Causes of Premature Postconflict Elections." Journal of Conflict Resolution 55(3):469–492.

———. 2013. "Time to Kill: The Impact of Election Timing on Postconflict Stability." Journal of Conflict Resolution 57(5):822–853.

Bratton, Michael. 2008. "Vote Buying and Violence in Nigerian Election Campaigns." Electoral Studies 27(4):621–632.

Burchard, Stephanie. 2015. Electoral Violence in Sub-Saharan Africa: Causes and Consequences. Lynne Rienner Publishers.

Chaturvedi, Ashish. 2005. "Rigging Elections with Violence." Public Choice 125(1–2):189–202.

Claes, Jonas. 2016. Electing Peace: Violence Prevention and Impact at the Polls. USIP.

Claes, Jonas and Inken von Borzyskowski. 2018. "What Works in Preventing Election Violence: Evidence from Kenya and Liberia." USIP Peaceworks.

Collier, Paul. 2009. Wars, Guns and Votes. Democracy in Dangerous Places. Harper Collins.

Collier, Paul and Pedro Vicente. 2012. "Violence, Bribery, and Fraud: The Political Economy of Elections in Sub-Saharan Africa." Public Choice 117–147.

Daxecker, Ursula, Elio Amicarelli, Alexander Jung. 2019. Electoral contention and violence (ECAV): A new dataset. Journal of Peace Research 56(5):714–723.

Daxecker, Ursula. 2012. "The Cost of Exposing Cheating: International Election Monitoring, Fraud, and Post-Election Violence in Africa." Journal of Peace Research 49(4):503–516.

———. 2014. "All Quiet on Election Day? International Election Observation and Incentives for Pre-Election Violence in AFRICAN Elections." Electoral Studies 34:232–243.

Dresden, Jennifer Raymond. 2017. "From Combatants to Candidates: Electoral Competition and the Legacy of Armed Conflict." Conflict Management and Peace Science 34(3):240–263.

Ebiede, Tarila Marclint. 2018. Ex-Militants and Electoral Violence in Nigeria's Niger Delta. In Violence in African Elections, ed. Mimmi Soderberg and Jesper Bjarnesen. University of Chicago Press, Chapter 6.

ECDPM. 2012. "Factsheet EEAS Mediation Support Project, Knowledge Product: Mediation and dialogue in Electoral Processes to Prevent and Mitigate Electoral Related Violence."

Englebert, Pierre and James Ron. 2004. "Primary Commodities and War: Congo-Brazzaville's Ambivalent Resource Curse." Comparative Politics 37(1):61–81.

Fischer, Jeff. 2002. "Electoral Conflict and Violence: A Strategy for Study and Prevention." IFES White Paper. URL: https://www.ifes.org/publications/electoral-conflict-and-violence-strategy-study-and-prevention

Fjelde, Hanne and Kristine Höglund. 2016a. "Electoral Institutions and Electoral Violence in Sub-Saharan Africa." British Journal of Political Science 46(2):297–320.

———. 2016b. "Electoral Violence: The Emergence of a Research Field." APSA Comparative Democratization Newsletter, July 2016, 1–11.

———. 2021. Introducing the Deadly Electoral Conflict Dataset (DECO). Journal of Conflict Resolution. https://doi.org/10.1177/00220027211021620.

Flores, Thomas and Irfan Nooruddin. 2012. "The Effect of Elections on Postconflict Peace and Reconstruction." Journal of Politics 74(2):558.

Flores, Thomas and Irfan Nooruddin. 2018. Elections in War and Peace. Cambridge University Press.

Gillies, David. 2011. Elections in Dangerous Places: Democracy and the Paradoxes of Peace-Building. McGill-Queen's University Press.

Gleditsch, Nils Petter, Peter Wallensteen, Mikael Eriksson, Margareta Sollenberg and Havard Strand. 2002. "Armed Conflict 1946-2001: A New Dataset." Journal of Peace Research 39(5):615–637.

Gutierrez-Romero, Roxana. 2014. "An Inquiry into the Use of Illegal Electoral Practices and Effects of Political Violence and Vote-Buying." Journal of Conflict Resolution 58(8):1500–1527.

Hafner-Burton, Emilie, Susan Hyde and Ryan Jablonski. 2014. "When Do Governments Resort to Election Violence?" British Journal of Political Science 44(1):149–179.

Hafner-Burton, Emilie, Susan Hyde and Ryan Jablonski. 2018. "Surviving Elections: Election Violence, Incumbent Victory and Post-Election Repercussions." British Journal of Political Science 48(2):459–488.

Hartzell, Caroline and Matthew Hoddie. 2015. "The Art of the Possible: Power Sharing and Post-Civil War Democracy." World Politics 67(1):37–71.

Höglund, Kristine, Anna Jarstad and Mimmi Söderberg Kovacs. 2009. "The Predicament of Elections in War-Torn Societies." Democratization 16(3):530–557.

Hyde, Susan and Nikolay Marinov. 2012. "Which Elections Can Be Lost?" Political Analysis 20(2):191–210.

International Crisis Group. 2007. "Nigeria's Elections: Avoiding a Political Crisis." Briefing (123) URL: https://www.crisisgroup.org/africa/west-africa/nigeria/nigeria-s-elections-avoiding-political-crisis.

Joshi, Madhav, Erik Melander and Jason Michael Quinn. 2017. "Sequencing the Peace: How the Order of Peace Agreement Implementation Can Reduce the Destabilizing Effects of Post-Accord Elections." Journal of Conflict Resolution 61(1):4–28.

Kammerud, Lisa. 2011. Merging Conflict Management with Electoral Practice: The IFES Experience. In Elections in Dangerous Places: Democracy and the Paradoxes of Peacebuilding, ed. David Gillies. London: McGill-Queen's University Press, 147–170.

Keels, Eric. 2017. "Oil Wealth, Post-conflict Elections, and Postwar Peace Failure." Journal of Conflict Resolution 61(5):1021–1045.

Kuhn, Patrick. 2015. "Do Contentious Elections Trigger Violence?" In Contentious Elections: From Ballots to Barricades, ed. Pippa Norris. Routledge, 89–110.

Kumar, Krishna. 1998. Postconflict Elections, Democratization, and International Assistance. Lynne Rienner Publishers.

Kumar, Krishna and Marina Ottaway. 1998. Postconflict Elections, Democratization, and International Assistance. Lynne Rienner.

Laakso, Liisa. 2009. Insights to Electoral Violence in Africa. In Votes, Money and Violence: Political Parties and Elections in Sub-Saharan Africa. KwaZulu-Natal Press, pp. 224–252.

Linder, Wolf and Andre Bachtiger. 2005. "What Drives Democratisation in Asia and Africa?" European Journal of Political Research 44(6):861–880.

Londregan, John and Andrea Vindigni. 2006. "Voting as a Credible Threat." Working Paper.

Makumbe, John. 2002. "Zimbabwe's Hijacked Election." Journal of Democracy 13(4):87–101.

Mallinder, Louise. 2019. Amnesties and Inclusive Political Settlements. PA-X Report: Transitional Justice Series. Edinburgh: Global Justice Academy, University of Edinburgh. URL: https://pure.qub.ac.uk/en/publications/amnesties-and-inclusive-political-settlements.

Masunungure, Eldred. 2011. "Zimbabwe's Militarized, Electoral Authoritarianism." Journal of International Affairs 65(1):47.

Matanock, Aila. 2018. "External Engagement: Explaining the Spread of Electoral Participation Provisions in Civil Conflict Settlements." International Studies Quarterly 62(3):656–670.

Matanock, Aila and Paul Staniland. 2018. "How and Why Armed Groups Participate in Elections." Perspectives on Politics 16(3):710–727.

Mehler, Andreas. 2009. Political Parties and Violence in Africa: Systematic Reflections Against Empirical Background. In Votes, Money and Violence: Political Parties and Elections in Sub-Saharan Africa. South Africa: University of KwaZulu-Natal Press, pp. 194–223.

Nilsson, Desire and Mimmi Söderberg Kovacs. 2005. "Breaking the Cycle of Violence? Promises and Pitfalls of the Liberian Peace Process." Civil Wars 7(4):396–414.

Opitz, Christian, Hanne Fjelde and Kristine Höglund. 2013. "Including Peace: The Influence of Electoral Management Bodies on Electoral Violence." Journal of Eastern African Studies 7(4):713–731.

Ottmann, Martin and Johannes Vüllers. 2015. "The Power-Sharing Event Dataset (PSED): A New Dataset on the Promises and Practices of Power-Sharing in Post-Conflict Countries." Conflict Management and Peace Science 32(3):327–350.

Reilly, Benjamin. 2017. "Elections and Post-Conflict Political Development."

Reiter, Dan. 2009. How Wars End. Princeton University Press.

Robinson, James and Ragnar Torvik. 2009. "The Real Swing Voter's Curse." American Economic Review 99(2):310–315.

Roque, Paula Cristina. 2009. "Angola's Faade Democracy." Journal of Democracy 20(4):137–150.

Sachikonye, Lloyd. 2011. When a State Turns on its Citizens: 60 Years of Institutionalised Violence in Zimbabwe. Harare: Weaver Press.

Schedler, Andreas. 2002. "Elections Without Democracy: The Menu of Manipulation." Journal of Democracy 13(2):36–50.

Seeberg, Merete Bech, Michael Wahman and Svend-Erik Skaaning. 2018. "Candidate Nomination, Intra-Party Democracy, and Election Violence in Africa." Democratization (3).

Southall, Roger. 2013. "How and Why Zanu-PF Won the 2013 Zimbabwe Elections." Strategic Review for Southern Africa 35(2):135.

Staniland, Paul. 2015. "Armed Groups and Militarized Elections." International Studies Quarterly 59(4):694–705.

Straus, Scott. 2011. "Its Sheer Horror Here: Patterns of Violence During the First Four Months of Cote d'Ivoire's Post-Electoral Crisis." African Affairs 110(440):481–489.

Straus, Scott and Charlie Taylor. 2012. Democratization and Electoral Violence in Sub- Saharan Africa, 1990–2008. In Voting in Fear: Electoral Violence in Sub-Saharan Africa. United States Institute of Peace, pp. 15–38.

Taylor, Charles, Jon Pevehouse and Scott Straus. 2017. "Perils of Pluralism: Electoral Violence and Incumbency in Sub-Saharan Africa." Journal of Peace Research 54(3):397–411.

United Nations. 2008. "United Nations Peacekeeping Operations: Principles and Guidelines."

———. 2009. "Elections and Conflict Prevention: A Guide to Analysis, Planing and Programming."

———. 2010. "Report of the Special Rapporteur on extrajudicial, summary or arbitrary executions, Philip Alston. A/HRC/14/24/Add.7."

———. 2011a. "European Commission UNDP Joint Task Force on Electoral Assistance. Thematic Workshop: Elections, Violence and Conflict Prevention. Summary Report, 20–24 June 2011."

———. 2011b. "Understanding Electoral Violence in Asia."

———. 2013. "United Nations Operation in Cote d'Ivoire—Post-Election Crisis."

USAID. 2010. "Electoral Security Framework. Technical Guidance Handbook for Democracy and Governance Officers."

———. 2013. "Best Practices in Electoral Security: A Guide for Democracy and Governance Programming."

USIP. 2010. "The Link Between DDR and SSR in Conflict-Affected Countries." URL: https://www.usip.org/publications/2010/05/link-between-ddr-and-ssr-conflict-affected-countries.

USIP. N.d. "Preventing Electoral Violence in Asia: Tools for Practitioners and Policymakers."

Wallsworth, Gregory. 2016. Political Participation and Political Violence. Dissertation, Michigan State University.

Walter, Barbara. 1999. "Designing Transitions from Civil War: Demobilization, Democratization, and Commitments to Peace." International Security 24(1):127–155.

Wilkinson, Steven. 2004. Votes and Violence: Electoral Competition and Ethnic Riots in India. Cambridge University Press.

Wilkinson, Steven and Christopher Haid. 2009. "Ethnic Violence as Campaign Expenditure: Riots, Competition, and Vote Swings in India." Working Paper.

CHAPTER 17

Disarmament, Demobilisation and Reintegration of Ex-Combatants

Alpaslan Özerdem

INTRODUCTION

The Disarmament, Demobilisation and Reintegration (DDR) of ex-combatants is one of the most sensitive and challenging aspects of post-accord peacebuilding processes due to its implications on security and power relations between the parties to the conflict. Moreover, the DDR of ex-combatants, particularly in environments where a large cohort of ex-combatants need to be integrated into civilian life, would have a wide range of economic, social, environmental, and cultural implications for receiving communities. Even if a peace process can withstand it, the failures of the DDR of ex-combatants would likely contribute to the transformation of political violence into criminality and cause significant security, economic and societal challenges for the post-conflict security.

A. Özerdem (✉)
Jimmy and Rosalynn Carter School for Peace and Conflict Resolution, George Mason University, Arlington, VA, USA
e-mail: aozerdem@gmu.edu

From Angola to El Salvador and South Africa, such a transformation of violence has resulted in a high level of criminality. At the same time, for the successful implementation of DDR programmes, the peacebuilding context would need to provide certain conditions in terms of stability in security, governance and socio-economic environment. They are not only important to get ex-combatants' buy-in to the DDR process but also for their long-term reintegration into the society. Due to such significant implications for peace and security, various aspects of DDR and its symbiotic relationship with peacebuilding have been extensively explored over the last two decades.[1]

In the conceptualisation of the relationship between DDR and peacebuilding, there are two main schools of thought that inform the way DDR challenges are perceived and responded to. The first approach is based on a security risk perspective in which ex-combatants are seen as a security risk both at a micro and macro level,[2] while the second one considers the issues as a development challenge.[3] According to the micro- and macro-insecurity framework, fear of personal violence and theft, namely micro-insecurity, may actually increase in the aftermath of an armed conflict for two basic reasons: first, if the demobilised combatants are not placed into employment, the lack of an income source increases their propensity to commit crimes; and second, ex-combatants tend to be unskilled, except in the use of weapons, which leads them to find themselves with a comparative advantage in criminal activities. The macro-insecurity aspect, on the other hand, argues that demobilisation may prove to be a potential threat to post-conflict peace and stability at national or even regional and global levels, if ex-combatants are deprived of economic opportunities and are socio-politically marginalised.

On the other hand, adopting a purely security-based perspective on DDR would mean that the reintegration approach could turn into a series of activities to keep ex-combatants 'busy' rather than targeting their effective socio-economic integration into society. This is ironically a high-risk approach as it is likely to alienate ex-combatants, forcing them to distance themselves from the DDR process and general peacebuilding activities. However, through timely and appropriate reintegration activities, it is not only possible to keep ex-combatants from the temptations of returning to fighting or resorting to crime and banditry but also to benefit from their direct contribution to the economy. In such a developmental perspective, ex-combatants are considered as individuals who have the potential to contribute to the general development in their community and country as a whole.[4]

In this chapter, the main objective is, therefore, to provide a general overview of ex-combatant DDR and its close-woven relationship with peacebuilding. Given the wide scope of activities that are undertaken within DDR, the chapter will focus only on some of the most critical issues such as inducements for disarmament, cantonment within demobilisation and the significance of community engagement in reintegration. The chapter will also focus on a number of procedural issues that play a significant role in the successful implementation of DDR processes such as the heterogeneity of ex-combatant caseloads, impact of preferential treatment of ex-combatants vis-a-vis community relations and engagement of local actors in the implementation of such programmes. However, before that, it is important to point out that the chapter will focus on 'formal' or programmatic types of DDR activities implemented by a wide range of international, national and local actors, rather than 'informal' or 'everyday' responses of reintegration that take place during and well after the end of such formal responses, while recognising that such everyday engagement plays an imperative role in reintegration outcomes in the long term.

Disarmament, Demobilisation and Reintegration

The United Nations' Integrated Disarmament, Demobilisation and Reintegration Standards (IDDRS) defines disarmament as the collection, control and disposal of small arms and light weapons and the development of responsible arms management programmes in a post-conflict context. Meanwhile, demobilisation is defined as a planned process by which the armed force of the government and/or opposition or factional forces either downsize or completely disband. Finally, reintegration is the process whereby former combatants and their families are integrated into the social, economic and political life of (civilian) communities.[5] It is important to note that these three phases are interrelated, rather than sequential, although they can be thought of as part of a sequence of activities that have to happen for a society to recover from armed conflict.[6]

As part of the liberal peace agenda, the international community has implemented DDR programmes in almost all post-accord contexts since the end of Cold War where it has undertaken state-building/peacebuilding initiatives, from Bosnia-Herzegovina, East Timor and Kosovo to Afghanistan, Liberia, Sierra Leone and South Sudan. As part of Security Sector Reform (SSR), DDR also occurred in a number of former Soviet and East European countries during their transformation from socialist regimes to liberal market economies. As shown in Table 17.1, it is possible to make a distinction between the two conventional DDR contexts of post-authoritarian/developmental (first generation) and post-conflict environments (second generation). Moreover, it is possible to identify DDR under combat conditions, as a third generation.[7] With such generational changes in DDR, while the UN agencies and departments (i.e. DPKO and UNDP), International Organisation for Migration and the World Bank, were the main leading agencies for DDR operations in the first and second generations, new actors such as NATO started to play a more active role in contexts like Kosovo and dominated the third-generation DDR operations. In terms of the overall cost of DDR programmes, a study by the Escola de Cultura de Pau at Barcelona Autonomous University shows that in 2008 there were 19 ongoing DDR

Table 17.1 The typology of DDR as part of SSR frameworks

	Context	Objective	Activities	Examples
First Generation	Post-authoritarian/ developmental context	Physical-security oriented	Professionalisation of the military	Eastern European countries in post-Cold War
Second Generation	'Post-conflict' environment	Contribute to SSR as part of statebuilding	Restructuring of new army/police force; reintegration of ex-combatants into civilian life	Bosnia-Herzegovina, Kosovo, East Timor, El Salvador, Sierra Leone, etc
Third Generation	Combat conditions	Contribute to post-conflict governance and ensuring physical security	Conventional SSR/DDR activities as in second-generation DDR with heavy involvement in ongoing combat	Afghanistan, Iraq

programmes globally, involving 1.1 million ex-combatants with a total cost of nearly US$ 1.6 billion.[8]

From a one-man-one-weapon approach in typical war-to-peace transition scenarios, the DDR processes were undertaken from primarily a security risk perspective through economic reintegration programmes. The preferential treatment of former combatants by setting quotas for places in the new army and police forces of such war-torn environments has become one of the key characteristics of those DDR programmes.[9] In a wider sense, the DDR process is considered a tool for statebuilding in which the state's monopoly on violence is the most significant concern. However, as pointed out by Munive and Stepputat, 'Instead of insisting on achieving the state's monopoly on violence, the agents of the global DDR regime may eventually improve chances for peace by considering different forms of violence management involving ANSAs [Armed "Non-Statutory Actors"], rather than focussing solely on their "elimination" through DDR programs'.[10] However, it is important to note that violence management involving ANSAs would require a careful engagement in a number of legal, institutional and ethical spheres. Furthermore, it is important to note that the overall securitisation of peacebuilding through a statebuilding approach is the primary example of the way the liberal peace response attempts to deal with the challenge of security and hence DDR in conflict-affected environments.[11]

Disarmament Inducements

Disarmament usually consists of four main phases: information collection and operational planning, weapons collection or retrieval operations, stockpile management and destruction/re-use.[12] Also, it is important to carefully determine the criteria on who is eligible to register as a combatant and what type of weapons are to be handed in, as this would have a significant impact on who might be excluded from and included in the programme. On the other hand, since each case has its own political, socio-cultural and economic conditions, the criteria should comply with the unique needs of the post-accord context concerned.[13]

Tanner suggests that there are three categories of UN disarmament missions based on the principles of consensus, coercion and compellence, undertaken within the wider context of peacekeeping missions.[14] However, in regard to the UN disarmament missions in the 1980s and early 1990s, the revealing aspect of debates within the UN was often the conspicuous lack of consideration of any inducements or persuasion to disarm, operating in tandem with coercion or compellence. Inducements, as understood by the UN peacekeeping missions, involved methods of bargaining for, or trading in, weapons. Inevitably, such an understanding led to the establishment of weapons-for-cash programmes in such contexts as El Salvador, Haiti, Liberia, Mozambique, Nicaragua and Somalia.[15]

There are some issues that require particular attention when using cash as an incentive in disarmament programmes, such as the cash amount offered per weapon. However, experience shows that weapons-for-cash programmes have a negligible effect on security, tend to attract old and unserviceable weapons, and often stimulate the creation of illegal arms markets, resulting in an influx of weapons into the society.[16] Berdal explains further that buy-back programmes have limited medium-term impact in reducing the number of weapons in countries that have (1) porous borders with countries with active weapons markets; (2) lack of capacity to enforce regulations on the open carrying and criminal use of weapons and (3) a political, economic or security climate which enhances the security and economic value of owning and using a weapon.[17] In some countries, the culture of the gun, which is often associated with masculinity, may also be another difficult barrier to overcome; Afghanistan is illustrative of such an environment. Overall, the most effective inducement and persuasion for combatants to disarm is a credible DDR programme that offers opportunities for new, non-violent livelihoods.[18]

Demobilisation with Cantonment

The aim of demobilisation is to transform the combatant identity into civilian status. In order to achieve this, registration, counting and monitoring and discharging of combatants are utilised as the main activities. In order to make ex-combatants ready to rejoin a community, and before the beginning of a formal reintegration programme, reinsertion packages that cover social, psychological, financial and training issues should be employed.[19]

One of the most significant challenges facing demobilisation concerns whether ex-combatants are already community-based or require assistance to survive upon reinsertion into receiving communities. If the caseload of ex-combatants is large, or if it is dispersed across a large geographical region, then the return to receiving communities may require logistical assistance, such as transportation. In order to provide reintegration assistance, the DDR process might need time to establish such programmes within the contexts of arrival for reintegration. Subsequently, a phased demobilisation might be required, allowing local communities enough time to absorb each group of demobilised combatants before the arrival of the next cohort. It is also likely that some ex-combatants will not have a community to return to, if they were abducted from their families when they were children, or if they have committed atrocities against their own communities. In such cases, they would need assistance to find an adoptive community for themselves.[20]

Cantonment is considered as an essential element within demobilisation based on a threefold rationale: first, it provides a number of operational opportunities, such as the registration and gathering of information and profiling of ex-combatants, their health screening for infectious diseases such as HIV/AIDS and the identification of vulnerable groups such as those with disabilities, child soldiers and female combatants. Cantonment can also provide opportunities for a thorough assessment of the capacities and needs of ex-combatants and the implementation of an effective targeting mechanism. Second, it allows for pre-discharge orientation sessions, which are intended to prepare ex-combatants and their families for the changed circumstances of civilian life and to furnish them with information on the DDR programme, including the benefits and opportunities available. Third, it may also have a political objective, particularly during the war-to-peace transition, of demonstrating a faction's willingness to demobilise some forces while retaining other forces in concentrated areas, where they can be remobilised if the peace agreement is not implemented.[21]

On the other hand, cantonment requires an extensive logistics operation to support ex-combatants and if adequate facilities are not provided, violent activities and rebellion can undermine the demobilisation and reintegration process, as well as the overall peace process.[22] Furthermore, the cost of such logistical operations can prove to be disproportionate to the resources available for subsequent reintegration activities. Cantonment might also attract communities of ex-combatants' families and develop into politically awkward semi-permanent settlements due to the socio-economic constraints of post-conflict environments for ex-combatants and their families to re-start their lives elsewhere.[23] Also, the cantonment of combatants reinforces the command structures that the process is intended to dissolve, and in the case of cantonment areas, the ex-combatants are concentrated and isolated from the community when the objective is, in fact, to dissipate and integrate them within the community. Therefore, as cantonment can prove detrimental to the effectiveness of the DDR programme by absorbing scarce resources and causing delays that undermine overall confidence in the process, it is important to explore possible alternatives to the cantonment of ex-combatants before deciding whether it constitutes an absolute necessity for demobilisation.

Reinsertion Assistance

Reinsertion of ex-combatants following demobilisation and prior to participation in a reintegration programme constitutes a crucial stage within the overall DDR process. The basic material needs of ex-combatants and their dependents can be divided into two areas: household consumption, such as food, clothes, health care and children's education, and household investment, such as shelter, agricultural tools and kitchen utensils.[24] The transitional safety net is often planned for a period of six months to a year after demobilisation and delivered through the provision of cash and/or goods. The cash assistance could be provided as a monthly amount or in a lump sum and needs to be tailored to meet the individual needs of the ex-combatant. Not all ex-combatants will require the same amount of reinsertion assistance; therefore, criteria for assistance need to be established and implemented in a transparent manner.[25]

Reinsertion assistance should be considered temporary, as reintegration requires a much more comprehensive response. Overall, five primary issues must be addressed when planning cash reinsertion assistance: the mobilisation of funds, differentiation criteria, size of the allowance, financial education and the development of a non-corruptible identification system. Experience indicates that criteria for differentiating the amounts paid to particular groups must be clearly and transparently established. This is particularly important in order to avoid discrimination, for example, against female ex-combatants. The amount of the allowance, as a general rule, should broadly correspond to the level of household income of the general population in order that it does not cause resentment within the community in which the ex-combatant will settle.[26]

Cash allowances should not be considered to be exclusive. For example, in Angola, in addition to cash, ex-combatants were provided with in-kind kit, including clothes, domestic tools, food and agricultural tools.[27] Free health services may be included in the reinsertion assistance package, especially if ex-combatants received free medical care during their period of military service. Any health support provided should be targeted at the family of the former combatant and includes children. However, depending upon the social context, it should be recognised that health support may be an element of the reinsertion assistance that potentially causes resentment among the community, especially if medical provision in the community is not freely available. It would, therefore, be preferable to channel funds through existing structures that benefit the community as a whole, rather than create DDR specific programmes.[28]

Community-Based Reintegration

The way in which the reintegration of ex-combatants is viewed by the donor community and implementing agencies will depend to a great degree on the philosophy underpinning the DDR programme and this will to some extent influence the way in which they are designed as well as the perceived success of such programmes. Therefore, it is particularly important that reintegration is perceived from a comprehensive perspective incorporating not only economic aspects but also social and political. It is possible to identify two main approaches to reintegration: (1) the one-man-one-weapon type approach in which the ex-combatant is the main focus of DDR and (2) community-based reintegration that contextualizes the reintegration experience within the receiving communities' socio-economic challenges, resources, capacities and capabilities. In order to adopt a community-based reintegration approach, the DDR programme must identify the most effective portfolio of activities with which to address the needs of the society. For peacebuilding to succeed, the second approach is preferable.[29]

Economic reintegration is seen as a way in which 'to equip former fighters with productive skills and employment so that they can return to civilian life'[30] and is viewed as important for the short-, medium- and long-term objectives of the DDR process.[31] Economic reintegration initiatives continue to be the main approach undertaken by DDR programmes around the world. The conventional approach to economic reintegration would incorporate some of the following types of activities: the provision of vocational training programmes, micro-enterprise development, labour intensive public works, rehabilitation of agriculture and employment opportunities through joining post-conflict security sector structures, among others.

From Mindanao and Kosovo to Liberia, Uganda and Ethiopia, such economic reintegration programmes often exhibit quick-fix characteristics, with poor infrastructure and inadequate reach-out. For example, vocational training programmes often fail to produce meaningful livelihood pathways, as the time spent for training is inadequate, its quality is poor and undertaken without any opportunity of practicing what is learned in the classroom environment. Micro-enterprises developed as part of economic reintegration evaporate as most ex-combatants do not have any previous experience of running a business.[32] Moreover, one of the correlates of DDR planning, which is often overlooked, is the overall economic situation in which programmes are attempted. This is a significant factor because the benefits of newly gained vocational skills or micro-enterprise schemes created as part of reintegration might only be realised if there is sufficient demand and absorptive capacity in the economy in general. The issues of corruption, economic insecurity and infrastructural challenges in the financial system can also undermine the utility of certain types of economic reintegration assistance. Therefore, it is essential to consider macro-economic indicators and issues of poverty in planning DDR responses.[33]

Political reintegration, 'the process through which the ex-combatant and his or her family become a full part of decision-making processes',[34] also forms an important component of the reintegration and peacebuilding process. Ex-combatants very often became involved with a military group because they identified with the politics of that group and opposed the politics of the government.[35] Assuring that they do not become a marginalised group and thus feel the need to return to arms is therefore instrumental in fostering stability and security.

There are not many examples of DDR experiences that incorporate specific political and social reintegration initiatives. The conventional thinking on reintegration assumes that once ex-combatants are provided with opportunities of employment and livelihoods, the other two types of reintegration will happen gradually. In fact, social reintegration gets the least attention from the DDR programmes, as political reintegration might be dealt with as part of wider negotiations and political settlements: the transformation of non-state armed groups into mainstream political parties is one means of political reintegration, as the cases of El Salvador (Farabundo Martí National Liberation Front), Mindanao (Moro

National Liberation Front) and Sudan (Sudan People's Liberation Army) demonstrated.[36]

Finally, effective social reintegration of ex-combatants is vital to the success of DDR programmes and the greater post-conflict reconstruction effort for a multitude of reasons. Upon returning to their home communities, ex-combatants are faced with a dramatically changed and changing social landscape, one defined by violence and destruction, and it is in this environment that their reintegration takes place. This issue is ever more salient for ex-combatants creating homes in new communities. The need for effective social reintegration becomes increasingly more apparent when one considers the fact that the identity of the ex-combatants and the community in relation to each other has undergone a transformation as a result of the conflict.[37]

KEY CONSIDERATIONS IN DDR IMPLEMENTATION

Heterogeneity of Ex-Combatant Caseloads

Ex-combatants form a heterogeneous group with varied characteristics and needs including men, women, boys and girls, and the gravity of these issues should not be overlooked as different groups may face different difficulties and obstacles in the DDR process. Assessing the diversity of caseloads, special attention needs to be given to the fate of ex-combatants, who have been disabled because of conflict, as well as female combatants and child soldiers. In addition to these three conventional categories of vulnerable groups within ex-combatant caseloads, Srivastava identifies three more vulnerable groups as: first, those who left the army before the peace agreement; second, those who were demobilised as senior personnel and finally, the families of combatants who have died in the conflict.[38] Each of these groups can be further sub-divided as ex-combatants who are from various sides in the conflict and those who were volunteered and forced to fight. However, the focus in this section will be mainly on female and child combatants as two specific vulnerable groups whose specific needs are often overlooked in DDR processes.

One of the characteristics of contemporary conflicts is that there has been an increase in the number of female combatants. However, as an International Labour Organisation (ILO) study of Ethiopia, Uganda, Zimbabwe and Mozambique shows, female combatants had reduced access to land, employment and training opportunities because the reintegration programmes did not ensure equal access to them as the most important policy element.[39] It is also argued that difficulties for female combatants can increase when they do not feel they are being accorded the same equality that they had as part of the army. For example, women as both fighters and war-affected civilians acquire new roles during the war. However, they are usually expected to return to their traditional roles after the war. Analysis of socio-economic data on ex-combatants in Guinea-Bissau and Eritrea has also shown that female ex-combatants were more vulnerable not only to sexual and gender-based violence but also to wider socio-economic challenges than their male counterparts.[40] Consequently, Tegegn emphasizes the importance of providing female ex-combatants with special assistance to enable them to participate fully and equally in social, economic and political life.[41]

When the needs of ex-combatants are assessed, it should be borne in mind that life choices made by women and girls may be quite different from those made by men and boys due to their different roles before, during and after conflict. In the same way, when it comes to demobilisation, specific gender requirements should be taken into account, especially if the phase requires the establishment of cantonment sites. In socio-economic reintegration once again, female ex-combatants would have different needs and expectations than male ex-combatants. Therefore, the reintegration process should ensure that traditional society structures do not result in reduced access to reintegration benefits for female ex-combatants such as not being able to attend vocational training courses because of childcare responsibilities or the need to travel long distances to reach training centres; cultural barriers to finding suitable employment and not having equal access to communal land and farming equipment. At the same time, the reintegration options that are open to female ex-combatants should include those vocational skills such as construction and driving that may not usually be considered as 'women's work' since such skills may have already been acquired during the conflict, and female ex-combatants may want to build on them.[42]

Similarly, in order to respond to the needs of former child soldiers, the World Bank presents three components as a prerequisite for their reintegration process: family reunification, psychological support and education and economic opportunity.[43] As well as facing a lack of specific programmes designed for their needs, one of the reasons child soldiers join in the outbreak of new conflicts is the intimidation they experienced after their demobilisation.[44] The transition from a military to civilian identity may also be much more difficult for child soldiers than adult combatants.[45] The DDR process is also likely to be more challenging for child soldiers than adult combatants. Identifying their families and facilitating reunification is usually a difficult task, as in some cases, child soldiers may not be welcomed by their families and communities because of what they were forced to do against their communities during the conflict. In respect of these particular requirements, it is also clear that the acceptance of families and communities and the means by which this can be fostered and reinforced need to form an integral component in any DDR programme directed at child soldiers. Furthermore, the provision of psychosocial care and support is often much more necessary for child soldiers than adult combatants in order to ensure that they can make the transition into a civilian identity successfully.[46]

Finally, the preceding requirements also necessitate a much longer term perspective for the DDR of child soldiers, as for example, according to an ILO study, the situation of girl former combatants is often more difficult than that of boys as girls are often used as sexual objects during the fighting, and consequently receive continued abuse after their demobilisation, making it difficult to reintegrate them into society. For example, because of their non-combatant roles as 'wives', messengers and cooks, most girl combatants tend to be invisible in DDR processes, or in cantonment sites they tend to face a high risk of sexual exploitation and young mothers and their children often experience a total rejection from their communities and experience continuing abuse and stigmatisation.[47] Consequently, it is necessary to monitor their reintegration process carefully, together with psychological counselling programmes to make sure that the process caters for their specific needs and concerns.[48]

Preferential Treatment of Ex-Combatants

Last presents a number of justifications for preferential treatment of ex-combatants. If ex-combatants cannot see a role for themselves in the post-conflict order, they may turn to banditry. It is particularly important that ex-combatants should not be seen returning to their communities empty-handed. Furthermore, targeted programmes may also be seen as a political payback for leaders who risked a great deal to bring their constituents into the peace process.[49] Supporting this view, the Bonn International Center for Conversion (BICC) asserts that ex-combatants require preferential treatment from a humanitarian point of view too, as they are out of a job and usually away from their home upon demobilisation.[50]

On the other hand, the preferential treatment of ex-combatants would also be likely to create resentment among other conflict-affected communities such as displaced persons who, like ex-combatants, face similar challenges in terms of access to land and means of livelihood. It is also necessary to note that there is no clear-cut difference between combatants and civilians in most armed conflicts, which can complicate such a targeted approach. Furthermore, receiving communities may also become resentful towards the preferential treatment of ex-combatants, especially if they are considered to have been responsible for wartime atrocities and destruction.[51]

Ball warns against the polarisation that ex-combatant-centred programmes can cause among conflict-affected populations and advises that these evolve into community-based programmes as early as possible, in order to be seen to benefit all the severely affected population.[52] The ILO, for example, recommends an inclusive approach that would contribute to the perception that peace will be built on social justice and the general welfare of all. In fact, it is crucial that ex-combatants actually avoid being given the label of 'ex-combatant'. It is asserted that ex-combatants should be encouraged to disperse rather than concentrate,[53] and it is important that ex-combatants would start to identify themselves as civilians as quickly as possible.

However, all too often, in order to ensure the participation of belligerent groups in the peacebuilding process, such preferential treatment is dictated by peace agreements. In such a context what needs to be done, therefore, is to strike a balance ensuring that 'ex-combatants should not receive more support than necessary to help them attain the standard of living of the communities in which they live'.[54] It is also possible that, while targeting ex-combatants as a preferential group for the recruitment of a new police force and army, and providing them with specific demobilisation benefits, reintegration programmes can be simultaneously designed to respond to the needs of the wider community around them. Emphasising this point, Ball notes that the community-based programmes actually ensure a greater opportunity for ex-combatants to be rapidly reintegrated.[55] In other words, ex-combatants should not be targeted in isolation for too long, but considered as individuals who are part of an extended family structure or even within their own wider community.

Role of Local Actors

Actors involved in the DDR process range from UN agencies, national and local government authorities, bilateral funding agencies and international financial institutions to international and local NGOs, community-based organisations and more importantly, ex-combatants themselves, their families and receiving communities. There is also a clear consensus in the literature that the assistance for DDR, particularly in the reintegration phase should be community-based and structured as part of general post-conflict recovery efforts.[56] The national ownership of DDR programmes is particularly critical as a number of legislative frameworks such as transitional justice and amnesty provisions; citizenship and nationality laws; weapons control and management; justice reform and legal provisions for new armed forces would all be necessary for the successful integration of DDR in the overall peacebuilding framework.[57] However, the international community in DDR programmes tends to be reluctant to empower local ownership of the process, as took place in Eritrea,[58] Mozambique[59] and Iraq.[60]

Reintegration programmes that are well-conceived and aimed at sustaining peacebuilding at the grassroots level would make it an essential requirement to take into consideration and build upon the existing knowledge of ex-combatants and their communities.[61] The value and significance of involving local actors in the planning and implementation of the reintegration process were clearly demonstrated in Somaliland. The National Demobilisation Commission (NDC) of Somaliland in 1993 included the direct involvement of war veterans and former combatants, which led to considerable improvements in the effectiveness of programme design and its delivery.[62] In the context of DDR in Haiti, MINUSTAH adopted a community-focussed Armed Violence Reduction and Prevention (ARVP) programme in order to disincentivise at-risk sections of the population from joining armed groups in the first place. Thus, the intervention was more suitable for Haiti's urban armed groups, which have more in common with street gangs than with rural rebel forces—the conventional targets of DDR.[63]

Conclusion

This chapter provided a general overview of DDR in its second and third generation form, highlighting a number of critical issues that play a significant role in its failures and successful outcomes. Overall, in relation to wider securitisation trends in the post-conflict peacebuilding environments, the third-generation DDR operations place their emphasis on security rather than development. This is the case even when their rhetoric makes so much reference to the reintegration of ex-combatants from a developmental perspective, as the reality on the ground sets the priorities on how to protect the well-being of intervening forces. The politics of DDR due to the implications of the process on power relations are also a prominent feature to consider, and it is important to recognise that they would likely be affected by many challenges, delays and disruptions. Furthermore, the importance of a community-centred approach rather than considering ex-combatants from a one-man-one-weapon perspective in isolation from their communities was highlighted. This would, in fact, serve better the overall goal of DDR, which is to make ex-combatants part of their communities. In other words, rather than adopting a technocratic approach, DDR processes would need to develop tailor-made responses according to specific characteristics of ex-combatants and their surrounding socio-political and economic environments.

The current practice of DDR tends to focus on economic reintegration of ex-combatants with much less attention on the challenges of social reintegration. This has been one of the main shortcomings of DDR processes in most post-accord contexts. The assumption of social reintegration that would happen as a trickle-down effect of economic reintegration is wrong, especially in such environments where there are serious trust deficiencies between ex-combatants and receiving communities due to the divisive nature of the conflict experienced. Everyday peacebuilding efforts of receiving communities and ex-combatants would need to be supported with a more targeted approach through social reintegration, paying specific attention on the challenges of trust-building, cohesion and cooperation.

Finally, it is also important to recognise that the challenges of third-generation DDR programmes such as those in Afghanistan and Iraq in terms of the impact of a continuing combat environment, might be even more challenging in such places as a post-conflict Syria in the future. This would partly be because of the excessive polarisation of armed groups and their numbers being in hundreds, and partly due to the transnational nature of some of them such as the Islamic State (Daesh). The DDR orthodoxy used by the international community in its current framework as explained in this chapter, may fall completely short in addressing disarmament, demobilisation and reintegration needs of ex-combatants and their receiving communities in such contexts, demanding significant revisions in the way such programmes are planned, funded and implemented.

Notes

1. M. Berdal, *Disarmament and Demobilisation After Civil Wars*, Adelphi Paper 303 (London: International Institute for Strategic Studies, 1996); N. Colletta, M. Kostner and I. Wiederhofer, *Case Studies in War-to-Peace Transition: The Demobilisation and Reintegration of Ex-Combatants in Ethiopia, Namibia and Uganda* (Washington, DC: World Bank, 1996); K. Kingma, 'Demobilizing and Reintegrating Soldiers: Lessons from Africa', in L. Reychler and T. Paffenholz (eds.) *Peacebuilding: A Field Guide* (London: Lynne Rienner Publishers, 2001) pp. 405–415; J. Gomes Porto and I. Parsons, *Sustaining the Peace in Angola: An Overview of Current Demobilisation, Disarmament and Reintegration, Article 27* (Bonn: Bonn International Center for Conversion, 2003); UN, *The Integrated Disarmament, Demobilisation and Reintegration Standards (IDDRS)* (New York: United Nations, 2006); M. Humphreys and J. Weinstein, 'Demobilisation and Reintegration', *Journal of Conflict Resolution*, 51, 4 (2007) pp. 531–567; A. Özerdem, *Post-war Recovery: Disarmament, Demobilisation and Reintegration* (London: I.B. Tauris, 2008); R. Muggah (ed.), *Security and Post-Conflict Reconstruction: Dealing with Fighters in the Aftermath of War* (Abingdon: Routledge, 2009); J. McMullin, *Ex-Combatants and the Post-Conflict State: Challenges of Reintegration* (London: Palgrave Macmillan, 2013); W. Kilroy, *Reintegration of Ex-Combatants After Conflict: Participatory Approaches in Sierra Leone and Liberia* (London: Palgrave Macmillan, 2015); O. Kaplan and E. Nussio, 'Explaining Recidivism of Ex-Combatants in Colombia', *Journal of Conflict Resolution*, (2016) https://doi.org/10.1177/0022002716644326; D.

B. Subedi, *Combatants to Civilians: Rehabilitation and Reintegration of Maoist Fighters in Nepal's Peace Process* (London: Palgrave Macmillan, 2018).
2. P. Collier, 'Demobilisation and Insecurity: A Study in the Economics of the Transition from War to Peace', *Journal of International Development*, 6, 3 (1994) pp. 343–351.
3. Berdal (1996), op. cit.
4. I. Nübler, *Human Resources Development and Utilization in Demobilisation and Reintegration Programs*, Paper 7 (Bonn: Bonn International Center for Conversion, 1997).
5. UN (2006), op. cit.
6. R. Bowd and A. Özerdem 'How to Assess Social Reintegration of Ex-Combatants', *Journal of Intervention and Peacebuilding* (2013) https://doi.org/10.1080/17502977.2012.727537.
7. R. Muggah and C. O'Donnell, 'Next Generation Disarmament, Demobilisation and Reintegration', *Stability: International Journal of Security and Development*, 4, 1 (2015), p.Art. 30. https://doi.org/10.5334/sta.fs.
8. W. Kilroy, *Reintegration of Ex-Combatants After Conflict: Participatory Approaches in Sierra Leone and Liberia* (London: Palgrave, 2015).
9. Özerdem (2008), op. cit.
10. J. Munive and F. Stepputat, 'Rethinking Disarmament, Demobilisation and Reintegration Programs', *Stability: International Journal of Security and Development*, 4, (1), p.Art. 30 (2015), p. 10. https://doi.org/10.5334/sta.fs.
11. A. Özerdem, 'Insurgency, Militias and DDR as Part of Security Sector Reconstruction in Iraq: How Not to Do It', *The Journal of Disaster Studies, Policy and Management*, S40–S59 (2010).
12. UN (2006), op. cit.
13. A. Özerdem, 'A Re-Conceptualisation of Ex-combatant Reintegration: "Social Reintegration" Approach', *Conflict, Security & Development*, 12, 1 (2012) pp. 51–73.
14. F. Tanner, 'Consensual versus Coercive Disarmament', in *Disarmament and Conflict Resolution Project—Managing Arms in Peace Processes: The Issues* (Geneva: United Nations Institute for Disarmament Research, 1996) pp. 169–204.

15. World Bank, *Demobilisation and Reintegration of Military Personnel: The Evidence from Seven Country Case Studies* (Washington, DC: World Bank, 1993).
16. Özerdem (2008), op. cit.
17. Berdal (1996), op. cit., p. 34.
18. M. Sedra, *Challenging the Warlord Culture: Security Sector Reform in Post-Taliban Afghanistan*, Paper 25 (Bonn: Bonn International Center for Conversion, 2002).
19. C. Gleichmann, M. Odenwald and K. Steenken, *Disarmament, Demobilisation and Reintegration: A Practical Field and Classroom Guide* (Frankfurt: GTZ, NODEFIC, PPC, SNDC, 2004).
20. M. Knight Mark and A. Özerdem, 'Guns, Camps and Cash: Disarmament, Demobilisation and Reinsertion of Former Combatants in Transitions from War to Peace', *Journal of Peace Research*, 41, 4 (2004) pp. 499–516.
21. DPKO, *Disarmament, Demobilisation and Reintegration of Ex-Combatants in a Peacekeeping Environment: Principles and Guidelines* (New York: Lessons Learned Unit, Department of Peacekeeping Operations, 1999).
22. K. Kingma, *Demobilisation and Reintegration of Ex-Combatants in Post-War and Transition Countries: Trends and Challenges of External Support* (Eschborn: GTZ, 2001).
23. D. Last, 'The Human Security Problem—Disarmament, Demobilisation and Reintegration', in *A Source Book on the State of the Art in Post-Conflict Rehabilitation*, unpublished report prepared by PRDU for Regional Socio-Economic Development Programme for Southern Lebanon (York: PRDU, University of York, 1999).
24. M. Kostner, *A Technical Note on the Design and Provision of Transitional Safety Nets for Demobilisation and Reintegration Programs* (Mimeo. Washington, DC: World Bank, 2001).
25. A. Özerdem and S. Podder, *Reinsertion Assistance and the Reintegration of Ex-Combatants in War to Peace Transitions*, Thematic Working Paper 4. https://bradscholars.brad.ac.uk/handle/10454/7311 (Bradford: University of Bradford, 2008).
26. Kostner (2001), op. cit.
27. Porto and Parsons (2003), op. cit.
28. Colletta et al. (1996), op. cit.
29. UN (2006), op. cit.

30. J. Ginifer, 'Reintegration of Ex-Combatants', in M. Malan et al., (eds.) *Sierra Leone: Building the Road to Recovery*, ISS Monograph Series 80, March, p. 43.
31. Özerdem (2008), op. cit.
32. A. Özerdem, 'Vocational Training of Former Kosovo Liberation Army Combatants: For What Purpose and End?', *Conflict, Security & Development*, 3, 3 (2003) pp. 383–405; M. Babiker and A. Özerdem, 'A Future Disarmament, Demobilisation and Reintegration Process in Sudan: Lessons Learned from Ethiopia, Mozambique and Uganda', *Conflict, Security & Development*, 3, 2 (2003) pp. 211–232; A. Özerdem and S. Podder, 'Grassroots and Rebellion: A Study on the Future of the Moro Struggle in Mindanao, Philippines', *Civil Wars*, 14, 4 (2012) pp. 521–545.
33. C. Maclay and A. Özerdem, '"Use" Them or "Lose" Them: Engaging Liberia's Disconnected Youth Through Socio-Political Integration', *International Peacekeeping*, 17, 3 (2010) pp. 343–360.
34. K. Kingma (ed.), *Demobilisation in Sub-Saharan Africa: The Development and Security Impacts* (New York: St. Martins, 2000) p. 28.
35. J. G. Porto, I. Parsons, and C. Alden, *From Soldiers to Citizens: The Social, Economic and Political Reintegration of UNITA Ex-Combatants* (Aldershot: Ashgate, 2007).
36. Özerdem (2008), op. cit.
37. Özerdem (2012), op. cit.
38. R. Srivastava, *Reintegrating Demobilised Combatants: A Report Exploring Options and Strategies for Training Related Intervention* (Geneva: International Labour Office, 1994).
39. Colletta et al. (1996), op. cit.
40. N. de Watteville, *Addressing Gender Issues in Demobilisation and Reintegration Programs*, Africa Region Working Article Series (Washington, DC: World Bank, 2002).
41. M. Tegegn, 'Demobilisation and Employment of Combatants: Two Perspectives', in M. Doornbos et al. (eds.) *Beyond Conflict in the Horn: The Prospects for Peace, Recovery and Development in Ethiopia, Eritrea and Sudan* (London: Institute of Social Sciences in association with James Currey, 1992) pp. 38–40.
42. UN (2006), op. cit.

43. World Bank, *Child Soldiers: Prevention, Demobilisation and Reintegration*, Dissemination Notes of Conflict Prevention and Reconstruction Unit, Number 3 (Washington, DC: The World Bank, 2002).
44. GTZ, *Demobilisation and Reintegration of Ex-Combatants in Postwar and Transition Countries: Trends and Challenges of External Support* (Eschborn: GTZ, 2001).
45. A. Özerdem and S. Podder (eds.), *Child Soldiers: From Recruitment to Reintegration* (London: Palgrave, 2011).
46. A. Özerdem, S. Podder, and E. Quitoriano, 'Identity, Ideology and Child Soldiering: Community and Youth Participation in Civil Conflict—A Study on the Moro Islamic Liberation Front, Mindanao, Philippines', *Civil Wars*, 12, 3 (2010) pp. 304–325.
47. ILO, *The Reintegration of Young Ex-Combatants into Civilian Life* (Geneva: International Labour Office, 1995).
48. Özerdem and Podder (2011), op. cit.
49. Last (1999), op. cit.
50. BICC, *Conversion Survey 1996: Global Disarmament, Demilitarisation and Demobilisation* (Oxford: Oxford University Press, 1996).
51. Kingma (2001), op. cit.
52. N. Ball, 'Demobilizing and Reintegrating Soldiers: Lessons from Africa', in K. Kumar (ed.) *Rebuilding Societies After Civil War—Critical Roles for International Assistance* (London: Lynne Rienner Publishers, 1997) pp. 85–105.
53. A. Mehreteab, *Veteran Combatants Do Not Fade Away: A Comparative Study on Two Demobilisation and Reintegration Exercises in Eritrea*, Paper 23 (Bonn: Bonn International Center for Conversion, 2002).
54. Kingma (2001), op. cit., p. 410.
55. Ball (1997), op. cit.
56. Kingma (2000), op. cit., Muggah (2009), op. cit., N. Wilen, 'A Hybrid Peace Through Locally Owned and Externally Financed SSR-DDR in Rwanda?' *Third World Quarterly*, 33, 7 (2012) pp. 1323–1336; A. Phayal, B. K. Prabin, and C. L. Thyne, 'What Makes an Ex-Combatant Happy? A Micro-Analysis of Disarmament, Demobilisation and Reintegration in South Sudan', *International Studies Quarterly*, 59, 4 (2015) pp. 654–668.
57. UN (2006), op. cit.

58. E.-M. Bruchhaus and A. Mehreteab, 'Leaving the Warm House: The Impact of Demobilisation in Eritrea', in K. Kingma (ed.) *Demobilisation in Sub-Saharan Africa: The Development and Security Impacts* (London: Macmillan Press, 2000) pp. 95–131.
59. I. B. Lundin, M. Chachiua, A. Gasper, H. Guebuza and G. Mbilana, 'Reducing Costs Through an Expensive Exercise', in K. Kingma (ed.) *Demobilisation in Sub-Saharan Africa: The Development and Security Impacts* (London: Macmillan Press, 2000).
60. Özerdem (2010), op. cit.
61. Kilroy (2015), op. cit.
62. Berdal (1996), op. cit.
63. M. Schuberth, 'Disarmament, Demobilisation and Reintegration in Unconventional Settings: The Case of MINUSTAH's Community Violence Reduction', *International Peacekeeping*, 24, 3 (2017) pp. 410–433.

CHAPTER 18

Security Sector Reform

Yuji Uesugi

INTRODUCTION

Security sector reform (SSR) is essentially a process of reconstructing, reconstituting or developing the security and justice sectors of a society, which includes both security and justice actors, such as the military, police, intelligence agencies, vigilante groups, civil defence forces, judicial and penal institutions and their oversight mechanisms such as the parliament, media, civil society and village councils.[1] While it is often the case that statutory institutions are identified as the main object of SSR, non-state actors such as rebel groups, tribal chiefs, customary courts and non-governmental organisations (NGOs) are increasingly recognised as key SSR stakeholders. The United Nations (UN) defines the goal of SSR as being 'the enhancement of effective and accountable security for the State and its peoples'.[2] It is this dual commitment to making security and justice sectors effective and accountable that distinguishes SSR from other types of security assistance.[3]

Y. Uesugi (✉)
Waseda University, Tokyo, Japan
e-mail: uesugi@waseda.jp

SSR encompasses three levels of reform activities: strategic, institutional and technical. What is required and affordable in each SSR setting will vary, so here is a typical, and inexhaustive, list of possible activities that fall into each category. At the strategic level, the constitution which sets the mandates and parameters of the security and justice sectors is often amended or replaced in the aftermath of a civil war. The constitutional reform is the most fundamental strategic reform activity usually undertaken in post-conflict peacebuilding as seen in Timor-Leste[4] and Nepal.[5] An equally important and commonly adopted practice is the immediate restoration of judicial independence in the government, particularly from its executive body. The organic laws of the military, police and civil defence institutions are either reformed or enacted normally as a part of SSR, through which the statutory security actors are placed under the rule of law and civilian control. Functional separation of the police from the military is often stipulated in a related regulation or policy. A national dialogue on security issues among a wide range of stakeholders can also be recognised as a strategic level SSR activity.

At the institutional level, the most common post-conflict SSR activities fall under the Disarmament, Demobilisation and Reintegration (DDR) rubric through which the reintegration of ex-combatants to civilian life is promoted. Through DDR an overly large security sector will be pared down to reduce wartime defence budgets. Sometimes, rebel and tribal forces are transformed or integrated into national security forces. Oversight mechanisms, including media and civil society organisations, are also reinforced or institutionalised during the SSR processes often aiming to improve budget transparency and/or to combat corruption. In some cases, an inter-ministerial council responsible for overseeing the security sector is established, while in other occasions, the judicial code of ethics is revised. In Timor-Leste, for example, the Parliamentary Committee B for Defence and Security was tasked with scrutinising the budget and spending of the statutory security actors, and an Anti-corruption Committee was organised to address the problem of government corruption, including the security sector.[6] In Timor-Leste, Liberia and Kosovo, institutional level SSR involved the inauguration of a new police academy together with new recruitment, training and promotion schemes to professionalise the national police forces.

The technical level activities are the most commonly pursued reform undertakings. At this level, various projects are carried out to develop the capacity of security and justice institutions and their oversight agencies. Under the banner of capacity building, workshops and seminars are provided to inform and socialise security personnel with a new set of knowledge and practices including human rights, civilian control, democracy and gender-mainstreaming. New curriculums for defence and police training can be developed and adopted at this level. As part of post-conflict police reform, for example, new techniques and theories for forensic investigation, criminal psychology, crowd control and community policing might be introduced. Tools for planning, budgeting, monitoring and evaluation are usually reviewed and often renewed for both the security and justice institutions and their oversight mechanisms.

These SSR activities can be classified in two distinctive ways: first, as a process of reform carried out by a state with or without outside support; and second, as an intervention policy and/or strategy of international peacebuilding actors. Existing literature covers both dimensions,[7] but the bulk of previous work has looked into the cases of international peacebuilding in Sierra Leone, Afghanistan, Liberia, Timor-Leste and Bosnia Herzegovina, all of which fall into the second category.[8] While SSR assistance by Western donors can be introduced in the context of post-conflict peacebuilding as well as in post-authoritarian transition/democratisation processes,[9] the focus of this chapter is on the former as the overarching theme of the book is to explore dimensions of international peacebuilding. In short, this chapter will focus on the theory and practice of SSR assistance in post-conflict peacebuilding of failed or fragile states.

Security assistance led by the United States (US) in the aftermath of its 'regime change' invasions of Afghanistan and Iraq is sometimes categorised as SSR.[10] In fact, it is the case of Afghanistan that tends to dominate much SSR analysis and discourse, and many criticisms of SSR are influenced by what happened in Afghanistan.[11] However, whether SSR assistance follows a peace process or conquest matters, and blurring this distinction invites false analogising between UN-sponsored peacebuilding and the US-led 'war on terror'.[12] Hence, security assistance led by the US operating under a 'war on terror' paradigm will be placed outside of the scope of this chapter.[13]

The objective of this chapter is fourfold. First, it attempts to outline the concept of SSR in the context of post-conflict peacebuilding. Second, by surveying challenges facing the implementation of SSR assistance, it intends to illuminate the 'conceptual-contextual divide'[14] or the 'policy-implementation gap'.[15] Third, by classifying existing criticism of SSR, it aims to demonstrate that SSR is a lasting and interactive process which is not suitable for many of the conventional SSR practices, characterised by linear, externally driven, short-term and technical activities.[16] Then, it seeks to argue that the concept of 'hybridity'[17] can facilitate our efforts to explore alternative approaches to SSR assistance that resonate with the multifaceted and 'adaptive' nature of SSR.[18]

Before proceeding, it is worth making clear the urgent need for SSR in societies emerging from violent conflict. The security sector is often dysfunctional and a co-constitutive of the ills of a divided or at-war polity and society. Authoritarian leaders often empower their security apparatus to keep them in position. The result might be a deeply corrupt system with little interest in serving the populace, or minority groups, and every interest in the perpetuation of the system. Perverse political economies can develop in which the conflict becomes the raison d'etre for the security forces and interior ministry. This civilianisation of the security sector often becomes a key challenge for a peace process and peace accord. The SSR challenge often operates in tandem with DDR tasks and the need to re-orient a society—and especially security personnel, militants and their support constituencies—towards a post-conflict future. As this chapter demonstrates, these tasks are often easier said than done. While SSR often involves changing the institutional infrastructure of the state, and high-level change in core ministries of the state, there should be no doubt about the ability of SSR (or lack of it) to impact everyday life. If everyday safety and security does not improve as a result of SSR (e.g. the ability to safely send children to school or crops to the market) then people cannot be blamed for withholding their support for the peace process or peace accord.

OUTLINING THE CONCEPT OF SSR

After the Cold War, the international community shifted its attention from inter-state wars to civil wars.[19] The UN was tasked to intervene in civil wars such as in Cambodia, El Salvador, Mozambique, Angola, Rwanda and Bosnia Herzegovina to help terminate deadly conflicts and undertake post-conflict peacebuilding. Post-conflict transitional security arrangements were negotiated and often included in peace agreements because these arrangements could dictate the post-conflict emerging order. For example, in Cambodia, disarmament of warring factions and the dispatch of UN peacekeeping forces to fill an anticipated security vacuum were agreed and stipulated in the Paris Peace Agreement of October 1991.

Nevertheless, it was not until the late 1990s when the United Kingdom (UK) introduced the concept of SSR as a distinct post-conflict peacebuilding policy for Sierra Leone that the theory and practice of SSR began to evolve in a formal sense. Fragile or failed states recovering from the scars of conflict, such as Sierra Leone, Liberia, Timor-Leste, Kosovo and Haiti, were often suffering from critical defects in their security and justice sectors. In many cases, security actors such as the military and police were bloated, corrupt, partisan and tainted by allegations of human rights abuses, which could cause a relapse of violence or pose serious 'human security'[20] threats to people on the ground. Therefore, it became imperative that the problematic security and justice sectors be reconstructed or reformed so that they could provide security and justice for the people and be held accountable for their actions.

Against a backdrop of the recognition of the needs of post-conflict states, Clare Short, then the UK Secretary of State for International Development, played an instrumental role in promoting the concept of SSR. SSR was conceived theoretically as a nexus between security and development,[21] and empirically its focus was on statebuilding with the aim of meeting the minimum standards of a Weberian state model of a monopoly of violence placed under democratic control.[22] The underlying assumption was that 'the state is the only actor capable of meeting the human security needs of the population'.[23]

During the Cold War, the security community of the West equipped and trained its allies in developing countries to be able to fight internal wars against communists and hold the line against a global communist expansion. The end of the Cold War, however, forced the security community to look for, or invent, new reasons to sustain their military spending and dodge the demand for peace dividend. In a cynical interpretation, they found SSR to be a convenient façade, which allowed them to support their former allies and enemies in post-conflict situations.[24]

On the other hand, the development community seized the opportunities of the post-Cold War world and claimed that SSR could offer the necessary foundations for further and sustainable development.[25] The fact that the term SSR was coined by development actors who often articulated SSR in terms of wider societal and political changes, suggests that they encroached on the conventional sphere of security actors such as military and intelligence agencies. Indeed, by inventing the concept of human security and linking it with a normative agenda of liberal peacebuilding,[26] the development community introduced a new approach to security assistance and engaged in post-conflict peacebuilding with an emphasis on the governance aspects of security and justice sectors, and with an aim to locate SSR within wider developmental agenda. For example, the United Nations Development Programme (UNDP) argued that poorly governed security and justice sectors can be the chief causes of insecurity in post-conflict states, and can perpetuate cycles of violence, conflict and criminality.[27]

The Organisation for Economic Cooperation and Development/Development Assistance Committee (OECD/DAC) published a landmark document in 2007 that instrumentalised the current mainstream SSR approach. The *OECD/DAC Handbook on Security System Reform (SSR): Supporting Security and Justice* defined SSR as a process in which a country seeks to 'increase [its] abilities to meet the range of security needs within their societies in a manner consistent with democratic norms and sound principles of governance, transparency and the rule of law'.[28] Such a liberal conception of SSR was echoed by the UN Secretary-General in his 2008 Report, emphasising that SSR should be undertaken 'without discrimination and with full respect for human rights and the rule of law'.[29]

The Geneva Centre for Security Governance (DCAF),[30] another norm entrepreneur in the field of SSR, has been at the spearhead of promoting the OECD/DAC model of SSR.[31] It characterises SSR as one approach (local ownership), with two objectives (effectiveness and accountability) and having three dimensions (political, holistic and technical).[32] Although it claims that 'local ownership'[33] should be the key approach to SSR assistance, external intervenors are tasked with safeguarding liberal values. For example, it argues that:

> SSR processes often take place in contexts in which external support to the process is desirable or even required because of limited local capacity or resources ... while it is important to respect local customs and traditions, external actors also need to ensure that these customs and traditions are consistent with international human rights norms and standards.[34]

The nature of SSR at the nexus between security and development can be found in the two abovementioned objectives of SSR. The emphasis on effectiveness mainly comes from the attributes of the security approach, and the focus on accountability is mainly influenced by the development approach. The underlying assumption is that if domestically powerful security actors capable of overthrowing the government or overwhelming counterforces in the society are not placed under proper supervision (civilian or democratic oversight), they can easily turn into security threats. Therefore, holding security actors accountable for their actions is of paramount importance in OECD/DAC's theory of SSR. That is why the OECD/DAC model emphasises democratic governance of the security sector.[35]

What makes SSR, in theory, different from conventional security assistance strategies of 'train-and-equip' is that it covers not only statutory security and justice actors (such as the military, police and judiciaries) but also non-statutory actors (such as militias, vigilante groups and customary courts), as well as oversight and management actors/institutions both statutory (such as the parliament, ministries and ombudsperson) and non-statutory (civil society organisations, media and academia). In other words, one of the distinctive features of the OECD/DAC model of SSR is its holistic scope of the reform objects.

Another important feature of SSR is its inherent political nature.[36] Because the development community is accustomed to providing technical assistance after an overall political settlement is reached by the conflict parties, there is a hidden risk that the political nature of SSR is neglected or underestimated. This is why SSR needs to be discussed during peace talks.[37] As SSR involves a renegotiation of the prevailing social contract,[38] it can constitute a fundamental pillar of a peace accord. While there is often broad commitment to the need to reform the security and justice sectors, conflict parties tend to disagree how such reforms should be implemented,[39] as they—both incumbent and insurgent—are often still operating under the logic of 'politics of survival'.[40] For them, it is critical that their sources of survival, i.e. armed forces, are kept intact, especially in the aftermath of civil war. International SSR assistance can be deemed political interference because it may affect the power-balance among the conflict parties and thus it can shape the outcome of peace talks. As a result, SSR is often renegotiated in the implementation phase, which makes a narrow technical approach insufficient.[41]

CHALLENGES OF IMPLEMENTATION

It is the coherent, holistic and integrated nature of SSR that makes its underlying principles meaningful in practice.[42] In fact, the concept of SSR was promoted originally to demonstrate the intrinsic interconnections of the security and justice sectors and to encourage integrated interventions.[43] If SSR is conceived as such and evaluated against its intrinsic criteria, the record of achievement on the ground is pretty poor. Although there are cases of the successful implementation of individual SSR projects, the integration of different SSR activities has rarely been materialised in practice.[44] Mark Downes, a deputy director of DCAF, admits this point by saying that 'it is difficult to find successful SSR examples'.[45]

The practice of SSR and the reality of SSR assistance on the ground have been divergent from the OECD/DAC principles and the DCAF guidelines. While the theory of SSR stems from liberal values and norms, the practice of international SSR assistance can be characterised as shallow, applying 'good enough' standards,[46] and limiting the scope of reform to statutory security institutions.[47] Such attributes can be traced in a series of post-conflict SSR assistance programmes carried out by the UN in Sierra Leone,[48] Liberia,[49] Rwanda,[50] Burundi,[51] Mozambique,[52] Bosnia-Herzegovina,[53] Nepal,[54] Timor-Leste,[55] Kosovo[56] and Haiti.[57]

Adequate resources and political will necessary for implementing the OECD/DAC model of SSR have never been marshalled on the ground, despite the fact that a sophisticated institutionalisation of SSR concepts took place in the post-conflict peacebuilding strategy of Western donors. This indicates that Western donors have never invested sufficiently in the implementation of the promises of the original SSR concept.[58]

Why do Western donors fail to follow the liberal conceptual guidelines promoted by the OECD/DAC? Why do they often abandon the pursuit of accountability and end up with the old custom of 'train-and-equip'?[59] Serious deviation from the OECD/DAC model has been identified as 'problems with implementation',[60] and problematised by Channa and Podder as a 'conceptual-contextual divide'[61] and Sedra as a 'policy-implementation gap'.[62]

Along with other factors found in complex realities and politically sensitive situations on the ground, the inherent political nature of SSR that brings the dilemma of local ownership to the fore, has caused Western donors to fall into the expedient practice of pursuing more achievable goals. According to the OECD/DAC model, external actors are expected to serve as a safeguard against illiberal customs and traditions which are not aligned with 'international' human rights norms and standards.[63] However, if Western donors insist on these liberal norms, they not only jeopardise the golden rule of local ownership[64] but they are more likely to face resistance from local elites, which could generate friction between them and their local counterparts. It is true that international support for a national government that engages in genuine SSR efforts is not automatically interpreted as a usurpation of national sovereignty and thus it is not seen as in violation of the principle of local ownership. Nonetheless, there is a tendency in post-conflict situations that local stakeholders are engaging in what can be seen as 'illiberal' practices. Some local elites are involved in illicit businesses and corruption and are not interested in ceasing these activities.[65] Even in a permissive environment where local stakeholders are generally supportive of international peacebuilding assistance, intrusive intervention into the core state apparatus of the security and justice sectors can induce resistance from the incumbent authority. Local leaders—both incumbent and insurgent—rarely want to cede control of their security forces to independent supervision. In many cases, national governments are inclined to see international SSR assistance as an opportunity to weaken their domestic opponents while receiving funds to upgrade their security forces.

Under such circumstances, in the worst-case scenario, imposing liberal SSR upon recalcitrant local actors could lead to political instability, something which SSR assistance aims to avoid or eliminate in the first place. Thus, Western donors are often forced to reconsider and bend their standards to adjust them to the local reality. At the same time, if Western donors, by respecting local ownership, introduce hesitantly and nominally an oversight and civilian control of security actors, there is a risk that security governance mechanisms would be watered-down and reshaped by local elites, as witnessed in the case of Timor-Leste and elsewhere.[66]

CRITICISM OF EXISTING SSR THEORY AND PRACTICE

SSR has been criticised by some scholars and experts who believe that it should be operated under altruistic motives and with an aim of achieving human security.[67] These critics have regarded orthodox approaches to SSR assistance as a failure and advocated alternative approaches.[68] Before moving on to the discussion of alternatives, let us examine why orthodox approaches to SSR assistance have been considered a failure. There are three possible explanations: (1) incompatibility with the local context; (2) inappropriate methods and timing and (3) rhetorical implementation.

Incompatibility with the Local Context

First, (some of) the contents of the OECD/DAC model were not appropriate for the local context, including the security environment, political situation, developmental stage or societal readiness for absorbing liberal norms, upon which SSR assistance was installed. For example, Albrecht and Buur argue that conventional prescriptions for strengthening the ability of state institutions to monopolise the means of violence are no longer either appropriate or realistic in the vast majority of fragile or post-conflict states in which SSR is undertaken.[69] This group of critics point to the Euro-centric nature of SSR assistance, which places Western or liberal values at the centre of its activities. They argue that Western donors, who are operating under assumptions about the self-evident superiority of liberal security orders, have no doubt that SSR essentially aims to make the security sector of post-conflict states look more like theirs.[70] Such a mindset and behaviour may not only be inappropriate for SSR assistance but also could cause unintended harm to a host society.

Inappropriate Methods and Timing

The second category of critics focuses on the methodology of SSR assistance. They criticise the manner through which SSR assistance so far has been delivered or introduced by external intervenors such as the UN and the EU. This group of critics can further be divided into two: one that resonates with the first category, denying universality of SSR inflected with liberal values of human rights and democracy, and the other that does not renounce the intrinsic liberal values underpinning the contents of assistance.

The former criticises the donor-driven nature of SSR assistance in which outside interveners, who may possess a wide range of technical expertise and be familiar with the OECD/DAC guidelines of SSR yet often lack sufficient knowledge of the local context, are tasked to design the blueprint for SSR, while local actors are used and consulted merely as informants.[71] Local actors are not allowed to design and plan the reform process of their own security and justice sectors as they are often seen as incapable (lack of capacity) or inappropriate (lack of neutrality), despite the fact that in theory local ownership is considered to be crucial to the success of SSR.[72] This perspective implies that if SSR assistance is realigned with the principle of local ownership, and designed through dialogue between local stakeholders and outside intervenors, the contents of SSR can be different from what the OECD/DAC theory prescribes.

The latter group of critics, who maintain that liberal SSR remains valid in other settings, can be sub-divided into three. The first set of criticisms revolves around the argument that the security situation is not ripe for SSR to be initiated. For example, Downes and Muggah argue that SSR may not be feasible or possible in post-conflict settings, and SSR could be a better fit in more normalised development environments where it can be more easily linked up with the governance agenda.[73] In other words, these critics do not dismiss the contents of liberal SSR assistance, but they argue that SSR needs to be implemented at the right time to be successful and thus some elements must be withheld until the situation becomes ripe for such an institutional reform agenda.[74]

Closely related to this ripeness criticism is what Paris presented as 'Institutionalisation before Liberalisation', which urges Western donors to help the host state build functioning institutions *before* they engage in liberal SSR assistance.[75] These critics argue that a more politically and culturally nuanced approach is effective in implementing a liberal SSR agenda.[76]

The third set of criticisms is against orthodox approaches to SSR that are characterised as technocratic, state-centric and gender-insensitive.[77] For example, Jackson argues that the failure to account for the politics of SSR, in terms of both local power relations and everyday political relationships underlying state structures, has tended to lead to a technocratic approach focused on improving the effectiveness of security institutions rather than on the politics that provide the context for security.[78] Some critics point out the fact that a 'hybrid political order',[79] in which informal and non-state actors such as tribal chief, rebel forces and customary courts provide security and justice for their constituents alongside the formal and statutory institutions, is a common reality across many post-conflict states, and underline the importance of including non-state actors, who have been neglected or considered to be replaced by the formal institutions, in SSR.[80] Despite the fact that the human security perspective, one of the fundamental principles of SSR, places the needs of the most vulnerable such as women and children at the centre of SSR assistance, in practice, however, gender has been marginalised in conventional approaches to SSR.[81] As is the case with non-state actors, the knowledge and capacity of women are often overlooked.[82]

Rhetorical Implementation

The third group of critics believes that the OECD/DAC model only exists in theory or what the intervenors said they would pursue under SSR assistance has remained merely rhetorical.[83] Much of the literature tends to treat outside intervenors such as the UN, the EU, the US and the UK as altruistic third parties seeking transformation on behalf of the most vulnerable or unrepresented segment of the population. The critics in this category, however, claim that Western donors have implemented SSR assistance programmes as a means to realise their strategic interests of transforming failed or fragile states into functioning members of an international system of liberal states.[84]

In a 'hyper-critical' analysis,[85] this amounts to a new form of Western or liberal imperialism that seeks to exploit or subjugate host societies.[86] While this view may fall into a trap of oversimplifying the complex motives of Western donors, it seems correct to assume that Western donors pursued at least two outcomes in their SSR assistance: 'rhetorical' OECD/DAC criteria and security for their own citizens at home.[87] From a Western donors' point of view, it is very doubtful whether SSR assistance can continue to be prioritised, if it does not serve their interests. A possible way to improve the practice of SSR assistance, therefore, is to make Western donors aware that sustainable SSR that guarantees the human security of the people within those states subject to SSR can in fact contribute to the maintenance of the international liberal order, which will benefit their citizens in the long-run.[88]

HYBRID SSR

Faced with a myriad of criticisms against the existing theory and practice of SSR, hybrid SSR emerged as a form of alternative approaches, which embrace both state and non-state actors, and recognising the complementary or supplementary roles of non-state actors in providing security and justice for the people in a post-conflict society.[89] It also acknowledges the merits of accommodating Western liberal principles with the local context when executing SSR assistance programmes. The main feature of hybrid SSR is that it is a continuous adaptation process to shape and reshape security sector actors, institutions, mechanisms, practices, standards and norms.

An emergent group of critical scholars, who stress the importance of 'contextual' factors which require cultural and political sensitivity, argue that the concept of 'hybridity'[90] helps us understand the dynamics of SSR processes by underlining the complexity and importance of the interplay between different actors involved in SSR.[91] In particular, they focus on interactions between outsiders and insiders on the one hand and, between state and society on the other. While the nexus between outside intervention and SSR is often restricted to the post-conflict statebuilding or peacebuilding phase, the dialogue between state and society will continue after such phases. Hence, the SSR process needs to be seen as a long-term endeavour encompassing constant contestation among national stakeholders as well as a series of multilateral negotiations between national leaders and their constituents, often communicating via local gatekeepers.[92] Furthermore, the political nature of SSR calls for time and patience from external actors engaged in SSR assistance.[93] It is imperative, therefore, that SSR be recognised as a constantly evolving process which requires sustained evaluation and ceaseless adaptation.[94] The outcome of SSR should be evaluated in the long-run and a minor improvement of the situation should not be denied outright as insufficient. This is because no matter how small the step made today may be, it may serve as a foundation for the future progress.

The perspective of the hybridity lens forces us to reconsider current theories and practices of SSR. The critical question is how external actors like the UN and the EU can improve their practice of SSR assistance so that they can bring about positive change. The hybridity lens elucidates possible answers to the following three practical questions: (1) how can SSR be implemented so that it can contribute to or facilitate political stability?; (2) should SSR be initiated under circumstances where political stability has not yet been restored? and (3) under what conditions should SSR be assisted by outside intervenors and how?

First and foremost, external intervenors must appreciate the inherent political nature of SSR. While there is no consensus on how the dilemma of local ownership can be overcome, external intervenors, if they wish to leave a positive impact on the process of SSR, must comprehend local contexts and behave in ways that support locally grounded initiatives of diverse local actors.[95]

On the second question, the answer is yes. The hybridity lens encourages us to attune to emerging hybrid political orders,[96] in which non-state security and justice actors are co-existing with statutory actors that are under construction or reform. While SSR assistance is not a panacea and sometimes it is not even an appropriate tool for restoring political stability, the hybridity lens helps us discover the intertwined reality that short-term stabilisation measures must be in line with the long-term goals of SSR.[97]

It is clear from the point of view of hybrid SSR that the external intervenors should support locally grounded initiatives rather than prioritising their own agenda over the needs and interests of local populations. Such an approach, however, may entail the preservation and reinforcement of certain 'illiberal' practices and values of the host society, which creates a new set of problems and dilemmas for Western donors.[98] Hybrid SSR, which eschews the Weberian state-centric model in favour of strengthening actually existing mechanisms of security provision, may require the reconciliation of possibly contradicting practices and principles.[99] For example, recent practices of SSR assistance began to employ a gender-sensitive approach, and provide special measures to address gender-based violence.[100] If hybrid SSR is to appreciate the roles of existing informal mechanisms including non-state actors, how can the gender-sensitive approach be reconciled with indigenous practices based on a different conception of gender roles which vary according to socio-economic, political and cultural contexts?

There is no easy answer to such a difficult question, but the hybridity lens reminds us that local contexts matter and so the outcome of SSR processes should be seen as the result of a complex interplay of multiple contextual elements including historical background, political dynamics, the personality of political and military leaders, etc. Therefore, it is short-sighted to engage with SSR processes in a manner that can be described as linear, externally driven, short-term and technical, i.e. all features found in orthodox SSR assistance practices. The hybridity lens also shows us that it is impossible to externally pre-design desirable outcomes and appropriate steps of SSR, and it is misleading to presuppose that the SSR process can be navigated by the external intervenors alone. This requires Western donors to consider a radical paradigm shift. Their mindset and behaviour need to be altered.

Conclusion

There has been much thinking on what constitutes the security and justice sectors and the technocratic details of SSR, but far less emphasis on the contexts within which SSR is likely to be implemented.[101] While it was not the purpose of this chapter to present case studies of SSR offering a detailed analysis of contextual factors, the chapter sought to portray SSR as part of an adaptative process. It demonstrated that recognising SSR as an adaptive and hybrid evolution can be a useful way to advance the theory and practice of SSR. A hybrid lens helps us find ways to address some of the criticisms levelled against orthodox approaches to SSR assistance.

In fact, the hybrid approach has already been endorsed by the OECD/DAC, which underscores the importance of 'deliberate strategies for supporting the marriage of indigenous, customary and communal institutions of governance with introduced, Western state institutions, with a view to creating constructive interaction and positive mutual accommodation'.[102] The critical question still remains, however: How and who (outsiders or insiders) are supposed to orchestrate all of that?

This chapter argues that if the SSR process, so far led predominantly by external actors, is to be realigned with the needs and interests of people on the ground, a new set of principles, approaches and values/norms that embraces and supports locally grown and grounded actors must replace the existing SSR architecture.[103] As discussed in this chapter, the existing architecture faces enormous implementation challenges. A new set of assumptions and approaches would rescue SSR from a flood of criticism and build a bridge between the theory and practice of SSR.

Notes

1. Uesugi (2014a, p. 5).
2. UN (2008, para. 17).
3. Mason (2016, p. 1).
4. Wallis (2014).
5. Dahal (2014).
6. Belo (2014, p. 161).
7. Uesugi (2014a).
8. Jackson and Bakrania (2018).
9. Uesugi (2014a), Jackson (2010), Hills (2010).

10. Lacher (2007, p. 247).
11. Sedra (2010a, p. 17).
12. Paris (2010, p. 348).
13. Sedra (2010a, p. 17).
14. Chanaa (2002), Podder (2013).
15. Sedra (2017).
16. Sedra (2018), Donais (2018), Jackson and Bakrania (2018).
17. Uesugi (2020), Mac Ginty (2011).
18. de Coning (2018), Donais (2018).
19. Kaldor (1998).
20. UNDP (1994).
21. Sedra (2017).
22. Sedra (2016, pp. 211–212).
23. Sedra (2010a, p. 26).
24. Sedra (2010a, p. 17).
25. Short (1999), DFID (2000).
26. Jackson and Bakrania (2018, p. 13).
27. UNDP (2003, pp. 5–6) cited in Sedra (2018, p. 52).
28. OECD (2007, p. 21).
29. UN (2008, para. 17).
30. DCAF used to be called as the Geneva Centre for Democratic Control of Armed Forces before it was renamed in 2019.
31. DCAF has published a number of influential documents on SSR. See for example, Hänggi and Scherrer (2008), Donais (2008), Born and Schnabel (2009).
32. DCAF-ISSAT (2012, pp. 6–7).
33. For a more comprehensive discussion on local ownership in SSR, see, for example, Donais (2008), Mobekk (2010a).
34. DCAF-ISSAT (2012, p. 8).
35. Ball (2010, p. 40).
36. Downes (2014).
37. Mason (2016).
38. Knight (2009) cited in Sedra (2018, p. 50).
39. DCAF (2019, p. 5), Mason (2016)
40. Peou (2018, p. 82).
41. Jackson and Bakrania (2018, p. 11).
42. Sedra (2018, p. 49).
43. Sedra (2018, p. 49).
44. Sedra (2018, p. 49).

45. Downes (2014).
46. Wallis (2017).
47. Sedra (2017).
48. Jackson and Albrecht (2010).
49. Ebo (2005).
50. Wilén (2012), Takeuchi (2011).
51. Banal and Scherrer (2008).
52. Lalá and Francisco (2006).
53. Marijan (2016).
54. Dahal (2014), Upreti and Vanhoutte (2009).
55. Uesugi (2014c), Dewhurst et al. (2016).
56. Scheye (2008), Holohan (2016), Sahin (2017).
57. Mobekk (2008), Baranyi (2019).
58. To fulfill the promise of the original SSR concept, Ball (2010, p. 41) suggested four principles.
59. Sedra (2016, p. 215), Ball (2010 p. 37).
60. Sedra (2010b, pp.107–109).
61. Chanaa (2002), Podder (2013).
62. Sedra (2017).
63. Wilson (2020), Denney (2012).
64. Moderan (2015).
65. DCAF (2019, pp. 7–8).
66. Uesugi (2014c), Uesugi (2018).
67. Molloy (2016, p. 201), Ball (2010, p. 32).
68. Sedra (2010a), Jackson (2018), Marijan (2017), Baranyi (2019), Dewhurst and Greising (2017).
69. Albrecht and Buur (2009, p. 397).
70. Donais (2018, p. 31).
71. Keethaponcalan (2020, p. 26).
72. DCAF-ISSAT (2012, p. 7).
73. Downes and Muggah (2010, p. 137), Sedra (2010a, p. 20).
74. Sedra (2010a, p. 21), Downes and Muggah (2010, p. 137); Uesugi (2014b, pp. 78–79).
75. Paris (2004).
76. DCAF-ISAT (2016).
77. Sedra (2018, p. 48), Mobekk (2010b).
78. Jackson (2018).
79. Boege et al. (2009).

80. Baker (2010), Lawrence (2012), Bagayoko et al. (2016), Donais (2017).
81. Mobekk (2010b), Griffiths (2011).
82. Mobekk (2010b, p. 280).
83. Nathan (2008, p. 19).
84. Jackson and Bakrania (2018)
85. Paris (2010, p. 338).
86. Chandler (2007).
87. Ball (2010, p. 39).
88. Ball (2010, p. 39).
89. Baker (2010), Lawrence (2012), Donais (2018),
90. Mac Ginty (2011), Mac Ginty and Sanghera (2012), Schroeder and Chappuis (2014), Uesugi (2020).
91. Bagayoko et al. (2016), Schroeder et al. (2014), Ansorg and Gordon (2019
92. Uesugi (2020).
93. DCAF-ISSAT (2012, p. 11).
94. De Coning (2018).
95. Clements and Uesugi (2020).
96. Boege et al. (2009), Baker (2010, p. 212).
97. Downes and Muggah (2010).
98. Donais (2017).
99. Donais (2017, p. 4).
100. Griffiths (2011, pp. 2–5).
101. Jackson (2018).
102. OECD (2011, p. 38).
103. Sedra (2010b, p. 102).

References

Albrecht, P., & Buur, L. (2009). An Uneasy Marriage: Non-State Actors and Police Reform. *Policing and Society*, 19(4), 390–405.

Ansorg, N., & Gordon, E. (2019). Co-operation, Contestation and Complexity in Post-Conflict Security Sector Reform. *Journal of Intervention and Statebuilding*, 13(1), 2–24.

Baker, B. (2010). The Future Is Non-State. In M. Sedra (Ed.), *The Future of Security Sector Reform* (pp. 208–228). CIGI. https://www.cigionline.org/sites/default/files/the_future_of_security_sector_reform.pdf.

Ball, N. (2010). The Evolution of the Security Sector Reform Agenda. In M. Sedra (Ed.), *The Future of Security Sector Reform* (pp. 29–44). CIGI. https://www.cigionline.org/sites/default/files/the_future_of_security_sector_reform.pdf.

Banal, L., & Scherrer, V. (2008). ONUB and the Importance of Local Ownership: The Case Study of Burundi. In H. Hänggi & V. Scherrer (Eds.), *Security Sector Reform and UN Integrated Missions: Experience from Burundi, the Democratic Republic of Congo, Haiti, and Kosovo* (pp. 29–66). DCAF/LIT.

Baranyi, S. (2019). Second-Generation SSR or Unending Violence in Haiti? *Stability: International Journal of Security and Development*, 8(1), 1–19. https://doi.org/10.5334/sta.668.

Bagayoko, N., Hutchful E., & Luckham R. (2016). Hybrid Security Governance in Africa: Rethinking the Foundations of Security, Justice and Legitimate Public Authority. *Conflict, Security & Development*, 16(1), 1–32. https://doi.org/10.1080/14678802.2016.1136137.

Belo, N. (2014). Peacebuilding and Security Sector Governance in Timor-Leste. In Y. Uesugi (Ed.), *Peacebuilding and Security Sector Governance in Asia* (pp. 149–173). DCAF/LIT.

Boege, V., Brown, A. M., & Clements, K. P. (2009). Hybrid Political Orders, Not Fragile States. *Peace Review*, 21(1), 13–21. https://doi.org/10.1080/10402650802689997.

Born, H., & Schnabel, A. (Eds.). (2009). *Security Sector Reform in Challenging Environments*. DCAF/LIT.

Chanaa, J. (2002). *Security Sector Reform: Issues, Challenges and Prospects*. Oxford University Press.

Chandler, D. (2007). The Security–Development Nexus and the Rise of 'Anti-Foreign Policy'. *Journal of International Relations and Development*, 10(4), 362–386.

Clements, K. P., & Uesugi, Y. (2020). Conclusion. In Y. Uesugi (Ed.), *Hybrid Peacebuilding in Asia* (pp. 139–152). Palgrave Macmillan. https://doi.org/10.1007/978-3-030-18865-8.

Dahal, S. H. (2014). Understanding the Security Sector of Nepal: Challenges and Prospects for Reform. In Y. Uesugi (Ed.), *Peacebuilding and Security Sector Governance in Asia* (pp. 105–124). DCAF/LIT.

DCAF. (2019). *Peace Processes*. SSR Backgrounder Series, DCAF. https://www.dcaf.ch/sites/default/files/publications/documents/DCAF_BG_18_Peace%20Processes.pdf.

DCAF-ISAT. (2012). *SSR in a Nutshell: Manual for Introductory Training on Security Sector Reform*. https://issat.dcaf.ch/download/2970/25352/ISSAT%20LEVEL%201%20TRAINING%20MANUAL%20-%20SSR%20IN%20A%20NUTSHELL%20-%205.3.pdf.

DCAF-ISAT. (2016). *TOP 10 TIPS SERIES for Security and Justice Sector Reform*. https://issat.dcaf.ch/download/107569/1909170/ISSAT_top_10_tips.pdf.

de Coning, C. (2018). Adaptive Peacebuilding. *International Affairs*, 94(2), 301–317. https://doi.org/10.1093/ia/iix251.

Denney, L. (2012). Liberal Chiefs or Illiberal Development? The Challenge of Engaging Chiefs in DFID's Security Sector Reform Programme in Sierra Leone. *Development Policy Review*, 31(1), 5–25. https://doi.org/10.1111/j.1467-7679.2013.00599.x.

Department for International Development (DFID). (2000). *Poverty and the Security Sector, Policy Statement*. UK Department for International Development.

Dewhurst, S., & Greising, L. (2017). *The Gradual Emergence of Second Generation Security Sector Reform in Timor-Leste*. CSG Papers. No. 16. https://secgovcentre.org/wp-content/uploads/2017/01/Second-Generation-SSR-in-Timor-Leste-January-2017.pdf.

Dewhurst, S., Saraiva, J., & Winch, B. (2016). *Assessing the Impact of Orthodox Security Sector Reform in Timor-Leste*. CSG Papers. No. 12. https://secgovcentre.org/wp-content/uploads/2017/01/Second-Generation-SSR-in-Timor-Leste-January-2017.pdf.

Donais, T. (2008). Understanding Local Ownership in Security Sector Reform. In T. Donais (Ed.), *Local Ownership and Security Sector Reform* (pp. 3–17). DCAF/LIT.

Donais, T. (2017). Engaging Non-State Security Providers: Whither the Rule of Law? *Stability: International Journal of Security and Development*, 6(1), 7–13. https://doi.org/10.5334/sta.553.

Donais, T. (2018). Security Sector Reform and the Challenge of Vertical Integration. *Journal of Intervention and Statebuilding*, 12(1), 31–47. https://doi.org/10.1080/17502977.2018.1426681.

Downes, M. (2014). *Is It Time to Rethink our Approach to Security Sector Reform?* DCAF, March 19. https://issat.dcaf.ch/Share/Blogs/ISSAT-Blog/Is-it-time-to-rethink-our-approach-to-Security-Sector-Reform.

Downes, M., & Muggah, R. (2010). Breathing Room: Interim Stabilization and Security Sector Reform in the Post-War Period. In M. Sedra (Ed.), *The Future of Security Sector Reform* (pp. 136–153). CIGI. https://www.cigionline.org/sites/default/files/the_future_of_security_sector_reform.pdf.

Ebo, A. (2005). *The Challenges and Opportunities of Security Sector Reform in Post-Conflict Liberia*. Geneva Centre for the Democratic Control of Armed Forces (DCAF) Occasional Paper No. 9. https://www.dcaf.ch/sites/default/files/publications/documents/op09_security_sector_reform_liberia.pdf.

Griffiths, C. (2011). *Mapping Study on Gender and Security Sector Reform Actors and Activities in Liberia* (A Doherty & Holvikivi A.

Eds.). DCAF. https://www.dcaf.ch/sites/default/files/publications/docume nts/Gender_mapping_Liberia_August2011.pdf.

Hänggi, H., & Scherrer, V. (Eds.). (2008). *Security Sector Reform and UN Integrated Missions: Experience from Burundi, the Democratic Republic of Congo, Haiti, and Kosovo.* DCAF/LIT.

Hills, A. (2010). Learning the Hard Wat: Implementing SSR in Africa's Post-Authoritarian States. In M. Sedra (Ed.), *The Future of Security Sector Reform* (pp. 177–191). CIGI. https://www.cigionline.org/sites/default/files/the_future_of_security_sector_reform.pdf.

Holohan, A. (2016). Peacebuilding and SSR in Kosovo: An Interactionist Perspective. *Global Crime,* 17(3–4), 331–351. https://doi.org/10.1080/17440572.2016.1197508.

Jackson, P. (2010). SSR and Post-Conflict Reconstruction: The Armed Wing of State Building. In M. Sedra (Ed.), *The Future of Security Sector Reform* (pp. 118–135). CIGI. https://www.cigionline.org/sites/default/files/the_future_of_security_sector_reform.pdf.

Jackson, P. (2018). Introduction: Second-Generation Security Sector Reform. *Journal of Intervention and Statebuilding,* 12(1), 1–10. https://doi.org/10.1080/17502977.2018.1426384.

Jackson, P., & Albrecht. P. (Eds.) (2010). *Security Sector Reform in Sierra Leone 1997–2007: Views from the Front Line.* DCAF/LIT

Jackson, P., & Bakrania, S. (2018). Is the Future of SSR Non-linear? *Journal of Intervention and Statebuilding,* 12(1), 11–30. https://doi.org/10.1080/17502977.2018.1426548.

Kaldor, M. (1998). *New and Old Wars: Organized Violence in a Global Era.* Polity Press.

Keethaponcalan, S. I. (2020). Asian Peacebuilding: Theory and Practice. In Y. Uesugi (Ed.), *Hybrid Peacebuilding in Asia* (pp. 15–35). Palgrave Macmillan. https://doi.org/10.1007/978-3-030-18865-8.

Knight, M. (2009). Security Sector Reform, Democracy, and the Social Contract from Implicit to Explicit. *Journal of Security Sector Management,* 7(1), 1–20.

Lacher, W. (2007). Iraq: Exception to, or Epitome of Contemporary Post-Conflict Reconstruction? *International Peacekeeping,* 14(2), 237–250.

Lalá, A. & Francisco, L. (2006). The Difficulties of Donor Coordination: Police and Judicial Reform in Mozambique. *Civil Wars,* 8(2), 163–180.

Lawrence, M. (2012). *Towards a Non-State Security Sector Reform Strategy.* SSR Issue Paper No. 8., CIGI. https://www.files.ethz.ch/isn/143235/SSR%20No%208_0.pdf.

Mac Ginty, R. (2011). *International Peacebuilding and Local Resistance: Hybrid Forms of Peace.* Palgrave Macmillan. https://doi.org/10.1057/9780230307032.

Mac Ginty, R., & Sanghera, G. (2012). Hybridity in Peacebuilding and Development: An Introduction. *Journal of Peacebuilding & Development*, 7(2), 3–8. https://doi.org/10.1080/15423166.2012.742800.

Marijan, B. (2016). *Assessing the Impact of Orthodox Security Sector Reform in Bosnia-Herzegovina*, CSG Papers, No. 9. https://secgovcentre.org/wp-content/uploads/2016/11/Assessing_Orthodox_SSR_in_Bosnia_Sept_2016.pdf.

Marijan, B. (2017). *The Gradual Emergence of Second Generation Security Sector Reform in Bosnia-Herzegovina*. CSG Papers, No. 13. https://secgovcentre.org/wp-content/uploads/2017/01/Second-Generation-SSR-in-Bosnia-Herzegovina-January-2017.pdf.

Mason, S. J. A. (2016). *Why Security Sector Reform Has to Be Negotiated*. CSS Analyses in Security Policy 194. Center for Security Studies. https://css.ethz.ch/content/dam/ethz/special-interest/gess/cis/center-for-securities-studies/pdfs/CSSAnalyse-194-EN.pdf.

Mobekk, E. (2008). MINUSTAH and the Need for a Context-Specific Strategy: The Case of Haiti. In H. Hänggi & V. Scherrer (Eds.), *Security Sector Reform and UN Integrated Missions: Experience from Burundi, the Democratic Republic of Congo, Haiti, and Kosovo* (pp. 113–168). DCAF/LIT.

Mobekk, E. (2010a). Security Sector Reform and the Challenges of Ownership. In M. Sedra (Ed.), *The Future of Security Sector Reform* (pp. 230–243). CIGI. https://www.cigionline.org/sites/default/files/the_future_of_security_sector_reform.pdf.

Mobekk, E. (2010b). Gender, Women and Security Sector Reform. *International Peacekeeping*, 17(2), 278–291. https://doi.org/10.1080/13533311003625142.

Moderan, O. (2015). Political Leadership and National Ownership of Security Sector Reform Processes. In O. Moderan (Ed.), *Toolkit for Security Sector Reform and Governance in West Africa*. DCAF. https://www.dcaf.ch/sites/default/files/publications/documents/SSRG-West-Africa-Toolkit-Tool-1-EN.pdf.

Molloy, D. (2016). *Disarmament, Demobilization, and Reintegration: Theory and Practice*, Lynne Rienner.

Nathan, L. (2008). The Challenge of Local Ownership of SSR: From Donor Rhetoric to Practice. In T. Donais (Ed.), *Local Ownership and Security Sector Reform* (pp. 19-36). DCAF/LIT.

OECD. (2007). *The OECD DAC Handbook on Security System Reform* (2007 edition). OECD. https://issat.dcaf.ch/download/478/3015/OECD%20DAC%20Handbook%20on%20SSR.pdf.

OECD. (2011). *Supporting Statebuilding in Situations of Conflict and Fragility: Policy Guidance*. DAC Guidelines and Reference Series, OECD Publishing. https://doi.org/10.1787/9789264074989-en.

Paris, R. (2004). *At War's End: Building Peace After Civil Conflict*. Cambridge University Press.
Paris, R. (2010). Saving Liberal Peacebuilding. *Review of International Studies*, 36(2), 337–365. https://doi.org/10.1017/S0260210510000057.
Peou, S. (2018). The Politics of Survival in Cambodia: National Security for Undemocratic Control. In B. Howe (Ed.), *National Security, Statecentricity, and Governance in East Asia* (pp. 81–105). Palgrave Macmillan. https://doi.org/10.1007/978-3-319-58974-9.
Podder, S. (2013). Bridging the "Conceptual–Contextual" Divide: Security Sector Reform in Liberia and UNMIL Transition. *Journal of Intervention and Statebuilding*, 7(3), 353–380. https://doi.org/10.1080/17502977.2013.770242.
Sahin, S. B. (2017). The Rhetoric and Practice of the 'Ownership' of Security Sector Reform Processes in Fragile Countries: The Case of Kosovo. *International Peacekeeping*, 24(3), 461–488. https://doi.org/10.1080/13533312.2016.1196107.
Scheye, E. (2008). UNMIK and the Significance of Effective Programme Management: The Case of Kosovo. In H. Hänggi & V. Scherrer (Eds.), *Security Sector Reform and UN Integrated Missions: Experience from Burundi, the Democratic Republic of Congo, Haiti, and Kosovo* (pp. 169–219). DCAF/LIT.
Schroeder, U. C., & Chappuis, F. (2014). New Perspectives on Security Sector Reform: The Role of Local Agency and Domestic Politics. *International Peacekeeping*, 21(2), 133–148. https://doi.org/10.1080/13533312.2014.910401.
Schroeder, U. C., Chappuis, F., & Kocak, D. (2014). Security Sector Reform and the Emergence of Hybrid Security Governance. *International Peacekeeping*, 21(2), 214–230. https://doi.org/10.1080/13533312.2014.910405.
Sedra, M. (2010a). Introduction: The Future of Security Sector Reform. In M. Sedra (Ed.), *The Future of Security Sector Reform* (pp. 16–27). CIGI. https://www.cigionline.org/sites/default/files/the_future_of_security_sector_reform.pdf.
Sedra, M. (2010b). Towards Second Generation Security Sector Reform. In M. Sedra (Ed.), *The Future of Security Sector Reform* (pp. 102–116). CIGI. https://www.cigionline.org/sites/default/files/the_future_of_security_sector_reform.pdf.
Sedra, M. (2016). 16 Security Sector Reform. In R. Mac Ginty (Ed.), *Routledge Handbook of Peacebuilding* (pp. 211–224). Routledge.
Sedra, M. (2017). *Security Sector Reform in Conflict-Affected Countries: The Evolution of a Model*. Routledge.
Sedra, M. (2018). Adapting Security Sector Reform to Ground-Level Realities: The Transition to a Second-Generation Model. *Journal of Intervention and Statebuilding*, 12(1), 48–63. https://doi.org/10.1080/17502977.2018.1426383.

Short, C. (1999). *Security Sector Reform and the Elimination of Poverty*. Centre for Defence Studies, King's College, London, March 9.

Takeuchi, S. (2011). *Gacaca and DDR: The Disputable Record of State-Building in Rwanda*, JICA-Ri Working Paper 32. https://www.jica.go.jp/jica-ri/publication/workingpaper/jrft3q00000023p7-att/JICA-RI_WP_No.32_2011_2.pdf.

Uesugi, Y. (2014a). Introduction. In Y. Uesugi (Ed.), *Peacebuilding and Security Sector Governance in Asia* (pp. 1–22). DCAF/LIT.

Uesugi, Y. (2014b). Conclusion. In Y. Uesugi (Ed.), *Peacebuilding and Security Sector Governance in Asia* (pp. 175–182). DCAF/LIT.

Uesugi, Y. (2014c). Security Sector Reform (SSR) in Timor-Leste: The Challenges of Respecting Local Ownership. *Asian Peacebuilding Initiatives*. http://peacebuilding.asia/1057/.

Uesugi, Y. (2018). Neo-authoritarian Peace in Timor-Leste. In B. Howe (Ed.), *National Security, Statecentricity, and Governance in East Asia* (pp. 107–126). Palgrave Macmillan. https://doi.org/10.1007/978-3-319-58974-9.

Uesugi, Y. (2020). Introduction. In Y. Uesugi (Ed.), *Hybrid Peacebuilding in Asia* (pp. 1–14). Palgrave Macmillan. https://doi.org/10.1007/978-3-030-18865-8.

United Nations (UN). (2008). *Securing Peace and Development: The Role of the United Nations in Supporting Security Sector Reform*. Report of the Secretary-General, A/62/659-S/2008/39 (23 January).

United Nations Development Programme (UNDP). (1994). *Human Development Report 1994*. Oxford University Press.

United Nations Development Programme (UNDP). (2003). *Security Sector Reform and Transitional Justice: A Crisis Post-Conflict Programmatic Approach*. UNDP.

Upreti, B. R. & Vanhoutte, P. (2009). Security Sector Reform in Nepal: Challenges and Opportunities. In H. Born & A. Schnabel (Eds.), *Security Sector Reform in Challenging Environments* (pp. 165–187). DCAF/LIT.

Wallis, J. (2014). *Constitution Making During State Building*. Cambridge University Press.

Wallis, J. (2017). Is 'Good Enough' Peacebuilding Good Enough? The Potential and Pitfalls of the Local Turn in Peacebuilding in Timor-Leste. *The Pacific Review*, 30(2), 251–269. https://doi.org/10.1080/09512748.2016.1220417.

Wilén, N. (2012). A Hybrid Peace through Locally Owned and Externally Financed SSR–DDR in Rwanda? *Third World Quarterly*, 33(7), 1323–1336. https://doi.org/10.1080/01436597.2012.691833.

Wilson, C. (2020). Illiberal Peacebuilding in India and Indonesia: The Dangers of the Hybrid Approach. In Y. Uesugi (Ed.), *Hybrid Peacebuilding in Asia* (pp. 115–138). Palgrave Macmillan. https://doi.org/10.1007/978-3-030-18865-8.

PART V

Peace Accords

CHAPTER 19

Peace Processes and Their Agreements

Christine Bell and Laura Wise

INTRODUCTION

As a conflict unfolds attempts to de-escalate and end it are typically ongoing: conflicts almost always co-exist with peace initiatives. However, the term 'peace process' has become associated with formal direct or indirect talks involving the main state and non-state protagonists to the conflict (sometimes termed 'track one' actors). The idea of the peace process emerged in its contemporary form at the end of the Cold War, and took hold as a new era emerged. Shifting East–West relationships created a number of dynamics which focused international attention on the need to resolve conflict arising within states. These included: a pressing need to address emergent conflict which accompanied the end of the Cold War; the apparent new potential to resolve other long-standing

C. Bell (✉) · L. Wise
School of Law, University of Edinburgh, Edinburgh, UK
e-mail: christine.bell@ed.ac.uk

L. Wise
e-mail: Laura.Wise@ed.ac.uk

conflicts fuelled by East–West proxy war dynamics; and a new international consensus to view intrastate conflict as a matter for international intervention using newly enabled UN tools.[1]

The peace process practice became characterized by four key elements all of which constituted a change from conflict resolution practices in the previous decades. The first element involved a focus on state/non-state negotiations aimed at reaching a new publicly available 'contract' in the form of a peace or transition agreement. Face-to-face attempts to end conflict by finding agreement on how to address its root causes replaced previous strategies such as quiet deals for armed-actor demobilization, or indirect attempts to cut away their support base by offering reform packages aimed at building support for 'moderates'. The second element comprised a common approach to settlement terms: ceasefires and commitments to end violence were linked to constitutional reform of the state aimed at inclusion. Non-state actors would commit to ending violence, in response to a reciprocal state commitment to end state violence and introduce radical reform of the state's institutions to be more inclusive of the non-state actors and the wider communities from which they were drawn. The third element saw international and regional organizations refocus their institutional formation over time, to support the new peace process practice as an internationalized practice. This was to result in: new peacebuilding organizations and mechanisms creating networks of practitioners; new international legal standards addressing peace processes and agreements; and new tool-kits, all aimed at better responding to intrastate conflict. The fourth element began as the idea that international legal standards relating to human rights and humanitarian law in some sense applied to this new practice, and over two decades from 1990 on, this idea developed into the emergence of new norms, and new articulations of how existing international law constrained peace mediation. A range of issues that had been understood to be within the preserve of the domestic state, started to be addressed by new international norms, relating to amnesties and transitional justice, to inclusion of women, to standards dealing with housing and return of refugees and displaced persons.

Over the last three decades, peace processes involving these four elements have become a key mechanism for resolving conflict, and this has led to extended negotiations in over 200 peace processes since 1990.[2] Some countries have had different processes over time (Colombia has had at least five distinct processes), or seen more than one conflict being addressed by more than one peace process simultaneously (the Philippines has had separate peace processes in Mindanao, and with the National Democratic Front, at the same time).[3] The practice has produced 1823 peace agreements, using a definition of a peace agreement as a 'formal, publicly available document produced after discussion with conflict protagonists and mutually agreed to by some or all of them, addressing conflict with a view to ending it'.[4] These agreements provide a rich documentary history of how societies have attempted end conflict. They provide information on: the types of joint commitment the parties to the conflict make to end conflict; the forms of ceasefires that are used to halt violence both temporarily and permanently; the types of permanent institutional reform and the pathways that become part of these commitments; and the type of social agendas for change that are articulated as necessary to rebuilding a social contract. A total of 83% of all peace agreements signed between 1990 and 2019 are related to intrastate conflicts, that is conflicts originating mainly within states, and only 4% in conflicts between states. Table 19.1 sets out these agreements in terms of level (whether interstate, intrastate or local), and Table 19.2 sets out their regional spread.[5]

This chapter is informed by a major quantitative and qualitative review of all peace agreements, in the period and provides a brief introduction to how peace processes unfold. We set out in general terms how peace processes and peace agreements are arrived at, and explore the function that formalized agreement plays in providing an exit from conflict. We use the discussion to understand how peace agreements support exits such, and the different types of agreement used to move forward at different stages of a peace process.

Table 19.1 Agreements by level of conflict and process

Agreement level	Number and percentage of agreements
Interstate agreements in interstate conflict	72 (4%)
Agreements in intrastate conflict	1509 (83%)
Local agreements	242 (13%)
Total	1823 (100%)

Table 19.2 Agreements by region

Region	Number and percentage of agreements
Africa (excluding MENA)	554 (30%)
Americas	195 (11%)
Asia Pacific	377 (21%)
Europe and Eurasia	410 (23%)
Middle East and North Africa	253 (14%)
Cross regional	34 (1%)
Total	1823 (100%)

In conclusion, we argue that the practice established in 1990 is now at a cross-roads and we point to a new global realignment that affects who intervenes, why and to what end, and to new forms of conflict, all of which stand to challenge established peace process practices and the assumptions that underpin them. We suggest the need to look beyond peace agreements as static points in conflict-to-peace transitions addressed at national conflict. We instead suggest that peace processes require multi-level peace processes across inter-related geopolitical, national, and local conflicts, and forms of adaptive management to deal with the interactions between these levels, to respond to what are best understood as 'complex conflict systems'.

Defining Peace Agreements: Beyond 'Handshake Moments'

In recent years, academic research examining peace agreements has grown exponentially, reflecting the post-Cold War increase in reaching mediated settlements to address violent, intrastate conflicts. Scholars and practitioners have grappled with questions around peace process design,[6] agreement longevity,[7] implementation,[8] and particularly issues of inclusion, driven by the idea that exclusion is a key driver of violent conflict something that has been adopted by policymakers, human rights actors, and peacebuilders alike.[9] However, despite this increased attention to the role of negotiated settlements in peacemaking practice, there remains no clear definition of what constitutes a peace agreement, or indeed what it should include in order to sustainably resolve violent conflict.

Within the field of peace and conflict research as a whole, an overfocus on comprehensive bargains, has driven analysis of peace processes.[10] Such grand bargains have been made across various well-known contexts such as South Africa (1994), Bosnia and Herzegovina (1995), Northern Ireland (1998), Burundi (2000), and have given rise to 'the popular image...of dark-suited men – and it is almost always men – emerging bleary-eyed from marathon negotiations'.[11] This image, however, is only a small part of the peacemaking story. A closer look at these 'peace agreements' reveals the quite different legal and political constructions of documents described as peace agreements. In South Africa, the main agreement took the form of an interim constitution primarily agreed by the African National Congress (ANC) and the then governing National Party, with the late add-in of other parties.[12] In Burundi, the Arusha Agreement was signed in 2000, but the main armed groups did not sign up to its commitments and it took two subsequent agreements to draw them into its framework at which point the agreements were constitutionalized.[13] In Bosnia, the comprehensive agreement—the 1995 Dayton Peace Agreement—is really 11 different agreements, all signed by different permutations of actors.[14] It was not the only comprehensive agreement in the process—early similar agreements had been signed and reneged on. Furthermore, we now know that the process had at least 44 written ceasefires[15]—some national and some very local—before that point; most failing to hold due to lack of credible commitment from the parties. In Northern Ireland, the main agreement was reached in 1998 between political parties rather than directly with armed groups—although an election had been contrived to ensure that even very small armed groups had political representatives at the talks (the election design also enabled women to form a political party and gain a place at the negotiation table).[16] A key Unionist political party, however, did not sign on to the agreement until years later when it came on board and negotiated the St Andrews Agreement, which extended and modified the original Belfast/Good Friday Agreement.[17]

Looking beyond comprehensive agreements, different types of agreements serve different stages and goals of a peace process: from ceasefire and pre-negotiation agreements, through framework agreements (sometimes in one big agreement, and sometimes negotiated issue-by-issue to build up a framework over time), to implementation and renegotiation agreements. Contrary to the best plans of mediators, there is no one sequence of staging that peace processes follow.[18] Parties often

Table 19.3 Agreements by stage of process

Stage of process	Number and percentage of agreements
Pre-negotiation or process agreements	508 (28%)
Framework agreements partial	456 (25%)
Framework agreements comprehensive	110 (6%)
Implementation/renegotiation agreements	330 (18%)
Ceasefire agreements	368 (20%)
Renewal agreements (short renewal of commitment to earlier agreements)	42 (3%)
Other	9 *
Total	1823 (100%)

Note 'other' constitutes a small number of agreements that do not easily fit in any category

renege on commitments, hostilities can resume, and talks can collapse. Peace processes do not necessarily neatly progress from ceasefire and pre-negotiation agreements to formal talks, nor does a ceasefire automatically pave the way for comprehensive negotiations, which parties then agree to implement. Nevertheless, peace agreements can be understood as falling into the following main types: pre-negotiation agreements, ceasefires, framework/substantive agreements, implementation/renegotiation agreements, and renewal agreements, see Table 19.3 for numbers. These will be discussed below.[19]

Pre-Negotiation Agreements

The path to a 'handshake moment' is usually prepared by a series of earlier deals, in which parties make commitments to both the process and the substance of other stages in the talks, often in an attempt to move from 'winning the war' to 'winning the peace', rather than in a spirit of compromise which involves letting go of their battlefield political goals.[20]

Some peace agreements are negotiated through secret talks and diplomatic back channels with the broader constituencies that they relate to only becoming aware of the document once parties and mediators determine that they have reached an appropriate moment to go public—or the secret process is unintentionally revealed.[21] The public talks that led to the Belfast Agreement in 1998, for example, were preceded by secret back-channel negotiations between representatives of the British government and the Irish Republican Army (IRA), which had happened at different moments during the then-thirty year conflict, when neither side could countenance public perception of being involved in a dialogue.[22] These talks intensified during the end of the 1980s and the Downing Street Declaration, made by the Prime Minister of the United Kingdom and the Taoiseach of the Republic of Ireland in 1993, responded to those peace talks, in essence launching the public phase of what was to become the peace process.[23] Similarly, secret talks in Norway between the government of Israel and the Palestinian Liberation Organization (PLO) produced the 1993 Oslo Accords. These took place outside the formal Madrid Conference talks which were ongoing but had not permitted the PLO to negotiate.[24] Back-channel negotiations from 1985 to 1990 between Nelson Mandela and South Africa's apartheid government of the time (initially without even the knowledge of the wider ANC leadership), paved the way to direct negotiations taking place with public knowledge.[25]

Although the rising use of smartphones, social media, and citizen journalism in the past decade may make it harder to keep negotiation efforts secret, the practice of closed talks persists. Pre-negotiation talks between the government of Colombia and the FARC-EP in Havana in 2012,[26] the confidential 'virtual peacemaking' between the government of Spain and ETA in 2011,[27] and the unofficial shuttle diplomacy between former U.S government officials and the Taliban from 2017 to 2018,[28] all demonstrate the contemporary appeal of such processes to parties in some of the world's most intractable conflicts. The decision to keep negotiations secret is often defended as necessary to reach an agreement, as parties can struggle to be seen to be compromising whilst conflict is ongoing, and may be more effective at reaching agreement if there are fewer competing interests on the table.[29]

Covert elite negotiations, however, have consequences for the inclusiveness of bargaining processes. Secret negotiations clearly exclude wider constituencies for peace and risk prioritizing the demands of armed actors over other sectoral interests. For a peace process to gain an element of legitimacy and public buy-in it must at some point become public and be conducted with a level of transparency and scrutiny.

However, whether conducted in secret or not, for conflict parties to begin to talk whilst hostilities are ongoing, they often have to agree on how they are prepared to talk with each other. Pre-negotiation agreements revolve around who will negotiate, with what status, and over what. Attempts by parties to insert their preferred negotiation outcome as preconditions to talks must be overcome. The resultant agreements often include details on how parties are going to hold or attend negotiations, such as the Joint Statements signed by the Peace Panels of the Government of the Philippines (GRP) and the Moro Islamic Liberation Front (MILF), prior to each round of exploratory talks facilitated by Malaysia that began in 2001.[30] Pre-negotiation texts can also refer to the principles parties can agree on to govern any subsequent process, such as the Agreed Basic Principles signed by parties to the conflict in Bosnia in September 1995 prior to comprehensive talks.[31] Or confidence-building measures can be agreed upon that allow parties to express their commitment to entering talks, such as the government of Yemen and Houthi rebels agreeing to swap prisoners in order to travel to Stockholm for talks in 2018.[32] Resolving these issues often leads to commitments that put in place pathway dependencies because agreements to the nature and substance of the political process to follow are often needed to secure a commitment to move from use of force and get parties to agree with talks. These substantive political commitments start to lock down the parameters of the peace process that emerges.

Despite being relatively overlooked in peace and conflict studies,[33] pre-negotiation agreements are often numerous and our review of peace processes globally between 1990 and 2019, indicate that 508 pre-negotiation texts were agreed as compared with 110 comprehensive agreements in the same period.[34] Qualitative analysis of provisions within these agreements shows us that they regularly go beyond procedural technicalities to set the agenda for later talks, with commitments used by negotiators as building blocks for grappling with highly contested issues, or by parties to advance key agendas that they are concerned could be lost if not included from the outset. For example, references to power-sharing appear in a fifth of pre-negotiation agreements sometimes as broad commitments and sometimes including specific details relating to form and function, even though we often associate the substantive details of power-sharing arrangements as something to be agreed as part of a broader package in comprehensive peace agreements. In several processes where power-sharing provisions were agreed in pre-negotiation texts, comprehensive agreements also provided for similar power-sharing arrangements, such as in Bosnia, Burundi, Nepal, Northern Ireland, and the Philippines.[35] Failure to include particular parties or agendas in pre-negotiation stages of peace processes may therefore make it harder to widen access later on. As a result of this realization, proponents of women's inclusion in peace processes and post-conflict politics under the mandate of United Nations Security Council Resolution 1325 have increasingly become concerned with influencing peace process agendas before and after the stages that negotiate framework agreements.[36]

Ceasefires

Ceasefire agreements are texts that primarily include commitments by parties to end their use of violence, whether for a temporary or an indefinite period. Sometimes they are agreed as part of a set of pre-negotiation commitments, often coupled with a commitment to a political process. Sometimes they can only be reached during talks-proper, when tied to more substantive commitments. Ceasefire commitments centrally define when violence will stop, and what constitutes a prohibited action, and how to achieve the immediate demobilization and cantonment of armed forces, ideally with some precision if they are to be effective. These basic commitments relating to the use of force, however, are often supplemented by confidence-building guarantees to raise the commitment costs for parties, and promote the durability of a break in hostilities.[37] Ceasefires are often a practical necessity if armed actors are to hold face-to-face talks, and politically necessary to reassure parties that no one side can use the focus on negotiations to gain a military advantage. They also can help build confidence in the process among the wider public. Prominent examples of ceasefire agreements that set the stage for talks on comprehensive issues include: the 2002 Cessation of Hostilities Framework Agreement between the Government of the Republic of Indonesia and the Free Aceh Movement; the 1990 Toncontin Agreement in Nicaragua; and the 1998 Arawa Agreement in Bougainville.[38] However, once reached, ceasefires can require extensive diplomatic and military resources to prevent the cessation from breaking down, or to stop parties from instrumentalizing ceasefires for their own gain elsewhere in the conflict zone.

There are also contexts in which—rather than use a ceasefire to launch discussions on a comprehensive settlement—parties commit and then reaffirm or develop their existing commitments to stop using violence, but without further attempts to address the issues at the heart of the conflict. In these processes, ceasefire agreements become formalized mechanisms to govern the principles of frozen conflict. A series of protocols agreed between Georgia, and the de facto government of Abkhazia since 1992 (often including Russia) produced commitments to managing the ceasefire line, including troop movements and establishing communications links between the two sides, in order to prevent violence from reoccurring.[39] High-level mediation efforts to resolve the impasse slowly continue; however, various iterations of this ceasefire regime to manage tensions have been in place since the last outbreak of war in 1998.

Other conflicts demonstrate that rather than being constrained by committing to ceasefires, actors sometimes find ways to use ceasefire regimes to advance their aims or shift conflict dynamics on the ground. In northeast Myanmar, ceasefire zones created by agreements between the government and armed groups in the early 1990s gave rise to what some have described as 'ceasefire capitalism', whereby political, military, and private actors utilize the zones to make territorial governance claims and facilitate resource exploitation in areas which were previously harder to access.[40] The Indian government's practice of selectively agreeing on ceasefires with some armed groups in northeast India, but not others, may have contributed to exacerbating conflict between non-state actors, by creating incentives for groups to use violence to outbid each other and gain access to negotiation processes, despite indefinitely containing the government's conflicts with its most challenging opponents.[41] More recently in Syria, localized ceasefires may have enabled parties to give themselves breathing room to re-allocate resources to other fronts, or consolidate territorial control through population evacuations as part of ceasefire agreement terms, which can also make future elimination strategies achievable.[42] These processes challenge us to think beyond ceasefires as merely having failed or succeeded, particularly regarding long-term implementation, and to consider broader contributions that ceasefire agreements can make to conflict, as well as peace.

Framework/Substantive Agreements

Substantive agreements are often considered as comprising comprehensive agreements that set out holistic attempts to end conflict. When we speak colloquially of peace agreements, often we use the term as a synonym for a comprehensive agreement. In these, parties agree on a substantive and holistic framework to resolve the conflict—no agreement can fully resolve all the issues in one go. Our peace agreement data shows, however, that core issues that need to be dealt with are often likely to be agreed on in a piecemeal manner, through what we term partial framework-substantive agreements: agreements that deal with substantive issues, 'but only deal with some of the issues in ways that appear to contemplate future agreements to complete'.[43]

There are several reasons for the overwhelming emphases on comprehensive peace accords. Firstly, talks on comprehensive peace agreements are highly publicized, and the images of former foes coming together offer highly symbolic events that overshadow the lesser-known steps to that moment. Images of the 'handshake moments' become shorthand for agreement to end the conflict, regardless of how many prior talks and arrangements preceded and followed these moments. Secondly, comprehensive agreements contain the results of comprehensive discussions on core issues driving conflict, and as such form quasi-constitutional documents (that is, they set out the principles and power-map for how the country is to be governed, and indeed some take the form of actual constitutions) which set out a new power-map for the country, with novel elements such as power-sharing and transitional justice, and so garner more attention. As a result, comprehensive agreements are often interpreted as a means of understanding the issues under discussion in a peace process, and as offering a blueprint of the type of society that the conflict parties are agreeing to transition towards in order to resolve the conflict. Framework agreements tend to be the most lengthy of all documents produced as part of peace processes, on average comprising 13 pages of text compared to ceasefire agreements, which average 3 pages.[44] The recent Final Agreement for Colombia in 2016, for example, comprised of 323 pages of text that provided for everything from human rights, cultural heritage, and transitional justice, to power-sharing institutions and security sector reform and is the longest peace agreement to date, closely followed by the 2005 Comprehensive Agreement between the Government of Sudan and the Sudan People's Liberation Army/Sudan People's Liberation Movement.[45]

However, even comprehensive agreements are often the result of incremental issue-by-issue processes: the examples of Colombia, Bougainville/Papua New Guinea, Mindanao/Philippines, and Sudan, all of which produced comprehensive accords, saw parties sign multiple agreements along the way, staging how they dealt with core issues such as governance, power-sharing, security sector reform, or transitional justice. The final accords also left the detail of some mechanisms or contemporaneously irreconcilable matters to later on in the process. This meant that issues could be dealt with one at a time so as to build the potential for agreement in situations of dispute and lack of trust.

Our review of framework agreements reveals three quite different approaches to peacemaking, which involve different types of deals that shape when and how substantive agreements are fashioned and how comprehensive they are. The first is that of a comprehensive agreement (whether built up gradually or reached in one moment) aiming to put in place a new set of arrangements for a national conflict, often in ways which promise to rework the political settlement for the country as a whole. This type of agreement is often used to address ethno-national conflicts and set out a quasi-constitutional power-map to institutionalize a new political settlement, and as noted above can be achieved in one agreement, or iteratively over time. The second type of agreement is that of a comprehensive agreement reached as regards sub-state conflict with national reach, and contemplating a new political settlement at the sub-state level. This type of agreement is also often used in situations of ethno-national conflict, where a minority population is concentrated in a sub-state region. It usually reconfigures the political settlement at the sub-state level leaving the national political settlement largely unaltered.[46] The third type of agreement, puts in place what we understand as 'interim transitional arrangements', whereby an agreement primarily between those representing the sides in the conflict aims to put in place elements of a transition.[47] These interim agreements do not necessarily contemplate any further final agreement, but rather that these transition processes will over time put in place the building blocks of democracy. Typically the agreement puts in place an interim power-sharing government including those with capacity to destabilize the country militarily, but uses that agreement to set up a wider more socially-owned transition process which over time is to lead to holding of elections and often a permanent new constitutional arrangement. Interim agreements often also put in place processes for revising or designing new constitutions, electoral reform, and providing for demobilization and military withdrawal. This type of agreement to interim arrangements is used to address situations of conflict in which lack of functioning democratic institutions or commitments is understood to be a key conflict issue, often coupled with deep political disagreement, and other forms of ethno-national or tribal division.

Each of these different types of process, have different design challenges and different implementation challenges.

Implementation/Renegotiation Agreements

The implementation stage of a peace process can sometimes be assumed to involve a technocratic process of putting earlier commitments made on paper into practice, requiring more effort from bureaucrats than from mediators. However, implementation agreements reflect the reality that implementing a peace agreement often requires new processes of negotiation and can become hotly contested as parties can see this stage as an opportunity to 'win the peace', by implementing selectively or not at all, particularly in contexts where there has been no clear military victory by one side or another.[48] Implementation issues arise with all stages and types of agreement, and implementation agreements can therefore follow an agreement at any stage of the process. At earlier stages of a peace process, they may be a necessary step to move from a pre-negotiation or ceasefire to engaging in comprehensive talks, as a more formal signifier that parties are committed to the process. However, implementation often becomes particularly critical after a framework or comprehensive agreement has been signed that sees the parties compromising on the core conflict issues.

Agreeing on implementation at this stage usually involves clarifying issues that were left unclear in the main peace agreement, and putting in place mechanisms to ensure delivery, and addressing new problems, or incorporating new actors who refused to sign up to the deal at the time and have capacity to destroy it. All of these efforts usually involve renegotiating the initial deal to some extent, as parties try to change the terms of the process—clawing back concessions made at an earlier stage. For example, if parties have previously committed to establishing commissions for resolving the status of contested territories, they may approach implementation as a chance to shape the commission's structure, mandate, and decision-making processes in order to gain control over said territory. If earlier stages of a process were restricted to core conflict parties, civil society organizations and other societal stakeholders may view the implementation phase as an opportunity to open up the process, by mobilizing for representation in institutions formed by implementation agreements, or in bodies whose sole function is to monitor implementation processes.[49]

Implementation can relate to peace agreement provisions in different ways: provisions can add detail on realizing earlier commitments on the same issue, or provisions can govern implementation of the agreement in its entirety. Willingness to build-in implementation mechanisms is often key to the parties demonstrating their credible commitment and that they are truly interested in substantive change based on compromise, rather than simply buying time until the process breaks down and conflict re-emerges.[50]

Renewal Agreements

Our collection of documents indicates that renewal agreements are often signed and can be considered as a form of implementation agreement. What we term 'renewal' agreements can be used at any stage in a peace process and involve agreements that are typically short documents that reaffirm parties' commitment to earlier agreed points. They are often signed at moments when the process is wavering and parties have essentially walked away from it, and can serve to reinvigorate or maintain momentum when processes become stalled, or to keep process mechanisms in place for longer than they had originally been intended. In the peace process between the government of the Philippines and the Moro Islamic Liberation Front, parties agreed several times to renew the mandate of an International Monitoring Team and the Ad Hoc Joint Action Group, both of which were confidence-building mechanisms to support the process.[51] Earlier agreements had established or provided terms of reference for these mechanisms, and provided that their mandates should be renewed yearly by the parties. The requirement for both parties to agree to this renewal resulted in agreements that can be viewed both as mandate extensions, and as signals of commitment from each party to continue to pursue their goals through a peace process, rather than armed conflict. Renewal agreements can feature at any stage of a process, because they affirm what came before, whether a pre-negotiation agreement or a comprehensive agreement. Whilst these agreements add little of substance, they bear witness to the need to sometimes re-start talks after breakdown by recommitting to previous terms.

PEACE AGREEMENTS AND COMPLEX CONFLICT SYSTEMS: PROCESSES 'ABOVE' AND 'BELOW' THE STATE

Peace processes are frequently assumed to involve governments negotiating with an armed opponent. However, many of the most intractable current conflicts take the form of what we suggest are better understood as complex conflict systems, rather than a singular 'conflict'. Increasingly, intrastate conflict involves an ever-more complicated intertwined set of local, national, and international conflicts whose connections with each other are difficult to unravel. Cases such as Libya, Syria, and South Sudan illustrate the ways in which conflict can involve a range of local actors with different conflict goals who have never been part of a unified opposition or even alliance but who form shifting alliances of convenience, and who operate with a fluid relationship to any national conflict actors. Local and national conflicts are often further embedded in an international geopolitical conflict dynamic, as states conduct proxy wars with each other by supporting armed groups engaged in intrastate conflict (which has always had internationalized dimensions). These geopolitical dynamics are reminiscent of the pre-Cold War days, but now reflect a changing and increasingly uncertain international legal order rather than earlier bi-polar certainties. A new global political marketplace of who intervenes in transition is in play, and competition over who will broker peace is itself contested because it is simultaneously a move for power within the conflict region, and a way to improve one's position vis-à-vis other states, in this uneasy global order.[52]

These changes deserve more elaboration than we can give here, but point to a need to think in fresh ways as to what a peace process needs to achieve in this new world. What types of agreement at what level are needed to respond to the contemporary multilevel conflict landscape? Do we need to now think of peace processes not as involving a comprehensive deal between a state and non-state actor to address a national political settlement, but requiring co-ordinated peace process*es* across local, national, and international levels? And can agreement at one of these levels achieve anything, if agreement cannot be achieved at other levels?

Above: Interstate Agreements for Intrastate Conflict

As regards international agreement, the involvement of actors from outside of conflict-affected societies is also a common feature of peace processes: over half of all peace agreements were signed by or negotiated in the presence of a third party,[53] many of which were representatives of the UN, current or former members of government, peacekeeping operations, international aid agencies, and religious organizations. Positioned as neutral facilitators, their role is often understood as a highly individualistic process dependent on the personality and skills of the mediator, or the concept of mediation driving the mediation team. However, mediator positions are also shaped by their organizational constraints and goals.

Peace processes to address conflict in Cambodia, Northern Ireland, and Afghanistan have not just used international third parties to mediate and support as third parties, but have seen external governments themselves make firm commitments in the peace process. These commitments are captured in agreements that are 'inter-state' in nature but respond to the relationship of the state parties not to interstate conflict as classically understood, but to the parties and people involved in intrastate conflict originating within existing (de facto or legal) state borders.[54] These agreements bind other states (often neighbouring states, but not exclusively) into the peace process in a way which goes beyond supporting peacemaking practices through political or financial resources, by creating a new architecture of commitments that can underwrite or supplement existing intrastate deals between conflict parties.

Why do governments sign interstate peace agreements which refer to conflict in a third-party state? These accords can serve a number of functions. They can aim to assist enforceability through making commitments legally binding through international law by making the agreement an interstate agreement and therefore a treaty—this was a device used in the Dayton Peace Agreement in Bosnia where states only signed the main body of the agreement and many of its annexes, sometimes in the role of underwriters of the armed groups at the heart of the conflict; they can encourage commitment from parties to the process at multiple levels by 'underwriting' their concerns and committing their own resources or non-interference, as was the case with interstate agreements that were signed as part of Cambodia's Paris Accords; they can involve third parties in other phases of the process, such as implementation.[55] These agreements can also recognize the role that international actors have played in sustaining the conflict and can involve primary commitments by those governments, such as to non-interference.

To give a fuller example, following the US-led coalition invasion of Afghanistan in 2001, various states and international organizations held a series of conferences in cities such as Berlin, London, and Paris.[56] In the outcome documents of these conferences, participants committed to support statebuilding, rule of law, development, reconstruction and human rights in Afghanistan, including as donors. There was a precedent of interstate agreement being used to resolve conflict in Afghanistan. In 1999, China, Iran, Pakistan, Tajikistan, Turkmenistan, Uzbekistan, Russia, and the US produced the 'Tashkent Declaration on Fundamental Principles for a Peaceful Settlement of the Conflict in Afghanistan' under the auspices of the UN, in which they pledged not to provide military support to any of the conflict parties, and set out blueprints for a possible UN-led peace process.[57] The composition of this group of states reflected the role that cross-border arms and drug trafficking, and political support for the Taliban by Pakistan were hindering attempts to bring parties to talks, and the interests that both the USA and Russia had in developments in Afghanistan. By 2001, however, the number of state parties, observer states, and the inclusion of organizations such as the World Bank and the Aga Khan Foundation, demonstrated how internationalized the conflict had become, and how tenuous the authority of the transitional Afghan administration was in practice.

'Below': Local Peace Processes

Conflicts also see local agreements being signed to address local dynamics of a wider conflict, or very localized conflicts that have a more tenuous or indirect relationship to the national conflict.[58] In Libya, South Sudan, Syria, and Yemen, whilst multiple attempts to reach national-level political settlements have faltered, local agreements—of different types—have attempted to address the local dynamics of conflict.[59] Sometimes these agreements are made between local groups and the state—through both national and local state agents, or can be made between different local groups, sometimes all on the 'same side' as regards the national conflict, and sometimes as local 'proxies' of national warring factions. The agreements reached formally or informally though these processes, are often much more concerned with the 'everyday' of how conflict re-manifests and what peace should look like.

Local peace process practices are diverse, and can draw on local forms of conflict resolution or channels for inter-communal dialogue. Although local processes primarily respond to incidences of violence within a limited geographic scope (as opposed to an entire conflict zone), the issues that they deal with often link to country-wide conflict dynamics.[60] Examination of local agreements indicates some common elements to the practice, such as that they often deal with very local conflict issues, for example cattle rustling, are signed by local actors, but who may remain connected to national actors for example as local branches of national groups or armies, and deal with the immediate locale. These processes can be mediated very communally at the local level, however, they can also be taken seriously by international mediators, because local conflicts are viewed as having the capacity to dismantle national agreements and act as a trigger for re-igniting a wider conflict.

Local peace processes do not necessarily involve 'peace agreements' as we understand them, and even when they do, the written text of these agreements can be secondary to the oral agreement, and operate more as a note between parties of what they have agreed, than as a public set of commitments. Local peace processes also sometimes take place in a largely unrecognized way, through ongoing peacebuilding activities, or through mechanisms designed to address the potential for conflict at the local level. For example, in Northern Ireland, a parades commission makes determination around marches with potential for sectarian violence, in processes that require forms of ongoing mediation and dialogue between groups, and although not termed 'local peace processes', these statutorily required mediations aim at a similar type of local agreement as to the conduct of any march, when crossing sectarian geographies.[61] In Bougainville, 'mass reconciliation ceremonies' and preparations for them, provide local processes of agreement between traditional leadership, state actors, erstwhile combatants, and civil society and address and attempt to restore a new re-balancing, of relationships considered to have become unbalanced through the conflict, area-by-area, often tied up with weapons disposal.[62] Whilst informal and undocumented and formal documented agreements may be useful, there are a diverse range of options for how local conflicts can be addressed—many of which will be highly culturally specific.

Conclusion: Current Challenges

The idea of a peace process often implicitly points to the idea of a journey to a destination in which the conflict will reach a point of resolution, and a new chapter of peace will begin. Peace processes often seem to oblige by delivering a comprehensive agreement to address the issues central to the conflict parties. However, peace processes require many different types of agreement over time, and the forms in which that agreement takes place will vary in order to respond to new conflict realities.

It is increasingly recognized that broader forms of social inclusion must accompany political-military deals if a peace agreement is to have legitimacy and be able to be sustained and built into a new social contract.[63] Mediators are now expected to include not just political parties and combatant groups, but a broader range of constituencies and groups, in peace process consultations, and to innovate as regards peace process design. This pressure has resulted in the appointment of women's advisory boards or technical committees as part of a talks process, innovative forms of public consultation, and new forms of sequencing processes to limit how much of the political settlement will be agreed upon by armed actors alone.[64] The challenges of supporting inclusion in multilevel complex contemporary processes include designing different strategies for different levels of peace process: strategies for inclusiveness at the geopolitical level, the national level and the local level, and ways to synthesize and connect peacemaking efforts between levels. However, the exhortation to 'inclusion' itself remains vague in terms of who is to be included in what stage of a peace process and how tensions between inclusion of groups at the heart of the conflict, and other constituencies and groups such as women, should be reconciled.[65] Understanding the complexity of peace processes through the documentary trails of the agreements that have sought to address them offers a new understanding of what reaching agreement on peace entails. It points to agreement not as something that happens in one moment, but more often emerging through an iterative process in which fragile agreement must be built slowly, and extended and reworked over time. Peace processes are messy and non-linear. Recognizing that they go backwards as well as forwards points to a need to approach implementation as a task of adaptive management, capable of responding to the new challenges that emerge, rather than trying to stick to timetables and timelines and build an idealized image of peace. Peace agreements must also be co-ordinated across different actors and levels of conflict: not just between the main protagonists in the conflict, but across local, national, and international stakeholders beyond these parties.

However, our peace agreement collection, with the complexity of its documentary trails, points to the creativity and innovation in peace process design. This creativity is possible and necessary in the search for conflict resolution, particularly when faced with the reality of ever-more complex and intractable conflict systems.

Acknowledgements This piece is an output of the Political Settlement Research Programme (PSRP), www.politicalsettlements.co.uk, and the new Peace and Conflict Resolution Evidence Platform, which is funded by the Foreign Commonwealth and Development Office, UK Aid, views are the authors' own. Thanks are also due to University of Edinburgh School of Law programme staff who read and commented and to the editors.

Notes

1. See further C. Bell (2008) On the Law of Peace: Peace Agreements and the Lex Pacificatoria (Oxford: Oxford University Press).
2. PA-X (2020) Peace Agreements Database and Access Tool, Version 3 (Edinburgh: Political Settlements Research Programme, University of Edinburgh), www.peaceagreements.org.
3. For timelines of these peace processes, search for country/entity (Colombia or Phillipines) on PA-X (2020) Peace Agreements Database and Access Tool, Version 3.
4. Christine Bell, Sanja Badanjak, Juline Beujouan, Tim Epple, Robert Forster, Astrid Jamar, Sean Molloy, Kevin McNicholl, Kathryn Nash, Jan Pospisil, Robert Wilson, and Laura Wise (2020) PA-X Peace Agreements Database and Dataset, Version 3. www.peaceagreements.org.
5. See at PA-X (2020) Peace Agreements Database and Access Tool, Version 3, www.peaceagreements.org. All peace agreements referenced in the chapter signed between January 1, 1990 and December 31, 2019 are available at this website.
6. See further, R. Badran (2013) 'Intrastate Peace Agreements and the Durability of Peace', *Conflict Management and Peace Science*, 31:2, 193–217.
7. See further, C. Hartzell, M. Hoddie, and D. Rothchild (2001) 'Stabilizing the Peace After Civil War: An Investigation of Some Key Variables', *International Organization*, 55:1, 183–208.
8. See further, M. Joshi, J.M. Quinn and P.M. Regan (2015) 'Annualized Implementation Data on Comprehensive Intrastate Peace Accords, 1989–2012', *Journal of Peace Research*, 52:4, 551–562; A. Jarstad and D. Nilsson (2008) 'From Words to Deeds: The Implementation of Power-Sharing Pacts in Peace Accords', *Conflict Management and Peace Science*, 25, 206–223. On the complexity of inclusion see, A.T. Hirblinger and D.M. Landau

(2020) 'Daring to Differ? Strategies of Inclusion in Peacemaking', *Security Dialogue*, Online First.
9. For reflection on the rise of the new 'inclusion projects' see C. Bell (2019) 'New Inclusion Project: Building Inclusive Peace Settlements', in Navigating Inclusion in Peace Processes, edited by Andy Carl (London: Conciliation Resources), pp. 11–17. See further, A. De Waal (2017) 'Inclusion in Peacemaking: From Moral Claim to Political Fact,' in The Fabric of Peace in Africa: Looking Beyond the State, edited by Pamela Aall and Chester A. Crocker (Waterloo: Centre for International Governance Innovation), pp. 165–185; J. Pospisil (2019) Peace in Political Unsettlement (Cham: Palgrave Macmillan).
10. See for example research published in 2018 that examines comprehensive peace agreements: K. DeRouen Jr., and I. Chowdhury (2018) 'Mediation, Peacekeeping and Civil War Peace Agreements', *Defence and Peace Economics*, 29:2, 130–146; J. Krause, W. Krause, and P. Bränfors (2018) 'Women's Participation in Peace Negotiations and the Durability of Peace', *International Interactions: Empirical and Theoretical Research in International Relations*, 44:6, 985–1016.
11. N. Caspersen (2017) Peace Agreements (Cambridge: Polity Press), p. 1.
12. South Africa, South African Constitution of 1993 (Interim Constitution), 18 November 1993, https://www.peaceagreements.org/view/407/.
13. Burundi, Arusha Peace and Reconciliation Agreement for Burundi, 28 August 2000, https://www.peaceagreements.org/view/306/; followed by the Global Ceasefire Agreement, 16 November 2003, https://www.peaceagreements.org/view/568/; and the Comprehensive Ceasefire Agreement between the Government of the Republic of Burundi and the Palipehutu—FNL, 7 September 2006, https://www.peaceagreements.org/view/336.
14. Bosnia and Herzegovina/Yugoslavia (former), General Framework Agreement for Peace in Bosnia and Herzegovina (Dayton Peace Agreement), 21 November 1995, https://www.peaceagreements.org/view/389/.
15. For a timeline of the ceasefires relating to the conflict in Bosnia and Herzegovina search for country/entity 'Bosnia and Herzegovina'

and agreement stage 'Ceasefired/related' on PA-X (2020) Peace Agreements Database and Access Tool, Version 3.
16. Ireland/United Kingdom/Northern Ireland, The Agreement Reached in the Multi-Party Negotiations (Good Friday Agreement or Belfast Agreement), 10 April 1998, https://www.peaceagreements.org/view/556/.
17. C. Bell (2008) On the Law of Peace.
18. For more on sequencing of peace agreement processes in processes that result in a peace agreement constitution, see C. Bell and K. Zulueta-Fülscher (2016) Sequencing Peace Agreements and Constitutions in the Political Settlement Process (Stockholm: International IDEA).
19. For full definitions of each peace agreement stage, see Bell et al. (2020) PA-X Codebook, Version 3.
20. C. Bell (2008) On the Law of Peace. For an account of the complex, multi-track pre-negotiation efforts in Rwanda before the Arusha process, see the chapter 'Early Peacemaking Efforts: Regional Prenegotiation' in B.D. Jones (2001) Peacemaking in Rwanda: The Dynamics of Failure (Boulder: Lynne Rienner Publishers).
21. A. Wanis-St. John (2006) 'Back-Channel Negotiation: International Bargaining in the Shadows', *Negotiation Journal*, 22:2, 119–144.
22. For a comprehensive account of the negotiations, see N. O Dochartaigh (2011) 'Together in the Middle: Back-Channel Negotiation in the Irish Peace Process', *Journal of Peace Research* 48:6, 767–780.
23. Ireland/United Kingdom/Northern Ireland, Joint Declaration Issued by The Prime Minister Rt John Major MP and the Taoiseach Mr. Albert Reynolds TD (Downing Street Declaration), 15 December 1993, https://www.peaceagreements.org/view/127/.
24. S. Behrendt (2007) The Secret Israeli-Palestinian Negotiations in Oslo: Their Success and Why the Process Ultimately Failed (Abingdon: Routledge).
25. D. Lieberfeld (1999) Talking with the Enemy: Negotiation and Threat Perception in South Africa and Israel/Palestine (Westport, CT: Praeger Publishers), pp. 42–43.

26. M. Schultze-Kraft (2019) Crimilegal Orders, Governance and Armed Conflict (Cham, Palgrave Pivot), p. 154.
27. T. Whitfield (2014) Endgame for ETA: Elusive Peace in the Basque Country (Oxford: Oxford University Press), p. 243.
28. S. Akerman (2018) Inside the Secret Taliban Talks to End America's Longest War, The Daily Beast, https://www.thedailybeast.com/inside-the-secret-taliban-talks-to-end-americas-longest-war, accessed 15 March 2019.
29. A. Wanis-St. John (2008) 'Peace Processes, Secret Negotiations and Civil Society: Dynamics of Inclusion and Exclusion', *International Negotiation*, 13, 1–9.
30. For example, see Philippines/Mindanao: Joint Statement—5th GRP-MILF Exploratory Talks, 28 March 2003, https://www.peaceagreements.org/view/191/; Joint Statement—6th GRP-MILF Exploratory Talks, 21 December 2004, https://www.peaceagreements.org/view/973/; Joint Statement—7th GRP-MILF Exploratory Talks, 20 April 2005, https://www.peaceagreements.org/view/974/.
31. Bosnia and Herzegovina/ Yugoslavia (former), Agreed Basic Principles signed on 8 September 1995 at Geneva, 8 September 1995, https://www.peaceagreements.org/view/77/.
32. P. Wintour (2018) 'Yemen's Warring Sides Agree to Prisoner Swap as Peace Talks Open', The Guardian, https://www.theguardian.com/world/2018/dec/06/yemen-talks-open-prisoner-swap-set-5000-people-free-un, accessed 15 March 2019.
33. For an important exception see, C. Buchanan (2019) Pathways to Peace Talks: Supporting Early Dialogue (London, Conciliation Resources, Accord Spotlight).
34. PA-X (2020) Peace Agreements Database and Access Tool, Version 3.
35. L. Wise (2018) 'Territorial Power-sharing and Inclusion in Peace Processes', PA-X Report, Power-Sharing Series (Edinburgh: Global Justice Academy, University of Edinburgh).
36. See for example UN Women (2018) 'Women's Meaningful Participation in Negotiating Peace and the Implementation of Peace Agreements: Report of the Expert Group Meeting', Convened by UN Women in preparation for the UN Secretary-General's report on Women and Peace and Security, 16–17 May 2018 (New York, United States: UN Women), p. 8.

37. See further V. P. Fortna (2004) Peace Time: Cease-fire Agreements and the Durability of Peace (Princeton: Princeton University Press); M. Åkebo (2017) Ceasefire Agreements and Peace Processes: A Comparative Study (Abingdon: Routledge); R. Forster (2019) 'Ceasefire Arrangements', PA-X Report (Edinburgh: Global Justice Academy, University of Edinburgh).
38. Indonesia/Aceh, Cessation of Hostilities Framework Agreement between the Government of the Republic of Indonesia and the Free Aceh Movement, 9 December 2002, https://www.peaceagreements.org/view/325/; Nicaragua, The Toncontin Agreement, 23 March 1990, https://www.peaceagreements.org/view/589/; Papua New Guinea/Bougainville, Agreement covering Implementation of the Ceasefire (Arawa Agreement), 30 April 1998, https://www.peaceagreements.org/view/557/.
39. For example, see Georgia/Russia (Abkhazia), Protocol of the Gali Meeting between the Georgian and Abkhaz Sides on the Issues of Stablization of the Situation in the Security Zone, 11 July 2000, https://www.peaceagreements.org/view/1773/.
40. K. Woods (2011) 'Ceasefire Capitalism: Military–Private Partnerships, Resource Concessions and Military–State Building in the Burma–China Borderlands', *Journal of Peasant Studies*, 38:4, 747–770.
41. A. Kolas, 2011, 'Naga Militancy and Violent Politics in the Shadow of Ceasefire', *Journal of Peace Research*, 48:6, 781–792.
42. I. Svensson and D. Cansin Karakus (2017) 'Between the Bombs: Exploring Partial Ceasefires in the Syrian Civil War, 2011–2017', *Terrorism and Political Violence*, 1–20.
43. Bell et al. (2020) PA-X Codebook, Version 3.
44. Average number of pages of all framework (partial and comprehensive) agreements and average number of all ceasefire agreements, 1990–2019. PA-X Version 3, metadata agreement length.
45. Colombia, Final Agreement to End the Armed Conflict and Build a Stable and Lasting Peace, 24 November 2016, https://www.peaceagreements.org/view/1845/.
46. See further, K. Zulueta-Fülscher and A. Welikala (2017) Substate Constitutions in Fragile and Conflict-affected Settings (Stockholm: International IDEA).

47. C. Bell and R. Forster (2019) Women and the Renegotiation of Transitional Governance Arrangements, PA-X Spotlight Gender Series (Edinburgh: Global Justice Academy).
48. C. Bell (2008) 'Negotiating Human Rights' in Contemporary Peacemaking Conflict, Peace Processes and Post-war Reconstruction, second edition, edited by John Darby and Roger Mac Ginty (Basingstoke: Palgrave Macmillan), p. 221.
49. See further, B. Paladini and S. Molloy (2019) 'More Inclusive Monitoring of Peace Agreement Implementation: Barometer Initiative in Colombia', in Navigating Inclusion in Peace Processes, edited by Andy Carl (London: Conciliation Resources), pp. 32–38.
50. See B. Walter (1997) The Critical Barrier to Civil War Settlement, International Organisation 5:1 at 335–364, on the importance of third party enforcement in intrastate conflicts, where non-state actors are expected to unilaterally give up the capacity for force.
51. For example see Philippines/Mindanao, Certification (Renewal of the International Monitoring Team mandate), 29 January 2015, https://www.peaceagreements.org/view/1350/; Certification (Renewal of Ad Hoc Joint Action Group mandate), 31 May 2015, https://www.peaceagreements.org/view/1351/.
52. On the new global political marketplace of transition, see T. Carothers and O. Samet-Marram (2015) The New Global Marketplace of Political Change (Washington, DC: Carnegie Endowment for, International Peace).
53. Based on third party signatory data, and secondary research when agreements are unsigned but agreed, 1990–2019. PA-X (2020) Peace Agreements Database and Access Tool, Version 3.
54. Bell et al. (2020) PA-X Codebook, Version 3.
55. See further, K. Nash, (2019) Interstate Agreements to End Intrastate Conflicts, PA-X Report (Edinburgh: Global Justice Academy, University of Edinburgh).
56. The composition of participating states and organisations changed between the different conferences. For example, representatives of 55 states and 25 international organizations were parties to the 2012 Tokyo Declaration Partnership for Self-Reliance in Afghanistan from Transition to Transformation (Tokyo Conference), whilst the 2004 Berlin Declaration (Berlin Conference) was

produced by 65 states and organisations. For a full list of the interstate agreements relating to Afghanistan see PA-X (2020) Peace Agreements Database and Access Tool, Version 3.

57. Afghanistan, Tashkent Declaration on Fundamental Principles for a Peaceful Settlement of the Conflict in Afghanistan, 19 July 1999, https://www.peaceagreements.org/view/553/
58. See further, J. Pospisil (2019) Peace in political unsettlement, pp. 190–195; L. Wise, R. Forster, and C. Bell (2019) Local Peace Processes: Opportunities and Challenges for Women's Engagement, PA-X Spotlight Gender Series (Edinburgh: Global Justice Academy).
59. For further on local agreements in Syria see R. Turkmani, M. Kaldor, W. Elhamwi, J. Ayo, and N. Hariri (2014) 'Hungry for Peace: Positives and Pitfalls of Local Truces and Ceasefires in Syria', *Security in Transition* (London: London School of Economics).
60. C. Buchold, J. Harlander, S. Quamber, and Ø Ege (2018) The End of the Big Peace? Opportunities for mediation (Oslo: Oslo Forum, Centre for Humanitarian Dialogue).
61. See further Parades Commission (2019) Frequently Asked Questions, https://www.paradescommission.org/, accessed 21 August 2019.
62. See further P. Reddy (2008) 'Reconciliation in Bougainville: Civil War, Peacekeeping and Restorative Justice', *Contemporary Justice Review*, 11:2, 117–130.
63. World Bank and United Nations (2018) Pathways for Peace: INCLUSIVE Approaches to Preventing Violent Conflict (Washington, DC: World Bank).
64. On these processes and the importance of inclusion generally see (London: Conciliation Resources).
65. See further for a good review of the literature, norms and issues, see A.T. Hirblinger and D.M. Landau (2020) supra.

CHAPTER 20

Power Sharing After Civil Wars: Matching Problems to Solutions

Timothy D. Sisk

Identity-related conflict is worsening in the contemporary global context. The Minority Rights Group (MRG), in its *Peoples Under Threat* global survey, notes increased identity-related conflict and threats to minorities and indigenous peoples worldwide.[1] In recent years, MRG has consistently reported worsening trends for the world's minorities and indigenous peoples with threats to culture, livelihoods, and rights to historical land as well as discrimination in access to education, healthcare, government services, and political representation. In recent years alarm bells for mass atrocities have been sounded for countries such as Afghanistan, South Sudan, Syria, and Somalia. Emerging and resurging conflicts along identity lines are noted in countries such as Azerbaijan, Cameroon, Macedonia, Indonesia, Kenya, South Africa, and Sri Lanka. Such conflicts can easily become a civil war. Overall, levels of intrastate conflict have risen since 2007 with a clear upward trend line emerging

T. D. Sisk (✉)
University of Denver, Denver, CO, USA
e-mail: timothy.sisk@du.edu

in 2010.[2] In these and still other contexts, such as Turkey, Indonesia, Kashmir, or Ukraine—which also saw worsening ethnic conditions in 2017 and 2018[3]—political systems globally are under serious strain from ethnic, religious, and sectarian mobilization.[4] While the "root causes" of such conflict typically lie in interactions among economic, political, and social factors, violence often emerges—or is organized along—identity-based lines. Contemporary technology only facilitates such identity-based violence. The 2019 MRG report focuses, for example, on the role of social media in contributing to social polarization and conflict dynamics.

The new wave of "ethnic" conflict raises key questions for contemporary peacemaking. In conflict settings where the badge of battle becomes more clearly ethnic or sectarian, external mediators have commonly looked to power sharing formulas to prevent, resolve, and build peace after violence. In Syria, the most injurious civil war of the twenty-first century, will a deeply divided Syria be able to avoid partition and create a non-sectarian future[5] or will ethnic power sharing be the basis of a settlement?

The Syria imbroglio, like other contemporary conflict contexts in which ethnic, racial, or religious identity differences are strong drivers, raises longstanding debates about peacemaking and the design of political institutions in deeply divided societies.

This chapter begins with an essential review of these longstanding—and still highly relevant—debates on power sharing, highlighting the differences between models of consociationalism (group-based power sharing) and centripetalism (an integrative approach). The following section reviews some recent findings on new debates around inclusivity in peace processes that envisage a "war-to-democracy" transition in relation to five areas: upstream inclusivity, rethinking presidentialism, electoral system choice and inclusivity, revisiting ethnic federalism, and strengthening social cohesion. These new factors are essential for mediators hoping to ameliorate identity-based conflicts.

Old Debates: Models of Democracy in Deeply Divided Societies

When partition is off the table as a solution to today's internal conflicts (as it generally is, despite some "frozen" conflicts in which self-determination remains the core dispute), some form of power sharing is often, if not always, a necessary element of a broader pact to end the war and pivot a country toward non-violent processing of social conflicts.[6] The turn to power sharing reflects a bargaining-based, institutional choice consideration that some combination of security, electoral, federal, or territorial, and group-rights guarantees can form the basis for a war-ending settlement, and that over time institutionalization of these guarantees can create permanent incentives for peace through inclusion, proportionality, decentralization, and fairer distribution of resources.[7] Yet, power sharing is not a single formula, and protagonists in conflict as well as mediators must make difficult choices among alternative institutional arrangements.[8] It is now well-appreciated that power sharing formulas can be hazardous to sustaining peace: they may reward those who perpetrated violence with a seat at the table of power, they may incentivize politicians to "play the ethnic card," and can structure politics along identity lines for generations to come.[9]

The Dangers of Majoritarianism

Advocates of power sharing in divided societies agree on the dangers of majoritarianism, citing the potential distortions in vote-to-seat outcomes, the inability of geographically dispersed minority parties to achieve representation, and—in the context of an ethnic party system—the likelihood that a single ethnic group or coalition of ethnic groups will govern to the detriment of others. Majoritarian systems seem to be especially vulnerable to elites who use identity politics as their organizing strategy, sowing fear and trumpeting nationalism as a deliberate electoral ploy.[10] Arend Lijphart, the most indefatigable critic of majoritarian and plurality electoral rules for divided societies (and indeed for other democracies), identifies the core problem when he refers to the potential for "majority dictatorship."[11] Donald Horowitz concurs, arguing in his seminal work, *Ethnic Groups in Conflict*, that under conditions of simple majority rule, "ethnic parties developed, majorities took power, and minorities took shelter. It was a fearful situation, in which the prospect of minority exclusion from government underpinned by ethnic voting, was potentially permanent…. Civil violence, military coups, and the advent of single-party regimes can all be traced to this problem of inclusion-exclusion."[12] Recent research on political parties in conflict-affected countries stresses the importance of designing incentives for inclusivity in political parties and for focusing on accountability and responsive government over the advancement of identity as such.[13]

Rejection of majoritarian democracy by power sharing advocates does not mean a rejection of democratic values. What distinguishes advocates of more consensus-oriented democracy, or power sharing, is the belief in the prospects for political or constitutional engineering to mitigate conflicts in divided societies. That is, they argue that the rules of the political game can be structured to institutionalize moderation on divisive ethnic themes, to contain the destructive tendencies, and to preempt the centrifugal forces created by ethnic politics. They do not assert that political engineering can eradicate deep enmities, but that appropriate institutions can nudge the political system in the direction of reduced conflict and greater governmental accountability. The common assumption is that choices over the basic rules of the game affect its outcomes. Horowitz writes, "Where there is some determination to play by the rules, the rules can restructure the system so the game itself changes."[14] While countries in recent years have emerged from conflict and done well in contexts of majoritarian democracy—notably Liberia, which has seen three rounds of majoritarian presidential elections since the Second Liberian Civil War ended in 2005—scholars routinely reject majoritarian rule institutions in societies with strong patterns of ethnic political mobilization as elections may merely be an ethnic census, with little hope of minority inclusion.[15]

The Consociation Formula

To mitigate the dangers of seemingly permanent minority exclusion, power sharing has been defined by Lijphart and others as a set of democratic principles that—when carried out through practices and institutions—provide each significant identity group or segment in a society representation and decision-making abilities on common issues and a degree of autonomy over issues of importance to the group. Lijphart's principles of power sharing—known as "consociational democracy" (derived from the Latin term consociatio, to associate in an alliance—was pathbreaking in its differentiation of coalescent democracy from majoritarian democracy.[16] War-ending peace agreements such as the 1989 Ta'if Accord for Lebanon, the 1995 Dayton Accords for Bosnia, or the 1998 Belfast/Good Friday Agreement for Northern Ireland are classically consociational in form. The bi-zonal, bi-federal solution Cyprus Reunification Plan proposed by the United Nations also reflected these characteristics.

Consociationalism, above all, relies on elite cooperation as the principal characteristic of successful conflict management in deeply divided societies.[17] Consociationalists suggest that even if there are deep communal differences, overarching integrative elite cooperation is a necessary and sufficient condition to assuage conflict. In the consociational approach, elites, or conflict group leaders, directly represent various societal segments and act to forge political ties at the center. Consociationalism relies on four principles:

- Inclusive executive branches, along the lines of a "grand coalition;"
- Proportionality in elections, public appointments, and fiscal matters;
- Territorial autonomy or non-territorial (group rights) autonomy, sometimes known as "corporate" autonomy; and
- Mutual or minority veto that enables minorities to exercise self-determination over matters of importance to the group, such as language, or education policy.

Consociational approaches, both in theory and in practice, have been deeply criticized as non-democratic (forming a government before electing it), reinforcing of ethnicity and nationalism at the expense of national unity, disadvantageous for women's representation, prone to gridlock, and rewarding of ethnic patronage networks. Moreover, there is a lack of clarity regarding the conditions which favour the adoption of consociational models, and whether it is possible to move beyond ethnic power sharing once it has been adopted.[18]

The Centripetalist Alternative

Scholars continue to differ deeply over whether the consociational power sharing approach (in which ethnic groups are usually represented through ethnically exclusive political parties) leads to better conflict management than the integrative or pluralist) approach, in which political organizations seek to transcend ethnic group differences.[19] The integrative approach sees as ideal the creation of pre-election coalitions between ethnic parties—or less commonly, the creation of broad multiethnic parties—on interests that transcend ethnic identities, such as common economic interests. Horowitz proposes a typology of five mechanisms aimed at reducing ethnic conflict that may be described as "centripetalism," which is an inward-spinning dynamic:

- Dispersions of power, often territorial, which "proliferate points of power so as to take the heat off of a single focal point;"
- Devolution of power and reservation of offices on an ethnic basis to foster intra-ethnic competition at the local level;
- Inducements for interethnic cooperation, such as electoral laws that effectively promote pre-election electoral coalitions through vote pooling;
- Policies to encourage alternative social alignments, such as social class or territory, by placing political emphasis on crosscutting cleavages;
- Reducing disparities between groups through managed distribution of resources.[20]

The centripetalist alternative can be seen in contexts such as Nigeria, where electoral rules for the presidency require broad-based political coalitions, the proliferation of states over time has broken down ethnic territorialization, and where ethnic political parties are disallowed. Other examples of centripetalism may be found in situations such as Sri Lanka, Fiji, Papua New Guinea, Kenya (in the 2010 constitution), and Northern Ireland (in its adoption of the Single Transferable Vote, or STV), and there is a continuing debate about their overall efficacy in inducing moderation.[21]

For policymakers, the debate among academics over approaches to power sharing may seem rather "academic"—filled with terminological exegeses, and irrelevant to the day-to-day decisions that must be made in dealing with contemporary ethnic crises. On the contrary, however, the power sharing debate continues to be critical to policymaking. The fundamental policy principles and specific policy recommendations that emanate from these two basic approaches to successful conflict management in a democratic framework—such as the type of electoral system that parties to a conflict should be encouraged to adopt—are starkly different. Understanding the differences and formulating appropriate policies may be critical—for disputants and international interveners alike—between successful ethnic conflict management, stagnation, and a cold peace (or "negative resilience," as the case of Lebanon has been described[22]) and costly violent confrontation. Thus, today in countries that had adopted consociationalism, much debate occurs on ways in which the original consociational bargain can be eventually overcome.

The old debates also continue to resound in contemporary contexts. Might it be possible in contexts such as Bosnia or Lebanon to move beyond consociationalism toward more integrative solutions? Has open-list proportional representation in South Africa contributed to the demise of a moderate center and the ethos of nonracialism and inclusion? Can territorial autonomy work to bring a definitive end to conflict in the Philippines? How effective will reserved congressional seats be for the FARC in the Colombian peace process? Can Iraq move beyond sectarianism in its ruling coalition? Can Nepal succeed in leaving behind a history of "ranked group" caste interactions and build a system of inclusion that remediates institutionalized discrimination, even as new ethnicity, religion, and caste-based mobilizations emerge? What options exist to resolve the language crisis in Cameroon? These old questions are also raised anew as Western societies grapple with increased multiculturalism and the rise of exclusive populisms, focusing on formal (citizenship and naturalization processes) and informal (consultative or interim) means of inclusion.[23]

NEW DEBATES: PROLIFERATING POINTS OF INCLUSION

While old debates on the efficacy and long-term effects of inclusivity in democracy continue, there are a host of new debates about ways to improve inclusivity in transitions to democracy in conflict-affected countries. The essential premise of the new debates is that neither stylistic model of power sharing can be said to be the best in all circumstances nor they are unlikely to be adopted by protagonists in conflict as a complete package of institutions or of underlying principles. Rather, what is needed is a spectrum of options ranging from the most consociational to the most integrative. The challenge is not to develop a single model of conflict-regulating practices, but rather to debate the merits and demerits of a menu of conflict-regulating practices that disputants and mediators can choose from and adapt to the intricacies and challenges of successfully regulating any given context.

In some instances a more consociational approach may lead to successful conflict regulation, whereas in other instances a more integrative approach may be best. In still other contexts, such as South Africa, prior experience with ethnic or racial representation (e.g., in the 1984 "Tricameral" constitution, which was based on apartheid social categorizations) means that ethnic power sharing as such is simply off the table. Whether any given institution or policy approach will contribute to success is highly dependent on the structure of ethnic relations, the specific patterns of ethnic politics in a given community, the historical development of a given conflict, the relationship between ethnic groups and the state, the attitudes and skills of political leaders, and the ability of groups in conflict to agree on the core principles underlying their political system.

Moments of transition offer opportunities to make these choices. A recent study of women's participation in constitution-making by Tamaru and O'Reilly showed that constitutional reform is both a common occurrence (they find 75 countries transitioned and undertook constitutional reform in the 25 years of 1990–2015) and that such processes have become much more participatory over time. They also find a failure to include women in these processes.[24] Broadening women's participation in such processes is one area where among scholars there is very little debate; the linkage between women's inclusion and more peaceful politics seems widely accepted with the causal mechanisms found in women's ability to build bridging social cohesion:

> Women repeatedly bridged divides in the negotiating process, contributing to peacebuilding and reconciliation in deeply divided societies, while also advancing consensus on key issues. They broadened societal participation and informed policymakers of citizens' diverse priorities for the constitution, helping to ensure greater traction for the emerging social contract.[25]

This section presents a short overview of six more contentious contemporary debates on democracy in contexts of deep identity-related divisions.

Upstream Inclusivity in Peace Processes

Building inclusivity into political settlements may require "upstream" inclusivity in peace processes. How inclusively should peace processes be structured, and does the timing of the inclusivity matter? This debate is central as some research has shown that greater involvement of civil society in peace negotiations leads in a path-dependent way to more durable peace over time.[26] Moreover, while much attention has been paid historically to ethnic participation as a means of inclusion, landmark global norms such as UN Security Council Resolution 1325 and the overall women, peace, and security agenda has highlighted inclusivity along gender lines as an essential element in re-making relations across identity groups: conflict dynamics transform gender relations and may create opportunities for crosscutting ties among women that bridge identity divides.[27]

On the one hand, there is argument (especially from a mostly political economy perspective) for the need for a political settlement among key elites to first guarantee peace and stability, with broadening of inclusivity over time.[28] Increasingly the focus on political settlements has gone further to evaluate inclusivity in peace processes and how inclusivity is reflected in peace agreements.[29] The argument for a narrow coalition in peacemaking relates to the debate on "spoilers," with some evidence in even celebrated peace processes such as South Africa or Nepal that, in the end, elite dynamics have mattered most. This focus on elite pact-making echoes the earlier findings of the transitology literature in democratization studies that, in the end, elite bargains are an essential stepping stone toward greater inclusivity over time.[30] Yet, they are also limited in that they tend to "paper over" local-level experiences and insecurities. Mehler found in an analysis of power sharing agreements that their effects are highly mixed in securing peace … they tend not to take into sufficient account local-level fears and provide for local-level security provisions.[31]

Yet, there is also a good argument for inclusivity that is upstream. Seminal work on civil society and peacebuilding has identified the functions of civil society's inclusion in peace processes including the promotion of intergroup social cohesion and has identified seven models of civil society participation in peace and transition processes in 11 country case studies. Indeed, Hellmüller and Zahar argue that in the stalled settlement talks on Syria, "Against the odds, progress can be observed at this level as Syrian society has become better organized and more tightly connected, and its voice in the process has grown stronger."[32]

Rethinking Presidentialism

Presidentialism-related crises capture news headlines from around the world. In DRC, Burundi, Gabon, Rwanda, and Uganda in Africa, for example, efforts to eliminate term limits and effectively allow "presidents for life" have either succeeded or stimulated devastating conflict. Presidencies in Zimbabwe and South Africa have ended with internal changes of regime in the context of misrule and corruption. The "perils of presidentialism" (as raised decades ago by Juan Linz[34]) is an ongoing debate in the literature on neo-patrimonialism. While it might be argued that presidential systems allow for the development of decisive coalitions for evenly distributed national development policies and that these can be inclusive—the presidency of Ellen Johnson Sirleaf in Liberia (2006–2018) supports this point—presidentialism more typically is fraught with problems such as vulnerability to excessive corruption, tendency toward electoral manipulation and fraud, capture of the military, and the development of deep patronage networks. Presidential systems—with executive branch authority highly centralized in one individual who is usually, but not always, directly elected—are more exclusive than parliamentary systems, particularly if the president is unambiguously identifiable as a member of any one community or interest.

Moments of transition may afford opportunities to design more inclusive executives. Parliamentary structures are an attractive option for divided societies. If structured with a broadly representative cabinet, such a structure can include many parties at the highest levels of government. Parliamentary government allows for many shades of possible political outcomes. When combined with a variable term (the government can be forced to resign when majority parliamentary support is withdrawn), it is a highly flexible arrangement. Broad-based executives are more easily created if the principle of proportionality is operational. The two most important proportionality practices are proportional representation in appointments, which often takes the form of the constitutionally entrenched reservation of offices on an ethnic or territorial basis, and a proportional representation electoral system. The use of special majorities on key issues in both cabinet and legislative institutions (for example, through innovative parliamentary rules) can serve this aim without reliance on grand coalitions or minority vetoes for named groups. Inclusive, legitimate, and authoritative arbiters of conflict such as broadly accepted commissions and judicial bodies are good examples of integrated administrative decision-making practices.

As the above discussion of centripetalism suggests, presidential systems can conceivably be constructed to ensure that candidates must present themselves as conciliatory broad-based leaders in order to be elected. A broad-minded Nelson Mandela-like individual, pursuing aims of national integration, can serve a symbolically important conflict-reducing role.

Inclusivity and Electoral System Choice

There is no perfect electoral system. For this reason, it appears that many countries affected by conflict, when tasked with the challenge of designing an electoral system anew, have either opted for unusual approaches (such as the adoption of the Single Transferable Vote in Afghanistan, which does not require political parties), simple approaches (such as List-Proportional Representation, or PR, in South Africa), or mixed approaches that combine single-member districts and PR (as in Nepal for its 2017 polls).

An appropriate electoral system in a divided society is arguably the most important mechanism through which parties in conflict can adopt a democratic conflict-regulating practice. This is true because, as the eminent Italian political scientist Giovanni Sartori has written, electoral systems are "the most specific manipulative element of politics."[35] The debate over which electoral system is best is complicated because electoral system design can be a very technical matter; the outcomes that flow from a specific choice are highly dependent on unknowns such as the spatial distribution of votes, shifting party alignments and inter-party pacts, voting behavior, ballot design, and myriad other variables.

Proportional representation (PR) can serve as the basis for determining the relative weight of various groups in terms of proportional representation in executive, legislative, and administrative arenas, especially when census data are inaccurate, suspicious, or absent. Moreover, some nation-wide PR systems do not require contentious boundary delimitation (districting). A critical issue is whether a simple PR system is expected to fragment the party system over time and what the implications of such fragmentation may be. A second issue is the appreciation that PR systems may not mitigate the effects of majority domination when the majority bloc is sufficiently cohesive.[36]

While a complete discussion of electoral systems is much beyond the present chapter, there remain good reasons to consider overall proportionality, and thus some form of PR, for electoral systems in conflict-affected countries. There is evidence that the use of quotas—formal and informal, and particularly in terms of political party recruitment and candidacy processes—has been effective in increasing women's participation.[37] Efforts to determine the extent to which the single transferable vote has contributed to peace in Northern Ireland as parties and candidates vie for seats in Stormont continue to be debated among scholars and practitioners.[38]

Revisiting Ethnic Federalism

The debate over ethnic federalism is an enduring one, and it is seen in modern manifestations in contexts such as Ethiopia, Nepal, Ukraine, and South Sudan. Under the right circumstances, the political needs of territorially concentrated ethnic groups, particularly minority groups, may be accommodated through grants of autonomy. Agreements are reached between the "rump" government and the autonomous units over issues such as economic and foreign relations and regional commerce. Decisions on these limited issues are made jointly. Critical variables are the degree of economic interdependence, the structure of fiscal relations, and the balance of dependency ... and the size of the country (an argument that has been made against ethnic federalism in Nepal).[39]

Ethnic federations require more extensive interaction than confederations at the central government level, and the allocation of powers between the central and regional governments is inevitably a difficult and ongoing balancing act. The management of the economy and the distribution of commonly held resources (for example, water or mineral rights) is critically important. Other thorny issues include boundary delimitation, the structure of security, the containment of secessionist tendencies, relations between subunits and foreign governments and international organizations, disparities across region or state in the adjudication of law, language, and education policy, and—perhaps most important—the status of minorities and majorities within any given region.

When groups are not territorially concentrated, or when the aim of federalism is to promote intragroup cleavages and foster alignments across groups, a mixed or crosscutting federal approach may serve to mitigate conflict and foster peace. Mixed federations are appropriate when one or two ethnic groups are mobilized, aggrieved, and territorially concentrated but other groups are more integrated; those territorially concentrated groups can be given special status or recognition while a nonethnic hue is preserved for the remainder of the polity. Noncommunal federalism can be especially appropriate when significant minority communities will reside in all of the subunits. Dangers occur in mixed federations when special status is conferred on one territory but not others (viz., Kashmir in India) and in noncommunal federations when some groups strive for greater territorial autonomy and such autonomy is not forthcoming.

While the broader debates on ethnic federalism continue, the focus in peacebuilding has turned to local dynamics and local action in newly decentralized state structures. Today, the peacebuilding literature speaks of the dilemmas in peacebuilding and of obstacles to international engagement as well as efforts to "turn to the local" to solve problems that continue to hinder building sustainable peace.[40] A cross-national study of local dynamics in eight countries undertaken by a consortium of US, Norwegian, Nepali, and South African researchers found that decentralization has multiple and often contradictory implications for peacebuilding. Rapidly changing local conditions in the aftermath of conflict mean that effective aid intervention must leverage local knowledge and adjust rapidly to secure appropriate local partners. The transformation of local governance following conflict can bring much benefit to local communities, including greater political representation for diverse groups and an environment for innovation. On the other hand, local government structures—whether formal state institutions or informal ones such as local peace committees—are well-known to be vulnerable to capture and corruption. The case studies confirmed that careful, local studies of subnational conflict dynamics are essential to effective interventions. Social, spatial, economic, and local-political assessments are needed to identify appropriate actors and practices to avoid capture by narrow interests.[41]

Strengthening Social Cohesion

Social cohesion recently has become a focus for peacebuilding actors working in countries affected by identity-based conflict.[42] Development strategies in fragile contexts target the nexus between state and society, with social cohesion and strengthening the social contract as primary aims for conflict-sensitive international engagement.[43] International peacebuilding networks have in recent years oriented themselves around the social cohesion concept to answer, in part, longstanding concerns that prior peacebuilding interventions were not sustainable because they were not based on a deep understanding of social dynamics.

Social cohesion programming has developed in both direct efforts to foster national networks and create infrastructures for peace, as well as through indirect approaches such as youth programming and "peace messaging." At the same time, the social cohesion concept has made strides through the development of country-level qualitative and quantitative studies of conditions, indicators, and attitudinal measures. Lessons have been learned regarding direct and indirect approaches, and coordinated work on strengthening social cohesion in conflict-affected countries has progressed. So too have regional approaches which focus on drivers of difference or cohesion across international boundaries.[44]

Conclusion

Although contemporary peacemakers have been persuasive and even coercive in attempts to coax leaders of warring parties into power sharing arrangements as a means of preventing or escaping violent conflict, it is ultimately up to the parties themselves to agree to accept a form of democracy that may be more, or less, inclusive. Rather than models as such, new debates increasingly focus on proliferation and overlapping mechanisms and opportunities for inclusivity.

There seems to be general agreement that consociational agreements, while potentially necessary to end wars, tend to become obsolete over time and they may require re-opening of the Pandora's box of peace agreement terms. Clearly, there are no easy answers to the puzzles of stabilizing societies after civil war and moving toward democracy as a system of sustainable conflict management. However, at least one piece of the puzzle is the ability of countries to renegotiate fundamental social contracts over time and of long-term international engagement to assist such processes. Some have suggested that at least one way to resolve the problem is to negotiate, in the first place, sunset clauses whereby the more fixed or rigid elements of power sharing expire over time.[45] Others admonish international policymakers to avoid rigid power sharing agreements.[46] While these are useful suggestions, they do not solve the fundamental dilemma of how to balance the initial demands for certainty through power sharing pacts with the uncertainty created in the renegotiation of social contracts over time.

For those emerging from conflict, there are certainly no one-size-fits-all forms of inclusive democratic governance. Interim power sharing or transitional governments, coupled with electoral processes that lead to constitution-making assemblies (as in South Africa or Nepal) seem to be an especially useful transitional approach in the immediate emergence from civil war. At the end of the day, what seems to matter most is the principle of inclusivity, and to match problems (assessment of specific conflict conditions) with the best-match or most-promising institutional solutions. It remains one of the critical challenges of the next generation of practitioners and scholars to demonstrate how further expansion of inclusivity has been tangibly achieved in contemporary conflict contexts.

Notes

1. Minority Rights Group International, *Peoples Under Threat 2019*, at: https://minorityrights.org/2019/06/03/peoples-under-threat-2019-the-role-of-social-media-in-exacerbating-violence/.
2. Marie Allansson, Erik Melander, and Lotta Themnér, "Organized Violence, 1989–2016," *Journal of Peace Research* 54 (4) (2017): 574–587; Monty G. Marshall and Gabrielle Elzinga-Marshall, *Global Report 2017: Conflict, Governance, and State Fragility*. Washington, DC: Center for Systemic Peace, 2017, available at: http://www.systemicpeace.org/vlibrary/GlobalReport2017.pdf; and Heidelberg Institute for International Conflict Research, *Conflict Barometer 2016*, at: https://hiik.de/conflict-barometer.
3. As featured in the analysis of the reporting of the International Crisis Group, which has published an analysis of each of these contexts: https://www.crisisgroup.org/. Recent trend analysis shows contemporary conflicts play out within majority-Muslim countries in which the protagonists are divided by the Shi'a-Sunni sectarian divide with its regional manifestations and interactions and its localized contexts (Gleditsch 2016; Hashemi and Postel 2017).
4. The 2017 World Bank/United Nations Development Report *Pathways for Peace: Inclusive Approaches to Preventing Conflict* reports that "More Countries Were Experiencing Violent Conflict in 2016 Than at Any Time in the Previous 30 Years," Washington, DC and New York: World Bank/UNDP, 2017: 12.

5. See the report of "The Day After" Project, which presents the outcome of a dialog project among Syrians in exile on a post-al Assad future in Syria facilitated by the United States Institute of Peace in early 2013. The report identifies as a key goal of the transitional process to "Establish citizenship and the equality of all citizens as decisive in relations between individuals and the state as opposed to sectarian, ethnic, or gender considerations." See the Report at: http://www.usip.org/publications/the-day-after-project.
6. Caroline Hartzell and Matthew Hodie, *Crafting Peace: Power-Sharing Institutions and the Negotiated Settlement of Civil Wars*. University Park, PA: Pennsylvania State University Press, 2007.
7. Philip Roeder and Donald Rothchild, eds., *Sustainable Peace: Power and Democracy after Civil War*. Ithaca, NY: Cornell University Press, 2005.
8. Recent research projects on power sharing include the special issue of the UNESCO's "Democracy and Power-Sharing in Multi-National States," *International Journal on Multicultural Societies* 8 (2) (2006), and the extensive work of the German Institute for Global and Area Studies (GIGA) project "Institutions for Sustainable Peace," available at: www.giga-hamburg.de/en/isp.
9. See Christine Bell, "Political Power Sharing and Inclusion: Peace and Transition Processes," PA-X Report, 2018, at: http://www.politicalsettlements.org/wp-content/uploads/2018/07/2018_Bell_PA-X-Political-Power-Sharing-Report.pdf.
10. For an earlier analysis of the ethnic entrepreneur problem as a driver of violence in the early 1990s, see Human Rights Watch, *Playing the 'Communal Card': Communal Violence and Human Rights*. New York: Human Rights Watch, 1995.
11. See Arend Lijphart, *Democracy in Plural Societies*. New Haven, CT: Yale University Press, 1977: 25–28, 114–118.
12. Donald Horowitz, *Ethnic Groups in Conflict*. Berkeley and Los Angeles: University of California Press, 1985: 629.
13. Benjamin Reilly and Per Nordlund, eds., *Political Parties in Conflict-Prone Societies*. Tokyo: United Nations University Press, 2008.
14. Ibid.: 601.
15. For an analysis of these dynamics in the run-up to the May 2018 elections in Iraq, see Margaret Coker and Falih Hassan, "ISIS Is

Weakened, but Iraq Election Could Unravel Hard-Won Stability," *The New York Times*, 30 January 2018, at: https://www.nytimes.com/2018/01/30/world/middleeast/iraq-election-abadi.html.
16. See Note 9.
17. Arend Lijphart, "Constitutional Design for Divided Societies," *Journal of Democracy* 15 (2) (2004): 96–109. The literature on consociational democracy is well developed.
18. Donald Horowitz, "Ethnic Power Sharing: Three Big Problems," *Journal of Democracy* 25 (2) (2014): 5–20.
19. For a recent overview of these debates, see Allison McCulloch and John McGarry, eds., *Power-Sharing: Empirical and Normative Challenges*. Abingdon: Routledge, 2017. See also Andreas Wimmer et al., eds., *Facing Ethnic Conflicts: Toward a New Realism*. Lanham: Rowman and Littlefield, 2004.
20. Horowitz, *Ethnic Groups in Conflict*: 597–600.
21. For an analysis, see Allison McCulloch, "Does Moderation Pay? Centripetalism in Deeply Divided Societies," *Ethnopolitics* 12 (1) (2012): 111–132.
22. Joy Aoun and Marie-Joëlle Zahar, "Lebanon: Confessionalism, Consociationalism, and Social Cohesion," in Fletcher Cox and Timothy D. Sisk, eds. *Peacebuilding in Deeply Divided Societies: Toward Social Cohesion?* London: Palgrave Macmillan, 2017.
23. See, for example, the work of the Raoul Wallenberg Institute on inclusive societies at: http://rwi.lu.se/what-we-do/focus-areas/inclusive-societies/; and International IDEA, "Migration, Social Polarization, Citizenship, and Mulicuturalism," in *The Global State of Democracy: Exploring Democracy's Resilience* (Chapter 7). Stockholm: International IDEA, 2017.
24. Nananko Tamaru and Marie O'Reilly, *How Women Influence Constitution Making After Conflict and Unrest*. Inclusive Security Research Report, January 2018, available at: https://www.inclusivesecurity.org/wp-content/uploads/2018/02/How-Women-Influence-Constitution-Making.pdf.
25. Tamaru and O'Reilly: 1.
26. Desirée Nilsson, "Anchoring the Peace: Civil Society Actors in Peace Accords and Durable Peace," *International Interactions: Empirical and Theoretical Research in International Relations* 38 (2) (2012): 243–266; and Thania Paffenholz, ed. *Civil Society &*

Peacebuilding: A Critical Assessment. Boulder: Lynne Rienner, 2009.
27. Marie Berry, *War, Women, and Power: From Violence to Mobilization in Rwanda and Bosnia-Herzegovina.* New York: Cambridge University Press, 2018.
28. See the analysis of pact-making in Anna Jarstad "Power Sharing: Former Enemies in Joint Government," in Anna K. Jarstad and Timothy D. Sisk, eds. *From War to Democracy: Dilemmas of Peacebuilding.* Cambridge: Cambridge University Press, 2008.
29. See the work of the project on political settlements at: http://www.politicalsettlements.org/.
30. Mahmoud Ould-Mohamedou and Timothy D. Sisk, eds., *Democratization in the 21st Century: Reviving Transitology.* Abindgon: Routledge, 2017.
31. Andreas Mehler, "Peace and Power Sharing in Africa: A Not so Obvious Relationship," *African Affairs* 108 (432) (2009): 453–473.
32. Sara Hellmüller and Marie-Joëlle Zahar, "Against the Odds: Civil Society in the Intra-Syrian Talks," International Peace Institute Issue Brief, March 2018, available at: https://www.ipinst.org/wp-content/uploads/2018/03/1803_Against-the-Odds.pdf.
33. Observers point to the "degradation" of the presidency in the United States, for example; see Robert Reich, "First 100 Days: Donald Trump and the Degradation of the Presidency," 23 April 2017, at: http://robertreich.org/post/159905075775.
34. Juan Linz, "The Perils of Presidentialism," *Journal of Democracy* 1 (1) (1990): 51–69.
35. Giovanni Sartori, "Political Development and Political Engineering," in J.D. Montgomery and A.O. Hirschman, eds. *Public Policy.* Cambridge: Harvard University Press, 1968: 273.
36. Matthijs Bogaards, "The Choice for Proportional Representation: Electoral System Design in Peace Agreements," *Civil Wars* 15 (2013): 71–87.
37. See, for example, Mark P. Jones, "Gender Quotas, Electoral Laws, and the Election of Women: Evidence from the Latin American Vanguard," *Comparative Political Studies* 42 (1) (2009): 56–81.
38. Transferable voting systems are complicated; to understand how the Northern Ireland system works, see the video prepared for an "Emoji" election by the BBC: http://www.bbc.com/news/av/

election-northern-ireland-2017-38911918/ni-assembly-election-how-does-the-stv-system-work.
39. Subindra Bogati and Timothy D. Sisk, "The Elusive 'New Nepal': Democratization, Ethnic Politics in a Plural Society," forthcoming for the project "Forging Resilient Social Contracts" (www.socialcontractsforpeacee.org).
40. For an analysis of this literature, see David Chandler, *Peacebuilding: The Twenty Years' Crisis, 1997–2017*. Cham, Switzerland: Palgrave Macmillan, 2017.
41. Astri Suhrke and Timothy D. Sisk, Final Report, "Innovations in Peacebuilding: International Norms and Local Dynamics in Conflict-affected Countries," Josef Korbel School of International Studies, March 2018. The final report is found at: https://www.du.edu/korbel/sie/research/sisk_innovations_in_peacebuilding.html.
42. Jane Jenson, Jane, "Defining and Measuring Social Cohesion," United Nations Research Institute for Social Development (UNRISD) and the Commonwealth Secretariat, 2010, available at: http://www.unrisd.org/80256B3C005BCCF9/%28httpPublications%29/170C271B7168CC30C12577D0004BA206?OpenDocument.
43. See, for example, International Dialogue on Peacebuilding and Statebuilding, *A New Deal for Engagement in Fragile States*. Paris: OECD Publishing, 2011; and Alexandre Marc et al., *Social Dynamics and Fragility: Engaging Societies in Responding to Fragile Situations*. Washington, DC: The World Bank, 2013.
44. Fletcher Cox and Timothy D. Sisk, eds. *Peacebuilding in Deeply Divided Societies: Toward Social Cohesion?* London: Palgrave.
45. For an up-to-date analysis of constitution-making and peacebuilding, see "Inclusive Peacebuilding in Conflict-Affected States: Designing for Democracy's Resilience," in International IDEA, *The Global State of Democracy: Exploring Democracy's Resilience* (Chapter 8).
46. S.G. Simonsen, "Addressing Ethnic Divisions in Post-Conflict Institution-Building: Lessons from Recent Cases," *Security Dialogue* 36 (3) (2005): 297–318.

CHAPTER 21

Peace Accords and Human Rights

Jan Pospisil

INTRODUCTION

Peace agreements and human rights are closely interwoven. About 70% of all peace agreements signed after 1990 refer to human rights or human rights-related issues. International practices of peacemaking and peacebuilding and multilaterally agreed peace processes that support operations such as peacekeeping, in particular, structurally rely on the human rights framework. The claim of the mutually reinforcing character of justice and peace developed into an internationally acclaimed policy agenda. Emerging norms such as the Responsibility to Protect (R2P) or human security refer to the human rights agenda of support for humanitarian interventions in ongoing armed conflict. As a consequence, human rights can nowadays be considered as one of the central normative backbones of negotiated peace settlements.

The multilateral success story of human rights-based approaches to peacemaking, however, is countered by critiques that argue that human

J. Pospisil (✉)
ASPR - Austrian Study Centre for Peace and Conflict Resolution, Vienna, Austria
e-mail: pospisil@aspr.ac.at

© The Author(s), under exclusive license to Springer Nature Switzerland AG 2022
R. Mac Ginty and A. Wanis-St. John (eds.), *Contemporary Peacemaking*, https://doi.org/10.1007/978-3-030-82962-9_21

rights function as an obstacle to—rather than a tool for—effective peacemaking. These critiques often refer to the questionable results of the human rights agenda in armed conflict. Human rights-based support for external armed intervention has contributed to a number of difficult and protracted situations. The examples of Libya, where the international armed intervention in 2011 was justified by the R2P norm, Iraq, where the UK government invoked a strong human rights agenda as a justification for regime change,[1] or, more recently and post facto, Afghanistan, where activists campaigned against the US withdrawal on human rights grounds, are cases in point.

Empirical evidence for the mainstreaming of human rights thinking and implementation in peace processes, whereby a thorough implementation of human rights would guarantee a more successful peace processes, is lacking. At the same time, human rights campaigns have contributed to the public rejection of comprehensive, carefully negotiated peace agreements. In Colombia in 2017, human rights advocates joined forces with hard-line politicians in their rejection of the peace accord struck between the government and the FARC, which was subsequently voted down in a referendum. The institutionalisation of international criminal law catalysed by the International Criminal Court (ICC), which is firmly embedded in human rights reasoning, has complicated peace processes by hampering the signing of a peace deal in Uganda (concerning the indictment of the leader of the Lord's Resistance Army, Joseph Kony) or by preventing international engagement with key players (for instance, the now ousted Omar al-Bashir in Sudan).

Human rights can be interpreted as a success story in providing the normative backbone of the indispensable justice-element in post-conflict transitions. At the same time, however, they may be understood as one of the spearheads of the international agenda of liberal peacemaking, which is nowadays widely criticised as having failed to achieve sustainable peace. These two interpretations demonstrate the normatively loaded contestation that human rights in peace accords often trigger. This chapter is not concerned with proving standpoints right or wrong. Instead, it takes stock of the empirical realities of how human rights are used in peace accords. In a second step, this chapter elaborates the main trade-offs between human rights-based justice claims and the transitional processes from armed conflict that are triggered by peace accords.

In doing so, this chapter, first, discusses the political and legal background of the relationship between peace accords and human rights along the different roles the normative framework takes in peacemaking efforts. Second, this chapter provides empirical insights on the role of human rights in peace accords as well as trends and trajectories of their utilisation. For this purpose, it relies on empirical data offered by the PA-X peace agreements database. Finally, the chapter discusses some of the tensions human rights generate in peace processes, namely human rights-based challenges to transitional justice and human rights-based challenges to power-sharing frameworks.

No Justice, No Peace—Revisited

The narrative that any peace accord must be firmly rooted in justice and, especially, in human rights has strong international traction. The United Nations has developed an extensive apparatus for sustaining this discourse. This apparatus works by declarations and assessments, by mandating of UN missions or missions by other regional organisations, and by the proliferation of human rights institutions. Regional organisations such as the African Union with the African Charter on Human and Peoples' Rights and the accompanying institutional structures have proliferated the narrative further. Human rights advocates and INGOs such as Human Rights Watch, which played an essential and partly disruptive role in contexts as different as Bosnia Herzegovina and Colombia, have become a vocal player in peace processes in recent years.

When assessing the role of human rights in the negotiation of peace agreements and in post-conflict transitions in general, three perspectives stand out: (1) the understanding of human rights violations as a root cause of armed conflict, because conflict parties might use the (perceived) denial of rights as a justification for the armed uprising, (2) the attempt to employ human rights law as a legal tool for legally regulating the consequences of armed conflict and post-conflict transitions, and (3) the interest of anchoring human rights as a form of global liberal governance. Peace processes and the often-related reconfiguration of a polity in a constitutional process, thus, are strong influenced by international human rights law.[2]

The assumption of the denial of human rights as a root cause of armed conflict is deeply embedded in the fundamental principles of liberal governance. This perspective holds that a peaceful polity rests on the indispensable implementation of human rights in its legal foundations. In turn, such liberal reasoning suggests that if a society is trapped in violent conflict, human rights implementation must have failed. Empirical research has not been able to substantiate a causal effect of human rights violations on triggering armed conflict. Moreover, attempts to translate other tangible root causes (like the withholding of political rights) into a human rights framework have been undertaken based on the empirical claim that repressive states are more prone to armed conflict.[3]

Conceptual reasoning has also been used to sustain the nexus between war and the denial of human rights. Mary Kaldor's 'new wars' hypothesis lays out deliberate human rights violations on a large scale as one of the new wars' key characteristics.[4] Christine Bell argues that human rights language can be applied 'for articulating the state's role in the root causes of the conflict'.[5] Irrespective of their potential structural role, it is widely undisputed that armed conflict unavoidably results in gross human rights violations.[6] Human rights-concerns thus need to be addressed when negotiating the conditions of ending armed violence and a possible framework for post-conflict transitions.

This requirement already points to the second perspective; the ability of human rights law to legally structure and regulate contexts of ongoing armed conflict and the often-violent post-conflict transitions. In doing so, human rights law runs in parallel with International Humanitarian Law (IHL), to an extent that even the UN General Assembly has framed one of its main resolutions concerning IHL in a human rights language ('Respect for Human Rights in Armed Conflicts', A/RES/2444, 19 December 1968). Nevertheless, the relationship is not straightforward. Noam Lubell, in an article for the International Committee of the Red Cross (ICRC), has argued that, while human rights law and IHL share many goals, 'they remain separate creatures'.[7] Especially the so-called humanitarian principles such as neutrality and impartiality, as they are enshrined in IHL, fundamentally contradict human rights law. After all, human rights can never be neutral against alleged perpetrators.

At the level of actual peace negotiations, human rights language can provide standards on which conflict parties might agree relatively easily due to strong international leverage. 'Human rights law thus assisted in presenting face-to-face negotiations as a neutral and moral option, rather than a radical new experiment'.[8] Applied in this way, human rights offer a pragmatic opportunity for actors to regain respectability. Commitments to human rights are even one of the major pathways to win international legitimacy since they represent a 'standard of civilization' which sets a benchmark for the behaviour of actors.[9] The high prevalence of human rights provisions in peace processes since 1990 is a consequence of these mechanisms. Yet, in order to be successful, the enforceability of human rights law needs to remain conditional and relative. When human rights turn into a threat for conflict actors, they almost certainly become contested and rejected. The purchase of human rights in peace negotiations rests in their pragmatic applicability which, however, at times contradicts the claim of universality inherent to international human rights law.

Finally, justice debates in peace negotiations can be seen as an opportunity to promote the international human rights agenda as a cornerstone of global liberal governance. Some human rights advocates attempt to use peace negotiations as a crucial opportunity to do so. Such negotiations offer a promising pathway for standard setting in the interest of global norm proliferation.[10] This logic seems straightforward at first glance, but it has two major disadvantages. First, a dogmatic approach to human rights may shrink mediation space and could even undermine the pragmatic applicability of human rights, one of the strengths the framework can offer in peace negotiations. Dogmatism thus turns human rights into another contested political project in a context characterised by fundamental political contestation. More radical parts of the human rights community might see such a political project as worth pursuing. However, it might well hinder the utilisation of human rights in peacemaking and could undermine its potential to reduce ongoing atrocities effectively.

Second, a dogmatic application weakens the human rights agenda in general. Its utilisation for openly interventionist concepts such as the Responsibility to Protect (R2P) has raised criticism of human rights being hypocritical and a justification for so-called 'humanitarian interventions' by an opportunistic yet opaque 'international community'.[11] In a historical context where humanitarian interventions have passed their prime and are heavily contested because of their normative implications,[12] linking peacemaking with global norm proliferation is likely to have negative consequences for both aims. It also contrasts with the empirical reality of an already existing healthy linkage between human rights and peace accords.

Human Rights Provisions in Peace Agreements

Peace agreements consistently refer to human rights across time and context. About 70% of all publicly available peace agreements signed since 1990 refer to human rights or contain human rights-related provisions. For a more thorough assessment of the particularities of human rights references in peace accords, the following part of this chapter analyses data provided by the PA-X peace agreements database produced and maintained by the University of Edinburgh.[13] The database consists of about 1600 peace agreements signed over the period from 1990 to the present day.[14] Since the agreements are coded along 12 major categories and 220 sub-categories—about 10% of the codes contain direct references to human rights. A comparative analysis, thus, reveals useful insights.[15]

Some of the most powerful patterns can be revealed by simple descriptive statistics. Figure 21.1 displays the percentage of human rights-related stipulations in peace agreements since 1990. The references remain stable across time until 2015. Surprisingly, in contrast to what one might expect, ceasefire agreements do not substantially diverge from this trend, which is mainly due to references to humanitarian issues with human rights implications. The trend within ceasefires, however, is more volatile compared to other peace agreements, mainly because the total number of ceasefire agreements is lower and the trajectory hence less stable. Overall, the high threshold shows that human rights are widely acknowledged as an indispensable prerequisite in peace negotiations and post-conflict transitions.

Fig. 21.1 Human rights references in peace agreements and ceasefire agreements, 1990–2018

Their usefulness in negotiations is due to their ability to provide an internationally recognised language for addressing contested issues without necessarily favouring the stronger party (Fig. 21.1).[16]

When looking at peace agreements (red lines in Figures), some significant drops in the percentage of human rights-related stipulations require further inquiry. The drop in the mid-1990s (1994–1998) is caused by the end of human rights-heavy peace processes in Central America, especially in Guatemala and Mexico, and the end of the peace negotiations in Bosnia Herzegovina which had produced a large number of agreements with references to human rights. Instead, peace agreements with the direct involvement of Russia, which commonly were weak on human rights, had been signed thereafter, especially in Moldova/Transnistria, Chechnya, Tajikistan and Georgia/Abkhazia. The agreements in the post-Soviet sphere lower the percentage.

Even more substantial is the significant decrease of references to human rights after 2015, from (including ceasefire agreements) 82% in 2015 to 50% in 2018. Part of the explanation might be an inconsistency of the data in recent years: the total number of signed peace agreements available in the PA-X database declines from 46 in 2015 to 24 in 2018. Therefore, with more agreements, many of them very short and often time-limited ceasefires, becoming available in upcoming years, the sharp drop might see a correction. But the numbers still suggest a tectonic shift: from 2015 to 2016 alone the percentage of peace agreements containing human rights provisions dropped by 20% (from 83 to 63%) while the total number of available agreements remains comparable (46–41). It appears that the global transformation towards a postliberal world order, which, inter alia, is signified by the disengagement of global liberal powers such as the US from peacemaking efforts in Syria, Yemen, or Libya, trickles down to the character of peace agreements. With the rise of states like Russia, Iran and Turkey especially in peacemaking efforts in the Middle East and North Africa (MENA) region, the role of human rights seems to fade.

The inconsistencies in the historical trajectory point to regional peculiarities in how human rights are addressed in peacemaking efforts. These differences also reflect broader trends in international politics. Table 21.1 lists the percentage of peace agreements containing human rights-related provisions across world regions. Peace agreements in the Americas contain the highest percentage of human rights provisions, confirming the influential role of the vibrant human rights community in the peace processes

Table 21.1 Regional patterns of human rights references in peace agreements

Region	Percentage of peace agreements referring to human rights issues (%)
The Americas	80
Africa	78
MENA	76
Europe	69
South Asia	69
Central Asia	68
Southeast Asia	60
Pacific	55

in Central America and, especially, in Colombia. The high numbers for Africa and the Middle East/North Africa (MENA) region can be explained by the high degree of international involvement many of the peace processes in these regions experience.

The comparably low portion of European peace agreements referring to human rights (68%), surprises at first glance. The empirical data provides a clear explanation: peace processes with substantial Russian involvement, such as in the Caucasus and the protracted conflicts in Eastern Europe, do not invoke human rights as regularly as other peace processes do. Less surprising is the low proportion of human rights references in Southeast Asia (58%). Traditionally, the region has been at the forefront of criticising or even denying the global human rights paradigm by referring to 'Asian values'.[17] In the realpolitik of peacebuilding, South Asia and Southeast Asia are the strongholds of what has been termed 'illiberal peacemaking' or 'authoritarian conflict management',[18] attempts to negotiate and implement peace that reject liberal international involvement and instead rely on principles of sovereignty and power-balancing. Sri Lanka and Myanmar are striking examples of this trend.[19]

These discrepancies also become visible when looking at individual peace processes. Figure 21.2 highlights some major peace processes since 1990 with respect to the *prevalence* of human rights provisions—the percentage of peace agreements explicitly referring to human rights—and *comprehensiveness*—how many different human rights-related issues are addressed in these agreements.[20] The level of comprehensiveness is high across contexts. Most peace processes deal with several different human rights issues and rarely remain at a level of only superficial references. Such comprehensiveness, however, does not necessarily confirm a high

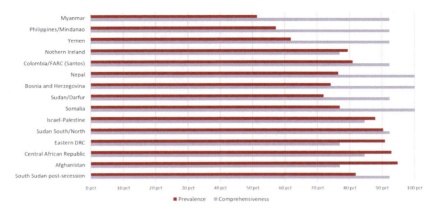

Fig. 21.2 Peace processes addressing human rights

acceptance of human rights: often, agreements refer to prevalent issues because of the need to address these issues and the capacity the human rights language provides to address them in a mutually acceptable way (e.g. citizenship rights or questions of mobility and access, see below).

Regarding the prevalence of human rights provisions, the individual peace processes confirm the regional trends shown above, especially the comparably strong utilisation of human rights in peace processes in sub-Saharan Africa, such as in South Sudan, Sudan, DRC or the Central African Republic. At the same time, most of these cases demonstrate that a strong commitment to human rights does not necessarily guarantee a successful and non-violent transformation of an ongoing armed conflict.

Issues and Institutions

The list of human rights-related issues addressed in peace agreements (see Fig. 21.3) confirms that human rights are predominantly applied either as a general reference for gaining international legitimacy or as a tool to support post-conflict transitions in key areas (such as the reform of the security sector or supporting civil society and free media). Concrete, hands-on topics such as provisions regarding mobility and access, media and communication, or issues regarding protection are among the most used categories. References to human rights institutions, in contrast, are rare.

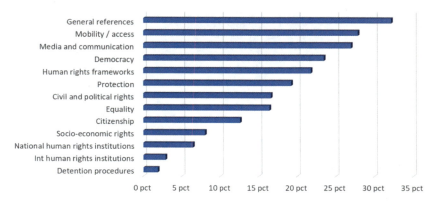

Fig. 21.3 Types of human rights provisions in peace agreements

Three types of human rights provisions can be distinguished: (1) stipulations addressing specific human rights-related concerns, with or without an explicit reference to human rights as a legal framework; (2) references to specific elements of human rights, mostly to use them for triggering specific reforms in transformational processes; and (3) efforts of implementing human rights institutionally.

In the utilisation of human rights for addressing concerns, general references to human rights and concrete commitments to issues such as mobility or protection often intertwine. For example, the Libyan Political Agreement, signed in Skhirat, Morocco, in December 2015, states

> *Until the decision on their disbanding and integration has been implemented and the status of their members has been settled, all armed formations shall commit themselves to the provisions of the Libyan legislations in force, international humanitarian law and the international human rights law, especially with regards to the protection of civilians and the provision of safe passage and freedom of movement for them.* (Libyan Political Agreement, 17 Dec 2015, Art 42)

This stipulation is typical for agreements negotiated in situations of ongoing armed conflict. In such emergency situations, negotiating parties and external actors aim to utilise human rights as a tool to implement safe passage agreements for relief, humanitarian agencies or Internally Displaced Person (IDP) populations, or even to settle on a (often spatially limited) truce. Co-references to IHL, for example to the humanitarian principles regarding the delivery of emergency relief, are common.[21]

Provisions invoking certain elements of human rights as a pathway for subsequent transformational change are diverse. If aiming to bring about structural change, such stipulations are usually embedded in a broader roadmap. The South Sudanese 'Revitalised Agreement on the Resolution of the Conflict in the Republic of South Sudan' (R-ARCSS), signed in Addis Ababa, Ethiopia, in September 2018, refers to human rights as a preliminary *'parameter of permanent constitution'*. The stipulation reads like a compact catalogue of contextualised civil rights: '*The Permanent Constitution-making Process shall be based on the principles of: ... Respecting ethnic and regional diversity and communal rights, including the right of communities to preserve their history, develop their language, promote their culture and expression of their identities*' (R-ARCSS, 12 Sept 2018, Art 6.2.5).

Only in rare instances are these provisions able to guarantee the implementation of such rights in a meaningful and thorough way. Nevertheless, they offer concerned individuals, communities and ethnopolitical groups something to relate to and to hold the main brokers of the South Sudanese political power play to account. If nothing else, the stipulations, in a positive sense, work as a potentially unsettling troublemaker possibly enabling stakeholders to claim specific rights in the course of a transformational process.

Finally, references to human rights institutions are mainly concerned with monitoring the implementation of human rights-related provisions. Observation schemes can include either national or multilateral institutions or both. The Nepalese Comprehensive Peace Accord (CPA) between the Nepalese government and the Maoist insurgents provides a prototypical example. When outlining the implementation procedures, the CPA refers to UN agencies—'*Both parties agree to give continuity to the task of monitoring provisions related to human rights mentioned in this agreement by the United Nations Office of the High Commissioner for Human Rights, Nepal*' (CPA, Nepal, 21 Nov 2006, Art 9.1)—as well as to the National Human Rights Commission for essentially the same task: '*The National Human Rights Commission will also carry out works related to the monitoring of human rights as mentioned in this agreement in addition to its duties as determined by law. In the course of implementing its duties, the Commission can receive the help of national and international human rights organizations after carrying out necessary coordination with them*' (CPA, Nepal, 21 Nov 2006, Art 9.4). The assignment of parallel responsibilities suggests that, in such cases, the international level works as a safety net for national frameworks, which still have to rely on a volatile institutional framework.

Virtually all references to international human rights institutions relate to monitoring tasks in the context of civilian protection, transitional justice or broader processes of political transition. The role of international human rights or criminal courts, in contrast, is marginal. Only three agreements, from Congo, Uganda and the Central African Republic, refer to the International Criminal Court (ICC) as having a potential role in post-conflict transitional justice processes. Such ignorance may be one indicator that human rights in their role as one of the main instruments of global liberal governance have indeed reached their 'endtimes'.[22]

Tensions Between Peace Agreements and Human Rights

Earlier sections in this chapter have already pointed to the substantial tensions a human rights-based approach in peacemaking can entail. In post-conflict transitions, these tensions mainly become apparent in the areas of transitional justice and post-conflict power-sharing.

The field of transitional justice developed as a human rights-based intervention to disturb the power bargaining in peace negotiations. Proponents were motivated by confronting the views of the belligerents with victim's perspectives.[23] Doing justice to them is essential for any sustainable post-conflict transition, it is argued. Furthermore, post-conflict periods in internal armed conflict were seen by some as an opportunity to implement the global human rights agenda nationally and regionally. Ruti G. Teitel, one of the activists at the forefront of the international transitional justice agenda, for instance, claims that the 'most vigorous enforcement of human rights law occurs in transitional periods'.[24]

The concrete tensions that arise between a human rights-focused application of transitional justice and the pragmatic compromises peacemaking often demands have been hotly debated. 'Targeting violators of human rights and bringing them to justice is essential. Accusation, however, comes more easily than making peace. The quest for justice for yesterday's victims of atrocities should not be pursued in such a manner that it makes today's living the dead of tomorrow'.[25] Pragmatic voices within the transitional justice field criticised the human rights dogmatism because of its blindness regarding opportunities and timing,[26] others interpreted its goals as 'irreconcilable'.[27]

What evolves are fundamentally different perspectives. 'The practical dilemmas actors face in peacebuilding can be quite different from those involved in the instauration of democratic citizenship and the transformation of an abusive state security apparatus'.[28] In discussing this challenge, Christine Bell has warned against the expansion of the transitional justice agenda to turn into a comprehensive wish list for manifold rights claims and democracy.[29] This suggestion remains valid a decade later.

The tensions between human rights and power-sharing arrangements in peace processes are fiercely disputed as well. Akin to transitional justice, a peacebuilding perspective wants to recognise human rights objections to power-sharing formula not as a principled problem, but as an issue of timing and tactics. The contestation concerns consociational arrangements post-conflict, where political and legal structures and the right of political representation become tied to often ethnically defined group identities. Since every identity-based definition of rights implies processes of exclusion along the same lines, these arrangements necessarily clash with the fundamental human rights principle of equality and non-discrimination.

Discussions on the relationship between human rights and power-sharing arrangements in recent years also involve courts and court decisions which substantially challenge institutional frameworks that evolved in peacemaking efforts.[30] Regarding Bosnia and Herzegovina, the case of Sejdić and Finci versus Bosnia Herzegovina before the European Court of Human Rights catalysed the debate. The applicants, supported by human rights advocacy groups such as Human Rights Watch, claimed a violation of their civil and political rights by the post-conflict framework laid out in the Dayton Peace Agreement and the Bosnian constitution it comprised. Sejdić and Finci, a Rom and a Jew, stated to be violated in their civil and political rights since the Dayton framework relates political representation and public sector employment opportunities to the membership of one of the three so-called constituent peoples (Bosniacs, Croats and Serbs).

In its decision from December 2009, the court ruled in favour of the applicants with just one dissenting opinion. The ruling has been heavily criticised by academic advocates of post-conflict power-sharing arrangements and by peacebuilding practitioners and diplomats.[31] The dissenting opinion by Judge Bonello criticised the judgement as well, stating that the court would behave like an 'uninvited guest'[32] ruling on a peace agreement involving many actors over which the court could not legitimately claim to have jurisdiction.

Such an opinion fails to consider that power-sharing arrangements are meant to be interim arrangements facilitating the transition to normal politics.[33] Like in Bosnia and Herzegovina, however, these interim arrangements tend to stick and become a permanent feature of enduring transitions, a formalised political unsettlement.[34] Under these circumstances, the argument of timing, which effectively translates into postponing thorough human rights implementation to later stages, does not have traction. It is, thus, difficult to imagine how courts and other institutions tasked with the implementation of *universal* rights can act with modesty. Modesty is not a feature of human rights. Making human rights implementation dependent on context implies to effectively terminate their universal project.[35]

Conclusion

The unresolvable tensions between peacemaking and human rights require us to focus on the practical gains offered by the utilisation of human rights in peacemaking. Such utilisation is always incomplete and full of limitations with respect to institutionalisation and the universal claims inherent to human rights. References to human rights, as hollow and weak as they often might seem, can enable stakeholders to put pressure on the state and its agents as well as on armed non-state actors to comply with transitional procedures.[36] As war gives way to a post-conflict transformation process, human rights can support the political and legal institutionalisation of a polity.[37] For example: a human rights commission, even if seen as a non-costly add-on to a peace agreement, may attain a surprisingly important role in the subsequent political process. Whereas a meaningful implementation of human rights-related stipulations cannot be guaranteed, they provide often crucial opportunities. Implementing human rights in peace accords, therefore, is mainly about opening optional pathways for change.

Human rights claims can disturb political bargaining and restrict the political space available in peace deals. It needs to be kept in mind that human rights are there to do so. Limiting political space by legal means is their *raison d'être*. The challenge, therefore, is how to navigate the clash of visions and to guarantee that the 'implementation of human rights commitments [is] to be supported in more politically aware ways'.[38] Such a politically aware way needs to reject the dogmatism and the dominance inherent in both peacemaking and human rights and to make the logics of both visions subordinate to a principled pragmatic way of transition. Human rights can also regain importance as a tool providing principles for pragmatist approaches.

Ultimately, the clash of visions between human rights and peacemaking does not need to be overcome. The danger of interventions by international legal institutions like the ECHR or the ICC is their power to overshoot by turning a potentially helpful disruption into an effective closure of the political space in which peace accords are made. This danger, however, lies beyond the immediate reality of peace negotiations. It is the concrete implications of the institutionalisation of global liberal governance that enforces an unhealthy uniformity to peace processes, which comes along with the risk of damaging them by the disability to adapt to their contextualities. Against this background, the current structural decline of global liberal governance may not be bad news. Instead, this decline might even support peacemaking by leaving justice issues, with the capacity to derail peace, unaddressed.

Database

PA-X, Peace Agreements Database, Political Settlements Research Programme, University of Edinburgh, www.peaceagreements.org/.

Funding Acknowledgement

This work was supported by the UK Department for International Development under Grant PO 6663 (Political Settlements Research Programme).

Notes

1. Thomas Cushman (2005) 'The Human Rights Case for the War in Iraq: A Consequentialist View', in Richard Ashby Wilson, ed., *Human Rights in the 'War on Terror'* (Cambridge: Cambridge University Press), pp. 78–107. Human rights groups advocated against the invocation of human rights to justify the invasion of Iraq, see: HRW—Human Rights Watch (2004) 'War

in Iraq: Not a Humanitarian Intervention', online commentary, 25 January 2004, https://www.hrw.org/news/2004/01/25/war-iraq-not-humanitarian-intervention [last accessed on 21 December 2019].
2. Jenna Sapiano (2019) 'Peace Settlements and Human Rights', in Marc Weller, Mark Retter and Andrea Varga, eds., *International Law and Peace Settlements* (Cambridge: Cambridge University Press); available as iCourts Working Paper, no. 161, 2019, p. 13.
3. Oskar N. T. Thoms and James Ron (2007) 'Do Human Rights Violations Cause Internal Conflict?', *Human Rights Quarterly* 29(3): 674–705. The authors also argue against a linear causality between human rights abuses and conflict likeliness because of the importance of contextual factors.
4. Mary Kaldor (2012) *New and Old Wars: Organised Violence in a Global Era*. 3rd edition (Cambridge: Polity Press), p. 2.
5. Christine Bell (2008) *On the Law of Peace: Peace Agreements and the Lex Pacificatoria* (Oxford: Oxford University Press), p. 33.
6. For example, OHCHR—UN Office of the High Commissioner for Human Rights (2011) *International Legal Protection of Human Rights in Armed Conflict* (New York, NY, and Geneva: United Nations).
7. Noam Lubell (2005) 'Challenges in Applying Human Rights Law to Armed Conflict', *International Review of the Red Cross* 87(860): 737–754, pp. 753–754.
8. Bell (2008), op. cit., p. 34.
9. Jacinta O'Hagan (2017) 'The Role of Civilization in the Globalization of International Society', in Tim Dunne and Christian Reus-Smit, eds., *The Globalization of International Society* (Oxford: Oxford University Press), pp. 185–203, pp. 200–201.
10. Jean Arnault (2014) 'Legitimacy and Peace Processes: International Norms and Local Realities', *Accord*, 25, Legitimacy and Peace Processes: From Coercion to Consent, 21–25, pp. 24–25.
11. David Chandler (2002) *From Kosovo to Kabul and Beyond: Human Rights and International Intervention* (London: Pluto Press), pp. 62–64. See also David Chandler (2006) *Empire in Denial: The Politics of State-Building* (London: Pluto Press) where the author refers to broader attempts of consolidating liberal democratic statebuilding including the implementation of human rights standards as 'empire in denial'.

12. Beate Jahn (2012) 'Humanitarian Intervention—What's in a Name?', *International Politics* 49(1): 36–58.
13. The database is open access and available under, www.peaceagreements.org.
14. The PA-X codebook defines peace agreements as 'formal, publicly-available documents, produced after discussion with conflict protagonists and mutually agreed to by some or all of them, addressing conflict with a view to ending it' (Bell et al. 2018: 1). For this analysis, only peace agreements referring to national or international peace processes have been used. Agreements confined to processes at the local level have been excluded from the analysis to ensure comparability.
15. The decision of PA-X to render all provisions related to the free movement of people, including the right of return, and the access of humanitarian relief as human rights-related issues might be unconventional but still legitimate. It reflects a broad interpretation of human rights, and breadth has to be kept in mind also in all quantitative assessments of the prevalence of human rights provisions in peace agreements based on PA-X.
16. Philipp Kastner (2015) *Legal Normativity in the Resolution of Internal Armed Conflict* (Cambridge, MA: Cambridge University Press).
17. Mark R. Thompson (2001) 'Whatever Happened to "Asian Values"?', *Journal of Democracy* 12(4): 154–165.
18. Claire Q. Smith (2014) 'Illiberal Peace-Building in Hybrid Political Orders: Managing Violence During Indonesia's Contested Political Transition', *Third World Quarterly* 35(8): 1509–1528; David Lewis, John Heathershaw, and Nick Megoran (2018) 'Illiberal Peace? Authoritarian Modes of Conflict Management', *Cooperation and Conflict* 53(4): 486–506.
19. Stefano Ruzza (2015) 'There are Two Sides to Every COIN: Of Economic and Military Means in Myanmar's Comprehensive Approach to Illiberal Peacebuilding', *European Journal of East Asian Studies* 14(1): 76–97.
20. These issues refer to the 13 human rights-related categories in the PA-X database, namely general references to human rights and the rule of law, equality, democracy, protection, human rights frameworks, civilian and political rights, socio-economic rights, national human rights institutions, regional or international human rights

institutions, mobility and access, detention procedures, media and communication and citizenship.
21. On the complex interrelation between international human rights law and humanitarian law see Christine Chinkin and Mary Kaldor (2017) *International Law and New Wars* (Cambridge: Cambridge University Press), pp. 265–281.
22. Stephen Hopgood (2013) *The Endtimes of Human Rights* (Ithaca, NY, and London: Cornell University Press).
23. See, for example, Kieran McEvoy and Kirsten McConnachie (2013) 'Victims and Transitional Justice: Voice, Agency and Blame', *Social & Legal Studies* 22(4): 489–513.
24. Ruti G. Teitel (2002) *Transitional Justice* (Oxford: Oxford University Press), p. 228.
25. Anonymous (1996) 'Human Rights in Peace Negotiations', *Human Rights Quarterly* 18(2): 249–258, p. 258.
26. Christine Bell (2009) 'Transitional Justice, Interdisciplinarity and the State of the "Field" or "Non-Field"', *International Journal of Transitional Justice* 3(1): 5–27.
27. Bronwyn Anne Leebaw (2008) 'The Irreconcilable Goals of Transitional Justice', *Human Rights Quarterly* 30(1): 95–118.
28. Paige Arthur (2009) 'How Transitions Reshaped Human Rights: A Conceptual History of Transitional Justice', *Human Rights Quarterly* 31(2): 321–367, p. 360.
29. Bell (2009) op. cit., pp. 25–26.
30. Richard H. Pildes (2008) 'Ethnic Identity and Democratic Institutions: A Dynamic Perspective', in Sujit Choudhry, ed., *Constitutional Design for Divided Societies: Integration or Accommodation?* (Oxford: Oxford University Press), pp. 173–201 and Sapiano (2019), op. cit.
31. For example, see, Christopher McCrudden and Brendan O'Leary (2013) 'Courts and Consociations, or How Human Rights Courts May De-stabilize Power-sharing Settlements', *European Journal of International Law* 24(2): 477–501.
32. ECHR—European Court of Human Rights. Grand Chamber (2009) *Case of Sejdić and Finci v. Bosnia and Herzegovina*. Judgement. Strasbourg, 22 December 2009, p. 54.
33. This is also confirmed by advocates such as McCrudden and O'Leary (2013), op. cit., p. 484.

34. Christine Bell and Jan Pospisil (2017) 'Navigating Inclusion in Transitions from Conflict: The Formalised Political Unsettlement', *Journal of International Development* 29(5): 576–593.
35. For a different view on this matter see Jack Donnelly (2007) 'The Relative Universality of Human Rights', *Human Rights Quarterly* 29(2): 281–306, who interprets the human rights' universality claim per se as relative.
36. Bell (2008), op. cit., p. 54.
37. Jan Pospisil (2019) *Peace in Political Unsettlement: Beyond Solving Conflict* (Cham: Palgrave Macmillan), pp. 116–117.
38. Christine Bell (2017) *Navigating Inclusion in Peace Settlements: Human Rights and the Creation of the Common Good* (London: The British Academy), p. 58.

CHAPTER 22

The Post-conflict Constitution as a Peace Agreement

Laurie Nathan

A great deal of research has been done on the durability of peace after the conclusion of a negotiated settlement in intra-state conflict.[1] This research concentrates on comprehensive peace agreements (CPAs) and ignores the peacemaking character and function of post-conflict constitutions (PCCs). With only a few exceptions, PCCs are not conceived as peace agreements in the scholarly literature.[2] Consequently, they are generally excluded from peace agreement databases.[3] In this chapter, I argue that PCCs should be regarded as peace agreements.

I define a PCC as a new or revised constitution enacted as part of efforts to end a violent conflict and prevent its recurrence. PCCs are a relatively common and widespread phenomenon. According to Widner, between 1975 and 2003 "nearly 200 new constitutions were drawn up in countries at risk of conflict, as part of peace processes and the adoption of multiparty political systems".[4] Since the end of the Cold War, PCCs

---

L. Nathan (✉)
University of Notre Dame, Notre Dame, IN, USA
e-mail: Laurie.N.Nathan.4@nd.edu

have included the constitutions of Burundi (2005), Cambodia (1993), East Timor (2002), El Salvador (1992), Iraq (2005), Kenya (2010), Macedonia (2001), Namibia (1990), Nepal (2015), South Africa (1996) and Sudan (2005). PCCs also take the form of interim constitutions, as in Burundi (1998 and 2001), Chad (1991), Central African Republic (2013), Democratic Republic of Congo (1994), Kosovo (2001), Nepal (2007) and South Africa (1993).

There are four reasons for viewing PCCs as peace agreements. First, the parties to a CPA themselves consider constitutional reform to be a vital means of entrenching their settlement and consolidating and maintaining peace in the long-term. They see the PCC as a legal form of their CPA. This is evident in the high proportion of CPAs that are associated with constitutional reform. As discussed below, a review of the CPAs contained in the Peace Accords Matrix reveals that the majority of these agreements expressly require constitutional reform; over two-thirds require either constitutional reform or adherence to a new constitution that shortly preceded the CPA; and nearly 90% expressly require constitutional and/or legislative reform.[5]

Second, a PCC offers the conflict parties greater assurance than a CPA that their opponent will adhere to the terms of a negotiated settlement and not return to war. Whereas a CPA has no legal status, a PCC has the constitutional status of supreme law and is therefore durable and enforceable. By virtue of this status, a PCC codifies and institutionalizes the CPA. Furthermore, many of the reforms typically envisaged in a CPA—such as those relating to electoral reform, judicial reform, security reform and respect for human rights and the rule of law—cannot come into effect unless they are enacted through the constitution or other law. I argue that a PCC thus mitigates the credible commitment problem, reassuring parties that are reluctant to conclude a peace agreement because they fear that their opponent will not honor its undertakings.

Third, the maintenance of peace is a core function of liberal constitutions in general. These constitutions perform this function by entrenching respect for human rights and the rule of law; establishing institutions for non-violent governance, dispute resolution and contestation of power; providing structures to ensure the safety, security and freedom of citizens; preventing discrimination against individuals and groups; and constraining the state's exercise of power. In addition to the peace maintenance function of liberal constitutions in general, PCCs can enable the transition from war to peace by addressing the incompatibilities that gave rise to the armed conflict and by normalizing and regulating non-violent politics and governance. The imperatives that lie at the heart of the post-conflict peacebuilding and statebuilding agenda—democratic governance, accountability, inclusiveness, responsiveness, the rule of law and respect for human rights[6]—are all constitutional as well as political matters.

Fourth, viewing PCCs as peace agreements is consistent with conventional definitions of a "peace agreement". Conceptually, the PCC is a peace agreement for the same reason that a CPA is a peace agreement: it is a negotiated contract that aims to resolve a conflict, end hostilities and prevent large-scale violence in the future. As a legal and more permanent expression of the preceding CPA, it fits naturally on a temporal spectrum of peace agreements. This does not imply that PCCs always ensure long-term peace. As with other types of peace agreement, such as CPAs and ceasefire accords, a PCC can fail to maintain peace or it can succeed partially or completely. As described in the concluding section of this chapter, a PCC can also generate and exacerbate conflict.

The argument that PCCs should be conceived as peace agreements has important implications for research on peace durability. This research is incomplete if it focuses exclusively on CPAs and ignores PCCs. Peace negotiations seldom end with the signing of a CPA. They frequently extend to a constitution-making phase, which might lead to political arrangements different from those envisaged in the CPA.[7] Because a PCC has the status of supreme law, moreover, it supersedes the CPA and becomes the definitive peace agreement. Conceiving PCCs as peace agreements opens up a rich area of academic and policy research on whether and how they ensure peace in practice.

This chapter aims to contribute to an understanding of intra-state peace agreements and to highlight the need for research on the peace maintenance role of PCCs. It is structured around the four reasons for viewing PCCs as peace agreements, namely the conflict parties' determination to constitutionalize CPAs; the PCC's features that address the commitment problem; the peace maintenance function of a constitution; and the PCC's consistency with standard definitions of a peace agreement. The concluding section sets out the research implications of the argument.

The Perspective of the Conflict Parties

The parties to a CPA tend to regard constitutional reform as a necessary corollary of their agreement. This is evident from the content of the 34 CPAs that comprise the Peace Accords Matrix. These CPAs, negotiated in civil conflicts between 1989 and 2012, were selected on the basis of the following criteria: the conflict resulted in at least 25 battle deaths per annum; the major parties to the conflict participated in the negotiations that produced the agreement; and the substantive issues underlying the conflict were addressed in the negotiations.[8]

A review of these CPAs reveals a consistent desire by the signatory parties to constitutionalize, or at least legalize, their agreement:

- Twenty of the 34 CPAs (58.8%) expressly require constitutional reform. In addition, three CPAs (8.8%) were followed by constitutional reform even though this was not expressly stipulated in the agreement. In another four cases (11.8%), the agreement requires adherence to a conflict resolution constitution adopted shortly before the CPA was concluded. In total, 27 CPAs (79.4%) are closely associated with constitutional reform (Appendix 1).
- Seven agreements (20.6%) are not associated with constitutional reform. Only two of these (5.9%) relate to national conflict and the other five address sub-national struggles for greater autonomy (Appendix 1). In all the sub-national cases, legislative reform was the preferred mode of legal institutionalization.
- If the inquiry is broadened to include legislative as well as constitutional reform, it transpires that 30 agreements (88.2%) expressly require constitutional and/or legislative reform.[9] Only four agreements (11.8%) do not refer to either constitutional or legislative reform.

It is clear from these statistics that the parties to a CPA generally envisage constitutional and/or legislative reform as a means of entrenching their commitment to peace and safeguarding and institutionalizing their negotiated settlement. The focus and extent of the required constitutional reform vary among the cases: the CPA can itself be a constitution (e.g. the 1993 interim constitution of South Africa); it can include a constitution (e.g. the 1995 General Framework Agreement for Peace in Bosnia and Herzegovina of 1995); it can require constitutional reform on particular issues (e.g. protection of ethnic minorities in the 2001 Ohrid Agreement for Macedonia); or it can call for constitutional reform without indicating a specific topic (e.g. the 1997 General Agreement on the Establishment of Peace and National Accord in Tajikistan).

The CPAs in the Peace Accords Matrix are a subset of the peace agreements negotiated in civil conflicts between 1989 and 2012, based on the criteria indicated above. By contrast, the UN Peace Agreements Database is less restrictive, covering agreements that "can be understood broadly as peace agreements and related material".[10] For the period 1989–2012, the UN database includes as many as 60 peace agreements that expressly require constitutional reform (Appendix 2). This figure confirms the prevalence of the conflict parties' determination to constitutionalize their peace agreement.

CREDIBLE COMMITMENT AND PEACE DURABILITY

In the political science literature on the durability of intra-state peace agreements, the dominant framework is bargaining theory with an emphasis on the commitment problem.[11] After a period of armed hostilities and a sustained drive to defeat an opponent, mutual enmity and mistrust among the conflict parties are very high. The parties fear that if they enter into negotiations and sign a peace agreement, their opponent might later renege on its commitments.[12] The breakdown of the agreement might leave the parties worse off than had they continued fighting.[13] This risk might cause them to reject negotiations or, if they engage in talks, to back away from concluding a settlement.[14]

There are no ironclad ways of overcoming the commitment dilemma. Nevertheless, previous research has identified a number of commonly utilized forms of protection, which can be grouped into two categories. The first comprises external third-party roles, including peacekeeping and monitoring and verifying compliance with a peace agreement.[15] The second category comprises political, military and territorial power-sharing arrangements, which can offer all sides protection against executive abuse of power and unilateral decision-making.[16]

Third-party security guarantees and power-sharing arrangements may mitigate the commitment problem but they are insufficient: the former are usually confined to the transition period, after which the domestic actors are left to their own devices; and strong domestic parties can easily abandon power-sharing arrangements that are not entrenched and enforceable. On the basis of commitment theory, we would therefore expect the conflict parties to pay serious attention to the domestic enforceability of power-sharing provisions and other safeguards contained in a CPA. In particular, we would expect them to incorporate the provisions of a CPA, which has no enduring enforceability, into a PCC, which in principle is enforceable through the courts. The validity of this expectation is confirmed by the statistics on constitutionalizing CPAs, presented above. Overlooked in the literature on peace agreements and credible commitment, constitutional reform is a major strategy for meeting the commitment challenge.

The parties to a CPA are no doubt savvy enough to know that a constitution is not a perfect solution to the commitment problem. Minorities groups, in particular, may be fearful that the executive will treat the constitution as "just a piece of paper". But for the reasons set out below, the parties are likely to see a PCC as a more credible commitment—a "stronger piece of paper"—than a CPA.

Legal status and enforceability. A number of scholars attribute legal status to peace agreements. For example, Bell maintains that substantive peace agreements typically have a legal-looking structure, with preambles, sections, articles and annexes, and typically employ legal-type language, referring to parties, signatories and binding obligations.[17] She concludes that "the parties mutually view [these agreements] as legal documents".[18] Badran claims that while peace agreements are not binding in the "traditional sense", they "enjoy a legal force".[19] Sapiano asserts that peace agreements are "political and legal pacts".[20]

For three reasons, these perspectives are not an accurate reflection of the legal status of peace agreements. First, they are not consistent with the outlook of the parties to a CPA. As noted above, the CPA parties frequently seek to legalize some or all of their agreement through constitutional or legislative reform. There would be no need for this if they believed that the CPA itself had legal status. By way of illustration, the Burundi parliament adopted the Arusha Peace and Reconciliation Agreement of 2000 as national legislation.[21] This move would have been wholly unnecessary had the Agreement been regarded as an enforceable legal text.

Second, the political process of concluding a CPA does not override or substitute for the formal process by which laws and constitutional amendments are approved by parliament.[22] Until the CPA is legalized, the existing laws and constitution remain in force. Hence the Arusha Agreement for Burundi states that the transitional National Assembly shall, as a matter of priority, amend or repeal legislation incompatible with the provisions of the Agreement and that, until amended or repealed, "all laws in force prior to the commencement of the transition shall remain in force".[23] Similarly, the 2005 CPA for Sudan requires the development of a new constitution but notes that before this constitution is adopted by the National Assembly, "the Parties agree that the legal status quo in their respective areas shall remain in force".[24]

Third, there are prominent instances where courts have refused to treat a CPA as a legal text. For example, when the Appeals Chamber of the Special Court for Sierra Leone was petitioned to review the validity of the amnesty conferred by the Lomé Peace Agreement of 1999, it declined to treat the agreement as binding law.[25] In 2015 the Burundi Constitutional Court was confronted with an inconsistency between the constitution and the Arusha Agreement regarding presidential term limits. The court observed that the Agreement was the "Constitution's bedrock" and had been adopted as national legislation.[26] Still, the Court resolved the inconsistency in favor of the Constitution. It held that the Agreement, although the bedrock of the Constitution, "is not supra-constitutional".[27] This assertion was politically controversial but legally sound. The Arusha Agreement itself declares that "the Constitution shall be the supreme law and must be upheld by the Legislature, the Executive and the Judiciary".[28]

Unlike a CPA, a PCC is formally binding and enforceable through the courts and it binds not only the CPA signatories but also the state, the executive and all persons and political actors in the country. By agreeing to incorporate some or all of the CPA into the PCC, the conflict parties strengthen their commitment to honor their undertakings, heightening their mutual confidence.

Effectuating the CPA. The significance of the PCC as a peace agreement lies not only in its capacity to endow the CPA with long-term enforceability. Certain categories of CPA provisions simply do not come into effect unless they are embedded in the constitution or other law. This is true, for example, of power-sharing arrangements such as territorial devolution of power and proportional representation voting systems; institutional reform such as reform of the judiciary, security services and administration; and respect for human rights and the rule of law. In the absence of constitutional or legislative enactment, these CPA provisions have no abiding value and do not address adequately the commitment problem.

In the absence of legalization, moreover, there is a risk that a court may declare the peace agreement invalid if it is deemed inconsistent with the prevailing constitution or laws. The Philippines offers an example of this scenario. In 2001 the government entered into negotiations with the Moro Islamic Liberation Front, resulting in the Memorandum of Agreement on Ancestral Domain that granted greater autonomy to the Moro people. The Supreme Court nullified the agreement on the following grounds: the legal obligation for consultation on such matters had not been met; the proposed association between the government and the envisaged Bangasamoro Juridical Entity ignored existing laws; and the memorandum was unconstitutional as it implied that the new juridical entity would attain independence.[29]

Durability. The durability of CPAs is intrinsically limited. Because their legal status is uncertain or non-existent, and because they are generally not subject to periodic amendment to reflect changing circumstances, they are not "living documents". As a result, their salience dwindles over time. A constitution, on the other hand, is supreme law, it is an enduring text and it can be revised according to specified procedures. Hence the PCC is not only a type of peace agreement but constitutes the definitive peace agreement.

This proposition can be illustrated with reference to the 1979 Lancaster House Agreement that ended the armed conflict in Zimbabwe and brought independence to the country. The Agreement contained significant compromises between the minority regime and the liberation movements. The most controversial of these was protection of white ownership of land for a period of ten years, restricting the new government's ability to address the inequalities and inequities of colonial and settler land distribution.[30] The only meaningful way to effectuate this protection and bind the government was through constitutionalization. The Agreement thus contained a summary of the independence constitution, which was duly incorporated into the new Constitution of 1980. As a result of this move, the compromise proved durable in the face of growing political tension over the lack of land reform. When the ten-year period ended, the government amended the Constitution and passed legislation enabling accelerated land acquisition and resettlement.[31]

Costs. Bargaining models of war termination invoke the idea of "costly signals", which are moves by the conflict parties that entail costly concessions or risks in order to convey a conciliatory attitude, build trust and reinforce the pledge to end hostilities.[32] In civil war peace processes, the most costly forms of signaling are disarmament and demobilization, which leave a party vulnerable to military attack. Consenting to incorporate CPA provisions into a constitution has a lower level of risk but it is nonetheless a meaningful signal of commitment to peace because the political costs are substantial. These costs include constraints on majority decisions and the government's freedom of action; subordination of the government to the courts; embedding the compromises of a negotiated settlement in supreme law; and antagonizing constituencies opposed to those compromises.

The conflict parties might also anticipate the relevance of long-term reputation costs. During the transition period after the signing of a CPA, international actors can ensure that the costs of violating the agreement are high. But the prominence of a CPA fades over time. In the medium- to long-term, the domestic and international political costs of reneging on peace commitments may be highest with respect to violating the constitution.

Legitimacy. In the midst of armed conflict, negotiations to forge a CPA tend to have fairly limited participation, with many such processes being dominated by the conflict parties. The process of designing and approving a PCC can be much broader. It can involve the citizenry and a multitude of political parties and interest groups, both informally through the media and public debate and formally through referenda and deliberation by parliaments or constituent assemblies.[33] In some circumstances, greater popular participation and greater representativeness of the deliberative bodies enhance the legitimacy of a PCC.[34]

The Peace Maintenance Function of a Constitution

A liberal constitution can be understood as a peace agreement regardless of whether it pertains to a post-conflict society. It serves this function in a number of ways, both tangible and intangible and both substantive and procedural: as a symbol and set of values, norms and aspirations that unite a nation; as a framework of principles, rules and mechanisms that require and facilitate non-violent political competition, resolution of disputes and management of grievances; as a system of governance based on the rule of law and respect for citizen's rights; and as a compact between citizens and the state that confers power on the state for the purpose of ensuring peace and order while at the same time constraining the exercise of that power.

This perspective reflects a long-standing, fundamental idea in liberal philosophy about the causes of domestic peace. As Paris puts it:

> The classical liberals of the eighteenth century were among the first to propose a link between constitutional limits on governmental power, respect for individual freedoms in the political and economic spheres, and peace. These thinkers maintained that protecting individual liberties and limiting the powers of the state would attenuate or even eliminate violent conflict.[35]

Exactly which features of liberal (and non-liberal) constitutions contribute significantly to the maintenance of peace in post-conflict societies is an empirical question. Danilovic and Clare distinguish between three concepts that are often conflated: "the protection of individual freedoms (liberalism), the rule of law and legal equality (constitutionalism), and representative rule (as embodied, for example, in modern democracy)".[36] The authors find that states that embrace liberal constitutionalism experience fewer civil wars than any other type of regime, including regimes measured on a strictly democratic scale regardless of their respect for civil liberties. Walter, focusing specifically on civil war recurrence, finds that "governments that are beholden to a formal constitution, that follow the rule of law, and that do not torture and repress their citizens are much less likely to face renewed violence in any form".[37]

In well-established democracies, the peace maintenance function of a constitution acquires a taken-for-granted character. Against the backdrop of armed conflict, however, the PCC can be a prominent blueprint of a radical transition from "normalized violent politics" to "normalized pacific politics". It encompasses an overarching normative and legal commitment to non-violent contestation of power, specifies the rules and procedures of the new political system, stipulates how these can be changed, provides for courts and other bodies to resolve disputes, and regulates legitimate use of force by the state. In the best-case scenario, these norms, procedures and mechanisms create the potential for the PCC to be a self-enforcing peace institution. Whereas the CPA is a static text with limited durability, the PCC is a collection of structures and processes that are dynamic, enduring and constantly in operation.

At a substantive level, PCCs are intended not only to end large-scale violence but also to prevent its recurrence. In this sense, they are mechanisms of structural conflict prevention. To a greater or lesser extent, they attempt to resolve or at least ameliorate the incompatibilities and grievances that gave rise to the preceding armed conflict. For example, the Angolan constitution of 1992 introduces multi-party democracy; the Burundi constitution of 2005 shares power between the Tutsi minority and Hutu majority communities; and the Macedonian constitution of 2001 affords special protection to the ethnic Albanian minority. The 1996 South African constitution seeks to overcome the structural problems of minority rule and racial discrimination in a number of ways: through the overarching construction of a constitutional democracy; through articles on universal franchise, dignity, equality, human rights, language, culture, land, affirmative action and non-discrimination; and through recognition of socio-economic rights related to adequate housing, food, water, education, health care and social security.

Addressing the incompatibilities that led to the prior armed conflict is a crucial peacemaking role of a PCC. While it might not be a sufficient condition for long-term peace, it could well be a necessary condition, especially where the conflict incompatibilities are embedded in the constitution of the *ancien regime*. In the nature of negotiated settlements, which often entail compromises and elite pacts, addressing the incompatibilities might not be done perfectly, but if it is not done adequately, the risk of recurrent violence will likely remain high.

Finally, the PCC's contribution to peace can be framed in terms of post-conflict peacebuilding, defined as a multifaceted endeavor to "identify and support structures which will tend to strengthen and solidify peace in order to avoid a relapse into conflict".[38] The peacebuilding agenda entails "building democratic governance, protecting human rights, strengthening the rule of law, and promoting sustainable development, equitable access to resources and environmental security".[39] It also covers statebuilding, which is concerned not only with state capacity but also with inclusive governance, engagement with citizens, accountability and responsiveness.[40] Whether PCCs can promote development, equity and environmental security is debatable, but there is no doubt that they are integral to the attainment of democratic governance, accountability, inclusiveness, responsiveness and respect for human rights and the rule of law.

Definition and Temporal Spectrum of Peace Agreements

Peace agreements can be defined as "contracts intended to end a violent conflict, or to significantly transform a conflict so that it can be more constructively addressed".[41] A more elaborate definition is that peace agreements are "formal documents that are publicly produced after discussion with all (or some of) the conflict's protagonists. They reflect a degree of agreement between those actors, primarily regarding the need to address and end physical violence".[42]

On the basis of these definitions, there is no conceptual difficulty in viewing PCCs as peace agreements (even if this is not the sole purpose of a PCC). PCCs are formal and public agreements among conflict parties and other actors, and their aims include ending violence and preventing its recurrence. This conception of a PCC's aims is not controversial in policy circles. For example, after the signing of the Comprehensive Peace Agreement for Nepal in 2006, the International Crisis Group observed that the "peace process [now] hinges on writing a constitution that permanently ends the conflict, addresses the widespread grievances that fuelled it and guards against the eruption of new violence".[43]

Peace agreements are not homogenous and can be differentiated on various grounds, such as whether they are comprehensive or partial and whether they are procedural or substantive.[44] It is also possible to draw a temporal distinction between peace agreements that are reached at different stages of a peacemaking process and have different purposes. An ideal-type breakdown would include, sequentially, a cessation of hostilities, a declaration of principles for negotiations, and a CPA. The PCC is often the next type of peace agreement in this sequence. It is intended to reinforce the CPA by conferring on the negotiated settlement the status of supreme law. By virtue of this status, the PCC becomes the definitive peace agreement.

By way of illustration, after the outbreak of armed conflict in Darfur in 2003, African mediators facilitated negotiations that led to the 2004 Agreement on Humanitarian Ceasefire on the Conflict in Darfur, the 2005 Declaration of Principles for the Resolution of the Sudanese

Conflict in Darfur and the 2006 Darfur Peace Agreement (DPA). Article 1 of the DPA requires the incorporation of the entire agreement into the national constitution. This did not happen because the DPA failed to end the conflict. By contrast, the civil war between the Sudanese government and the Sudan People's Liberation Movement ended through a sequence of agreements that culminated in the CPA of 2005. The CPA states that the parties shall give "legal and constitutional effect to the arrangements agreed therein" and establish a constitutional review commission to develop an interim national constitution based on the agreement.[45] This process proceeded quickly. The 2005 Constitution of Sudan constitutionalizes the CPA in its entirety by stipulating that the CPA "is deemed to have been duly incorporated in this Constitution; any provisions of the Comprehensive Peace Agreement which are not expressly incorporated herein shall be considered as part of this Constitution".[46]

Conclusion

The argument that PCCs should be viewed as peace agreements is consistent with the way CPA parties see these documents, as well as with standard definitions of peace agreements. A PCC meets the criteria for a peace agreement even if it is more than that. Like a CPA, it is a contract that aims to end hostilities and prevent a recurrence of violence. But unlike a CPA, it has the status of supreme law. It therefore supersedes the CPA and becomes the definitive peace agreement.

The conclusion to be drawn from this argument is not that PCCs always succeed in maintaining peace but that their role in this regard should be examined more extensively than has been the case to date. The core question would be exactly the vital question that drives research on CPAs: what factors and what content make these agreements most likely to lead to the establishment and maintenance of peace? From a policy perspective, the critical issues have little to do with the technical dimensions of constitution-drafting and everything to do with the politics of constitutional processes, substance, compromises, institutions and fidelity. While every situation is unique, domestic and international policymakers could learn a great deal from comparative research on these issues.

Tackling the core research question would be an important corrective to existing studies on the relationship between CPAs and durable peace, which take no account of the PCC as an intervening variable that has an *independent effect on peace*. This corrective is analytically necessary for three reasons, related respectively to the process, content and effects of constitutional reform. First, conflict resolution processes do not end with the technical implementation of a CPA. They often extend into a constitution-making phase, which is a new site of political struggle. This phase can be fraught with tension and disputes.[47] The contestation is especially severe where elites have not reached agreement on the underlying political settlement.[48] Examples of protracted and conflictual constitution-making processes over the past decade include Nepal,[49] as well as Libya, Somalia and Yemen.[50]

Second, the content of a PCC may be quite different from that of the preceding CPA.[51] This is because the CPA parties may have made promises they never intended to keep; they may have buyer's remorse; they may be struggling to sell the CPA compromises to their constituents; the balance of power between the signatories may have changed; non-signatory parties may be involved in the constitution-making endeavor; and international pressure may have eased. Where the content of the PCC differs from that of the CPA, it is the former that has an abiding effect.

Third, as discussed in this chapter, a PCC can contribute to the establishment and maintenance of peace. In summary, a PCC can address the incompatibilities that led to the preceding violent conflict; codify the transition from "normalized violent politics" to "normalized pacific politics"; unify a divided nation around a set of common values, symbols, aspirations and norms; lay the foundation for the rule of law, respect for human rights and protection of minorities; constrain the power of the state; reform the security services, the judiciary and other institutions; provide for regular, free and fair elections; and enable non-violent resolution of political disputes.

A PCC is also a significant intervening variable if, conversely, it generates conflict. There are several ways in which this might happen: the process of constitution writing can intensify ethnic conflict[52]; constitutionalized power-sharing arrangements can exacerbate social divisions and create dysfunctional electoral or governance systems[53]; a PCC can fail to resolve adequately the incompatibilities and structural problems that gave rise to the preceding armed conflict; and compromises deemed necessary to achieve a negotiated settlement can later become a source of tension. For example, the land compromise included in the Lancaster House Agreement for Zimbabwe and subsequently entrenched in the

PCC became a major source of political tension that reverberated long after the constitutional protection of white-owned land was removed.[54]

Finally, it should be noted that PCCs do not constitute a homogenous category. This chapter has focused on PCCs emanating from negotiated settlements but new constitutions can also be promulgated after a military victory (e.g. the Rwanda constitution of 2003). Further distinctions can be drawn between interim and final constitutions[55]; between constitutional reform that precedes, follows and takes the place of a CPA; between comprehensive and partial constitutional reform; between reforms directed at national versus sub-national conflict; and between reforms with varying degrees of conformity to liberal and democratic norms. Other relevant variables are the inclusiveness of the process of constitution-making,[56] and the influence of external actors in this process.[57] Ultimately, a PCC's contribution to peace depends on how it is applied and enforced. By investigating the peace maintenance role of PCCs in light of these distinctions and variables, research could generate valuable theoretical and policy insights on peace durability after civil war termination.

Appendix 1

Relationship Between CPAs in the Peace Accords Matrix and Post-conflict Constitutions

CPAs Associated with PCCs (79.4% of 34 CPAs)
CPA Requires PCC (58.8% of 34 CPAs)
- Bosnia and Herzegovina, General Framework Agreement for Peace in Bosnia and Herzegovina, 1995.
- Burundi, Arusha Peace and Reconciliation Agreement for Burundi, 2000.
- Cambodia, Framework for a Comprehensive Settlement of the Cambodia Conflict, 1991.
- Congo, Agreement on Ending Hostilities in the Republic of Congo, 1999.
- Cote d'Ivoire, Ouagadougou Political Agreement, 2007.
- Djibouti, Agreement for Reform and Civil Concord, 2001.
- El Salvador, Peace Agreement (Mexico Agreement), 1991.
- Guatemala, Agreement on a Firm and Lasting Peace, 1996
- Lebanon, Taif Accord, 1989.

- Macedonia, Framework Agreement, 2001.
- Mozambique, General Peace Agreement for Mozambique, 1992.
- Nepal, Comprehensive Peace Accord, 2006.
- Papua New Guinea, Bougainville Peace Agreement, 2001.
- Rwanda, Peace Agreement between the Government of the Republic of Rwanda and the Rwandese Patriotic Front, 1993.
- Sierra Leone, Peace Agreement between the Government of Sierra Leone and the Revolutionary United Front of Sierra Leone (Lomé Agreement), 1999.
- South Africa, Constitution of the Republic of South Africa (Interim Constitution), 1993.
- Sudan, Comprehensive Peace Agreement between the Government of the Republic of Sudan and the Sudan People's Liberation Movement/Army, 2005.
- Tajikistan, General Agreement on the Establishment of Peace and National Accord in Tajikistan, 1997.
- Timor-Leste (East Timor), Agreement between Republic of Indonesia and Portuguese Republic on the Question of East Timor.
- United Kingdom, Good Friday Agreement, 1998.

CPA Followed by PCC Although Not Expressly Required (8.8% of 34 CPAs)

- Croatia, Basic Agreement on the Region of Eastern Slavonia, Baranja and Western Sirmium (Erdut Agreement), 1995.
- Guinea-Bissau, Agreement between the Government of Guinea-Bissau and the Self-Proclaimed Military Junta (Abuja Peace Agreement), 1998.
- Liberia, Peace Agreement between the Government of Liberia, the Liberians United for Reconciliation and Democracy, the Movement for Democracy in Liberia and the Political Parties, 2003.

CPA Requires Adherence to Preceding PCC (11.8% of 34 CPAs)

- Angola, Lusaka Protocol, 1994.
- Djibouti, Agreement on Peace and Reconciliation, 1994.
- Mali, National Pact Concluded between the Govt. of Mali and the Unified Movements and Fronts of Azawad Giving Expression to the Special Status of Northern Mali, 1992.

- Niger, Agreement Establishing Permanent Peace between the Government of the Republic of Niger and the Organization de La Résistance Armée (ORA), 1995.

CPAs Not Associated with PCCs (20.6% of 34 CPAs)
CPA Relates to National Conflict (5.9% of 34 CPAs)
- Angola, Luena Memorandum of Understanding, 2002.
- Sierra Leone, Peace Agreement between the Government of the Republic of Sierra Leone and the Revolutionary United Front of Sierra Leone (Abidjan Agreement), 1996.

CPA Relates to Regional Conflict (14.7% of 34 CPAs)
- Bangladesh, Chittagong Hill Tracts Peace Accord, 1997.
- India, Memorandum of Settlement (Bodo Accord), 1993.
- Indonesia, Memorandum of Understanding between the Government of the Republic of Indonesia and the Free Aceh Movement, 2005.
- Philippines, Mindanao Final Agreement, 1996.
- Senegal, General Peace Agreement between the Government of the Republic of Senegal and Le Mouvement des Forces Démocratiques de la Casamance (MFDC), 2004.

Appendix 2

Other CPAs That Require Constitutional Reform

In addition to the CPAs in the Peace Accords Matrix that require constitutional reform, the following peace agreements in the UN Peacemaker database (https://peacemaker.un.org/document-search) also stipulate the need for constitutional reform:

- Afghanistan, Afghan Peace Accord (Islamabad Accord), 1993.
- Afghanistan, Agreement on Provisional Arrangements in Afghanistan Pending the Re-establishment of Permanent Government Institutions, 2001.
- Angola, Bicesse Accords, 1991.

- Burundi, Agreement Embodying a Convention on Governance between the Forces for Democratic Change and the Political Parties of the Opposition, 1994.
- Burundi, The Global Ceasefire Agreement, 2003.
- Burundi, Accord de partage de pouvoir au Burundi, 2004.
- Colombia, Acuerdo Final entre el Gobierno Nacional y el Movimiento Armado Quintin Lame, 1991.
- Colombia, Acuerdo Político entre el Gobierno Nacional, los Partidos Políticos, el M-19, y la Iglesia Católica en Calidad de Tutora Moral y Espiritual del Proceso, 1990.
- Colombia, Acuerdo Final entre el Gobierno Nacional y el Ejército Popular de Liberación, 1991.
- Colombia, Acuerdo Final entre el Gobierno Nacional y el Partido Revolucionario de los Trabajadores, 1991.
- Comoros, Accord cadre pour la reconciliation aux Comores (Accord de Fomboni), 2001.
- Cote d'Ivoire, Linas-Marcoussis Agreement, 2003.
- Democratic Republic of the Congo, Global and Inclusive Agreement on Transition in the Democratic Republic of Congo (Pretoria Agreement), 2002.
- Democratic Republic of the Congo, Inter-Congolese Political Negotiations: The Final Act (Sun City Agreement), 2003.
- Gabon, Accords de Paris, 1994.
- Georgia, Declaration on Measures for a Political Settlement of the Georgian/Abkhaz Conflict, 1994.
- India, Memorandum on Settlement of Bodoland Territorial Council (BTC), 2003.
- Kenya, Kenya National Dialogue and Reconciliation—Longer-Term Issues and Solutions: Constitutional Review, 2008.
- Kosovo, Serbia, Interim Agreement for Peace and Self-Government in Kosovo (Rambouillet Accords), 1999.
- Madagascar, Charte de la transition, 2009.
- Maldives, Roadmap for a Possible Way Forward, 2012.
- Mexico, San Andrés Larráinzar Agreements, 1996.
- Papua New Guinea, Charter of Mirigini for a New Bougainville, 1994.
- Papua New Guinea, Loloata Understanding, 2000.
- Philippines, Framework Agreement on the Bangsamoro, 2012.

- Russian Federation, Agreement on the Basic Principles of Relations between the Russian Federation and the Chechen Republic, 1995.
- Solomon Islands, Townsville Peace Agreement, 2000.
- Somalia, Cairo Declaration on Somalia, 1997.
- Somalia, Declaration on Cessation of Hostilities and the Structures and Principles of the Somalia National Reconciliation Process, 2002.
- Somalia, Decisions of the High Level Committee (Djibouti Agreement), 2008.
- Somalia, Agreement between the Transitional Federal Government and the Puntland Regional State of Somalia (Galcayo Agreement), 2009.
- Somalia, Protocol Establishing the Somali National Constituent Assembly, 2012.
- Sudan, Sudan Peace Agreement, 1997.
- Sudan, Agreement between the Government of Sudan and the National Democratic Alliance (Cairo Agreement), 2005.
- Sudan, Eastern Sudan Peace Agreement, 2006.
- Sudan, Doha Document for Peace in Darfur (DDPD), 2011.
- Togo, Dialogue inter-Togolais: accord politique global, 2006.
- Yemen, Agreement Establishing a Union between the State of the Yemen Arab Republic and the State of the People's Democratic Republic of Yemen, 1990.
- Yemen, Agreement on the Implementation Mechanism for the Transition Process in Yemen in Accordance with the Initiative of the Gulf Cooperation Council (GCC), 2011.
- Zimbabwe, Agreement between the Zimbabwe African National Union-Patriotic Front (ZANU-PF) and the Two Movement for Democratic Change (MDC) Formations, on Resolving the Challenges Facing Zimbabwe, 2008.

Notes

1. For example, Walter, *Committing to Peace*; Hartzell, 'Explaining the Stability of Negotiated Settlements'; Hartzell and Hoddie, 'Institutionalizing Peace'; Mattes and Savun, 'Fostering Peace after Civil War'; Joshi and Quinn, 'Is the Sum Greater than the Parts?'.
2. An exception is Samuels, who focuses on the design and process of developing a post-conflict constitution, which "can be partly a peace agreement and partly a framework setting up the rules by

which the new democracy will operate" (see Samuels, 'Post-conflict Peace-Building', 664). Bell observes that some peace agreements take the form of a constitution or incorporate a constitution, but she does not view PCCs in general as a category of peace agreement (see Bell, 'Peace Agreements', 391–4).
3. The relevant databases do not adopt a consistent and systematic approach to the inclusion of PCCs. South Africa's interim constitution of 1993 is the only PCC included in the peace agreement databases of the Peace Accords Matrix (https://peaceaccords.nd.edu/) and the Uppsala Conflict Data Program (www.pcr.uu.se/research/ucdp/datasets/). Libya's transitional constitution of 2011 is the only PCC in the UN Peacemaker database of peace agreements (https://peacemaker.un.org/document-search). The PA-X database, which has over 1500 peace agreements, includes 17 constitutions but does not explain why these PCCs, and not others, were selected (https://www.peaceagreements.org/search?s=list).
4. Widner, 'Constitution Writing and Conflict Resolution', 1.
5. The Peace Accords Matrix is available at https://peaceaccords.nd.edu/.
6. Menocal, 'State Building for Peace'; OECD, *Supporting Statebuilding*.
7. Lanz, Nathan and Raffoul, 'Negotiations, Continued'.
8. Joshi, Quinn and Regan, 'Annualized Implementation Data', 552.
9. With further research, it would be possible to account for the variation between those CPAs requiring only constitutional reform, those requiring only legislative reform and those requiring both. The relevant factors include the constitutional character of the country; the legitimacy and adequacy of the existing constitution; the causes of the conflict; the nature of the negotiated solutions in the CPA; the balance of power between the CPA parties; the orientation of the drafters of the CPA; and the role of external actors in the design of the CPA.
10. The UN Peace Agreements Database is available at http://peacemaker.un.org/document-search.
11. For example, Walter, *Committing to Peace*; Mattes and Savun, 'Fostering Peace after Civil War'; Joshi and Quinn, 'Is the Sum Greater than the Parts?'.
12. Hartzell and Hoddie, 'Institutionalizing Peace', 321.
13. Walter, 'The Critical Barrier to Civil War Settlement', 338–9.

14. Walter, 'The Critical Barrier to Civil War Settlement', 339–40.
15. Walter, 'The Critical Barrier to Civil War Settlement'; Fortna, 'Does Peacekeeping Keep Peace?'; Mattes and Savun, 'Fostering Peace after Civil War'.
16. Hartzell and Hoddie, 'Institutionalizing Peace', 321.
17. Bell, 'Peace Agreements', 378.
18. Bell, 'Peace Agreements', 378.
19. Badran, 'Intrastate Peace Agreements', 196.
20. Sapiano, 'Courting Peace', 132.
21. Law No. 1/017 on the Adoption of the Arusha Peace and Reconciliation Agreement for Burundi, 1 December 2000.
22. The 1995 Constitution of Bosnia and Herzegovina is an exception to the general pattern of constitutionalizing a CPA through the requisite *legal* process. The Constitution was contained in Annex 4 of the 1995 General Framework Agreement for Peace in Bosnia and Herzegovina. It came into being, superseding the existing constitution, upon the signing of the Agreement, without complying with the prevailing constitutional requirements for parliamentary adoption (see Yee, 'The New Constitution of Bosnia and Herzegovina').
23. Arusha Peace and Reconciliation Agreement, Protocol II, article 16.
24. Republic of Sudan, Interim National Constitution, Chapter 2, article 2.12.8.
25. Appeals Chamber of the Special Court for Sierra Leone.
26. Constitutional Court of Burundi, 'Judgment no. RCCB 303'.
27. Constitutional Court of Burundi, 'Judgment no. RCCB 303', 4.
28. Arusha Peace and Reconciliation Agreement, article 3(30).
29. Gatmaytan, 'Judicial Review of Peace Initiatives'.
30. Palmer, 'Land Reform in Zimbabwe'.
31. Coldham, 'Land Acquisition Act'.
32. Kydd, 'Trust, Reassurance, and Cooperation'; Jarstad and Nilsson, 'From Words to Deeds'.
33. Benomar, 'Constitution-Making after Conflict'; Widner, 'Constitution Writing and Conflict Resolution'.
34. Benomar, 'Constitution-Making after Conflict'; Samuels, 'Post-Conflict Peace-Building and Constitution-Making'.
35. Paris, 'Bringing the Leviathan Back In', 425–6.
36. Danilovic and Clare, 'The Kantian Liberal Peace', 399.

37. Walter, 'Conflict Relapse and the Sustainability', 3; Walter, 'Why Bad Governance Leads to Repeat Civil'.
38. United Nations, 'An Agenda for Peace'.
39. Menocal, 'State Building for Peace', 1717.
40. Menocal, 'State Building for Peace'; OECD, *Supporting Statebuilding*.
41. Yawanarajah and Ouellet, 'Peace Agreements'.
42. Bell and Zulueta-Fülscher, 'Sequencing Peace Agreements', 18.
43. International Crisis Group, 'Nepal's Constitutional Process', i.
44. Högbladh, 'Peace Agreement Dataset Codebook', 10.
45. Comprehensive Peace Agreement between the Government of the Republic of Sudan, Chapter 2, article 2.12.2).
46. Republic of Sudan, Interim National Constitution, article 225.
47. Hart, 'Constitution-Making'.
48. Bell and Zulueta-Fülscher, 'Sequencing Peace Agreements', 31–44.
49. Thapa and Ramsbotham, 'Two Steps Forward'.
50. Bell and Zulueta-Fülscher, 'Sequencing Peace Agreements'.
51. On Nepal, as an example, see Thapa and Ramsbotham, 'Two Steps Forward'.
52. Widner, 'Constitution Writing and Conflict Resolution', 1.
53. Samuels, 'Post-Conflict Peace-Building and Constitution-Making', 671.
54. Moyo, 'The Evolution of Zimbabwe's Land Acquisition'.
55. Alston and Ginsburg, 'Playing for Constitutional Time'.
56. For example, Widner, 'Constitution Writing and Conflict Resolution'.
57. For example, Dann and Al-Ali, 'The Internationalized *Pouvoir Constituant*'.

References

Alston, Eric, and Tom Ginsburg (2017) 'Playing for Constitutional Time: Interim Constitutions and Transitional Provisions', in Frank Fagan and Saul Levmore (eds.), *The Timing of Lawmaking*, Cheltenham: Edward Elgar, pp. 110–129.

Appeals Chamber of the Special Court for Sierra Leone (2004) 'Decision on Challenge to Jurisdiction: Lomé Accord Amnesty', 13 March.

Arusha Peace and Reconciliation Agreement for Burundi (2000).
Badran, Ramzi (2014) 'Intrastate Peace Agreements and the Durability of Peace', *Conflict Management and Peace Science* 31(2): 193–217.
Bell, Christine (2006) 'Peace Agreements: Their Nature and Legal Status', *American Journal of International Law* 100(2): 373–412.
Bell, Christine, and Kimana Zulueta-Fülscher (2016) 'Sequencing Peace Agreements and Constitutions in the Political Settlement Process', *Policy Paper* 13, International Idea, Stockholm.
Benomar, Jamal (2004) 'Constitution-Making after Conflict: Lessons for Iraq', *Journal of Democracy* 15(2): 81–95.
Coldham, Simon (1993) 'Land Acquisition Act, 1992 of Zimbabwe', *Journal of African Law* 37(1): 82–88.
Comprehensive Peace Agreement between the Government of the Republic of Sudan and the Sudan People's Liberation Movement/Army (2005).
Constitutional Court of Burundi (2015) 'Judgment no. RCCB 303', translation commissioned by the Pan African Lawyers' Union. Available at https://lawyersofafrica.org/wp-content/uploads/2015/05/Judgment-of-Burundi-Constitutional-Court-ENGLISH-Translation.pdf.
Danilovic, Vesna, and Joe Clare (2007) 'The Kantian Liberal Peace (Revisited)', *American Journal of Political Science* 51(2): 397–414.
Dann, Philipp, and Zaid Al-Ali (2006) 'The Internationalized *Pouvoir Constituant*—Constitution-Making Under External Influence in Iraq, Sudan and East Timor', in Armin von Bogdandy and Rudiger Wolfrum (eds.), *Max Planck Yearbook of United Nations Law*, vol. 10, Leiden: Martinus Nijhoff, pp. 423–463.
Darfur Peace Agreement (2006). Available at http://www.un.org/zh/focus/southernsudan/pdf/dpa.pdf.
Fearon, James (2004) 'Why Do Some Civil Wars Last So Much Longer Than Others?', *Journal of Peace Research* 41(3): 275–301.
Fortna, Virginia (2004) 'Does Peacekeeping Keep Peace? International Intervention and the Duration of Peace After Civil Wars', *International Studies Quarterly* 48(2): 269–292.
Gatmaytan, Dante (2016) 'Judicial Review of Peace Initiatives', *Pacific Basin Law Journal* 34(1): 47–68.
Hart, Vivien (2001) 'Constitution-Making and the Transformation of Conflict', *Peace & Change* 26(2): 153–176.
Hartzell, Caroline (1999) 'Explaining the Stability of Negotiated Settlements to Intrastate Wars', *Journal of Conflict Resolution* 43(1): 3–22.
Hartzell, Caroline, and Matthew Hoddie (2003) 'Institutionalizing Peace: Power Sharing and Post-Civil War Conflict Management', *American Journal of Political Science* 47(2): 318–332.

Högbladh, Stina (2012) 'Peace Agreement Dataset Codebook', Uppsala Conflict Data Program. Available at http://ucdp.uu.se/downloads/peace/ucdp-codebook-peace-agreements.pdf.

International Crisis Group (2007) 'Nepal's Constitutional Process', *Asia Report* 128.

Jarstad, Anna, and Desirée Nilsson (2008) 'From Words to Deeds: The Implementation of Power-Sharing Pacts in Peace Accords', *Conflict Management and Peace Science* 25(3): 206–223.

Joshi, Madhav, and Jason Michael Quinn (2015) 'Is the Sum Greater than the Parts? The Terms of Civil War Peace Agreements and the Commitment Problem Revisited', *Negotiation Journal* 31(1): 7–30.

Joshi, Madhav, Jason Michael Quinn, and Patrick Regan (2015) 'Annualized Implementation Data on Comprehensive Intrastate Peace Accords, 1989–2012', *Journal of Peace Research* 52(4): 551–562.

Kydd, Andrew (2000) 'Trust, Reassurance, and Cooperation', *International Organization* 54(2): 325–357.

Lanz, David, Laurie Nathan, and Alexandre Raffoul (2019) 'Negotiations, Continued: Ensuring the Positive Performance of Power-Sharing Arrangements', *Special Report* 455, United States Institute of Peace.

Mattes, Michaela, and Burcu Savun (2009) 'Fostering Peace After Civil War: Commitment Problems and Agreement Design', *International Studies Quarterly* 53(3): 737–759.

Menocal, Alina (2011) 'State Building for Peace: A New Paradigm for International Engagement in Post-Conflict Fragile States?', *Third World Quarterly* 32(10): 1715–1736.

Moyo, Sam (2006) 'The Evolution of Zimbabwe's Land Acquisition', in Mandivamba Rukuni, Patrick Tawonezvi, and Carl Eicher with Mabel Munyuki-Hungwe and Prosper Matondi (eds.), *Zimbabwe's Agricultural Revolution Revisited*, Harare: University of Zimbabwe, pp. 143–163.

OECD (2011) *Supporting Statebuilding in Situations of Conflict and Fragility: Policy Guidance*, DAC Guidelines and Reference Series, Paris: Organisation for Economic Co-Operation and Development.

Palmer, Robin (1990) 'Land Reform in Zimbabwe, 1980–1990', *African Affairs* 89(355): 163–181.

Paris, Roland (2006) 'Bringing the Leviathan Back In: Classical Versus Contemporary Studies of the Liberal Peace', *International Studies Review* 8(3): 425–440.

Republic of Sudan (2005) 'Interim National Constitution of the Republic of Sudan'.

Samuels, Kirsti (2006) 'Post-Conflict Peace-Building and Constitution-Making', *Chicago Journal of International Law* 6(2): 663–682.

Sapiano, Jenna (2017) 'Courting Peace: Judicial Review and Peace Jurisprudence', *Global Constitutionalism* 6(1): 131–165.

Thapa, Deepak, and Alexander Ramsbotham, eds. (2017) 'Two Steps Forward, One Step Back: The Nepal Peace Process', *ACCORD* 26, Conciliation Resources.

United Nations (1992) An Agenda for Peace. Preventive Diplomacy, Peacemaking and Peace-Keeping, UN doc. A/47/277.

Walter, Barbara (1997) 'The Critical Barrier to Civil War Settlement', *International Organization* 51(3): 335–364.

Walter, Barbara (2002) *Committing to Peace: The Successful Settlement of Civil Wars*, Princeton: Princeton University Press.

Walter, Barbara (2010) 'Conflict Relapse and the Sustainability of Post-Conflict Peace', Background Paper, *World Development Report 2011*. Available at http://web.worldbank.org/archive/website01306/web/pdf/wdr%20background%20paper_walter_04dbd.pdf.

Walter, Barbara (2015) 'Why Bad Governance Leads to Repeat Civil War', *Journal of Conflict Resolution* 59(7): 1242–1272.

Widner, Jennifer (2005) 'Constitution Writing and Conflict Resolution', *Research Paper* 2005/51, UNU-WIDER, United Nations University.

Yawanarajah, Nita, and Julien Ouellet (2003) *Peace Agreements, Beyond Intractability Website*. Available at http://www.beyondintractability.org/essay/structuring-peace-agree.

Yee, Sienho (1996) 'The New Constitution of Bosnia and Herzegovina', *European Journal of International Law* 7: 176–192.

PART VI

Implementation and Reconstruction

CHAPTER 23

Transitional Justice and Peacemaking/Peacebuilding

Roddy Brett and Lina Malagón

INTRODUCTION

States and societies do not tend to follow a linear or sequential logic in the aftermath of conflict: poor quality peace, post-accord violence and conflict recidivism occur regularly in the wake of armed conflict and initially successful negotiations.[1] According to a wide range of scholarship, between 40 and 60 per cent of conflicts relapse at least once after a

---

Many of the ideas in the this chapter are explored in more depth in the monograph R. Brett, *The Path Towards Reconciliation After Colombia's War: Understanding the Roles of Victims and Perpetrators* (University of Pennsylvania Press, 2022).

R. Brett (✉)
University of Bristol, Bristol, UK
e-mail: Roddy.brett@bristol.ac.uk

L. Malagón
Ulster University, Belfast, UK

settlement has been reached.² The critical timeframe for conflict relapse is between five to ten years; for example, an estimated 60 per cent of all armed conflicts settled during the early 2000s recurred within five years.³ Significantly, even in those cases where recidivism does not take place, the quality of peace achieved has often been low and the peace dividend meagre, leading to situations of so-called 'no war, no peace'.⁴ Within this context, international actors, states and civil society have struggled to develop effective practices through which to address the causes, consequences and legacies of political violence; the transitional justice paradigm increasingly represents an example of such interventions.

From the mid-1980s, Transitional Justice (TJ) emerged as a developing set of practices, theories, mechanisms and concerns aimed at confronting and dealing with past human rights violations, specifically those that had been perpetrated principally during the authoritarian episodes that had characterised the Cold War regimes, in particular in Latin America and Eastern Europe.⁵ After the 1980s, the application of TJ interventions has expanded, and the paradigm has gradually shifted away from its original orientation towards authoritarian regimes and post-authoritarian societies.⁶ TJ mechanisms have since become increasingly employed in conflict and post-conflict settings, as well, more recently, as within established democracies.⁷ Consequently, the TJ paradigm has gradually become an integral component of the liberal peace repertoire, embedded within the dominant global peacemaking and peacebuilding architecture, and intrinsic in that regard to peace negotiations and to post-conflict state and nation-building.⁸ The framework of rights that has undergirded TJ interventions since the 1980s—victims' rights to truth, justice, reparation and non-repetition—has thus itself become pivotal to mainstream peacemaking and peacebuilding initiatives, and critical to the global dissemination of those norms linked to liberalism and neoliberalism.⁹

After the 2000s, a growing interest in the perspective of victims of political violence has increased, evident in academic studies and other forms of practical application in the field. Broader processes such as the creation of a victim's trust fund at the International Criminal Court (ICC) established by the Statute and Rules of Procedure and Evidence, the increased focus on the rights of victims in UN mechanisms and practices and the worldwide establishment of distinct reparations programs also shaped this development.¹⁰ This so-called *victims' turn* in transitional justice has provoked a broader discussion on the approach and scope of transitional justice and peacebuilding practices, in particular as regards the scope for the participatory and bottom-up construction of TJ measures and programmes that would incorporate victims' demands.[11] In recent years, policymakers and scholars have furthermore discussed the need to implement a transformative approach for transitional justice and peacebuilding, in order to redress grievances of civil and political rights, in tandem with those rights that speak to the socio-economic and structural root causes and consequences of violent conflict. Scholarship has debated a more diverse concept of TJ that would be contingent upon a notion of so-called transformative justice. Transformative justice has drawn upon a more complex understanding of human rights in relation to the framework typically employed in transitional justice and peacebuilding with the aim of remedying structural violations of economic, social and cultural violations.[12] This type of justice would require innovative, specifically focused tools which would be contemplated as having a longer term application than those mechanisms typically employed in conventional transitional justice programs.[13]

This chapter traces the development of the transitional justice paradigm, with particular reference to its relevance for making and building peace in post-authoritarian and post-conflict societies. The chapter begins by documenting the emergence of the TJ paradigm in the 1980s, before turning to an analysis of its subsequent evolution towards becoming incorporated as an integral component of peace negotiations and post-conflict reconstruction processes. The chapter ends with a discussion of how, over the last decade, TJ has undergone a further shift in emphasis, specifically with regard to the mentioned 'victims' turn'—the direct inclusion of victims in the design and implementation of TJ mechanisms—what the implications of said transformation have been both for the paradigm itself and for peacemaking and peacebuilding, and the inclusion of a transformative approach of TJ mechanisms in practice.

THE EMERGENCE AND CONSOLIDATION OF TRANSITIONAL JUSTICE

In the aftermath of the atrocities of the Second World War and of the Nuremburg and Tokyo courts that sought to respond to them, international treaties, such as the Genocide Convention (1945) and the Universal Declaration of Human Rights (1948), were formulated within the framework of the newly established United Nations System. The urgent drive to establish said treaties was linked to the emerging exceptional and international interest in the creation of a global rights framework. Subsequently, with the end of the Cold War in the late 1980s and the accompanying increase in political will at international level to support Peace Keeping Operations and to sustain the numerous transitions from authoritarian rule, in particular in Latin America and Eastern Europe, demands to establish effective conflict resolution strategies and mechanisms grew. The United Nations *Agenda for Peace*, launched in 1992, represented a first attempt through which to situate such practices in a normative framework to intervene in the new post-Cold War internal conflicts. Significantly, this context also precipitated the beginning of the emergent push towards the 'universalisation' of international rights and justice norms, which would become crucial to the subsequent expansion of the transitional justice paradigm.[14] Accordingly, for Teitel (2000: 217), in this environment, the recognition of massive and systematic wrongdoing as a common feature of state and non-state repression gave rise to the emergence of justice mechanisms that involved individual and collective processes of acknowledgment of responsibility and accountability.

A decade later, in 2002, the victim's trust fund at the International Criminal Court (ICC) was established by the Statute and Rules of Procedure and Evidence, which possessed the option of granting individual or collective reparations. Said mechanism opened the door to the active participation of victims in the procedures of the ICC. For its part, in 2004, the United Nations Secretary-General issued the report *The Rule of Law and Transitional Justice in Conflict and Post-Conflict Societies*, with the view to protecting and promoting justice and the rule of law in conflict and post-conflict societies.[15] On this occasion, the Secretary-General encouraged the explicit articulation between transitional justice with peacemaking and peacebuilding initiatives undertaken by the UN through concrete actions, such as ensuring participation of UN experts on these topics within peace processes and peacekeeping operations and promoting TJ, peacemaking and peacebuilding within the international normative framework of human rights. Over the following years, the UN consolidated a set of mechanisms to promote TJ. In 2005, a set of principles concerning the right to a remedy and reparations for victims of gross human rights violations was adopted by the General Assembly of the United Nations.[16] In 2011, the Human Rights Council appointed a Special Rapporteur on the Promotion of Truth, Justice, Reparation and Guarantees of Non-Recurrence.[17] Thereby, the emergence of TJ was linked then to a growing global interest in a world order based upon peace, liberalism and the rule of law, in short, to a global justice norm,[18] shaped by the gradual diffusion of norms and practices in human rights and conflict transformation, described by Engstrom as the 'global accountability regime'.[19] In this sense, the TJ paradigm focused upon the legacy of mass atrocities in authoritarian countries undergoing liberalising transition,[20] as victims, states and international actors struggled with how to address and redress the impact of past violence in societies characterised by large-scale violations of human rights and humanitarian law and acutely weak, compromised or even non-existent judicial systems.[21]

TJ practices accordingly became commonplace in countries transitioning from dictatorial regimes and internal armed conflict to democratic civilian rule in Latin America, Africa, the Middle East and Asia, during and in the wake of the so-called Third Wave of Democratisation in the 1980s. Such developments, it is argued, gave 'meaning to accountability within broader context of political democratisation'.[22] TJ practices, including in particular institutional initiatives,[23] were thus associated with periods of political change, and operationalised in contexts characterised by histories of impunity, the ongoing political power of authoritarian elites, weak legal systems, widespread crimes and political instability.[24]

The initial focus of TJ was to develop and support mechanisms, both judicial and non-judicial, formulated by states and international actors oriented not only towards achieving accountability for past crimes (trials, truth commissions), but also victim-oriented restorative justice initiatives (reparations, monuments, public memory projects) and mechanisms of security and peace (amnesties, pardons, constitutional amendments, institutional reform).[25] The fundamental objectives of TJ practices were thus driven by the push to guarantee the restitution of the individual and collective dimensions of victims' rights (the rights to truth, justice, reparation and non-repetition) and, arguably, by efforts to craft sustainable peace and interpersonal reconciliation in the aftermath of gross human rights violations and protracted political violence.[26] In this regard, the paradigm was characterised by a core focus upon accountability for victims. Nevertheless, whilst the protection of victims and the guarantee of victims' rights represented a central aim of initial TJ interventions, a primary constraining factor during this time was the degree to which TJ practices, in particular accountability and justice for past crimes, were subordinated to the task of maintaining the stability and impetus of fragile political transitions.[27] Initially then, the prerogatives and interests of high-level political and armed actors often outranked victims' demands in diverse contexts, in the so-called Peace versus Justice debate, as victims' interests in accountability were traded against the interests of the armed actors in attaining power and benefitting from amnesty.[28]

Societies frequently experience a tension between victims' groups demanding accountability through TJ measures and the demands of other actors, including some victims' organisations, focused on the desire to forget and turn the page. For example, after the dictatorships in the Southern Cone, states adopted self-amnesties and general and unconditional amnesties in forgive and forget laws during the 1970s and 1980s, which impeded the recognition of justice for the victims. Since then, victims' organisations have worked for the repeal of the laws and the explicit promotion of victims' rights. International human rights jurisprudence which requires the absolute prohibition of blanket amnesties has also since been adopted, representing a thorn in the side for those powerful actors seeking impunity/immunity for past crimes.[29] In 1998 in Argentina, for example, the National Congress repealed the Full Stop Law (Law 23.492, 1986) and Due Obedience Law (23.521, 1987), which had conferred effective amnesty upon state actors, opening the way for future prosecutions. In 2003, the executive issued Law 25,779, by which the laws were annulled, and, two years later, in 2005, the Supreme Court of Justice declared the amnesty laws unconstitutional. In Chile, in 1998, the Supreme Court of Justice decided similarly not to apply the Amnesty Decree (Decree-Law 2191, 1978) in cases of human rights violations. It was not the same case in Brazil. In 2010 the Supreme Court of Justice resolved that the Amnesty Law (Law 6.683, 1979) was constitutional (Allegation of Non-Compliance with Fundamental Precept 153). This decision led to the Brazilian states being condemned by the Interamerican Court of Human Rights in 2010.[30] In Uruguay, Uruguayans voted in referendums (1989 and 2009) and decided on both occasions to keep the Law on the Expiration of the Punitive Claims of the State (Law 15.848, 1986), which was finally repealed in 2011.

In the case of Colombia, a core aspect of the recent peace process between the Government and the guerrilla group the Revolutionary Armed Forces of Colombia (FARC-EP) (2012–2016) was the discussion around diverse elements of transitional justice. The issue of amnesty, for example, was central to the FARC-EP guerrilla and a make or break theme for their giving up the armed struggle; in other words, the FARC-EP were unlikely to negotiate terms if a significant possibility existed for guerrilla fighters to end up in prison. There was scope at the negotiating table; however, to discuss amnesty for both state security forces and the guerrilla and, in the end, a workable amnesty was reached, which included the provisions of amnesty for rebels who had signed the final peace agreement and had been accused or condemned specifically for political crimes and related offences. In contrast, it was agreed that crimes which were not eligible for amnesty or pardon would be submitted to the Special Jurisdiction for Peace (JEP), which would be able to impose three types of sanctions or punishments: (a) ordinary sanctions characterised by a minimum of five to eight years of effective restriction of freedom and rights, not imprisonment; (b) restorative sanctions which would involve participation in projects at local level and (c) alternative sanctions which would be imposed upon those who acknowledged responsibility later in the legal process. Alternative sanctions would involve deprivation of freedom—including prison—of between five to eight years.

However, for broader Colombian society, the acceptance of amnesty for the FARC-EP was extremely problematic, both emotionally and politically. During the last two decades of the conflict, the FARC-EP began to use kidnapping and car, animal and collar bombs as a military strategy, strategies which had a disproportionate effect upon civilians. At the same time, the guerrilla also became involved in illicit drug production and trafficking. As a consequence, public support for the guerrilla waned significantly. Whilst state and paramilitary actors carried out similarly grotesque attacks and were also involved in illicit drug production and trafficking,[31] the emphatic focus of the media upon guerrilla violence ultimately played a key role in crafting negative public opinion of the guerrilla. Consequently, discussion of amnesty for the guerrilla, whatever the terms of such a provision were likely to be, confronted enormous opposition from public and media actors and represented a key obstacle to the peace process. This issue ultimately played out in the October 2016 plebiscite, when those powerful actors opposing the peace process, including former President Uribe and his political party the Democratic Centre, galvanised public opinion, stating that amnesty for the FARC-EP was an affront to victims and an unacceptable injustice. As a consequence, the package of agreements was initially rejected in the plebiscite, and had to be rapidly renegotiated before being approved by Congress in late November.

Shifting Parameters for the Transitional Justice Paradigm

Scholarship specifically assessing the factors that shape the complex and multiple paths taken by post-conflict societies, in particular of their capacity to prevent recidivism and secure quality peace, have tended then to focus upon state-building, governance and institutionalisation, security and DDR, economic stabilisation and development. Joshi and Wallensteen identify a series of dimensions key to quality peace: post-war security; governance; economic restructuring; the strengthening of civil society and the promotion of social cohesion. However, somewhat unusually, the authors also include *transitional justice and reconciliation*[32] as a key requirement for quality peace. Joshi and Wallensteen's assertion reflects the claims by a range of TJ scholars and policymakers that TJ mechanisms (TJMs) and their objectives represent core tenets of sustainable peace. In this regard, scholars have argued that truth-telling,[33] reparations[34] and justice initiatives (whether juridical or not)[35] represent central pillars of successful peacebuilding and reconciliation, evidencing a clear nexus between TJ and liberal peace politics.[36]

Over time, a considerable range of practices and measures emerged across a wide spectrum of countries, and became employed by a broad range of actors—governments, local and national institutions, non-governmental organisations, international organisations—consolidating the development of the TJ field through laws, policies and programmes.[37] The first trials for perpetrators of human rights violations embedded within transitional contexts had occurred after the end of the authoritarian regimes in Greece and Portugal in the 1970s. However, TJ would reach a turning point in the wake of the trials of the members of Argentina's former military junta in 1985—what Sikkink refers to as the 'cascade effect'. Successive trials followed in Bolivia, Guatemala, Panama, Chile and Haiti, a process that would reach its zenith with the high-profile arrest of former Chilean dictator General Augusto Pinochet in London in 1998. During the same period, victims' increasing demands to uncover the truth pertaining to the violations which they and their families had suffered at the hands of armed actors began to wield significant impact. In 1983, for example, the newly elected civilian government of President Raúl Alfonsín in Argentina established the National Commission on the Disappearance of Persons (CONADEP). CONADEP's final report, *Núnca Más* (Never

Again), was publicly presented in September 1984, setting a key precedent for subsequent truth commissions, including those in EL Salvador (1992), South Africa (1996), Guatemala (1998) and East Timor (2001), amongst others.

According to Sikkink,[38] during the 1990s, the so-called 'justice cascade' represented a key moment for the evolution of TJ. During this decade, international and national norms and mechanisms with the objective of ensuring individual criminal accountability for perpetrators of human rights violations were gradually consolidated. Sikkink notes that in the 1990s, the cascade effect that had begun in the 1980s was reinforced with the creation of the ad-hoc International Criminal Tribunal for the Former Yugoslavia (ICTY), the International Criminal Tribunal for Rwanda (ICTR) and, ultimately, the ratification of the International Criminal Court (ICC).[39] A related wave of domestic and international criminal justice trials took place for human rights violations committed by individual perpetrators. In parallel with this process, the arrest of General Pinochet in the UK in 1998, ushered in the so-called 'Pinochet effect', the detention itself making a bold statement that impunity could no longer be the expected norm for individual perpetrators of gross human rights violations. The arrest of Pinochet then made a resounding statement that third countries could hold foreign leaders accountable and bring them to justice through their own legal systems, marking the clear operationalisation of the principle of universal jurisdiction. In this respect then, for Sikkink, the overriding characteristic of the justice cascade became the consolidation of a framework through which to guarantee mechanisms aimed at ensuring individual criminal accountability for human rights violations, a framework reinforced by international standards and norms that provided the legal basis for the expansion of TJ. Nevertheless, despite this legalistic approach, TJ developed as a multidisciplinary theory and practice drawing upon past experiences of other states and regimes across the world. In the words of McEvoy, TJ became 'normalised, institutionalised and mainstreamed'.[40]

Reparations measures for victims of political violence have also been adopted during transitions. Initially, the transitional justice agenda focused largely on violations of civil and political rights, providing economic compensation for homicides, disappearance, torture or arbitrary detention or exile. Occasionally said measures included health and education services for the survivors and families of victims of those violations.[41] Said practices were implemented through the decisions of courts and via administrative programmes. For example, after Argentina's violent dictatorship (1975–1983), a broad policy of economic reparations was gradually approved in the transition between 1983 and 1999. During the 1990s, other political transitions would similarly adopt economic compensation for victims. For example, between 1990 and 2003, Chile carried out a programme of reparations to redress the atrocities committed by the military regime (1973–1990).[42] In 1995, Brazil issued the Law of Victims of Political Assassination and Disappearance—other violations were not included—after a robust campaign by civil society organisations and victims against an amnesty that had been granted to political prisoners and was followed by the acknowledgement of serious human rights violations by state agents (1964–1985).[43] In the case of Peru, a truth commission was created focused upon overcoming the atrocities committed by the military regime (1980–2000). In its 2003 report, the TC recommended the creation of a reparation programme, which was ultimately approved in 2005; in 2010 the government announced the beginning of economic compensation to victims.[44]

Within the context of peace processes, reparations measures have, moreover, been included, for example, as recommendations in the report of truth commissions. For example, after the peace negotiations in El Salvador between the government and the rebel movement, the Farabundo Martí National Liberation Front (FMLN), the 1993 report of the truth commission recommended providing reparations to victims of the political violence carried out between 1980 and 1991. In Guatemala, the 1996 peace accords between the government and the guerrilla group, the Guatemalan National Revolutionary Unity (URNG), provided provision for the creation of a truth commission. In its 1999 report, it recommended the adoption of measures to compensate and repair the victims of the conflict (1960–1996). However, the Congress refused to issue a law; consequently, the government subsequently adopted a Governmental Accord in 2003, creating the programme for ten years, which was extended for a further ten years until 2023.[45] The South African Truth and Reconciliation Commission, headed by the Committee on Reparations and Rehabilitation (CRR), recommended in its 1998 report, for example, the adoption of a reparations programme for victims of the Apartheid regimen (1948–1990). However, only in 2003 was a reduced version of the original reparations policy demanded by the TC adopted.[46] In 2004, two years after the war, the Truth and Reconciliation Commission (TRC) for Sierra Leone recommended the implementation of a comprehensive reparations programme for the victims of the conflict (1991–2002). This TC was included in the 1999 Peace agreement between the Armed Forces Revolutionary Council (AFRC)/Revolutionary United Front (RUF) rebels and the government represented by the Kabbah regime.

In recent years, other conflicts, such as the cases of Uganda, Democratic Republic of Congo (DRC) and Kenya,[47] have seen reparation programmes incorporated as part of a 'package' of transitional justice measures. Such measures have arguably been used by governments to give the appearance of taking appropriate remedy for victims to overcome political violence. Nevertheless, a so-called 'implementation gap' has often arisen, characterised as a problem of 'scandalous proportions' by the UN Special Rapporteur on Transitional Justice.[48]

Programmes and measures worldwide have, in fact, faced similar shortcomings to a greater or lesser extent. The absence of adequate budgets for the comprehensive implementation of the measures, governments' lack of political will to make consistent and comprehensive measures of reparation, the lack of coordination between state entities to meet the victims' needs, political instability, the continuity of political violence and human rights violations that generate new victims, the lack of victims' participation, the exclusion of entire categories of victims on the basis of political considerations and the gender insensitivity of many reparation programmes have been common problems that the programmes have faced. Consequently, the achievements of said programmes have been minimum or null, evidencing that reparations are often unfeasible in practice.[49]

TRANSITIONAL JUSTICE AND PEACEBUILDING

Since the end of the Cold War, the closure of armed conflicts through negotiated peace settlements has become more frequent, levelling out, in part, the historical tendency towards conflict termination resulting from military victory.[50] In the aftermath of the launch of the United Nations *Agenda for Peace*, and in parallel with the *justice cascade*, international peace support initiatives have moved away from their previous emphasis upon peacekeeping, as policymakers and states have sought to meet the challenges brought by changing patterns of conflict and violence and address more effectively their causes and consequences. The development of policies oriented towards redressing the impact of political violence and atrocities upon non-combatants has become a priority in this regard, as has the question of how to deal with victims and perpetrators of political violence.[51] International actors, including IGOs and INGOs, and individual states have since formulated increasingly complex multi-level and multi-dimensional strategies, which seek to craft sustainable peace and improve its quality through ambitious peacemaking efforts and peace-building and state-building programmes.[52] Significantly, TJ practice and thinking have become core components of these strategies.

TJ has gradually become an integral component of the liberal peace repertoire, intrinsic to post-conflict state-building and embedded within the predominant global peacemaking and peacebuilding architecture. Engagement with TJ concerns during peace negotiations and in post-conflict peacebuilding practice have meant a shift away from the paradigm's original domain of authoritarian transition and post-authoritarian societies.[53] Accordingly, peace negotiations oriented towards the closure of internal armed conflict and civil war are now increasingly likely to incorporate the paradigm as a mechanism through which to frame discussions of provisions integral to the respective peace agenda, in particular with regard to justice provisions for perpetrators and rights provisions for victims.[54] Whilst victims' rights have consequently become pivotal to mainstream peacemaking and peacebuilding initiatives then,[55] the rights framework upon which the liberal peace paradigm was initially forged (fundamental human rights; individual civil and political rights) has, in turn, been extended, as victims' rights frameworks have begun to shape spheres of peacemaking and peacebuilding directly. As it has been incorporated into the liberal peacemaking framework, so TJ has been consolidated as a staple of peace negotiations and post-conflict reconstruction, central both to disarmament, demobilisation and reintegration (DDR) and to broader provisions relating to democratisation, state-building, reconciliation and human rights protection.[56] For example, amnesty provisions consistently represent a core theme determining whether negotiations commence and subsequently stay on track, or whether actors return to armed struggle. As conflict parties and mediators negotiate what kind of justice regime perpetrators may face, discussions relating to amnesty for armed actors (whether state or non-state) or the nature of justice provisions for human rights violations have become framed within the language of TJ. Armed actors are not likely to negotiate in order to end up behind bars, and framing demands for immunity and amnesty within TJ language may confer them with a veneer of legitimacy. Since the Rome Statute and the International Criminal Court have come into force, blanket amnesties are no longer accepted as legitimate outcomes of peace negotiations—international crimes such as genocide and crimes against humanity cannot be 'amnestied'. However, amnesties for certain crimes—such as sedition and rebellion—are often granted as part of a peace settlement, and increasingly likely to be combined with other provisions to satisfy victims' rights, such as mechanisms to guarantee the rights to truth and reparation. In this regard, peace negotiations addressing the satisfaction of broader victims' rights, such as the rights to truth, reparation and non-repetition, have been grounded in the TJ paradigm.

Since the 1990s, reflecting the provisions within the Agenda for Peace and wider developments within the normative frameworks relative to human rights, victims' rights, peacebuilding and TJ, the nature and scope of peace negotiations have evolved. As they have adopted an increasingly ambitious and thematically broad remit,[57] so peace negotiations often address an extensive spectrum of issues over and above demobilisation, disarmament and reintegration (DDR). Themes including governance, political participation, power sharing, security sector reform, human rights, human security, reconciliation, economic reform and local development are frequently the subject of formal negotiations between armed actors. As perpetrators (states, armed groups), international actors and victims themselves struggle to come to terms with the causes and consequences of violence in post-conflict states, so transitional justice has itself become a key component of peace negotiations. To this end, organizations such as the International Centre for Transitional Justice and Swisspeace (through its strategy *Dealing with the Past*—DwP) have sought to guarantee the effective incorporation of TJ into conflict transformation frameworks. Swisspeace, for example, has urged negotiators and mediators to recognise 'the value of incorporating transitional justice principles and mechanisms as early as possible' in mediation processes.[58] In this regard, the approach seeks to institutionalise TJ as a normative framework to which mediators are bound and expected to promote during mediation processes. Building on the more limited framework of the UN Guidance for Effective Mediation, Guidance Principles and framework for United Nations approach to transitional justice processes and mechanisms,[59] the strategy aims to guarantee that equipping UN mediators with relevant human rights and transitional justice expertise within the UN system, and ensuring participation of UN human rights experts during peace negotiations, including potentially during the pre-negotiation phase.

Within this historical context, since the 1990s, there has been a growing acknowledgment by policymakers and scholars alike that TJ may play a role in crafting sustainable peace,[60] although it is not a sole indicator of it. In this regard, scholarship has identified a constituent relationship between peacebuilding and the pursuit of justice,[61] arguing that both TJ and peacebuilding work on similar assumptions pertaining to adequate post-conflict institutional arrangements—such as democratic politics—which may generate sustainable peace.[62] As a result, ambitious arguments have been made that identify a causal logic linking TJ paradigm to the broader remit of peacebuilding. Scholars have posited that TJ processes are integral to peacebuilding and reconciliation, given their potential to recover truth and bring healing at the individual and societal levels, whilst also potentially providing victims with justice, reforming state institutions, strengthening the rule of law and guaranteeing the non-repetition of human rights violations. Olsen et al. are perhaps more cautious, arguing that, at best, transitional justice practices may wield an important impact upon human rights protection measures and democratic consolidation by building capacities and strengthening institutions, elements themselves integral to Liberal Peacebuilding. However, Backer goes further, positing that transitional justice mechanisms may lead to coexistence and social harmony and thus establish shared values and norms integral to sustainable peace; such a process may balance power between groups, whilst at once institutionalising intergroup trust and collaboration. In this regard, Backer posits that a 'vital synergy' can in fact exist between TJ and quality peace.[63] Similarly, broader discussions have contended that truth-telling,[64] reparations[65] and justice guarantees[66] represent key pillars of peacebuilding and may contribute to reconciliation.[67] LaPlante, for example, identifies symbiotic relationship between TJ and peacebuilding, contending that sustainable peace is an intrinsic goal of transitional justice.[68] Lambourne goes perhaps further still, contending that the contribution of the TJ paradigm to peacebuilding is essential, given both its causal link to intergroup reconciliation (a key aspect of sustainable peace) and the necessarily 'transformative' role that TJ ought to play in building sustainable and just peace.[69]

Scholars have specifically further argued that top-down TJ mechanisms, in particular truth-telling mechanisms, may go at least some way towards precipitating reconciliation and fostering conditions for peace, despite the severe challenges faced, such as the extant legacy of violence, culture of fear, lack of trust and ongoing structural inequalities in transitional contexts.[70] Formal truth commissions, it is contended, may go some way towards establishing the truth about the past, provide a public platform for victims, inform and catalyse public debate, recommend victim reparation and legal and institutional reforms, whilst at the same time generating intergroup empathy, tolerance and understanding by allowing conflicting parties to witness each other's grievances and suffering.[71] Scholarship has also focused upon whether the effective implementation of TJ mechanisms may lead to individual/collective healing and reconciliation between formerly warring parties and their constituencies and between victims and perpetrators and, in turn, contribute to self-enforcing peace.[72] Hayner, for example, has argued that transitional justice processes can contribute to sustainable peace through truth recovery, fostering reconciliation, healing at individual and national levels, the provision of justice for victims, the strengthening of the rule of law and the guarantee of non-repetition.[73] Freeman and Hayner have in fact gone as far as to argue that 'Historical accounting via truth-telling is one of the most important steps in the reconciliation process'.[74]

In general then, scholarship exploring both theoretical aspects of TJ and a wide range of empirical case studies has pursued the argument that the implementation of truth commissions, reparations programmes, and the prosecution of perpetrators[75] contribute to sustainable peace and reconciliation.[76] Nevertheless, in a significant contribution to the debate, however, Mendeloff critiques the assumption that TJ mechanisms lead inexorably to sustainable peace and reconciliation.[77] Mendeloff correctly argues that such lofty objectives have not been borne out by empirical experience, including particularly at community level, where intergroup prejudice often persists and the objectives at the core of TJ do not reflect local demands and interests.[78]

As a consequence of the growing links between TJ and peacemaking/peacebuilding, engagement with the issue has become increasingly prevalent during peace negotiations; the challenge for negotiators and mediators in this regard has been how and when to address TJ during negotiations. In an initial analysis of those peace agreements (available in English, French, Russian, Spanish, Portuguese and Arabic) signed across all regional contexts between 1975 and 2019, many of which were subject to external mediation, there were over 300 episodes in which agreements incorporated the topic of transitional justice, either directly or indirectly (see Table 23.1). Significantly, TJ was employed within said agreements to refer to a series of considerably broad provisions, amongst them.[79]

This brief sample evidences how, in spite of the increasing visibility of the theme of TJ within the context of peace negotiations, there has been little consensual understanding of or agreement upon its core meaning or objectives within said context, over and above its generic relevance to the resolution of intergroup antagonism and conflict management. The concept has accordingly been employed to refer to a considerably broad set of provisions situated within the overall framework of the liberal peace paradigm and, specifically, its objective of establishing 'new structures for governance' and mechanisms for the management of intergroup differences 'on a minimally cooperative basis'.[80] Said interventions posit that intergroup antagonisms are best addressed through the institutionalization of, on the one hand, democratic frameworks that seek to foster and

Table 23.1 Transitional justice provisions in peace agreements

Provisions	Peace agreements
Reconciliation and governance/power-sharing	Burundi 2000; Central African Republic 1997; Northern Ireland 1998
Reconciliation	Libya 2015; South Africa 1991
Democratization, political participation and inclusion through amnesty	El Salvador 1992; Georgia/Abkhazia 1994; Guatemala 1996; Somalia 2004
Human rights and international humanitarian law	Mali 2013; South Africa 1991; Sudan 2005; Central African Republic 2015; South Sudan 2015
Amnesty, truth-telling mechanisms and reparations	Bosnia and Herzegovina 1995; Burundi 2006; Colombia 2016; Democratic Republic of Congo 2013; El Salvador 1991; Guatemala 1996; Iraq 2010; Ivory Coast 2007; Libya 2015; Mali 2015; Nepal 2006; Sudan 2011
Demobilization, disarmament and reintegration	Colombia 2004; Guatemala 1996; Liberia 2003; Sierra Leone 1999; Uganda 2008
Healing (by traditional mechanisms or otherwise)	Democratic Republic of Congo 2013; Nepal 2006; Solomon Islands 2000; South Sudan 2015; Uganda 2007
Victims' rights	Colombia 2015/16; Nepal 2006

guarantee mutual cooperation[81] and, on the other, initiatives that aim to redress the wrongs of the past through the transitional justice paradigm.[82] Both approaches ultimately seek to transform intergroup relations based on antagonism, distrust, disrespect and violent interaction by engendering trust, compromise, cooperation and respect and by establishing mechanisms to deal with past abuses.

Transitional Justice in Peacemaking and Peacebuilding at the Local Level

Over the last few decades, there has also been an increase in discussions on the way in which formal mechanisms of TJ are adopted, designed, approved and implemented, as well as their accountability potential. Such discussions have increasingly taken place at the local rather than international level. Scholars and practitioners/activists have convincingly evidenced how the implementation of TJ is not an apolitical issue, in part responding to demands from local actors for inclusion in TJ processes. Specifically, local actors have claimed that TJ practices often lack legitimacy, local ownership and effective participation.[83] As a result, multiple authors have highlighted the failure of formal TJMs as part of peacemaking strategies, particularly when implemented as one-size-fits-all models and argued against the instrumental use by states of TJ mechanisms to privilege state interests.[84]

As a consequence of said debates, a more hybrid structure has emerged for TJ mechanisms, according to which formal systems and local practise coexist, pursuing with the common goals of achieving justice and supporting a successful transition. Important examples of the implementation of exclusively local mechanisms have been studied in order to understand and compare results with cases where internationally standardised, top-down TJ measures were implemented. In the case of Rwanda, for example, a local-dispute resolution mechanism called Gacaca was created independently from the international TJ toolkit measures. It sought to apply practices of conflict resolution at the local level via the participation of the actors involved. For instance, combatants were called to give their confessions regarding violent events, victims could accuse perpetrators, and testimonies were also collected throughout the country and in each community, with the aim of seeking accountability including for lower level perpetrators.[85] However, as Waldorf[86] has explained, this local mechanism still reproduced several of the problems that are associated with the formal mechanisms of TJ, such as state-led top-down implementation that was modified multiple times to respond to external and internal needs and pressures. With each change, the model became less participatory, more formalised and increasingly coercive. In some cases, the model arguably led to greater obstacles for reconciliation between communities and contributed to conflicts between local powers. Similar conclusions were reached in other cases where local models were applied, such as in Burundi, Uganda and the Republic of Congo.[87]

Based on these experiences, specific TJ practices and TJ within peacebuilding contexts have sought to combine the formal mechanisms promoted by international agencies, including the UN, with the needs, priorities and local demands for justice.[88] In this way, an approach that recognizes the necessity of bottom-up construction has been, in part, advanced. This research does not ignore the tensions and challenges that academics and practitioners highlight about such efforts. However, as different authors have pointed out, the extremes that separate one model from another do not lead to desirable results or represent experiences to be replicated.[89] In this sense, the inclusion approach of formal TJMs as a viable means to achieve greater civil and political rights for victims and the promotion of their economic, social and cultural rights is successful only when it encourages the understanding, participation and inclusion of the local context in which it is applied.

Transitional Justice and Peacebuilding: Closing Remarks

As discussed in this chapter, peace processes and post-conflict reconstruction interventions have progressively and explicitly incorporated discussions over how to address the legacies of past violence, leading, in practice, to the adoption of specific TJ provisions within peace accords and the almost inevitable inclusion of TJ provisions within liberal peacebuilding operations. Transitional Justice is now part of the 'checklist' of peacemaking and peacebuilding interventions, given the assumption that enduring peace rests upon 'dealing with the past', as well as other fundamental elements of liberal peacebuilding.[90] Not only has TJ become operationally situated within and, at times, conflated with liberal peacebuilding architecture; the very achievement of peace has also increasingly become understood by many scholars and practitioners as contingent upon effectively *dealing with the past*. Nevertheless, as has been argued in this chapter, such lofty claims have not been borne out in practice. Transitional Justice practices have not led inexorably to self-sustaining peace, and have, at times, in fact challenged fragile transitions, manifest, for example, in the confrontation between those actors seeking accountability and those habitually powerful actors and sectors struggling to maintain both historical power and impunity. Reparations programmes have themselves enjoyed low levels of success, neither compensating victims of violence in a meaningful manner, nor leading to broader transformation. Whilst important changes have taken place as regards the locus of agency in TJ debates and practices—in short, the so-called 'victims' turn'—locally led TJ measures have tended not to be able to escape from the instrumentalization or control by elite actors. Whilst significant changes have on paper taken place with respect to which actors participate in the design and implementation of TJ mechanisms within the context of peacemaking then, in practice, as yet such changes have not led to lasting and meaningful transformation; in short, the contention that TJ leads to peace has not been significantly proven. Nevertheless, victims and survivors continue to seek more meaningful response from both TJ and liberal peacebuildingframeworks, suggesting that the nature of both paradigms will continue to evolve over time.

Notes

1. C. Cheng, J. Goodhand and P. Meehan, *Synthesis Paper: Securing and Sustaining Elite Bargains that Reduce Violent Conflict* (London: Stabilisation Unit, 2018).
2. R. Caplan, *Measuring Peace: Principles, Practices and Politics* (Oxford: Oxford University Press, 2019); C. Call, *Why Peace Fails: The Causes and Prevention of Civil War Recurrence* (Washington, DC: Georgetown University Press, 2012); R. Mac Ginty and J. Darby, *Contemporary Peacemaking: Conflict, Peace Processes and Post-War Reconstruction* (2nd revised edition, Palgrave Macmillan UK, 2008).
3. C. Cheng, J. Goodhand and P. Meehan, *Synthesis Paper: Securing and Sustaining Elite Bargains that Reduce Violent Conflict* (London: Stabilisation Unit, 2018).
4. R. Mac Ginty, *No War, No Peace: The Rejuvenation of Stalled Peace Processes and Peace Accords* (Palgrave Macmillan, 2006); J. Madhav

and P. Wallensteen, *Understanding Quality Peace: Peacebuilding after Civil War* (London: Routledge, 2018).
5. M. Minow, *Between Vengeance and Forgiveness: Facing History after Genocide and Mass Violence* (Boston: Beacon Press, 2000); R. Teitel, *Transitional Justice in a New Era* (26 Fordham Int'l L.J. 893, 2002–2003); L. Arriaza and N. Roht-Arriaza, 'Social Reconstruction as a Local Process', *International Journal of Transitional Justice*, vol. 2, no. 2 (July 2008) pp. 152–172.
6. M. Minow, *Between Vengeance and Forgiveness: Facing History after Genocide and Mass Violence* (Boston: Beacon Press, 2000); R. Teitel, *Transitional Justice in a New Era* (26 Fordham Int'l L.J. 893, 2002–2003); L. Arriaza and N. Roht-Arriaza, 'Social Reconstruction as a Local Process', *International Journal of Transitional Justice*, vol. 2, no. 2 (July 2008) pp. 152–172; R. Shaw, 'Rethinking Truth and Reconciliation Commissions: Lessons from Sierra Leone. Special Report', *Unites States Institute of Peace* (Washington, DC, 2005); C. Bell, 'Transitional Justice, Interdisciplinarity and the State of the "Field" or "Non-Field"', *International Journal of Transitional Justice*, vol. 3, no. 1 (March 2009) pp. 5–27; S. Robins, 'Mapping a Future for Transitional Justice by Learning from Its Past', *International Journal of Transitional Justice*, vol. 9, no. 1 (March 2015) pp. 181–190.
7. K. McEvoy, 'Beyond Legalism: Towards a Thicker Understanding of Transitional Justice', *Journal of Law and Society*, vol. 34 (2007) pp. 411–440; P. Lundy and M. McGovern 'Whose Justice? Rethinking Transitional Justice from the Bottom Up', *Journal of Law and Society*, vol. 35 (2008) pp. 265–292; J. García-Godos, C. L. Sriram, J. Herman and O. Martin-Ortega (eds.), *Transitional Justice and Peacebuilding: Victims and Ex-Combatants* (London: Routledge, 2013); R. Duthie, 'Toward a Development-Sensitive Approach to Transitional Justice', *International Journal of Transitional Justice*, vol. 2, no. 3 (2008) pp. 292–309; P. Gready, *The Era of Transitional Justice: The Aftermath of the Truth and Reconciliation Commission in South Africa and Beyond* (London: Routledge, A GlassHouse Book, 2010).
8. C. L. Sriram, 'Justice as Peace? Liberal Peacebuilding and Strategies of Transitional Justice', *Global Society*, vol. 21, no. 4 (2007) pp. 579–591; R. Brett and L. Malagón, 'Overcoming the Original Sin of the Original Condition: How Reparations May Contribute

to Emancipatory Peacebuilding', *Human Rights Review*, vol. 14, no. 3 (2013) pp. 257–271; R. Carranza, 'Plunder and Pain: Should Transitional Justice Engage with Corruption and Economic Crimes?', *International Journal of Transitional Justice*, vol. 2, no. 3 (December 2008) pp. 310–330; W. Lambourne, 'Transitional Justice and Peacebuilding after Mass Violence', *International Journal of Transitional Justice*, vol. 3, no. 1 (2009) pp. 28–48; P. Firchow and R. Mac Ginty, 'Reparations and Peacebuilding: Issues and Controversies', *Human Rights Review*, vol. 14 (2013) pp. 231–239.
9. S. Robins, 'Failing Victims? The Limits of Transitional Justice in Addressing the Needs of Victims of Violations', *Human Rights and International Legal Discourse*. White Rose Research Online. University of York (2017) pp. 41–58: 56.
10. P. Engstrom, 'Transitional Justice and Ongoing Conflicts', in J. García-Godos, C. L. Sriram, J. Herman and O. Martin-Ortega (eds.), *Transitional Justice and Peacebuilding: Victims and Ex-Combatants* (London: Routledge, 2013) p. 45.
11. R. Brett and L. Malagón, 'Overcoming the Original Sin of the Original Condition: How Reparations May Contribute to Emancipatory Peacebuilding', *Human Rights Review*, vol. 14, no. 3 (2013) pp. 257–271.
12. P. Gready and S. Robins, 'From Transitional to Transformative Justice: A New Agenda for Practice', *International Journal of Transitional Justice*, vol. 8, no. 3 (November 2014) pp. 339–361.
13. M. Evans, 'Structural Violence, Socioeconomic Rights, and Transformative Justice', *Journal of Human Rights*, vol. 15, no. 1 (2016) pp. 1–20.
14. R. Teitel, *Transitional Justice* (New York: Oxford University Press, 2000) pp. 11–15.
15. United Nations Secretary General, 'The Rule of Law and Transitional Justice in Conflict and Post-Conflict Societies', August 23, 2004.
16. United Nations General Assembly, A/RES/60/147. 'Basic Principles and Guidelines on the Right to a Remedy and Reparation for Victims of Gross Violations of International Human Rights Law and Serious Violations of International Humanitarian Law', March 21, 2006.

17. Human Rights Council. A/HRC/RES/18/7. 'Resolution adopted by the Human Rights Council 18/7. Special Rapporteur on the promotion of truth, justice, reparation and guarantees of non-recurrence'.
18. P. Lundy and M. McGovern, 'Whose Justice? Rethinking Transitional Justice from the Bottom Up', *Journal of Law and Society*, vol. 35 (2008) pp. 265–292: 268.
19. P. Engstrom, 'Transitional Justice and Ongoing Conflicts', in J. García-Godos, C. L. Sriram, J. Herman and O. Martin-Ortega (eds.), *Transitional Justice and Peacebuilding: Victims and Ex-Combatants* (London: Routledge, 2013) p. 41.
20. P. Hayner, *Unspeakable Truths: Facing the Challenge of Truth Commissions* (Oxford: Routledge, 2011); N. Aiken, *Identity, Reconciliation and Transitional Justice: Overcoming Intractability in Divided Societies* (Oxon: Routledge, 2013).
21. R. Teitel, *Transitional Justice in a New Era* (26 Fordham Int'l L.J. 893, 2002–2003); R. Shaw, 'Rethinking Truth and Reconciliation Commissions: Lessons from Sierra Leone. Special Report', *Unites States Institute of Peace* (Washington, DC, 2005); C. Bell, 'Transitional Justice, Interdisciplinarity and the State of the "Field" or "Non-Field"', *International Journal of Transitional Justice*, vol. 3, no. 1 (March 2009) pp. 5–27; S. Robins, 'Mapping a Future for Transitional Justice by Learning from Its Past', *International Journal of Transitional Justice*, vol. 9, no. 1 (March 2015) pp. 181–190.
22. Ibid.
23. T. Olsen, L. Payne, and A. Reiter, *Transitional Justice in Balance: Comparing Processes, Weighing Efficacy* (Washington, DC: United State Institute of Peace Press, 2010) p. 9; N. Roht-Arriaza, 'The New Landscape of Transitional Justice', in N. Roht-Arriaza and J. Mariezcurrena (eds.), *Transitional Justice in the Twenty-First Century* (New York: Cambridge University Press, N., 2006).
24. R. Teitel, *Transitional Justice* (New York: Oxford University Press, 2000); C. Bell, 'Transitional Justice, Interdisciplinarity and the State of the "Field" or "Non-Field"', *International Journal of Transitional Justice*, vol. 3, no. 1 (March 2009) pp. 5–27.
25. K. Sikkink, *The Justice Cascade: How Human Rights Prosecutions Are Changing World Politics* (Norton Series in World Politics. New York: W. W. Norton, K. 2011); T. Olsen, L. Payne, and A. Reiter,

Transitional Justice in Balance: Comparing Processes, Weighing Efficacy (Washington, DC: United State Institute of Peace Press, 2010).
26. R. Teitel, *Transitional Justice* (New York: Oxford University Press, 2000).
27. J. Zalaquett, 'Balancing Ethical Imperatives and Political Constraints: The Dilemma of New Democracies confronting Past Human Rights Violations', *Hastings Law Journal*, no. 43 (1992) pp. 1427–1438.
28. C. L. Sriram, 'Liberal Peacebuilding and Transitional Justice: What Place for Socioeconomic Concerns?', *Justice and Economic Violence in Transition*. Springer, New York, NY (2014) pp. 27–49.
29. See Inter-American Court of Human Rights, Judgment of March 14, 2001, Case of Barrios Altos v. Perú. Serie C No. 75.
30. Inter-American Court of Human Rights, 24 November 2010. Available at http://www.corteidh.or.cr/docs/casos/articulos/seriec_219_esp.pdf (Consulted 18 January 2021).
31. According to the report of the Historical Memory Group (GMH), created by the transitional justice mechanism, the Law 975, 2005, the paramilitary groups were the main perpetrators of massacres and selective assassinations across the country during the armed conflict. They also practiced sexual violence, selective assassinations, forced disappearances, torture and brutality, threats, massive forced displacements and economic blockades against civilians. The state agents often committed assassinations and forced disappearances. The Group focusses on the regular collusion and omission of members of the Security Forces and their 'alliances with powerful groups that defend economic and political interests through violent methods, or greedily seek access to more land and/or resources' GMH (2013: 44–46) ¡Basta Ya! Colombia: Memorias de guerra y dignidad. Bogotá: Imprenta Nacional. http://centrodememoriahistorica.gov.co/descargas/informes2016/basta-ya-ingles/BASTA-YA-ingles.pdf (Consulted 18 January 2021).
32. J. Madhav and P. Wallensteen, *Understanding Quality Peace: Peacebuilding after Civil War* (London: Routledge, 2018). Our emphasis.
33. M. Minow, *Between Vengenance and Forgiveness: Facing History after Genocide and Mass Violence* (Boston: Beacon Press, 2000).

34. P. Firchow, 'Do Reparations Repair Relationships? Setting the Stage for Reconciliation in Colombia', *International Journal of Transitional Justice*, vol. 11, no. 2 (2017) pp. 315–338.
35. W. Lambourne, 'Transitional Justice and Peacebuilding after Mass Violence', *International Journal of Transitional Justice*, vol. 3 no. 1 (2009) pp. 28–48.
36. K. McEvoy, 'Beyond Legalism: Towards a Thicker Understanding of Transitional Justice', *Journal of Law and Society*, vol. 34 (2007) pp. 411–440; P. Lundy and M. McGovern, 'Whose Justice? Rethinking Transitional Justice from the Bottom Up', *Journal of Law and Society*, vol. 35 (2008) pp. 265–292; J. García-Godos, C. L. Sriram, J. Herman and O. Martin-Ortega (eds.), *Transitional Justice and Peacebuilding: Victims and Ex-Combatants* (London: Routledge, 2013).
37. See S. Buckley-Zistel, B. T. Koloma, C. Braun and F. Mieth, *Transitional Justice Theories* (London: Routledge, 2014) pp. 5–7; N. Kritz, *Transitional Justice: How Emerging Democracies Reckon with Former Regimes* (Washington, DC: United States Institute of Peace Press, 1995); R. Alonso, J. Argomaniz, C. Joyce, O. Lynch and A. Serrano, 'Best Practice Recommendations for Supporting Victims of Terrorism', in J. Argomaniz and O. Lynch (eds.), *Victims and Perpetrators of Terrorism: Exploring Identities, Roles and Narratives* (London: Routledge, 2018); W. Lambourne, 'Transitional Justice and Peacebuilding after Mass Violence', *International Journal of Transitional Justice*, vol. 3, no. 1 (2009) pp. 28–48.
38. K. Sikkink, *The Justice Cascade: How Human Rights Prosecutions Are Changing World Politics* (Norton Series in World Politics. New York: W. W. Norton, K. 2011).
39. See also N. Roht-Arriaza and J. Mariezcurrena (eds.), *Transitional Justice in the Twenty-First Century* (New York: Cambridge University Press, 2006) p. 7; C. Corradetti, N. Eisikovits and J. Volpe Rotondi, 'Introduction', in C. Corradetti, N. Eisikovits and J. Volpe Rotondi (eds.), *Theorizing Transitional Justice* (London: Routledge, 2015) p. 2; See also Par Engstrom, 'Transitional Justice and Ongoing Conflicts', in J. García-Godos, C. L. Sriram, J. Herman and O. Martin-Ortega (eds.), *Transitional Justice and Peacebuilding. Victims and Ex-Combatants* (London: Routledge, 2013).

40. K. McEvoy, 'Beyond Legalism: Towards a Thicker Understanding of Transitional Justice', *Journal of Law and Society*, vol. 34 (2007) pp. 411–440.
41. N. Roht-Arriaza, 'Reparations and Economic, Social, and Cultural Rights', in *Justice and Economic Violence in Transition* (New York, NY: Springer, 2014) pp. 109–138.
42. See L. Roniger and M. Sznajder, *The Legacy of Human Rights Violations in the Southern Cone: Argentina, Chile and Uruguay* (Oxford University Press, 2003).
43. See L. Fletcher, 'Comparative Country Studies Regarding Truth, Justice, and Reparations for Gross Human Rights Violations: Brazil, Chile, and Guatemala' (IHRLC Working Paper Series No. 2, UC Berkeley Public Law Research Paper No. 2758973, April 1, 2014). Available at http://dx.doi.org/10.2139/ssrn.2758973 (Consulted 20 January 2021).
44. See L. Laplante and K. Theidon, 'Truth with Consequences: Justice and Reparations in Post-Truth Commission Peru', *29 Hum. Rts.*, Q. 228 (2007).
45. See D. Martínez and L. Gómez, 'A Promise to Be Fulfilled: Reparations for Victims of the Armed Conflict in Guatemala' (August 2019). Available at https://reparations.qub.ac.uk/assets/uploads/Guatemalan-Report-ENG-LR.pdf (Consulted 20 January 2021).
46. See C. Colvin, 'Overview of the Reparations Program in South Africa', in P. De Greiff, (ed.), *The Handbook of Reparations* (Oxford University Press, 2006).
47. See A. Macdonald, '"Somehow This Whole Process Became So Artificial": Exploring the Transitional Justice Implementation Gap in Uganda', *International Journal of Transitional Justice*, vol. 13, no. 2 (July 2019) pp. 225–248.
48. United Nations General Assembly, A/69/518, 14 October 2014.
49. Ibid.
50. B. Conley-Zilkic, *How Mass Atrocities End: Studies from Guatemala, Burundi, Indonesia, Sudan, Bosnia Herzegovina and Iraq* (New York: Cambridge University Press, 2016).
51. See R. English, *Modern War: A Very Short Introduction* (United Kingdom: OUP Oxford, 2013) contests the argument that the targeting of civilians is a new phenomenon, arguing that this has been an historically consistent modality of war. See also L.

Vaughan, A. Roberts, J. Welsh and D. Zaum *The United Nations Security Council and War: The Evolution of Thought and War* (Oxford University Press, 2010).

52. C. Cheng, J. Goodhand and P. Meehan, *Synthesis Paper: Securing and Sustaining Elite Bargains that Reduce Violent Conflict* (London: Stabilisation Unit, 2018); O. Ramsbotham, H. Miall, and T. Woodhouse, *Contemporary Conflict Resolution* (Polity, 2011, April 11); J. Madhav and P. Wallensteen, *Understanding Quality Peace: Peacebuilding after Civil War* (London: Routledge, 2018).

53. L. Laplante 'On the Indivisibility of Rights: Truth Commissions, Reparations, and the Right to Development', *Yale Human Rights and Development Law Journal*, vol. 10 (2007) pp. 141–177; Z. Miller, 'Effects of Invisibility: In Search of the 'Economic' in Transitional Justice', *International Journal of Transitional Justice*, vol. 2, no. 3 (December 2008) pp. 266–291; I. Muvingi, 'Sitting on Powder Kegs: Socioeconomic Rights in Transitional Societies', *International Journal of Transitional Justice*, vol. 3, no. 2 (2009) pp. 163–182; L. Fletcher and H. Weinstein, 'Violence and Social Repair: Rethinking the Contribution of Justice to Reconciliation', *Human Rights Quarterly*, vol. 24 (2002) pp. 573–639.

54. C. L. Sriram, 'Justice as Peace? Liberal Peacebuilding and Strategies of Transitional Justice', *Global Society*, vol. 21, no. 4 (2007) pp. 579–591; R. Brett and L. Malagón, 'Overcoming the Original Sin of the Original Condition: How Reparations May Contribute to Emancipatory Peacebuilding', *Human Rights Review*, vol. 14, no. 3 (2013) pp. 257–271; R. Carranza, 'Plunder and Pain: Should Transitional Justice Engage with Corruption and Economic Crimes?', *International Journal of Transitional Justice*, vol. 2, no. 3 (December 2008) pp. 310–330; W. Lambourne, 'Transitional Justice and Peacebuilding after Mass Violence', *International Journal of Transitional Justice*, vol. 3, no. 1 (2009) pp. 28–48.

55. S. Robins, 'Failing Victims? The Limits of Transitional Justice in Addressing the Needs of Victims of Violations', *Human Rights and International Legal Discourse*. White Rose Research Online. University of York (2017) pp. 41–58.

56. L. Laplante, 'On the Indivisibility of Rights: Truth Commissions, Reparations, and the Right to Development', *Yale Human Rights and Development Law Journal*, vol. 10 (2007) pp. 141–177; Z.

Miller, 'Effects of Invisibility: In Search of the "Economic" in Transitional Justice', *International Journal of Transitional Justice*, vol. 2, no. 3 (December 2008) pp. 266–291; I. Muvingi, 'Sitting on Powder Kegs: Socioeconomic Rights in Transitional Societies', *International Journal of Transitional Justice*, vol. 3, no. 2 (2009) pp. 163–182.
57. R. Brett, 'The Role of Civil Society Actors in Peacemaking: The Case of Guatemala', *Journal of Peacebuilding & Development*, vol. 12, no. 1 (2017) pp. 49–64.
58. J. Pring, 'From Transitional Justice to Dealing with the Past: The Role of Norms in International Peace Mediation', *Essential*, University of Basel, Swisspeace, no. 4 (2017) p. 3. Available at https://www.swisspeace.ch/assets/publications/downloads/Essentials/6bb4d5497a/From-Transitional-Justice-to-Dealing-with-the-Past-The-Role-of-Norms-in-International-Peace-Mediation-Essential-17-swisspeace.pdf (Consulted 20 January 2021).
59. United Nations General Assembly, A/RES/60/147. 'Basic Principles and Guidelines on the Right to a Remedy and Reparation for Victims of Gross Violations of International Human Rights Law and Serious Violations of International Humanitarian Law', March 21, 2006.
60. J. P. Lederach, *Building Peace: Sustainable Reconciliation in Divided Societies* (Washington, DC: United States Institute of Peace Press, 1997); W. Lambourne, 'Transitional Justice and Peacebuilding after Mass Violence', *International Journal of Transitional Justice*, vol. 3, no. 1 (2009) pp. 28–48; K. Andrieu, 'Civilizing Peacebuilding: Transitional Justice, Civil Society and the Liberal Paradigm', *Security Dialogue*, vol. 41, no. 5 (2010) pp. 537–558: 538; D. Bar-Tal, 'The Challenges of Social and Political Psychology in Pursuit of Peace: Personal Account', *Peace and Conflict: Journal of Peace Psychology*, vol. 25, no. 3 (2019) pp. 182–197.
61. R. Kerr, 'Peace through Justice? The International Criminal Tribunal for the Former Yugoslavia', *Southeast European and Black Sea Studies*, vol. 7, no. 3 (2007) pp. 373–385: 373.
62. C. L. Sriram, 'Justice as Peace? Liberal Peacebuilding and Strategies of Transitional Justice', *Global Society*, vol. 21, no. 4 (2007) pp. 579–591: 579.

63. D. Backer, 'Factoring Transitional Justice into the Quality Peace Equation', *Understanding Quality Peace* (Routledge, 2018, January 29) pp. 121–134: 131.
64. T. A. Borer (ed.), *Telling the Truths: Truth Telling and Peace Building in Post-Conflict Societies* (University of Notre Dame, Notre Dame Press, 2006).
65. P. Firchow, 'Do Reparations Repair Relationships? Setting the Stage for Reconciliation in Colombia', *International Journal of Transitional Justice*, vol. 11, no. 2 (2017) pp. 315–338.
66. W. Lambourne, 'Transitional Justice and Peacebuilding after Mass Violence', *International Journal of Transitional Justice*, vol. 3, no. 1 (2009) pp. 28–48.
67. D. Mendeloff, 'Truth-Seeking, Truth-Telling, and Post-Conflict Peacebuilding: Curb the Enthusiasm?', *International Studies Review*, vol. 3, no. 6 (2004) pp. 355–380: 355; M. B. Hirsch, M. MacKenzie, M. Sesay, 'Measuring the Impacts of Truth and Reconciliation Commissions: Placing the Global "Success" of TRCs in Local Perspective', *Cooperation and Conflict*, Sept, vol. 47, no. 3 (2012) pp. 386–403.
68. L. Laplante, 'Transitional Justice and Peace Building for the Future: Diagnosing and Addressing the Socioeconomic Roots of Violence Through a Human Rights and Intergenerational Framework', *Sustainable Development, International Criminal Justice, and Treaty Implementation* (Cambridge University Press, 2013) p. 281.
69. W. Lambourne, 'Transitional Justice and Peacebuilding after Mass Violence', *International Journal of Transitional Justice*, vol. 3, no. 1 (2009) pp. 28–48.
70. M. Minow, *Between Vengeance and Forgiveness: Facing History after Genocide and Mass Violence* (Boston: Beacon Press, 2000); P. Hayner, *Unspeakable Truths: Transitional Justice and the Challenge of Truth Commissions* (London: Routledge, 2001); P. Hayner, *Unspeakable Truths: Facing the Challenge of Truth Commissions* (Oxford: Routledge, 2011).
71. D. Mendeloff, 'Truth-Seeking, Truth-Telling, and Post-Conflict Peacebuilding: Curb the Enthusiasm?', *International Studies Review*, vol. 3, no. 6 (2004) pp. 355–380.

72. See B. Hamber and R. Wilson, 'Symbolic Closure Through Memory, Reparation and Revenge in Post-Conflict Societies', *Journal of Human Rights*, vol. 1, no. 1 (2002) pp. 35–53.
73. P. Hayner, *Unspeakable Truths: Transitional Justice and the Challenge of Truth Commissions* (London: Routledge, 2001).
74. M. Freeman and P. B. Hayner, *Truth-Telling: Reconciliation after Violent Conflict: A Handbook* (Stockholm: International Institute for Democracy and Electoral Assistance, 2003) pp. 597–655.
75. A key debate in this regard has been the so-called peace versus justice debate in C. L. Sriram and S. Pillay (eds.), *Peace Versus Justice? The Dilemma of Transitional Justice in Africa* (Scottsville: University of KwaZulu-Naatal Press, 2010); see also J. Pring, 'From Transitional Justice to Dealing with the Past: The Role of Norms in International Peace Mediation', *Essential*, University of Basel, Swisspeace, no. 4 (2017). Available at https://www.swisspeace.ch/assets/publications/downloads/Essentials/6bb4d5497a/From-Transitional-Justice-to-Dealing-with-the-Past-The-Role-of-Norms-in-International-Peace-Mediation-Essential-17-swisspeace.pdf (Consulted 20 January 2021).
76. D. Mendeloff, 'Truth-Seeking, Truth-Telling, and Post-Conflict Peacebuilding: Curb the Enthusiasm?', *International Studies Review*, vol. 3, no. 6 (2004) pp. 355–380.
77. In his research, Mendeloff (2004: 357–359) contests the arguments that TJ (1) encourages social healing and reconciliation; (2) promotes justice; (3) allows for the establishment of an official historical record; (4) serves a public education function; (5) aids institutional reform; (6) helps promote democracy; (7) pre-empts future atrocities; and (8) deters future atrocities.
78. R. Shaw, L. Waldorf with P. Hazan (eds.), *Localizing Transitional Justice: Interventions and Priorities after Mass Violence* (Stanford: Stanford University Press, 2010); See also J. Hughes, 'Agency Versus Structure in Reconciliation', *Ethnic and Racial Studies*, vol. 41, no. 4 (2018) pp. 624–642.
79. See Language of Peace Dataset (Marc Weller): analysis based upon 2798 paragraphs within 255 Peace Agreements between 1975 and 2018 (in English and Spanish). See https://www.languageofpeace.org/#/. Accessed 22/01/2021.
80. J. Madhav and P. Wallensteen, *Understanding Quality Peace: Peacebuilding after Civil War* (London: Routledge, 2018).

81. C. Cheng, J. Goodhand and P. Meehan, *Synthesis Paper: Securing and Sustaining Elite Bargains that Reduce Violent Conflict* (London: Stabilisation Unit, 2018); J. Madhav and P. Wallensteen, *Understanding Quality Peace: Peacebuilding after Civil War* (London: Routledge, 2018); See also D. Bloomfield, T. Barns and L. Huyse, *Reconciliation after Violent Conflict: A Handbook* (Stockholm: International IDEA, 2003).
82. In fact, Bloomfield (2003: 12) has gone as far as arguing that an interdependent relationship exists between reconciliation and democracy, situating the former firmly within the remit of the liberal peace paradigm.
83. P. Lundy and M. McGovern, 'Whose Justice? Rethinking Transitional Justice from the Bottom Up', *Journal of Law and Society*, vol. 35 (2008) pp. 265–292; L. Fletcher and H. Weinstein, 'Violence and Social Repair: Rethinking the Contribution of Justice to Reconciliation', *Human Rights Quarterly*, vol. 24 (2002) pp. 573–639.
84. L. Arriaza and N. Roht-Arriaza, 'Weaving Braid of Histories: Local Post-Armed Conflict Initiatives in Guatemala', in R. Shaw, L. Waldorf with P. Hazan (eds.), *Localizing Transitional Justice: Interventions and Priorities after Mass Violence* (Stanford Studies in Human Rights. Stanford, CA: Stanford University Press, 2010); R. Duthie, 'Afterword: The Consequences of Transitional Justice in Particular Contexts', in L. A. Hinton (ed.), *Transitional Justice: Global Mechanisms and Local Realities after Genocide and Mass Violence* (New Jersey: Rutgers University Press, 2011) pp. 249–255.
85. P. Clark, *The Gacaca Courts, Post-Genocide Justice and Reconciliation in Rwanda: Justice Without Lawyers* (Oxford: University of Oxford, 2011); J. Burnet, 'Justice Truth, Reconciliation, and Revenge in Rwanda's Gacaca', in L. A. Hinton (ed.), *Transitional Justice: Global Mechanisms and Local Realities after Genocide and Mass Violence* (New Jersey: Rutgers University Press, 2011).
86. L. Waldorf, '"Like Jews Waiting for Jesus": Posthumous Justice in Post/Genocide Rwuanda', in R. Shaw, L. Waldorf with P. Hazan (eds.), *Localizing Transitional Justice: Interventions and Priorities after Mass Violence* (Stanford, CA: Stanford University Press, 2010) pp.183–202.

87. A. Nee and P. Uvin, 'Silence and Dialogue: Burundians Alternatives to Transitional Justice', in R. Shaw, L. Waldorf, with P. Hazan, *Localizing Transitional Justice: Interventions and Priorities after Mass Violence* (Stanford: Stanford University Press, 2010); S. Finnstrom, 'Reconciliation Grown Bitter? War, Redistribution and Ritual Action in Northern Uganda', in R. Shaw, L. Waldorf with Hazan P. (eds.), *Localizing Transitional Justice: Interventions and Priorities after Mass Violence* (Stanford Studies in Human Rights. Stanford, CA: Stanford University Press, 2010).
88. A. Robben, 'Testimonies, Truths, and Transitional Justice in Argentina and Chile', in L. A. Hinton (ed.), *Transitional Justice: Global Mechanisms and Local Realities after Genocide and Mass Violence* (New Brunswick: Rutgers University Press, 2011); L. A. Hinton, *Transitional Justice: Global Mechanisms and Local Realities after Genocide and Mass Violence* (New Jersey: Rutgers University Press, 2011); L. Arriaza and N. Roht-Arriaza, 'Weaving Braid of Histories: Local Post-Armed Conflict Initiatives in Guatemala', in R. Shaw, L. Waldorf with P. Hazan (eds.), *Localizing Transitional Justice: Interventions and Priorities after Mass Violence* (Stanford Studies in Human Rights. Stanford, CA: Stanford University Press, 2010).
89. M. Sieff and L. Vinjamuri, 'Prosecuting War Criminals: The Case for Decentralisation', *Conflict, Security & Development*, vol. 2, no. 2 (2002) pp. 103–113; P. Gready, 'Analysis: Reconceptualising Transitional Justice: Embedded and Distanced Justice', *Conflict, Security and Development*, vol. 5, no. 1 (2005) pp. 3–21.
90. D. Sharp, 'Beyond the Post-Conflict Checklist; Linking Peacebuilding and Transitional Justice Through the Lens of Critique', *Chicago Journal of International Law* (2013). See also A. L. Bronwyn, 'The Irreconcilable Goals of Transitional Justice', *Human Rights Quarterly*, vol. 30, no. 1 (February 2008) pp. 95–118; K. Andrieu, 'Civilizing Peacebuilding: Transitional Justice, Civil Society and the Liberal Paradigm', *Security Dialogue*, vol. 41, no. 5 (2010) pp. 537–558: 538.

CHAPTER 24

Peace Education as a Peacemaking Tool in Conflict Zones

Alexander Cromwell

Peace education can complement the peacemaking process at various stages of conflict escalation and de-escalation.[1] Its particular utility is in addressing the animosity that conflicting groups feel toward each other as a result of histories of violence and perceived (or actual) injustice. Peace education is, therefore, a useful prevention tool because it can increase understanding between groups with prejudice towards one another before their mutual animosity escalates to violence. Actors have also used peace education during protracted conflicts to improve the attitudes of a portion of the population with the hope that such activities will lay the foundation for a peacemaking process.[2] Additionally, peace education can complement peace processes by facilitating parallel positive interactions across difference at the grassroots level, which helps to support an infrastructure

A. Cromwell (✉)
Elliott School of International Affairs, George Washington University, Washington, DC, USA
e-mail: acromwell@gwu.edu

for peace should an agreement be signed.[3] Finally, because peace education counters deeply rooted prejudice and helps to rebuild trust between previously warring communities, it is an essential piece of any post-conflict reconstruction process.

However, peace education is not without its challenges. The quintessential test confronting peace education mirrors the challenge faced by actors involved in peace processes—that of sustainability. In the same way that the signing of a peace agreement only marks the beginning of a peace process,[4] facilitating a peace education program is only the first step for altering the dynamics between conflicting groups in conflict contexts. A fundamental concern in such instances is, therefore, how to sustain participants' transformations over the long term.[5] Moreover, scholars question how micro-level transformations that individuals experience in these programs affect peace efforts at the macro-level of society.[6] These considerations are paramount in understanding how peace education can contribute to peacemaking processes. They also illuminate the practices necessary to make peace education a useful tool to complement interventions at different stages of conflict escalation.

This chapter provides prescriptive elements on how to maximize impact in peace education given the challenges of sustainability and scaling impact beyond initial program participants. It argues that the processes of peace education—including both how the content is taught and the overall structure of the program—are key to making these programs have the most impact. Moreover, peacemakers will be most effective in integrating peace education into peace processes when they become aware of the theories of change that drive peace education and how to combine these theories to engage populations at different stages in conflict.

THE ROLE OF EDUCATION IN PEACEBUILDING AND CONFLICT ESCALATION

Peace education programs are designed to cultivate knowledge, skills, attitudes, beliefs, and behaviors that create a culture of peace.[7] In support of this ideal, UN General Assembly Resolution 52/13 (A/RES/52/13) states that a culture of peace is made up of attitudes, behaviors, and values that reject violence, address root causes to avert conflicts, and use negotiation and discussion to resolve issues.[8] Such a culture of peace aligns with peace writ large as an overarching vision for the broader outcome that can result from including education in peacebuilding processes.

Proponents of this approach argue that peace education programs seek to counter the culture of violence that permeates today's society and to move toward a culture of peace.[9] According to Galtung, cultural violence is "any aspect of a culture that can be used to legitimize violence in its direct or structural form."[10] Direct violence is committed from one person to another, and structural violence is instituted by the system in which people live.[11] A culture of peace is the normalization of practices that counter direct and structural violence, fostering direct peace, in the form of collaborative, nonviolent interactions between people, and structural peace, embodied by egalitarian societies where individuals can meet their basic needs.[12]

This approach is particularly important given the ways in which education is routinely conceptualized in post-conflict settings. Governments and international actors tend to focus on simply getting students back into schools, with the sole purpose of preparing these students to compete in the economic marketplace.[13] Doing so misses an opportunity to repair relations across conflict differences and to teach peace-oriented values. Michael Karlberg explains that Western-liberal norms, which emphasize competition as a key organizing force for society, constrain individuals' thinking about the possibility for building cooperative societies.[14] This tendency leads post-conflict governments, with the support of the international community, to reestablish education with the singular goal of promoting economic agency. A focus on a culture of peace results in education that moves away from this emphasis on economic competition and reorients itself around societal cooperation.

Education does not always contribute to peace.[15] Conflicting parties often use education to further divide populations.[16] Schools are primary sites for nation building, meaning that violent or repressive governments or sectors of society that operate schools may tightly control curriculum and use the education system to perpetuate norms supporting militarism and violence.[17] For example, isolating opposing groups into separate educational spaces and teaching only one narrative of history that blames another group reifies conflictual identities and exacerbates tensions between disputing groups.[18] Conflict can further marginalize disadvantaged groups by providing unequal access to education[19] or through the destruction of schools serving these populations.[20] Therefore, education can be used to escalate conflict, and actors considering education as a peacebuilding tool must be aware of its potential negative effects.

Despite the negative uses of education, educational interventions are important peacebuilding endeavors. Anna Knutzen and Alan Smith identify three ways that education can contribute to peacebuilding.[21] First, the termination of conflict allows governments to direct funds to education that were previously used to finance conflict, resulting in a "peace dividend." Moreover, rebuilding the education sector can develop citizens' trust in government institutions because they see concrete improvements in society after the conflict.[22] Second, attending to cleavages between conflicting groups and developing teacher training and curricula addressing group inequalities can also contribute to peace. For example, the purpose of peace education in ethnopolitical conflict contexts is to build relationships between such adversarial groups to transform how they view each other.[23] Third, students can learn and prioritize nonviolent methods for resolving conflicts. The public sector must also be reformed to address institutionalized societal inequalities contributing to nonviolence through equitable education for all. The second and third contributions of peace education are the focal points of this chapter.

THEORIES OF CHANGE IN PEACE EDUCATION

Peace education does not have a uniform approach.[24] Programs encompass a number of themes, including but not limited to human rights, conflict resolution education, critical media literacy, environmental education, nonviolence education, international education, and disarmament education.[25] Programs also take many forms in the formal and informal sector, such as youth summer camps, coexistence and dialogue programs, public school courses, peer mediation programs, community initiatives, weekend workshops, and integrated classrooms.[26]

Susan Allen identified three theories of change that explain transformations resulting from peace education: "building bridges," "culture of peace," and "shifts in consciousness."[27] Table 24.1 outlines common theories of change aligning with these three theories that are most relevant to the impact that peace education can have on peacebuilding. Structural theories have been adapted to focus on the education sector.

Table 24.1 Peace education theories of change

	Peace education theories of change			
	Building bridges	Culture of peace (personal)	Culture of peace (Structural)	Shifts in consciousness
Two Faces of Education in Ethnic Conflict (Bush and Saltarelli 2000)[a]	Changing the rules of the game: humanizing the other through positive contact builds relationships between groups and changes how identity groups interact with one another	Demilitarization of the mind: discounts violence as the best way to resolve issues; problems between groups can be resolved without violence	Delegitimization of violent force as a means of addressing problems: delegitimizes violent systems of authority, and re-legitimizes alternative authority structures; maintains the capability to work in the context by building on local initiatives	Problematization: cultivating critical thinking and curiosity about assumptions Articulation of alternatives: helping participants realize they have choices and they can create changes in their communities
Designing for Results (Church and Rogers 2006)[b]	Healthy Relationships and Connections Theory: bringing together conflicting groups heals divisions and dismantles stereotypes and prejudice between these groups	Reduction of Violence Theory: teaching nonviolent methods to resolve conflicts will reduce violence	Institutional Development Theory: establishing strong and equitable institutions that distribute resources in a just manner will balance society	Individual Change Theory: bottom-up process focused on personal transformations in consciousness eventually leading to broader social change

(continued)

Table 24.1 (continued)

	Peace education theories of change				
	Building bridges	Culture of peace (personal)	Culture of peace (Structural)	Shifts in consciousness	
Encouraging Effective Evaluation (OECD 2007)[c]	*Healthy Relationships and Connections*: bringing together conflicting groups repairs societal cleavages and removes prejudice between these groups	*Culture of Peace*: teaching values that renounce violence and promote dialogue will result in individuals addressing conflicts nonviolently	*Culture of Peace*: addressing the root causes of the conflict can contribute to lasting peace	*Individual Change*: empowering the individual through stimulating consciousness transformations to build peace	
The Role of Education in Peacebuilding (UNICEF 2011)[d]	*Social*: encounters between conflicting groups improve attitudes of students towards these groups to ameliorate future conflict	*Security*: education in a violence-free setting teaches nonviolent skills for conflict resolution	*Economic*: fair and equal access to education for all groups will support societal peace *Social*: addressing unequal access to resources and opportunities can transform society for peace	*Governance*: teaching youth their rights and duties will help them contribute to their societies	

	Peace education theories of change			
	Building bridges	Culture of peace (personal)	Culture of peace (Structural)	Shifts in consciousness
Theories & Indicators of Change (Babbitt et al. 2013)[e]	Social/Cultural Contact: facilitating contact between individuals in opposing groups will remove stereotypes and improve relationships, resulting in decreased conflict	Culture of Peace: shifting attitudes to support peaceful resolution of conflict will counter a "culture of war"	Statebuilding Theory of Change: developing dependable institutions (particularly in terms of education) leads citizens to not use violence to meet their needs	N/A

[a] Bush and Saltarelli, *The Two Faces of Education in Ethnic Conflict*, 27–30
[b] Cheyanne Church and Mark M. Rogers, *Designing for Results: Integrating Monitoring and Evaluation in Conflict Transformation Programs* (Washington, DC: Search for Common Ground, 2006),
[c] OECD, *Encouraging Effective Evaluation of Conflict Prevention and Peacebuilding Activities: Toward DAC Guidance* (Paris: OECD DAC, 2008), 86–87
[d] UNICEF, *The Role of Education in Peacebuilding*, 34–35
[e] Eileen Babbitt, Diana Chigas, and Robert Wilkinson, *Theories and Indicators of Change Briefing Paper: Concepts and Primers for Conflict Management and Mitigation* (Washington, DC: United States Agency for International Development, 2013), 18–21

Building Bridges Theory

As illustrated in the "building bridges" column of the table, this theory focuses on facilitating transformations in attitudes between conflicting groups with the aim of building positive relationships between these groups.[28] It corresponds to Knutzen and Smith's proposed second impact that education can have on peacebuilding because of its emphasis on addressing group divisions. This approach is based on intergroup contact theory, which suggests that facilitating contact between members of conflicting groups will reduce prejudice.[29] While the overarching goal of peace education is facilitating transformations in youth that support the building of a culture of peace, building bridges theory is essential for programs that take place in identity-based or intractable conflict contexts because the negative feelings between conflicting groups are so profound in these situations.[30]

Culture of Peace Theory

Although transformations described by all three theories of change contribute to building a culture of peace, "culture of peace" theory focuses specifically on cultural transformations at the individual and structural level. This attention to both the personal and the structural is reflected in the table's organization. The theory aligns with Knutzen and Smith's third proposed contribution. It suggests that, to stimulate a societal shift towards a culture of peace, individuals' attitudes about the possibility for resolving conflicts peacefully should be transformed.[31] Societal structures must also be shifted to further support these attitudinal transformations. Relating this theory to peace education, instructors should teach nonviolent approaches for solving disputes and educational institutions must be reformed to reflect equity and nonviolence.

Shifts in Consciousness Theory

The third theory—"shifts in consciousness"—argues that personal transformations in consciousness through reflection, dissonance, and other experiences can lead individuals to develop their peacebuilding capacity, and when this occurs on a large scale, it can result in social change.[32] Thus, the cells in this theory's column of the table emphasize that individual transformations lead to action for peace. Supporting this idea,

Sharri Plonski argues that cultivating participants' capability for social change through individual transformation is the purpose of peace education.[33] Additionally, this theory aligns with Monisha Bajaj's goal for peace education: developing "transformative optimism" in support of cultivating action for peace.[34] She adapts the term from Cesar Augusto Rossatto,[35] describing it as having an awareness of the structural challenges that one's community faces, while still believing in one's ability to create change despite these challenges. These consciousness transformations can lead to participants' future social change activities.

TRANSFORMATIONS RESULTING FROM PEACE EDUCATION

Drawing from the literature on peace education, Table 24.2 lists transformations that can occur in successful peace education programs. The table outlines specific transformations in knowledge, beliefs, attitudes, emotions, behaviors, and skills that move participants toward a culture of peace and organizes these transformations around the three theories of change explored in the previous section: building bridges theory, culture of peace theory, and shifts in consciousness theory. Transformations described in Darla Deardorff's model of intercultural competence[36] have been modified to focus toward groups with which individuals are in conflict.

TEACHER TRAINING AND PROGRAMMATIC FACTORS

Fitzduff and Jean argue that teacher training is more important for effective peace education than designing new curricula because ample content already exists on topics in peace and conflict studies.[38] Moreover, even the best curriculum will likely be ineffective if put in the hands of incapable teachers.[39] This is not to say that curricula should not be developed or adapted for specific conflict settings; it is particularly important that a curriculum is adjusted to resonate with the local context.[40] However, Fitzduff and Jean suggest that training educators is an effective short-term method for improving peace education, particularly given the challenges of passing legislation on curriculum reform. This idea is further supported by research in post-conflict societies in West Africa, which illustrates that because of the lack of resources in these contexts, students' learning is more dependent on the teachers than the curricula.[41] Furthermore, given the challenges many teachers face in post-conflict societies, such

Table 24.2 Transformations resulting from peace education[37]

	Building bridges	Culture of peace	Shifts in consciousness
Cognitive Transformations/Knowledge	1. Knowledge about the opposing group (Carstarphen 2004; Pettigrew and Tropp 2008) 2. Cultural self-awareness (Deardorff 2006)	1. Conflict resolution concepts (Romano 2011) 2. Knowledge of human rights (Tibbitts 2008)	1. Self-knowledge and understanding of self in relation to others (Allen Nan 2010)
Cognitive Transformations/Beliefs	1. Breaking stereotypes about the outgroup (Harris and Morrison 2012; Salomon 2002) 2. Humanization of the 'other' (Ross 2014; Salomon 2008) 3. Out-group variability (Pettigrew et al. 2011)	1. Belief in the possibility of peace (Allen Nan 2010)	1. Transformative optimism, peacebuilding capacity (Bajaj 2008; Jäger 2014) 2. Self-efficacy (Bandura 1977; Ross 2017) 3. Self-confidence (Dwyer and Peters 2004; Ross 2017)
Cognitive Transformations/Attitudes	1. Cognitive empathy: understanding the perspective of the group that one is in conflict with (Bar-Tal et al. 2010) 2. Prejudice reduction, positive out-group attitudes (Pettigrew and Tropp 2008) 3. Respect toward the opposing group (Deardorff 2006) 4. Openness towards the opposing group (Deardorff 2006)	1. Attitudes toward peace that reject violence (de Rivera 2008; Gopin 2009)	1. Transformative learning: shift in frame of reference (Deardorff 2006; Mezirow 1997) 2. Conscientization (Freire 2000) 3. Vision of a positive future (Gopin 2012; Lederach 2005; Ross 2017) 4. Motivation to engage in social change activities (Cromwell 2019; Lazarus 2015; Ross 2017) 5. Self-awareness (Deardorff 2006)

	Building bridges	Culture of peace	Shifts in consciousness
Emotional Transformations/Affective Development	1. Affective empathy: being able to imagine how the person is feeling in their situation (Salomon 2008; Swart et al. 2011) 2. Reduced intergroup anxiety (Pettigrew and Tropp 2008) 3. Decrease in hate and fear towards the other group (Church and Rogers 2006; Rosen and Perkins 2013)	1. Learning to manage emotions to approach conflict nonviolently (Goleman 2006; Gopin 2004)	1. High-intensity dissonance (Kiely 2005) 2. Critical emotional praxis (Zembylas 2009)
Behavioral Transformations	1. Developing relationships with individuals from opposing groups (Lederach 1997; Pettigrew 1998; Rosen and Perkins 2013) 2. Acknowledgement/sharing personal stories (Bar-On 2002; Lederach 1997; Salomon 2008) 3. Peacebuilding activity across conflict groups (Lazarus 2011)	1. Behaviors that reject violence (de Rivera 2008) 2. Changing social norms to reflect a culture of peace (Allen Nan 2010; OECD 2007)	1. Peacebuilding activity (Lazarus 2011) 2. Leadership outreach projects (Wehrenfennig et al. 2015) 3. Projects empowering youth in participants' local communities (Cromwell 2019)
Skills	1. Building networks across conflict groups (Ross 2017) 2. Skills for dialogue with the "other" (Wehrenfennig et al. 2015)	1. Conflict resolution skills (mediation, facilitation, etc.) (Johnson and Johnson 1996) 2. Dialogue and negotiation skills (de Rivera 2008)	1. Critical reflection (Bar-Tal et al. 2010; Mezirow 1997) 2. Listening, observing, and evaluating (Deardorff 2006) 3. Activist skills (Ross 2017) 4. Leadership skills (Wehrenfennig et al. 2015)

as confronting their own experiences with violence and meeting national guidelines for standardized tests with few resources, pedagogical training and institutional support are key for their efficacy as peace educators.[42]

Teachers must also be convinced of the value of peace education. For example, although Kenya's government developed a "Peace Education Programme" for schools throughout the country, many educators did not actually teach this subject because students were not being tested on it.[43] Teachers' tendency not to teach this content was also a result of instructors lacking materials and training in peace education pedagogy.[44] Therefore, peace educators must first experience the transformative effects of this pedagogy firsthand, and be trained on how to use such pedagogy, before they can both understand its value and effectively teach it to others.[45]

Additionally, studies illustrate that programmatic factors influence the success of peace education programs.[46] The next sections describe considerations for teacher training and program structures related to each of the three theories of change.

Facilitating Transformations that Build Bridges

Transformations explained by building bridges theory result from participants' encounters with outgroup members. Ifat Maoz identified four models of "encounter" programs with Jewish and Palestinian citizens of Israel: Coexistence, Joint Projects, Confrontation, and Narrative.[47] Two of these models, the Coexistence Model and the Joint Projects Model, emphasize how contact can strengthen interpersonal relationships across the divide.[48] Coexistence Model-based programs seek to have participants experience *decategorization*[49] from their conflictual identities through positive interpersonal interactions with outgroup members that highlight individual similarities. The Joint Projects model is based on participants *recategorizing* themselves into a superordinate identity[50] that connects them together based on collaborative activities. However, these programs are critiqued because if participants' respective group identities are not salient during the contact, these interactions will not generalize beyond individuals to other outgroup members.[51]

Contrary to this approach, programs using the Confrontation Model facilitate disagreements as the groups directly tackle the asymmetrical qualities of the conflict, meaning that group identities are salient throughout the process. However, such direct confrontations can damage relationships when conflicts escalate during these discussions.[52] In the Narrative Model, participants from different groups share personal stories that enhance empathy and relationships across the divide, while also teaching participants about the struggles experienced by groups on both sides.[53] Learning about these struggles is thought to help positive contact generalize beyond interpersonal relationships to how individuals view the opposing group.[54]

These models all relate to building bridges theory because they are based on contact across lines of difference—although the Confrontation Model emphasizes structural change through empowering the marginalized group and increasing the dominant group's awareness of their privilege.[55] Many initiatives combine variations of these models in their programming.[56] One such program is Seeds of Peace, which brings youth representing opposing sides from the Israeli–Palestinian conflict and other conflicts to Maine for three weeks. It utilizes a "mixed-model encounter" approach, providing opportunities for participants to connect individually through summer camp activities while also addressing the conflict through daily cross-group dialogues.[57]

Two other factors to consider in such programs are providing unstructured time for informal relationship-building and developing equitable organizational structures to model participants' interactions across difference.[58] Regarding the first factor, according to studies examining interactions between Israeli Jews and Palestinians across multiple integrated schools, although these interactions were generally positive, very few students visited each other outside of school time.[59] This lack of informal interaction inhibited participants' ability to build close relationships. For the second factor, comparing two organizations working with Jewish and Palestinian citizens of Israel, Karen Ross found that one organization closed down because of its structural inequalities that contradicted its mission, such as having Palestinians as translators rather than as co-facilitators with their Jewish counterparts.[60]

Facilitating Transformations to Build a Culture of Peace

If attitudinal and behavioral shifts away from a culture of violence towards a culture of peace are to occur, peace education pedagogy must reflect its content.[61] Thus, as students increase their knowledge of peace and conflict, learn about the value of approaching conflicts nonviolently, and develop negotiation and dialogue skills,[62] educators should model these processes in their interactions with students.[63] For example, the use of corporal punishment in Kenya during the implementation of its Peace Education Programme hindered faculty members' ability to teach nonviolence to their students.[64] Therefore, peace educators should embody the values and attitudes they wish to impart to their students.

Facilitating Shifts in Consciousness

Shifts in consciousness theory builds on the work of Paulo Freire, who advocated for helping individuals to develop *conscientization*, an awareness of their consciousness, through "problem-posing education."[65] As Freire explains: "In problem-posing education, people [...] come to see the world not as a static reality but as a reality in process, in transformation."[66] He argues that the process of dialogue opens up participants' awareness of the fluid nature of their surroundings and stimulates critical thinking that helps them to recognize their ability to engage in action. Research on peace education with Pakistani youth illustrated that participants recognized the importance of discussion-oriented classes for developing confidence in their opinions.[67] When their teachers acknowledged the value of their contributions, these participants asked critical questions and realized that they could transform the world around them because it was not fixed.[68] In other words, alumni developed a sense of transformative optimism—a belief in their ability to create change despite the challenges they faced.[69] Peace educators can implement this process to empower participants to become change agents in their communities.

Peace education that facilitates shifts in consciousness also typically includes experiential components. Engaging in action in one's surroundings and reflecting on that action is key to facilitating these transformations.[70] For example, in informal peace education programs bringing Pakistani youth to the United States, participants attributed their increased motivation to work for social change to their experiences in the US engaging in community service, learning how to take initiative in communities there, and experiencing the program staff's and their host families' caring attitudes toward them.[71] Research on volunteering shows that in general, the more that people volunteer, the more likely it will be that they keep volunteering.[72] Therefore, peace education that incorporates aspects of service or volunteering can influence youth to improve their communities.

COMBINING THEORIES OF CHANGE

Because of the multiple root causes of conflict, focusing on only one of these theories of change limits the effectiveness of potential programs. For starters, one downfall of the building bridges approach is that it does not adequately focus on social change, and in some cases, it can even subdue marginalized groups through superficial friendships with the "other."[73] This flaw can be addressed through incorporating shifts in consciousness theory with building bridges theory by providing opportunities for individuals to recognize their capacity for social change. Karen Ross further argues that such programs also need to specifically focus on structural inequalities in the conflict and provide concrete organizing skills that participants can use beyond their program attendance to work for improving their communities.[74] Below I explore examples of programs that illustrate the value of combining these theories of change for creating sustainable and impactful transformations at different conflict stages.

Sustaining Transformations

Sustaining transformations is particularly challenging in protracted conflict settings. For example, Ifat Maoz found that, throughout their lifetime, roughly sixteen percent of Jewish Israelis had attended some sort of peace education or dialogue program with Israeli Arabs. However, only 38.5 percent of the Jewish Israelis that attended these programs believed that having such an experience led them to develop more positive attitudes toward these groups.[75] This means that only roughly six percent of the overall Jewish Israeli population believed that they had experienced a positive impact from dialogue with the "other." Similar to Karen Ross' findings in her research, Maoz attributed this drawback to unequal staffing roles between the Jewish Israeli and Arab Israeli personnel of these programs. It may also be that these programs did not emphasize shifts in conscious in addition to building bridges and provide enough opportunities for alumni to engage in concrete action that would reinforce their initial transformations resulting from building bridges. Ned Lazarus' longitudinal (1993–2010) study of Israelis and Palestinians in Seeds of Peace found that the greatest predictor of long-term positive effects from this program was how well-developed the follow-on activities were.[76] In other words, the program's focus on action in addition to building bridges helped some youth to sustain their transformations, even in the face of resurging conflict during the Al-Aqsa Intifada, which lasted from 2000 until 2005.

Many programs also incorporate shifts in consciousness by encouraging participants to implement a community project after they complete the initial program.[77] In one such program, alumni in Pakistan developed interfaith harmony projects to address the long-standing religious conflicts present in their communities.[78] This approach reflects a cycle of learning through these experiences, emblematic of Freire's conceptualization of praxis[79] and Kolb's experiential learning model.[80] In both models, individuals engage in community action and learn from reflection on this action. They then engage in future action that is informed by these previous activities. Programs that include community service and leadership components start this cycle while participants are still attending the program. Using this approach increases participants' likelihood to engage in action once they return to their communities because of their shifts in consciousness related to this action. Many Pakistani alumni exemplified this cycle because they completed community service during the program and then worked on multiple projects after their return from the program.[81] These experiences sustained and deepened the transformations that alumni initially experienced.

Scaling Peace Education Impact to Support Peacemaking

Combining theories of change to include shifts in consciousness and providing opportunities for future action also led to community impact at different stages of conflict. This phenomenon was most apparent in the post-conflict experiences of Sierra Leone and Mozambique. In Sierra Leone, peace education programs using this approach changed some communities' negative perceptions of youth. This change was particularly important because the rampant and brutal violence committed by the Revolutionary United Front and other fighting forces during the war led individuals in many communities to fear youth.[82] Michael Wessells describes a program that brought together ex-combatant and noncombatant youth to collaboratively engage in community service projects building infrastructure that the community needed.[83] The program transformed how these youth viewed each other through the collaborative contact that they experienced. Additionally, when community members witnessed ex-combatant youth choosing to engage in such constructive acts for the community, instead of meeting their needs through violence and crime, it shifted these community members' perceptions of them and helped to earn their trust.[84] This programming repaired relationships and built peace at the community level. The example illustrates how peace education can impact communities beyond their direct participants both in terms of infrastructure built through community service and how the act of community service can transform community perceptions across lines of difference.

In Mozambique, ProPaz implemented a peace education program providing former youth associated with fighting forces with leadership and conflict resolution skills training.[85] Bringing together these youth also bridged the divide across former combatant groups. One hundred and fifty of these participants were also trained as "peace promoters" and tasked with going to other communities to facilitate peacebuilding dialogues there. In one such dialogue, community members expressed that the presence of land mines hurt the community because their children were afraid to walk around the neighborhood. The dialogue created understanding between community members and ex-combatants and motivated these ex-combatants to inform police where land mines had been planted, which resulted in many landmines being removed. Interestingly, the program focused more on the shifts in consciousness and culture of peace theories in its approach, but facilitators created space for dialogue, which built bridges across group differences. The program's focus on "peace promoters" was essential for increasing the impact that it was able to have in this post-conflict context.

Peace education is also particularly important in contexts that don't fit neatly into phases such as "post-conflict" and have various ongoing regionalized conflicts and tensions.[86] Lebanon is one such conflict. UNICEF's Education for Peace program in Lebanon took place between 1988 and 1993 and included 600 youth.[87] The program began before the civil war ended in October 1989 with the signing of the Taif agreement and continued into the post-conflict peacebuilding process. However, various conflicts have continued in Lebanon as a result of political and sectarian tensions, regional conflicts, and terrorism.[88] Thus, analyzing this case sheds light on the impact of peace education in contexts that transcend clear categorizations. The program connected youth together from opposing groups and showed them how to teach younger children the same lessons they were being taught through creative activities. In other words, it had a building bridges component and a shifts in consciousness component. The focus on educating and taking care of children led program participants and alumni to share their learning with younger community members. Zeena Zakharia explains that many civil society actors whom she met during her research in 2011 attribute their peacebuilding work to Education for Peace, although they did not directly participate in the program. She describes the head of a civil society organization who did not participate in the program but worked with someone who had. When she interviewed him, he stated: "everything I learned about peacebuilding I learned from those camps."[89] He also explained: "Look around at all of the NGOs [non-governmental organizations] in Lebanon, and you will find that they all go back to those camps."[90] Thus, moving past simply transforming how participants viewed each other, and intentionally focusing on how these participants could teach others what they had learned, led to impact beyond the program's initial participants.

Peace education supports the broader process of rebuilding relationships across conflict divides at various conflict stages. This rebuilding of relationships is essential for setting the foundation to transform conflict, or to reconstruct a peaceful society after the conclusion of a formal peace process. Moreover, as argued throughout this chapter, combining theories of change to emphasize shifts in consciousness and action for peace will extend this impact. "Talk is cheap," as the popular saying goes. Motivating participants to engage in action moves past feel-good dialogue in peace education and pushes participants to put their money where their mouth is, so to speak. This focus on action also reminds peace educators to consider how to staff these programs so that the opposing sides of the conflict are equally represented and empowered. By practicing what they preach through their organizational models, peace educators can encourage participants to do the same.

CONCLUSION

Peace education programs are important peacebuilding initiatives that can contribute to peacemaking. This chapter described three common theories of change guiding peace education and the types of transformations typically associated with these theories. It also highlighted best practices for facilitating transformations related to each of these theories and the importance of combining the theories to sustain and maximize program impact. Particularly in programs in which participants need to build bridges across a conflict divide, careful intentionality in choosing program processes, training teachers, developing the organization's structure, and providing space for unstructured time are paramount for amplifying impact. Moreover, the combination of shifts in consciousness with building bridges facilitates transformations in participants that can lead to their action for social change. Consequently, programs are most likely to result in long-term impact when they train teachers and develop program structures that emphasize discussion, leadership, and experiential learning components leading to participants' increased motivation and transformative optimism. Furthermore, programs' specific focus on action that participants could take in terms of projects and community dialogues, educating younger community members, or community service all contributed to sustaining their transformations and increasing their community impact. Programs that consider such factors can effectively contribute to peacemaking in societies at multiple conflict phases, from creating a general foundation for a peace process to helping repair relationships following a peace agreement.

Acknowledgements I would like to thank the editors of this volume for their helpful feedback and support throughout the process of writing this chapter. I am also particularly grateful to Anthony Wanis-St. John for his mentorship during my time at American University. I am also thankful to Susan Hirsch and Arthur Romano for their large role in shaping the ideas in this chapter. And I am grateful to Daniel Boerger and Harry Nitzberg for their detailed edits and revisions throughout this process. Portions of this chapter originally appeared in my dissertation: Alexander Cromwell, "Building a Culture of Peace: The Long-Term Effects of Encounter-Based Peace Education with Pakistani Youth" (PhD diss., George Mason University, Fairfax, 2019), ProQuest Dissertations and Theses Global.

Notes

1. Zeena Zakharia, "Peace Education and Peacebuilding across the Conflict Continuum: Insights from Lebanon," in *Peace Education: International Perspectives*, ed. Monisha Bajaj and Maria Hantzopoulos (London: Bloomsbury, 2016), 86.
2. Deepak Malhotra and Sumanasiri Liyanage, "Long-Term Effects of Peace Workshops in Protracted Conflicts," *The Journal of Conflict Resolution* 49, no. 6 (2005): 919.

3. John Paul Lederach, *The Moral Imagination: The Art and Soul of Building Peace* (New York: Oxford University Press, 2005), 43–49.
4. See the introduction to this volume. See also Lederach, *The Moral Imagination*, 43–49.
5. Gavriel Salomon, "Four Challenges Facing Peace Education in Regions of Intractable Conflict," *Peace and Conflict* 17, no. 1 (2011): 46–59; Ned Lazarus, "EVALUATING SEEDS OF PEACE: Assessing Long-Term Impact in Volatile Context," in *Peace Education Evaluation: Learning from Experience and Exploring Prospects*, ed. Celina Del Felice, Aaron Karako, and Andria Wisler (Charlotte: Information Age Publishing, 2015), 163–178.
6. Esra Çuhadar Gürkaynak, Bruce Dayton, and Thania Paffenholz, "Evaluation in Conflict Resolution and Peacebuilding," in *Handbook of Conflict Analysis and Resolution*, ed. Dennis J.D. Sandole, Sean Byrne, Ingrid Sandole-Staroste, and Jessica Senehi (New York: Routledge, 2008), 272–284; Marc Howard Ross, "Peace Education and Political Science," in *Handbook on Peace Education*, ed. Gavriel Salomon and Ed Cairns (New York: Psychology Press, 2010), 121–133.
7. Susan Fountain, "Peace Education in UNICEF," (UNICEF, 1999); Gavriel Salomon and Ed Cairns, eds., *Handbook on Peace Education* (New York: Psychology Press, 2010).
8. United Nations General Assembly Resolution A/RES/52/13, "Culture of Peace," January 15, 1998; Joseph de Rivera, ed., *Handbook on Building Cultures of Peace* (New York: Routledge, 2008), 2.
9. See, for example, Salomon and Cairns, *Handbook on Peace Education*, 5; Kevin Kester, "Education for Peace: Content Form and Structure: Mobilizing Youth for Civic Engagement," *Peace and Conflict Review* 4, no. 2 (2010): 2.
10. Johan Galtung, "Cultural Violence," *Journal of Peace Research* 27, no. 3 (1990): 291.
11. Johan Galtung, "Violence, Peace, and Peace Research," *Journal of Peace Research* 6, no. 3 (1969): 167–191.
12. Galtung, "Cultural Violence," 291.
13. Alan Smith, "Education in the Twenty-First Century: Conflict, Reconstruction and Reconciliation," *Compare: A Journal of*

Comparative and International Education 35, no. 4 (December 2005): 384–385.
14. Michael Karlberg, "The Power of Discourse and the Discourse of Power: Pursuing Peace through Discourse Intervention," *International Journal of Peace Studies* 10, no. 1 (Spring/Summer 2005): 14–16.
15. Pamela R. Aall, Jeffrey W. Helsing, and Alan C. Tidwell, "Addressing Conflict Through Education," in *Peacemaking in International Conflict: Methods & Techniques*, ed. I. William Zartman (Washington, DC: United States Institute of Peace, 2007), 327–353.
16. Kenneth Bush and Diana Saltarelli, *The Two Faces of Education in Ethnic Conflict* (FL: UNICEF Innocenti Research Centre, 2000), 33; Michelle J. Bellino, Julia Paulson, and Elizabeth Anderson Worden. "Working through Difficult Pasts: Toward Thick Democracy and Transitional Justice in Education," *Comparative Education* 53, no. 3 (2017): 321–322.
17. UNICEF, *The Role of Education in Peacebuilding: Literature Review* (UNICEF, 2011); Bush and Saltarelli, *The Two Faces of Education in Ethnic Conflict*, 28.
18. Giuditta Fontana, *Education Policy and Power-Sharing in Post-Conflict Societies: Lebanon, Northern Ireland, and Macedonia* (London: Palgrave, 2017).
19. Felisa L. Tibbitts and Gail Weldon, "History Curriculum and Teacher Training: Shaping a Democratic Future in Post-Apartheid South Africa," *Comparative Education* 53, no. 3 (2017): 442–461.
20. UNESCO, "The Hidden Crisis: Armed Conflict and Education," *Education for All Global Monitoring Report* (UNESCO, 2011); Bush and Saltarelli, *The Two Faces of Education in Ethnic Conflict*, 11.
21. Anna Knutzen and Alan Smith, *UNICEF Peacebuilding, Education and Advocacy Programme: Uganda Conflict Analysis* (New York: UNICEF, 2012), 9.
22. Knutzen and Smith, *UNICEF Peacebuilding, Education and Advocacy Programme*, 9.
23. Gavriel Salomon, "Peace Education: Its Nature, Nurture and the Challenges It Faces," in *Handbook on Building Cultures of Peace*, ed. Joseph de Rivera (New York: Springer, 2008), 111.

24. Salomon, "Peace Education: Its Nature, Nurture and the Challenges it Faces," 107–108.
25. Arthur Romano, *Education for Peace: A Resource Guide for Educators and the Community* (Newark: Center for the Study of Genocide, Conflict Resolution, and Human Rights, Rutgers, The State University of New Jersey, 2011), 9–10.
26. Zvi Bekerman and Claire McGlynn, "Introduction," in *Addressing Ethnic Conflict Through Peace Education: International Perspectives*, ed. Zvi Bekerman and Claire McGlynn (New York: Palgrave Macmillan, 2007), 1–5.
27. Susan Allen Nan, *Theories of Change and Indicator Development in Conflict Management and Mitigation* (Washington, DC: United States Agency for International Development, 2010), Appendix A.
28. Allen Nan, *Theories of Change and Indicator Development in Conflict Management and Mitigation*, Appendix A.
29. Miles Hewstone and Rupert Brown, "Contact Is Not Enough: An Intergroup Perspective on the 'Contact Hypothesis'," in *Contact and Conflict in Intergroup Encounters*, ed. Miles Hewstone and Rupert Brown (Oxford: Basil Blackwell, 1986), 1–44.
30. Salomon, "Peace Education: Its Nature, Nurture and the Challenges It Faces," 109–111.
31. Allen Nan, *Theories of Change and Indicator Development in Conflict Management and Mitigation*, Appendix A.
32. Allen Nan, *Theories of Change and Indicator Development in Conflict Management and Mitigation*, Appendix A.
33. Sharri Plonski, "Developing Agency through Peacebuilding in the Midst of Intractable Conflict: The Case of Israel and Palestine," *Compare: A Journal of Comparative and International Education* 35, no. 4 (2005): 393–409.
34. Monisha Bajaj, "Introduction," in *Encyclopedia of Peace Education*, ed. Monisha Bajaj (Charlotte: Information Age Publishing, 2008), 4.
35. Cesar Augusto Rossatto, *Engaging Paulo Freire's Pedagogy of Possibility* (Oxford: Rowman and Littlefield, 2005), 81–88.
36. Darla K. Deardorff, "Identification and Assessment of Intercultural Competence as a Student Outcome of Internationalization," *Journal of Studies in International Education* 10, no. 3 (2006): 241–266.

37. An earlier version of this table appeared in my dissertation: Cromwell, "Building a Culture of Peace," 42.
38. Mari Fitzduff and Isabella Jean, *Peace Education: State of the Field and Lessons Learned from USIP Grantmaking* (Washington, DC: United States Institute of Peace, 2011), 10–11.
39. Fitzduff and Jean, *Peace Education*, 10–11.
40. Monisha Bajaj and Maria Hantzopolous, eds., *Peace Education: International Perspectives* (London: Bloomsbury, 2016); Bush and Saltarelli, *The Two Faces of Education in Ethnic Conflict*, 27.
41. Susan Shepler and James H. Williams, "Understanding Sierra Leonean and Liberian Teachers' Views on Discussing Past Wars in their Classrooms," *Comparative Education* 53, no. 3 (2017): 426–427.
42. Bellino, Paulson, and Worden, "Working through Difficult Pasts," 321–322.
43. Mary Mendenhall and Nivedita Chopra, "Educating for Peace in Kenya: Insights and Lessons Learned from Peace Education Initiatives across the Country," in *Peace Education: International Perspectives*, ed. Monisha Bajaj and Maria Hantzopoulos (London: Bloomsbury, 2016), 96.
44. Mendenhall and Chopra, "Educating for Peace in Kenya," 97.
45. Tibbitts and Weldon, "History Curriculum and Teacher Training"; Mendenhall and Chopra, "Educating for Peace in Kenya," 96–97.
46. Karen Ross, *Youth Encounter Programs in Israel: Pedagogy, Identity, & Social Change* (Syracuse: Syracuse University Press, 2017), 147; Lazarus, "EVALUATING SEEDS OF PEACE," 170.
47. Ifat Maoz, "Does Contact Work in Protracted Asymmetrical Conflict? Appraising 20 Years of Reconciliation-Aimed Encounters between Israeli Jews and Palestinians," *Journal of Peace Research* 48, no. 1 (2011): 118.
48. Karen Ross, "Narratives of Belonging (and Not): Inter-group Contact in Israel and the Formation of Ethno-National Identity Claims," *International Journal of Intercultural Relations* 42, no. 1 (2014): 39–40.
49. David A. Wilder, "Social Categorization: Implications for Creation and Reduction of Intergroup Bias," in *Advances in Experimental Social Psychology* 19, ed. Leonard Berkowitz (Orlando: Academic Press, 1986), 291–355.

50. John Dovidio, Samuel Gaertner, and Kerry Kawakami, "Intergroup Contact: Past, Present, and Future," *Group Processes & Intergroup Relations* 6, no. 1 (2003): 5–21.
51. Hewstone and Brown, "Contact Is Not Enough," 1–44.
52. Maoz, "Does Contact Work in Protracted Asymmetrical Conflict?" 120.
53. Maoz, "Does Contact Work in Protracted Asymmetrical Conflict?" 120.
54. Dan Bar-On, "Conciliation through Storytelling: Beyond Victimhood," in *Peace Education: The Concept, Principles, and Practices around the World*, ed. Gavriel Salomon and Baruch Nevo (Mahwah: Lawrence Erlbaum Associates Publishers, 2002), 109–116.
55. Ross, "Narratives of Belonging (and Not)," 39–40.
56. Ross, "Narratives of Belonging (and Not)," 40.
57. Edie Maddy-Weitzman, "Waging Peace in the Holy Land: A Qualitative Study of Seeds of Peace, 1993–2004" (PhD diss., Boston University, 2005); Ned Lazarus, "Evaluating Peace Education in the Oslo-Intifada Generation: A Long-Term Impact Study of Seeds of Peace 1993–2010" (PhD diss., American University, 2011), 23.
58. Ross, *Youth Encounter Programs in Israel*, 152; Ilham Nasser and Mohammed Abu-Nimer, "Peace Education in a Bilingual and Biethnic School for Palestinians and Jews in Israel: Lessons and Challenges," in *Addressing Ethnic Conflict through Peace Education*, ed. Zvi Bekerman and Claire McGlynn (New York: Palgrave Macmillan, 2007), 113–117.
59. Nasser and Abu-Nimer, "Peace Education in a Bilingual and Biethnic School for Palestinians and Jews in Israel," 113.
60. Ross, *Youth Encounter Programs in Israel*, 55.
61. Johan Galtung, "Form and Content of Peace Education," in *Encyclopedia of Peace Education*, ed. Monisha Bajaj (Charlotte: Information Age Publishing, 2008), 49–58.
62. de Rivera, *Handbook on Building Cultures of Peace*, 2.
63. Romano, *Education for Peace*, 6.
64. Solvor Mjøberg Lauritzen, "Building Peace Through Education in a Post-Conflict Environment: A Case Study Exploring Perceptions of Best Practices," *International Journal of Educational Development* 51 (2016): 77–83.

65. Paulo Freire, *Pedagogy of the Oppressed* (New York: Continuum, 2000), 79.
66. Freire, *Pedagogy of the Oppressed*, 83.
67. Cromwell, "Building a Culture of Peace," 217–223.
68. Cromwell, "Building a Culture of Peace," 217–223.
69. Bajaj, "Introduction," 4.
70. Freire, *Pedagogy of the Oppressed*, 79; David A. Kolb, *Experiential Learning: Experience as the Source of Learning and Development*, 2nd ed. (Upper Saddle River: Pearson, 2015), 50–52.
71. Alexander Cromwell, "How Peace Education Motivates Youth Peacebuilding: Examples from Pakistan," *International Journal of Educational Development* 66 (2019): 66.
72. Barbara A. Butrica, Richard W. Johnson, and Sheila R. Zedlewski, "Volunteer Dynamics of Older Americans," *The Journals of Gerontology: Series B* 64B, no. 5 (2009): 644–655.
73. Maoz, "Does Contact Work in Protracted Asymmetrical Conflict?" 122.
74. Ross, *Youth Encounter Programs in Israel*, 152–153.
75. Ifat Maoz, "Educating for Peace through Planned Encounters between Jews and Arabs in Israel: A Reappraisal of Effectiveness," in *Handbook on Peace Education*, ed. Gavriel Salomon and Ed Cairns (New York: Psychology Press, 2010), 303–313.
76. Lazarus, "EVALUATING SEEDS OF PEACE," 170.
77. Cromwell, "Building a Culture of Peace," 260; Daniel Wehrenfennig, Daniel Brunstetter, and Johanna Solomon, "The Olive Tree Initiative: Lessons Learned about Peace Education through Experiential Learning," in *Peace Education Evaluation: Learning from Experience and Exploring Prospects*, ed. Celina Del Felice, Aaron Karako, and Andria Wisler (Charlotte: Information Age Publishing, 2015), 179–192.
78. Cromwell, "Building a Culture of Peace," 287.
79. Freire, *Pedagogy of the Oppressed*, 84.
80. Kolb, *Experiential Learning*, 51.
81. Cromwell, "Building a Culture of Peace," 259.
82. Michael Wessells and Davidson Jonah, "Recruitment and Reintegration of Former Youth Soldiers in Sierra Leone: Challenges of Reconciliation and Post-accord Peacebuilding," in *Troublemakers or Peacemakers? Youth in Post-Accord Peacebuilding*, ed. Siobhan

McEvoy-Levy (Notre Dame: University of Notre Dame Press, 2006), 27–47.
83. Michael Wessells, "Child Soldiers, Peace Education, and Postconflict Reconstruction for Peace," *Theory into Practice* 44, no. 4 (2005): 363–369.
84. Wessells, "Child Soldiers, Peace Education, and Postconflict Reconzstruction for Peace."
85. Stephanie Schwartz, *Youth in Post-Conflict Reconstruction: Agents of Change* (Washington, DC: United States Institute of Peace Press, 2010), 53–54.
86. Zakharia, "Peace Education and Peacebuilding across the Conflict Continuum," 86.
87. Zakharia, "Peace Education and Peacebuilding across the Conflict Continuum," 83.
88. "Political Instability in Lebanon," Council on Foreign Relations, accessed September 30, 2019, https://www.cfr.org/interactive/global-conflict-tracker/conflict/political-instability-lebanon.
89. Zakharia, "Peace Education and Peacebuilding across the Conflict Continuum," 84.
90. Zakharia, "Peace Education and Peacebuilding across the Conflict Continuum," 84.

CHAPTER 25

Post-accord Crime and Violence

Christina Steenkamp

INTRODUCTION

One of the basic expectations of peace accords is that they will reduce levels of violence in the emerging post-war society. However, in reality, most post-accord societies continue to experience alarmingly high levels of violence and run the risk of becoming even more insecure environments than when it was at war. It is all too easy to find examples. In Northern Ireland, violent attacks on the security forces and so-called 'punishment' attacks on civilians continue despite decades of 'peace' after the Good Friday Agreement was signed in 1998. In South Africa, violent crime and homicide rates rose significantly after the end of Apartheid in 1994. Electoral violence continues to plague polls in Kenya after the National Accord and Reconciliation Agreement of 2008. And after Latin America's much feted peace deal in Colombia in 2016 between the government and the Revolutionary Armed Forces of Colombia (FARC), violence between armed groups has continued and at least 500 people have been killed in the period up to mid-2019 and 210,000 displaced.[1]

C. Steenkamp (✉)
Oxford Brookes University, Oxford, UK
e-mail: csteenkamp@brookes.ac.uk

The ubiquity of post-accord violence raises some important questions: *what* forms does the violence take; *who* are responsible for this violence, *why* does violence continue at such high levels and *how* does it affect post-war societies? This chapter will address each of these questions in turn. Firstly, it will identify three types of violence in post-accord contexts: violence with political, economic and social aims. Secondly, the chapter will illustrate how different groups can be responsible for violence and emphasis will be on the role of the state, organised groups, the community and individuals as perpetrators of violence. Thirdly, the chapter will consider the reasons for continuing violence and lastly, it will consider the effects of post-accord violence.

In answering each of these questions, a central theme emerges: that post-accord violence does not stand in isolation from conditions and factors which characterised either the war or the peace. This violence that follows peace accords is shaped by both the previous experience of war, and by the peace process and the implementation of the accords. The chapter will show how the perpetrators of violence can be either inherited from the war, or be the products of the peace process. Equally, the causes of violence are related to conditions caused by war and by peace and the types of violence that characterise post-accord contexts often have their genesis in the wartime society.

For a long time, the academic attention to violence in the aftermath of peace accords focused on single case studies, with El Salvador, Guatemala, Bosnia-Herzegovina, South Africa, Northern Ireland and Israel/Palestine receiving particular attention. Whilst this literature undoubtedly made important contributions to understanding continuing physical insecurity in these particular societies, a more holistic account of post-accord violence across regions and countries—and indeed, across time—only started emerging over the last decade and remains rare.[2] These studies identify the shared causes, manifestations and consequences of post-accord violence, irrespective of geographical location, and emphasise how it is found in almost all post-accord contexts. This literature produces a more nuanced understanding of the dynamics of the post-peace accord period as a distinct, and indeed hugely vulnerable, phase in a conflict or peace process.

The argument in this chapter will be illustrated with evidence from post-accord societies since the end of the Cold War. Civil wars are the most common form of violent conflict in the post-1990 period.[3] Accompanying this trend, there has been a significant increase in the number of peace accords aimed at addressing these conflicts: between 1990 and 2016 more than 1500 peace accords have been signed worldwide.[4] The evidence in this chapter comes from civil wars which have been ended—at least officially or temporarily—by substantive peace accords. Unsurprisingly, this is hugely relevant to the violence discussed in this chapter: the violence takes place in a context where there has been no military victory by one side over the other. Rather, violence takes place in the wake of a peace process which (in most cases) included a process of multi-party negotiations and the reaching of a comprehensive peace accord which addresses not only the cessation of violence, but also tackles at least some of the underlying causes of the conflict. As such, these comprehensive (or substantive) peace accords are different from ceasefire accords—the latter are a type of pre-negotiation accord which is specifically aimed at pausing direct violence and they typically precede negotiations for comprehensive peace accords.[5] Comprehensive peace accords provide a consideration of the political, social and economic dimensions and consequences of the conflict and contain at least some ideas of how to structure the post-war society. Ideally, a comprehensive peace accord provides guidance to restructure and transform society in order to prevent a return to war. Sadly, but not surprising, not all accords become fully implemented and almost half of all peace accords are indeed likely to fail.[6]

THE CONTEXT OF POST-ACCORD VIOLENCE

There are some assumptions and caveats to consider in any discussion of post-accord violence. The term 'post-war' violence implies that this violence happens once the conflict is over. This is problematic because it assumes that all peace accords are somehow inherently fair and offer legitimate and appropriate tools for managing the political divisions which underpinned the conflict in the first place. This is not necessarily the case and peace accords are prone to failure. In the Central African Republic (CAR), for example, the latest in a series of eight peace accords between government and rebel groups were signed in February 2019—after all previous seven accords since the conflict started in 2013 had failed. The previous seven attempts at ending the conflict decisively clearly had little impact.[7] And the prognosis for the eighth accord was not good: just one month later, there were already reports emerging of renewed fighting between insurgent groups.[8]

Peace accords often collapse and presage a return to war, instead of securing long-term political stability, prosperity and physical security for civilians. This raises an important question about whether 'post-war' violence is really taking place in a post-conflict context. To what extent is post-accord violence actually post-war violence, or is it simply a continuation of the violent conflict? It may simply be a gear-shift in the conflict, or be a continuation of old animosities at a community level which have been little affected by an elite-level accord. Post-accord violence may thus, at its core, be little more than a continuation of the struggle for political power. It is therefore more accurate to refer to this violence as post-accord violence rather than using the more optimistic term 'post-war' violence.

Secondly, there is a tendency to uniformly condemn the violence that occurs in the wake of peace accords. It is seen as a 'problem' which needs to be addressed so that it does not derail the political deal. The underlying assumption is that the peace accord is inherently legitimate and that the violence is unwarranted. Most peace accords since the end of the Cold War have been designed, negotiated and implemented in line with the assumptions of Liberal Peacebuilding. Consequently, proponents of the Liberal Peace are likely to see any opposition to the infrastructure of such peace accords as illegitimate.[9] This does not recognise that the perpetrators of post-accord violence may have, in their view, legitimate reasons for rejecting this particular vision of a post-war society that is contained in the accord. Or, in another example that will be discussed later, it ignores the discrepancy between international norms about what constitutes legitimate economic activity (i.e. what is 'crime') versus local permissive norms that may facilitate involvement in the 'illegal' economy. Post-accord violence—as with all violence—is thus further complicated by competing and clashing interpretations surrounding its legitimacy.

In addition, post-accord violence takes place in a context of raised popular expectations about the peace dividend—and this includes popular expectations about increased physical safety. When levels of violent crime, homicide rates and gang wars increase, when armed groups continue to carry out inter-ethnic attacks and the state periodically assassinates its political opponents, it could lead to popular disillusionment—and potentially rejection—of the political deal.

It is important to recognise that patterns of violence vary substantially across post-war societies. Post-civil war Lebanon after the signing of the Ta'if accords in 1998, for example, displayed relatively high levels of political violence, but levels of violent crime remained low.[10] In contrast, in

Liberia after the civil war ended in 2003, post-war violence took the form of violent crime with very low levels of politically motivated violence.[11] There is thus considerable variation across cases and regions in terms of the types, causes and perpetrators of post-accord violence. The following sections will further unpack this diversity in forms of violence.

TYPES OF POST-ACCORD VIOLENCE

This discussion will illustrate how different types of violence which are common to post-accord societies could have political, economic or social goals. It is, of course, entirely possible and likely that one act of violence, such as attacks on returning refugees, could have multiple goals: it could be politically motivated insofar as returning refugees are seen to challenge the political power balance in a town or it could be economically motivated as they put pressure on limited economic resources.

Post-accord violence has political aims when it intends to change the balance of political power in society. Violence can be used at various stages of a peace process, for example, to influence the reaching of an accord, or it could be used to impact on the implementation of the peace accord.

Violence which aims to directly derail or influence the outcomes of a peace process is known as spoiler violence where force is used by 'leaders and parties who believe that peace emerging from negotiations threatens their power, worldview, and interests, and use violence to undermine attempts to achieve it'.[12] Spoiler violence is often used in parallel to peace negotiations and serve political aims by destabilising or manipulating the process of political bargaining and compromise. Spoilers pursue various aims during the negotiations and they could be participants in the peace process (so-called 'inside spoilers') or they could be 'outside' spoilers who have shunned inclusion in the political process.[13] However, the concept of 'spoiling' could also apply to the post-accord phase when groups use violence to explicitly challenge the terms of the accord.

The New Irish Republican Army (IRA) is a good example of a spoiler who rejects the 1998 Good Friday Agreement which ended 30 years of violent civil conflict in Northern Ireland. Since the signing of the accord, there have been a range of so-called dissident republican groups who rejected the accord and the peace process because it does not secure the unification of Northern Ireland with the Republic of Ireland.[14] Since 1998, dissident republican groups have killed several members of the security forces across Northern Ireland.[15] A new dissident group, the New IRA, became particularly prominent in recent years. The New IRA was formed in 2012 and have since been involved in killings, gun and bomb attacks on security forces and vigilante violence against its own community.[16] By 2019, there were fears that the organisation was absorbing other dissident republican groups and posed an increasing danger to political stability in Northern Ireland, particularly in a context of a suspended regional assembly at Stormont and the prospective return of a 'hard' border between Northern Ireland and the Republic of Ireland as part of Brexit negotiations.[17] Dissident republican violence shows how, despite the persistence of a peace accord, spoiler groups (who are unwilling to give up on their original political goals—in this case, a united Ireland) can continue to challenge the political agreement and be a significant source of violence in a post-accord society.

Politically motivated violence can also thwart the implementation of the peace accord. Elections are often enshrined in peace accords and this could provide more opportunities for politically motivated violence. The Nepalese conflict between the government and Maoist insurgents ended with the signing of a comprehensive peace accord in November 2006. Under the terms of the accord, regular elections would take place to choose the national assembly. However, subsequent elections have been marred by the use of violence by different political groupings, not least groups associated with the former Maoist insurgents.[18] More than 10 years after the signing of the accord, elections remained marred by violence such as the 56 violent clashes, explosions and vandalism across Nepal in the election period of 5–7 December 2017.[19] Electoral violence in the aftermath of peace accords can have clear political objectives insofar as it aims to affect the competition for political power (see the chapter by Borzyskowski and Saunders in this volume). This violence can be the result of new post-war conditions, for example, when refugees or those who were internally displaced return to their villages to vote and this creates political tensions in the community.[20] However, it often shares close links with the war: elections provide new opportunities for former political and ethnic rivalries to express themselves (often violently) and the political parties involved are often the same (or closely related to) the protagonists in the war and who have not yet fully disarmed or demobilised.[21]

Another common type of post-accord violence, which is not explicitly politically motivated, is violent crime. Violent crime is closely associated with organised crime and youth gangs, especially in Central America.[22]

Several states in Central America are also post-peace accord societies, with Guatemala, El Salvador, Nicaragua and Honduras engaging in peace processes in the 1990s. Peace has brought neither economic prosperity, nor safety for these post-accord societies. Drug cartels cooperate with street gangs (called *maras*) in the trafficking and selling of illicit drugs.[23] The reasons for the prevalence of the *maras* in Central America include weak state institutions which are unable to deter involvement in crime; a policy of forced repatriation of refugees (some with criminal links to gangs in the US) from cities in the US; a normalisation of violence as a result of the wars and the circulation of small arms in society; high numbers of socio-economically disadvantaged young men who are drawn into gangs; a context of severe poverty and economic inequality and lastly, the geography of the region and its centrality in drug trafficking routes.[24] The competition between cartels and gangs to control the lucrative smuggling routes between narcotics producing countries in Latin America and the main consumer markets in the USA have led to extraordinary high levels of violence. Gang violence—as an example of post-accord violence—is largely economic. It is undoubtedly linked to the social and political factors described above, but gang violence in Central America is largely underpinned by the financial profits from the lucrative trade in narcotics.

It would be wrong to assume that violent crime cannot be highly politically charged, especially so in post-war environments. A good example is the violent attacks on (mostly white) farmers in post-Apartheid South Africa. Since the end of Apartheid in 1994, thousands of (mostly white) farmers and members of their families have been killed on farms and smallholdings in South Africa in what are commonly referred to as 'farm attacks'. The figures are disputed, but in the 10 years between 1993 and 2003, some 1500 people—mostly white Afrikaners—were killed in farm attacks.[25] Some years later, official Police statistics recorded 140 murders and 1069 farm attacks in 2001/2.[26] These rates are extremely low when compared with national homicide rates, but these farm attacks are politically highly charged: Evidence shows that the vast majority of farm attacks are motivated by robbery,[27] but—because the perpetrators are mostly black Africans—white Afrikaners interpret the violence as a form of persecution, ethnic targeting and with the intention to repossess their land.[28] This interpretation of farm attacks holds negative consequences for reconciliation between different groups and it shows how violent crime can carry huge political meaning in post-accord environments.

Another common type of violence that often characterises post-war settings is vigilante violence. This form of socially motivated violence is focused on maintaining or structuring social relations and order rather than to influence configurations of political power or achieve material gain. Since 1996, post-war Guatemala remains one of the most violent countries in the world, with high levels of organised crime and gang-related violence. In the immediate aftermath of the peace accord, between 1999 and 2006, Guatemala's murder rate increased by 120 per cent and reached a shocking 108 murders per 100,000 civilians in the capital city.[29] In response to these rising levels of violent crime and the failure of state responses, communities increasingly took matters into their own hands. Since the 1996 peace accords, vigilante violence in the form of lynching by mobs, known as *linchamientos*, have increased exponentially.[30] These vigilante groups in Guatemala are, in some ways, relics from configurations of violence during the conflict. During the conflict, the Guatemalan state co-opted members of rural communities into paramilitary structures (so-called Civil Self-Defence Patrols) to 'protect' these communities against communist infiltrators.[31] After the conflict, these paramilitary structures persisted in local practices and former paramilitary leaders are often involved in the lynching of alleged criminals.[32] Furthermore, the practice of lynching also stems from the public executions of 'criminals' by both guerrilla and army forces during the war—often by setting victims alight.[33] This illustrates how the conditions and practices entrenched during the war (in this case, the practice of lynching by guerrillas and the army, and the militarisation of rural communities) and conditions from the post-peace period (the rise of violent crime and the state's perceived inability to respond effectively), interact to produce high levels of violence.

This section has shown how the violence that follows on from peace accords can, generally speaking, take three forms based on the motivations that underpin them: it can be classified as political, economic or social violence. In reality, as explained at the start of the section, these distinctions might not be so obvious: an act of violence could hold multiple motivations and serve multiple goals simultaneously. Yet, it is important to recognise that these different types of violence are linked with a variety of factors and perpetrators which either stem from the conflict itself, or are the direct result of the peace process. In many ways, peace accords' failure to deliver the expected or desired political, social or economic benefits to the wider society is responsible for these different forms of violence.

The Perpetrators of Post-accord Violence

The examples discussed above point to the existence of a wide range of perpetrators who carry out violence in post-accord contexts. These range from organised groups to individuals, from the state to the community. It will become clear that the perpetrators of post-accord violence are rarely the products of the peace process, but indeed, often predate and survive the peace accord.

Organised groups who engage in violence include paramilitary groups or criminal gangs, as discussed earlier. These groups may have existed—and indeed, have directly participated in—the conflict, such as the National Liberation Army (ELN) in Colombia which killed 21 people and wounded 68 others in January 2019 alone—just three years after the peace accords between the Revolutionary Armed Forces of Colombia (FARC) and the government.[34] Alternatively, they could be the products of the peace process itself (such as the dissident republican groups in Northern Ireland). Their links to organised crime and their potential to mobilise and recruit local populations make violence by these groups particularly significant after peace accords.

Of course, individuals carry out violence without belonging to a larger economic or political organisation (although they may share the views of such an existing group). They could carry out 'lone wolf' terror attacks, which could be seen as spoiler violence with political motivations.[35] A good example is the assassination of Israeli prime minister Yitzhak Rabin in 1995 (after the Oslo peace accords between the Palestinian Liberation Organisation and the Israeli government) by the Israeli far-right sympathiser Yigal Amir.[36] Individuals can also be opportunistic and engage in violent crime in a context of lowered opportunity costs due to the state's limited law enforcement capacity.

The state is often a major protagonist in the violent conflict, and can continue to be a significant perpetrator of insecurity afterwards. Post-accord states could use violence to assassinate political opponents or suppress political opponents. State violence is usually carried out by the state's own institutions such as the security forces, but it could also employ other groups to carry out violence on its behalf. The state's continued involvement in various forms of violence in post-accord settings is particularly stark in Central America.[37] The Salvadoran state has long been accused of carrying out extrajudicial killings targeted at gangs and other 'antisocial' elements.[38] By 2003 there was evidence that a new generation of state-affiliated death squads have emerged to kill gang members.[39] In Honduras too, death squads aligned to the state were still targeting street children and youth gangs well after the end of the conflict in the late 1980s.[40]

The community also remains a common perpetrator of post-accord violence, as the earlier example of Guatemalan *linchamientos* illustrated. Here violence springs from the community itself, rather than from a (semi) permanent non-state armed group. Vigilante violence often seem spontaneous and reactionary. In South African townships, mob vigilantism has become a feature of daily life in response to high levels of crime and the state's incapacity to respond effectively. Again, however, the 'mob' is not always entirely spontaneous: in South African instances of vigilantism the punishment of crime suspects is often led by local community organisations called 'street committees'.[41] These street committees originated during Apartheid's low intensity conflict to function as sites of local-level democratic decision-making. They became some of the building blocks of the post-Apartheid 'community policing' approach which emphasised the role of community structures in local policing—and which is widely seen as a contributing factor to the prevalence of community-based vigilantism in South Africa.[42] This illustrates how even non-violent community structures which preceded the peace accords can be active in committing violence in its wake.

Another example of the community as a perpetrator of post-accord violence can be found in post-war Bosnia-Herzegovina. Attacks on returning refugees (whose return to villages and towns are provided for in the terms of the accord) by ethnically divergent groups in the community were common in the first few years after the Dayton accords in 1995.[43] For example, when 800 Bosnian Muslims and Croats returned to their former homes in a Serbian controlled town of Doboj in 1996, it led to a violent confrontation involving 1500 Serbs.[44]

Apparently spontaneous community-driven violence can mask involvement by armed organised groups. So-called 'recreational rioting' by youths in Northern Ireland illustrates how seemingly impulsive community-based violence can be closely linked with armed groups. The persistent pattern of rioting between Catholic and Protestant youths on the streets of Northern Irish cities in the summer months, especially, have been labelled 'recreational' as it is seen to be devoid of political motivation and rather, be underpinned by youthful boredom.[45] However, in reality, there is substantial evidence that paramilitary armed groups are often active behind the scenes to direct and manage the communal rioting between youths of opposing communities.[46] The behind-the-scenes involvement of organised armed groups in violence by the community testifies to the central role that these groups continue to play in the daily lives of their communities, despite pressure to disarm and demobilise.

This section has showed how the perpetrators of post-accord violence are varied and range from individual acts of opportunistic low-level crime, to orchestrated campaigns of violence by armed groups, to extrajudicial state killings and seemingly spontaneous mob violence in the community. Many of these perpetrators have originated during the conflict and managed to outlive the peace accords.

THE CAUSES OF POST-ACCORD VIOLENCE

Unsurprisingly, violence that follows peace accords has multiple causes. Many of these causes are related to either the preceding conflict, or the dynamics of the peace process (or both).[47] The timing of post-accord violence is crucial in understanding its causes: this is violence that takes place in the immediate aftermath of (often prolonged) periods of violent conflict. The violence is the result of conditions which have been created during the conflict, as well as conditions associated with the transition from war to peace. It can sometimes be tricky to identify the accurate causes of violence. Berdal[48] points out that economic factors often stimulate post-accord violence, but that these causal conditions can be subordinate to political and ideological factors. It is tempting for policy-makers to simplify the causality of violence by focusing on one economic set of conditions, but this can ignore the complex interaction between political, ideological and economic factors.

Violent crime that is related to organised crime has its underlying causes in the political economy of a particular society. Post-accord environments present conditions which can be highly favourable to organised crime, such as limited law enforcement, high levels of corruption and the availability of resources and networks which can be utilised by organised crime groups. However, these organised crime networks are rarely unique to the post-accord context. Indeed, they are instrumental in determining viability, intensity and longevity of the war itself. The relationship between organised crime and violent conflict has been the subject of a growing body of literature investigating this crime-conflict nexus.[49] Most armed groups are, in one way or another and to varying degrees, involved in the illicit economy during the conflict because it provides them with funds to buy weapons, pay combatants and control populations. Equally, already existing organised crime groups cooperate with political protagonists in a conflict because it provides them with recruits, access to markets and political influence. These illicit economic networks, trafficking routes and corrupt liaisons often persist into the post-accord phase, where they expand and play an even greater role in the ways the state and society function.

Organised crime is closely associated with corruption, and it is worth emphasising how violent conflict can establish corrupt practices which persist once the war has ended. Iraq provides a good example of how corruption, organised crime and conflict interact. Saddam Hussain's regime in Iraq became heavily involved in the shadow economy in an attempt to circumvent international sanctions in the 1980s and 1990s. The state's involvement in such sanction-busting activities created fertile ground for corruption to become endemic.[50] These high levels of corruption have persisted after the 2003 US-led invasion of Iraq and the overthrow of the regime. Le Billon argues that liberal peacebuilding, in particular, is particularly conducive to corruption due to the uncertainties (such as the threat of dismissal and electoral loss) and economic opportunities (such as the availability of imported goods; aid and improved transportation links) which accompany the transition from war to peace.[51] Ex-combatants could also view their newly acquired appointments in the civil service (and the accompanying opportunities to supplement their salaries) as reward for their previous sacrifices. In post-Saddam Iraq, officials in the Health Ministry cooperated with organised crime syndicates to pilfer medical supplies and drugs intended for hospitals at every stage of the supply chain.[52] In addition, ordinary civilians often have little choice but to participate in these shadow economies and the corrupt relationships which underpin them, in order to secure everyday goods and services. Incidentally, this may provide caution against hasty post-war anti-corruption policies: corruption and the illegal economy with which it co-exists, provides local populations with a level of political, social and economic security and stability in uncertain times. Radical interventions to tackle corruption—in the absence of viable economic alternative livelihoods—may leave sections of the population particularly vulnerable.[53]

The economic conditions which underpin crime and violence may have been inherited from the conflict, but could also be the result of a particular model of peacebuilding. Low levels of economic development and high levels of unemployment make involvement in criminal groups or activities an attractive option for civilians. Neoliberal economic reforms, another key component of the Liberal Peace paradigm, are notorious for exacerbating existing economic cleavages and inequalities and increasing the economic burden on the most vulnerable sections of society.[54] Peacebuilding and the post-war period also create new opportunities and spaces for illegal economic activity due to improvements in the import and export of goods, greater freedom of movement and limited institutional capacity to curb crime. If peace accords are unable to provide an improvement in the economic lives of civilians, it could push them towards the illegal economy to make ends meet—especially when such activity is not viewed as being 'illicit' (i.e. not in conflict with local custom or morality).[55]

A major contributing factor in post-accord violence is the inability and ineffectiveness of state institutions in societies emerging from violent conflict. There is an absence of state institutions that can inhibit and regulate the use of force, whilst providing security and stability to its citizens.[56] This context of limited state capacity in delivering social, political and economic good and services provides fertile ground for crime and violence. Democratisation and its associated freedoms and rights (which are often part of the Liberal Peace package) create new spaces and freedom for organised crime and other illegal and violent actors to operate with relative impunity.[57] There is often a push for multi-party competitive elections (a key component of liberal democracy) before sufficient levels of security, political stability or institutional capacity have been established. This can lead to further lawlessness and corruption as organised criminal groups use the institutional vacuum to form alliances with new political incumbents.[58] An ineffective justice system can lead to the increased popularity of vigilante justice where civilians become perpetrators of violence themselves.[59]

Security sector reform (SSR) and a downscaling of the security services often take place under the terms of the peace accord, but this can significantly weaken the post-accord state's ability to respond to violent crime. In Guatemala, for example, the reduction of the security services' abilities and mission was a necessary concession to get the leftist opposition groups to the negotiating table. The resulting large number of influential ex-soldiers with few economic prospects and the incompetence of the remaining security apparatus undoubtedly contributed to the country's alarmingly high post-accord violent crime rates.[60]

A cultural permissiveness towards the use of violence can also contribute to the use of violence, both during the conflict and afterwards. A so-called culture of violence (the social norms and values which allow and justify the use of violence) is both a result of prolonged exposure to violence and a cause of further violence.[61] Various factors, which are closely associated with armed conflict, can encourage a culture of violence: a hyper-inflated masculinity is often promoted during conflict in order to foster a warrior culture; and states and non-state armed groups justify, reward and encourage the use of violence by civilians and against civilians. As society becomes accustomed to the widespread use of violence during a protracted civil war, violence becomes a legitimate and acceptable response to solving everyday conflicts. A culture of violence is thus both a consequence and a necessary condition of intrastate armed conflict.[62] This impact lingers on after the war: Civilians became desensitised to violence and, because norms and values are slow to change, this permissive context continues into the post-accord society.

However, much more work still needs to be done on the manifestations and causes of a culture of violence. Berdal,[63] for example, points out that some countries do not exhibit high levels of post-war violence across the board, despite the brutality of the previous conflict. This suggests that the link between prolonged exposure to violence and the use of violence might not be as automatic as the culture of violence literature implies.

A last obvious cause of violence after peace agreements is the availability of weapons and the presence of poorly demobilised ex-combatants in society. The link between post-war violence and wartime violence is particularly stark here: it is common knowledge that Disarmament, Demobilisation and Reintegration (DDR) projects are rarely successful in completely removing all weapons from society and helping combatants make the transition back to civilian life.[64] Weapons which fuelled the conflict often remain in circulation after the conflict and are used in crimes committed in the post-war period. Equally, the release of large numbers of (mostly) young men who are ill-prepared for civilian life into communities can lead to increased criminal and political violence.[65] Ex-combatants might also harbour particular expectations about the peace dividend, which could remain unmet. In East Timor the struggle against

Indonesian occupation ended when independence was granted in 1999, but the state's failure to provide the expected support and employment to war veterans was a major cause of the violent riots that rocked Dili in December 2004.[66] Large numbers of frustrated ex-combatants in a postwar society provide fertile ground for continuing political and criminal violence. The inadequate demilitarisation of wartime special military and security forces means that these state-affiliated organisations outlive the peace process and can become increasingly involved in organised crime and violence after the war.[67]

The causes of violence that follow in the wake of peace accords are varied, but they tend to be closely connected to the violent conflict. The availability of weapons, the presence of large numbers of ex-combatants, adverse economic conditions, weak state institutions and the presence of organised crime groups are all factors and conditions which predate the peace process. However, there are certain causes of post-accord violence which are directly related to the peace accords: for example, the promotion of a neoliberal economic agenda which either leave unjust structures and processes in place, or further exacerbate poverty and economic inequality. Either outcome can lead to popular frustration with the 'peace'.

The Implications of Post-accord Violence

Unsurprisingly, post-accord violence poses many risks to states and societies emerging from conflict. Firstly, it could be a sign that the conflict is not really finished and that the peace process is doomed to failure. Violence is also indicative of the failure of peace accords to reverse patterns of socio-economic decline.

Secondly, it places significant pressure on the state to respond to violence by apprehending and prosecuting perpetrators at a time when policing and defence budgets are under pressure, and judicial reforms are perhaps beginning to take place and police forces are undergoing significant restructuring processes. States are under pressure to abandon longer term development projects in favour of dramatic immediate interventions in crime, which addresses the symptoms rather than the causes of violent crime. This could lead to popular support for those parties which advocate a rejection of the peace deal and a return to conflict. It could also lead to support for groups who are seen to resist physical insecurity by using violence themselves, as evident from the examples of vigilante violence. High levels of insecurity can lead to popular calls for the death penalty, a restriction on human rights and the introduction of draconian measures to 'fight crime'. In El Salvador, for example, post-accord violence dominates electoral politics and political parties promote populist policies of crime management. The hugely popular *Mano Dura* (meaning 'strong-handed') crime policy in El Salvador encapsulated an iron-fisted approach to crime management, including giving the military a role in policing crime and suspending due process of law in certain cases.[68] This emphasis on crime management in policymaking also happens at the expense of policies and debates which address other urgent issues facing the post-accord society.

Thirdly, continued post-accord violence further embeds violent and armed groups in the structures and daily lives of communities. This has a spiral effect where violence and insecurity make civilians more reliant on violent entrepreneurs in their quest for protection, who in turn, have more opportunities for further violence.

Fourth, post-accord violence affects social capital. Social capital refers to the bonds of trust and networks which exist between individuals and groups in a society and which is essential for community development and cohesion.[69] War generally destroys social capital (or is the consequence of low levels of social capital—particularly between groups in society), but it is extremely sought-after for societies who engage in reconciliation and social reconstruction activities.[70] Continuing high levels of violence after war can inhibit the building of trust and cooperation between previously antagonistic groups in society. The examples of farm attacks in South Africa are a good illustration of how post-accord violence can cause a particular ethnic group to consider themselves as being deliberately selected as targets, thus creating distrust and fear towards other groups in society.

Conclusion

Post-accord violence is common in societies that emerge from prolonged period of war. This chapter has shown how it often has its genesis in the conditions created by the war—and, ironically, by the conditions of the peace. Violence that occurs after peace accords have been signed is thus the product of both the preceding conflict and the peace process. This is particularly evident in *who* carried out the violence as the main protagonists during the conflicts often survive the conflict and continue their use of violence afterwards—possibly with an ostensibly different purpose. The *causes* of continuing violence are often similar to the factors which caused the war in the first place. Equally, the perpetrators of violence often pursue similar aims with their use of violence before and after the peace accord.

Post-accord violence rarely appears out of the blue. It is more likely to be a continuation of the use of force by perpetrators of violence during the conflict who have managed to survive the peace process. These actors can continue using violence, often in pursuit of the same objectives and for the same reasons as before. This is not to say that the processes of peacebuilding are not influential in causing and determining the nature of post-accord violence—far from it. Peace processes and the implementation of peace accords create novel conditions and generate new actors which are also conducive to violence. The Liberal Peace, in particular, has much to answer for in this regard: it promotes neo-liberal economic policies which nurture violent and organised crime and promotes a liberal democracy which encourages premature elections in unstable societies. Peacebuilding should not be a blunt instrument with which we tackle post-accord violence. Strategies aimed at reducing violence should be adapted to its specific manifestations and conditions and policymakers may have to be pragmatic in their approach to violence. This may mean collaborating—in the short term, at least—with alternative structures and groups in society which serve the social, political and economic needs of local populations. For example, organised crime groups are well known to play an important role in the daily life and survival of communities. Rather than adopting harsh anti-corruption and anti-crime strategies which would strip local populations of the only (however imperfect) safety net they have, it might be more effective to explore ways in which such forms and the providers of non-state governance could be incorporated into peacebuilding efforts. Over the longer term, though, it remains imperative that peacebuilding addresses the root causes of post-accord violence and find ways to transform the actors who perpetuate this violence.

In the end, continuing high levels of violence after war and the inability of the state to respond effectively can lead to a popular disaffection with the peace dividend. It raises questions about the quality of peace that followed the peace accord when high levels of physical insecurity persist: if peace is not the absence of direct violence, then what is it? This continued physical insecurity and its various links to the previous conflict also illustrates the impotence of many peace accords to translate into positive change in the social, economic and political fortunes of civilians.

Notes

1. Casey, N. (2019) 'Colombia's Peace Deal Promised a New Era: So Why Are These Rebels Rearming?' *New York Times*, 17 May. Available at https://www.nytimes.com/2019/05/17/world/americas/colombia-farc-peace-deal.html (accessed 12 June 2019).
2. Examples include Boyle, M.J. (2014) *Violence After War: Explaining Instability in Post-Conflict States* (Baltimore: JHU Press); Darby, J. (ed.) (2006) *Violence and Reconstruction* (Notre Dame: Notre Dame University); Steenkamp, C. (2014) *Violent Societies: Networks of Violence in Civil War and Peace* (Basingstoke: Palgrave); Suhrke, A., and Berdal, Mats (eds.) (2012) *The Peace in Between: Post-War Violence and Peacebuilding* (Abingdon: Routledge).
3. Allansson, M., Melander, E., and Themnér, L. (2017) Organized Violence, 1989–2016. *Journal of Peace Research*, 54(4), pp. 574–587.
4. *Peace Agreements Database*. (2019) Edinburgh University. Available at https://www.peaceagreements.org/ (accessed 10 June 2019).
5. Bell, C. (2003) *Peace Agreements and Human Rights* (Oxford: Oxford University Press), p. 21.
6. Högbladh, S. (2011) Peace Agreements 1975–2011-Updating the UCDP Peace Agreement Dataset. *States in Armed Conflict*, 55, p. 51.
7. Diatta, M. (2019) 'Will the Latest Central African Republic Peace Deal Hold?', *ISS Today*, 25 February. Available at https://issafrica.org/iss-today/will-the-latest-central-african-republic-peace-deal-hold (accessed 10 June 2019).
8. Mudge, L. (2019) 'Just One Month in, Optimism About CAR's Peace Deal Is Fading', *Human Rights Watch*, 19 March. Available at https://www.hrw.org/news/2019/03/19/just-one-month-optimism-around-cars-peace-deal-fading (accessed 12 June 2019).

9. Newman, E., and Richmond, O.P. (2006) *The Impact of Spoilers on Peace Processes and Peacebuilding*. Policy Brief no. 2 (Tokyo: United Nations University), p. 103.
10. Knudsen, A., and N. Yassin. (2012) 'Political Violence in Post-Civil War Lebanon', in Suhrke, A., and Berdal, M. (eds.). *The Peace in Between: Post-War Violence and Peacebuilding* (Abingdon: Routledge). The authors argue that patterns of political violence in Lebanon have changed over the course of the conflict and post-accord period, for example, with much of the inter-ethnic violence during the war making way for political assassinations in the post-accord period.
11. Wimpelmann Chaudhary, T. (2012) in Suhrke, A., and Berdal, M. (eds.). *The Peace in Between: Post-War Violence and Peacebuilding* (Abingdon: Routledge).
12. Stedman, S.J. (1997) Spoiler Problems in Peace Processes. *International Security*, 22(2), p. 5.
13. Stedman, S.J. (1997) Spoiler Problems in Peace Processes. *International Security*, 22(2), pp. 5–53.
14. Tonge, J. (2014) A Campaign Without End?: 'Dissident' Republican Violence in Northern Ireland. *Political Insight*, 5(1), pp. 14–17; Horgan, J., and Morrison, J.F. (2011) Here to Stay? The Rising Threat of Violent Dissident Republicanism in Northern Ireland. *Terrorism and Political Violence*, 23(4), pp. 642–669; Morrison, J.F., and Horgan, J. (2016) Reloading the Armalite? Victims and Targets of Violent Dissident Irish Republicanism, 2007–2015. *Terrorism and Political Violence*, 28(3), pp. 576–597.
15. Tonge, J. (2014) A Campaign Without End?: 'Dissident' Republican Violence in Northern Ireland. *Political Insight*, 5(1), pp. 14–17.
16. Moriarty, G. (2019) 'Who Are the New IRA and What Have They Done?', *Irish Times*, 23 April. Available at https://www.irishtimes.com/news/ireland/irish-news/who-are-the-new-ira-and-what-have-they-done-1.3869569 (accessed 15 June 2019).
17. *The Week*. (2019) 'What Is the New IRA and How Much Danger Does It Pose?', 23 April. Available at https://www.theweek.co.uk/72541/what-is-the-new-ira-and-how-dangerous-is-it (accessed 15 June 2019).

18. Joshi, M. (2014) Post-accord Political Violence, Elections, and Peace Processes: Evidence from Nepal. *Civil Wars*, *16*(3), pp. 276–299.
19. Nepal Monitor. (2017) Fact Sheet: Electoral Violence and Contestation During Nepal's Second Phase—House of Representative and Provincial Assembly Elections. Available at https://www.nepalmonitor.org/blog/2017/12/10/fact-sheet-nepals-second-phase-house-of-representative-and-provincial-assembly-elections/ (accessed 10 January 2019).
20. Höglund, K. (2008) 'Violence in War-to-Democracy Transitions', in Jarstad, A.K. and Sisk, T.D. (eds.). *From War to Democracy: Dilemmas of Peacebuilding* (Cambridge: Cambridge University Press), p. 85; Höglund, K. (2009) Electoral Violence in Conflict-Ridden Societies: Concepts, Causes, and Consequences. *Terrorism and Political Violence*, *21*(3), pp. 412–427.
21. Dunning, T. (2011) Fighting and Voting: Violent Conflict and Electoral Politics. *Journal of Conflict Resolution*, *55*(3), pp. 327–339.
22. Bruneau, T., Dammert, L., and Skinner, E. (2011) *Maras: Gang Violence and Security in Central America* (Austin: University of Texas Press); Frühling, H.H., Tulchin, J.S., and Golding, H. (eds.). (2003) *Crime and Violence in Latin America: Citizen Security, Democracy, and the State* (Washington, DC: Woodrow Wilson Center Press).
23. Pérez, O.J. (2013) Gang Violence and Insecurity in Contemporary Central America. *Bulletin of Latin American Research*, *32*(s1), p. 225; Levenson, D.T. (2013) 'What Happened to the Revolution? Guatemala City's *Maras* from Life to Death', in McAllister, C., and Nelson, D.M. (eds.). *War by Other Means: Aftermath in Post-Genocide Guatemala* (Durham, NC: Duke University Press).
24. Bruneau, T., Dammert, L., and Skinner, E. (2011) *Maras: Gang Violence and Security in Central America* (Austin: University of Texas Press), pp. 8–10; Pérez, O.J. (2013) Gang Violence and Insecurity in Contemporary Central America. *Bulletin of Latin American Research*, *32*(s1), pp. 222–227.
25. Carroll, R. (2003) 'South African Farm Attacks "Not Racial"', *The Guardian*, 26 September. Available at https://www.theguardian.com/world/2003/sep/26/southafrica.rorycarroll (accessed 10 June 2019).

26. This was the year when police statistics started recording farm attacks as a separate category of violent crime. More information can be found in Burger, J. (2018) *Policy Brief: Violence Crime on Farms and Smallholdings in South Africa.* Pretoria: Institute for Security Studies. Available online at https://issafrica.s3.amazonaws.com/site/uploads/pb115-4.pdf (accessed 10 June 2019), p. 4.
27. Carroll, R. (2003) 'South African Farm Attacks "Not Racial"', *The Guardian*, 26 September. Available at https://www.theguardian.com/world/2003/sep/26/southafrica.rorycarroll (accessed 10 June 2019).
28. Chothia, F. (2018) 'South Africa: The Groups Playing on the Fears of a "White Genocide"', *BBC News*, 1 September. Available at https://www.bbc.co.uk/news/world-africa-45336840 (accessed 10 June 2019); Verwey, C., and Quayle, M. (2012) Whiteness, Racism, and Afrikaner Identity in Post-Apartheid South Africa. *African Affairs, 111*(445), pp. 551–575.
29. Cited in Brands, H. (2011) Crime, Irregular Warfare, and Institutional Failure in Latin America: Guatemala as a Case Study. *Studies in Conflict & Terrorism, 34*(3), p. 231.
30. Handy, J. (2004) Chicken Thieves, Witches, and Judges: Vigilante Justice and Customary Law in Guatemala. *Journal of Latin American Studies, 36*(3), pp. 533–561; Weston, G. (2019) *Guatemalan Vigilantism and the Global (Re)Production of Collective Violence: A Tale of Two Lynchings* (Abingdon: Routledge); Núñez, D. (2017) 'There Are No Lynchings Here', in Santamaría, Gema, and Carey, David (eds.). *Violence and Crime in Latin America: Representations and Politics* (University of Oklahoma); Burrell, J. (2013) 'After Lynching', in McAllister, C., and Nelson, D.M. (eds.). *War by Other Means: Aftermath in Post-Genocide Guatemala* (Duke University Press).
31. Esparza, M. (2017) *Silenced Communities: Legacies of Militarization and Militarism in a Rural Guatemalan Town* (New York: Berghahn Books), pp. 47–67.
32. Godoy, A.S. (2002) Lynchings and the Democratization of Terror in Postwar Guatemala: Implications for Human Rights. *Human Rights Quarterly, 24*(3), pp. 648–649; Weston, G. (2019) *Guatemalan Vigilantism and the Global (Re)Production of Collective Violence: A Tale of Two Lynchings* (Abingdon: Routledge).

33. Godoy, A.S. (2002) Lynchings and the Democratization of Terror in Postwar Guatemala: Implications for Human Rights. *Human Rights Quarterly*, *24*(3), p. 653.
34. Casey, N. (2019) 'Colombia's Peace Deal Promised a New Era. So Why Are These Rebels Rearming?' *New York Times*, 17 May. Available at https://www.nytimes.com/2019/05/17/world/americas/colombia-farc-peace-deal.html (accessed 12 June 2019); Gonzålez, J., and Casey, N. (2019) 'Colombia Car Bombing Suspect Belonged to Rebel Group, Government Says', *The New York Times*, 18 January. Available at https://www.nytimes.com/2019/01/18/world/americas/atentado-bogota-colombia-bombing-eln.html (accessed 12 June 2019).
35. Excellent overviews of the motivations and manifestations of lone-wolf terrorism can be found in Spaaij, R. (2010) The Enigma of Lone Wolf Terrorism: An Assessment. *Studies in Conflict & Terrorism*, *33*(9), pp. 854–870; Spaaij, R. (2011) *Understanding Lone Wolf Terrorism: Global Patterns, Motivations and Prevention* (Springer Science & Business Media).
36. Spaaij, R. (2010) The Enigma of Lone Wolf Terrorism: An Assessment. *Studies in Conflict & Terrorism*, *33*(9), p. 862.
37. Cruz, J.M. (2016) State and Criminal Violence in Latin America. *Crime, Law and Social Change*, *66*(4), pp. 375–396.
38. Lakhani, N. (2017) 'We Fear Soldiers More Than Gangsters': El Salvador's 'Iron Fist' Policy Turns Deadly', *The Guardian*, 6 Febuary. Available at https://www.theguardian.com/world/2017/feb/06/el-salvador-gangs-police-violence-distrito-italia (accessed 12 June 2019); Hume, M. (2007) Mano Dura: El Salvador Responds to Gangs. *Development in Practice*, *17*(6), pp. 739–751.
39. Hume, M. (2007) Mano Dura: El Salvador Responds to Gangs. *Development in Practice*, *17*(6), p. 745; Cruz, J.M. (2011) Criminal Violence and Democratization in Central America: The Survival of the Violent State. *Latin American Politics and Society*, *53*(4), p. 17.
40. In Cruz, J.M. (2011) Criminal Violence and Democratization in Central America: The Survival of the Violent State. *Latin American Politics and Society*, *53*(4), p. 5.
41. Singh, A.M. (2016) *Policing and Crime Control in Post-Apartheid South Africa* (London: Routledge). Introduction.

42. Super, G.J. (2016) Punishment, Violence, and Grassroots Democracy in South Africa—The Politics of Populist Punitiveness. *Punishment & Society, 18*(3), pp. 325–345.
43. Berdal, M., Collantes-Celador, G., and Zupcevic Buzadzic, M. (2012) 'Post-War Violence in Bosnia and Herzegovina', in Suhrke, A., and Berdal, Mats (eds.). *The Peace in Between: Post-War Violence and Peacebuilding* (Abingdon: Routledge), p. 81.
44. Human Rights Watch. (1997) Human Rights Watch World Report 1997—Bosnia and Herzegovina, 1 January 1997. Available at: https://www.refworld.org/docid/3ae6a8ab0.html (accessed 18 June 2019).
45. Jarman, N., and O'Halloran, C. (2001) Recreational Rioting: Young People, Interface Areas and Violence. *Child Care in Practice, 7*(1), pp. 2–16.
46. Leonard, M. (2010) What's Recreational About 'Recreational Rioting'? Children on the Streets in Belfast. *Children & Society, 24*(1), p. 46.
47. Steenkamp, C. (2011) In the Shadows of War and Peace: Making Sense of Violence After Peace Accords. *Conflict, Security & Development, 11*(3), pp. 357–383.
48. Berdal, M. (2012) 'Reflections on Post-War Violence and Peacebuilding', in Suhrke, A., and Berdal, Mats (eds.). *The Peace in Between: Post-War Violence and Peacebuilding* (Abingdon: Routledge), p. 319.
49. De Boer, J., and Bosetti, L. (2015) The Crime-Conflict 'Nexus': State of the Evidence. *Occasional Paper*, 5.
50. Pugh, M. (2004) Rubbing Salt into War Wounds: Shadow Economies and Peacebuilding in Bosnia and Kosovo. *Problems of Post-Communism, 51*(3), p. 54; Le Billon, P. (2008) Corrupting Peace? Peacebuilding and Post-Conflict Corruption. *International Peacekeeping, 15*(3), pp. 344–361.
51. Le Billon, P. (2008) Corrupting Peace? Peacebuilding and Post-Conflict Corruption. *International Peacekeeping, 15*(3), p. 346.
52. Looney, R.E. (2008) Reconstruction and Peacebuilding Under Extreme Adversity: The Problem of Pervasive Corruption in Iraq. *International Peacekeeping, 15*(3), p. 427.
53. Le Billon, P. (2008) Corrupting Peace? Peacebuilding and Post-Conflict Corruption. *International Peacekeeping, 15*(3), p. 355.

54. Howarth, K. (2014) Connecting the Dots: Liberal Peace and Post-Conflict Violence and Crime. *Progress in Development Studies*, *14*(3), pp. 261–273; Pugh, M., Cooper, N., and Turner, M. eds. (2016) *Whose Peace? Critical Perspectives on the Political Economy of Peacebuilding* (Basingstoke: Palgrave Macmillan).
55. Le Billon, P. (2008) Corrupting Peace? Peacebuilding and Post-Conflict Corruption. *International Peacekeeping*, *15*(3), p. 355.
56. Berdal, M. (2012) 'Reflections on Post-War Violence and Peacebuilding', in Suhrke, A., and Berdal, Mats (eds.). *The Peace in Between: Post-War Violence and Peacebuilding* (Abingdon: Routledge), p. 314.
57. Call, C. (2003) Democratisation, War and State-Building: Constructing the Rule of Law in El Salvador. *Journal of Latin American Studies*, *35*, pp. 827–862.
58. Cockayne, J. (2017) Can Organised Crime Shape Post-War Transitions? Evidence from Sicily. *Third World Thematics: A TWQ Journal*, p. 5.
59. Suhrke, A. (2012) 'The Peace in Between', in Suhrke, A., and Berdal, M. (eds). *The Peace in Between: Post-War Violence and Peacebuilding* (Abingdon: Routledge), p. 19.
60. Brands, H. (2011) Crime, Irregular Warfare, and Institutional Failure in Latin America: Guatemala as a Case Study. *Studies in Conflict & Terrorism*, *34*(3), p. 232; Richani, 2010, p. 435.
61. Steenkamp, C. (2005) The Legacy of War: Conceptualizing a 'Culture of Violence' to Explain Violence After Peace Accords. *The Round Table*, *94*(379), pp. 253–267; Waldmann, P. (2007) 'Is There a Culture of Violence in Colombia?' *Terrorism and Political Violence*, 19, pp. 593–609; Steenkamp, C. (2014) *Violent Societies: Networks of Violence in Civil War and Peace* (Basingstoke: Palgrave), see Chapter 5.
62. Steenkamp, C. (2014) *Violent Societies: Networks of Violence in Civil War and Peace* (Basingstoke: Palgrave), p. 140.
63. Berdal, M. (2012) 'Reflections on Post-War Violence and Peacebuilding', in Suhrke, A., and Berdal, Mats (eds.). *The Peace in Between: Post-War Violence and Peacebuilding* (Abingdon: Routledge), p. 313.
64. Giustozzi, A. (ed.) (2016) *Post-Conflict Disarmament, Demobilization and Reintegration: Bringing State-Building Back in*

(Abingdon: Routledge); Molloy, D. (2017) *Disarmament, Demobilization, and Reintegration: Theory and Practice* (Boulder: Kumarian Press), p. 1.
65. Berdal, M. (2012) 'Reflections on Post-War Violence and Peacebuilding', in Suhrke, A., and Berdal, Mats (eds.). *The Peace in Between: Post-War Violence and Peacebuilding* (Abingdon: Routledge), p. 316.
66. Babo-Soares, D. (2012) 'Conflict and Violence in Post-Independence East Timor', in Suhrke, A., and Berdal, Mats (eds.). *The Peace in Between: Post-War Violence and Peacebuilding* (Abingdon: Routledge), p. 217.
67. Berdal, M. (2012) 'Reflections on Post-War Violence and Peacebuilding', in Suhrke, A., and Berdal, Mats (eds.). *The Peace in Between: Post-War Violence and Peacebuilding* (Abingdon: Routledge), p. 317.
68. Holland, A.C. (2013) Right on Crime? Conservative Party Politics and 'Mano Dura' Policies in El Salvador. *Latin American Research Review*, pp. 44–67.
69. Putnam, R.D. (2001) *Bowling Alone: The Collapse and Revival of American Community* (New York: Simon and Schuster).
70. Cox, M. (ed.) (2008) *Social Capital and Peace-Building: Creating and Resolving Conflict with Trust and Social Networks* (Abingdon: Routledge).

BIBLIOGRAPHY

Allansson, M., Melander, E., and Themnér, L. (2017). Organized Violence, 1989–2016. *Journal of Peace Research*, 54(4), 574–587.
Babo-Soares, D. (2012). 'Conflict and Violence in Post-Independence East Timor', in Suhrke, A., and Berdal, Mats (eds.). *The Peace in Between: Post-War Violence and Peacebuilding* (Abingdon: Routledge).
Bell, C. (2003). *Peace Agreements and Human Rights* (Oxford: Oxford University Press).
Berdal, M. (2012). 'Reflections on Post-War Violence and Peacebuilding', in Suhrke, A., and Berdal, Mats (eds.). *The Peace in Between: Post-War Violence and Peacebuilding* (Abingdon: Routledge).
Berdal, M., Collantes-Celador, G., and Zupcevic Buzadzic, M. (2012). 'Post-War Violence in Bosnia and Herzegovina', in Suhrke, A., and Berdal, Mats

(eds.). *The Peace in Between: Post-War Violence and Peacebuilding* (Abingdon: Routledge).

Boyle, M.J. (2014). *Violence After War: Explaining Instability in Post-Conflict States*. (Baltimore: JHU Press).

Brands, H. (2011). Crime, Irregular Warfare, and Institutional Failure in Latin America: Guatemala as a Case Study. *Studies in Conflict & Terrorism*, 34(3), 228–247.

Bruneau, T., Dammert, L., and Skinner, E. (2011). *Maras: Gang Violence and Security in Central America* (Austin: University of Texas Press).

Burger, J. (2018). *Policy Brief: Violence Crime on Farms and Smallholdings in South Africa*. Pretoria: Institute for Security Studies. Available online at https://issafrica.s3.amazonaws.com/site/uploads/pb115-4.pdf (accessed 10 June 2019).

Burrell, J. (2013). 'After Lynching', in McAllister, C., and Nelson, D.M. (eds.). *War by Other Means: Aftermath in Post-Genocide Guatemala*. (Durham, NC: Duke University Press).

Call, C. (2003). Democratisation, War and State-Building: Constructing the Rule of Law in El Salvador. *Journal of Latin American Studies*, 35, 827–862.

Carroll, R. (2003). 'South African Farm Attacks "Not Racial"', *The Guardian*, 26 September. Available at https://www.theguardian.com/world/2003/sep/26/southafrica.rorycarroll (accessed 10 June 2019).

Casey, N. (2019). 'Colombia's Peace Deal Promised a New Era: So Why Are These Rebels Rearming?' *New York Times*, 17 May. Available at https://www.nytimes.com/2019/05/17/world/americas/colombia-farc-peace-deal.html (accessed 12 June 2019).

Chothia, F. (2018). 'South Africa: The Groups Playing on the Fears of a "White Genocide"', *BBC News*, 1 September. Available at https://www.bbc.co.uk/news/world-africa-45336840 (accessed 10 June 2019).

Cockayne, J. (2017). Can Organised Crime Shape Post-War Transitions? Evidence from Sicily. *Third World Thematics: A TWQ Journal*, 1–19.

Cox, M. (ed.). (2008). *Social Capital and Peace-Building: Creating and Resolving Conflict with Trust and Social Networks* (Abingdon: Routledge).

Cruz, J.M. (2011). Criminal Violence and Democratization in Central America: The Survival of the Violent State. *Latin American Politics and Society*, 53(4), 1–33.

Darby, J. (ed.) (2006). *Violence and Reconstruction* (Notre Dame: Notre Dame University).

De Boer, J., and Bosetti, L. (2015). The Crime-Conflict 'Nexus': State of the Evidence. *Occasional Paper*, 5. (Tokyo: United Nations University Centre for Policy Research).

Diatta, M. (2019). 'Will the Latest Central African Republic Peace Deal Hold?' *ISS Today*, 25 February. Available at https://issafrica.org/iss-today/will-the-latest-central-african-republic-peace-deal-hold (accessed 10 June 2019).

Dunning, T. (2011). Fighting and Voting: Violent Conflict and Electoral Politics. *Journal of Conflict Resolution*, 55(3), 327–339.

Esparza, M. (2017). *Silenced Communities: Legacies of Militarization and Militarism in a Rural Guatemalan Town* (New York: Berghahn Books).

Frühling, H.H., Tulchin, J.S., and Golding, H. (eds.). (2003). *Crime and Violence in Latin America: Citizen Security, Democracy, and the State* (Washington, DC: Woodrow Wilson Center Press).

Giustozzi, A. (ed.). (2016). *Post-Conflict Disarmament, Demobilization and Reintegration: Bringing State-Building Back in.* (Abingdon: Routledge).

Godoy, A.S. (2002). Lynchings and the Democratization of Terror in Postwar Guatemala: Implications for Human Rights. *Human Rights Quarterly*, 24(3), 640–661.

Gonzålez, J., and Casey, N. (2019). 'Colombia Car Bombing Suspect Belonged to Rebel Group, Government Says', *The New York Times*, 18 January. Available at https://www.nytimes.com/2019/01/18/world/americas/atentado-bogota-colombia-bombing-eln.html (accessed 12 June 2019).

Handy, J. (2004). Chicken Thieves, Witches, and Judges: Vigilante Justice and Customary Law in Guatemala. *Journal of Latin American Studies*, 36(3), 533–561.

Högbladh, S. (2011). Peace Agreements 1975–2011-Updating the UCDP Peace Agreement Dataset. *States in Armed Conflict*, 55, 85–105.

Höglund, K. (2009). Electoral Violence in Conflict-Ridden Societies: Concepts, Causes, and Consequences. *Terrorism and Political Violence*, 21(3), 412–427.

Holland, A.C. (2013). Right on Crime? Conservative Party Politics and "Mano Dura" Policies in El Salvador. *Latin American Research Review*, 44–67.

Horgan, J., and Morrison, J.F. (2011). Here to Stay? The Rising Threat of Violent Dissident Republicanism in Northern Ireland. *Terrorism and Political Violence*, 23(4), 642–669.

Howarth, K. (2014). Connecting the Dots: Liberal Peace and Post-Conflict Violence and Crime. *Progress in Development Studies*, 14(3), 261–273.

Human Rights Watch. (1997). Human Rights Watch World Report 1997—Bosnia and Herzegovina, 1 January 1997. Available at: https://www.refworld.org/docid/3ae6a8ab0.html (accessed 18 June 2019).

Hume, M. (2007). Mano Dura: El Salvador Responds to Gangs. *Development in Practice*, 17(6), 739–751.

Jarman, N., and O'Halloran, C. (2001). Recreational Rioting: Young People, Interface Areas and Violence. *Child Care in Practice*, 7(1), 2–16.

Jarstad, A.K., and Sisk, T.D. (eds.). (2008). *From War to Democracy: Dilemmas of Peacebuilding* (Cambridge: Cambridge University Press).

Joshi, M. (2014). Post-Accord Political Violence, Elections, and Peace Processes: Evidence from Nepal. *Civil Wars*, *16*(3), 276–299.

Knudsen, A., and Yassin, N. (2012). 'Political Violence in Post-Civil War Lebanon', in Suhrke, A., and Berdal, M. (eds.). *The Peace in Between: Post-War Violence and Peacebuilding* (Abingdon: Routledge).

Lakhani, N. (2017). 'We Fear Soldiers More Than Gangsters': El Salvador's 'Iron Fist' Policy Turns Deadly', *The Guardian*, 6 Feburary. Available at https://www.theguardian.com/world/2017/feb/06/el-salvador-gangs-police-violence-distrito-italia (accessed 12 June 2019).

Le Billon, P. (2008). Corrupting Peace? Peacebuilding and Post-Conflict Corruption. *International Peacekeeping*, *15*(3), 344–361.

Leonard, M. (2010). What's Recreational About 'Recreational Rioting'? Children on the Streets in Belfast. *Children & Society*, *24*(1), 38–49.

Levenson, D.T. (2013). 'What Happened to the Revolution? Guatemala City's *Maras* from Life to Death', in McAllister, C., and Nelson, D.M. (eds.). *War by Other Means: Aftermath in Post-Genocide Guatemala* (Duke University Press).

Looney, R.E. (2008). Reconstruction and Peacebuilding Under Extreme Adversity: The Problem of Pervasive Corruption in Iraq. *International Peacekeeping*, *15*(3), 424–440.

Molloy, D. (2017). *Disarmament, Demobilization, and Reintegration: Theory and Practice*. (Boulder: Kumarian Press).

Moriarty, G. (2019). 'Who Are the New IRA and What Have They Done?' *Irish Times*, 23 April. Available at https://www.irishtimes.com/news/ireland/irish-news/who-are-the-new-ira-and-what-have-they-done-1.3869569 (accessed 15 June 2019).

Morrison, J.F., and Horgan, J. (2016). Reloading the Armalite? Victims and Targets of Violent Dissident Irish Republicanism, 2007–2015. *Terrorism and Political Violence*, *28*(3), 576–597.

Mudge, L. (2019). 'Just One Month in, Optimism About CAR's Peace Deal Is Fading', *Human Rights Watch*, 19 March. Available at https://www.hrw.org/news/2019/03/19/just-one-month-optimism-around-cars-peace-deal-fading (accessed 12 June 2019).

Nepal Monitor. (2017). Fact Sheet: Electoral Violence and Contestation During Nepal's Second Phase—House of Representative and Provincial Assembly Elections. Available at https://www.nepalmonitor.org/blog/2017/12/10/fact-sheet-nepals-second-phase-house-of-representative-and-provincial-assembly-elections/ (accessed 10 January 2019).

Newman, E., and Richmond, O.P. (2006). *The Impact of Spoilers on Peace Processes and Peacebuilding*. Policy Brief no. 2. Tokyo: United Nations University.

Núñez, D. (2017). 9 "There Are No Lynchings Here", in Santamaría, Gema, and Carey, David (eds.). *Violence and Crime in Latin America: Representations and Politics* (Norman: University of Oklahoma).
Peace Agreements Database. (2019). Edinburgh University. Available at https://www.peaceagreements.org/ (accessed 10 June 2019).
Pérez, O.J. (2013). Gang Violence and Insecurity in Contemporary Central America. *Bulletin of Latin American Research*, *32*(s1), 217–234.
Pugh, M. (2004). Rubbing Salt into War Wounds: Shadow Economies and Peacebuilding in Bosnia and Kosovo. *Problems of Post-Communism*, *51*(3), 53–60.
Pugh, M., Cooper, N., and Turner, M. (eds.). (2016). *Whose Peace? Critical Perspectives on the Political Economy of Peacebuilding* (Basingstoke: Palgrave Macmillan).
Putnam, R.D. (2001). *Bowling Alone: The Collapse and Revival of American Community.* (New York: Simon and Schuster).
Richani, N. (2010). State Capacity in Postconflict Settings: Explaining Criminal Violence in El Salvador and Guatemala. *Civil Wars*, *12*(4), 431–455
Singh, A.M. (2016). *Policing and Crime Control in Post-Apartheid South Africa.* (London: Routledge).
Spaaij, R. (2010). The Enigma of Lone Wolf Terrorism: An Assessment. *Studies in Conflict & Terrorism*, *33*(9), 854–870.
Spaaij, R. (2011). *Understanding Lone Wolf Terrorism: Global Patterns, Motivations and Prevention.* Springer Science & Business Media.
Stedman, S.J. (1997). Spoiler Problems in Peace Processes. *International Security*, *22*(2), 5–53.
Steenkamp, C. (2005). The Legacy of War: Conceptualizing a 'Culture of Violence' to Explain Violence After Peace Accords. *The Round Table*, *94*(379), 253–267.
Steenkamp, C. (2011). In the Shadows of War and Peace: Making Sense of Violence After Peace Accords. *Conflict, Security & Development*, *11*(3), 357–383.
Steenkamp, C. (2014). *Violent Societies. Networks of Violence in Civil War and Peace* (Basingstoke: Palgrave).
Suhrke, A. (2012). 'The Peace in Between', in Suhrke, A., and Berdal, M. (eds.). *The Peace in Between: Post-War Violence and Peacebuilding* (Abingdon: Routledge).
Super, G.J. (2016). Punishment, Violence, and Grassroots Democracy in South Africa—The Politics of Populist Punitiveness. *Punishment & Society*, *18*(3), 325–345.
The Week. (2019). 'What Is the New IRA and How Much Danger Does It Post?' 23 April. Available at https://www.theweek.co.uk/72541/what-is-the-new-ira-and-how-dangerous-is-it (accessed 15 June 2019).

Tonge, J. (2014). A Campaign Without End?: 'Dissident' Republican Violence in Northern Ireland. *Political Insight*, 5(1), 14–17.
Verwey, C., and Quayle, M. (2012). Whiteness, Racism, and Afrikaner Identity in Post-Apartheid South Africa. *African Affairs*, 111(445), 551–575.
Waldmann, P. (2007). 'Is There a Culture of Violence in Colombia?' *Terrorism and Political Violence*, 19, 593–609.
Weston, G. (2019). *Guatemalan Vigilantism and the Global (Re)Production of Collective Violence: A Tale of Two Lynchings*. (Abingdon: Routledge).
Wimpelmann Chaudhary, T. (2012). 'The Political Economies of Violence in Post-War Liberia', in Suhrke, A., and Berdal, M. (eds.). *The Peace in Between: Post-War Violence and Peacebuilding* (Abingdon: Routledge).

CHAPTER 26

Everyday Economic Experiences and Peace Processes

Birte Vogel

INTRODUCTION

Economics and the economy are often seen as something detached from everyday lives. Something that requires a math-heavy degree and follows the rules and laws of hard sciences like physics. Yet, all of us engage with economic activities on a daily basis by working, buying groceries or spending money in the pub. The economic environment these activities take place in, property rights, tax rates or the legal rights and protection granted to employees, among many others, impacts the experience of these activities. The distortion and destruction of this economic environment is one of the consequences of war, and its reconstruction a vital part of peace processes. This chapter argues that everyday experiences of economic reconstruction matter to the outcome of peace processes because (1) they can impact the trust of people in peace processes and

---

B. Vogel (✉)
University of Manchester, Manchester, UK
e-mail: Birte.vogel@manchester.ac.uk

© The Author(s), under exclusive license to Springer Nature Switzerland AG 2022
R. Mac Ginty and A. Wanis-St. John (eds.), *Contemporary Peacemaking*,
https://doi.org/10.1007/978-3-030-82962-9_26

its perception as something 'positive'; (2) they can impact the legitimacy of (new) institutions and the state more generally; and last, (3) they impact the possibility of future conflicts. Peace processes need not only address the current conflict but build mechanisms that prevent future violent conflicts. It is well-established that economic and socio-economic inequality can be a prime cause, or catalyst, for new violent conflicts.[1] As such, peace processes must pay close attention to the post-conflict economy formation process and its translation into, and implications for, everyday lives. This means looking beyond macroeconomic data and focusing on the everyday experiences of conflict-affected societies.

The importance for economic reconstruction is not a new realisation. John Maynard Keynes was one of the first economists to argue for economic post-war reconstruction at the end of the First World War. He warned participants at the conference of Versailles, where the peace treaty was negotiated, that the 'policy of reducing Germany to servitude for a generation, of degrading the lives of millions of human beings, and of depriving a whole nation of happiness should be abhorrent and detestable'.[2] Keynes had moral reservations about placing exceptionally high monthly reparation payments on Germany, forcing the government to cut pensions and services. He also, from an economic point of view, predicted negative effects for the global economy, and ultimately the sustainability of peace in Europe. He suggested, that the only way out of this misery would be another war. Keynes' arguments were largely ignored, and Europe found itself soon in the midst of the Second World War. The 'Germany as a victim' narrative proved to be very useful for Nazi mobilisation. The implementation of the European Recovery Program (ERP)—better known as the Marshall Plan—at the end of the Second World War represented the opposite approach. Under the umbrella of the ERP, the United States invested billions to rebuild war-torn European regions and economies.[3] Fast-forward a century from Versailles: economic reconstruction efforts are now an essential part of peace processes, peace accords and peacebuilding interventions, and a key part of what is known as the liberal peace agenda.[4]

Although this chapter focuses on the experiences of economic reconstruction, it is important to briefly think about what peacemakers have to seek to undo. Violent conflicts, and in particular civil wars, have negative consequences on local economies. They can destroy or damage large parts of a county's resources, including not only physical infrastructure (roads, bridges, buildings), institutional capacity that deals with economic affairs, moving of assets abroad, but also the labour force (death, injuries, migration).[5] Conflict can further lead to inflation, the black marketisation of good, the rise of militia-led control over resources vital to everyday life, the (illegal) enrichment of armed actors whether state or non-state[6] and the creation of extra-legal economies.[7] Many of these dynamics mean that some actors are invested in conflict rather than peace.

It is against this background that economic reconstruction efforts are implemented. Within the liberal peace framework, economic reconstruction rests on some key principles: macroeconomic discipline, privatisation of businesses and global integration.[8] The aim, in theory, is to put states in the best possible position to address the economic and social challenges connected to building peace. The focus, both in policy and academic research, however, is frequently at the macroeconomic level. Reforms and polices are designed to stimulate positive macroeconomic effects, measured primarily through Gross Domestic Product (GDP) growth rates, in the immediate phase after signing peace agreements, or the end of violent conflict. According to World Bank Statistics, countries usually see a spike in annual GDP growth rates immediately after hostilities end[9] and reconstruction begins.

All selected countries in the Table 26.1 confirm significantly higher annual GDP growth rates at the latest in year one after the end of the conflict. In some cases, the peace process had reduced violence and growth started in the year the conflict ended (year 0 in the table), or, as in the case of Sierra Leone, the peace agreement was signed in January

Table 26.1 Annual GDP growth rates[10] in selected countries a year before (−1), the year of end of hostilities (0) and the three years after the official end of the conflict (1–3)

	−1 (%)	0 (%)	1 (%)	2 (%)	3 (%)	2018
Bosnia Herzegovina (1994–1998)	n/a	20.8	89	34.4	15.6	3.1
Iraq (2010–2014)	6.4	7.5	13.9	7.6	0.7	0.6
Lebanon (1998–1993)	−42.5	26.5	49.4	16.4	10.8	0.2
Liberia (2002–2006)	3.8	−30.1	2.6	5.3	8.0	1.2
Nepal (2005–2009)	3.5	3.4	3.4	6.1	4.5	6.3
Rwanda (1993–1997)	−8.1	−50.2	35.2	12.7	13.8	8.7
Sierra Leone (2001–2005)	−6.3	26.4	9.3	6.6	4.5	3.7
Sri Lanka (2008–2013)	5.9	3.5	8	8.4	9.0	3.2

enabling year 0 to already be a prosper period. For instance, in the first two years after the end of violent conflict in 2009 Sri Lanka has seen GDP growth rates of over 8%, Bosnia and Herzegovina (BiH) averaged with a GDP growth rate of over 5% from the signing of the Dayton peace agreement in 1995[11] to the early 2000s.

Yet, Selby argues, 'peace processes are disparate and divergent in their economic and social impacts—benefiting some while harming others, or at the very least, [...] they might leave [some] behind'.[12] GDP growth rates says little about the distribution of economic benefits per se, and a closer look often reveals that top-down reconstruction and economic pro-peace interventions do not trickle down to conflict-affected communities and ordinary people at large. Instead reforms favour growth and the private sector over labour conditions and welfare programmes.[13] This chapter engages with what happens at the micro-level of society. It argues that people's everyday experience of national economies and their livelihood situations have significant bearings on the quality and durability of peace, and the legitimacy of the peace process more generally. It does so by first outlining the current approach to economic reconstruction, focusing on two key theories of the liberal framework: (1) that market liberalisation and trade integration promote peace; and (2) that growth leads to development, peace and stabilisation. There are two main criticisms to make about these assumptions: First, the underlying theories are developed in response to conflicts between states. Scholarship so far knows little about how they work out in intra-state conflict and national peace processes. Second, on a policy level, the resulting formal programmes often only target the macro-level or are connected to urban centres and do not reach down to all levels of society. The chapter then looks at the challenges to connect these theories to the economic and socio-economic needs on the local and community-level in conflict-affected societies, in particular with focus on intra-state conflicts that have gained prominence over inter-state conflict in the past decades. Following from this, the chapter outlines some local experiences of economic reconstruction reforms based on research in Bosnia and Herzegovina and Sri Lanka and shows the implications of economic reconstruction on the perception of the peace process. It is worth noting that both countries begin their economic post-war reconstruction from different starting points. The conflict in BiH ended with the signing of the Dayton Peace Agreement in 1995, and a transition from a planned to a market economy. The agreement was heavily supported and facilitated by international actors. While Sri Lanka experienced an extended peace process in the early 2000s, the conflict ended as a result of military suppression and a violent defeat of the Tamil Tigers in 2009. Yet, international aid agencies have been supporting the post-war phase with a range of different socio-economic peacebuilding and development programmes in both countries, while BiH, as suggested, also experienced major structural reforms.

THE THEORY OF ECONOMIC RECONSTRUCTION

Economics and the economy have always been a vital part of conflict and war. Material inequality, disputes over resources and 'greed' are frequently cited as root cause of conflict.[14] Likewise, economic factors encourage people to join national armies and rebel forces and provide a breeding ground for ethno-nationalist and religious radicalisation. Consequently, peace processes, peace accords and peacebuilding intervention are accompanied by a range of economic (re-)construction activities that should address the above problems. The leading policy documents guiding (economic) reconstruction efforts have long been the *Washington Consensus* (1989) and the United Nations (UN) Secretary-General's well-known report *An Agenda for Peace* (1992) and represent a normative merger of development and security in their approaches. While principles of the Washington Consensus today are largely regarded as too stringent and unsuitable for post-conflict societies, many of the reforms now aim at poverty reduction and try to connect to the Sustainable Development Goals (SDGs).[15] Thus, programmes have traditionally been better equipped for the context of development rather than conflict and state fragility. This is reflected in the general approaches of international financial institutions (IFIs) such as the International Monetary Fund (IMF) or the World Bank. IFIs have only recently adopted specific policies towards post-conflict reconstruction.[16] The World Bank, for instance, originally only provided short-term emergency recovery assistance in the immediate aftermath of shocks such as natural disasters, and later violent conflict.[17] It was not before the late 1990s that they linked emergency assistance with general and long-term development objectives and specific policies for conflict-affected societies.[18] There is a growing awareness that economic reforms and initiatives need to be seen as part of the wider peacebuilding efforts, and not separate from them. This should be mirrored at the operational level, where a systematic cooperation among the UN, the World Bank and the IMF on peace- and state-building issues are still lacking.[19]

On the ground, economic reconstruction programmes come in various forms, and have complex and diverse objectives that make economic reforms inseparable from its political, institutional and social counterparts. Most commonly, economic reconstruction consists of a set of macroeconomic reforms that aim at growth and stabilisation rather than peace. This includes structural adjustment and technical assistance programmes, the privatisation of state enterprises and services, elimination and formalisation of war and shadow economies, market deregulation, infrastructure investments, new bilateral trade agreements and ultimately the integration into the global economy more broadly.[20] In particular since the 1990s, conflict-affected countries such as Afghanistan, Bosnia and Herzegovina or Kosovo have seen deep economic and regulatory reforms led by the UN, or the United States in case of Iraq, in cooperation with the above-discussed IFIs. Criticism points to the inherent power dynamics and conditions that come with international loans that have profound impact on national policies and often leave receiving countries little choice but to comply.[21]

Economic and political processes are deeply interwoven, yet policy and scholarship too often regard them as separate. This is connected to current methodological orthodoxy as econometric analysis and modelling has conventionally been restricted to quantitative economic variables leaving little room for political assumptions.[22] Assistance-receiving countries are highly dependent on external money for reform activities,[23] making them subject to the conditionality of donors and economic visions that are largely modelled on Western experiences and practices.[24] This phase of post-conflict economy formation, which can be understood as the time when new economic systems emerge in an interaction between formal and informal processes that occur in a period after violent conflict ends, and include the introduction, adjustment or abolition of economic practices, institutions and rules that shape the transformation of the socio-economic fabric in a post-agreement phase.[25] The new economic systems that emerge at the end of violent conflict often leaves little room for the economic history, practices and traditions of conflict-affected countries but align with Western models of capitalism.[26] As such, there is a danger that post-war reconstruction is treated as ahistorical. Countries, however, have their own economic legacies, and formal and informal practices of how business is done, and economic interactions are organised. That often includes a set of formal and informal rules of the market.[27] Post-war economic systems are not starting from scratch but need to find ways to integrate and respect some of these practices and memories. In former Yugoslavia, for example, the shift from a planned economy to a market economy was not only a formal change of the organisation of economic activities but had significant implications on how people experienced the system pre- and post-war. The new system no longer connected to experiences of significant workers' rights and self-management of the workspace through workers' councils, and effectively reduced the space for interethnic collaboration that used to be facilitated through the councils.[28] Thus, economic reconstruction shares some of the criticisms levelled at the 'liberal peace project' more generally, such as cultural blindness, a focus on institutions and a technocratic approach to economic, social and institutional reforms rather than a contextualised engagement with the diverse local dynamics and the power structure that are guiding them.[29]

Below, I review two key claims of economic reconstruction efforts that are concerned with macroeconomic developments. I will discuss the idea that market liberalisation and trade integration lead to peace. I will then turn to the idea that growth leads to development, which in turn supports peace and stability. Both claims are implicitly or explicitly based on theories that assume conflict to be an affair between sovereign nation states only. However, many contemporary peace processes are not between states but between communities. They are often localised, regional and concerned with the relationships between different ethnic, religious, cultural, tribal and other groups. This has implications for how we need to read these theories, and at the same time, justifies why the focus should shift from macroeconomic data to the everyday experiences of economic reconstruction.

'Market Liberalisation and Trade Integration Promote Peace'

Theories of economic reconstruction assume that *market liberalisation and trade integration promote peace*. A core assumption on economic liberalism is that increased international trade, commerce and foreign direct investment will lead to global economic interdependence, and a reliance on the free movement of goods, people and capital. This changes the incentive structures for states towards cooperation rather than war, as both sides profit from this relationship. Consequently, cooperation lessens the chances of relapse into conflict, and strengthens the prospects of sustainable peace instead.[30] Accordingly, economic liberalization has become central to liberal peacebuilding discourses. The above is by no means a new argument made under the liberal peace umbrella, but has been advanced by economists and philosophers such as Adam Smith or Emanuel Kant as early as the eighteenth century. Smith, for instance, argued that the greatest source of interstate peace was indeed trade and not democracy pointing to the complex web of relations trade and commerce build between nation states.[31] Since then, various scholars have confirmed a positive correlation between economic interdependence, and peace and security.[32] The European Union is regularly cited as one of the biggest success stories of peace based on economic interdependence. However, what is easily overlooked is that the European Union not only had a process of economic, but also one of political integration.

What if peace processes take place between communities rather than states? Studies that engage with trade integration among communities or in disputed territories have not confirmed the same effects per se. In Cyprus, for instance, the EU-promoted Green Line Regulation should have encouraged economic interdependence between Greek and Turkish Cypriot communities. However, the data shows that trade volumes have not gone up significantly since its introduction in 2004.[33] Instead, consumers and small-scale traders alike avoid engaging in trade with the 'other side' for complex, often conflict-related, reasons. This includes a wish not to financially strengthen other communities, or in the Cypriot case, to support an 'illegal state' in the North with their taxes. In this vein, it is also worth remembering that economic interdependence only means that both sides should have economic advantages. It says little about how fairly these advantages are distributed between the two sides, let alone within each unit of analysis (which can be a state, a region or a community).

'Growth Leads to Development, Leads to Peace and Stability'

Current academic and, in particular, policy literature is keen to emphasise the correlation between growth, development and peace and stability. In theory, economic growth and development should lead to foreign direct investment, and increased employment opportunities. However, a careful reading of the literature shows that this is less often as clear-cut as assumed. While there is good evidence between the low levels of economic development and state fragility, economic growth and development do not necessarily lead to a way out of fragility and conflict.[34] Indeed, growth and development, for some, can increase pre-existing horizontal inequalities and contribute to old tensions, or contribute to new ones, if growth is not managed through adequate policies. A focus on macroeconomic growth rates says relatively little about how different communities experience reforms. To better understand in-country inequalities, it is helpful to look at the Gini coefficient, or Gini index, currently the most commonly used index to measure inequality. The lower the coefficient, the better are resources distributed within a country. It is worth noting that the index is criticised for relying on imperfect data; it mainly is gathered through self-reported household data via surveys. High-income households tend to op-out of such surveys or underreport their income.[35] Data is also only available for a few years per country, and represents relative and not absolute wealth. For example, Iraq has a comparable Gini coefficient to Sweden (0.295 and 0.292, respectively),[36] yet absolute income, and relatedly, quality of life, access to social services and economic opportunities in both countries are different. Hence, the Gini index is by no means a perfect or accurate tool to understand inequality, but it can indicate some general trends about resource allocation within society.

From the Fig. 26.1 it becomes evident that some of the same countries that showed spiking GDP growth rates in the post-war period (Table 26.1) have largely not seen a decreasing Gini coefficient. Instead, most

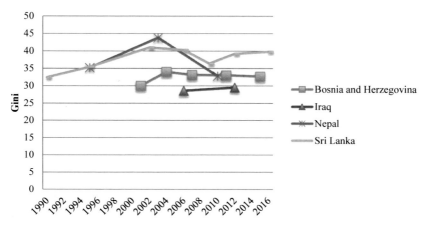

Fig. 26.1 Change of Gini Index over time

countries show an increase of inequality over time. Bosnia and Herzegovina's Gini coefficient increased from 0.3 in 2001 to 0.327 in 2015. Likewise, while Sri Lanka saw an increase from 0.364 to 0.398 since the end of the war. The only country to beat this trend is Nepal where inequality decreased since the end of the civil war in 2006. The overall increase of Gini indices across countries, however, indicates that despite economic growth rates inequality could not be reduced, and, ultimately, that the profits of the post-war period did not 'trickle-down' equally. To understand who the 'winners' and 'losers' of economic reforms are, it requires an intersectional approach that takes different identity markers and vulnerabilities into account. The combination of gender, class, ethnic identity, religion, age and geographical location determine how the economic reforms impact on people's life beyond the aggregated data of GDP growth at the national level. In sum, post-war economic growth is often slow and poorly distributed, and tends to remain at the elite level of society. It is often limited to capital cities or urban areas meaning that rural communities are even more detached from the possible benefits of the peace process.[37] Further, the empirical data shows that inequality often does not foster competition but instead undermines the legitimacy of the state and the peace process in the eye of local populations, or as Pugh argues: 'there is no clear correlation between raw economic growth and peace, rather a relationship between wealth distribution and conflict'.[38] It is against this background that the chapter turns to the experiences of economic reconstruction beyond macroeconomic numbers.

Experiences of Economic Reconstruction

A Disappointing Economic Experience of 'Peace'

Taking the experience of economic reconstruction rather than GDP rates as a starting point for evaluating the impact of economic reconstruction efforts on peace processes can uncover very different narratives to those of 'development' and 'interdependence'. When interviewing people in conflict-affected societies about their main concerns of the post-war phase, the lack of employment opportunities is often the main issue to be raised. In former Yugoslavia, the transition and post-war reconstruction was particularly challenging. The end of the war in 1995 not only brought a phase of re-building the economic system, but of re-imagining it within the capitalist and neo-liberal frameworks favoured by Western donors. The experience of the economic post-war order has been, for many, one of austerity. In September 2018, 46.7% of the youth were unemployed, one of the highest rates in the world.[39] Many young people have decided to move abroad in search for the 'better life' that was promised with the structural reforms in BiH. This has implications for the economy: many of the best-qualified professionals leave the country in search for better opportunities and futures contributing to the well-known problem of 'brain-drain'. Most importantly, it impacts on the social and family structures in conflict-affected areas. A mother and restaurant owner interviewed in Sarajevo in 2016, for example, paints a picture of a city where she sees little ethnic conflict these days, but many families are separated by economic necessity. The lack of economic opportunities motivated the son to move abroad and the daughter to relocate to another city.[40] She blames the corrupt political system and the international community for the separation of her family. Stories like hers are common in Sarajevo, and show that many in the local population perceive the 'peace process' as negative despite the end of conflict hostilities.

The shortcomings of post-war reconstruction are not only located in economic reforms, but also socio-economic peacebuilding programmes that were meant to supplement structural reforms and fill the gaps. To respond to the problem of the benefits of large macroeconomic reforms not trickling down, micro-finance has emerged as one innovative tool to directly empower and connect to people in conflict-affected societies. The idea is to give small loans, often with low interest rates, to selected individuals who are either seen as particularly vulnerable, for example, based on their ethnicity, gender or location, or particularly promising in getting into the local and global economy.[41] In many instances, it is regarded as a tool to 'empower' people in an environment that is usually determined by a shrinking or absent welfare state and social security system.[42] It often plays on the notion that the poor are resilient or creative entrepreneurs that just need the financial means to get started. In reality, the absence of functioning social protection mechanisms leads to situations where local populations have to 'get creative' about how they survive and manage their daily lives. In BiH, to stay with the previous example, micro-finance was promoted as a way to support female entrepreneurism and get women back into the market.[43] The reality, however, is that women took out loans to support their children's education, buy clothes or cover basic needs.[44] Similar experiences were shared with me in Sri Lanka. NGO employees there described micro-credit programmes, in particular those run by private actors, as a 'trap' for rural communities in which people fear indebtedness and must fund their own basic needs in the absence of state assistance. Representatives of development agencies even made a link between increasing suicide rates and the programme.[45] Experiences such as those described above can lead to a lack of trust in the peace process, and makes the experience of 'peace' one of personal struggle, economic precariousness and insecurity.

Donors and post-conflict development programmes in Sri Lanka have created what many in the NGO and business sector refer to as a 'degree culture'.[46] The country has seen considerable investment into education since the end of the civil war in 2009. That has created two problems: a large segment of the populations has obtained degrees and extra certifications. This process has created expectations for many to obtain better-paid and more responsible employment. However, there was little demand in the local economy for highly qualified employees, meaning that many recently trained and graduated people did in fact not find a job that they deemed suitable. Second, owners of small- and medium-sized businesses, the type of businesses that employ about 90% of the population, struggle to find workers that are willing to work basic factory or hospitality jobs. This leaves industry searching for employees for low- and mid-level jobs, while, at the same time, immigration laws are restrictive. Here, peacebuilding and development programmes explicitly have created expectations of better employment opportunities that in fact do not exist. This does not only contribute to the personal disappointments, but at the same time weakens the local business sector. For many, peace has brought neither progress nor 'a better life'.

Losing Legitimacy

These negative personal experiences of economic post-war reconstruction and macroeconomic reforms, as argued in the introduction, can have an impact on the legitimacy of those actors in charge of the peace process, as well as the process itself. Notions of state legitimacy often draw on Weber's tripartite framework of legal, traditional and charismatic authority.[47] Recent debates have shown that a more complex understanding of legitimacy is needed in conflict-affected societies that take different levels and sources of legitimacy into account.[48] When it comes to economics, state investment in public goods and social welfare is seen as the main source of government legitimacy.[49] The economic everyday should also be seen as one of multiple sites of legitimacy that constitute state legitimacy after conflict. The economic experience of post-war reconstruction is thus vital to consider. It can either demonstrate that the state is capable of keeping, or creating, a (new) social contract. Or, in other cases, the state is seen as incapable of delivering the promise of an improved quality of life. The latter can have negative implications for the peace process. In 2014, for example, BiH witnessed large-scale protests about the generally poor economic situation. Protests were in favour of a more socially equal and inclusive agenda and against a privatisation process that was widely perceived to have been mismanaged.[50] There was also frustration at the lack of any comprehensive plan for the country's socio-economic recovery. According to one observer, the protests were against a 'sense of futurelessness'.[51] Many attributed their daily economic challenges—directly or indirectly—to international reconstruction efforts.[52] The poorly handled privatisation of state companies, and the austerity measures resulting from International Monetary Fund loans impacted on peoples living conditions. Average monthly wages only increased from 622 Euros in 2010 to 665 Euros in 2016.[53] Increasing taxes, food prices and inflation mean that many effectively earn less. During the protest, thus, citizens claimed that most economic benefits of the post-war period were enjoyed exclusively by political and economic elites only.

Conclusion

This chapter has shown that despite positive GDP growth rates and billions in international investment, the experience of peace and the peace process, for many, remains one of austerity and livelihood struggles. These experiences are in stark contrast to the expectations political elites raise at the signing of peace agreements. However, if everyday peace is about how life is lived and enacted, then people's economic condition is vital. This has a direct bearing on the quality of peace. Bosnia is 'at peace' but people are disillusioned with what peace means in terms of their living conditions. While BiH at a state level now might be better integrated into a global economy, many people's economic everyday is hardly worth keeping the peace for. A major reason for this is the inability of formal economic structures and dynamics to fulfil their aspirations. Likewise, socio-economic peacebuilding programmes do not necessarily help to address the gap between aspirations and reality. Microfinance, for instance, has been evaluated negatively by development agencies, at least in Sri Lanka. It has supported recipients' short-term needs in the absence of sustainable and shared economic growth and an absent welfare state, but likewise caused new long-term problems when recipients find themselves unable to repay their loan. One could say social peace is operating on a loan system.

Other programmes, such as investment in education, often missed the needs of the local employment market and left both participants and employers frustrated with the outcomes. This points to the general problem that (economic) development programmes that support the SGDs—of which economic justice is a key aspect—often do not speak to each other, or have contradictory aims. While development programming might focus on the poor, reconstruction efforts at the same time usually support market liberalisation, privatisation and austerity—processes that often adversely affect already underprivileged communities. These are not only a question of social and socio-economic justice but also of political order. BiH demonstrates how international reforms aimed at macroeconomic changes fundamentally failed to connect to the everyday resulting in a legitimacy crisis for both international actors and a state that was already dysfunctional in the eyes of Bosnian citizens.

There are a couple of key lessons that can be taken from the above. To start with, approaches towards understanding and evaluating economics and economic reconstruction need to be driven by more than macroeconomic analysis and quantitative data that tend to marginalize other forms of economic experiences and knowledges. Consequently, economic reconstruction should focus on the everyday too while not neglecting the macroeconomic and structural dimensions. That would, for example, mean investment in economic projects beyond the national level, connecting to local economic history, practices and actual rather than assumed needs. To quote a positive example, local bazaars in Iraq have become an important space for everyday peacebuilding, as they fulfil both an economic and a social function in bringing communities together and supporting livelihoods.[54] An investment in, and restoration of, such places thus could have a positive impact on the experience of economic reconstruction. This underlines that the social, political and economic are interlinked and not working in silos. Last, if economic reconstruction is about more than reemerging from, and overcoming, old conflicts, but about building the foundations for a sustainable peace, it needs to move from peacebuilding to social justice. The current focus on the macro-level tends to overlook, or ignore, questions of socio-economic inequality that can be a source for future violent conflicts.

Notes

1. See, for example: Collier, P., and Hoeffler, A. (1998). On Economic Causes of Civil War. *Oxford Economic Papers, 50*(4), 563–573; Collier, P. (1999). On the Economic Consequences of Civil War. *Oxford Economic Papers, 51*(1), 168–183; Ohlson, T. (2008). Understanding Causes of War and Peace. *European Journal of International Relations, 14*(1), 133–160.
2. John Maynard Keynes, *The Economic Consequences of the Peace*.
3. The US motivation was not necessarily that they learnt from the problem of the First World War, but they also wanted to ensure that Europe would not gravitate towards communism and the Soviet Union. The argument here is obviously more complex than this chapter has space to discuss.
4. See, for example, Richmond, O. (2001). *Maintaining Order, Making Peace*. Springer; Paris, R. (2004). *At War's End: Building Peace After Civil Conflict*. Cambridge University Press.
5. Collier, *The Economic Consequences of Civil War*, op. cit.
6. Pugh, M. C., Cooper, N., Pugh, M., and Goodhand, J. (2004). *War Economies in a Regional Context: Challenges of Transformation*. Lynne Rienner Publishers.
7. Nordstrom, C. (2003). Casting Long Shadows: War, Peace, and Extra-Legal Economies. In *Contemporary Peacemaking*, 2nd edition (pp. 289–299). London: Palgrave Macmillan; Nordstrom, C. (2004). *Shadows of War: Violence, Power, and International Profiteering in the Twenty-First Century*. University of California Press.
8. Pugh, M. (2006). Post-War Economies and the New York Dissensus. *Conflict, Security & Development, 6*(3), 269–289, p. 269.
9. I specifically focus on civil wars.
10. All data available via the World Bank Group at https://data.worldbank.org/indicator/ny.gdp.mktp.cd, last accesses 20 June 2019.

11. I excluded the years 1996–1998 from this average, as the transition of the country's economic system led to initial spikes of over 88 and 34% in the first two years.
12. Selby, J. (2008). The Political Economy of Peace processes. In *Whose Peace? Critical Perspectives on the Political Economy of Peacebuilding* (pp. 11–29). London: Palgrave Macmillan, p. 11.
13. Herring, Herring E. (2008). Neoliberalism Versus Peacebuilding in Iraq. In *Whose Peace? Critical Perspectives on the Political Economy of Peacebuilding* (pp. 47–64). London: Palgrave Macmillan, p. 47, see also Pugh (2006), op. cit.
14. Collier and Hoeffler (1998), op. cit.
15. Pugh, M. (2006). Post-War Economies and the New York Dissensus. *Conflict, Security & Development*, 6(3), 269–289, p. 273.
16. See for example, *The New Deal for Engagement in Fragile States* (2011) or the World Bank's *World Development Report 2011: Conflict, Security and Development* or the *Operational Policy and Bank Procedures 2.30 on Development Cooperation and Conflict*.
17. Viterbo, A. (2018). The Role of the International Financial Institutions in Fragile and Conflict-Affected Countries. In *Peace Maintenance in Africa* (pp. 111–134). Cham: Springer.
18. Ibid.
19. Viterbo, International Financial Institutions, op. cit.
20. For a good overview see Peterson, J. H. (2014). *Building a Peace Economy? Liberal Peacebuilding and the Development-Security Industry*. Manchester University Press.
21. Pugh (2006), op. cit.
22. Carbonnier, G. (2002). The Competing Agendas of Economic Reform and Peace Process: A Politico-Economic Model Applied to Guatemala. *World Development*, 30(8), 1323–1339.
23. del Castillo, Graciana. (2008). *Rebuilding War-Torn States: The Challenge of Post-Conflict Economic Reconstruction*. Oxford University Press.
24. Pugh (2006), op. cit.
25. Distler, W., Stavrevska, E., and Vogel. B. (2018). Economies of Peace: Economy Formation Processes and Outcomes in Conflict-Affected Societies. *Civil Wars*, 22(2), 139–150. See page 139.
26. Ibid.

27. Charman, A., and Petersen, L. (2015). A Transnational Space of Business: The Informal Economy of Ivory Park, Johannesburg. In *Mean Streets, Migration, Xenophobia and Informality in South Africa*, edited by J. Crush, A. Chikanda, and C. Skinner (pp. 78–99). Waterloo: Southern African Migration Programme.
28. Ramović, J. (2018). Looking into the Past to See the Future? Lessons Learned from Self-Management for Economies in Post-Conflict Societies of the Former Yugoslavia. *Civil Wars, 20*(2), 171–192.
29. Mac Ginty, R., and Richmond, O. P. (2013). The Local Turn in Peace Building: A Critical Agenda for Peace. *Third World Quarterly, 34*(5), 763–783.
30. Gartzke, E. (2007). The Capitalists Peace. *American Journal of Political Science, 51*(1), 166–191.
31. Smith, A. (1776). *Wealth of Nations*.
32. Doyle, M. W. (1983). Kant, Liberal Legacies and Foreign Affairs, Part I, *Philosophy and Public Affairs, 12*(3); Spiegel, H. (1991). *The Growth of Economic Thought*. Durham: Duke University Press; Gartzke, E. (2007). The Capitalists Peace. *American Journal of Political Science, 51*(1), 166–191.
33. Gokcekus, O., Henson, J., Nottebaum, D., and Wanis-St John, A. (2012). Impediments to Trade Across the Green Line in Cyprus: Classic Barriers and Mistrust. *Journal of Peace Research, 49*(6), 863–872.
34. Hinds, R. (2015). *Economic Growth and Fragility* (GSDRC Helpdesk Research Report 1214). Birmingham, UK: GSDRC, University of Birmingham.
35. Simson, R., and Savage, M. (2019). The Global Significance of National Inequality Decline. *Third World Quarterly*, online first https://doi.org/10.1080/01436597.2019.1662287.
36. World Bank data, https://data.worldbank.org/indicator/SI.POV.GINI?most_recent_value_desc=false, last accessed 25 October 2019.
37. Narain, V. (2009). Growing City, Shrinking Hinterland: Land Acquisition, Transition and Conflict in Peri-Urban Gurgaon, India. *Environment and Urbanization, 21*(2), 501–512.
38. Pugh, *Post-War Economies*, op. cit., p. 270.
39. World Bank data from September 2018: youth is defined as people between 15 and 24 years. The general employment rate in the

country was 20.8%. Data available from https://data.worldbank.org/indicator/sl.uem.totl.zs.
40. Restaurant owner, personal conversation, 25 March 2016, Sarajevo, BiH.
41. Doyle, K. (1998). *Microfinance in the Wake of Conflict: Challenges and Opportunities*. Bethesda, MD: Microenterprise Best Practices, available from http://www.gdrc.org/icm/disasters/conflict.pdf, last accessed 25 October 2019.
42. Stavrevska, E. B. (2018). The Mother, the Wife, the Entrepreneur? Women's Agency and Microfinance in a Disappearing Post-Conflict Welfare State Context. *Civil Wars*, 20(2), 193–216.
43. Ibid.
44. Ibid.
45. NGO Employee 'Livelihood Programme', Personal Interview, 15 February 2019, Colombo, Sri Lanka.
46. NGO Employee 'Youth Empowerment', Personal Interview, 16 February 2019, Colombo, Sri Lanka.
47. Weber, M. (1976). *Wirtschaft und Gesellschaft*, 5th edition (ed. J. Winckelmann). Tübingen: Mohr.
48. Boege, V. (2014). Vying for Legitimacy in Post-Conflict Situations: The Bougainville Case. *Peacebuilding*, 2(3), 237–252.
49. Taydas, Z., and Peksen, D. (2012). Can States Buy Peace? Social Welfare Spending and Civil Conflicts. *Journal of Peace Research*, 49(2), 273–287.
50. *The Guardian*. (2014). Bosnians Aren't Arguing About National Identity Now: This Is an Economic War, available from https://www.theguardian.com/commentisfree/2014/feb/12/bosnians-economic-war-tuzla-protests, last accessed 25 October 2019.
51. Kurtović, L. (2015). 'Who Sows Hunger, Reaps Rage': On Protest, Indignation and Redistributive Justice in Post-Dayton Bosnia-Herzegovina. *Southeast European and Black Sea Studies*, 15(4), 639–659, p. 639.
52. Lidén, K., Mikhelidze, N., Stavrevska, E. B., and Vogel, B. (2016). EU Support to Civil Society Organizations in Conflict-Ridden Countries: A Governance Perspective from Bosnia and Herzegovina, Cyprus and Georgia. *International Peacekeeping*, 23(2), 274–301, p. 290.
53. Western Balkans Labor Market Trends 2018, available from http://documents.worldbank.org/curated/en/565231521435

487923/pdf/124354-Western-Balkans-Labor-market-trends-2018-final.pdf, p. 83, last accessed 26 October 2019.
54. O'Driscoll, D. (2019). Building Everyday Peace in Kirkuk, Iraq—The Potential of Locally Focused Interventions. *SIPRI Policy Paper*, No. 52, available from https://www.sipri.org/publications/2019/sipri-policy-papers/building-everyday-peace-kirkuk-iraq-potential-locally-focused-interventions.

# PART VII

Conclusion

CHAPTER 27

Conclusion: Peace Processes, Past, Present, and Future

Anthony Wanis-St. John and Roger Mac Ginty

Around 40 peace processes were underway in the year 2020, and there were hundreds of such processes underway in the past two decades.[1] While many resulted in agreements, some of these were minor, temporary, and highly localized. A good number of these peace agreements were comprehensive, landmark accords that brought significant national and regional change. Taken together, this peacemaking represents an enormous learning opportunity through which peacemaking and peace-support efforts by political and militant leaders, governments, international organizations, and civil society can be analyzed. The period saw innovations in peacemaking, the forging of new norms, and new legal

---

A. Wanis-St. John
School of International Service, American
University School of International Service, Washington, DC, USA
e-mail: wanis@american.edu

R. Mac Ginty (✉)
Durham University, Durham, UK
e-mail: roger.macginty@durham.ac.uk

© The Author(s), under exclusive license to Springer Nature Switzerland AG 2022
R. Mac Ginty and A. Wanis-St. John (eds.), *Contemporary Peacemaking*, https://doi.org/10.1007/978-3-030-82962-9_27

frameworks, not least in relation to the Women, Peace, and Security agenda. Peace processes and accords in some contexts encouraged political leaders in other areas to investigate negotiated outcomes. There also appears to be a much greater understanding among international organizations of the links between development and conflict, and the need for peace processes and peace agreements to address the development and governance issues that often drive conflict.

As we advance in our understanding of how to make and sustain peace, the challenges to peacemaking have also become more confounding and dire. Despite the sheer number of peace agreements, it is worth noting that the notion of a negotiated settlement—that is, ending or tamping violent conflict through negotiation rather than through military victory—does not have universal acceptance. Indeed, there have been very significant examples of a refusal to negotiate and the pursuit of what has been called 'authoritarian conflict management'.[2] A major trend has been a drift towards 'stabilisation' or international strategies that prioritize stability above more emancipatory aims linked to democracy or rights. While the 'liberal peace' of the 1990s and 2000s often involved quite expansive international interventions, the trend since then has been towards more limited forms of intervention. In some cases, peacebuilding programmes have been co-opted as part of security-led approaches. And if the classic cleavage of rebels versus the state were not challenging enough to resolve by negotiation, the panorama has become even more difficult when popular uprisings against repressive governments combine with competing local and transnational militant groups, and multiple and self-serving foreign interventions. The situation in Libya, for example, exemplifies all of these challenges in the context of two rival governments.[3] Myanmar, Democratic Republic of the Congo, and Syria also have such dynamics.

The origins of any peace process or agreement—changes in the geo-political or regional situation, initiatives from civil society, secret meetings, chance encounters between significant actors—are often unrecognized at the time. It is even more difficult to determine when a peace process has succeeded, but it is clearly not the final signature on a peace accord. The function of an accord is to identify general principles and parameters of agreement, as well as indicate the specific solutions the parties aspire to implement. Implementation challenges may prolong the peace process cycle for many years, during which functioning institutions must be established and reforms carried through. During that time, it is hoped that certain things will emerge: better norms of political dialogue, non-sectarian and more inclusive politics, as well as transformations of cultural and structural violence.

This chapter will follow the cycle of peace processes through four phases: (1) pre-negotiation; (2) the management of the process, including negotiations and violence; (3) peace accords; and (4) post-accord reconstruction and conflict transformation. It is worth noting, however, that peace processes are not strictly linear; progress may be made on one issue while, at the same time, there are set-backs in relation to other issues. If every peace process had to wait for a complete ending to violence, few would get off the ground. Each peace process will have its own sequencing, and it is worth thinking of peace process events (for example, the start of negotiations between adversaries) as well as wider demographic, economic, or societal trends that occur over the longer term. Sometimes it is possible to tackle traditional 'post-settlement' tasks such as decommissioning and disarmament early in the process, and the momentum created by this may assist the move towards negotiations. Our decision to divide peace processes into four phases is mainly an aid to comprehensibility. We then conclude the chapter by presenting eleven propositions about the nature and problems of contemporary peace processes. The propositions are necessarily tentative in that to some extent they are speculative and to some extent they are prescriptive and normative.

Getting into Talks: Pre-negotiation

Conflicting parties rarely want to reach a settlement at the same time. During the war in Bosnia during 1993 and 1994, for example, the willingness of Muslims, Serbs, or Croats to engage in negotiation was determined primarily by their fortunes on the field of war and the resulting territorial gains or losses. By definition, these conditions never coincide for all parties. The result is a pendulum-like swing, with ethnic rivals proposing talks in turn, but rarely at the same time. Windows of opportunity, when all parties are simultaneously prepared to negotiate, are rare and of limited duration. Yet it is only during such relatively infrequent opportunities that a settlement may be attempted.

The central metaphor in determining these opportunities is Zartman's concept of a 'ripe moment', when the parties' reach a mutually hurting stalemate (MHS) and 'find themselves locked in a conflict from which they cannot escalate to victory and this deadlock is painful to both of them'. Zartman also documented the dynamics that render civil wars highly resistant to ripeness.[4] While the concept has been criticized by some as too passive, Zartman insists that 'unripeness should not constitute an excuse for second or third parties' inaction'.

When compromise is in the air, other metaphors may be applied. Imagine the set of factors required to end violence—'Track-two' approaches (nongovernmental contact by such mediators as the business community, academics, or churches), secret talks, a ceasefire, agreement to negotiate, mediation, demilitarization, decommissioning—as a circle of dominoes standing like the stones at Stonehenge. The ending of violent conflict ultimately requires the movement of all the dominoes, but the process can be triggered initially by moving one of them forward, creating a momentum which nudges its neighbour along, and so on to the next one, and the next. The momentum depends on readiness to exploit temporary advantages. The effects of the 2004 tsunami, for example, stimulated peace moves in Aceh and Sri Lanka, but only contributed to agreement in the former case.

Most often the process requires a combination of more than one of these triggers to create momentum. Then the momentum itself, by providing the opportunity for opponents to work together, can become an agent in the process. The peace processes in Turkey, Colombia, South Africa, Northern Ireland, and Israel–Palestine all began with secret talks. These have certain advantages over traditional diplomacy as a preliminary to substantive talks: the formal barriers imposed by protocol are dropped; the temperature of the water and the temper of one's opponents may be tested with limited risk; 'what-if' scenarios can be floated without commitment. Secret talks can be a useful transition process for those who rose to leadership as security or insurgent leaders, and who often have little or no experience in the art of compromise. As du Toit noted, secret talks have 'low exit costs'.[5] As such they offer no guarantee of success. Initial secret talks between jailed Kurdish leader Abdullah Ocalan and the Turkish government did lead to further negotiations but that process collapsed. They have low 'entry costs' as well, as the heavy preconditions to negotiation are often absent in back channels, and the parties may well wish to deny their internal hardliners any chance to oppose negotiations that are otherwise sorely needed.[6]

Occasionally, the move from secret to open negotiations is managed by the protagonists themselves. Far more often, as Christopher Mitchell points out, a third party becomes involved. Intermediaries such as the business community, the churches, and academics were active in South Africa and Northern Ireland. Mediators, such as the Norwegian academics and diplomats who were critical in starting the Oslo and Sri Lankan talks, often play a more effective role during the preliminaries of a peace process than later.

It is not uncommon for the state and non-state actors to form a temporary alliance at the intra-group level. In Northern Ireland, the pro-united Ireland parties and the Irish government reached a loose understanding in advance of negotiation. Similar developments occurred in the Basque Country and Corsica. To some extent, under President Trump, the United States and the Taliban formed an unlikely alliance committed to direct talks, while the Afghan government sat warily on the sidelines, although this seems due to U.S.–Taliban shared interest in a U.S. withdrawal, rather than any commitment to a peaceful, inclusively governed Afghanistan. When a militant revolutionary movement shifts towards a broader approach which includes constitutional parties from their own identity group, it is a strong indicator of ripeness for negotiations. These alliances help to compensate for the asymmetrical nature of negotiations, where the initial advantage leans towards the government side.

In the suspicious climate that accompanies the early stages of pre-negotiation, confidence-building measures can reassure opponents, but they carry high risks. Confidence-building measures are concessions by one side to encourage movement from the other—the declaration of a ceasefire, the inclusion of militants in talks, decommissioning of weapons. Symbolic gestures by Nelson Mandela to white South Africans greatly eased the first stages of negotiations. The danger is that premature concessions may be 'banked' rather than reciprocated by the recipients. This has been a constant factor in ceasefires agreed in Colombia, and in the Syria civil war, whereby governments use the ceasefires to gain advantage before a renewed offensive. The general lesson is that unilateral confidence-building gestures should only be conceded rarely. In the case of Moldova, confidence-building measures over twenty five years seem to have become an entrenched part of the conflict landscape and have not produced the desired momentum towards substantive peace talks.[7]

Managing the Process: Dealing with Negotiations and Violence

During the years of violence preceding peace negotiations, cross-ethnic communications diminish and hostile stereotypes become entrenched. Opposing aspirations are expressed in mutually exclusive terms. The belief grows that one's opponents are cohesive, devious, and successful, while one's own side is divided, frustrated, and victimized. These are not ideal conditions for negotiations and are too often mirrored.

How can confidence be built at this stage in the fledgling process, and rules and procedures established to move it forward? The Colombian peace process marked a significant shift by the Colombian government by recognizing FARC (Revolutionary Armed forces of Colombia) as a legitimate negotiating partner and—de facto—recognizing the failures of the Colombian state to legitimately represent all its peoples. In Colombia, somewhat unusually, violence took place while the peace talks continued in Havana. In most other cases, the fact that negotiations take place at all presumes an acceptance, often implicit, that the representatives of militants have been admitted to negotiations in return for giving up violence. Their inclusion, whatever pressures it imposes on the process, admits militants to the common enterprise and applies a moral pressure on them to preserve the process in the face of violence from dissidents or spoiler groups. In cases like the Central African Republic, shepherding fourteen armed groups into a process was no mean feat but there was also a sense that some armed groups experienced a fear of missing out.

The decision to include militants does not presume that the mechanics of their admission has been agreed. They are often required to pass 'good behaviour' tests. Probation periods were set before Sinn Féin was admitted to talks in Northern Ireland, and Ariel Sharon's insistence in 2002 that negotiations with Palestinians could not start until violence had ended for two weeks created an effective stalemate. In 2019 an Afghan government spokesperson said, 'If we are going to give the Taliban the privilege of peace negotiations, they need to prove how much control they have over their commanders and fighters'.[8] A period of one month was set as the test the Taliban had to meet. In Northern Ireland the Mitchell Principles were devised, and imposed, as conditions for entry to talks and for punishing breaches by militant groups associated with the negotiating parties.[9] Such good behaviour tests may indeed encourage parties to take decisive steps to build confidence, but they can also become deterrents to negotiation if they demand in advance what might be one of the outcomes of the process. The disparate Syrian opposition groups have long insisted on the departure of President Assad as a precondition to negotiation, which offered Assad a convenient excuse to reject such talks.

As a general rule, secrecy diminishes in importance as negotiations proceed. The need to prepare communities for the forthcoming compromises increases. An excess of early publicity entrenches differences before an agreement can be reached. An excess of secrecy not only encourages conspiracy interpretations but also fails to prepare public opinion for the necessary compromises. Of course, secrecy and transparency are not so easily controlled. It is also worth noting that the news media is often more interested in conflict and violence than peace. In a sense, it is easier to talk up threats than the prospects of a peace that might be tentative. Moreover, social media adds a dimension to the dissemination of peace process information. The Colombian peace process was accompanied by an anti-peace process Twitter tirade from former president Uribe, making it difficult for the Colombian government to win over public support for its risky initiative.[10]

A key part of any talks process will be the agenda and discussion papers that might accompany that agenda. Shuttle diplomacy may be needed to establish the preconditions and ground rules for talks. If these can be agreed, proximity talks are often necessary before the participants are willing to meet in plenary sessions. An important issue in all of this is power. More precisely, what actors have the power to impose their agenda, discussion papers, or preconditions on a talks process. In some cases, governments will have the power, trappings of state apparatus, and legitimacy to impose conditions and rules. In other cases, insurgent groups may wield significant power as well. External actors are often essential in navigating between opponents, offering technical expertise and sometimes financial incentives, and attempting to impose an official status on a talks process. It is sometimes the case that non-state actors lack the experience and ability to develop discussion papers and other preparatory material that could otherwise help them and their counterparts better understand their priorities and the trade-offs among them.

The issues under negotiation are distinctive to each conflict, but some themes are constant. The early release of prisoners is almost always a sine qua non for militants engaged in talks; it is also a highly emotive reminder to victims of violence that their sensibilities have been pushed into the background in the interests of securing peace. Reforms in policing, security, and the administration of justice are also constant features if an accord is agreed. Protection for human rights, recognition of identity concerns, and aspirations towards economic reform have become increasingly common topics in talks processes. In general, there has been a broadening of peace process agendas reflecting an increasing recognition that peace is a development issue as well as one concerning security and territory. There has also been a conscious lending and borrowing between cases, whereby initiatives and techniques from one peace process have been adopted in another peace process. Increased capacity and expertise from peace-focused international organizations and INGOs has helped with this, as has the professionalization of the peacebuilding sector and the growth of a cadre of peacebuilding professionals.

Time frames and deadlines are essential to maintain momentum, and deserve greater attention. Just as some actors have the power to set a peace process agenda, or act as gatekeepers to talks processes, some actors will have power over timing and deadlines. Often these timescapes are linked to the political cycle—especially elections. Deadlines are often imposed to provide focus and urgency to negotiations. Essentially though, deadlines are almost always artificial constructions and parties extend them if it suits their needs. In some cases, ceasefires are reached but there seems to be little urgency by one or more actors to move to serious negotiations. In both India and Myanmar non-state armed actors have signed ceasefire agreements but there have not been serious talks. The government benefits from a decline in violence and a reduction in the readiness of the armed groups, and often the armed groups profit from what has been termed 'ceasefire economies'.[11]

One by-product of establishing deadlines is that negotiations sometimes advance in surges rather than by gradual increments. This encourages the emergence of a brinkmanship style of negotiation. This approach carries obvious risks but has some incidental benefits. It confirms to a divided community that its leaders are fighting a tough fight, thus helping to prepare them for the compromises to come. The help is often necessary, for the interests of leaders and their supporters may diverge as a deal nears completion. By that time it is often more difficult for the negotiators to leave the process than to stay in it—they might have reached process bias. By the more optimistic reading, their engagement in a common enterprise creates a common bond; more cynically, the failure of the peace process and a return to war places those who initiated the strategy in danger (sometimes physical danger) from more zealous elements within their own community as the Armenia–Azerbaijan case consistently demonstrates.

The process of making an accord is usually played out to a background of violence. It may even be perpetrated by some of those engaged in the negotiations. The Colombian peace process did not involve a prior ceasefire (although there were several unilateral and temporary ones) and continuing 'battlefield' actions risked affecting, if not derailing, the peace talks, including the killing of the FARC's top commander while secret talks were underway in 2011. US–Taliban talks involved intermittent partial ceasefires as confidence-building measures but not a halt to violent operations.[12] Israel has a long history of seeking to alter in its favour the 'facts on the ground' prior to negotiations such as through the construction of Israeli settlements on occupied Palestinian territory. If nothing else, behavior like this illustrates that peace negotiations can be an extension of conflict.

Spoiler violence presents a considerable threat to peace processes and accords. The intention is to destabilize pro-peace initiatives by undermining those from the in-group who are engaged in negotiations, and to goad opponents into reaction. Given the uncertainties of peace processes, and the prospect of compromise, public opinion may well be insecure and so spoilers can thrive in such an atmosphere. Much depends on the capability of spoilers and the extent to which the various camps in a peace process have been able to maintain discipline and prevent splintering. Much also depends on the success of demobilization, disarmament, and reintegration programmes and the general post-accord economic prospects. If the post-accord economy is able to offer alternative livelihoods then the prospects of peace will be enhanced. A key problem in many post-accord societies, well-discussed by Christina Steenkamp in this volume, is the rise of crime—especially violent theft. This can have a real impact on the lived experience of communities in post-accord societies leading to a disaffection with 'the peace'.

Peace Accords

Before the point is reached when a peace accord is being negotiated, a fundamental question needs to be addressed. Can the central grievances be resolved within the existing national framework, or do they require secession and autonomy? The question reveals the centrality of statehood in questions of peace and conflict. Can the existing state be modified, perhaps through constitutional engineering or the extension of rights, or is a breakaway necessary or acceptable? Complete secession is relatively rare with Kosovo, Eritrea, South Sudan, and Timor Leste providing examples, although there continue to be numerous demands for secession (such as Somaliland, Nagorno-Karabakh, Assam in India, Catalonia, and possibly Northern Syria's Kurds). A more usual route is for the state to seek to remain intact but in a modified form, exemplified by the federal relationship between the Kurdish Regional Government and Iraq. In cases like Spain and India, the central state is wary of any secessionism lest one instance leads to more. States must often judge how much autonomy they can grant to minority groups while still holding the state together. It is a delicate balance as autonomy can take on a life of its own and lead to unanticipated outcomes. Devolution of power from London to Scotland was meant to satiate Scottish demands for independence. If anything, it has fueled them. As mentioned earlier, we may also highlight 'authoritarian' secessions, such as the Russian-supported separations of Donbas from Ukraine, or South Ossetia from Georgia, which only postpone the same questions of rights, affiliation, citizenship and sovereignty.

Powersharing has proved to be a common way of retaining the state in a unitary form but managing relations within it. As discussed by Timothy Sisk in this volume, it offers a mechanism for representation and decision-making, especially for those who have traditionally been excluded and whose grievances may have led to violence. Powersharing has often been regarded as an interim arrangement that allows parties to deal with the business of government and avoid difficult decisions on constitutional issues. The hope of many consociational arrangements is that the meta conflict will wither away as parties get on with day-to-day governing. The report card on Northern Ireland is mixed: adversarial parties are capable of dealing with each other on day-to-day governing issues. But they still hold very divergent views on their preferred constitutional outcome and despite decades of proximity to one another in the governing chamber their enmity has not lessened. In some cases powersharing has led to a distortion of government. In South Sudan, for example, the size of the National Legislative Assembly has been extended, and extended again, as a way of accommodating disaffected constituencies. Inclusion and good governance are not always compatible.

The political is usually only one part of a peace accord. Also important are rights (particularly the rights of minorities or those who have held a collective grievance) and dealing with the past. In many cases human rights institutions are established or enhanced. A peace accord may lead to a new, or amended, constitution in which rights (as well as new distributions of power) might attain a prominent role, as explained by Laurie Nathan, in his chapter here on post-conflict constitutions. It is worth being mindful of the possible gap between de jure rights and protections and the extent to which institutions and populations take these with due seriousness. The Nepalese constitution, for example, is a beacon of rights, especially economic rights. But the extent to which the government is able to protect those rights, and fulfil other peace process provisions, is limited. A key issue in the possible gap between the stated intentions in a peace accord and the delivery of those intentions is the extent to which an agreement is accepted by various constituencies and stakeholders. Important here is the extent to which the parties in negotiations have engaged in expectation management and prepared the ground for change and compromise. The democratic validation of peace accords through referenda or post-accord elections have been important in encouraging ownership of a post-accord polity. In a sense, a post-accord referendum could take the form of a social contract or commitment by voters to give a peace accord a chance—although it can also be used to oppose accords. Both of these aspects are explored here by Joana Amaral in her chapter on peacemaking referendums. Indeed, the performativity of holding a peace accord referendum, or a post-accord election, is important in signaling democratic intentions and capability.

Reconstruction and Conflict Transformation

A significant number of peace accords have failed or have seriously undelivered. Explanations of why so many peace processes and peace accords fail to survive, mature, or bring about positive peace include:

> the weakness of many post-war and post-accord states, many of them with serious economic inequality and weak institutions;
> flaws in the process, which may not have included all the fundamental issues in dispute, or all the key actors, thereby prolonging and even extending the dispute;
> the failure of leaders to carry their followers in the agreement period, especially if the benefits expected to flow from an agreement are disappointing, delayed, or reframed as losses;

failure to implement the agreement—a particular problem when agreements are vague and therefore require post-agreement negotiations;

the corrosive effects of post-accord violence;

failure to deliver the economic buttressing necessary for post-war reconstruction;

the emergence of unanticipated (some of them un-anticipatable) developments, such as a 'natural' disaster that illustrates government incapacity;

failure to demobilize and disarm combatants, who may continue to victimize the population even if they are no longer organized as a fighting force;

failure to develop a political culture of dialogue in which the parties accept each other as legitimate actors and can resolve their differences through nonviolent means of contestation.

The disappointment, however, mainly arises from a mistaken view that a peace agreement marks the end of a peace process. Certainly, it means that a peace process has passed a significant symbolic milestone on the road to stability, moving the journey on to the different but no less difficult implementation stage. In order to secure the agreement, it is tempting for negotiators to defer some sensitive issues for post-accord attention, laying minefields for the future in the interests of short-term gain. During the Oslo negotiations, for example, five critical issues, including Jerusalem, settlements and refugee return, were 'blackboxed' to enable the two sides to move forward on other less inflexible issues such as the gradual withdrawal of Israeli forces from Palestine and the emergence of a Palestinian Authority. Failures in implementing the interim withdrawals and the Israeli reluctance to curb settlement activity contributed strongly to the death of that peace process. In Northern Ireland, the post-war years were dogged by the deferred issues of policing and the decommissioning of weapons held by militant organizations. The dismantling of war machines is often a dominant theme. The transfer of ex-militant activists into the police and security forces is a highly visible statement that there has been a qualitative shift in the conflict. It was also a tangible demonstration of commitment to fair employment practices. Yet the integration of ex-militants into the security forces is not always possible or even desirable.

The need to move smoothly from an elite-driven political settlement towards a more fair and democratic society cannot be exaggerated. In South Africa, the inability to deliver either economic regeneration, 'everyday' security, accountable governance, and greater social equality led to a growing sense of disillusion with peace itself. In the former Yugoslavia, it is fair to say that although there has not been a return to war, many electors are sullen and disillusioned with the polity. Concrete benefits from a peace accord may seem slim if unemployment or emigration are the most realistic prospects for young people. While a post-accord state might be politically viable, in the sense that it seeks to satiate the identity demands of people, it may not be economically viable. Despite oil reserves, South Sudan—which gained independence in 2011—has faced prolonged humanitarian crises, factional armed violence, and food insecurity. Given a World Bank projection that 'poverty levels are expected to remain extremely high', it is unsurprising if people ask questions about the dividend from independence.[13]

Post-settlement administrations also inherit the problems left by years of violence and confrontation. Truth commissions have become a common but far from universal approach to confront past violence, with mixed records of success. Latin American truth commissions and the Truth and Reconciliation Commission in South Africa attempted to address the hurts of victims as a basis for reconciliation. The controversy surrounding these bodies demonstrates that it may take as long to repair community dysfunction as it took to create it—decades rather than years. Northern Ireland has had no serious attempt at reconciliation in the decades since the 1998 Good Friday Agreement. Among other things, this points to the sensitivity and highly political nature of the issue. Yet in Northern Ireland and in many other post-accord locations there has been what can be called 'social reconciliation', or individuals and communities 'getting on with things'. This has not involved formal reconciliation initiatives and ceremonies. Instead, in Cambodia, northern Uganda, Bosnia and many other locations that have transitioned from outright violence, people have had to get on with the business of life: getting the kids to school, holding down a job, setting up a business. In the process, inter-group conciliation may have happened—organically, informally and without ceremony. In a sense, this is civil society—as distinct from civil society organizations. The latter have been increasingly important players in peace processes, often encouraging parties to investigate peace initiatives, to include important issues (like victims or minorities), and playing a large role in post-accord peacebuilding.[14] Very often international organizations sub-contract to civil society organizations.[15] Working through civil society organizations offers the promise of getting closer to communities and by-passing governments that are, perhaps, partisan, corrupt, or incapable. Certainly the past two decades have seen the rapid growth of a professionalized transnational peacebuilding community of practice (some would call it an industry). Peacebuilding NGOs have been criticized for being donor-led, metropolitan, dominated by actors from the global north, and often promoting a particularly shallow version of 'local participation'. But the existence of such a large peacebuilding sector is revealing of the limitations of other sectors, namely international organizations and governments.

A key factor facing all peace accords is the need to transform the accord from a document agreed between elites to a working social contract that is embodied and lived through everyday life among the populace. In other words, how can a peace accord be 'owned' beyond the elites who drew it up and take on a life of its own? Recent research has begun to explore how populations grapple with the state and non-state armed groups in order to obtain the fruits of peace accords.[16]

Work on the Women, Peace, and Security agenda has shown just how elitist peace negotiations can be, and how opening them up to women, minorities, refugees, and victims can bring a new, more inclusive, dimension to peace talks. Certainly 'inclusion' is a prominent term among many organizations working for peace. But beyond formal and funded pro-peace projects and programmes, it is worth thinking about how peace can be engaged with, shared, enjoyed, and promoted on a day-to-day basis in communities. This everyday peace is often low-key and tentative. It may take the form of inter-group civility or business relations. It may involve small acts of sociality, reciprocity, and solidarity. These acts, as seemingly inconsequential as individuals from formerly warring parties sharing the same queue at a bakery, are the glue that hold societies together.[17] They represent an everyday co-existence that might, under the right circumstances, develop into something more substantive. This sort of everyday peace might be criticized as 'negative peace' but sometimes the enmity held in communities is so deep that this is all that can be expected. In such circumstances, a peace accord and associated provisions and institutions are crucial to provide the security and protections that will permit inter-group interaction to take place.

It would seem that more research is required to identify how to advance peace accords towards sustainable peace and reconciliation. A genuine transformation away from a conflict ethos,[18] and the infrastructure that maintains such an infrastructure, would seem to require a good many contingent factors: supportive international and regional environment; an economy that can deliver and share a peace dividend; an ability to balance justice and the difficult legacies of conflict and victimhood, with peace; political parties and constituencies mature enough to prioritize long-term conciliation over short-term gains; and an absence of spoiling and in-group 'outbidding'.[19] When listed in this manner, the tasks facing peacebuilders seem insurmountable. Yet, societies have made effective war to peace transitions. While none of these transitions has been without problems, it is worth stating that lives have been saved and improved—on a vast scale—because of organized attempts to make peace. Peacemaking is worth doing, and it is worth doing as well as possible.

Eleven Propositions

If peace processes are so shaped by their individual characteristics, is it possible to extract general guidelines for peacemakers from the substantial modern history of peace processes? Clearly each conflict and peacemaking attempt will have its own specific characteristics, but it is possible to offer tentative generalizable lessons. We propose eleven propositions.

Proposition 1 *A lasting agreement is impossible unless it actively involves those with the power to bring it down by violence and who enjoy some measure of legitimate representation.*

Is it possible to make a settlement without including parties with militant associations? The greatest initial obstacle to an inclusive peace process is the unwillingness of constitutional politicians to deal with parties associated with violence. The distaste of some parties in dealing with others they deem as incorrigible or gratuitously violent is understandable. The strategy of ignoring demands for talks has been very common (for example, Turkey in relation to the Kurds or Spain in relation to the Basques or Catalans). It is often a sign that a government is powerful enough to ignore such demands, but it does condemn a government to a long-term, and often draining, policy of suppression and feigned ignorance. An alternative to an inclusive peace process might include a partial peace process in which certain parties or factions are kept out of negotiations. The danger of doing so is that the excluded party or parties are incentivized to wreck the process from the outside and greatly increase the lethality and duration of conflict. Some governments find it challenging to negotiate with fragmented militant groups. The Colombian peace process with the FARC is being followed up by negotiations with the previously excluded ELN. The Philippines has had partially successful peace negotiations with the MNLF and only later with the MILF. Each set of negotiations is likely to tackle the same issues and might have gotten the parties to peace sooner had the negotiations been inclusive.[20] Another alternative is to avoid a negotiating process altogether and seek to suppress opponents. Such a strategy worked for Sri Lanka in 2008–2009 with its defeat of Tamil separatists but the human rights cost was appalling. And there are cases in which both partial exclusion and repression entangle the negotiations. The Palestinian–Israeli conflict has long been predicated on many layers of exclusion of various Palestinian groups, and Israel has always kept the threat and use of force 'on the table'.

It seems difficult to conceive of a successful peace process from which veto-holders are excluded. The phrase 'you don't make peace with your friends' (attributed to a number of political leaders) seems relevant. It underlines the importance of persuading governments to engage with their opponents in the first place. Such initial conversations would usually be conducted via a back channel. Of course, including (possibly formerly) militant groups in negotiations is difficult. The question arises about how to respond when more extreme groups continue or resume campaigns of violence. The relationship between governments and militants presents an uncomfortable moral ambiguity. Having accepted the principle of amnesties for earlier 'terrorists' in order to attract them into negotiation, negotiators might then assume a stern approach to the use of violence in the future. At the same time, they must also keep the door open to the inclusion of late converts. At that point, the creation of a mechanism is necessary to regulate the process—criteria for admission to talks, the conditions for expulsion, and the future inclusion of spoilers.

The reality is that total inclusion is never possible. There are always zealots who will not compromise. The more numerous and compromising the moderates on each side, the greater the likelihood that the extremes can be marginalized. Therefore, the demand for inclusive talks is always a qualified one. Just as the principle of 'sufficient consensus'[21] was adopted in South Africa in recognition of the impossibility of progress if all participants had veto powers, it is necessary to apply a principle of 'sufficient inclusion' in relation to militant organizations. This does not mean the inclusion of all parties using or threatening to use violence. The principle of 'sufficient inclusion' is that a peace process should include both or all actors who represent a significant proportion of their community and all actors who have the ability to destroy an agreement. The two groups are often coterminous. Some cases pose serious challenges to the principle of sufficient inclusion: in Syria the armed and unarmed opposition to the government have proven resistant to all efforts at unity needed in order to streamline their inclusion in negotiations. This is in part due to the vast array of parties—themselves mutually incompatible—that compose the opposition and who frequently split, reform, and morph into new groups. Afghanistan's post US withdrawal political future was meant to include the Taliban in a power sharing arrangement, yet exclude some of the legacy warlords of the past, and the ISIS–Khorasan faction that arose only a few years ago.[22] Some research suggests that peace processes themselves worsen existing splits among rebels, and thus vastly increase the likelihood that rebels will fragment into new groups and complicate peacemaking.[23]

Proposition 2 *The absence of violence is not a prerequisite for peace. Negotiations are. Successful peace negotiations must anticipate and manage the problem of continuing violence.*

Agreement by violent groups to negotiate is never unanimous. As excluded or fragmented militant groups enter the process, further breakaway spoilers might emerge. The actions of spoilers move increasingly towards the margins during and after the process of peace negotiations. This raises the question of how spoiler violence will be tackled after a peace accord, especially if a new political dispensation includes former militants.

At some point during the process, when all the splinter groups likely to join the process have done so, two rumps may remain—those engaged in crime for personal advantage and ideological zealots. They pose different problems. The most common strategy is to criminalize the former and to confront them through a reformed police force and justice system acceptable across the community. Post-accord crime, however, continues to afflict a large number of cases. It is much more difficult for ex-militants to turn against groups who share their general orientation but have refused to buy into the peace process. One key aspect is the size of the spoiler group and the seriousness of its threat to the peace process. If the spoilers carry significant popular support the authority of negotiators is seriously circumscribed. The ANC's dominance of political protest in South Africa made condemnation a lot easier.

A successful peace process is organic and cumulative. The public euphoria following the ending of violence contrasts with the mutual suspicion of the early negotiations. Constitutional politicians are forced to negotiate with people they regard as criminals, often at the risk of alienating their voting support. They tend to overlook the risks facing the militants who have entered negotiations, and whose position is severely undermined if the talks collapse. In a number of peace processes, tests were imposed before militants were admitted into talks. The reasons for the tests are understandable, but they can actually be (or be seen as) a delaying tactic.

If the process survives the first nervous contacts, it may strengthen. Sometimes it is reinforced by internal pressure from public opinion. Working relationships often develop between the negotiators as they concentrate on the practical minutiae of negotiations and become better acquainted with the boundaries within which their opponents operate. The process of achieving this position locks those involved in negotiation in an uncomfortable process bias embrace. As negotiations progress, the participants become more attracted to the positive rewards of a historic breakthrough. It becomes increasingly difficult for any of them to contemplate a return to the earlier violence. Failure to make progress would rule out another initiative for the near future. It would also probably mean the end of their political careers and, sometimes, threaten their lives.

One of the greatest challenges to this dynamic is continuing violence from dissidents, from rival militant groups, from militias, and from governments themselves. Some of the violence may even be sponsored by the negotiators themselves for strategic advantage. Persistent stalemates during the negotiations will strengthen the internal cohesion of competing parties and erode the common ground between them. This underlines the importance of maintaining forward momentum in negotiations, presenting evidence of advantages for all parties. Generally speaking, the further the process develops and results in effective implementation and positive changes in people's lives, the stronger its shock absorbent facility and the more capable its ability to withstand the atrocities designed to undermine it. The policy implication is to focus economic and political support on the initial stages of the process.

Proposition 3 *Peace processes are deals: they require trade-offs.*

Peace negotiations are complex and multi-faceted, involving a range of teams negotiating across a range of constitutional, security, political, economic, and cultural issues. This 'disaggregation'—the conduct of negotiations through plenaries and sub-groups, each dealing with a different issue and reporting according to a different time frame—is perhaps unavoidable.[24] Certainly the task of negotiating across multiple issues and using multiple negotiating teams who might be working to different timeframes vastly complicates any peace process, especially if communication across these teams is dysfunctional. It could be that progress is made more easily on some issues more than others. Agreement on difficult issues might be deferred, perhaps raising the prospect of difficult post-agreement negotiations. But in some cases, parties in negotiations have reached a rough equivalence on issues. For example, one party might give way on an issue that is important to its supporters, while another party reciprocates on an issue that has traction with its support base. UN mediation in the 1992 Chapultepec Accords in El Salvador meant that 'compliance with specific undertakings by one side would be contingent upon compliance with specific undertakings by the other side'.[25]

Crucial to pacific outcomes in peace processes is an understanding among all sides that concessions must be made. This is difficult because the narratives used in conflicts, particularly those used at an intra-group level, are often couched in a zero-sum language. If one party has spent years demonizing another party as incorrigible, it is difficult to then be seen to make concessions to that side. The reciprocation mentioned above helps. But to fulfil the potential of a peace process and accord, it is helpful if parties move beyond a purely transactional model and instead embrace a way of thinking that accepts loss and gain in the mix. This is easier said than done and much depends on the messaging that parties direct towards their base. In addition, it may require that parties abandon extreme preconditions that only serve as a barrier to negotiation, and to prioritize their desired outcomes so that trades and linkages among them are possible. Mediators need to encourage and understand those priorities and rankings among issues within each side and across the table, so that they can creatively contribute bridging proposals and creative solutions.

Proposition 4 *During peace negotiations, the primary function of leaders is to deliver their own people. Assisting their opponents in the process is secondary.*

Peace accords are negotiated by the elites of both power holders and seekers, who must then persuade their followers to endorse it through an election or referendum. Power seekers who abandon violence and enter talks are vulnerable to accusations of betrayal. Peace processes are often the site of appeals to emotions, and potential spoilers will be keen to exploit this. There are similar constraints on power holders. As mentioned in the last proposition, parties involved in peace processes need to lay the groundwork among their supporters. This is difficult as many peace processes are secret, especially in their earlier phases. In fact, the overreliance on secrecy in order to reach agreements may come at the expense of building support among followers.

Both power holders and power seekers may have to go through difficult transitions. The power holders—usually the state—enter negotiation because they recognize the inevitability of change before their followers do; their main difficulty is to convince their supporters that the resulting changes are minimal and some governments shirk this task. The power seekers—usually militant leaders—get into negotiation because they recognize the advantages of negotiation before their followers do; their main difficulty is to convince their supporters that the negotiations are achieving major concessions from the state. If the process moves too slowly, it hurts the power seekers. If it moves too speedily, it hurts the power holders. Spoilers more readily mobilize against a peace process and its implementation stages when these are drawn out or delayed.

In navigating this complex journey, the primary function of leaders is to deliver their own followers. It is true that both sets of leaders are more likely to recognize the difficulties of their opponents as negotiations evolve. They also come to realize that a peace process cannot be completed unless their opponents also have enough to satisfy their followers. This mutual dependency is in tension with the risk that assisting their opponents may alienate their own supporters. The reality is that the loss of their followers is a greater threat to party leaders than the collapse of the process.

27 CONCLUSION: PEACE PROCESSES, PAST, PRESENT, AND FUTURE 605

Propositions 5 and 6 *If a peace agreement is to stick, initiatives are needed to re-integrate members of the security forces and paramilitary groups into society. Such initiatives must be integrated with moves to address the needs of the victims of violence.*

The problem of re-integrating ex-militants into society is sharpened by their ability to undermine the peace process. In some cases the problem is partially addressed by transferring ex-guerrillas into the regular army and police force. Such an option is not always open, yet prudence demands that those who were engaged in the war must be provided with jobs and training. The ending of violence leaves a high risk inheritance. The shrinkage of the security industry—army, police, prison officers, private security guards—brings on to the unemployment register people skilled in the use of arms. A similar risk of redundancy faces the militants whose lives have been devoted to armed resistance. Their speedy return to civil society is essential, less because they deserve a reward than because they have the means to destabilize the peace process. While the need to demobilize fighters after war has long been understood, the psychosocial needs of former combatants should be anticipated in any peace process in order for their return to civil society to succeed.

Historically, two distinct approaches have been applied to the victims of violence—what John Groom has called the Nuremberg Tribunal way and the South African way.[26] These can be summarized as justice versus peace. The judicial route, through the punishment of war crimes, continues through the International Criminal Court, although that body has been criticized for the selective nature of the cases it pursues. The other version, through truth and reconciliation initiatives, can be time-consuming and costly. There have been significant advances in approaches to transitional and transformation justice in recent years, and a wider recognition of the need to focus on victims and victimhood. This is necessarily sensitive as parties to a conflict may regard their own side as victims and the other side as perpetrators. A parity of victimhood requires a significant shift in public and political opinion, again requiring the preparation of constituencies. This was handled in an innovative way in the Colombian peace process in that victims' delegations were invited to take part in the negotiations in Havana and a truth commission was established even before that. Importantly the issue was not left to the end of a peace process.

Issues such as amnesties, the release of prisoners (especially high-profile prisoners), memorialization, and compensation all risk re-igniting division and hindering a move towards a new type of politics. War memorials, for example, need careful treatment in divided societies if they are to avoid becoming shrines to division rather than to common suffering. Reparations too can provoke rather than ease tensions if the amounts are perceived to be low, or to have been gained illegitimately, or they are unaccompanied by investigations of atrocities. Even after reparations were instituted by law in Chile, and accepted by the victims' relatives, there were few prosecutions against the military, because they were protected by the 1978 Amnesty law. In general, the efficacy of truth and reconciliation commissions is heavily determined by timing and local sensitivities. It may have been appropriate to the needs of Chile and South Africa, but each society must find a form appropriate to its traditions and circumstances. Whatever the circumstances, the needs of victims should be confronted at a much earlier stage than has often been the case in peace processes. In the case of Cambodia after the Paris Peace Accords, a Cambodian court was created to address the genocide, with the support of the UN. Despite its hybrid nature, the court failed to do much more than indict five Khmer Rouge associates, only three of whom were convicted of genocide and crimes against humanity.[27] It is a challenge to assure an appropriate balance of justice with forgiveness, accountability with reconciliation, of memory with forgetting. Peace processes may both innovate and borrow experiences from others.

Proposition 7 *A peace process does not end with a peace accord.*

There are no rules about the best time to reach formal agreement during a peace process. Some peace processes can become elongated. The negotiators of the 1648 Treaty of Westphalia took years to reach agreement and outstayed the welcome of the townspeople who were hosting them. Echoing this, in 2021 hundreds of South Sudanese politicians were asked to leave a luxury hotel complex after three years of unpaid bills and little prospect of an agreement.[28] At some stage—preferably sooner rather than later—a peace process needs to be a viable vehicle to reach an accord.

If negotiators wait until all major issues have been agreed, the process may collapse from mutual distrust or violence before they reach a conclusion. If they defer complex and divisive issues for later resolution, it will be more difficult to contain negotiations as mutual fears and suspicions flourish among the uncertainty. In either case, post-settlement euphoria may be followed by post-agreement tristesse, and the all-important momentum lost. A common pattern has been for peace processes and peace accords to be greeted by some level of excitement and support but for this to ebb away over time as some issues drag and positive change is slow in coming. It is fair to say that some peace processes 'fail' after apparent political agreement has been reached through an accord. They fail in the sense that populations become disaffected and do not see a peace dividend in terms of their everyday security or livelihood.

As a final point, it is worth asking when does a post-conflict or post-peace accord society lose the 'post' and just become a society? For example, is Bosnia–Herzegovina always destined to be called 'post-conflict' even though the Dayton Accords were reached decades ago? Academics and peacebuilding practitioners have a role to play in this as their use of the label 'post-conflict' risks reinforcing a status that might be more descriptive of the past than the present. Unless of course the wartime leaders fail to transform their political cultures and become little more than warlords in suits.

Proposition 8 *Peace is a development issue.*

The issues that have the most chance of making an impact on people's lives inhabit the social and economic realm. These issues require serious attention during mainstream political negotiations lest the gap between public expectation and reality remain unfulfilled in the fragile post-accord years. Failure to address these 'bread and butter' issues may lead to a public disenchantment that overshadows political or constitutional compromises. In sum, peace processes must embrace development issues.

According to a popular story, King William of Orange crossed the river Boyne by boat during a famous Irish battle in 1690. The boatman asked him how the battle was progressing. 'What is it to you?' replied the King, 'You'll still be boatman whoever wins'. The lesson for those involved in contemporary peace processes is that poverty, inequality, and social exclusion require serious attention (as part of any peace initiative). Uneven development is a major contributory cause of conflict. If a peace accord fails to address serious inequality and provides few routes of economic opportunity then the accord itself may lead to a new cycle of violence.

Notwithstanding complex constitutional transformations, the main problems facing many people in South Sudan, Colombia, and other post-peace accord areas are economic, if not humanitarian. To speak of 'haves' and 'have nots' may sound antiquated, but when having nothing threatens peace, it becomes salient. More concerning, if peace processes enshrine lucrative arrangements for certain sectors, the result is that new grievances will be created or old ones perpetuated. In South Sudan, the years after independence in 2011 have been fraught with war, drought, and economic hardship. Per capita Gross Domestic Product fell from $1111 in 2014 to less than $200 in 2017.[29]

Just as war affects different sections of society in different ways, peace has a differential impact. Peace will often impact upon men and women, young people and the elderly, urban and rural dwellers in different ways. It is no coincidence that wartime population displacement usually has the greatest impact on the most vulnerable, usually the elderly, infirm, and dependent. Peace processes need to focus on the variations within society and not necessarily minister to those who can shout the loudest, often men and those who retain their arms. On top of structural inequalities within societies, the international economic system has the capacity to undermine peace. While the international community may promise a peace dividend, the reality of currency flows, uneven trading relationships and competition can hamper post-accord development. It is beyond question that wars generate illicit economies and economic exploitation of the most vulnerable, and peace processes should seek to reverse such wartime injustices.

Proposition 9 *Inclusive peace processes not only embrace the meaningful participation of the typically excluded—women, all victims of war, unarmed opposition groups—they also integrate robust civil society roles that go beyond tokenism.*

In the last decade or so, there has been a growing emphasis on documenting and analyzing the roles that civil society can play in peacemaking. Cases illustrate mediation roles, protective roles, advocacy roles, among others. Civil society groups sometimes form alliances that demand an end to violence. They also influence the negotiation agenda of peace processes, to insure that the needs of society generally are addressed, and not sacrificed in order to privilege warlords, power brokers, and other wartime elites. Furthermore, they build support for peace, often taking on the critical task we describe in Proposition 4—that of preparing publics for a turn to peaceful coexistence although it must be acknowledged that there also exist 'uncivil' societies who either self-mobilize or are supported by outside actors, for the purpose of fomenting hatred, espousing maximal demands and generally furthering divisiveness. This is more important than the mere presence of a handful of women or members of civil society among the delegates to peace talks. While this may symbolize inclusion, meaningful participation is concerned with agendas, redressing wartime grievances, and building public awareness to hold leaders accountable for their peacemaking promises and commitments.

Proposition 10 *The absence of war is not peace.*

A significant number of peace processes become stalled after a ceasefire has been reached. The protagonists are able to enjoy the benefits of an end to direct violence, but they lack an impetus to reach a comprehensive peace agreement. The result can be a 'no war, no peace' situation in which the peace process is stuck. International peace support in the form of donor conferences or recognition of the legitimacy of militant groups can inadvertently reinforce these 'no war, no peace' situations by removing incentives for parties to enter into serious negotiations on core issues of contention. At certain stages in the Sri Lankan, Colombian, and Oslo peace processes antagonists were content to bank the benefits of an absence of war but saw little advantage in pushing for peace. The danger with 'no war, no peace' situations, as evidenced by the three cases just mentioned, is that violence creeps back into the void left by the absence of a dynamic peace process. Certainly in recent years, the cold peace between Armenia and Azerbaijan ignited into hot and violent war, with needless loss of life, in part because a ceasefire negotiated two decades ago had not been consolidated with a comprehensive settlement of the Artsakh/Nagorno–Karabakh dispute. In fact, Armenia's seizure of Artsakh/Nagorno–Karabakh and adjoining Azeri territory in 1994 may have unripened the conflict, with Armenian citizens and diaspora preferring the post war status quo instead of a Minsk Group-mediated settlement.

'No war, no peace' situations are also apparent in some post-peace accord societies in which the peace accord fails to address the core issues of the conflict. Despite being long-standing, the Dayton Accords and the Good Friday Agreement have failed to address the conflicting nationalisms and identities that underpin division. The Colombian peace accord has not fully resolved land tenure, a key driver of the political economy that sustained the conflict. While the peace accord may have success in stanching violence, instituting a new political dispensation, and kick-starting reconstruction, it may fail to deal with underlying grievances and so be prone to a resumption of violence. The widespread murder of community leaders and social activists in Colombia is evidence of a peace accord that only goes so far.

A final type of 'no war, no peace' situation is visible in situations whereby the conflict is mainly confined to a specific geographic region of a larger state. With the conflict effectively compartmentalized, governments and large sections of the population and economy of the United Kingdom, Spain, India, Colombia, and Sri Lanka have been relatively insulated from the civil war. Therefore, while one part of the population enjoys the 'peace', the other endures the war or repression. Through its security wall and cantonment-type policies, Israel has quite successfully separated itself from its Palestinian neighbours. The obvious danger of such situations is that governments and others can maintain a fiction of peace or normalcy in the territory it controls and ignore, as best it can, tension and resentment that affects others.

Proposition 11 *Indigenous approaches to dispute resolution are often more appropriate than international 'best practice'.*

The involvement of external actors in peace processes brings the risk of a standardization of peacemaking techniques and reconstruction programmes. In some cases, international 'best practice' may be culturally inappropriate, unsustainable, and resemble a top-down imposition that makes little connection with the bulk of the population. For example, techniques honed to ameliorate the symptoms of psycho-social trauma among adolescents in in US urban areas may have little application to child soldiers in West Africa. Yet the transfer of Western ideas and practice is a persistent trend in contemporary peacemaking. It is a trend with potentially serious cultural implications in reshaping how citizens in war-affected states interact with each other, their state, and the market. This is not to deny the very real potential advantages accruing from international practice, expertise, and resources. But while it is useful to look for guidance from comparative examples, no magic template applies to all peace processes. Instead, it seems sensible that local and international actors be open to a wide range of peacemaking techniques and feel free to adopt and adapt dispute resolution techniques according to local circumstances. At the same time, neither local populations nor Western peacemakers should fetishize indigenous practices that may be culturally 'appropriate' while also masking structural and cultural violence that may be locally contested.

NOTES

1. I. Navarro Milián, J.M. Royo Aspa, J. Urgell García, P. Urrutia Arestizábal, A. Villellas Ariño, and M. Villellas Ariño (2021) Peace Talks in Focus 2020: Report on Trends and Scenarios, Barcelona, Icaria.
2. J. Heathershaw and C. Owen (2019) 'Authoritarian Conflict Management', *Conflict, Security and Development*, 19(3): 269–273.
3. R.M. Perito (2016) 'Libya: A Post-Arab Spring Test for Security Sector Reform', Centre for Security Governance, CSG Papers. No. 8.
4. I.W. Zartman, ed. *Elusive Peace: Negotiating an End to Civil Wars* (Brookings Institution Press, 1995).
5. P. du Toit, 'South Africa: In Search of Post-Settlement Peace', in J. Darby & R. Mac Ginty (eds), *The Management of Peace Processes* (London: Macmillan, 2000), p. 19.
6. A. Wanis-St. John, *Back Channel Negotiation: Secrecy in the Middle East Peace Process* (Syracuse University Press, 2011).
7. N. Kemoklidze and S. Wolff (2020) 'Trade as a Confidence-Building Measure in Protracted Conflicts: The Cases of Georgia and Moldova Compared', *Eurasian Geography and Economics*, 61(3): 305–332.
8. Cited in M. Masal, 'Afghan Government Demands Ceasefire Before Any Taliban Talks', *New York Times* (29 October 2019).
9. The 1996 Mitchell Report, named after US Senator George Mitchell, chair of the International Body on Arms Decommissioning, laid down conditions for all negotiators. Before participants were admitted to all-party negotiations they were required to agree to six principles, including their commitment: to democratic and exclusively peaceful means of resolving political issues; to the total disarmament of all paramilitaries; that such disarmament must be verifiable by an independent commission; to renounce and oppose any effort to use force or the threat of force to influence the course of the outcome of all-party negotiations; to abide by the letter of any agreement reached in all-party negotiations and to resort to democratic and exclusively peaceful methods in trying to alter any aspect of that outcome with which they may disagree; and 'to take effective steps' to end 'punishment' killings and beatings.

10. J. Partlow, 'Ex-president Uribe Wages One-Man Twitter War Against Colombia Peace Deal', *Washington Post* (25 September 2015). Accessed at: https://www.washingtonpost.com/news/worldviews/wp/2015/09/25/ex-president-uribe-wages-one-man-twitter-war-against-colombia-peace-deal/.
11. D. Brenner (2015) 'Ashes of Co-optation: From Armed Group Fragmentation to the Rebuilding of Popular Insurgency in Myanmar', *Conflict, Security & Development*, 15(4): 337–358, at p. 338.
12. K. Manson and S. Findlay, 'US and Taliban Agree Ceasefire in Step Towards Peace Deal', *Financial Times* (15 February 2020). Accessed at https://www.ft.com/content/e56d3e94-4f53-11ea-95a0-43d18ec715f5.
13. World Bank, 'The World Bank in South Sudan', *World Bank* (13 October 2020). Accessed at https://www.worldbank.org/en/country/southsudan/overview.
14. Thania Paffenholz, 'Civil Society and Peacebuilding: Summary of Results from a Comparative Research Project', CCDP Working Paper 4 (Geneva: CCDP, 2009).
15. Oliver P. Richmond and Henry F. Carey, *Subcontracting Peace: The Challenges of NGO Peacebuilding* (Aldershot: Ashgate, 2005).
16. A. Arjona (2016) 'Institutions, Civilian Resistance, and Wartime Social Order: A Process-Driven Natural Experiment in the Colombian Civil War', *Latin American Politics and Society*, 58(3): 99–122; Noah Rosen, Converting Peace Processes into Local Peace in Colombia, doctoral dissertation (in progress), American University, School of International Service, 2021.
17. Roger Mac Ginty, *Everyday Peace: How So-Called Ordinary People Can Disrupt Violent Conflict* (Oxford: Oxford University Press, 2021).
18. D. Bar-Tal (2000) 'From Intractable Conflict Through Conflict Resolution to Reconciliation: Psychological Analysis', *Political Psychology*, 21(2): 351–365.
19. C.I. Zuber and E. Szöcsik (2015) 'Ethnic Outbidding and Nested Competition: Explaining the Extremism of Ethnonational Minority Parties in Europe', *European Journal of Political Research*, 54(4): 784–801.
20. S. Ghais (2019) 'Consequences of Excluding Armed Groups from Peace Negotiations: Chad and the Philippines', *International Negotiation*, 24(1): 61–90.

21. The condition of 'sufficient consensus' is defined by Friedman thus: 'consensus was sufficient if the process could move on the backing of only those who supported a proposal. Disagreement would be recorded; dissenters could remain in the process, await its outcome, and then decide whether to support it' in S. Friedman, 'Afterword: The Brief Miracle', in S. Friedman & D. Atkinson (eds), *South African Review: 7 The Small Miracle—South Africa's Negotiated Settlement* (Johannesburg: Ravan Press, 1994), p. 22.
22. Islamic State-Khorasan Backgrounder, Center for Strategic and International Studies, November 9, 2018.
23. A. Duursma and F. Fliervoet (2020) 'Fueling Factionalism? The Impact of Peace Processes on Rebel Fragmentation in Civil Wars', *Journal of Conflict Resolution*, 65(4): 788–812.
24. D. Bloomfield, C. Nupen, and P. Harris, 'Negotiation Process', in P. Harris & B. Reilly (eds), *Democracy and Deep-Rooted Conflict: Options for Negotiators* (Sweden: Institute for Democracy and Electoral Assistance, 1998).
25. F. Osler Hampson, *Nurturing Peace: Why Peace Settlements Succeed or Fail* (Washington, DC: United States Institute of Peace Press, 1996), p. 153.
26. J. Groom, 'Coming Out of Violence: Ten Troubling Questions', *Proceedings of the International Peace Studies Symposium, Coming Out of War and Ethnic Violence* (Okinawa: Okinawa International University, 1996).
27. Extraordinary Chambers in the Courts of Cambodia (ECCC), http://www.eccc.gov.kh/en/about-eccc/introduction.
28. C. Newkey-Burden (2021) 'Peace Talk Politicians Kicked Out of Hotels Over $50 m Unpaid Bill', *The Week*, 9 February. Accessed at https://www.theweek.co.uk/951925/sudanese-politicians-kicked-out-peace-talk-hotels-unpaid-bills.
29. World Bank, op. cit.

INDEX

A

Afghanistan, 8, 31, 57, 61, 76, 79, 80, 86, 93, 96, 107, 159, 167, 189, 190, 192, 195, 237, 263, 265, 291, 298, 315, 336, 338, 348, 357, 396, 397, 405–407, 417, 428, 568, 589, 601

African Union (AU), 87, 93–96, 98, 217, 218, 223, 429

Al-Qaeda, 58, 97, 223, 293

Apartheid, 4, 133, 141, 144, 189, 387, 414, 484, 533, 539, 542

Armenia, 593, 609

Artsakh, 609

Asylum, 14, 160–163, 169, 173

Authoritarian conflict management, 9, 586

Azerbaijan, 24, 407, 593, 609

B

Back channel negotiations, 265, 267, 386

Basque Country, 46, 199, 589

Bosnia, 19, 26, 34, 167, 189, 190, 216, 218, 299, 336, 357, 358, 362, 385, 388, 396, 401, 403, 410, 413, 429, 433, 439, 440, 450, 467, 490, 534, 542, 555, 568, 572, 575, 580, 587, 597, 607

Burundi, 93, 94, 164, 170, 201, 247, 292, 362, 385, 388, 401, 416, 448, 452, 453, 457, 467, 490, 492

C

Cambodia, 8, 189, 190, 358, 396, 448, 597, 606

Ceasefire, 6, 9, 28, 52, 88, 89, 91, 92, 94–96, 165, 184–187, 201, 208, 222, 223, 240, 291, 295–297, 300, 301, 307, 313, 321, 382, 383, 385, 386, 389–391, 393, 401, 404, 432, 433, 449, 458, 535, 588, 589, 592, 593, 609

Centripetalism, 408, 412, 417, 423

© The Editor(s) (if applicable) and The Author(s), under exclusive license to Springer Nature Switzerland AG 2022
R. Mac Ginty and A. Wanis-St. John (eds.), *Contemporary Peacemaking*,
https://doi.org/10.1007/978-3-030-82962-9

Chad, 217, 218, 240, 242, 244, 246, 448
Children, 52, 167, 170, 183, 339–341, 345, 358, 366, 523, 542, 573
Civil society, 2, 8, 10, 12, 14, 56, 68, 71, 72, 74, 75, 98, 99, 108–110, 114, 148, 150, 151, 165, 189, 190, 222, 230, 236–243, 246, 250, 251, 253, 270, 295, 314, 316, 319, 355, 356, 361, 393, 398, 414, 415, 435, 476, 482, 484, 524, 580, 585, 586, 597, 598, 605, 608, 609
Cold War, 86, 87, 89, 91, 133, 204, 336, 358, 359, 381, 384, 395, 447, 476, 478, 485, 534, 536
Colombia, 7, 44, 96, 107, 111, 113, 141, 143, 147, 149, 185, 189, 200, 229, 238, 251, 252, 270, 292, 307, 315, 382, 387, 391, 400, 404, 405, 428, 429, 434, 480, 490, 533, 541, 588–590, 607, 610
Community-based organizations (CBOs), 71, 347
Conflict analysis, 12, 55–80, 230
Conflict management, 5, 6, 9, 13, 28, 33, 34, 126, 129, 130, 213, 218, 228, 230, 253, 263, 411, 412, 420, 443, 490
Conflict prevention, 79, 121, 124, 129, 130, 132, 208, 316, 457
Conflict resolution, 6, 14, 32, 79, 99, 122–125, 128–130, 133–135, 141, 146, 164, 170, 171, 209, 214, 290, 294, 297, 300, 382, 397, 399, 450, 460, 478, 491, 510, 512, 516, 517, 523
Conflict transformation, 6, 13, 56, 70, 72, 124, 133, 208, 440, 479, 487, 587, 595

Consociation, 411, 413, 439
consociationalism, 16, 408, 411, 413
Cote D'Ivoire, 93
Crime, 17, 62, 88, 96, 111, 240, 299, 300, 302, 334, 479–481, 487, 523, 533, 536–549, 593, 601, 605, 606
Culture of peace, 170, 508–517, 519, 523
Cyprus, 9, 27, 34, 94, 141, 143–145, 147, 150, 221, 410, 570, 580

D
Darfur, 9, 92, 93, 175, 214, 222, 223, 291, 458, 459
Dayton Peace Accord, 52
Deadlines, 24, 181, 183, 187–189, 192, 193, 592
Democratic republic of Congo (DRC), 92, 107, 111, 416, 435, 448, 485, 490, 586
Diaspora, 173, 232, 609
Disarmament, 2, 3, 15, 92, 96, 187, 299, 317, 333, 335, 337, 338, 349, 352, 356, 358, 455, 486, 487, 490, 510, 546, 587, 593, 611
Displacement, 14, 107, 159, 160, 162, 164, 165, 171, 172, 497, 608
Donors, 56, 72, 75–77, 90, 189–191, 251, 294, 357, 362–366, 368, 397, 568, 573, 574, 609

E
East Timor, 8, 90, 133, 139, 141, 143, 146, 336, 448, 483, 546
Education, 57, 63, 134, 160, 169, 170, 191, 319, 321, 340, 344, 407, 411, 418, 457, 483, 503,

507–516, 518–524, 573, 574, 576
Ejército de Liberación Nacional (ELN), 252, 292, 541, 600
Elections, 84, 92, 94, 151, 160, 166, 167, 171, 183, 220, 239, 240, 247, 307–324, 392, 410, 411, 422, 460, 538, 545, 549, 552
election violence, 98, 308–313, 315–317, 319–322
Eritrea, 27, 167, 344, 347, 594
Ethiopia, 26, 201, 342, 343, 352, 418, 437
Ethnic Armed Organizations (EAOs), 215, 222, 223, 252
European Union (EU), 34, 62, 151, 204, 217, 219, 246, 294, 300, 364, 366, 367, 570, 580
Everyday peace, 348, 575, 581, 598
Extremists, 68, 161, 247–249, 253, 293

F

Facilitator, 60, 200, 205, 209, 294, 396, 519, 523
Faith-based organizations, 71
Federalism, 408, 418, 419
Former combatants, 11, 317, 322, 333–349, 356, 522, 523, 544, 546, 547, 605
Frente Popular para la Liberación de Saguia el-Hamra y de Río de Oro (POLISARIO), 144
Fuerzas Armadas Revolucionarias de Colombia (FARC), 590, 593, 600

G

Gender, 3, 10, 11, 20, 70, 104–106, 109–115, 119, 344, 366, 368, 415, 422, 485, 572, 573

Georgia, 39, 389, 404, 433, 490, 580, 594
Guatemala, 7, 96, 118, 141, 143–145, 147, 165, 215, 236, 292, 296, 303, 315, 433, 482–484, 490, 499, 504, 505, 534, 539, 540, 545, 553, 578

I

Inclusion, 6, 10–14, 104–107, 110–112, 114, 117, 131, 146, 148, 149, 162, 164, 169, 222, 235–239, 242, 243, 246, 253, 382, 384, 388, 397, 399–401, 406, 409, 410, 413–415, 466, 477, 490–492, 537, 589, 590, 594, 598, 600, 601, 609
India, 6, 9, 56, 91, 123, 134, 187, 194, 244, 296, 307, 390, 419, 579, 592, 594, 610
Indigenous approaches, 13, 121, 129
Internally displaced persons (IDPs), 8, 164, 172, 436
International Court of Justice (ICJ), 85, 143
International Criminal Court (ICC), 299, 428, 438, 441, 476, 478, 483, 487, 605
International Non-Governmental Organisations (INGOs), 10, 11, 183, 189–191, 290, 294, 295, 429, 486, 592
Iraq, 8, 19, 27, 57, 62, 78, 93, 97, 141, 143, 145, 167, 189, 190, 192, 224, 265, 336, 347, 348, 357, 413, 422, 428, 441, 448, 490, 544, 555, 568, 571, 576, 578, 594
Islamic State (ISIS), 223, 224, 248, 349
Islamic State-Khorasan (ISIS-K), 601, 613

Israel, 4, 9, 27, 30, 62, 87, 218, 263, 264, 291, 387, 518, 519, 534, 593, 600, 610

K

Kenya, 56, 80, 84, 87, 95, 98, 169, 206, 214, 308, 319–321, 407, 412, 448, 485, 518, 520, 533
Khmer Rouge, 606
Kosovo, 8, 9, 19, 90, 167, 189, 217, 221, 296, 299, 336, 342, 356, 359, 362, 448, 555, 568, 594
Kurds, 18, 594, 599
 Kurdish Regional Government (KRG), 594

L

Leadership, 7, 27, 28, 58, 71, 73, 74, 98, 107, 123, 124, 148, 171, 214, 215, 220–222, 225–227, 252, 263, 387, 398, 517, 522, 523, 525, 588
League of Arab States, 87
Lebanon, 19, 90, 96, 163, 168–171, 193, 243, 351, 410, 412, 413, 523–525, 536, 551
Lederach, John Paul, 13, 31, 41, 53, 122, 136, 206, 211, 281, 501, 516, 517, 526
Legitimacy, 5, 94, 105, 111, 112, 133, 134, 145, 147, 148, 151–153, 209, 220, 227, 237, 244, 251, 262, 265, 270, 272–274, 276, 298, 300, 301, 307, 315, 323, 387, 399, 430, 435, 442, 455, 466, 487, 491, 536, 564, 566, 572, 574–576, 580, 591, 609
Liberal Peace, 8, 84, 133, 189–191, 194, 335, 337, 360, 428, 476, 482, 486, 488, 490, 492, 493, 504, 536, 544, 545, 549, 564, 565, 569, 570, 586
Liberia, 8, 91, 93, 164, 189, 194, 237, 239, 240, 242, 246, 251, 254, 296, 308, 311, 314, 319–322, 336, 338, 342, 356, 357, 359, 362, 410, 416, 490, 537, 565
Libya, 6, 8, 9, 19, 93, 99, 190, 221, 241, 249, 395, 397, 428, 433, 460, 466, 490, 586

M

Malaysia, 218, 219, 249, 388
Mali, 9, 92, 107, 205, 214, 221, 222, 293, 490
Mediation, 1, 3, 10, 13, 14, 24, 26, 29, 31, 33, 37, 44, 48, 49, 60, 83, 85, 89, 90, 93–96, 98, 99, 101, 127, 142, 152, 171, 200–204, 206, 207, 209, 210, 213–219, 223, 225–230, 253, 295, 300, 301, 382, 390, 396, 398, 431, 487, 490, 510, 517, 588, 603, 608
Moldova, 433, 589
Morocco, 144, 436
Moro Islamic Liberation Front (MILF), 219, 221, 222, 224, 244–246, 251, 254, 294, 353, 388, 394, 454
Mozambique, 27, 91, 206, 211, 214, 311, 338, 343, 347, 352, 358, 362, 522, 523
Mutually hurting stalemate (MHS), 24–30, 32–35, 223, 225, 587
Myanmar, 14, 94, 107, 165, 171, 186, 187, 189, 194, 214, 215, 222, 223, 252, 390, 434, 586, 592

N

Nagorno-Karabakh, 40, 144, 153, 176, 594, 609
Negotiations, 2, 3, 5–7, 10, 11, 13–15, 24–39, 44–46, 48–50, 52, 60, 68, 70, 84, 90, 98, 104–112, 117, 142–153, 160, 164, 165, 167, 171, 183–188, 199, 207–209, 214, 215, 217, 218, 222–228, 230, 235–237, 239–255, 261–271, 274–277, 289–295, 297–302, 322, 342, 367, 382, 385–387, 389, 390, 393, 402, 414, 429–433, 438, 441, 449–451, 454, 455, 458, 475–477, 484, 486–490, 508, 517, 519, 535, 537, 538, 586–593, 595, 596, 598, 600–604, 606, 608, 609
Nepal, 118, 356, 362, 388, 413, 415, 417, 418, 421, 437, 438, 448, 458, 460, 468, 490, 538, 552, 565, 572
Nigeria, 96, 412
Non-Governmental Organisations (NGOs), 55, 57, 61, 73, 76, 80, 108, 190, 216, 219, 253, 290, 294, 347, 355, 482, 524, 573, 574, 580
Nonviolence, 125, 129, 510, 514, 520
  nonviolent movements, 252, 253
North Atlantic Treaty Organisation (NATO), 8, 30, 271, 298, 299, 336
Northern Ireland, 6, 7, 27, 44, 46, 105, 118, 141, 143, 146, 147, 149, 151, 184, 187, 204, 218, 219, 226, 227, 233, 236, 251, 263, 268–270, 272, 279, 281, 295, 301, 385, 388, 396, 398, 402, 410, 412, 418, 424, 490, 533, 534, 537, 538, 541, 542, 551, 588–590, 594, 596, 597

O

Organization for Economic Co-operation and Development (OECD), 71, 72, 79, 360–366, 369, 370, 372, 425, 466, 468, 512, 513, 517
Organization of American States (OAS), 143, 202

P

Pakistan, 27, 126, 134, 138, 159, 167, 264, 397, 522
Palestine, 87, 94, 222, 237, 263, 264, 268, 402, 534, 596
Participation, participatory approaches, 10, 11, 71, 72, 77, 93, 103–110, 112–115, 122, 126, 135, 144, 147, 160, 162, 164–169, 171, 224, 228, 236–238, 240–242, 270, 307, 315, 318, 340, 346, 414, 415, 418, 455, 477, 478, 481, 485, 487, 488, 490–492, 598, 609
Participatory Rural Appraisal (PRA), 56, 72
Peace, 577–579
  peace accords, peace agreements, 89, 91, 104–107, 109–114, 117, 118, 143–145, 147–149, 151, 152, 165, 166, 170, 181–184, 186–189, 193, 194, 206, 221–223, 226, 236, 240–243, 245, 246, 248, 251, 252, 254, 263, 265, 269, 270, 289, 290, 292, 299–301, 317, 318, 321, 322, 339, 343, 346, 358, 361, 383–386, 388, 390, 391, 393, 395, 396, 398–400,

402, 405, 410, 415, 420, 427–429, 431–436, 438–441, 443, 447–455, 458, 459, 466, 481, 484, 485, 489, 490, 492, 508, 525, 533–538, 540–543, 545–550, 555, 556
peacebuilding, 3, 9–11, 45, 46, 49–51, 53, 55–57, 59, 61, 64, 65, 67, 68, 71, 73–76, 79, 80, 83, 84, 88, 90–92, 94, 104, 105, 109, 111, 112, 117, 133, 160, 168–172, 193, 209, 270, 298, 307, 321, 333–337, 341, 342, 346–348, 356–360, 362, 363, 367, 382, 398, 414, 415, 419, 427, 434, 439, 449, 457, 476–478, 482, 486–489, 491–493, 495, 500, 501, 509, 510, 514, 516, 517, 523, 524, 544, 545, 549, 564, 567, 569, 573–578, 586, 592, 598, 607
peace education, 13, 17, 57, 170, 507–516, 518–524
peacekeeping, 8, 83–86, 89–94, 99, 101, 194, 217, 296–299, 305, 321, 337, 338, 358, 395, 406, 427, 451, 478, 485
peacemaking, 1–3, 7, 9–16, 37, 60, 83–100, 110, 121–135, 142–150, 152, 153, 160, 202, 205, 213–217, 220, 225, 226, 228, 238, 251, 262, 267, 308, 316, 317, 320, 321, 384, 385, 387, 392, 396, 399, 408, 415, 427–429, 431, 433, 438–441, 447, 457, 458, 476, 478, 486, 489, 491–493, 507, 508, 522, 524, 525, 585, 586, 595, 601, 608, 610
Philippines, 27, 46, 107, 112, 113, 119, 218, 219, 222, 224, 229, 237, 240–242, 244–248, 250, 251, 294, 307, 383, 388, 391, 394, 403, 405, 413, 454, 600
Power, 27, 35, 51, 63, 66, 72, 74, 75, 83, 85, 86, 93, 95, 96, 106, 111, 113, 126, 132, 148, 152, 160–162, 168, 181–183, 186–188, 192, 200, 207, 219–221, 224, 236, 237, 239, 240, 242, 253, 262, 264, 272, 274, 281, 291, 295, 297, 310, 311, 313, 314, 316, 318, 322, 333, 348, 361, 365, 395, 409, 418, 433, 437, 438, 441, 448, 451, 453, 456, 457, 460, 466, 479, 480, 488, 492, 493, 536–538, 540, 568, 569
power sharing, 84, 143, 148, 239, 317, 388, 391, 392, 408–415, 420–422, 429, 438–440, 451, 453, 460, 487, 490
Practitioners, 2, 13, 24, 26, 30, 31, 34, 37, 44–46, 56, 60, 152, 184, 192, 206, 229, 317, 382, 384, 418, 421, 439, 491, 492, 607
Pre-negotiation, 36, 105, 106, 117, 183, 184, 187, 207, 209, 211, 226, 244, 295, 385–389, 393, 394, 402, 488, 535, 587, 589

Q
Quebec, 143

R
Referendums, 2, 7, 12, 14, 113, 141–153, 167, 251, 270, 428, 480, 595, 604
Refugees, 7, 8, 14, 61, 159–172, 202, 382, 537–539, 542, 598
Religion, 64, 74, 80, 413, 572
Repatriation, 7, 14, 160, 162–168, 171, 175, 539

Resettlement, 160, 162–164, 171, 454
Resilience, 58, 64, 98, 99, 412
Returnee, 164–166, 170
Revolutionary Armed Forces of Colombia/Fuerzas Armadas Revolucionarias de Colombia (FARC), 96, 143, 149, 220, 238, 251, 252, 292, 413, 428, 480, 481, 533, 541, 590
Rhodesia, 27
Ripeness, 13, 23, 25–37, 39, 44–49, 51, 52, 202, 203, 221, 223, 227, 365, 588, 589
Rohingya, 171, 215
Russia, 26, 27, 62, 85, 91, 95, 216, 218, 219, 397, 404, 433
Rwanda, 93, 133, 141, 143, 161, 170, 189, 190, 193, 205, 296, 358, 362, 402, 416, 461, 483, 491, 565

S

Secrecy
 and exclusion, 6, 266
 secret channel, 267, 272
 secret contact, 264–267, 270, 275, 276
 secret negotiation, 261–263, 268, 271, 387
Security sector reform (SSR), 2, 15, 68, 183, 189, 317, 321, 322, 336, 355–371, 391, 487, 545
Sexual and gender-based violence, 10, 344, 368
Sierra Leone, 8, 91, 93, 189, 190, 300, 306, 311, 336, 357, 359, 362, 453, 467, 485, 490, 494, 496, 522, 565
Somalia, 19, 44, 61, 80, 91, 93, 94, 200, 205, 338, 407, 460, 490

South Africa, 4, 27, 29, 31, 32, 107, 133, 141, 144, 145, 189, 226, 236, 263, 264, 268, 302, 334, 385, 387, 401, 402, 407, 413, 415–417, 421, 448, 450, 457, 466, 483, 490, 533, 534, 539, 542, 548, 579, 588, 589, 597, 601, 602, 606
South Sudan, 9, 92, 94, 107, 109, 117, 141, 143, 159, 167, 169, 189, 214, 218, 220–222, 229, 336, 395, 397, 407, 418, 435, 437, 490, 594, 597, 607, 608
Spoiler, 149, 228, 230, 243, 247, 252, 267, 291, 295, 303, 304, 415, 537, 538, 541, 590, 593, 600–602, 604
Sri Lanka, 26, 187, 199, 200, 206, 300, 307, 407, 412, 434, 565–567, 572–574, 576, 580, 588, 600, 610
Statebuilding, 3, 8, 189, 190, 195, 336, 337, 359, 367, 396, 442, 449, 486
Sudan, 27, 92, 94, 189, 222, 246, 291, 299, 343, 391, 428, 435, 448, 453, 459, 490
Sustainability, 48, 49, 97, 270, 508, 564
Symbolism, 50, 104, 105, 111, 123, 130, 134, 152, 247, 291, 391, 417, 455, 460
Syria, 6, 14, 19, 26, 27, 30, 31, 34, 36, 84, 87, 88, 94, 95, 107, 109, 110, 114, 159, 166, 167, 169–171, 214, 217–219, 221–223, 228, 263, 265, 293, 348, 390, 395, 397, 406–408, 415, 422, 433, 586, 589, 601
Systems approach, 58, 77

T

Tajikistan, 218, 229, 397, 433, 451

Taliban, 8, 80, 192, 237, 265, 266, 271, 291, 298, 315, 387, 397, 589, 590, 593, 601

Tamil Tigers, Liberation Tigers of Tamil Eelam (LTTE), 300, 301, 567

Tanzania, 126, 138, 163, 164

Time, 2, 3, 9, 14, 16, 23, 26, 30, 36, 44–51, 53, 56, 58, 60, 61, 63, 66, 67, 72–75, 80, 84, 87, 88, 90, 91, 96, 98, 104, 105, 107–110, 112, 126, 128, 150, 164, 181–183, 187, 188, 191, 192, 199, 206–208, 216, 217, 222, 224, 227, 229, 230, 237, 239–241, 243–245, 249, 251, 253, 264, 266, 270–272, 274–276, 291, 294, 297, 299, 300, 315–317, 320, 334, 339, 342, 344, 363, 365, 367, 382, 383, 385, 387, 392–394, 398, 399, 409, 412, 414, 415, 417, 420, 421, 428, 432, 435, 454–456, 479, 481, 482, 489, 492, 493, 519, 525, 534, 544, 547, 568, 569, 572, 574, 576, 586, 587, 600, 607, 610

Timor-Leste/East Timor, 111, 133, 356, 357, 359, 362, 363

Track two, Track II, 206, 268

Transitional Justice (TJ), 2, 13, 16, 111, 133, 166, 347, 382, 391, 429, 438, 439, 476–480, 482, 483, 485–494, 497, 501, 503

Turkey, 4, 9, 18, 27, 62, 150, 159, 170, 294, 408, 433, 588, 599

U

Uganda, 80, 109, 159, 162, 164, 299, 342, 343, 352, 416, 428, 438, 485, 490, 492, 597

Ukraine, 408, 418, 594

United Kingdom (UK), 8, 9, 57, 88, 146, 163, 219, 226, 294, 359, 366, 402, 428, 483, 610

United Nations, 7, 12, 19

United National Secretary General, 29, 104, 116, 118, 174, 214, 217, 495

United Nations Department of Political Affairs, 89

United Nations High Commissioner for Refugees, 174, 177

United Nations Security Council, 8, 26, 85–89, 92–94, 99, 103, 117, 161, 164, 166, 169, 177, 217, 219, 228, 389, 415

United Nations Mission for the Referendum in Western Sahara (MINURSO), 144

United States (US), 19, 33, 62, 78, 85, 88, 90, 95, 163, 187, 192, 205, 219, 223, 228, 264–268, 271, 273, 301, 302, 337, 357, 366, 428, 433, 520, 564, 568, 589

V

Violence, 1, 2, 4, 6, 9, 11, 12, 15, 17, 28, 32, 44, 46, 47, 50, 58, 66, 68, 70, 80, 84, 87, 91, 95, 97–99, 111, 113, 118, 122, 125–127, 129–132, 135, 141, 145, 146, 153, 159, 182, 184–186, 200, 203, 208, 243, 245, 247–249, 252, 289–302, 304, 308–323, 333, 334, 337, 359, 360, 364, 382, 383, 389, 390, 397, 398, 408, 409, 422,

430, 443, 449, 456–459, 475, 476, 479, 481, 483–485, 487, 489, 492, 493, 497, 507–509, 511–513, 516–519, 522, 533–543, 545–549, 551, 552, 554–556, 565, 587, 590–594, 596, 597, 599–602, 604–610
Voting, 145, 152, 153, 166–168, 176, 319, 409, 417, 424, 453, 602

W

Western Sahara, 94, 144, 242
Women, 10, 20, 71, 74, 80, 94, 103–115, 133, 166, 236, 237, 239, 241, 343, 344, 366, 382, 385, 388, 399, 411, 414, 415, 418, 598, 608, 609
Women, peace and security, 13, 103, 104, 111, 112, 403, 586, 598

Y

Yemen, 6, 9, 32, 94, 95, 107, 188, 194, 214, 222, 388, 397, 433, 460

Z

Zartman, I. William, 13, 37–42, 44, 53, 202, 203, 210, 223, 227, 232–234, 247, 255, 304, 527, 587, 588, 611